Sweet & Maxwell's

Family Law Statutes 2003/04

AUSTRALIA
Law Book Co.
Sydney

CANADA and USA
Carswell
Toronto

HONG KONG
Sweet & Maxwell Asia

NEW ZEALAND
Brookers
Wellington

SINGAPORE and MALAYSIA
Sweet & Maxwell Asia
Singapore and Kuala Lumpur

Sweet & Maxwell's

Family Law Statutes 2003/04

1st Edition

Professor Michael Freeman, LL.M
Barrister
Professor of English Law, University College London

LONDON
SWEET & MAXWELL
2003

Published in 2003 by Sweet & Maxwell Ltd
of 100 Avenue Road, London NW3 3PF
Typeset by Sweet & Maxwell Ltd, 100 Avenue Road, London NW3 3PF
and Mendip Communications Ltd, Frome, Somerset
Printed in Great Britain by Ashford Colour Printers Hants

No natural forests were destroyed to make this product; only farmed timber was used and replanted

ISBN 0 421 797 304

Grateful acknowledgement is made to the UN for permission to reproduce the UN Convention on the Rights of the Child.

PREFACE

Though many of its principles are deeply embedded within the common law, the framework of Family Law is now essentially statutory. All students of the subject must be familiar with a range of statutes dealing with such matters as marriage, nullity and divorce and their financial consequences, children, and domestic violence.

This book is a compilation of the essential statutory material with legislation dating from 1882 to 2002. Amendments, additions and repeals are carefully documented in footnotes. It is believed that this will be of assistance to students and their teachers.

Not everyone will agree with the selection of statutory material. It is, however, my experience that Family Law courses do not now include much probate or succession emphasis, and care has accordingly been taken to keep this material down to a bare minimum. By way of contrast, there is some 'medical law' material, including parts of the Human Fertilisation and Embryology Act 1990 because increasingly attention is being drawn to this, if only for comparative purposes, in Family Law courses. The contours of Family Law have shifted and, doubtless, will continue to shift.

A decision has been taken not to include the Adoption Act 1976 and to print in full the new Adoption and Children Act 2002. The assumption is made that courses run in 2003-2004 will treat the 2002 Act as if it is in operation and substitute it for the 1976 Act. This may prove foolhardy: how many courses taught the divorce part of the Family Law Act 1996 for two to three years before it was abandoned? I, nevertheless, believe I have made the right decision this time.

As with any new collection, opinions will differ on content. I would be interested in hearing from those who use this book whether there is material which they believe should be included and is currently not, and indeed whether there is anything included which they think should not be. In addition to statutes, the book includes the very important United Nations Convention on the Rights of the Child.

I hope the addition of an Index will be found helpful.

Since the statutes are not annotated, they will be admitted to most Family Law examinations. The book should thus serve the dual function of study guide and examination aide.

I am grateful to the editorial staff of Sweet and Maxwell for the assistance they gave me with the preparation of this volume. I also wish to express my thanks to my very capable secretary, Alison Compton, whose help in the preparation of this volume was also invaluable.

Professor Michael Freeman
July 1, 2003

CONTENTS

CHRONOLOGICAL CONTENTS

STATUTES

INTERNATIONAL MATERIALS

ALPHABETICAL CONTENTS

STATUTES

INTERNATIONAL MATERIALS

Married Women's Property Act 1882

(45 AND 46 VICT. C. 75)

Questions between husband and wife as to property to be decided in a summary way

17. In any question between husband and wife as to the title to or possession of property, either party, [...][1], may apply by summons or otherwise in a summary way to the High Court or such County Court as may be prescribed and the Court may, on such application (which may be heard in private), make such order with respect to the property as it thinks fit. **1-001**

Law of Property Act 1925

(15 AND 16 GEO. 5 C. 20)

PART I

GENERAL PRINCIPLES AS TO LEGAL ESTATES, EQUITABLE INTERESTS AND POWERS

Undivided Shares and Joint Ownership

Joint tenancies

36.—(1) Where a legal estate (not being settled land) is beneficially limited to or held in trust for any persons as joint tenants, the same shall be held [in trust][2], in like manner as if the persons beneficially entitled were tenants in common, but not so as to sever their joint tenancy in equity. **2-001**

(2) No severance of a joint tenancy of a legal estate, so as to create a tenancy in common in land, shall be permissible, whether by operation of law or otherwise, but this subsection does not affect the right of a joint tenant to release his interest to the other joint tenants, or the right to server a joint tenancy in an equitable interest whether or not the legal estate is vested in the joint tenants:

Provided that, where a legal estate (not being settled land) is vested in joint tenants beneficially, and any tenant desires to sever the joint tenancy in equity, he shall give to the other joint tenants a notice in writing of such desire or do such other acts or things as would, in the case of personal estate, have been effectual to sever the tenancy in equity, and thereupon [the land shall be held in trust on terms][3] which would have been requisite for giving effect to the beneficial interests if there had been an actual severance.

---

[1] Words repealed by Statute Law (Repeals) Act 1969 c.52 Sch 1 Pt III

[2] Words substituted by Trusts of Land and Appointment of Trustees Act 1996 c.47 Sch 2 para 4 (2)

[3] Words substituted by Trusts of Land and Appointment of Trustees Act 1996 c.47 Sch 2 para 4 (3) (b)

[Nothing in this Act affects the right of a survivor of joint tenants, who is solely and beneficially interested, to deal with his legal estate as if it were not held [in trust][1].][2]

(3) Without prejudice to the right of a joint tenant to release his interest to the other joint tenants no severance of a mortgage term or trust estate, so as to create a tenancy in common, shall be permissible.

PART II

CONTRACTS, CONVEYANCES AND OTHER INSTRUMENTS

Conveyances and other Instruments

Conveyances to be by deed

2-002 **52.**—(1) All conveyances of land or of any interest therein are void for the purpose of conveying or creating a legal estate unless made by deed.

(2) This section does not apply to—

(a) assents by a personal representative;

(b) disclaimers made in accordance with [sections 178 to 180 or sections 315 to 319 of the Insolvency Act 1986][3], or not required to be evidenced in writing;

(c) surrenders by operation of law, including surrenders which may, by law, be effected without writing;

(d) leases or tenancies or other assurances not required by law to be made in writing;

(e) receipts [other than those falling within section 115 below][4];

(f) vesting orders of the court or other competent authority;

(g) conveyances taking effect by operation of law.

Instruments required to be in writing

2-003 **53.**—(1) Subject to the provision hereinafter contained with respect to the creation of interests in land by parol—

(a) no interest in land can be created or disposed of except by writing signed by the person creating or conveying the same, or by his agent thereunto lawfully authorised in writing, or by will, or by operation of law;

(b) a declaration of trust respecting any land or any interest therein must be manifested and proved by some writing signed by some person who is able to declare such trust or by his will;

(c) a disposition of an equitable interest or trust subsisting at the time of the disposition, must be in writing signed by the person disposing of the same, or by his agent thereunto lawfully authorised in writing or by will.

(2) This section does not affect the creation or operation of resulting, implied or constructive trusts.

---

[1] Words substituted by Trusts of Land and Appointment of Trustees Act 1996 c.47 Sch 2 para 4 (3) (a)

[2] Words added by Law of Property (Amendment) Act 1926 c.11 Sch

[3] Words substituted by virtue of Insolvency Act 1985 c.65 s 235 (1) Sch 8 para 4 and Insolvency Act 1986 c.45 ss 437, 439 (2) Sch 11 para 10, Sch 14

[4] Words substituted by Law of Property (Miscellaneous Provisions) Act 1989 c.34 s 1 (8) Sch 1

PART XI

MISCELLANEOUS

Miscellaneous

Presumption of survivorship in regard to claims to property

184. In all cases where, after the commencement of this Act, two or more persons have died in circumstances rendering it uncertain which of them survived the other or others, such deaths shall (subject to any order of the court), for all purposes affecting the title to property, be presumed to have occurred in order of seniority, and accordingly the younger shall be deemed to have survived the elder. **2-004**

Administration of Estates Act 1925

(15 AND 16 GEO. 5 C. 23)

PART IV

DISTRIBUTION OF RESIDUARY ESTATE

Succession to real and personal estate on intestacy

46.—(1) The residuary estate of an intestate shall be distributed in the manner or be held on the trusts mentioned in this section, namely:— **3-001**

[(i) If the intestate leaves a husband or wife, then in accordance with the following table:

If the intestate—

(1) leaves— (a) no issue, and (b) no parent, or brother or sister of the whole blood, or issue of a brother or sister of the whole blood.	the residuary estate shall be held in trust for the surviving husband or wife absolutely.
(2) leaves issue (whether or not persons mentioned in sub-paragraph (b) above also survive)	the surviving husband or wife shall take the personal chattels absolutely and, in addition, the residuary estate of the intestate (other than the personal chattels) shall stand charged with the payment of a [fixed net sum][1], free of death duties and costs, to the surviving husband or wife with interest thereon from the date of the death [...][2] [at

such rate as the Lord Chancellor may specify by order][3] until paid or appropriated, and, subject to providing for that sum and the interest thereon, the residuary estate (other than the personal chattels) shall be held—

(a) as to one half upon trust for the surviving husband or wife during his or her life, and, subject to such life interest, on the statutory trusts for the issue of the intestate, and

(b) as to the other half, on the statutory trusts for the issue of the intestate.

(3) leaves one or more of the following, that is to say, a parent, a brother or sister of the whole blood, or issue of a brother or sister of the whole blood, but leaves no issue

the surviving husband or wife shall take the personal chattels absolutely and, in addition, the residuary estate of the intestate (other than the personal chattels) shall stand charged with the payment of a [fixed net sum][4], free of death duties and costs, to the surviving husband or wife with interest thereon from the date of the death [...][5] [at such rate as the Lord Chancellor may specify by order][6] until paid or appropriated, and, subject to providing for that sum and the interest thereon, the residuary estate (other than the personal chattels) shall be held—

(a) as to one half in trust for the surviving husband or wife absolutely, and

(b) as to the other half—

(i) where the intestate leaves one parent or both parents (whether or not brothers or sisters of the intestate or their issue also survive) in trust for the parent absolutely or, as the case may be, for the two parents in equal shares absolutely,

(ii) where the intestate leaves no parent, on the statutory trusts for the brothers and sisters of the whole blood of the intestate.][7]

[1] Words substituted by Family Provision Act 1966 c.35 s 1 (2) (a)
[2] Words repealed by Statute Law (Repeals) Act 1981 c.19 s 1 (1) Sch 1 Pt I
[3] Words substituted by Administration of Justice Act 1977 c.38 s 28 (1)
[4] Words substituted by Family Provision Act 1966 c.35 s 1 (2) (a)
[5] Words repealed by Statute Law (Repeals) Act 1981 c.19 s 1 (1) Sch 1 Pt I
[6] Words substituted by Administration of Justice Act 1977 c.38 s 28 (1)
[7] Substituted by Intestates' Estates Act 1952 c.64 s 1 (2)

[The fixed net sums referred to in paragraphs (2) and (3) of this Table shall be of the amounts provided by or under section 1 of the Family Provision Act 1966][1]

[1] Words added by Family Provision Act 1966 c.35 s 1 (2) (a)

(ii) If the intestate leaves issue but no husband or wife, the residuary estate of the intestate shall be held on the statutory trusts for the issue of the intestate;

(iii) If the intestate leaves [no husband or wife and][1] no issue but both parents, then, [...][2] the residuary estate of the intestate shall be held in trust for the father and mother in equal shares absolutely;

(iv) If the intestate leaves [no husband or wife and][3] no issue but one parent, then, [...][4] the residuary estate of the intestate shall be held in trust for the surviving father or mother absolutely;

(v) If the intestate leaves no [husband or wife and no issue and no][5] parent, then [...][6] the residuary estate of the intestate shall be held in trust for the following persons living at the death of the intestate, and in the following order and manner, namely:—

First, on the statutory trusts for the brothers and sisters of the whole blood of the intestate; but if no person takes an absolutely vested interest under such trusts, then

Secondly, on the statutory trusts for the brothers and sisters of the half blood of the intestate; but if no person takes an absolutely vested interest under such trusts; then

Thirdly, for the grandparents of the intestate and, if more than one survive the intestate, in equal shares; but if there is no member of this class; then

Fourthly, on the statutory trusts for the uncles and aunts of the intestate (being brothers or sisters of the whole blood of a parent of the intestate); but if no person takes an absolutely vested interest under such trusts; then

Fifthly, on the statutory trusts for the uncles and aunts of the intestate (being brothers or sisters of the half blood of a parent of the intestate); [...][7];

(vi) In default of any person taking an absolute interest under the foregoing provisions, the residuary estate of the intestate shall belong to the Crown or to the Duchy of Lancaster or to the Duke of Cornwall for the time being, as the case may be, as bona vacantia, and in lieu of any right to escheat.

The Crown or the said Duchy or the said Duke may (without prejudice to the powers reserved by section nine of the Civil List Act, 1910, or any other powers), out of the whole or any part of the property devolving on them respectively, provide, in accordance with the existing practice, for dependants, whether kindred or not, of the intestate, and other persons for whom the intestate might reasonably have been expected to make provision.

[(1A) The power to make orders under subsection (1) above shall be exercisable by statutory instrument subject to annulment in pursuance of a resolution of either House of Parliament; and any such order may be varied or revoked by a subsequent order made under the power.][8]

[1] Words inserted by Intestates' Estates Act 1952 c.64 s 1 (3) (a)
[2] Words repealed by Intestates' Estates Act 1952 c.64 s 1 (3) (a)
[3] Words inserted by Intestates' Estates Act 1952 c.64 s 1 (3) (a)
[4] Words repealed by Intestates' Estate Act 1952 c.64 s 1 (3) (a)
[5] Words substituted by Intestates' Estates Act 1952 c.64 s 1 (3) (b) (i)
[6] Words repealed by Intestates' Estates Act 1952 c.64 s 1 (3) (b) (ii)
[7] Words repealed by Intestates' Estates Act 1952 c.64 s 1 (3) (b) (ii)
[8] Inserted by Administration of Justice Act 1977 c.38 s 28 (1) (b)

(2) A husband and wife shall for all purposes of distribution or division under the foregoing provisions of this section be treated as two persons.

[[(2A) Where the intestate's husband or wife survived the intestate but died before the end of the period of 28 days beginning with the day on which the intestate died, this section shall have effect as respects the intestate as if the husband or wife had not survived the intestate.][1]

(3) Where the intestate and the intestate's husband or wife have died in circumstances rendering in uncertain which of them survived the other and the intestate's husband or wife is by virtue of section one hundred and eighty-four of the Law of Property Act, 1925, deemed to have survived the intestate, this section shall, nevertheless, have effect as respects the intestate as if the husband or wife had not survived the intestate.][2]

[(4) The interest payable on [the fixed net sum][3] payable to a surviving husband or wife shall be primarily payable out of income.][4]

Statutory trusts in favour of issue and other classes of relatives of intestate

3-002 **47.**—(1) Where under this Part of this Act the residuary estate of an intestate, or any part thereof, is directed to be held on the statutory trusts for the issue of the intestate, the same shall be held upon the following trusts, namely:—

(i) In trust, in equal shares if more than one, for all or any the children or child of the intestate, living at the death of the intestate, who attain the age of [eighteen years][5] or marry under that age, and for all or any of the issue living at the death of the intestate who attain the age of [eighteen years][6] or marry under that age of any child of the intestate who predeceases the intestate, such issue to take through all degrees, according to their stocks, in equal shares if more than one, the share which their parent would have taken if living at the death of the intestate, and so that no issue shall take whose parent is living at the death of the intestate and so capable of taking;

(ii) The statutory power of advancement, and the statutory provisions which relate to maintenance and accumulation of surplus income, shall apply, but when an infant marries such infant shall be entitled to give valid receipts for the income of the infant's share or interest;

(iii) [...][7]

(iv) The personal representatives may permit any infant contingently interested to have the use and enjoyment of any personal chattels in such manner and subject to such conditions (if any) as the personal representatives may consider reasonable, and without being liable to account for any consequential loss.

(2) If the trusts in favour of the issue of the intestate fail by reason of no child or other issue attaining an absolutely vested interest—

(a) the residuary estate of the intestate and the income thereof and all statutory accumulations, if any, of the income thereof, or so much thereof as may not have been paid or applied under any power affecting the same, shall go, devolve and be held under the provisions of this

[1] Added by Law Reform (Succession) Act 1995 c.41 s 1 (1)
[2] Added by Intestates' Estates Act 1952 c.64 s 1 (4)
[3] Words substituted by Family Provision Act 1966 c.35 s 1 (2) (b)
[4] Added by Intestates' Estates Act 1952 c.64 s 1 (4)
[5] Words substituted by Family Law Reform Act 1969 c.46 s 3 (2)
[6] Words substituted by Family Law Reform Act 1969 c.46 s 3 (2)
[7] Repealed by Law Reform (Succession) Act 1995 c.41 Sch 1 para 1

Part of this Act as if the intestate had died without leaving issue living at the death of the intestate;

(b) references in this Part of this Act to the intestate "leaving no issue" shall be construed as "leaving no issue who attain an absolutely vested interest";

(c) references in this Part of this Act to the intestate "leaving issue" or "leaving a child or other issue" shall be construed as "leaving issue who attain an absolutely vested interest."

(3) Where under this Part of this Act the residuary estate of an intestate or any part thereof is directed to be held on the statutory trusts for any class of relatives of the intestate, other than issue of the intestate, the same shall be held on trusts corresponding to the statutory trusts for the issue of the intestate (other than the provision for bringing any money or property into account) as if such trusts (other than as aforesaid) were repeated with the substitution of references to the members or member of that class for references to the children or child of the intestate.

[(4) References in paragraph(i) of subsection(1) of the last foregoing section to the intestate leaving, or not leaving, a member of the class consisting of brothers or sisters of the whole blood of the intestate and issue of brothers or sisters of the whole blood of the intestate shall be construed as references to the intestate leaving, or not leaving, a member of that class who attains an absolutely vested interest.][1]

(5) [...][2]

[Right of surviving spouse to have own life interest redeemed

47A.—(1) Where a surviving husband or wife is entitled to a life interest in part of the residuary estate, and so elects, the personal representative shall purchase or redeem the life interest by paying the capital value thereof to the tenant for life, or the persons deriving title under the tenant for life, and the costs of the transaction; and thereupon the residuary estate of the intestate may be dealt with and distributed free from the life interest. **3-003**

(2) [...][3]

(3) An election under this section shall only be exercisable if at the time of the election the whole of the said part of the residuary estate consists of property in possession, but, for the purposes of this section, a life interest in property partly in possession and partly not in possession may be treated as consisting of two separate life interests in those respective parts of the property.

[(3A) The capital value shall be reckoned in such manner as the Lord Chancellor may by order direct, and an order under this subsection may include transitional provisions.

(3B) The power to make orders under subsection (3A) above shall be exercisable by statutory instrument subject to annulment in pursuance of a resolution of either House of Parliament; and any such order may be varied or revoked by a subsequent order made under the power.][4]

(4) [...][5]

[1] Added by Intestates' Estates Act 1952 c.64 s 1 (3) (c)
[2] Repealed by Family Provision Act 1966 c.35 s 9 Sch 2
[3] Repealed by Administration of Justice Act 1977 c.38 s 28 (2) Sch 5 Pt VI
[4] Inserted by Administration of Justice Act 1977 c.38 s 28
[5] Repealed by Administration of Justice Act 1977 c.38 s 28 (2) Sch 5 Pt VI

(5) An election under this section shall be exercisable only within the period of twelve months from the date on which representation with respect to the estate of the intestate is first taken out:

Provided that if the surviving husband or wife satisfies the court that the limitation to the said period of twelve months will operate unfairly—

(a) in consequence of the representation first taken out being probate of a will subsequently revoked on the ground that the will was invalid or,

(b) in consequence of a question whether a person had an interest in the estate, or as to the nature of an interest in the estate, not having been determined at the time when representation was first taken out, or

(c) in consequence of some other circumstances affecting the administration or distribution of the estate,

the court may extend the said period.

(6) An election under this section shall be exercisable, except where the tenant for life is the sole personal representative, by notifying the personal representative (or, where there are two or more personal representatives of whom one is the tenant for life all of them except the tenant for life) in writing; and a notification in writing under this subsection shall not be revocable except with the consent of the personal representative.

(7) Where the tenant for life is the sole personal representative an election under this section shall not be effective unless written notice thereof is given to the [[Senior Registrar][1] of the Family Division of the High Court][2] within the period within which it must be made; and provision may be made by probate rules for keeping a record of such notices and making that record available to the public.

In this subsection the expression "probate rules" means rules [of court made under section 127 of the Supreme Court Act 1981][3].

(8) An election under this section by a tenant for life who is an infant shall be as valid and binding as it would be if the tenant for life were of age; but the personal representative shall, instead of paying the capital value of the life interest to the tenant for life, deal with it in the same manner as with any other part of the residuary estate to which the tenant for life is absolutely entitled.

(9) In considering for the purposes of the foregoing provisions of this section the question when representation was first taken out, a grant limited to settled land or to trust property shall be left out of account and a grant limited to real estate or to personal estate shall be left out of account unless a grant limited to the remainder of the estate has previously been made or is made at the same time.][4]

---

[1] Words substituted by Supreme Court Act 1981 c.54 s 152 (1) Sch 5
[2] Words substituted by Administration of Justice Act 1970 c.31 Sch 2 para 4
[3] Words substituted by Supreme Court Act 1981 c.54 s 152 (1) Sch 5
[4] Added by Intestates' Estates Act 1952 c.64 s 2 (b)

Children and Young Persons Act 1933

(23 AND 24 GEO. 5 C. 12)

PART I

PREVENTION OF CRUELTY AND EXPOSURE TO MORAL AND PHYSICAL DANGER

Offences

Cruelty to persons under sixteen

1.—(1) If any person who has attained the age of sixteen years and has [has responsibility for][1] any child or young person under that age, wilfully assaults, ill-treated, neglects, abandons, or exposes him, or causes or procures him to be assaulted, ill-treated, neglected, abandoned, or exposed, in a manner likely to cause him unnecessary suffering or injury to health (including injury to or loss of sight, or hearing, or limb, or organ of the body, and any mental derangement), that person shall be guilty of a misdemeanor, and shall be liable— **4-001**

(a) on conviction on indictment, to a fine [...][2] or alternatively, [...][3], or in addition thereto, to imprisonment for any term not exceeding [ten][4] years;

(b) on summary conviction, to a fine not exceeding [£400][5] pounds, or alternatively, [...][6], or in addition thereto, to imprisonment for any term not exceeding six months.

(2) For the purposes of this section—

(a) a parent or other person legally liable to maintain a child or young person [, or the legal guardian of a child or young person,][7] shall be deemed to have neglected him in a manner likely to cause injury to his health if he has failed to provide adequate food, clothing, medical aid or lodging for him, or if, having been unable otherwise to provide such food, clothing, medical aid or lodging, he has failed to take steps to procure it to be provided under [the enactments applicable in that behalf][8];

(b) where it is proved that the death of an infant under three years of age was caused by suffocation (not being suffocation caused by disease or the presence of any foreign body in the throat or air passages of the infant) while the infant was in bed with some other person who has attained the age of sixteen years, that other person shall, if he was, when he went to bed, under the influence of drink, be deemed to have neglected the infant in a manner likely to cause injury to its health.

(3) A person may be convicted of an offence under this section—

[1] Words substituted by Children Act 1989 c.41 Sch 13 para 2
[2] Words repealed by Children Act 1975 c.72 Sch 4 Pt III
[3] Words repealed by Children and Young Persons Act 1963 c.37 s 64 Sch 5
[4] Words substituted by Criminal Justice Act 1988 c.33 s 45 (1) (2)
[5] Words substituted by Children Act 1975 c.72 Sch 3 para 1
[6] Words repealed by Children and Young Persons Act 1963 c.37 s 64 Sch 5
[7] Words inserted by Children Act 1989 c.41 Sch 12 para 2
[8] Words substituted by S.I. 1951/174 (1951 I, p. 1369), Sch

(a) notwithstanding that actual suffering or injury to health, or the likelihood of actual suffering or injury to health, was obviated by the action of another person;

(b) notwithstanding the death of the child or young person in question.

(4) [...][1]

(5) [...][2]

(6) [...][3]

(7) Nothing in this section shall be construed as affecting the right of any parent, [or (subject to section 548 of the Education Act 1996) any other person,][4] having the lawful control or charge of a child or young person to administer punishment to him.

Supplemental

[Interpretation of Part I

4-002 **17.**—(1) For the purposes of this Part of this Act, the following shall be presumed to have responsibility for a child or young person—

(a) any person who—

(i) has parental responsibility for him (within the meaning of the Children Act 1989); or

(ii) is otherwise legally liable to maintain him; and

(b) any person who has care of him.

(2) A person who is presumed to be responsible for a child or young person by virtue of subsection (1)(a) shall not be taken to have ceased to be responsible for him by reason only that he does not have care of him.][5]

Law Reform (Married Women and Tortfeasors) Act 1935

(25 AND 26 GEO. 5 C. 30)

PART I

CAPACITY, PROPERTY, AND LIABILITIES OF MARRIED WOMEN; AND LIABILITIES OF HUSBANDS

Capacity of married women

5-001 **1.** Subject to the provisions of this Part of this Act, [...][6] a married woman shall—

(a) be capable of acquiring, holding, and disposing of, any property; and

(b) be capable of rendering herself, and being rendered, liable in respect of any tort, contract, debt, or obligation; and

[1] Repealed by Criminal Law Act 1967 c.58 s 12 Sch 3 Pt III
[2] Repealed by Criminal Justice Act 1988 c.33 s 170 (2) Sch 16
[3] Repealed by Criminal Justice Act 1988 c.33 s 170 (2) Sch 16
[4] Words substituted by School Standards and Framework Act 1998 c.31 Sch 30 para 1
[5] Substituted by Children Act 1989 c.41 Sch 13 para 5
[6] Words repealed by Law Reform (Husband and Wife) Act 1962 c.48 Sch 1

(c) be capable of suing and being sued, either in tort or in contract or otherwise; and

(d) be subject to the law relating to bankruptcy and to the enforcement of judgments and orders,

in all respects as if she were a feme sole.

Property of married women

2.—(1) Subject to the provisions of this Part of this Act all property which— **5-002**

(a) immediately before the passing of this Act was the separate property of a married woman or held for her separate use in equity; or

(b) belongs at the time of her marriage to a woman married after the passing of this Act; or

(c) after the passing of this Act is acquired by or devolves upon a married woman,

shall belong to her in all respects as if she were a feme sole and may be disposed of accordingly:[...][1]

(2) [...][2]

(3) [...][3]

Abolition of husband's liability for wife's torts and ante-nuptial contracts debts and obligations

3. Subject to the provisions of this Part of this Act, the husband of a married **5-003**
woman shall not, by reason only of his being her husband, be liable—

(a) in respect of any tort committed by her whether before or after the marriage, or in respect of any contract entered into, or debt or obligation incurred, by her before the marriage; or

(b) to be sued, or made a party to any legal proceeding brought, in respect of any such tort, contract, debt, or obligation.

Marriage Act 1949

(12 AND 13 GEO. 6 C. 76)

PART I

RESTRICTIONS ON MARRIAGE

Marriages within prohibited degrees

1.—(1) A marriage solemnized between a man and any of the persons **6-001**
mentioned in the first column of Part I of the First Schedule to this Act, or between a woman and any of the persons mentioned in the second column of the said Part I, shall be void.

[(2) Subject to subsection (3) of this section, a marriage solemnized between a man and any of the persons mentioned in the first column of Part II of the First

---

[1] Words repealed by Married Women (Restraint upon Anticipation) Act 1949 c.78 s 1 Sch 2

[2] Repealed by Married Women (Restraint upon Anticipation) Act 1949 c.78 s 1 Sch 2

[3] Repealed by Married Women (Restraint upon Anticipation) Act 1949 c.78 s 1 Sch 2

Schedule to this Act, or between a woman and any of the persons mentioned in the second column of the said Part II, shall be void.

(3) Any such marriage as is mentioned in subsection (2) of this section shall not be void by reason only of affinity if both the parties to the marriage have attained the age of twenty-one at the time of the marriage and the younger party has not at any time before attaining the age of eighteen been a child of the family in relation to the other party.

(4) Subject to subsection (5) of this section, a marriage solemnized between a man and any of the persons mentioned in the first column of Part III of the First Schedule to this Act or between a woman and any of the persons mentioned in the second column of the said Part III shall be void.

(5) Any such marriage as is mentioned in subsection (4) of this section shall not be void by reason only of affinity if both the parties to the marriage have attained the age of twenty-one at the time of the marriage and the marriage is solemnized—

(a) in the case of a marriage between a man and the mother of a former wife of his, after the death of both the former wife and the father of the former wife;

(b) in the case of a marriage between a man and the former wife of his son, after the death of both his son and the mother of his son;

(c) in the case of a marriage between a woman and the father of a former husband of hers, after the death of both the former husband and the mother of the former husband;

(d) in the case of a marriage between a woman and a former husband of her daughter, after the death of both of her daughter and the father of her daughter.][1]

Marriages of persons under sixteen

6-002 **2.** A marriage solemnized between persons either of whom is under the age of sixteen shall be void.

Marriages of persons under twenty-one

6-003 **3.**—(1) Where the marriage of [a child][2], not being a widower or widow, is intended to be solemnized on the authority of [certificates][3] issued by a superintendent registrar under Part III of this Act, [...][4]the consent of the person or persons specified in [subsection (1A) of this section][5] shall be required [...][6]:

Provided that—

(a) if the superintendent registrar is satisfied that the consent of any person whose consent is so required cannot be obtained by reason of absence or inaccessibility or by reason of his being under any disability, the necessity for the consent of that person shall be dispensed with, if there is any other person whose consent is also required; and if the consent of no other person is required, the Registrar General may dispense with the necessity of obtaining any consent, or the court may, on application being made, consent to the marriage, and the consent of

[1] Inserted by Marriage (Prohibited Degrees of Relationship) Act 1986 c.16 s 1 (6) Sch 1 para 2
[2] Words substituted by Family Law Reform Act 1987 c.42 ss 33 (1), 34 (2) (5) Sch 2 para 9
[3] Words substituted by Immigration and Asylum Act 1999 c.33 Sch 14 para 4 (a)
[4] Words repealed by Immigration and Asylum Act 1999 c.33 Sch 16 para 1
[5] Words substituted by Children Act 1989 c.41 Sch 12 para 5 (1)
[6] Words repealed by Children Act 1989 c.41 Sch 15 para 1

the court so given shall have the same effect as if it had been given by the person whose consent cannot be so obtained;

(b) if any person whose consent is required refuses his consent, the court may, on application being made, consent to the marriage, and the consent of the court so given shall have the same effect as if it had been given by the person whose consent is refused.

[(1A) The consents are—

(a) subject to paragraphs (b) to (d) of this subsection, the consent of—

(i) each parent (if any) of the child who has parental responsibility for him; and

(ii) each guardian (if any) of the child;

(b) where a residence order is in force with respect to the child, the consent of the person or persons with whom he lives, or is to live, as a result of the order (in substitution for the consents mentioned in paragraph (a) of this subsection);

(c) where a care order is in force with respect to the child, the consent of the local authority designated in the order (in addition to the consents mentioned in paragraph (a) of this subsection);

(d) where neither paragraph (b) nor (c) of this subsection applies but a residence order was in force with respect to the child immediately before he reached the age of sixteen, the consent of the person or persons with whom he lived, or was to live, as a result of the order (in substitution for the consents mentioned in paragraph (a) of this subsection).

(1B) In this section 'guardian of a child', 'parental responsibility', 'residence order' and 'care order' have the same meaning as in the Children Act 1989.][1]

(2) The last foregoing subsection shall apply to marriages intended to be solemnized on the authority of a common licence, with the substitution of references to the ecclesiastical authority by whom the licence was granted for references to the superintendent registrar, and with the substitution of a reference to the Master of the Faculties for the reference to the Registrar General.

(3) Where the marriage of [a child][2], not being a widower or widow, is intended to be solemnized after the publications of banns of matrimony then, if any person whose consent to the marriage would have been required under this section in the case of a marriage intended to be solemnized otherwise than after the publication of the banns, openly and publicly declares or causes to be declared, in the church or chapel in which the banns are published, at the time of the publication, his dissent from the intended marriage, the publication of banns shall be void.

(4) A clergyman shall not be liable to ecclesiastical censure for solemnizing the marriage of [a child][3] after the publication of banns without the consent of the parents or guardians of [the child][4] unless he had notice of the dissent of any person who is entitled to give notice of dissent under the last foregoing subsection.

[1] Inserted by Children Act 1989 c.41 Sch 12 para 5 (2)
[2] Words substituted by Family Law Reform Act 1987 c.42 ss 33 (1), 34 (2), (5) Sch 2 para 9
[3] Words substituted by Family Law Reform Act 1987 c.42 ss 33 (1), 34 (2), (5) Sch 2 para 9
[4] Words substituted by Family Law Reform Act 1987 c.42 ss 33 (1), 34 (2), (5) Sch 2 para 9

(5) For the purposes of this section, "the court" means the High Court, [the county court of the district in which any applicant or respondent resides][1], or a court of summary jurisdiction [[appointed for the commission area [...][2]][3][...][4] in which any applicant or respondent resides][5], and rules of court may be made for enabling applications under this section—

(a) if made to the High Court, to be heard in chambers;

(b) if made to the county court, to be heard and determined by the registrar subject to appeal to the judge;

(c) if made to a court of summary jurisdiction, to be heard and determined otherwise than in open court.

and shall provide that, where an application is made in consequence of a refusal to give consent, notice of the application shall be served on the person who has refused consent.

(6) Nothing in this section shall dispense with the necessity of obtaining the consent of the High Court to the marriage of a ward of court.

Hours for solemnization of marriages

6-004 **4.** A marriage may be solemnized at any time between the hours of eight in the forenoon and six in the afternoon.

PART II

MARRIAGE ACCORDING TO RITES OF THE CHURCH OF ENGLAND

Preliminary

Methods of authorising marriages

6-005 **5.** A marriages according to the rites of the Church of England may be solemnized—

(a) after the publication of banns of matrimony;

(b) on the authority of a special licence of marriage granted by the Archbishop of Canterbury or any other person by virtue of the Ecclesiastical Licences Act, 1533 (in this Act referred to as a "special licence");

(c) on the authority of a licence of marriage (other than a special licence) granted by an ecclesiastical authority having power to grant such a licence (in this Act referred to as a "common licence"); or

(d) on the authority of [certificates][6] issued by a superintendent registrar under Part III of this Act.

[except that paragraph (a) of this section shall not apply in relation to the solemnization of any marriage mentioned in subsection (2) of section 1 of this Act.][7]

[1] Words substituted by Family Law Reform Act 1969 c.46 s 2 (2)
[2] Words repealed by Access to Justice Act 1999 c.22 Sch 15 (V) (1) para 1
[3] Words substituted by Domestic Proceedings and Magistrates' Courts Act 1978 c.22 s 89 (2) (a) Sch 2 para 9
[4] Words repealed by Access to Justice Act 1999 c.22 Sch 15 (V) (1) para 1
[5] Words inserted by Family Law Reform Act 1969 c.46 s 2 (2)
[6] Word substituted by Immigration and Asylum Act 1999 c.33 Sch 14 para 5
[7] Words inserted by Marriage (Prohibited Degrees of Relationship) Act 1986 c.16 s 1 (4), (6) Sch 1 para 3

[Marriages between certain persons related by affinity

5A. No clergyman shall be obliged— **6-006**

(a) to solemnize a marriage which, apart from the Marriage (Prohibited Degrees of Relationship) Act 1986, would have been void by reason of the relationship of the persons to be married; or

(b) to permit such a marriage to be solemnized in the church or chapel of which he is the minister.][1]

Marriage by banns

Place of publication of banns

6.—(1) Subject to the provisions of this Act, where a marriage is intended to be solemnized after the publication of banns of matrimony, the banns shall be published— **6-007**

(a) if the persons to be married reside in the same parish, in the parish church of that parish;

(b) if the persons to be married do not reside in the same parish, in the parish church of each parish in which one of them resides:

Provided that if either of the persons to be married resides in a chapelry or in a district specified in a licence granted under section twenty of this Act, the banns may be published in an authorised chapel of that chapelry or district instead of in the parish church of the parish in which that person resides.

(4) Banns of matrimony may be published in any parish church or authorised chapel which is the usual place of worship of the persons to be married or of one of them although neither of those persons resides in the parish or chapelry to which the church or chapel belongs:

Provided that the publication of banns by virtue of this subsection shall be in addition to and not in substitution for the publication of banns required by subsection (1) of this section.

Time and manner of publication of banns

7.—(1) Subject to the provisions of section nine of this Act, banns of matrimony shall be published on three Sundays preceding the solemnization of the marriage during morning service or, if there is no morning service on a Sunday on which the banns are to be published, during evening service. **6-008**

(2) Banns of matrimony shall be published in an audible manner and in accordance with the form of words prescribed by the rubric prefixed to the office of matrimony in the Book of Common Prayer, and all the other rules prescribed by the said rubric concerning the publication of banns and the solemnization of matrimony shall, so far as they are consistent with the provisions of this Part of this Act, be duly observed.

(3) The parochial church council of a parish shall provide for every church and chapel in the parish in which marriages may be solemnized, a register book of banns made of durable materials and marked in the manner directed by section fifty-four of this Act for the register book of marriages, and all banns shall be published from the said register book of banns by the officiating clergyman, and not from loose papers, and after each publication the entry in the register book shall be signed by the officiating clergyman, or by some person under his direction.

[1] Inserted by Marriage (Prohibited Degrees ofRelationship) Act 1986 c.16 s 3

Notice to clergyman before publication of banns

6-009 **8.** No clergyman shall be obliged to publish banns of matrimony unless the persons to be married, at least seven days before the date on which they wish the banns to be published for the first time, deliver or cause to be delivered to him a notice in writing, dated on the day on which it is so delivered, stating the christian name and surname and the place of residence of each of them, and the period during which each of them has resided at his or her place of residence.

Persons by whom banns may be published

6-010 **9.**—(1) Subject to the provisions of this section and of section fourteen of this Act, it shall not be lawful for any person other than a clergyman to publish banns of matrimony.

(2) Where on any Sunday in any church or other building in which banns of matrimony may be published a clergyman does not officiate at the service at which it is usual in that church or building to publish banns, the banns may be published—

(a) by a clergyman at some other service at which banns of matrimony may be published; or

(b) by a layman during the course of a public reading authorised by the bishop of the diocese of a portion or portions of the service of morning or evening prayer, the public reading being at the hour when the service at which it is usual to publish banns is commonly held or at such other hour as the bishop may authorise;

Provided that banns shall not be published by a layman unless the incumbent or minister in charge of the said church or building, or some other clergyman nominated in that behalf by the bishop, has made or authorised to be made the requisite entry in the register book of banns of the said church or building.

(3) Where a layman publishes banns of matrimony by virtue of this section the layman shall sign the register book of banns provided under section seven of this Act and for that purpose shall be deemed to be the officiating clergyman within the meaning of that section.

Solemnization of marriage after publication of banns

6-011 **12.**—(1) Subject to the provisions of this Part of this Act, where banns of matrimony have been published, the marriage shall be solemnized in the church or chapel or, as the case may be, one of the churches or chapels in which the banns have been published.

(2) Where a marriage is not solemnized within three months after the completion of the publication of the banns, that publication shall be void and no clergyman shall solemnize the marriage on the authority thereof.

Marriage by Common Licence

Places in which marriages may be solemnized by common licence

6-012 **15.**—(1) Subject to the provisions of this Part of this Act, a common licence shall not be granted for the solemnization of a marriage in any church or chapel other than—

(a) the parish church of the parish, or an authorised chapel of the ecclesiastical district, in which one of the persons to be married has had his or her usual place of residence for fifteen days immediately before the grant of the licence; or

(b) a parish church or authorised chapel which is the usual place of worship of the persons to be married or of one of them.

(2) For the purposes of this section, any parish in which there is no parish church or chapel belonging thereto or no church or chapel in which divine service is usually solemnized every Sunday, and any extra-parochial place which has no authorised chapel, shall be deemed to belong to any adjoining parish or chapelry.

Provisions as to common licences

16.—(1) A common licence shall not be granted unless one of the persons to be married has sworn before a person having authority to grant such a licence— **6-013**

(a) that he or she believes that there is no impediment of kindred or alliance or any other lawful cause, nor any suit commenced in any court, to bar or hinder the solemnization of the marriage in accordance with the licence;

(b) that one of the persons to be married has had his or her usual place of residence in the parish or other ecclesiastical district in which the marriage is to be solemnized for fifteen days immediately before the grant of the licence or that the parish church or authorised chapel in which the marriage is to be solemnized is the usual place of worship of those persons or of one of them;

(c) where one of the persons to be married is [a child][1] and is not a widower or widow, that the consent of the person or persons whose consent to the marriage is required under section three of this Act has been obtained, that the necessity of obtaining any such consent has been dispensed with under that section, that the court has consented to the marriage under that section, or that there is no person whose consent to the marriage is so required.

[(1A) A common licence shall not be granted for the solemnization of a marriage mentioned in subsection (2) of section 1 of this Act unless—

(a) the person having authority to grant the licence is satisfied by the production of evidence that both the persons to be married have attained the age of twenty-one; and

(b) he has received a declaration in writing made by each of those persons specifying their affinal relationship and declaring that the younger of those persons has not at any time before attaining the age of eighteen been a child of the family in relation to the other.

(1B) In the case of a marriage mentioned insubsection (4) of section 1 of this Act which by virtue of subsection (5) of that section is valid only if at the time of the marriage both the parties to the marriage have attained the age of twenty-one and the death has taken place of two other persons related to those parties in the manner mentioned in the said subsection (5), a common licence shall not be granted for the solemnization of the marriage unless the person having authority to grant the licence is satisfied by the production of evidence—

(a) that both the parties to the marriage have attained the age of twenty-one; and

(b) that both those other persons are dead.][2]

---

[1] Words substituted by Family Law Reform Act 1987 c.42 ss 33 (1), 34 (2) (5) Sch 2 para 9

[2] Inserted by Marriage (Prohibited Degrees of Relationship) Act 1986 c.16 s 1 (4) (6) Sch 1 para 4 (a)

(2) [Subject to subsection (2A) of this section][1] if any caveat is entered against the grant of a common licence, the caveat having been duly signed by or on behalf of the person by whom it is entered and stating his place of residence and the ground of objection on which the caveat is founded, no licence shall be granted until the caveat or a copy thereof is transmitted to the ecclesiastical judge out of whose office the licence is to issue, and the judge has certified to the registrar of the diocese that he has examined into the matter of the caveat and is satisfied that it ought not to obstruct the grant of the licence, or until the caveat is withdrawn by the person who entered it.

[(2A) Where in the case of a marriage mentioned in subsection (2) of section 1 of this Act a caveat is entered under subsection (2) of this section on the ground that the persons to be married have not both attained the age of twenty-one or that one of those persons has at any time before attaining the age of eighteen been a child of the family in relation to the other, then, notwithstanding that the caveat is withdrawn by the person who entered it, no licence shall be issued unless the judge has certified that he has examined into that ground of objection and is satisfied that that ground ought not to obstruct the grant of the licence.

(2B) In the case of a marriage mentioned in subsection (2) of section 1 of this Act, one of the persons to be married may apply to the ecclesiastical judge out of whose office the licence is to issue for a declaration that, both those persons having attained the age of twenty-one and the younger of those persons not having at any time before attaining the age of eighteen been a child of the family in relation to the other, there is no impediment of affinity to the solemnization of the marriage; and where any such declaration is obtained the common licence may be granted notwithstanding that no declaration has been made under the said subsection (1A).][2]

(3) Where a marriage is not solemnized within three months after the grant of a common licence, the licence shall be void and no clergyman shall solemnize the marriage on the authority thereof.

Marriage under superintendent registrar's certificate

Marriage under superintendent registrar's certificate

6-014 **17.** A marriage according to the rites of the Church of England may be solemnized on the authority of [certificates][3] of a superintendent registrar in force under Part III of this Act in any church or chapel in which banns of matrimony may be published [or in the case of a marriage in pursuance of section 26(1)(dd) of this Act the place specified in the [notices of marriage and certificates][4] as the place where the marriage is to be solemnized][5]:

Provided that a marriage shall not be solemnized as aforesaid in any such church or chapel without the consent of the minister thereof [(wherever the marriage is solemnized)][6] or by any person other than a clergyman.

[1] Words inserted by Marriage (Prohibited Degrees of Relationship) Act 1986 c.16 s 1(4) (6) Sch 1 para 4(b)

[2] Inserted by Marriage (Prohibited Degrees of Relationship) Act 1986 c.16 s 1 (4) (6) Sch 1 para 4 (c)

[3] Words substituted by Immigration and Asylum Act 1999 c.33 Sch 14 para 6 (a)

[4] Words substituted by Immigration and Asylum Act 1999 c.33 Sch 14 para 6 (b)

[5] Words inserted by Marriage Act 1983 c.32 s 1 (7) Sch 1 para 2 (a)

[6] Words inserted by Marriage Act 1983 c.32 s 1 (7) Sch 1 para 2 (b)

Miscellaneous Provisions

Witnesses

22. All marriages solemnized according to the rites of the Church of England shall be solemnized in the presence of two or more witnesses in addition to the clergyman by whom the marriage is solemnized. 6-015

Void marriages

25. If any persons knowingly and wilfully intermarry according to the rites of the Church of England (otherwise than by special licence)— 6-016

(a) [except in the case of a marriage in pursuance of section 26(1)(dd) of this Act,][1] in any place other than a church or other building in which banns may be published;

(b) without banns having been duly published, a common licence having been obtained, or [certificates][2] having been duly issued under Part III of this Act by a superintendent registrar to whom due notice of marriage has been given; or

(c) on the authority of a publication of banns which is void by virtue of subsection (3) of section three or subsection (2) of section twelve of this Act, on the authority of a common licence which is void by virtue of subsection (3) of section sixteen of this Act, or on the authority of [certificates of a superintendent registrar which are][3] void by virtue of subsection (2) of section thirty-three of this Act;

(d) in the case of a marriage on the authority of [certificates][4] of a superintendent registrar, in any place other than the church [building or other place specified in the [notices of marriage and certificates][5] as the place where the marriage is to be solemnized][6];

or if they knowingly and wilfully consent to or acquiesce in the solemnization of the marriage by any person who is not in Holy Orders, the marriage shall be void.

PART III

MARRIAGE UNDER SUPERINTENDENT REGISTRAR'S CERTIFICATE

Issue of certificates

Marriages which may be solemnized on authority of superintendent registrar's certificate

26.—(1) Subject to the provisions of this Part of this Act, the following marriages may be solemnized on the authority of [two certificates][7] of a superintendent registrar— 6-017

[1] Words inserted by Marriage Act 1983 c.32 s 1 (7) Sch 1 para 3 (a)
[2] Words substituted by Immigration and Asylum Act 1999 c.33 Sch 14 para 7 (a)
[3] Words substituted by Immigration and Asylum Act 1999 c.33 Sch 14 para 7 (b)
[4] Words substituted by Immigration and Asylum Act 1999 c.33 Sch 14 para 7 (c)
[5] Words substituted by Immigration and Asylum Act 1999 c.33 Sch 14 para 7 (c)
[6] Words substituted by Marriage Act 1983 c.32 s 1 (7) Sch 1 para 3 (b)
[7] Words substituted by Immigration and Asylum Act 1999 c.33 Pt IX s 161 (3)

(a) a marriage in a registered building according to such form and ceremony as the persons to be married see fit to adopt;
(b) a marriage in the office of a superintendent registrar:
[(bb) a marriage on approved premises;][1]
(c) a marriage according to the usages of the Society of Friends (commonly called Quakers);
(d) a marriage between two persons professing the Jewish religion according to the usages of the Jews;
[(dd) the marriage (other than a marriage in pursuance of paragraph (c) or (d) above) of a person who is house-bound or is a detained person at the place where he or she usually resides;][2]
(e) a marriage according to the rites of the Church of England [in any church or chapel in which banns of matrimony may be published][3].

(2) [...][4]

Notice of marriage

6-018 **27.**—(1) Where a marriage is intended to be solemnized on the authority of [certificates][5] of a superintendent registrar [...][6], notice of marriage in the prescribed form shall be given—
(a) if the persons to be married have resided in the same registration district for the period of seven days immediately before the giving of the notice, by [each][7] of those persons to the superintendent registrar of that district;
(b) if the persons to be married have not resided in the same registration district for the said period of seven days as aforesaid, by [each][8] of those persons to the superintendent registrar of [the registration district in which he or she has resided][9] for that period.

(2) [...][10]

(3) A notice of marriage shall state the name and surname, marital status, occupation [, place of residence and nationality][11] of each of the persons to be married and [in the case of a marriage intended to be solemnized at a person's residence in pursuance of section 26(1)(dd) of this Act, which residence is to be the place of solemnization of the marriage and, in any other case,][12] [the church or other building or premises in or on which][13] the marriage is to be solemnized and—
(a) [...][14] shall state the period, not being less than seven days, during which each of the persons to be married has resided in his or her place of residence;

---

[1] Added by Marriage Act 1994 c.34 s 1 (1)
[2] Inserted by Marriage Act 1983 c.32 s 1 (7) Sch 1 para 4 (a)
[3] Words inserted by Marriage Act 1983 c.32 s 1 (7) Sch 1 para 4 (a)
[4] Repealed by Immigration and Asylum Act 1999 c.33 Sch 16 para 1
[5] Words substituted by Immigration and Asylum Act 1999 c.33 Sch 14 para 8
[6] Words repealed by Immigration and Asylum Act 1999 c.33 Sch 16 para 1
[7] Word substituted by Immigration and Asylum Act 1999 c.33 Pt IX s 161 (1) (a)
[8] Words substituted by Immigration and Asylum Act 1999 c.33 Pt IX s 161 (1) (b)
[9] Words substituted by Immigration and Asylum Act 1999 c.33 Pt IX s 161 (1) (b)
[10] Repealed by Immigration and Asylum Act 1999 c.33 Sch 16 para 1
[11] Words substituted by Immigration and Asylum Act 1999 c.33 Pt IX s 161 (2)
[12] Words inserted by Marriage Act 1983 c.32 s 1 (7) Sch 1 para 5 (a)
[13] Words substituted by Marriage Act 1994 c.34 Sch 1 para 2
[14] Words repealed by Immigration and Asylum Act 1999 c.33 Sch 16 para 1

(b) [...][1] Provided that if either of the persons to be married has resided in the place stated in the notice for more than one month, the notice may state that he or she has resided there for more than one month.

(4) The superintendent registrar shall file all notices of marriage and keep them with the records of his office, and shall [subject to section 27A of this Act][2] also forthwith enter the particulars given in every such notice, together with the date of the notice and the name of the person by whom the notice was given, in a book (in this Act referred to as "the marriage notice book") furnished to him for that purpose by the Registrar General, and the marriage notice book shall be open for inspection free of charge at all reasonable hours.

(5) If the persons to be married wish to be married in the presence of a registrar in a registered building for which an authorised person has been appointed, they shall, at the time when notice of marriage is given to the superintendent registrar under this section, give notice to him that they require a registrar to be present at the marriage.

[Additional information required in certain cases

27A.—(1) This section applies in relation to any marriage intended to be solemnized at a person's residence in pursuance of section 26(1)(dd) of this Act, and in the following provisions of this section that person is referred to as "the relevant person". **6-019**

(2) Where the relevant person is not a detained person, [each notice][3] of marriage required by section 27 of this Act shall be accompanied by a medical statement relating to that person made not more than fourteen days before the date on which the notice is given.

(3) Where the relevant person is a detained person, [each notice][4] of marriage required by section 27 of this Act shall be accompanied by a statement made in the prescribed form by the responsible authority not more than twenty-one days before the date on which notice of the marriage is given under section 27—

(a) identifying the establishment where the person is detained; and

(b) stating that the responsible authority has no objection to that establishment being specified in the notice of marriage as the place where that marriage is to be solemnized.

(4) [Each person][5] who gives notice of the marriage to the superintendent registrar in accordance with section 27 of this Act shall given the superintendent registrar the prescribed particulars, in the prescribed form, of the person by or before whom the marriage is intended to be solemnized.

(5) The superintendent registrar shall not enter the particulars given in the notice of the marriage in the marriage notice book until he has received the statement and the particulars required by subsections (2) or (3) and (4) of this section.

(6) The fact that a superintendent registrar has received a statement under subsection (2) or (as the case may be) (3) of this section shall be entered in the marriage notice book together with the particulars given in the notice of marriage and any such statement together with the form received under subsection (4) of this section shall be filed and kept with the records of the office

[1] Repealed by Immigration and Asylum Act 1999 c.33 Sch 16 para 1
[2] Words inserted by Marriage Act 1983 c.32 s 1 (7) Sch 1 para 5 (b)
[3] Words substituted by Immigration and Asylum Act 1999 c.33 Sch 14 para 9 (a)
[4] Words substituted by Immigration and Asylum Act 1999 c.33 Sch 14 para 9 (a)
[5] Words substituted by Immigration and Asylum Act 1999 c.33 Sch 14 para 9 (b)

of the superintendent register or, where notice of marriage is required to be given to two superintendent registrars, of [each][1] of them.

(7) In this section—

"medical statement", in relation to any person, means a statement made in the prescribed form by a registered medical practitioner that in his opinion at the time the statement is made—

(a) by reason of illness or disability, he or she ought not to move or be moved from the place where he or she is at that time, and

(b) it is likely that it will be the case for at least the following three months that by reason of the illness or disability he or she ought not to move or be moved from that place; and

"registered medical practitioner" has the meaning given by Schedule 1 to the Interpretation Act 1978; and

"responsible authority" means—

(a) if the person is detained in a hospital (within the meaning of Part II of the Mental Health Act 1983), the managers of that hospital (within the meaning of section 145(1) of that Act); or

(b) if the person is detained in a prison or other place to which the Prison Act 1952 applies, the governor or other officer for the time being in charge of that prison or other place.][2]

[Provisions relating to section 1(3) marriages

6-020 **27B.**—(1) This section applies in relation to any marriage mentioned in subsection (2) of section 1 of this Act which is intended to be solemnized on the authority of [certificates][3] of a superintendent registrar.

(2) The superintendent registrar shall not enter notice of the marriage in the marriage notice book unless—

(a) he is satisfied by the production of evidence that both the persons to be married have attained the age of twenty-one; and

(b) he has received a declaration made in the prescribed form by each of those persons, each declaration having been signed and attested in the prescribed manner, specifying their affinal relationship and declaring that the younger of those persons has not at any time before attaining the age of eighteen been a child of the family in relation to the other.

(3) The fact that a superintendent registrar has received a declaration under subsection (2) of this section shall be entered in the marriage notice book together with the particulars given in the notice of marriage and any such declaration shall be filed and kept with the records of the office of the superintendent registrar or, where notice of marriages is required to be given to two superintendent registrars, of each of them.

(4) Where the superintendent registrar receives from some person other than the persons to be married a written statement signed by that person which alleges that the declaration made under subsection (2) of this section is false in a material particular, the superintendent registrar shall not issue a certificate [...][4] unless a declaration is obtained from the High Court under subsection (5) of this section.

[1] Word substituted by Immigration and Asylum Act 1999 c.33 Sch 14 para 9 (c)
[2] Inserted by Marriage Act 1983 c.32 s 1(7) Sch 1 para 6
[3] Words substituted by Immigration and Asylum Act 1999 c.33 Sch 14 para 10 (a)
[4] Words repealed by Immigration and Asylum Act 1999 c.33 Sch 16 para 1

(5) Either of the persons to be married may, whether or not any statement has been received by the superintendent registrar under subsection (4) of this section, apply to the High Court for a declaration that, both those persons having attained the age of twenty-one and the younger of those persons not having at any time before attaining the age of eighteen been a child of the family in relation to the other, there is no impediment of affinity to the solemnization of the marriage; and where such a declaration is obtained the superintendent registrar may enter notice of the marriage in the marriage notice book and may issue a certificate [...][1] whether or not any declaration has been made under subsection (2) of this section.

(6) Section 29 of this Act shall not apply in relation to a marriage to which this section applies, except so far as a caveat against the issue of a certificate [...][2] for the marriage is entered under that section on a ground other than the relationship of the persons to be married.][3]

[Provisions relating to section 1(5) marriages

27C. In the case of a marriage mentioned in subsection (4) of section 1 of this Act which by virtue of subsection (5) of that section is valid only if at the time of the marriage both the parties to the marriage have attained the age of twenty-one and the death has taken place of two other persons related to those parties in the manner mentioned in the said subsection (5), the superintendent registrar shall not enter notice of the marriage in the marriage notice book unless satisfied by the production of evidence— **6-021**

(a) that both the parties to the marriage have attained the age of twenty-one, and

(b) that both those other persons are dead.][4]

Declaration to accompany notice of marriage

28.—(1) No certificate [...][5] for marriage shall be issued by a superintendent registrar unless the notice of marriage is accompanied by a solemn declaration in writing, in the body or at the foot of the notice, made and signed at the time of the giving of the notice by the person by whom the notice is given and attested as mentioned in subsection (2) of this section— **6-022**

(a) that he or she believes that there is no impediment of kindred or alliance or other lawful hindrance to the marriage;

[(b) that the persons to be married have for the period of 7 days immediately before the giving of the notice had their usual places of residence within the registration district or registration districts in which notice is given;][6]

(c) where one of the persons to be married is [a child][7] and is not a widower or widow, that the consent of the person or persons whose consent to the marriage is required under section three of this Act has been obtained, that the necessity of obtaining any such consent has been dispensed with under that section, that the court has consented to the

[1] Words repealed by Immigration and Asylum Act 1999 c.33 Sch 16 para 1

[2] Words repealed by Immigration and Asylum Act 1999 c.33 Sch 16 para 1

[3] Inserted by Marriage (Prohibited Degrees of Relationship) Act 1986 c.16 s 1 (4) (6) Sch 1 para 5

[4] Inserted by Marriage (Prohibited Degrees of Relationship) Act 1986 c.16 s 1 (4) (6) Sch 1 para 5

[5] Words repealed by Immigration and Asylum Act 1999 c.33 Sch 16 para 1

[6] Substituted by Immigration and Asylum Act 1999 c.33 Sch 14 para 11

[7] Words substituted by Family Law Reform Act 1987 c.42 ss 33 (1), 34 (2) (5) Sch 2 para 9

marriage under that section, or that there is no person whose consent to the marriage is so required.

(2) Any such declaration as aforesaid shall be signed by the person giving the notice of marriage in the presence of the superintendent registrar to whom the notice is given or his deputy, or in the presence of a registrar of births and deaths or of marriages for the registration district in which the person giving the notice resides or his deputy, and that superintendent registrar, deputy superintendent registrar, registrar or deputy registrar, as the case may be, shall attest the declaration by adding thereto his name, description and place of residence.

Marriage under certificate without licence

6-023 **31.**—(1) Where a marriage is intended to be solemnized on the authority of [certificates][1] of a superintendent registrar [...][2], the superintendent registrar to whom notice of marriage has been given shall suspend or affix in some conspicuous place in his office, for [15][3] successive days next after the day on which the notice was entered in the marriage book, the notice of marriage, or an exact copy signed by him of the particulars thereof as entered in the marriage notice book.

(2) At the expiration of the said period of [15][4] days the superintendent registrar, on the request of the person by whom the notice of marriage was given, shall issue a certificate in the prescribed form unless—

[(a) the superintendent registrar is not satisfied that there is no lawful impediment to the issue of the certificate; or][5]

(b) the issue of the certificate has been forbidden under the last foregoing section by any person authorised in that behalf.

(3) Every such certificate shall set out the particulars contained in the notice of marriage and the day on which the notice was entered in the marriage notice book and shall contain a statement that the issue of the certificate has not been forbidden as aforesaid.

(4) No marriage shall be solemnized on the production of [certificates][6] of a superintendent registrar [...][7] until after the expiration of the [waiting period in relation to each notice of marriage][8].

[(4A) "The waiting period", in relation to a notice of marriage, means—

(a) the period of 15 days, or

(b) such shorter period as may be determined by the Registrar General under subsection (5A) or by a superintendent registrar under any provision of regulations made under subsection (5D),

after the day on which the notice of marriage was entered in the marriage notice book.][9]

(5) Where a marriage is to be solemnized in a registered building for which an authorised person has been appointed and no notice requiring a registrar to be present at the marriage has been given to the superintendent registrar under subsection (5) of section twenty-seven of this Act, the superintendent registrar shall, when issuing a certificate under this section, give to [the person by whom

[1] Words substituted by Immigration and Asylum Act 1999 c.33 Sch 14 para 14 (a)
[2] Words repealed by Immigration and Asylum Act 1999 c.33 Sch 16 para 1
[3] Figure substituted by Immigration and Asylum Act 1999 c.33 Pt IX s 160 (4) (a)
[4] Figure substituted by Immigration and Asylum Act 1999 c.33 Pt IX s 160 (4) (b)
[5] Substituted by Immigration and Asylum Act 1999 c.33 Pt IX s 163 (1)
[6] Words substituted by Immigration and Asylum Act 1999 c.33 Sch 14 para 14 (a)
[7] Words repealed by Immigration and Asylum Act 1999 c.33 Sch 16 para 1
[8] Words substituted by Immigration and Asylum Act 1999 c.33 Pt IX s 160 (4) (c)
[9] Added by Immigration and Asylum Act 1999 c.33 Pt IX s 160 (5)

notice of marriage was given][1] printed instructions in the prescribed form for the due solemnization of the marriage.

[(5A) If, on a application made to the Registrar General, he is satisfied that there are compelling reasons for reducing the 15 day period because of the exceptional circumstances of the case, he may reduce that period to such shorter period as he considers appropriate.

(5B) "The 15 day period" means the period of 15 days mentioned in subsections (1) and (2).

(5C) If the Registrar General reduces the 15 day period in a particular case, the reference to 15 days in section 75(3)(a) is to be treated, in relation to that case, as a reference to the reduced period.]

[Appeal on refusal under section 31(2)(a)

31A.—(1) If, relying on section 31(2)(a), a superintendent registrar refuses to issue a certificate, the person applying for it may appeal to the Registrar General. **6-024**

(2) On such an appeal, the Registrar General must—

(a) confirm the refusal; or

(b) direct that a certificate be issued.

(3) If—

(a) relying on section 31(2)(a), a superintendent registrar refuses to issue a certificate as a result of a representation made to him, and

(b) on an appeal against the refusal, the Registrar General declares the representation to have been frivolous and to be such that it ought not to obstruct the issue of a certificate,

the person making the representation is liable for the costs of the proceedings before the Registrar General and for damages recoverable by the applicant for the certificate.

(4) For the purpose of enabling a person to recover any such costs and damages, a copy of the declaration of the Registrar General purporting to be sealed with the seal of the General Register Office is evidence that the Registrar General has declared the representation to have been frivolous and to be such that it ought not to obstruct the issue of a certificate.][2]

32. [...][3] **6-025**

[Period of validity of certificate

33.—(1) A marriage may be solemnized on the authority of certificates of a superintendent registrar at any time within the period which is the applicable period in relation to that marriage. **6-026**

(2) If the marriage is not solemnized within the applicable period—

(a) the notices of marriage and the certificates are void; and

(b) no person may solemnize the marriage on the authority of those certificates.

(3) The applicable period, in relation to a marriage, is the period beginning with the day on which the notice of marriage was entered in the marriage notice book and ending—

(a) in the case of a marriage which is to be solemnized in pursuance of section 26(1)(dd), 37 or 38, on the expiry of three months; and

---

[1] Words substituted by Immigration and Asylum Act 1999 c.33 Sch 14 para 14 (b)

[2] Added by Immigration and Asylum Act 1999 c.33 Pt IX s 163 (2)

[3] Repealed by Immigration and Asylum Act 1999 c.33 Sch 16 para 1

(b) in the case of any other marriage, on the expiry of twelve months.

(4) If the notices of marriage given by each person to be married are not given on the same date, the applicable period is to be calculated by reference to the earlier of the two dates.][1]

[Marriages normally to be solemnized in registration district in which one party resides

6-027 **34.** Subject to section 35, a superintendent registrar may not issue a certificate for the solemnization of a marriage elsewhere than within a registration district in which one of the persons to be married has resided for 7 days immediately before the giving of the notice of marriage.][2]

Marriages in registration district in which neither party resides

6-028 **35.**—(1) A superintendent registrar may issue a certificate [...][3] for the solemnization of a marriage in a registered building which is not within a registration district in which either of the persons to be married resides, where the person giving the notice of marriage declares by endorsement thereon in the prescribed form—

[(a) that the persons to be married desire the marriage to be solemnized according to a specified form, rite or ceremony, being a form, rite or ceremony of a body or denomination of Christians or other persons meeting for religious worship to which one of them professes to belong.][4]

(b) that, to the best of his or her belief, there is not within the registration district in which one of them resides any registered building in which marriage is solemnized according to that form, rite or ceremony;

(c) the registration district nearest to the residence of that person in which there is a registered building in which marriage may be so solemnized; and

(d) the registered building in that district in which the marriage is intended to be solemnized;

and where any such certificate [is issued in respect of each of the persons to be married][5], the marriage may be solemnized in the registered building stated in the notice.

[(2) A superintendent registrar may issue a certificate [...][6]for the solemnization of a marriage in a registered building which is the usual place of worship of the persons to be married, or of one of them, notwithstanding that the building is not within a registration district in which either of those persons resides.][7]

[(2A) A superintendent registrar may issue a certificate [...][8]for the solemnization of a marriage in the office of another superintendent registrar, notwithstanding that the office is not within a registration district in which either of the persons to be married resides.

(2B) A superintendent registrar may issue a certificate [...][9]for the solemnization of a marriage on approved premises, notwithstanding that the premises are

[1] Substituted by Immigration and Asylum Act 1999 c.33 Sch 14 para 15
[2] Substituted by Immigration and Asylum Act 1999 c.33 Sch 14 para 16
[3] Words repealed by Immigration and Asylum Act 1999 c.33 Sch 16 para 1
[4] Substituted by Marriage Act 1949 (Amendment) Act 1954 c.47 s 2
[5] Words substituted by Immigration and Asylum Act 1999 c.33 Sch 14 para 17 (2) (b)
[6] Words repealed by Immigration and Asylum Act 1999 c.33 Sch 16 para 1
[7] Substituted by Marriage Act 1949 (Amendment) Act 1954 c.47 s 1
[8] Words repealed by Immigration and Asylum Act 1999 c.33 Sch 16 para 1
[9] Words repealed by Immigration and Asylum Act 1999 c.33 Sch 16 para 1

not within a registration district in which either of the persons to be married resides.][1]

(3) A superintendent registrar may issue a certificate for the solemnization of a marriage in any parish church or authorised chapel which is the usual place of worship of the persons to be married, or of one of them, notwithstanding that the church or chapel is not within a registration district in which either of those persons resides.

(4) A superintendent registrar may issue a certificate [...][2]for the solemnization of a marriage according to the usages of the Society of Friends or in accordance with the usages of persons professing the Jewish religion, notwithstanding that the building or place in which the marriage is to be solemnized is not within a registration district in which either of the persons to be married resides.

(5) Where a marriage is intended to be solemnized on the authority of [certificates][3] of a superintendent registrar issued under subsection (2) or subsection (3) of this section, [each notice][4] of marriage given to the superintendent registrar and [each certificate][5] issued by the superintendent registrar shall state, in addition to the description of the registered building or, as the case may be, the parish church or authorised chapel, in which the marriage is to be solemnized, that it is the usual place of worship of the persons to be married or of one of them and, in the latter case, shall state the name of the person whose usual place of worship it is.[...][6]

Marriages in registered buildings

Solemnization of marriage in registered building

44.—(1) Subject to the provisions of this section, where [the notices of marriage and certificates][7] issued by a superintendent registrar state that a marriage between the persons named therein is intended to be solemnized in a registered building, the marriage may be solemnized in that building according to such form and ceremony as those persons may see fit to adopt: **6-029**

Provided that no marriage shall be solemnized in any registered building without the consent of the minister or of one of the trustees, owners, deacons or managers thereof, or in the case of a registered building of the Roman Catholic Church, without the consent of the officiating minister thereof.

(2) Subject to the provisions of this section, a marriage solemnized in a registered building shall be solemnized with open doors in the presence of two or more witnesses and in the presence of either—

(a) a registrar of the registration district in which the registered building is situated, or

(b) an authorised person whose name and address have been certified in accordance with the last foregoing section by the trustees or governing body of that registered building or of some other registered building in the same registration district.

1 Added by Marriage Act 1994 c.34 s 2 (1)
2 Words repealed by Immigration and Asylum Act 1999 c.33 Sch 16 para 1
3 Words substituted by Immigration and Asylum Act 1999 c.33 Sch 14 para 17 (5) (a)
4 Words substituted by Immigration and Asylum Act 1999 c.33 Sch 14 para 17 (5) (b)
5 Words substituted by Immigration and Asylum Act 1999 c.33 Sch 14 para 17 (5) (c)
6 Repealed by Immigration and Asylum Act 1999 c.33 Sch 16 para 1
7 Words substituted by Immigration and Asylum Act 1999 c.33 Sch 14 para 23

(3) Where a marriage is solemnized in a registered building each of the persons contracting the marriage shall, in some part of the ceremony and in the presence of the witnesses and the registrar or authorised person, make the following declaration:—

"I do solemnly declare that I know not of any lawful impediment why, I, AB, may not be joined in matrimony to CD"

and each of them shall say to the other:—

"I call upon these persons here present to witness that I, AB, do take thee, CD, to be my lawful wedded wife [or husband]":

Provided that if the marriage is solemnized in the a presence of an authorised person without the presence of a registrar, the persons to be married, instead of saying each to the other the last-mentioned form of words, may say:—

"I, AB, do take thee, CD, to be my wedded wife [or husband]".

[(3A) As an alternative to the declaration set out in subsection (3) of this section the persons contracting the marriage may make the requisite declaration either—

(a) by saying "I declare that I know of no legal reason why I [*name*] may not be joined in marriage to [*name*]"; or

(b) by replying "I am" to the question put to them successively "Are you [*name*] free lawfully to marry [*name*]?";

and as an alternative to the words of contract set out in that subsection the persons to be married may say to each other "I [*name*] take you [*or* thee] [*name*] to be my wedded wife [*or* husband]".][1]

Marriages in register offices

Solemnization of marriage in register office

6-030 **45.**—(1) Where a marriage is intended to be solemnized on the authority of [certificates][2] of a superintendent registrar, the persons to be married may state in the [notices][3] of marriage that they wish to be married in the office of the superintendent registrar or one of the superintendent registrars, as the case may be, to whom notice of marriage is given, and where any such [notices have][4] been given and the [certificates][5] have been issued accordingly, the marriage may be solemnized in the said office, with open doors, in the presence of the superintendent registrar and a registrar of the registration district of that superintendent registrar and in the presence of two witnesses, and the persons to be married shall make the declarations and use the form of words set out in [subsection (3) or (3A)][6] of the last foregoing section in the case of marriages in registered buildings [...][7].

(2) No religious service shall be used at any marriage solemnized in the office of a superintendent registrar.

[1] Substituted by Marriage Ceremony (Prescribed Words) Act 1996 c.34 s 1 (1)
[2] Words substituted by Immigration and Asylum Act 1999 c.33 Sch 14 para 24 (a)
[3] Word substituted by Immigration and Asylum Act 1999 c.33 Sch 14 para 24 (b)
[4] Words substituted by Immigration and Asylum Act 1999 c.33 Sch 14 para 24 (c)
[5] Words substituted by Immigration and Asylum Act 1999 c.33 Sch 14 para 24 (d)
[6] Words added by Marriage Ceremony (Prescribed Words) Act 1996 c.34 s 1 (2) (a)
[7] Words repealed by Marriage Ceremony (Prescribed Words) Act 1996 c.34 s 1 (2)

[Solemnization of certain marriages

45A.—(1) This section applies to marriages solemnized, otherwise that according to the rites of the Church of England, in pursuance of section 26(1)(dd) of this Act at the place where a person usually resides. **6-031**

(2) The marriage may be solemnized according to a relevant form, rite or ceremony in the presence of a registrar of the registration district in which the place where the marriage is solemnized is situated and of two witnesses and each of the persons contracting the marriage shall make the declaration and use the form of words set out in [subsection (3) or (3A) of section 44][1] of this Act in the case of marriages in registered buildings [...][2].

(3) Where the marriages is not solemnized in pursuance of subsection (2) of this section it shall be solemnized in the presence of the superintendent registrar and a registrar of the registration district in which the place where the marriage is solemnized is situated and in the presence of two witnesses, and the persons to be married shall make the declarations and use the form of words set out in [subsection (3) or (3A) of section 44][3] of this Act in the case of marriages in registered buildings [...][4].

(4) No religious service shall be used at any marriage solemnized in the presence of a superintendent registrar.

(5) In subsection (2) of this section a "relevant form, rite or ceremony" means a form, rite or ceremony of a body of persons who meet for religious worship in any registered building being a form, rite or ceremony in accordance with which members of that body are married in any such registered building.][5]

Register office marriage followed by religious ceremony

46.—(1) If the parties to a marriage [solemnized in the presence of a superintendent registrar][6] desire to add the religious ceremony ordained or used by the church or persuasion of which they are members, they may present themselves, after giving notice of their intention so to do, to the clergyman or minister of the church or persuasion of which they are members, and the clergyman or minister, upon the production of a certificate of their marriage before the superintendent registrar and upon the payment of the customary fees (if any), may, if he sees fit, read or celebrate in the church or chapel of which he is the regular minister the marriage service of the church or persuasion to which be belongs or nominate some other minister to do so. **6-032**

(2) Nothing in the reading or celebration of a marriage service under this section shall supersede or invalidate any marriage previously [solemnized in the presence of a superintendent registrar][7], and the reading or celebration shall not be entered as a marriage in any marriage register book kept under Part IV of this Act.

(3) No person who is not entitled to solemnize marriages according to the rites of the Church of England shall by virtue of this section be entitled to read or celebrate the marriage service in any church or chapel of the Church of England.

[1] Words added by Marriage Ceremony (Prescribed Words) Act 1996 c.34 s 1 (2) (a)
[2] Words repealed by Marriage Ceremony (Prescribed Words) Act 1996 c.34 s 1 (2)
[3] Words added by Marriage Ceremony (Prescribed Words) Act 1996 c.34 s 1 (2) (a)
[4] Words repealed by Marriage Ceremony (Prescribed Words) Act 1996 c.34 s 1 (2)
[5] Inserted by Marriage Act 1983 c.32 s 1(7) Sch 1 para 11
[6] Word substituted by Marriage Act 1983 c.32 s 1(7) Sch 1 para 12
[7] Word substituted by Marriage Act 1983 c.32 s 1(7) Sch 1 para 12

[Approval of premises

6-033 **46A.**—(1) The [Chancellor of the Exchequer][1] may by regulations make provision for and in connection with the approval by local authorities of premises for the solemnization of marriages in pursuance of section 26(1)(bb) of this Act

(2) The matters dealt with by the regulations may include—

(a) the kinds of premises in respect of which approvals may be granted;

(b) the procedure to be followed in relation to applications for approval;

(c) the consideration to be taken into account by a local authority in determining whether to approve any premises;

(d) the duration and renewal of approvals;

(e) the conditions that must or may be imposed by a local authority on granting or renewing an approval;

(f) the determination and charging by local authorities of fees in respect of applications for the approval of premises and in respect of the renewal of approvals;

(g) the circumstances in which a local authority must or may revoke an approval;

(h) the review of any decision to refuse an approval or the renewal of an approval, to impose conditions on granting or renewing an approval or to revoke an approval;

(i) the notification to the Registrar General of all approvals granted, renewed or revoked;

(j) the keeping by local authorities of registers of approved premises;

(k) the issue by the Registrar General of guidance supplementing the provision made by the regulations.

(3) In this section "local authority" means a county council, metropolitan district council or London borough council.][2]

[Solemnization of marriage on approved premises

6-034 **46B.**—(1) Any marriage on approved premises in pursuance of section 26(1)(bb) of this Act shall be solemnized in the presence of—

(a) two witnesses, and

(b) the superintendent registrar and a registrar of the registration district in which the premises are situated.

(2) Without prejudice to the width of section 46A(2)(e) of this Act, the [Chancellor of the Exchequer][3] shall exercise his power to provide for the imposition of conditions as there mentioned so as to secure that members of the public are permitted to attend any marriage solemnized on approved premises in pursuance of section 26(1)(bb) of this Act.

(3) Each of the persons contracting such a marriage shall make the declaration and use the form of words set out in [section 44(3) or (3A)][4] of this Act in the case of marriages in registered buildings [...][5].

(4) No religious service shall be used at a marriage on approved premises in pursuance of section 26(1)(bb) of this Act.][6]

[1] Words substituted by SI 1996/273 Sch 2 para 10
[2] Added by Marriage Act 1994 c.34 s 1 (2)
[3] Words substituted by SI 1996/273 Sch 2 para 10
[4] Words added by Marriage Ceremony (Prescribed Words) Act 1996 c.34 s 1 (2) (b)
[5] Words repealed by Marriage Ceremony (Prescribed Words) Act 1996 c.34 s 1 (2)
[6] Added by Marriage Act 1994 c.34 s 1 (2)

Miscellaneous Provisions

Void marriages

49. If any persons knowingly and wilfully intermarry under the provisions of this Part of this Act— **6-035**

(a) without having given due notice of marriage to the superintendent registrar;

(b) without a certificate for marriage having been duly issued [, in respect of each of the persons to be married,][1] by the superintendent registrar to whom notice of marriage was given;

(c) [...][2]

(d) on the authority of [certificates which are][3] void by virtue of subsection (2) of section thirty-three of this Act;

(e) in any place other than the church, chapel, registered building, office or other place specified in the [notices][4] of marriage and [certificates][5] of the superintendent registrar;

[(ee) in the case of a marriage purporting to be in pursuance of section 26(1)(bb) of this Act, on any premises that at the time the marriage is solemnized are not approved premises;][6]

(f) in the case of a marriage in a registered building (not being a marriage in the presence of an authorised person), in the absence of a registrar of the registration district in which the registered building is situated; [...][7]

(g) in the case of a marriage in the office of a superintendent registrar, in the absence of the superintendent registrar or of a registrar of the registration district of that superintendent registrar;[...][8]

[[(gg) in the case of a marriage on approved premises, in the absence of the superintendent registrar of the registration district in which the premises are situated or in the absence of a registrar of that district; or][9]

(h) in the case of a marriage to which section 45A of this Act applies, in the absence of any superintendent registrar or registrar whose presence at that marriage is required by that section;][10]

the marriage shall be void.

PART VI

GENERAL

Offences relating to solemnization of marriages

75.—(1) Any person who knowingly and wilfully— **6-036**

(a) solemnizes a marriage at any other time than between the hours of eight in the forenoon and six in the afternoon (not being a marriage by

[1] Words inserted by Immigration and Asylum Act 1999 c.33 Sch 14 para 27 (a)
[2] Repealed by Immigration and Asylum Act 1999 c.33 Sch 16 para 1
[3] Words substituted by Immigration and Asylum Act 1999 c.33 Sch 14 para 27 (c)
[4] Words substituted by Immigration and Asylum Act 1999 c.33 Sch 14 para 27 (d)
[5] Words substituted by Immigration and Asylum Act 1999 c.33 Sch 14 para 27 (d)
[6] Added by Marriage Act 1994 c.34 Sch 1 para 3 (a)
[7] Word repealed by Marriage Act 1994 c.34 Sch 1 para 3 (b)
[8] Word repealed by Marriage Act 1994 c.34 Sch 1 para 3 (b)
[9] Added by Marriage Act 1994 c.34 Sch 1 para 3 (c)
[10] Inserted by Marriage Act 1983 c.32 s 1(7) Sch 1 para 13

special licence, a marriage according to the usages of the Society of Friends or a marriage between two persons professing the Jewish religion according to the usages of the Jews);

(b) solemnizes a marriage according to the rites of the Church of England without bans of matrimony having been duly published (not being a marriage solemnized on the authority of a special licence, a common licence or [certificates][1] of a superintendent registrar);

(c) solemnizes a marriage according to the said rites (not being a marriage by special licence [or a marriage in pursuance of section 26(1)(dd) of this Act][2]) in any place other than a church or other building in which banns may be published;

(d) solemnizes a marriage according to the said rites falsely pretending to be in Holy Orders;

shall be guilty of felony and shall be liable to imprisonment for a term not exceeding fourteen years.

(2) Any person who knowingly and wilfully—

(a) solemnizes a marriage (not being a marriage by special licence, a marriage according to the usages of the Society of Friends or a marriage between two persons professing the Jewish religion according to the usages of the Jews) in any place other than—

(i) a church or other building in which marriages may be solemnized according to the rites of the Church of England, or

(ii) the registered building [office [approved premises][3] or person's residence specified as the place where the marriage was to be solemnized][4] in the [notices of marriage and certificates][5] required under Part III of this Act;

[(aa) solemnizes a marriage purporting to be in pursuance of section 26(1)(bb) of this Act on premises that are not approved premises;][6]

(b) solemnizes a marriage in any such registered building as aforesaid (not being a marriage in the presence of an authorised person) in the absence of a registrar of the district in which the registered building is situated;

[(bb) solemnizes a marriage in pursuance of section 26(1)(dd) of this Act, otherwise than according to the rites of the Church of England, in the absence of a registrar of the registration district in which the place where the marriage is solemnized is situated;][7]

(c) solemnizes a marriage in the office of a superintendent registrar in the absence of a registrar of the district in which the office is situated;

[(cc) solemnizes a marriage on approved premises in pursuance of section 26(1)(bb) of this Act in the absence of a registrar of the district in which the premises are situated;][8]

1 Words substituted by Immigration and Asylum Act 1999 c.33 Sch 14 para 30 (2)
2 Words inserted by Marriage Act 1983 c.32 s 1 (7) Sch 1 para 20 (a)
3 Words inserted by Marriage Act 1994 c.34 Sch 1 para 7 (a)
4 Words substituted by Marriage Act 1983 c.32 s 1 (7) Sch 1 para 20 (b)
5 Words substituted by Immigration and Asylum Act 1999 c.33 Sch 14 para 30 (3) (a)
6 Added by Marriage Act 1994 c.34 Sch 1 para 7 (b)
7 Inserted by Marriage Act 1983 c.32 s 1 (7) Sch 1 para 20 (c)
8 Added by Marriage Act 1994 c.34 Sch 1 para 7 (c)

(d) solemnizes a marriage on the authority of [certificates][1] of a superintendent registrar [before the expiry of the waiting period in relation to each notice of marriage][2]; or

(e) solemnizes a marriage on the authority of [certificates][3] of a superintendent registrar after the expiration of [the period which is, in relation to that marriage, the applicable period for the purposes of section 33 of this Act][4];

shall be guilty of felony and shall be liable to imprisonment for a term not exceeding five years.

[(2A) In subsection (2)(d) "the waiting period" has the same meaning as in section 31(4A).][5]

(3) A superintendent registrar who knowingly and wilfully—

[(a) issues any certificate for marriage before the expiry of 15 days from the day on which the notice of marriage was entered in the marriage notice book;][6]

(b) issues any certificate [...][7] for marriage after the expiration of [the period which is, in relation to that marriage, the applicable period for the purposes of section 33 of this Act][8];

(c) issues any certificate the issue of which has been forbidden under section thirty of this Act by any person entitled to forbid the issue of such a certificate; or

(d) solemnizes or permits to be solemnized in his office [or, in the case of a marriage in pursuance of [section 26(1)(bb) or (dd)][9] of this Act, in any other place][10] any marriage which is void by virtue of any of the provisions of Part III of this Act;

shall be guilty of felony and shall be liable to imprisonment for a term not exceeding five years.

(4) No prosecution under this section shall be commenced after the expiration of three years from the commission of the offence.

Interpretation

78.—(1) In this Act, except where the context otherwise required, the following expressions have the meanings hereby respectively assigned to them, that is to say— **6-037**

["approved premises" means premises approved in accordance with regulations under section 46A of this Act as premises on which marriages may be solemnized in pursuance of section 26(1)(bb) of this Act;][11]

"authorised chapel" means—

(a) in relation to a chapelry, a chapel of the chapelry in which banns of matrimony could lawfully be published immediately before the passing of the Marriage Act, 1823, or in which banns may be published and marriages may be solemnized by virtue of section

[1] Words substituted by Immigration and Asylum Act 1999 c.33 Sch 14 para 30 (3) (b)
[2] Words substituted by Immigration and Asylum Act 1999 c.33 Sch 14 para 30 (3) (b)
[3] Words substituted by Immigration and Asylum Act 1999 c.33 Sch 14 para 30 (3) (c)
[4] Words substituted by SI 1997/986 Art 2 (4) (a)
[5] Added by Immigration and Asylum Act 1999 c.33 Sch 14 para 30 (4)
[6] Substituted by Immigration and Asylum Act 1999 c.33 Sch 14 para 30 (5)
[7] Words repealed by Immigration and Asylum Act 1999 c.33 Sch 16 para 1
[8] Words substituted by SI 1997/986 Art 2 (4) (b)
[9] Words substituted by Marriage Act 1994 c.34 Sch 1 para 7 (d)
[10] Words inserted by Marriage Act 1983 c.32 s 1(7) Sch 1 para 20 (d)
[11] Definition inserted by Marriage Act 1994 c.34 Sch 1 para 8

two of the Marriages Confirmation Act, 1825, or of an authorisation given under section three of the Marriage Act, 1823;

(b) in relation to an extra-parochial place, a church or chapel of that place in which banns may be published and marriages may be solemnized by virtue of section two of the Marriages Confirmation Act, 1825, or of an authorisation given under section three of the Marriage Act, 1823, or section twenty-one of this Act;

(c) in relation to a district specified in a licence granted under section twenty of this Act, the chapel in which banns may be published and marriages may be solemnized by virtue of that licence;

"authorised person" has the meaning assigned to it by section forty-three of this Act;

"brother" includes a brother of the half blood;

["child of the family", in relation to any person, means a child who has lived in the same household as that person and been treated by that persons as a child of his family][1]

"clergyman" means a clerk in Holy Orders of the Church of England;

"common licence" has the meaning assigned to it by section five of this Act;

"ecclesiastical district," in relation to a district other than a parish, means a district specified in a licence granted under section twenty of this Act, a chapelry or an extra-parochial place;

["child" means a person under the age of eighteen;][2]

"marriage notice book" has the meaning assigned to it by section twenty-seven of this Act;

"parish" means an ecclesiastical parish and includes a district constituted under the Church Building Acts, 1818 to 1884, notwithstanding that the district has not become a new parish by virtue of section fourteen of the New Parishes Act, 1856, or section five of the New Parishes Measure, 1943, being a district to which Acts of Parliament relating to the publication of banns of matrimony and the solemnization of marriages were applied by the said Church Building Acts as if the district had been an ancient parish, and the expression "parish church" shall be construed accordingly;

"prescribed" means prescribed by regulations made under section seventy-four of this Act;

"registered building" means a building registered under Part III of this Act;

"registrar" means a registrar of marriages;

"Registrar General" means the Registrar General of Births, Deaths and Marriages in England;

"registration district" means the district of a superintendent registrar;

"sister" includes a sister of the half blood;

"special licence" has the meaning assigned to it by section five of this Act;

"superintendent registrar" means a superintendent registrar of births, deaths and marriages;

[1] Definition inserted by Marriage (Prohibited Degrees of Relationship) Act 1986 c.16 s 1 (4), (6) Sch 1 para 7

[2] Definition substituted by Family Law Reform Act 1987 c.42 ss 33 (1), 34 (2), (5) Sch 2 para 10 (a)

"trustees or governing body," in relation to Roman Catholic registered buildings, includes a bishop or vicar general of the diocese.[...][1]

(2) Any reference in this Act to the Church of England shall, unless the context otherwise required, be construed as including a reference to the Church in Wales.

[(3) For the purposes of this Act a person is house-bound if—

(a) [each notice][2] of his or her marriage given in accordance with section 27 of this Act is accompanied by a medical statement (within the meaning of section 27A(7) of this Act) made, not more than fourteen days before the date on which that notice was given, in relation to that person; and

(b) he or she is not a detained person.

(4) For the purposes of this Act a person is a detained person if he or she is for the time being detained—

(a) otherwise than by virtue of section 2, 4, 5, 35, 36 or 136 of the Mental Health Act 1983 (short term detentions), as a patient in a hospital; or

(b) in a prison or other place to which the Prison Act 1952 applies,

and in paragraph (a) above "patient" and "hospital" have the same meanings as in Part II of the Mental Health Act 1983.

(5) For the purposes of this Act a person who is house-bound or is a detained a person shall be taken, if he or she would not otherwise be, to be resident and usually resident at the place where he or she is for the time being.][3]

SCHEDULES

Section 1 First SCHEDULE

Kindred and Affinity

Prohibited degrees of relationship

Mother	Father
[Adoptive mother or former adoptive mother][1]	[Adoptive father or former adoptive father][2]
Daughter	Son
[Adoptive daughter or former adoptive daughter][3]	[Adoptive son or former adoptive son][4]
Father's mother	Father's father
Mother's mother	Mother's father
Son's daughter	Son's son
Daughter's daughter	Daughter's son
Sister	Brother
[...][5]	
Father's sister	Father's brother
Mother's sister	Mother's brother

[1] Repealed by Children Act 1989 c.41 Sch 15 para 1
[2] Words substituted by Immigration and Asylum Act 1999 c.33 Sch 14 para 31
[3] Inserted by Marriage Act 1983 c.32 s 1 (7) Sch 1 para 21

Brother's daughter	Brother's son
Sister's daughter	Sister's son

[1] Entry inserted by Children Act 1975 c.72 s 108 (1) (a) Sch 3 para 8
[2] Entry inserted by Children Act 1975 c.72 s 108 (1) (a) Sch 3 para 8
[3] Entry inserted by Children Act 1975 c.72 s 108 (1) (a) Sch 3 para 8
[4] Entry inserted by Children Act 1975 c.72 s 108 (1) (a) Sch 3 para 8
[5] Entries repealed by Marriage (Prohibited Degrees of Relationship) Act 1986 c.16 s 1 (4), (6) Sch 1 para 8 (a)

DEGREES OF AFFINITY REFERRED TO IN SECTION 1(2) AND (3) OF THIS ACT

[Daughter of former wife	Son of former husband
Former wife of father	Former husband of mother
Former wife of father's father	Former husband of father's mother
Former wife of mother's father	Former husband of mother's mother
Daughter of son of former wife	Son of son of former husband
Daughter of daughter of former wife	Son of daughter of former husband][1]

[1] Inserted by Marriage (Prohibited Degrees of Relationship) Act 1986 c.16 s 1 (4), (6) Sch 1 para 8 (b)

DEGREES OF AFFINITY REFERRED TO IN SECTION 1(4) AND (5) OF THIS ACT

[Mother of former wife	Father of former husband
Former wife of son	Former husband of daughter][1]

[1] Inserted by Marriage (Prohibited Degrees of Relationship) Act 1986 c.16 s 1 (4), (6) Sch 1 para 8 (b)

Intestates' Estates Act 1952

(15 AND 16 GEO. 6 AND 1 ELIZ. 2 C. 64)

PART I

AMENDMENTS OF LAW OF INTESTATE SUCCESSION

Rights of surviving spouse as respects the matrimonial home

7-001 **5.** The Second Schedule to this Act shall have effect for enabling the surviving husband or wife of a person dying intestate after the commencement of this Act to acquire the matrimonial home.

SCHEDULES

Section 5 Second SCHEDULE

RIGHTS OF SURVIVING SPOUSE AS RESPECTS THE MATRIMONIAL HOME

1.—(1) Subject to the provisions of this Schedule, where the residuary estate of the intestate comprises an interest in a dwelling-house in which the surviving husband or wife was resident at the time of the intestate's death, the surviving husband or wife may require the personal representative, in exercise of the power conferred by section forty-one of the principal Act (and with due regard to the requirements of that section as to valuation) to appropriate the said interest in the dwelling-house in or towards satisfaction of any absolute interest of the surviving husband or wife in the real and personal estate of the intestate. **7-002**

(2) The right conferred by this paragraph shall not be exercisable where the interest is—

(a) a tenancy which at the date of the death of the intestate was a tenancy which would determine within the period of two years from that date; or

(b) a tenancy which the landlord by notice given after that date could determine within the remainder of that period.

(3) Nothing in subsection (5) of section forty-one of the principal Act (which requires the personal representative, in making an appropriation to any person under that section, to have regard to the rights of others) shall prevent the personal representative from giving effect to the right conferred by this paragraph.

(4) The reference in this paragraph to an absolute interest in the real and personal estate of the intestate includes a reference to the capital value of a life interest which the surviving husband or wife has under this Act elected to have redeemed.

(5) Where part of a building was, at the date of the death of the intestate, occupied as a separate dwelling, that dwelling shall for the purposes of this Schedule be treated as a dwelling-house.

2. Where—(a) the dwelling-house forms part of a building and an interest in the whole of the building is comprised in the residuary estate; or **7-003**

(b) the dwelling-house is held with agricultural land and an interest in the agricultural land is comprised in the residuary estate; or

(c) the whole or a part of the dwelling-house was at the time of the intestate's death used as a hotel or lodging house; or

(d) a part of the dwelling-house was at the time of the intestate's death used for purposes other than domestic purposes,

the right conferred by paragraph 1 of this Schedule shall not be exercisable unless the court, on being satisfied that the exercise of that right is not likely to diminish the value of assets in the residuary estate (other than the said interest in the dwelling-house) or make them more difficult to dispose of, so orders.

3.—(1) The right conferred by paragraph 1 of this Schedule— **7-004**

(a) shall not be exercisable after the expiration of twelve months from the first taking out of representation with respect to the intestate's estate;

(b) shall not be exercisable after the death of the surviving husband or wife;

(c) shall be exercisable, except where the surviving husband or wife is the sole personal representative, by notifying the personal representative (or, where there are two or more personal representatives of whom one is the surviving husband or wife, all of them except the surviving husband or wife) in writing.

(2) A notification in writing under paragraph (c) of the foregoing sub-paragraph shall not be revocable except with the consent of the personal representative; but the surviving husband or wife may require the personal representative to have the said interest in the dwelling-house valued in accordance with section forty-one of the principal Act and to inform him or her of the result of that valuation before he or she decides whether to exercise the right.

(3) Subsection (9) of the section forty-seven A added to the principal Act by section two of this Act shall apply for the purposes of the construction of the reference in this paragraph to the first taking out of representation, and the proviso to subsection (5) of that section shall apply for the purpose of enabling the surviving husband or wife to apply for an extension of the period of twelve months mentioned in this paragraph.

4.—(1) During the period of twelve months mentioned in paragraph 3 of this Schedule the personal representative shall not without the written consent of the surviving husband or wife sell or otherwise dispose of the said interest in the dwelling-house except in the course of administration owing to want of other assets. **7-005**

(2) An application to the court under paragraph 2 of this Schedule may be made by the personal representative as well as by the surviving husband or wife, and if, on an application under that paragraph, the court does not order that the right conferred by paragraph 1 of this Schedule shall be exercisable by the surviving husband or wife, the court may authorise the personal representative to dispose of the said interest in the dwelling-house within the said period of twelve months.

(3) Where the court under sub-paragraph (3), of paragraph 3 of this Schedule extends the said period of twelve months, the court may direct that this paragraph shall apply in relation to the extended period as it applied in relation to the original period of twelve months.

(4) This paragraph shall not apply where the surviving husband or wife is the sole personal representative or one of two or more personal representatives.

(5) Nothing in this paragraph shall confer any right on the surviving husband or wife as against a purchaser from the personal representative.

7-006 **5.**—(1) Where the surviving husband or wife is one of two or more personal representatives, the rule that a trustee may not be a purchaser of trust property shall not prevent the surviving husband or wife from purchasing out of the estate of the intestate an interest in a dwelling-house in which the surviving husband or wife was resident at the time of the intestate's death.

(2) The power of appropriation under section forty-one of the principal Act shall include power to appropriate an interest in a dwelling-house in which the surviving husband or wife was resident at the time of the intestate's death partly in satisfaction of an interest of the surviving husband or wife in the real and personal estate of the intestate and partly in return for a payment of money by the surviving husband or wife to the personal representative.

7-007 **6.**—(1) Where the surviving husband or wife is a person of unsound mind or a defective, a requirement or consent under this Schedule may be made or given on his or her behalf by the committee or receiver, if any, or, where there is no committee or receiver, by the court.

(2) A requirement or consent made or given under this Schedule by a surviving husband or wife who is an infant shall be as valid and binding as it would be if he or she were of age; and, as respects an appropriation in pursuance of paragraph 1 of this Schedule, the provisions of section forty-one of the principal Act as to obtaining the consent of the infant's parent or guardian, or of the court on behalf of the infant, shall not apply.

7-008 **7.**—(1) Except where the context otherwise requires, references in this Schedule to a dwelling-house include references to any garden or portion of ground attached to and usually occupied with the dwelling-house or otherwise required for the amenity or convenience of the dwelling-house.

(2) This Schedule shall be construed as one with Part IV of the principal Act.

Maintenance Orders Act 1958

(6 AND 7 ELIZ. 2 C. 39)

PART I

REGISTRATION, ENFORCEMENT AND VARIATION OF CERTAIN MAINTENANCE ORDERS

Application of Part I

8-001 **1.**—(1) The provisions of this Part of this Act shall have effect for the purpose of enabling maintenance orders to which this Part of this Act applies to be registered—

(a) in the case of an order made by the High Court or a county court, in a magistrates' court; and

(b) in the case of an order made by a magistrates' court, in the High Court,

and, subject to those provisions, while so registered—

(i) to be enforced in like manner as an order made by the court of registration; and

(ii) in the case of an order registered in a magistrates' court, to be varied by a magistrates' court.

[(1A) In the following provisions of this Act "maintenance order" means any order specified in Schedule 8 to the Administration of Justice Act 1970.][1]

(2) This Part of this Act applies to maintenance orders made by the High Court, a county court or a magistrates' court, other than orders registered under Part II of the Maintenance Orders Act, 1950.

(3) Without prejudice to the provisions of section twenty-one of this Act, in this Part of this Act, unless the context otherwise requires, the following expressions have the following meanings—

"High Court order", "county court order" and "magistrates' court order" meanan order made by the High Court, a county court or a magistrates' court, as the case may be;

"order" means a maintenance order to which this Part of this Act applies;

"original court" and "court of registration", in relation to an order, mean the court by which the order was made or, as the case may be, the court in which the order is registered;

"registered" means registered in accordance with the provisions of this Part of this Act, and "registration" shall be construed accordingly;

and for the purposes of this Part of this Act an order for the payment by the defendant of any costs incurred in proceedings relating to a maintenance order, being an order for the payment of costs made while the maintenance order is not registered, shall be deemed to form part of that maintenance order.

[(4) For the purposes of this section a maintenance order [which is registered in a magistrates' court under Part I of the Maintenance Orders (Reciprocal Enforcement) Act 1972 or Part I of the Civil Jurisdiction and Judgments Act 1982][2] [or Council Regulation (EC) No. 44/2001 of 22nd December 2000 on jurisdiction and the recognition and enforcement of judgments in civil and commercial matters][3] shall be deemed to be a maintenance order made by that court.][4]

Registration of orders

2.—(1) A person entitled to receive payments under a High Court or county court order may apply for the registration of the order to the original court, and the court may, if it thinks fit, grant the application. **8-002**

(2) Where an application for the registration of such an order is granted—

(a) no proceedings shall be begun, and no writ, warrant or other process shall be issued, for the enforcement of the order before the registration of the order or the expiration of the prescribed period from the grant of the application, whichever first occurs; and

(b) the original court shall, on being satisfied within the period aforesaid by the person who made the application that no such proceedings or process begun or issued before the grant of the application remain pending or in force, cause a certified copy of the order to be sent to the

---

1 Added by Administration of Justice Act 1970 c.31 s 27 (3)

2 Words substituted by Civil Jurisdiction and Judgments Act 1982 c.27 ss 15 (4), 36 (6), 52 Sch 12 Pt I para 3

3 Words inserted by SI 2001/3929 Sch 3 para 5

4 Added by Maintenance Orders (Reciprocal Enforcement) Act 1972 c.18 Sch para 4

[justices' chief executive for][1] the magistrates' court acting for the petty sessions area in which the defendant appears to be;

but if at the expiration of the period aforesaid the original court has not been so satisfied, the grant of the application shall become void.

(3) A person entitled to receive payments under a magistrates' court order who considers that the order could be more effectively enforced if it were registered may apply for the registration of the order to the original court, and the court [may, if it thinks fit, grant the application][2].

[(3A) Without prejudice to subsection (3) of this section, where a magistrates' court order provides both for the payment of a lump sum and for the making of periodical payments, a person entitled to receive a lump sum under the order who considers that, so far as it relates to that sum, the order could be more effectively enforced if it were registered may apply to the original court for the registration of the order so far as it so relates, and the court may, if it thinks fit, grant the application.

(3B) Where an application under subsection (3A) of this section is granted in the case of a magistrates' court order, the provisions of this Part of this Act shall have effect in relation to that order as if so far as it relates to the payment of a lump sum it were a separate order.][3]

(4) Where an application for the registration of a magistrates' court order is granted—

(a) no proceedings for the enforcement of the order shall be begun before the registration takes place and no warrant or other process for the enforcement thereof shall be issued in consequence of any such proceedings begun before the grant of the application; and

(b) [...][4]

(c) the original court shall, on being satisfied in the prescribed manner that no process for the enforcement of the order issued before the grant of the application remains in force, cause a certified copy of the order to be sent to the prescribed officer of the High Court.

(5) The officer [of, or justices' chief executive for,][5] a court who receives a certified copy of an order sent to him under this section shall cause the order to be registered in that court.

[(6) Where a magistrates' court order is registered under this Part of this Act in the High Court, then—

(a) if payments under the magistrates' court order are required to be made (otherwise than to [a justices' chief executive][6]) by any method of payment falling within section 59(6) of the Magistrates' Courts Act 1980 (standing order, etc.), any order requiring payment by that method shall continue to have effect after registration;

(b) any order by virtue of which sums payable under the magistrates' court order are required to be paid to [a justices' chief executive][7] (whether or not by any method of payment falling within section 59(6) of that Act) on behalf of the person entitled thereto shall cease to have effect.

[1] Words substituted by Access to Justice Act 1999 c.22 Sch 13 para 26 (2)
[2] Words substituted by Civil Jurisdiction and Judgments Act 1982 c.27 ss 37 (1), 52 Sch 11 Pt I para 2 (2)
[3] Inserted by Civil Jurisdiction and JudgmentsAct 1982 c.27 ss 37 (1), 52 Sch 11 Pt I para 2 (3)
[4] Repealed by Access to Justice Act 1999 c.22 Sch 15 (V) (8) para 1
[5] Words substituted by Access to Justice Act 1999 c.22 Sch 13 para 26 (3)
[6] Words substituted by Access to Justice Act 1999 c.22 Sch 13 para 26 (4)
[7] Words substituted by Access to Justice Act 1999 c.22 Sch 13 para 26 (4)

(6ZA) Where a High Court or county court order is registered under this Part of this Act in a magistrates' court, then—

(a) if a means of payment order (within the meaning of section 1(7) of the Maintenance Enforcement Act 1991) has effect in relation to the order in question, it shall continue to have effect after registration; and

(b) in any other case, the magistrates' court shall order that all payments to be made under the order in question (including any arrears accrued before registration) shall be made to [a justices' chief executive][1].

(6ZB) Any such order as to payment—

(a) as is referred to in paragraph (a) of subsection (6) of this section may be revoked, suspended, revived or varied by an exercise of the powers conferred by section 4A of this Act; and

(b) as is referred to in paragraph (a) or (b) of subsection (6ZA) of this section may be varied or revoked by an exercise of the powers conferred by section 3(2A) or (2B) or section 4(2A), (5A) or (5B) of this Act.

(6ZC) Where by virtue of the provisions of this section or any order under subsection (6ZA)(b) of this section payments under an order cease to be or become payable to [a justices' chief executive][2], the person liable to make the payments shall, until he is given the prescribed notice to that effect, be deemed to comply with the order if he makes payments in accordance with the order and any order under subsection (6ZA)(b) of this section of which he has received such notice.][3]

(7) In this section "certified copy" in relation to an order of a court means a copy certified by the proper officer of the court to be a true copy of the order or of the official record thereof.

Enforcement of registered orders

3.—(1) Subject to the provisions of [section 2A of this Act and][4]this section, a registered order shall be enforceable in all respects as if it had been made by the court of registration and as if that court had had jurisdiction to make it; and proceedings for or with respect to the enforcement of a registered order may be taken accordingly. **8-003**

[(2) [Subject to the provisions of subsections (2A) to (3) of this section][5], an order registered in magistrates' court shall be enforceable as a magistrates' court maintenance order within the meaning of section 150(1) of the Magistrates' Courts Act 1980.][6]

[(2A) Where an order registered in a magistrates' court is an order other than one deemed to be made by the High Court by virtue of section 1(2) of this Act, section 76 of the Magistrates' Courts Act 1980 (enforcement of sums adjudged to be paid) shall have effect as if for subsections (4) to (6) there were substituted the following subsections—

> "(4) Where proceedings are brought for the enforcement of a magistrates' court maintenance order under this section, the court may vary the order by exercising one of its powers under paragraphs (a) to (d) of section 59(3) above.
>
> (5) In deciding which of the powers under paragraphs (a) to (d) of section 59(3) above it is to exercise, the court shall have regard to any representations made by the debtor and the creditor (which expressions have the same meaning as they have in section 59 above).

[1] Words substituted by Access to Justice Act 1999 c.22 Sch 13 para 26 (5)

[2] Words substituted by Access to Justice Act 1999 c.22 Sch 13 para 26 (6)

[3] Substituted by Maintenance Enforcement Act 1991 c.17 Sch 1 para 7

[4] Words inserted by Civil Jurisdiction and JudgmentsAct 1982 c.27 ss 37 (1), 52 Sch 11 Pt II para 6 (3)

[5] Words substituted by Maintenance Enforcement Act 1991 c.17 Sch 1 para 8 (1)

[6] Substituted by Family Law Reform Act 1987 c.42 s 33 (1) Sch 2 para 18

(6) Subsection (4) of section 59 above shall apply for the purposes of subsection (4) above as it applies for the purposes of that section."

(2B) Where an order registered in a magistrates' court is an order deemed to be made by the High Court by virtue of section 1(2) of this Act, sections 76 and 93 of the Magistrates' Courts Act 1980 (enforcement of sums adjudged to be paid and complaint for arrears) shall have effect subject to the modifications specified in subsections (2ZA) and (2ZB) of section 18 of the Maintenance Orders Act 1950 (enforcement of registered orders).][1]

(3) Where an order remains or becomes registered after the discharge of the order, no proceedings shall be taken by virtue of that registration except in respect of arrears which were due under the order at the time of the discharge and have not been remitted.

[(3A) Any person under an obligation to make payments under an order registered in a magistrates' court shall give notice of any change of address to the [justices' chief executive for][2] the court; and any person who without reasonable excuse fails to give such a notice shall be liable on summary conviction to a fine not exceeding level 2 on the standard scale [...][3]][4]

(4) Except as provided by this section, no proceedings shall be taken for or with respect to the enforcement of a registered order.

Variation of orders registered in magistrates' courts

8-004 **4.**—(1) The provisions of this section shall have effect with respect to the variation of orders registered in magistrates' courts, and references in this section to registered orders shall be construed accordingly.

(2) Subject to the following provisions of this section—

(a) the court of registration may exercise the same jurisdiction to vary any rate of payments specified by a registered order (other than jurisdiction in a case where a party to the order is not present in England when the application for variation is made) as is exercisable, apart from this subsection, by the original court; and

(b) a rate of payments specified by a registered order shall not be varied except by the court of registration or any other magistrates' court to which the jurisdiction conferred by the foregoing paragraph is extended by rules of court.

[(2A) The power of a magistrates' court to vary a registered order under subsection (2) of this section shall include power, if the court is satisfied that payment has not been made in accordance with the order, to vary the order by exercising one of its powers under paragraphs (a) to (d) of section 59(3) of the Magistrates' Courts Act 1980.

(2B) Subsection (4) of section 59 of that Act shall apply for the purposes of subsection (2A) of this section as it applies for the purposes of that section.

(2C) In deciding which of the powers under paragraphs (a) to (d) of section 59(3) of that Act it is to exercise, the court shall have regard to any representations made by the debtor and the creditor (which expressions have the same meaning as they have in section 59 of that Act).][5]

(3) [...][6]

[1] Added by Maintenance Enforcement Act 1991 c.17 Sch 1 para 8 (2)
[2] Words substituted by Access to Justice Act 1999 c.22 Sch 13 para 27
[3] Words repealed by Statute Law (Repeals) Act 1993 c.50 Sch 1 (XIV) para 1
[4] Inserted by Matrimonial and Family Proceedings Act 1984 c.42 ss 46 (1), 48 Sch 1 para 4
[5] Added by Maintenance Enforcement Act 1991 c.17 Sch 1 para 9 (1)
[6] Repealed by Administration of Justice Act 1970 c.31 s 48 (2) Sch 11

(4) If it appears to the court to which an application is made by virtue of subsection (2) of this section for the variation of a rate of payments specified by a registered order [that it is for any reason][1] appropriate to remit the application to the original court, the first-mentioned court shall so remit the application, and the original court shall thereupon deal with the application as if the order were not registered.

(5) Nothing in subsection (2) of this section shall affect the jurisdiction of the original court to vary a rate of payments specified by a registered order if an application for the variation of that rate is made to that court—

(a) in proceedings for a variation of provisions of the order which do not specify a rate of payments; or

(b) at a time when a party to the order is not present in England.

[(5A) Subject to the following provisions of this section, subsections (4) to (11) of section 60 of the Magistrates' Courts Act 1980 (power of clerk and court to vary maintenance orders) shall apply in relation to a registered order (other than one deemed to be made by the High Court by virtue of section 1(2) of this Act) as they apply in relation to a maintenance order made by a magistrates' court (disregarding section 23(2) of the Domestic Proceedings and Magistrates' Court Act 1978 and section 15(2) of the Children Act 1989) but—

(a) as if in subsection (8) after the words "the court which may" there were inserted "subject to subsection (10) below"; and

(b) as if for subsections (9) and (10) there were substituted the following subsections—

"(9) Subsections (4) of section 59 above shall apply for the purposes of subsection (8) above as it applies for the purposes of that section.

(10) In deciding which of the powers under paragraphs (a) to (d) of section 59(3) above it is to exercise, the court shall have regard to any representations made by the debtor and the creditor."

(5B) Subject to the following provisions of this section, subsections (4) to (11) of section 60 of the Magistrates' Courts Act 1980 (power of clerk and court to vary maintenance orders) shall apply in relation to a registered order deemed to be made by the High Court by virtue of section 1(2) of this Act as they apply in relation to a maintenance order made by a magistrates' court (disregarding section 23(2) of the Domestic Proceedings and Magistrates' Courts Act 1978 and section 15(2) of the Children Act 1989) but—

(a) as if in subsection (4) for paragraph (b) there were substituted—

"(b) payments under the order are required to be made to [a justices' chief executive][2] by any method of payment falling within section 59(6) above (standing order, etc.)";

[...][3] after the words "the court" there were inserted "which made the order";

(b) as if in subsection (5) for the words "to the [justices' chief executive for the court][4]" there were substituted "in accordance with paragraph (a) of subsection (9) below";

(c) as if in subsection (7), paragraph (c) and the word "and" immediately preceding it were omitted;

(d) as if in subsection (8) for the words "paragraphs (a) to (d) of section 59(3) above" there were substituted "subsection (9) below";

(e) as if for subsections (9) and (10) there were substituted the following subsections—

[1] Words substituted by Administration of Justice Act 1970 c.31 s 48 (3)
[2] Words substituted by Access to Justice Act 1999 c.22 Sch 13 para 28 (2)
[3] Words repealed by Access to Justice Act 1999 c.22 Sch 15 (V) (7) para 1
[4] Words substituted by Access to Justice Act 1999 c.22 Sch 13 para 28 (3)

"(9) The powers of the court are—

(a) the power to order that payments under the order be made directly to [a justices' chief executive][1];

(b) the power to order that payments under the order be made to the clerk of the court, or to [a justices' chief executive][2], by such method of payment falling within section 59(6) above (standing order, etc.) as may be specified;

(c) the power to make an attachment of earnings order under the Attachment of Earnings Act 1971 to secure payments under the order.

(10) In deciding which of the powers under subsection (9) above it is to exercise, the court shall have regard to any representations made by the debtor.

(10A) Subsection (4) of section 59 above (power of court to require debtor to open account) shall apply for the purposes of subsection (9) above as it applies for the purposes of that section but as if for paragraph (a) there were substituted—

(a) the court proposes to exercise its power under paragraph (b) of section 60(9) below"][3]

(6) No application for any variation of a registered order shall be made to any court while proceedings for any variation of the order are pending in any other court.

[(6B) No application for any variation of a registered order shall be made to any court in respect of an order for periodical or other payments made under Part III of the Matrimonial and Family Proceedings Act 1984.][4]

(7) Where a magistrates' court, in exercise of the jurisdiction conferred by subsection (2) of this section, varies or refuses to vary a registered order, an appeal from the variation or refusal shall lie to the High Court[...][5].

[Variation etc. of orders registered

8-005 **4A.**—(1) The provisions of this section shall have effect with respect to orders registered in the High Court other than maintenance orders deemed to be made by a magistrates' court by virtue of section 1(4) of this Act, and the reference in subsection (2) of this section to a registered order shall be construed accordingly.

(2) The High Court may exercise the same powers in relation to a registered order as are exercisable by the High Court under section 1 of the Maintenance Enforcement Act 1991 in relation to a qualifying periodical maintenance order (within the meaning of that section) which has been made by the High Court, including the power under subsection (7) of that section to revoke, suspend, revive or vary—

(a) any such order as is referred to in paragraph (a) of section 2(6) of this Act which continues to have effect by virtue of that paragraph; and

(b) any means of payment order (within the meaning of section 1(7) of that Act of 1991) made by virtue of the provisions of this section.][6]

---

[1] Words substituted by Access to Justice Act 1999 c.22 Sch 13 para 28 (4) (b)
[2] Words substituted by Access to Justice Act 1999 c.22 Sch 13 para 28 (4) (b)
[3] Added by Maintenance Enforcement Act 1991 c.17 Sch 1 para 9 (2)
[4] Inserted by Matrimonial and Family Proceedings Act 1984 c.42 ss 46 (1), 48 Sch 1 para 5
[5] Words repealedby Administration of Justice Act 1977 c.38 s 32 (4) Sch 5 Pt IV
[6] Added by Maintenance Enforcement Act 1991 c.17 Sch 1 para 10

Law Reform (Husband and Wife) Act 1962

(10 AND 11 ELIZ. 2 C. 48)

Actions in tort between husband and wife

1.—(1) Subject to the provisions of this section, each of the parties to a marriage shall have the like right of action in tort against the other as if they were not married. **9-001**

(2) Where an action in tort is brought by one of the parties to a marriage against the other during the subsistence of the marriage, the court may stay the action if it appears—

(a) that no substantial benefit would accrue to either party from the continuation of the proceedings; or

(b) that the question or questions in issue could more conveniently be disposed of on an application made under section seventeen of the Married Women's Property Act 1882 (determination of questions between husband and wife as to the title to or possession of property);

and without prejudice to paragraph (b) of this subsection the court may, in such an action, either exercise any power which could be exercised on an application under the said section seventeen, or give such directions as it thinks fit for the disposal under that section of any question arising in the proceedings.

(3) [...][1]

Short title, repeal, interpretation, saving and extent

3.—(2) [...][2] **9-002**

(3) The references in subsection (1) of section one and subsection (1) of section two of this Act to the parties to a marriage include references to the persons who were parties to a marriage which has been dissolved.

(4) This Act does not apply to any cause of action which arose, or would but for the subsistence of a marriage have arisen, before the commencement of this Act.

Married Women's Property Act 1964

CHAPTER 19

Money and property derived from housekeeping allowance

1. If any question arises as to the right of a husband or wife to money derived from any allowance made by the husband for the expenses of the matrimonial home or for similar purposes, or to any property acquired out of such money, the **10-001**

[1] Repealed by SI 1998/2940 art 4

[2] Repealed by Statute Law (Repeals) Act 1974 c.22 Sch Pt XI

money or property shall, in the absence of any agreement between them to the contrary, be treated as belonging to the husband and the wife in equal shares.

Theft Act 1968

CHAPTER 60

General and consequential provisions

Husband and wife

11-001 **30.**—(1) This Act shall apply in relation to the parties to a marriage, and to property belonging to the wife or husband whether or not by reason of an interest derived from the marriage, as it would apply if they were not married and any such interest subsisted independently of the marriage.

(2) Subject to subsection (4) below, a person shall have the same right to bring proceedings against that person's wife or husband for any offence (whether under this Act or otherwise) as if they were not married, and a person bringing any such proceedings shall be competent to give evidence for the prosecution at every stage of the proceedings.

(3) [...][1]

(4) Proceedings shall not be instituted against a person for any offence of stealing or doing unlawful damage to property which at the time of the offence belongs to that person's wife or husband, or for any attempt, incitement or conspiracy to commit such an offence, unless the proceedings are instituted by or with the consent of the Director of Public Prosecutions:

Provided that—

(a) this subsection shall not apply to proceedings against a person for an offence—

(i) if that person is charged with committing the offence jointly with the wife or husband; or

(ii) if by virtue of any judicial decree or order (wherever made) that person and the wife or husband are at the time of the offence under no obligation to cohabit;[...][2]

(b) [...][3]

[(5) Notwithstanding [section 6 of the Prosecution of Offences Act 1979][4] subsection (4) of this section shall apply—

(a) to an arrest (if without warrant) made by the wife or husband, and

(b) to a warrant of arrest issued on an information laid by the wife or husband.][5]

[1] Repealed by Police and Criminal Evidence Act 1984 c.60 s 119 Sch 7 Pt I
[2] Word repealed by Criminal Jurisdiction Act 1975 c.59 Sch 6 Pt I
[3] Repealed by Criminal Jurisdiction Act 1975 c.59 Sch 6 Pt I
[4] Words substituted by Prosecution of Offences Act 1979 c.31 Sch 1
[5] Added by Criminal Jurisdiction Act 1975 c.59 Sch 5 para 2 (1)

Effect on civil proceedings and rights

31.—(1) A person shall not be excused, by reason that to do so may incriminate that person or the wife or husband of that person of an offence under this Act— **11-002**

(a) from answering any question put to that person in proceedings for the recovery or administration of any property, for the execution of any trust or for an account of any property or dealings with property; or

(b) from complying with any order made in any such proceedings;

but no statement or admission made by a person in answering a question put or complying with an order made as aforesaid shall, in proceedings for an offence under this Act, be admissible in evidence against that person or (unless they married after the making of the statement or admission) against the wife or husband of that person.

(2) Notwithstanding any enactment to the contrary, where property has been stolen or obtained by fraud or other wrongful means, the title to that or any other property shall not be affected by reason only of the conviction of the offender.

Civil Evidence Act 1968

CHAPTER 64

PART II

MISCELLANEOUS AND GENERAL

Convictions, etc. as evidence in civil proceedings

Findings of adultery and paternity as evidence in civil proceedings

12.—(1) In any civil proceedings— **12-001**

(a) the fact that a person has been found guilty of adultery in any matrimonial proceedings; and

[(b) the fact that a person has been found to be the father of a child in relevant proceedings before any court in England and Wales or has been adjudged to be the father of a child in affiliation proceedings before any court in the United Kingdom;][1]

shall (subject to subsection (3) below) be admissible in evidence for the purpose of proving, where to do so is relevant to any issue in those civil proceedings, that he committed the adultery to which the finding relates or, as the case may be, is (or was) the father of that child, whether or not he offered any defence to the allegation of adultery or paternity and whether or not he is a party to the civil proceedings; but no finding or adjudication other than a subsisting one shall be admissible in evidence by virtue of this section.

(2) In any civil proceedings in which by virtue of this section a person is proved to have been found guilty of adultery as mentioned in subsection (1)(a)

---

[1] Substituted by Family Law Reform Act 1987 c.42 ss 29 (1) (2), 33 (2) Sch 3 paras 1, 6

above or [to have been found or adjudged][1]to be the father of a child as mentioned in subsection (1)(b) above—

(a) he shall be taken to have committed the adultery to which the finding relates or, as the case may be, to be (or have been) the father of that child, unless the contrary is proved; and

(b) without prejudice to the reception of any other admissible evidence for the purpose of identifying the facts on which the finding or adjudication was based, the contents of any document which was before the court, or which contains any pronouncement of the court, in the [other proceedings][2]in question shall be admissible in evidence for that purpose.

(3) Nothing in this section shall prejudice the operation of any enactment whereby a finding of fact in any matrimonial or affiliation proceedings is for the purposes of any other proceedings made conclusive evidence of any fact.

(4) Subsection (4) of section 11 of this Act shall apply for the purposes of this section as if the reference to subsection (2) were a reference to subsection (2) of this section.

[(5) In this section—

"matrimonial proceedings" means any matrimonial cause in the High Court or a county court in England and Wales or in the High Court in Northern Ireland, any consistorial action in Scotland, or any appeal arising out of any such cause or action;

'relevant proceedings' means—

(a) proceedings on a complaint under section 42 of the National Assistance Act 1948 or section 26 of the Social Security Act 1986;

(b) proceedings under the Children Act 1989;

(c) proceedings which would have been relevant proceedings for the purposes of this section in the form in which it was in force before the passing of the Children Act 1989[;][3]

[...][4]

"affiliation proceedings" means, in relation to Scotland, any action of affiliation and aliment;

and in this subsection "consistorial action" does not include an action of aliment only between husband and wife raised in the Court of Session or an action of interim aliment raised in the sheriff court.]

Privilege

Privilege against incrimination of self or spouse

12-002 **14.**—(1) The right of a person in any legal proceedings other than criminal proceedings to refuse to answer any question or produce any document or thing if to do so would tend to expose that person to proceedings for an offence or for the recovery of a penalty—

(a) shall apply only as regards criminal offence under the law of any part of the United Kingdom and penalties provided for by such law; and

(b) shall include a like right to refuse to answer any question or produce any document or thing if to do so would tend to expose the husband or wife of that person to proceedings for any such criminal offence or for the recovery of any such penalty.

[1] Words substituted by Family Law Reform Act 1987 c.42 ss 29 (3), 33 (2) Sch 3 paras 1, 6
[2] Words substituted by Family Law Reform Act 1987 c.42 ss 29 (3), 33 (2) Sch 3 paras 1, 6
[3] Added by Child Support Act 1991 c.48 s 27 (5)
[4] Repealed by Child Support, Pensions and Social Security Act 2000 c.19 Sch 9 (IX) para 1

(2) In so far as any existing enactment conferring (in whatever words) powers of inspection or investigation confers on a person (in whatever words) any right otherwise than in criminal proceedings to refuse to answer any question or give any evidence tending to incriminate that person, subsection (1) above shall apply to that right as it applies to the right described in that subsection; and every such existing enactment shall be construed accordingly.

(3) In so far as any existing enactment provides (in whatever words) that in any proceedings other than criminal proceedings a person shall not be excused from answering any question or giving any evidence on the ground that to do so may incriminate that person, that enactment shall be construed as providing also that in such proceedings a person shall not be excused from answering any question or giving any evidence on the ground that to do so may incriminate the husband or wife of that person.

(4) Where any existing enactment (however worded) that—

(a) confers powers of inspection or investigation; or

(b) provides as mentioned in subsection (3) above,

further provides (in whatever words) that any answer or evidence given by a person shall not be admissible in evidence against that person in any proceedings or class of proceedings (however described, and whether criminal or not), that enactment shall be construed as providing also that any answer or evidence given by that person shall not be admissible in evidence against the husband or wife of that person in the proceedings or class of proceedings in question.

(5) In this section "existing enactment" means any enactment passed before this Act; and the references to giving evidence are references to giving evidence in any manner, whether by furnishing information, making discovery, producing documents or otherwise.

Family Law Reform Act 1969

CHAPTER 46

PART I

REDUCTION OF AGE OF MAJORITY AND RELATED PROVISIONS

Reduction of age of majority from 21 to 18

1.—(1) As from the date on which this section comes into force a person shall attain full age on attaining the age of eighteen instead of on attaining the age of twenty-one; and a person shall attain full age on that date if he has then already attained the age of eighteen but not the age of twenty-one. **13-001**

(2) The foregoing subsection applies for the purposes of any rule of law, and, in the absence of a definition or of any indication of a contrary intention, for the construction of "full age", "infant", "infancy", "minor", "minority" and similar expressions in—

(a) any statutory provision, whether passed or made before, on or after the date on which this section comes into force; and

(b) any deed, will or other instrument of whatever nature (not being a statutory provision) made on or after that date.

(3) In the statutory provisions specified in Schedule 1 to this Act for any reference to the age of twenty-one years there shall be substituted a reference to the age of eighteen years; but the amendment by this subsection of the provisions specified in Part II of that Schedule shall be without prejudice to any power of amending or revoking those provisions.

(4) This section does not affect the construction of any such expression as is referred to in subsection (2) of this section in any of the statutory provisions described in Schedule 2 to this Act, and the transitional provisions and savings contained in Schedule 3 to this Act shall have effect in relation to this section.

(5) The Lord Chancellor may by order made by statutory instrument amend any provision in any local enactment passed on or before the date on which this section comes into force (not being a provision described in paragraph 2 of Schedule 2 to this Act) by substituting a reference to the age of eighteen years for any reference therein to the age of twenty-one years; and any statutory instrument containing an order under this subsection shall be subject to annulment in pursuance of a resolution of either House of Parliament.

(6) In this section "statutory provision" means any enactment (including, except where the context otherwise requires, this Act) and any order, rule, regulation, byelaw or other instrument made in the exercise of a power conferred by any enactment.

(7) Notwithstanding any rule of law, a will or codicil executed before the date on which this section comes into force shall not be treated for the purposes of this section as made on or after that date by reason only that the will or codicil is confirmed by a codicil executed on or after that date.

Provisions relating to marriage

13-002 **2.**—(1) [...][1]

(2) [...][2]

(3) Where for the purpose of obtaining a certificate [...][3] for marriage under Part III of the said Act of 1949 a person declares that the consent of any person or persons whose consent to the marriage is required under the said section 3 has been obtained, the superintendent registrar may refuse to issue the certificate [...][4] for marriage unless satisfied by the production of written evidence that the consent of that person or of those persons has in fact been obtained.

(4) In this section any expression which is also used in the said Act of 1949 has the same meaning as in that Act.

Consent by persons over 16 to surgical, medical and dental treatment

13-003 **8.**—(1) The consent of a minor who has attained the age of sixteen years to any surgical, medical or dental treatment which, in the absence of consent, would constitute a trespass to his person, shall be as effective as it would be if he were of full age; and where a minor has by virtue of this section given an effective consent to any treatment it shall not be necessary to obtain any consent for it from his parent or guardian.

[1] Textually amends Foreign Marriage Act 1892 c.23 s 7 (c), Marriage with Foreigners Act 1906 c.40 Sch Pt I para 2 (c) and Marriage Act 1949 c.76 s 78 (1)

[2] Textually amends Marriage Act 1949 c.76 s 3 (5)

[3] Words repealed by Immigration and Asylum Act 1999 c.33 Sch 16 para 1

[4] Words repealed by Immigration and Asylum Act 1999 c.33 Sch 16 para 1

(2) In this section "surgical, medical or dental treatment" includes any procedure undertaken for the purposes of diagnosis, and this section applies to any procedure (including, in particular, the administration of an anaesthetic) which is ancillary to any treatment as it applies to that treatment.

(3) Nothing in this section shall be construed as making ineffective any consent which would have been effective if this section had not been enacted.

Time at which a person attains a particular age

9.—(1) The time at which a person attains a particular age expressed in years shall be the commencement of the relevant anniversary of the date of his birth. **13-004**

(2) This section applies only where the relevant anniversary falls on a date after that on which this section comes into force, and, in relation to any enactment, deed, will or other instrument, has effect subject to any provision therein.

Persons under full age may be described as minors instead of infants

12. A person who is not of full age may be described as a minor instead of as an infant, and accordingly in this Act "minor" means such a person as aforesaid. **13-005**

13. [...][1] **13-006**

PART III

PROVISIONS FOR USE OF BLOOD TESTS IN DETERMINING PATERNITY

Power of court to require use of blood tests

20.—[[(1) In any civil proceedings in which the parentage of any person falls to be determined, the court may, either of its own motion or on an application by any party to the proceedings, give a direction— **13-007**

(a) for the use of scientific tests to ascertain whether such tests show that a party to the proceedings is or is not the father or mother of that person; and

(b) for the taking, within a period specified in the direction, of bodily samples from all or any of the following, namely, that person, any party who is alleged to be the father or mother of that person and any other party to the proceedings;

and the court may at any time revoke or vary a direction previously given by it under this subsection.][2]][3]

[(1A) Tests required by a direction under this section may only be carried out by a body which has been accredited for the purposes of this section by–

(a) the Lord Chancellor, or

(b) a body appointed by him for the purpose.][4]

[1] Repealed by Northern Ireland Constitution Act 1973 c.36 s 41 (1) Sch 6 Pt I

[2] Substituted by Family Law Reform Act 1987 c.42 Pt IV s 23 (1)

[3] Substituted by Courts and Legal Services Act 1990 c.41 Sch 16 (I) para 3

[4] Substituted by Child Support, Pensions and Social Security Act 2000 c.19 Pt V s 82 (2) (a)

[(2) The [individual][1] carrying out scientific tests in pursuance of a direction under subsection (1) [("the tester")][2]above shall make to the court a report in which he shall state—

(a) the results of the tests;

(b) whether any party to whom the report relates is or is not excluded by the results from being the father or mother of the person whose parentage is to be determined; and

(c) in relation to any party who is not so excluded, the value, if any, of the results in determining whether that party is the father or mother of that person;

and the report shall be received by the court as evidence in the proceedings of the matters stated in it.

(2A) Where the proceedings in which the parentage of any person falls to be determined are proceedings on an application under section 56 of the Family Law Act 1986, any reference in subsection (1) or (2) of this section to any party to the proceedings shall include a reference to any person named in the application.][3]

(3) A report under subsection (2) of this section shall be in the form prescribed by regulations made under section 22 of this Act.

(4) Where a report has been made to a court under subsection (2) of this section, any party may, with the leave of the court, or shall, if the court so directs, obtain form [the tester][4] a written statement explaining or amplifying any statement made in the report, and that statement shall be deemed for the purposes of this section (except subsection (3) thereof) to form part of the report made to the court.

(5) Where a direction is given under this section in any proceedings, a party to the proceedings, unless the court otherwise directs, shall not be entitled to call as a witness [the tester, or any other][5] person by whom any thing necessary for the purpose of enabling those tests to be carried out was done, unless within fourteen days after receiving a copy of the report he serves notice on the other parties to the proceedings, or on such of them as the court may direct, of his intention to call [the tester or that other person][6]; and where [the tester or][7]any such person is called as a witness the party who called him shall be entitled to cross-examine him.

(6) Where a direction is given under this section the party on whose application the direction is given shall pay the cost of taking and testing [bodily samples][8] for the purpose of giving effect to the direction (including any expenses reasonably incurred by any person in taking any steps required of him for the

[1] Words substituted by Child Support, Pensions and Social Security Act 2000 c.19 Pt V s 82 (2) (b) (i)

[2] Words inserted by Child Support, Pensions and Social Security Act 2000 c.19 Pt V s 82 (2) (b) (ii)

[3] Subsections (1), (2) and (2A) substituted for subsections (1) and (2) by Family Law Reform Act 1987 c.42 Pt IV s 23 (1)

[4] Words substituted by Child Support, Pensions and Social Security Act 2000 c.19 Pt V s 82 (2) (c)

[5] Words substituted by Child Support, Pensions and Social Security Act 2000 c.19 Pt V s 82 (2) (d) (i)

[6] Words substituted by Child Support, Pensions and Social Security Act 2000 c.19 Pt V s 82 (2) (d) (ii)

[7] Words added by Child Support, Pensions and Social Security Act 2000 c.19 Pt V s 82 (2) (d) (iii)

[8] Words substituted by Family Law Reform Act 1987 c.42 Sch 2 para 21

purpose), and of making a report to the court under this section, but the amount paid shall be treated as costs incurred by him in the proceedings.

Consents, etc., required for taking of blood samples

21.—(1) Subject to the provisions of subsections (3) and (4) of this section, a [bodily sample][1] which is required to be taken from any person for the purpose of giving effect to a direction under section 20 of this Act shall not be taken from that person except with his consent. **13-008**

(2) The consent of a minor who has attained the age of sixteen years to the taking from himself of a [bodily sample][2] shall be as effective as it would be if he were of full age; and where a minor has by virtue of this subsection given an effective consent to the taking of a [bodily sample][3] it shall not be necessary to obtain any consent for it from any other person.

(3) A [bodily sample][4] may be taken from a person under the age of sixteen years, not being such a person as is referred to in subsection (4) of this section[-][5]

[(a) if the person who has the care and control of him consents; or

(b) where that person does not consent, if the court considers that it would be in his best interests for the sample to be taken.][6]

(4) A [bodily sample][7] may be taken from a person who is suffering from mental disorder within the meaning of [the Mental Health Act 1983][8] and is incapable of understanding the nature and purpose of [scientific tests][9] if the person who has the care and control of him consents and the medical practitioner in whose care he is has certified that the taking of a [bodily sample][10] from him will not be prejudicial to his proper care and treatment.

(5) The foregoing provisions of this section are without prejudice to the provisions of section 23 of this Act.

Failure to comply with direction for taking blood tests

23.—(1) Where a court gives a direction under section 20 of this Act and any person fails to take any step required of him for the purpose of giving effect to the direction, the court may draw such inferences, if any, from that fact as appear proper in the circumstances. **13-009**

(2) Where in any proceedings in which the [parentage][11] of any person falls to be determined by the court hearing the proceedings there is a presumption of law that that person is legitimate, then if—

(a) a direction is given under section 20 of this Act in those proceedings, and

(b) any party who is claiming any relief in the proceedings and who for the purpose of obtaining that relief is entitled to rely on the presumption fails to take any step required of him for the purpose of giving effect to the direction.

---

[1] Words substituted by Family Law Reform Act 1987 c.42 Sch 2 para 22
[2] Words substituted by Family Law Reform Act 1987 c.42 Sch 2 para 22
[3] Words substituted by Family Law Reform Act 1987 c.42 Sch 2 para 22
[4] Words substituted by Family Law Reform Act 1987 c.42 Sch 2 para 22
[5] Substituted by Child Support, Pensions and Social Security Act 2000 c.19 Pt V s 82 (3)
[6] Substituted by Child Support, Pensions and Social Security Act 2000 c.19 Pt V s 82 (3)
[7] Words substituted by Family Law Reform Act 1987 c.42 Sch 2 para 22
[8] Words substituted by Mental Health Act 1983 c.20 ss 146, 147, 148 Sch 4 para 25
[9] Words substituted by Family Law Reform Act 1987 c.42 Sch 2 para 22
[10] Words substituted by Family Law Reform Act 1987 c.42 Sch 2 para 22
[11] Word substituted by Family Law Reform Act 1987 c.42 Sch 2 para 24 (a)

the court may adjourn the hearing for such period as it thinks fit to enable that party to take that step, and if at the end of that period he has failed without reasonable cause to take it the court may, without prejudice to subsection (1) of this section, dismiss his claim for relief notwithstanding the absence of evidence to rebut the presumption.

(3) Where any person named in a direction under section 20 of this Act fails to consent to the taking of a [bodily sample][1] from himself or from any person named in the direction of whom he has the care and control, he shall be deemed for the purposes of this section to have failed to take a step required of him for the purpose of giving effect to the direction.

Interpretation of Part III

13-010 **25.** In this Part of this Act the following expressions have the meanings hereby respectively assigned to them, that is to say—

["bodily sample" means a sample of bodily fluid or bodily tissue taken for the purpose of scientific tests;][2]

"excluded" means excluded subject to the occurrence of mutation [to section 27 of the Family Law Reform Act 1987 and to sections 27 to 29 of the Human Fertilisation and Embryology Act 1990][3];

["scientific tests" means scientific tests carried out under this Part of this Act and made with the object of ascertaining the inheritable characteristics of bodily fluids or bodily tissue.][4]

PART IV

MISCELLANEOUS AND GENERAL

Rebuttal of presumption as to legitimacy and illegitimacy

13-011 **26.** Any presumption of law as to the legitimacy or illegitimacy of any person may in any civil proceedings be rebutted by evidence which shows that it is more probable than not that that person is illegitimate or legitimate, as the case may be, and it shall not be necessary to prove that fact beyond reasonable doubt in order to rebut the presumption.

---

[1] Words substituted by Family Law Reform Act 1987 c.42 Sch 2 para 24 (b)
[2] Substituted by Family Law Reform Act 1987 c.42 Pt IV s 23 (2) (a)
[3] Words inserted by Human Fertilisation and Embryology Act 1990 c.37 ss 39 (3), 43 (2), 49 (5) Sch 4 para 1
[4] Added by Family Law Reform Act 1987 c.42 Pt IV s 23 (2) (b)

Law Reform (Miscellaneous Provisions) Act 1970

CHAPTER 33

Legal consequences of termination of contract to marry

Engagements to marry not enforceable at law

1.—(1) An agreement between two persons to marry one another shall not under the law of England and Wales have effect as a contract giving rise to legal rights and no action shall lie in England and Wales for breach of such an agreement, whatever the law applicable to the agreement. **14-001**

(2) This section shall have effect in relation to agreements entered into before it comes into force, except that it shall not affect any action commenced before it comes into force.

Property of engaged couples

2.—(1) Where an agreement to marry is terminated, any rule of law relating to the rights of husbands and wives in relation to property in which either or both has or have a beneficial interest, including any such rule as explained by section 37 of the Matrimonial Proceedings and Property Act 1970, shall apply, in relation to any property in which either or both of the parties to the agreement had a beneficial interest while the agreement was in force, as it applies in relation to property in which a husband or wife has a beneficial interest. **14-002**

(2) Where an agreement to marry is terminated, section 17 of the Married Women's Property Act 1882 and section 7 of the Matrimonial Causes (Property and Maintenance) Act 1958 (which sections confer power on a judge of the High Court or a county court to settle disputes between husband and wife about property) shall apply, as if the parties were married, to any dispute between, or claim by, one of them in relation to property in which either or both had a beneficial interest while the agreement was in force; but an application made by virtue of this section to the judge under the said section 17, as originally enacted or as extended by the said section 7, shall be made within three years of the termination of the agreement.

Gifts between engaged couples

3.—(1) A party to an agreement to marry who makes a gift of property to the other party to the agreement on the condition (express or implied) that it shall be returned if the agreement is terminated shall not be prevented from recovering the property by reason only of his having terminated the agreement. **14-003**

(2) The gift of an engagement ring shall be presumed to be an absolute gift; this presumption may be rebutted by proving that the ring was given on the condition, express or implied, that it should be returned if the marriage did not take place for any reason.

Enticement of spouse, etc

Abolition of actions for enticement, seduction and harbouring of spouse or child

5. No person shall be liable in tort under the law of England and Wales— **14-004**

(a) to any other person on the ground only of his having induced the wife or husband of that other person to leave or remain apart from the other spouse;
(b) to a parent (or person standing in the place of a parent) on the ground only of his having deprived the parent (or other person) of the services of his or her child by raping, seducing or enticing that child; or
(c) to any other person for harbouring the wife or child of that other person,

except in the case of a cause of action accruing before this Act comes into force if an action in respect thereof has been begun before this Act comes into force.

Marriage (Registrar General's Licence) Act 1970

CHAPTER 34

Marriages which may be solemnised by Registrar General's licence

15-001 **1.**—(1) Subject to the provisions of subsection (2) below, any marriage which may be solemnised on the authority of [certificates][1] of a superintendent registrar may be solemnised on the authority of the Registrar General's licence [elsewhere than at a registered building, the office of a superintendent registrar or approved premises][2]:

Provided that any such marriage shall not be solemnised according to the rites of the Church of England or the Church in Wales.

(2) The Registrar General shall not issue any licence for the solemnising of a marriage as is mentioned in subsection (1) above unless he is satisfied that one of the persons to be married is seriously ill and is not expected to recover and cannot be moved to a place at which under the provisions of the Marriage Act 1949 (hereinafter called the "principal Act") the marriage could be solemnised [(disregarding for this purpose the provisions of that Act relating to marriages in pursuance of section 26(1)(dd) of that Act)][3].

Notice of marriage

15-002 **2.**—(1) Where a marriage is intended to be solemnised on the authority of the Registrar General's licence, notice shall be given in the prescribed form by either of the persons to be married to the superintendent registrar of the registration district in which it is intended that the marriage shall be solemnised, and the notice shall state by or before whom it is intended that the marriage shall be solemnised.

(2) The provisions of section 27(4) of the principal Act (which relate to entries in the marriage notice book) shall apply to notices of marriage on the authority of the Registrar General's licence.

(3) The provisions of section 28 of the principal Act (declaration to accompany notice of marriage) shall apply to the giving of notice under this Act with the exception of paragraph (b) of subsection (1) of that section and with the

[1] Words substituted by Immigration and Asylum Act 1999 c.33 Sch 14 para 39
[2] Words substituted by Marriage Act 1994 c.34 Sch 1 para 9
[3] Words inserted by MarriageAct 1983 c.32 s 2 (3)

modification that in section 28(2) references to the registrar of births and deaths or of marriages and deputy registrar shall be omitted.

Evidence of capacity, consent etc., to be produced

3. The person giving notice to the superintendent registrar under the provisions of the foregoing section shall produce to the superintendent registrar such evidence as the Registrar General may require to satisfy him— **15-003**

(a) that there is no lawful impediment to the marriage;

(b) that the consent of any person whose consent to the marriage is required under section 3 of the principal Act, [...][1] has been duly given; and

(c) that there is sufficient reason why a licence should be granted;

(d) that the conditions contained in section 1(2) of this Act are satisfied and that the person in respect of whom such conditions are satisfied is able to and does understand the nature and purport of the marriage ceremony:

Provided that the certificate of a registered medical practitioner shall be sufficient evidence of any or all of the matters in subsection (1)(d) of this section referred to.

Application to be reported to Registrar General

4. Upon receipt of any notice and evidence as mentioned in sections 2 and 3 above respectively the superintendent registrar shall inform the Registrar General and shall comply with any directions he may give for verifying the evidence given. **15-004**

Caveat against issue of Registrar General's licence

5. The provisions of section 29 of the principal Act (caveat against issue of certificate [...][2]) shall apply to the issue of a licence by the Registrar General with the modification that a caveat may be entered with either the superintendent registrar or the Registrar General and in either case it shall be for the Registrar General to examine into the matter of the caveat and to decide whether or not the licence should be granted and his decision shall be final, and with a further modification that the references to the superintendent registrar in that section shall refer to the superintendent registrar of the registration district in which the marriage is intended to be solemnised. **15-005**

Marriage of persons under eighteen

6. The provisions of section 3 of the principal Act (marriage of persons under 18) shall apply for the purposes of this Act to a marriage intended to be solemnised by Registrar General's licence as they apply to a marriage intended to be solemnised on the authority of [certificates][3] of a superintendent registrar under Part III of the principal Act with the modification that if the consent of any person whose consent is required under that Act cannot be obtained by reason of absence or inaccessibility or by reason of his being under any disability, the superintendent registrar shall not be required to dispense with the necessity for the consent of that person and the Registrar General may dispense with the necessity of obtaining the consent of that person, whether or not there is any other person whose consent is also required. **15-006**

[1] Words repealed by Children Act 1989 c.41 Sch 15 para 1

[2] Words repealed by Immigration and Asylum Act 1999 c.33 Sch 16 para 1

[3] Words substituted by Immigration and Asylum Act 1999 c.33 Sch 14 para 41

Issue of licence by Registrar General

15-007 **7.** Where the marriage is intended to be solemnised on the authority of the Registrar General and he is satisfied that sufficient grounds exist why a licence should be granted he shall issue a licence in the prescribed form unless—

(a) any lawful impediment to the issue of the licence has been shown to his satisfaction to exist; or

(b) the issue of the licence has been forbidden under section 30 of the principal Act.

Period of validity of licence

15-008 **8.**—(1) A marriage may be solemnised on the authority of the Registrar General's licence at any time within one month from the day on which the notice of marriage was entered in the marriage notice book.

(2) If the marriage is not solemnised within the said period of one month, the notice of marriage and the licence shall be void, and no person shall solemnise the marriage on the authority thereof.

Place of solemnisation

15-009 **9.** A marriage on the authority of the Registrar General's licence shall be solemnised in the place stated in the notice of marriage.

Manner of solemnisation

15-010 **10.**—(1) Any marriage to be solemnised on the authority of the Registrar General's licence shall be solemnised at the wish of the persons to be married either—

(a) according to such form or ceremony, not being the rites or ceremonies of the Church of England or the Church in Wales, as the persons to be married shall see fit to adopt, or

(b) by civil ceremony.

(2) Except where the marriage is solemnised according to the usages of the Society of Friends or is a marriage between two persons professing the Jewish religion according to the usages of the Jews, it shall be solemnised in the presence of a registrar:

Provided that where the marriage is to be by civil ceremony it shall be solemnised in the presence of the superintendent registrar as well as the registrar.

(3) Except where the marriage is solemnised according to the usages of the Society of Friends or is a marriage between two persons professing the Jewish religion according to the usages of the Jews, the persons to be married shall in some part of the ceremony in the presence of two or more witnesses and the registrar and, where appropriate, the superintendent registrar, make the declaration and say to one another the words prescribed by [section 44(3) or (3A)][1] of the principal Act.

(4) No person who is a clergyman within the meaning of section 78 of the principal Act shall solemnise any marriage which is solemnised on the authority of the Registrar General.

Civil marriage followed by religious ceremony

15-011 **11.**—(1) If the parties to a marriage solemnised on the authority of the Registrar General's licence before a superintendent registrar desire to add the

[1] Words added by Marriage Ceremony (Prescribed Words) Act 1996 c.34 s 1 (2) (b)

religious ceremony ordained or used by the church or persuasion of which they are members and have given notice of their desire so to do a clergyman or minister of that church or persuasion upon the production of a certificate of their marriage before the superintendent registrar and upon the payment of the customary fees (if any), may, if he sees fit, read or celebrate in the presence of the parties to the marriage the marriage service of the church or persuasion to which he belongs or nominate some other minister to do so.

(2) The provisions of section 46(2) and (3) of the principal Act shall apply to such a reading or celebration as they apply to the reading or celebration of a marriage service following a marriage solemnised in the office of a superintendent registrar.

Void marriages

13. The provisions of section 49 of the principal Act (void marriages) shall apply to a marriage under the authority of the Registrar General's licence:— **15-012**

(a) with the substitution in paragraph (b) for the words from "[certificates][1] for marriage" onwards of the words "[a Registrar][2] General's licence";

(b) [...][3]

(c) with the substitution for paragraph (d) of the words "on the authority of a licence which is void by virtue of section 8(2) of the Marriage (Registrar General's Licence) Act 1970";

(d) with the substitution for paragraph (e) of the words "in any place other than the place specified in the notice of marriage and the Registrar General's licence";

(e) with the substitution for paragraphs (f) and (g) of the words "in the absence of a registrar or, where the marriage is by civil ceremony, of a superintendent registrar, except where the marriage is solemnised according to the usages of the Society of Friends or is a marriage between two persons professing the Jewish religion according to the usages of the Jews".

Documentary authority for marriage

14. Where a marriage is to be solemnised on the authority of the Registrar General's licence a document issued by the superintendent registrar stating that the Registrar General's licence has been granted and that authority for the marriage to be solemnised has been given shall be delivered before the marriage to the following person, that is to say— **15-013**

(a) if the marriage is to be solemnised according to the usages of the Society of Friends, the registering officer of that Society for the place where the marriage is to be solemnised;

(b) if the marriage is to be solemnised according to the usages of persons professing the Jewish religion, the officer of the synagogue by whom the marriage is required to be registered under Part IV of the principal Act;

(c) in any other case, the registrar in whose presence the marriage is to be solemnised.

[1] Words substituted by Immigration and Asylum Act 1999 c.33 Sch 14 para 42 (a)
[2] Words substituted by Immigration and Asylum Act 1999 c.33 Sch 14 para 42 (a)
[3] Repealed by Immigration and Asylum Act 1999 c.33 Sch 16 para 1

Registration of marriages

15-014 **15.** A marriage solemnised on the authority of the Registrar General's licence shall be registered in accordance with the provisions of the principal Act which apply to the registration of marriages solemnised in the presence of a registrar or according to the usages of the Society of Friends or of persons professing the Jewish religion.

Offences

15-015 **16.**—(1) It shall be an offence knowingly and wilfully—

(a) to solemnise a marriage by Registrar General's licence in any place other than the place specified in the licence;

(b) to solemnise a marriage by Registrar General's licence without the presence of a registrar except in the case of a marriage according to the usages of the Society of Friends or a marriage between two persons professing the Jewish religion according to the usages of the Jews;

(c) to solemnise a marriage by Registrar General's licence after the expiration of one month from the date of entry of the notice of marriage in the marriage notice book;

(d) to give false information by way of evidence as required by section 3 of this Act;

(e) to give a false certificate as provided for in section 3(1)(d) of this Act;

and any person found guilty of any of the above-mentioned offences shall be liable on summary conviction to a fine not exceeding £100 or on indictment to a fine not exceeding £500 or to imprisonment not exceeding three years or to both such fine and such imprisonment.

(2) A superintendent registrar who knowingly and wilfully solemnises or permits to be solemnised in his presence, or a registrar who knowingly and wilfully registers a marriage by Registrar General's licence which is void by virtue of Part III of the principal Act as amended by this Act shall be guilty of an offence and shall be liable on summary conviction to a fine not exceeding £100 or on indictment to a fine not exceeding £500 or to imprisonment not exceeding three years or to both such fine and such imprisonment.

(3) No prosecution under this section shall be commenced after the expiration of three years from the commission of the offence.

(4) The provisions of sections 75(1)(a) and 75(2)(a) of the principal Act shall not apply to a marriage solemnised on the authority of the Registrar General's licence.

Matrimonial Proceedings and Property Act 1970

CHAPTER 45

PART II

MISCELLANEOUS PROVISIONS

Provisions relating to property of married persons

Contributions by spouse in money or money's worth to the improvement of property

37. It is hereby declared that where a husband or wife contributes in money or money's worth to the improvement of real or personal property in which or in the proceeds of sale of which either or both of them has or have a beneficial interest, the husband or wife so contributing shall, if the contribution is of a substantial nature and subject to any agreement between them to the contrary express or implied, be treated as having then acquired by virtue of his or her contribution a share or an enlarged share, as the case may be, in that beneficial interest of such an extent as may have been then agreed or, in default of such agreement, as may seem in all the circumstances just to any court before which the question of the existence or extent of the beneficial interest of the husband or wife arises (whether in proceedings between them or in any other proceedings). **16-001**

Extension of s. 17 of Married Women's Property Act 1882

39. An application may be made to the High Court or a county court under section 17 of the Married Women's Property Act 1882 (powers of the court in disputes between husband and wife about property) (including that section as extended by section 7 of the Matrimonial Causes (Property and Maintenance) Act 1958) by either of the parties to a marriage notwithstanding that their marriage has been dissolved or annulled so long as the application is made within the period of three years beginning with the date on which the marriage was dissolved or annulled; and references in the said section 17 and the said section 7 to a husband or a wife shall be construed accordingly. **16-002**

Attachment of Earnings Act 1971

CHAPTER 32

Cases in which attachment is available

Courts with power to attach earnings

1.—(1) The High Court may make an attachment of earnings order to secure payments under a High Court maintenance order. **17-001**

(2) A county court may make an attachment of earnings order to secure—

(a) payments under a High Court or a county court maintenance order;
(b) the payment of a judgment debt, other than a debt of less than £5 or such other sum as may be prescribed by county court rules; or
(c) payments under an administration order.

(3) A magistrates' court may make an attachment of earnings order to secure—

(a) payments under a magistrates' court maintenance order;
(b) the payment of any sum adjudged to be paid by a conviction or treated (by any enactment relating to the collection and enforcement of fines, costs, compensation or forfeited recognisances) as so adjudged to be paid; or
(c) the payment of any sum required to be paid by an [order under section 17(2) of the Access to Justice Act 1999][1].

(4) The following provisions of this Act apply, except where otherwise stated, to attachment of earnings orders made, or to be made, by any court.

(5) Any power conferred by this Act to make an attachment of earnings order includes a power to make such an order to secure the discharge of liabilities arising before the coming into force of this Act.

Principal definitions

17-002 **2.** In this Act—

(a) "maintenance order" means any order specified in Schedule 1 to this Act and includes such an order which has been discharged if any arrears are recoverable thereunder;
(b) "High Court maintenance order", "county court maintenance order" and "magistrates' court maintenance order" mean respectively a maintenance order enforceable by the High Court, a county court and a magistrates' court;
(c) "judgment debt" means a sum payable under—
    (i) a judgment or order enforceable by a court in England and Wales (not being a magistrates' court);
    (ii) an order of a magistrates' court for the payment of money recoverable summarily as a civil debt; or
    (iii) an order of any court which is enforceable as if it were for the payment of money so recoverable,

    but does not include any sum payable under a maintenance order or an administration order;
(d) "the relevant adjudication", in relation to any payment secured or to be secured by an attachment of earnings order, means the conviction, judgment, order or other adjudication from which there arises the liability to make the payment; and
(e) "the debtor", in relation to an attachment of earnings order, or to proceedings in which a court has power to make an attachment of earnings order, or to proceedings arising out of such an order, means the person by whom payment is required by the relevant adjudication to be made.

Application for order and conditions of court's power to make it

17-003 **3.**—(1) The following persons may apply for an attachment of earnings order:—

[1] Words substituted by Access to Justice Act 1999 c.22 Sch 4 para 8

(a) the person to whom payment under the relevant adjudication is required to be made (whether directly or through an officer of any court);

(b) where the relevant adjudication is an administration order, any one of the creditors scheduled to the order;

(c) without prejudice to paragraph (a) above, where the application is to a magistrates' court for an order to secure maintenance payments, and there is in force an order under [section 59(1) of the Magistrates' Courts Act 1980"][1], or section 19(2) of the Maintenance Orders Act 1950, that those payments be made to the clerk of a magistrates' court, the clerk of that court;

(d) in the following cases the debtor—

(i) where the application is to a magistrates' court;

or

(ii) where the application is to the High Court or a county court for an order to secure maintenance payments.

(2) An application for an attachment of earnings order to secure maintenance payments shall not be made, except by the debtor, unless at least fifteen days have elapsed since the making of the related maintenance order.

(3) For an attachment of earnings order to be made on the application of any person other than the debtor it must appear to the court that the debtor has failed to make one or more payments required by the relevant adjudication.

(4) Where proceedings are brought—

(a) in the High Court or a county court for the enforcement of a maintenance order by committal under section 5 of the Debtors Act 1869; or

(b) in a magistrates' court for the enforcement of a maintenance order under ["section 76 of the Magistrates' Courts Act 1980"][2] (distress or committal),

then, subject to subsection (5) below, the court may make an attachment of earnings order to secure payments under the maintenance order, instead of dealing with the case under section 5 of the said Act of 1869 or, as the case may be, section 64 of the said Act of 1952.

(5) The court shall not, except on the application of the debtor, make an attachment of earnings order to secure payments under a maintenance order if it appears to it that the debtor's failure to make payments in accordance with the maintenance order is not due to his wilful refusal or culpable neglect.

(6) Where proceedings are brought in a county court for an order of committal under section 5 of the Debtors Act 1869 in respect of a judgment debt for any of the taxes, contributions or liabilities specified in Schedule 2 to this Act, the court may, in any circumstances in which it has power to make such an order, make instead an attachment of earnings order to secure the payment of the judgment debt.

(7) A county court shall not make an attachment of earnings order to secure the payment of a judgment debt if there is in force an order or warrant for the debtor's committal, under section 5 of the Debtors Act 1869, in respect of that debt; but in any such case the court may discharge the order or warrant with a view to making an attachment of earnings order instead.

[1] Words substituted by Magistrates' Courts Act 1980 c.43 s 154 Sch 7 para 97 (a)

[2] Words substituted by Magistrates' Courts Act 1980 c.43 s 154 Sch 7 para 97 (b)

Administration orders in the county court

Extension of power to make administration order

17-004 **4.**—(1) Where, on an application to a county court for an attachment of earnings order to secure the payment of a judgment debt, it appears to the court that the debtor also has other debts, the court—

(a) shall consider whether the case may be one in which all the debtor's liabilities should be dealt with together and that for that purpose [an administration order should be made][1]; and

(b) if of opinion that it may be such a case, shall have power (whether or not it makes the attachment of earnings order applied for), with a view to making an administration order, to order the debtor to furnish to the court a list of all his creditors and the amounts which he owes to them respectively.

(2) If, on receipt of the list referred to in subsection (1)(b) above, it appears to the court that the debtor's whole indebtedness amounts to not more than the amount [which for the time being is the county court limit for the purposes of section 112 of the County Courts Act 1984][2] (limit of total indebtedness governing county court's power to make administration order on application of debtor), the court may make such an order in respect of the debtor's estate.

[(2A) Subsection (2) above is subject to section 112(3) and (4) of the County Courts Act 1984 (which require that, before an administration order is made, notice is to be given to all the creditors and thereafter restricts the right of any creditor to institute bankruptcy proceedings).][3]

(3) [...][4]

(4) Nothing in this section is to be taken as prejudicing any right of a debtor to apply, under [section 112 of the County Courts Act 1984][5] for an administration order.

Attachment of earnings to secure payments under administration order

17-005 **5.**—(1) Where a county court makes an administration order in respect of a debtor's estate, it may also make an attachment of earnings order to secure the payments required by the administration order.

(2) At any time when an administration order is in force a county court may (with or without an application) make an attachment of earnings order to secure the payments required by the administration order, if it appears to the court that the debtor has failed to make any such payment.

(3) The power of a county court under this section to make an attachment of earnings order to secure the payments required by an administration order shall, where the debtor is already subject to an attachment of earnings order to secure the payment of a judgment debt, include power to direct that the last-mentioned order shall take effect (with or without variation under section 9 of this Act) as an order to secure the payments required by the administration order.

---

[1] Words substituted by Insolvency Act 1976 c.60 s 13 (2)

[2] Words substituted by County Courts Act 1984 c.28 s 148 (1) Sch 2 para 40 (a)

[3] Substituted by County Courts Act 1984 c.28 s 148 (1) Sch 2 para 40 (b)

[4] Repealed by Insolvency Act 1976 c.60 s 13 (1) Sch 3

[5] Words substituted by County Courts Act 1984 c.28 s 148 (1) Sch 2 para 40 (c)

Consequences of attachment order

Effect and contents of order

6.—(1) An attachment of earnings order shall be an order directed to a person who appears to the court to have the debtor in his employment and shall operate as an instruction to that person— **17-006**

(a) to make periodical deductions from the debtor's earnings in accordance with Part I of Schedule 3 to this Act; and

(b) at such times as the order may require, or as the court may allow, to pay the amounts deducted to the collecting officer of the court, as specified in the order.

(2) For the purposes of this Act, the relationship of employer and employee shall be treated as subsisting between two persons if one of them as a principal and not as a servant or agent, pays to the other any sums defined as earnings by section 24 of this Act.

(3) An attachment of earnings order shall contain prescribed particulars enabling the debtor to be identified by the employer.

(4) Except where it is made to secure maintenance payments, the order shall specify the whole amount payable under the relevant adjudication (or so much of that amount as remains unpaid), including any relevant costs.

(5) The order shall specify—

(a) the normal deduction rate, that is to say, the rate (expressed as a sum of money per week, month or other period) at which the court thinks it reasonable for the debtor's earnings to be applied to meeting his liability under the relevant adjudication; and

(b) the protected earnings rate, that is to say the rate (so expressed) below which, having regard to the debtor's resources and needs, the court thinks it reasonable that the earnings actually paid to him should not be reduced.

(6) In the case of an order made to secure payments under a maintenance order (not being an order for the payment of a lump sum), the normal deduction rate—

(a) shall be determined after taking account of any right or liability of the debtor to deduct income tax when making the payments; and

(b) shall not exceed the rate which appears to the court necessary for the purpose of—

(i) securing payment of the sums falling due from time to time under the maintenance order, and

(ii) securing payment within a reasonable period of any sums already due and unpaid under the maintenance order.

(7) For the purposes of an attachment of earnings order, the collecting officer of the court shall be (subject to later variation of the order under section 9 of this Act)—

(a) in the case of an order made by the High Court, either—

(i) the proper officer of the High Court, or

(ii) the [appropriate officer][1] of such county court as the order may specify;

(b) in the case of an order made by a county court, the [appropriate officer][2] of that court; and

---

[1] Words substituted by Administration of Justice Act 1977 c.38 s 19 (5) (a)

[2] Words substituted by Administration of Justice Act 1977 c.38 s 19 (5) (a)

(c) in the case of an order made by a magistrates' court, the [justices' chief executive for that court or for][1] another magistrates' court specified in the order.

[(8) In subsection (7) above "appropriate officer"means an officer designated by the Lord Chancellor.][2]

Compliance with order by employer

17-007 7.—(1) Where an attachment of earnings order has been made, the employer shall, if he has been served with the order, comply with it; but he shall be under no liability for non-compliance before seven days have elapsed since the service.

(2) Where a person is served with an attachment of earnings order directed to him and he has not the debtor in his employment, or the debtor subsequently ceases to be in his employment, he shall (in either case), within ten days from the date of service or, as the case may be, the cesser, give notice of that fact to the court.

Interrelation with alternative remedies open to creditor

17-008 **8.**—(1) Where an attachment of earnings order has been made to secure maintenance payments, no order or warrant of commitment shall be issued in consequence of any proceedings for the enforcement of the related maintenance order begun before the making of the attachment of earnings order.

(2) Where a county court has made an attachment of earnings order to secure the payment of a judgment debt—

(a) no order or warrant of commitment shall be issued in consequence of any proceedings for the enforcement of the debt begun before the making of the attachment of earnings order; and

(b) so long as the order is in force, no execution for the recovery of the debt shall issue against any property of the debtor without the leave of the county court.

(3) An attachment of earnings order made to secure maintenance payments shall cease to have effect upon the making of an order of commitment or the issue of a warrant of commitment for the enforcement of the related maintenance order, or upon the exercise for that purpose of the power conferred on a magistrates' court by [section 77(2) of the Magistrates' Courts Act 1980][3] to postpone the issue of such a warrant.

(4) An attachment of earnings order made to secure the payment of a judgment debt shall cease to have effect on the making of an order of commitment or the issue of a warrant of commitment for the enforcement of the debt.

(5) An attachment of earnings order made to secure any payment specified in section 1(3)(b) or (c) of this Act shall cease to have effect on the issue of a warrant committing the debtor to prison for default in making that payment.

Subsequent proceedings

Variation, lapse and discharge of orders

17-009 **9.**—(1) The court may make an order discharging or varying an attachment of earnings order.

[1] Words substituted by Access to Justice Act 1999 c.22 Sch 13 para 66
[2] Added by Administration of Justice Act 1977 c.38 s 19 (5) (b)
[3] Words substituted by Magistrates' Courts Act 1980 c.43 s 154 Sch 7 para 98

(2) Where an order is varied, the employer shall, if he has been served with notice of the variation, comply with the order as varied; but he shall be under no liability for non-compliance before seven days have elapsed since the service.

(3) Rules of court may make provision—

(a) as to the circumstances in which an attachment of earnings order may be varied or discharged by the court of its own motion;

(b) in the case of an attachment of earnings order made by a magistrates' court, for enabling a single justice, on an application made by the debtor on the ground of a material change in his resources and needs since the order was made or last varied, to vary the order for a period of not more than four weeks by an increase of the protected earnings rate.

(4) Where an attachment of earnings order has been made and the person to whom it is directed ceases to have the debtor in his employment, the order shall lapse (except as respects deduction from earnings paid after the cesser and payment to the collecting officer of amounts deducted at any time) and be of no effect unless and until the court again directs it to a person (whether the same as before or another) who appears to the court to have the debtor in his employment.

(5) The lapse of an order under subsection (4) above shall not prevent its being treated as remaining in force for other purposes.

Attachment order in respect of maintenance payments to cease to have effect on the occurrence of certain events

11.—(1) An attachment of earnings order made to secure maintenance payments shall cease to have effect— **17-010**

(a) upon the grant of an application for registration of the related maintenance order under section 2 of the Maintenance Orders Act 1958 (which provides for the registration in a magistrates' court of a High Court or county court maintenance order, and for registration in the High Court of a magistrates' court maintenance order);

(b) where the related maintenance order is registered under Part I of the said Act of 1958, upon the giving of notice with respect thereto under section 5 of that Act (notice with view to cancellation of registration);

(c) subject to subsection (3) below, upon the discharge of the related maintenance order while it is not registered under Part I of the said Act of 1958;

(d) upon the related maintenance order ceasing to be registered in a court in England or Wales, or becoming registered in a court in Scotland or Northern Ireland, under Part II of the Maintenance Orders Act 1950.

(2) Subsection (1)(a) above shall have effect, in the case of an application for registration under section 2(1) of the said Act of 1958, notwithstanding that the grant of the application may subsequently become void under subsection (2) of that section.

(3) Where the related maintenance order is discharged as mentioned in subsection (1)(c) above and it appears to the court discharging the order that arrears thereunder will remain to be recovered after the discharge, that court may, if it thinks fit, direct that subsection (1) shall not apply.

Administrative provisions

Power of court to obtain statements of earnings etc

17-011 **14.**—(1) Where in any proceedings a court has power to make an attachment of earnings order, it may—

(a) order the debtor to give to the court, within a specified period, a statement signed by him of—

(i) the name and address of any person by whom earnings are paid to him;

(ii) specified particulars as to his earnings and anticipated earnings, and as to his resources and needs; and

(iii) specified particulars for the purpose of enabling the debtor to be identified by any employer of his;

(b) order any person appearing to the court to have the debtor in his employment to give to the court, within a specified period, a statement signed by him or on his behalf of specified particulars of the debtor's earnings and anticipated earnings.

(2) Where an attachment of earnings order has been made, the court may at any time thereafter while the order is in force

[(a) make such an order as is described in subsection (1)(a) or (b)above; and

(b) order the debtor to attend before it on a day and at a time specified in the order to give the information described in subsection (1)(a) above.][1]

(3) In the case of an application to a magistrates' court for an attachment of earnings order, or for the variation or discharge of such an order, the power to make an order under subsection (1) or (2) above shall be exercisable also, before the hearing of the application, by a single justice.

(4) Without prejudice to subsections (1) to (3) above, rules of court may provide that where notice of an application for an attachment of earnings order is served on the debtor, it shall include a requirement that he shall give to the court, within such period and in such manner as may be prescribed, a statement in writing of the matters specified in subsection (1)(a) above and of any other prescribed matters which are, or may be, relevant under section 6 of this Act to the determination of the normal deduction rate and the protected earnings rate to be specified in any order made on the application.

(5) In any proceedings in which a court has power to make an attachment of earnings order, and in any proceedings for the making, variation or discharge of such an order, a document purporting to be a statement given to the court in compliance with an order under subsection (1)(a) or (b) above, or with any such requirement of a notice of application for an attachment of earnings order as is mentioned in subsection (4) above, shall, in the absence of proof to the contrary, be deemed to be a statement so given and shall be evidence of the facts stated therein.

Miscellaneous provisions

Enforcement provisions

17-012 **23.**—(1) If, after being served with notice of an application to a county court for an attachment of earnings order or for the variation of such an order [or with

[1] Substituted by Administration of Justice Act 1982 c.53 s 53 (1)

an order made under section 14(2)(b) above][1], the debtor fails to attend on the day and at the time specified for any hearing of the application, the court may adjourn the hearing and order him to attend at a specified time on another day; and if the debtor—

(a) fails to attend at that time on that day; or

(b) attends, but refuses to be sworn or give evidence,

he may be ordered by the judge to be imprisoned for not more than fourteen days.

[(1A) In any case where the judge has power to make an order of imprisonment under subsection (1) for failure to attend,he may, in lieu of or in addition to making that order, order the debtor to be arrested and brought before the court either forthwith or at such time as the judge may direct.][2]

(2) Subject to this section, a person commits an offence if—

(a) being required by section 7(1) or 9(2) of this Act to comply with an attachment of earnings order, he fails to do so; or

(b) being required by section 7(2) of this Act to give a notice for the purposes of that subsection, he fails to give it, or fails to give it within the time required by that subsection; or

(c) he fails to comply with an order under section 14(1) of this Act or with any such requirement of a notice of application for an attachment of earnings order as is mentioned in section 14(4), or fails (in either case) to comply within the time required by the order or notice; or

(d) he fails to comply with section 15 of this Act; or

(e) he gives a notice for the purposes of section 7(2) of this Act, or a notification for the purposes of section 15, which he knows to be false in a material particular, or recklessly gives such a notice or notification which is false in a material particular; or

(f) in purported compliance with section 7(2) or 15 of this Act, or with an order under section 14(1), or with any such requirement of a notice of application for an attachment of earnings order as is mentioned in section 14(4), he makes any statement which he knows to be false in a material particular, or recklessly makes any statement which is false in a material particular.

(3) Where a person commits an offence under subsection (2) above in relation to proceedings in, or to an attachment of earnings order made by, the High Court or a county court, he shall be liable on summary conviction to a fine of not more than [level 2 on the standard scale][3] or he may be ordered by a judge of the High Court or the county court judge (as the case may be) to pay a fine of not more than [£250][4] or, in the case of an offence specified in subsection (4) below, to be imprisoned for not more than fourteen days; and where a person commits an offence under subsection (2) otherwise than as mentioned above in this subsection, he shall be liable on summary conviction to a fine of not more than [level 2 on the standard scale][5].

(4) The offences referred to above in the case of which a judge may impose imprisonment are—

[1] Words inserted by Administration of Justice Act 1982 c.53 s 53 (2) (a)
[2] Inserted by Contempt of Court Act 1981 c.49 s 14 (5) Sch 2 Pt III para 6
[3] Words substituted by Criminal Justice Act 1982 c.48 ss 38, 46
[4] Figure substituted by Criminal Justice Act 1991 c.53 Sch 4 (I) para 1
[5] Words substituted by Criminal Justice Act 1982 c.48 ss 38, 46

(a) an offence under subsection (2)(c) or (d), if committed by the debtor; and

(b) an offence under subsection (2)(e) or (f), whether committed by the debtor or any other person.

(5) It shall be a defence—

(a) for a person charged with an offence under subsection (2)(a) above to prove that he took all reasonable steps to comply with the attachment of earnings order in question;

(b) for a person charged with an offence under subsection (2)(b) to prove that he did not know, and could not reasonably be expected to know, that the debtor was not in his employment, or (as the case may be) had ceased to be so, and that he gave the required notice as soon as reasonably practicable after the fact came to his knowledge.

(6) Where a person is convicted or dealt with for an offence under subsection (2)(a), the court may order him to pay, to whoever is the collecting officer of the court for the purposes of the attachment of earnings order in question, any sums deducted by that person from the debtor's earnings and not already paid to the collecting officer.

(7) Where under this section a person is ordered by a judge of the High Court or a county court judge to be imprisoned, the judge may at any time revoke the order and, if the person is already in custody, order his discharge.

(8) Any fine imposed by a judge of the High Court under subsection (3) above and any sums ordered by the High Court to be paid under subsection (6) above shall be recoverable in the same way as a fine imposed by that court in the exercise of its jurisdiction to punish for contempt of court; [section 129 of the County Courts Act 1984][1] (enforcement of fines) shall apply to payment of a fine imposed by a county court judge under subsection (3) and of any sums ordered by a county court judge to be paid under subsection (6); and any sum ordered by a magistrates' court to be paid under subsection (6) shall be recoverable as a sum adjudged to be paid on a conviction by that court.

(9) For the purposes of section 13 of the Administration of Justice Act 1960 (appeal in cases of contempt of court), subsection (3) above shall be treated as an enactment enabling the High Court or a county court to deal with an offence under subsection (2) above as if it were contempt of court.

(10) In this section references to proceedings in a court are to proceedings in which that court has power to make an attachment of earnings order or has made such an order.

[(11) A district judge, assistant district judge or deputy district judge shall have the same powers under this section as a judge of a county court.][2]

Meaning of "earnings"

17-013 **24.**—(1) For the purposes of this Act, but subject to the following subsection, "earnings" are any sums payable to a person—

(a) by way of wages or salary (including any fees, bonus, commission, overtime pay or other emoluments payable in addition to wages or salary or payable under a contract of service);

(b) by way of pension (including an annuity in respect of past services, whether or not rendered to the person paying the annuity, and including periodical payments by way of compensation for the loss, abolition or

[1] Words substituted by County Courts Act 1984 c.28 s 148 (1) Sch 2 para 41

[2] Subsection inserted by Courts and Legal Services Act 1990 c.41 s 125 (2) Sch 17 para 6

relinquishment, or diminution in the emoluments, of any office or employment);

[(c) by way of statutory sick pay.][1]

(2) The following shall not be treated as earnings:—

(a) sums payable by any public department of the Government of Northern Ireland or of a territory outside the United Kingdom;

(b) pay or allowances payable to the debtor as a member of Her Majesty's forces [other than pay or allowances payable by his employer to him as a special member of a reserve force (within the meaning of the Reserve Forces Act 1996)][2];

(c) pension, allowances or benefit payable under any [enactment relating to social security;][3]

(d) pension or allowances payable in respect of disablement or disability;

(e) [except in relation to a maintenance order][4] wages payable to a person as a seaman, other than wages payable to him as a seaman of a fishing boat.

[(f) guaranteed minimum pension within the meaning of the [Pension Schemes Act 1993][5].][6]

Matrimonial Causes Act 1973

CHAPTER 18

PART I

DIVORCE, NULLITY AND OTHER MATRIMONIAL SUITS

Divorce

Divorce on breakdown of marriage

1.—(1) Subject to section 3 below, a petition for divorce may be presented to the court by either party to a marriage on the ground that the marriage has broken down irretrievably. **18-001**

(2) The court hearing a petition for divorce shall not hold the marriage to have broken down irretrievably unless the petitioner satisfies the court of one or more of the following facts, that is to say—

(a) that the respondent has committed adultery and the petitioner finds it intolerable to live with the respondent;

(b) that the respondent has behaved in such a way that the petitioner cannot reasonably be expected to live with the respondent;

---

1 Inserted by Social Security Act 1985 c.53 s 21 Sch 4 para 1

2 Words inserted by SI 1998/3086 reg 6 (1)

3 Words substituted by Social Security Act 1986 c.50 s 86 Sch 10 Pt VI para 102

4 Words inserted by Merchant Shipping Act 1979 c.39 s 39 (1)

5 Words substituted by Pension Schemes Act 1993 c.48 Sch 8 para 4

6 Inserted by Social Security Pensions Act 1975 c.60 Sch 4 Pt I para 15

(c) that the respondent has deserted the petitioner for a continuous period of at least two years immediately preceding the presentation of the petition;

(d) that the parties to the marriage have lived apart for a continuous period of at least two years immediately preceding the presentation of the petition (hereafter in this Act referred to as "two years' separation") and the respondent consents to a decree being granted;

(e) that the parties to the marriage have lived apart for a continuous period of at least five years immediately preceding the presentation of the petition (hereafter in this Act referred to as "five years' separation").

(3) On a petition for divorce it shall be the duty of the court to inquire, so far as it reasonably can, into the facts alleged by the petitioner and into any facts alleged by the respondent.

(4) If the court is satisfied on the evidence of any such fact as is mentioned in subsection (2) above, then, unless it is satisfied on all the evidence that the marriage has not broken down irretrievably, it shall, subject to [section 5][1] below, grant a decree of divorce.

(5) Every decree of divorce shall in the first instance be a decree nisi and shall not be made absolute before the expiration of six months from its grant unless the High Court by general order from time to time fixes a shorter period, or unless in any particular case the court in which the proceedings are for the time being pending from time to time by special order fixes a shorter period than the period otherwise applicable for the time being by virtue of this subsection.

Supplemental provisions as to facts raising presumption of breakdown

18-002 **2.**—(1) One party to a marriage shall not be entitled to rely for the purposes of section 1(2)(a) above on adultery committed by the other if, after it became known to him that the other had committed that adultery, the parties have lived with each other for a period exceeding, or periods together exceeding, six months.

(2) Where the parties to a marriage have lived with each other after it became known to one party that the other had committed adultery, but subsection (1) above does not apply, in any proceedings for divorce in which the petitioner relies on that adultery the fact that the parties have lived with each other after that time shall be disregarded in determining for the purposes of section 1(2)(a) above whether the petitioner finds it intolerable to live with the respondent.

(3) Where in any proceedings for divorce the petitioner alleges that the respondent has behaved in such a way that the petitioner cannot reasonably be expected to live with him, but the parties to the marriage have lived with each other for a period or periods after the date of the occurrence of the final incident relied on by the petitioner and held by the court to support his allegation, that fact shall be disregarded in determining for the purposes of section 1(2)(b) above whether the petitioner cannot reasonably be expected to live with the respondent if the length of that period or of those periods together was six months or less.

(4) For the purposes of section 1(2)(c) above the court may treat a period of desertion as having continued at a time when the deserting party was incapable of continuing the necessary intention if the evidence before the court is such that,

[1] Words substituted (with saving) by Matrimonial and Family Proceedings Act 1984 c.42 ss 46 (1), 48 (3) Sch 1, Sch 2 para 10

had that party not been so incapable, the court would have inferred that his desertion continued at that time.

(5) In considering for the purposes of section 1(2) above whether the period for which the respondent has deserted the petitioner or the period for which the parties to a marriage have lived apart has been continuous, no account shall be taken of any one period (not exceeding six months) or of any two or more periods (not exceeding six months in all) during which the parties resumed living with each other, but no period during which the parties lived with each other shall count as part of the period of desertion or of the period for which the parties to the marriage lived apart, as the case may be.

(6) For the purposes of section 1(2)(d) and (e) above and this section a husband and wife shall be treated as living apart unless they are living with each other in the same household, and references in this section to the parties to a marriage living with each other shall be construed as references to their living with each other in the same household.

(7) Provision shall be made by rules of court for the purpose of ensuring that where in pursuance of section 1(2)(d) above the petitioner alleges that the respondent consents to a decree being granted the respondent has been given such information as will enable him to understand the consequences to him of his consenting to a decree being granted and the steps which he must take to indicate that he consents to the grant of a decree.

[Bar on petitions for divorce within one year of marriage

3.—(1) No petition for divorce shall be presented to the court before the expiration of the period of one year from the date of the marriage. **18-003**

(2) Nothing in this section shall prohibit the presentation of a petition based on matters which occurred before the expiration of that period.][1]

Divorce not precluded by previous judicial separation

4.—(1) A person shall not be prevented from presenting a petition for divorce, or the court from granting a decree of divorce, by reason only that the petitioner or respondent has at any time, on the same facts or substantially the same facts as those proved in support of the petition, been granted a decree of judicial separation or an order under, or having effect as if made under, the Matrimonial Proceedings (Magistrates' Courts) Act 1960 [or Part I of the Domestic Proceedings and Magistrates' Courts Act 1978][2] or any corresponding enactments in force in Northern Ireland, the Isle of Man or any of the Channel Islands. **18-004**

(2) On a petition for divorce in such a case as is mentioned in subsection (1) above, the court may treat the decree or order as sufficient proof of any adultery, desertion or other fact by reference to which it was granted, but shall not grant a decree of divorce without receiving evidence from the petitioner.

(3) Where a petition for divorce in such a case follows a decree of judicial separation or [(subject to sub-section (5) below)][3] an order containing a provision exempting one party to the marriage from the obligation to cohabit with the other, for the purposes of that petition a period of desertion immediately

[1] Substituted (with saving) by Matrimonial and Family Proceedings Act 1984 c.42 ss 1, 46 (1), 48 (2) Sch 2

[2] Words inserted by Domestic Proceedings and Magistrates' Courts Act 1978 c.22 s 89 (2) Sch 2 para 38

[3] Words inserted by Domestic Proceedings and Magistrates' Courts Act 1978 c.22 ss 62 (a), 89 (2)

preceding the institution of the proceedings for the decree or order shall, if the parties have not resumed cohabitation and the decree or order has been continuously in force since it was granted, be deemed immediately to precede the presentation of the petition.

[(4) For the purposes of section 1(2)(c) above the court may treat as a period during which the respondent has deserted the petitioner any of the following periods, that is to say—

(a) any period during which there is in force an injunction granted by the High Court or a county court which excludes the respondent from the matrimonial home;

(b) any period during which there is in force an order made by the High Court or a county court under—[section 1 or 9 of the Matrimonial Homes Act 1983][1]

which prohibits the exercise by the respondent of the right to occupy a dwelling-house in which the applicant and the respondent have or at any time have had a matrimonial home;

(c) any period during which there is in force an order made by a magistrates' court under section 16(3) of the Domestic Proceedings and Magistrates' Courts Act 1978 which requires the respondent to leave the matrimonial home or prohibits the respondent from entering the matrimonial home.

(5) Where—

(a) a petition for divorce is presented after the date on which Part I of the Domestic Proceedings and Magistrates' Courts Act 1978 comes into force, and

(b) an order made under the Matrimonial Proceedings (Magistrates' Courts) Act 1960 containing a provision exempting the petitioner from the obligation to cohabit with the respondent is in force on that date,

then, for the purposes of section 1(2)(c) above, the court may treat a period during which such a provision was included in that order (whether before or after that date) as a period during which the respondent has deserted the petitioner.][2]

Refusal of decree in five year separation cases on grounds of grave hardship to respondent

18-005 **5.**—(1) The respondent to a petition for divorce in which the petitioner alleges five years' separation may oppose the grant of a decree on the ground that the dissolution of the marriage will result in grave financial or other hardship to him and that it would in all the circumstances be wrong to dissolve the marriage.

(2) Where the grant of a decree is opposed by virtue of this section, then—

(a) if the court finds that the petitioner is entitled to rely in support of his petition on the fact of five years' separation and makes no such finding as to any other fact mentioned in section 1(2) above, and

(b) if apart from this section the court would grant a decree on the petition,

the court shall consider all the circumstances, including the conduct of the parties to the marriage and the interests of those parties and of any children or other persons concerned, and if of opinion that the dissolution of the marriage will result in grave financial or other hardship to the respondent and that it would

[1] Words substituted by Matrimonial Homes Act 1983 c.19 ss 12, 13 Sch 2
[2] Added by Domestic Proceedings and Magistrates' Courts Act 1978 c.22 ss 62 (b), 89 (2)

in all the circumstances be wrong to dissolve the marriage it shall dismiss the petition.

(3) For the purposes of this section hardship shall include the loss of the chance of acquiring any benefit which the respondent might acquire if the marriage were not dissolved.

Attempts at reconciliation of parties to marriage

6.—(1) Provision shall be made by rules of court for requiring the solicitor acting for a petitioner for divorce to certify whether he has discussed with the petitioner the possibility of a reconciliation and given him the names and addresses of persons qualified to help effect a reconciliation between parties to a marriage who have become estranged. **18-006**

(2) If at any stage of proceedings for divorce it appears to the court that there is a reasonable possibility of a reconciliation between the parties to the marriage, the court may adjourn the proceedings for such period as it thinks fit to enable attempts to be made to effect such a reconciliation.

The power conferred by the foregoing provision is additional to any other power of the court to adjourn proceedings.

Consideration by the court of certain agreements or arrangements

7. Provision may be made by rules of court for enabling the parties to a marriage, or either of them, on application made either before or after the presentation of a petition for divorce, to refer to the court any agreement or arrangement made or proposed to be made between them, being an agreement or arrangement which relates to, arises out of, or is connected with, the proceedings for divorce which are contemplated or, as the case may be, have begun, and for enabling the court to express an opinion, should it think it desirable to do so, as to the reasonableness of the agreement or arrangement and to give such directions, if any, in the matter as it thinks fit. **18-007**

Intervention of Queen's Proctor

8.—(1) In the case of a petition for divorce— **18-008**

(a) the court may, if it thinks fit, direct all necessary papers in the matter to be sent to the Queen's Proctor, who shall under the directions of the Attorney-General instruct counsel to argue before the court any question in relation to the matter which the court considers it necessary or expedient to have fully argued;

(b) any person may at any time during the progress of the proceedings or before the decree nisi is made absolute give information to the Queen's Proctor on any matter material to the due decision of the case, and the Queen's Proctor may thereupon take such steps as the Attorney-General considers necessary or expedient.

(2) Where the Queen's Proctor intervenes or shows cause against a decree nisi in any proceedings for divorce, the court may make such order as may be just as to the payment by other parties to the proceedings of the costs incurred by him in so doing or as to the payment by him of any costs incurred by any of those parties by reason of his so doing.

(3) The Queen's Proctor shall be entitled to charge as part of the expenses of his office—

(a) the costs of any proceedings under subsection (1)(a) above;

(b) where his reasonable costs of intervening or showing cause as mentioned in subsection (2) above are not fully satisfied by any order under that subsection, the amount of the difference;

(c) if the Treasury so directs, any costs which he pays to any parties under an order made under subsection (2).

Proceedings after decree nisi: general powers of court

18-009 **9.**—(1) Where a decree of divorce has been granted but not made absolute, then, without prejudice to section 8 above, any person (excluding a party to the proceedings other than the Queen's Proctor) may show cause why the decree should not be made absolute by reason of material facts not having been brought before the court; and in such a case the court may—

(a) notwithstanding anything in section 1(5) above (but subject to sections 10(2) to (4) and 41 below) make the decree absolute; or

(b) rescind the decree; or

(c) require further inquiry; or

(d) otherwise deal with the case as it thinks fit.

(2) Where a decree of divorce has been granted and no application for it to be made absolute has been made by the party to whom it was granted, then, at any time after the expiration of three months from the earliest date on which that party could have made such an application, the party against whom it was granted may make an application to the court, and on that application the court may exercise any of the powers mentioned in paragraphs (a) to (d) of subsection (1) above.

Proceedings after decree nisi: special protection for respondent in separation cases

18-010 **10.**—(1) Where in any case the court has granted a decree of divorce on the basis of a finding that the petitioner was entitled to rely in support of his petition on the fact of two years' separation coupled with the respondent's consent to a decree being granted and has made no such finding as to any other fact mentioned in section 1(2) above, the court may, on an application made by the respondent at any time before the decree is made absolute, rescind the decree if it is satisfied that the petitioner misled the respondent (whether intentionally or unintentionally) about any matter which the respondent took into account in deciding to give his consent.

(2) The following provisions of this section apply where—

(a) the respondent to a petition for divorce in which the petitioner alleged two years' or five years' separation coupled, in the former case, with the respondent's consent to a decree being granted, has applied to the court for consideration under subsection (3) below of his financial position after the divorce; and

(b) the court has granted a decree on the petition on the basis of a finding that the petitioner was entitled to rely in support of his petition on the fact of two years' or five years' separation (as the case may be) and has made no such finding as to any other fact mentioned in section 1(2) above.

(3) The court hearing an application by the respondent under subsection (2) above shall consider all the circumstances, including the age, health, conduct, earning capacity, financial resources and financial obligations of each of the parties, and the financial position of the respondent, as having regard to the divorce, it is likely to be after the death of the petitioner should the petitioner die

first; and, subject to subsection (4) below, the court shall not make the decree absolute unless it is satisfied—

(a) that the petitioner should not be required to make any financial provision for the respondent, or

(b) that the financial provision made by the petitioner for the respondent is reasonable and fair or the best that can be made in the circumstances.

(4) The court may if it thinks fit makes the decree absolute notwithstanding the requirements of subsection (3) above if—

(a) it appears that there are circumstances making it desirable that the decree should be made absolute without delay, and

(b) the court has obtained a satisfactory undertaking from the petitioner that he will make such financial provision for the respondent as the court may approve.

[Proceedings after decree nisi: religious marriage

10A—(1) This section applies if a decree of divorce has been granted but not made absolute and the parties to the marriage concerned— **18-011**

(a) were married in accordance with—

(i) the usages of the Jews, or

(ii) any other prescribed religious usages; and

(b) must co-operate if the marriage is to be dissolved in accordance with those usages.

(2) On the application of either party, the court may order that a decree of divorce is not to be made absolute until a declaration made by both parties that they have taken such steps as are required to dissolve the marriage in accordance with those usages is produced to the court.

(3) An order under subsection (2)—

(a) may be made only if the court is satisfied that in all the circumstances of the case it is just and reasonable to do so; and

(b) may be revoked at any time.

(4) A declaration of a kind mentioned in subsection (2)—

(a) must be in a specified form;

(b) must, in specified cases, be accompanied by such documents as may be specified; and

(c) must, in specified cases, satisfy such other requirements as may be specified.

(5) The validity of a decree of divorce made by reference to such a declaration is not to be affected by any inaccuracy in that declaration.

(6) "Prescribed" means prescribed in an order made by the Lord Chancellor and such an order—

(a) must be made by statutory instrument;

(b) shall be subject to annulment in pursuance of a resolution of either House of Parliament.

(7) "Specified" means specified in rules of court.][1]

[1] Added by Divorce (Religious Marriages) Act 2002 c.27 s 1 (1)

Nullity

Grounds on which a marriage is void

18-012 **11.** A marriage celebrated after 31st July 1971 shall be void on the following grounds only, that is to say—

(a) that it is not a valid marriage under the provisions of [the [Marriage Acts 1949 to 1986][1]][2] (that is to say where—
  (i) the parties are within the prohibited degrees of relationship;
  (ii) either party is under the age of sixteen; or
  (iii) the parties have intermarried in disregard of certain requirements as to the formation of marriage);

(b) that at the time of the marriage either party was already lawfully married;

(c) that the parties are not respectively male and female;

(d) in the case of a polygamous marriage entered into outside England and Wales, that either party was at the time of the marriage domiciled in England and Wales.

For the purposes of paragraph (d) of this subsection a marriage [is not polygamous if][3] at its inception neither party has any spouse additional to the other.

Grounds on which a marriage is voidable

18-013 **12.** A marriage celebrated after 31st July 1971 shall be voidable on the following grounds only, that is to say—

(a) that the marriage has not been consummated owing to the incapacity of either party to consummate it;

(b) that the marriage has not been consummated owing to the wilful refusal of the respondent to consummate it;

(c) that either party to the marriage did not validly consent to it, whether in consequence of duress, mistake, unsoundness of mind or otherwise;

(d) that at the time of the marriage either party, though capable of giving a valid consent, was suffering (whether continuously or intermittently) from mental disorder within the meaning of [the Mental Health Act 1983][4] of such a kind or to such an extent as to be unfitted for marriage;

(e) that at the time of the marriage the respondent was suffering from venereal disease in a communicable form;

(f) that at the time of the marriage the respondent was pregnant by some person other than the petitioner.

Bars to relief where marriage is voidable

18-014 **13.**—(1) The court shall not, in proceedings instituted after 31st July 1971, grant a decree of nullity on the ground that a marriage is voidable if the respondent satisfies the court—

(a) that the petitioner, with knowledge that it was open to him to have the marriage avoided, so conducted himself in relation to the respondent as

[1] Words substituted by Marriage (Prohibited Degrees of Relationship) Act 1986 c.16 s 6 (4)
[2] Words substituted by virtue of Marriage Act 1983 c.32 s 12 (1)
[3] Words substituted by Private International Law (Miscellaneous Provisions) Act 1995 c.42 Sch 1 para 2 (2)
[4] Words substituted by Mental Health Act 1983 c.20 ss 146, 147, 148 Sch 4 para 34

to lead the respondent reasonably to believe that he would not seek to do so; and

(b) that it would be unjust to the respondent to grant the decree.

[(2) Without prejudice to subsection (1) above, the court shall not grant a decree of nullity by virtue of section 12 above on the grounds mentioned in paragraph (c), (d), (e) or (f) of that section unless—

(a) it is satisfied that proceedings were instituted within the period of three years from the date of the marriage, or

(b) leave for the institution of proceedings after the expiration of that period has been granted under subsection (4) below.][1]

(3) Without prejudice to subsections (1) and (2) above, the court shall not grant a decree of nullity by virtue of section 12 above on the grounds mentioned in paragraph (e) or (f) of that section unless it is satisfied that the petitioner was at the time of the marriage ignorant of the facts alleged.

[(4) In the case of proceedings for the grant of a decree of a nullity by virtue of section 12 above on the grounds mentioned in paragraph (c), (d), (e) or (f) of that section, a judge of the court may, on an application made to him, grant leave for the institution of proceedings after the expiration of the period of three years from the date of the marriage if—

(a) he is satisfied that the petitioner has at some time during that period suffered from mental disorder within the meaning of the Mental Health Act 1983, and

(b) he considers that in all the circumstances of the case it would be just to grant leave for the institution of proceedings.

(5) An application for leave under subsection (4) above may be made after the expiration of the period of three years from the date of the marriage.][2]

Marriages governed by foreign law or celebrated abroad under English law

14.—(1) Where, apart from this Act, any matter affecting the validity of a marriage would fall to be determined (in accordance with the rules of private international law) by reference to the law of a country outside England and Wales, nothing in section 11, 12 or 13(1) above shall— **18-015**

(a) preclude the determination of that matter as aforesaid; or

(b) require the application to the marriage of the grounds or bar there mentioned except so far as applicable in accordance with those rules.

(2) In the case of a marriage which purports to have been celebrated under the Foreign Marriage Acts 1892 to 1947 or has taken place outside England and Wales and purports to be a marriage under common law, section 11 above is without prejudice to any ground on which the marriage may be void under those Acts or, as the case may be, by virtue of the rules governing the celebration of marriages outside England and Wales under common law.

Application of ss. 1(5), 8 and 9 to nullity proceedings

15. Sections 1(5), 8 and 9 above shall apply in relation to proceedings for nullity of marriage as if for any reference in those provisions to divorce there were substituted a reference to nullity of marriage. **18-016**

Effect of decree of nullity in case of voidable marriage

16. A decree of nullity granted after 31st July 1971 in respect of a voidable marriage shall operate to annul the marriage only as respects any time after the **18-017**

[1] Substituted by Matrimonial and Family Proceedings Act 1984 c.42 ss 2 (2), 48 (2)

[2] Inserted by Matrimonial and Family Proceedings Act 1984 c.42 ss 2 (3), 48 (2)

decree has been made absolute, and the marriage shall, notwithstanding the decree, be treated as if it had existed up to that time.

Other matrimonial suits

Judicial separation

18-018 **17.**—(1) A petition for judicial separation may be presented to the court by either party to a marriage on the ground that any such fact as is mentioned in section 1(2) above exists, and the provisions of section 2 above shall apply accordingly for the purposes of a petition for judicial separation alleging any such fact, as they apply in relation to a petition for divorce alleging that fact.

(2) On a petition for judicial separation it shall be the duty of the court to inquire, so far as it reasonably can, into the facts alleged by the petitioner and into any facts alleged by the respondent, but the court shall not be concerned to consider whether the marriage has broken down irretrievably, and if it is satisfied on the evidence of any such fact as is mentioned in section 1(2) above it shall, subject to section 41 below, grant a decree of judicial separation.

(3) Sections 6 and 7 above shall apply for the purpose of encouraging the reconciliation of parties to proceedings for judicial separation and of enabling the parties to a marriage to refer to the court for its opinion an agreement or arrangement relevant to actual or contemplated proceedings for judicial separation, as they apply in relation to proceedings for divorce.

Effects of judicial separation

18-019 **18.**—(1) Where the court grants a decree of judicial separation it shall no longer be obligatory for the petitioner to cohabit with the respondent.

(2) If while a decree of judicial separation is in force and the separation is continuing either of the parties to the marriage dies intestate as respects all or any of his or her real or personal property, the property as respects which he or she died intestate shall devolve as if the other party to the marriage had then been dead.

(3) Notwithstanding anything in section 2(1)(a) of the Matrimonial Proceedings (Magistrates' Courts) Act 1960, a provision in force under an order made, or having effect as if made, under that section exempting one party to a marriage from the obligation to cohabit with the other shall not have effect as a decree of judicial separation for the purposes of subsection (2) above.

Presumption of death and dissolution of marriage

18-020 **19.**—(1) Any married person who alleges that reasonable grounds exist for supposing that the other party to the marriage is dead may, [...][1] present a petition to the court to have it presumed that the other party is dead and to have the marriage dissolved, and the court may, if satisfied that such reasonable grounds exist, grant a decree of presumption of death and dissolution of the marriage.

(2) [...][2]

(3) In any proceedings under this section the fact that for a period of seven years or more the other party to the marriage has been continually absent from the petitioner and the petitioner has no reason to believe that the other party has been living within that time shall be evidence that the other party is dead until the contrary is proved.

[1] Words repealed by Domicile and Matrimonial Proceedings Act 1973 c.45 s 17 (2) Sch 6
[2] Repealed by Domicile and Matrimonial Proceedings Act 1973 c.45 s 17 (2) Sch 6

(4) Sections 1(5), 8 and 9 above shall apply to a petition and a decree under this section as they apply to a petition for divorce and a decree of divorce respectively.

(5) [...][1]

(6) It is hereby declared that neither collusion nor any other conduct on the part of the petitioner which has at any time been a bar to relief in matrimonial proceedings constitutes a bar to the grant of a decree under this section.

General

Relief for respondent in divorce proceedings

20. If in any proceedings for divorce the respondent alleges and proves any such fact as is mentioned in subsection (2) of section 1 above (treating the respondent as the petitioner and the petitioner as the respondent for the purposes of that subsection) the court may give to the respondent the relief to which he would have been entitled if he had presented a petition seeking that relief. **18-021**

PART II

FINANCIAL RELIEF FOR PARTIES TO MARRIAGE AND CHILDREN OF FAMILY

Financial provision and property adjustment orders

Financial provision and property adjustment orders

21.—(1) The financial provision orders for the purposes of this Act are the orders for periodical or lump sum provision available (subject to the provisions of this Act) under section 23 below for the purpose of adjusting the financial position of the parties to a marriage and any children of the family in connection with proceedings for divorce, nullity of marriage or judicial separation and under section 27(6) below on proof of neglect by one party to a marriage to provide, or to make a proper contribution towards, reasonable maintenance for the other or a child of the family, that is to say— **18-022**

(a) any order for periodical payments in favour of a party to a marriage under section 23(1)(a) or 27(6)(a) or in favour of a child of the family under section 23(1)(d), (2) or (4) or 27(6)(d);

(b) any order for secured periodical payments in favour of a party to a marriage under section 23(1)(b) or 27(6)(b) or in favour of a child of the family under section 23(1)(e), (2) or (4) or 27(6)(e); and

(c) any order for lump sum provision in favour of a party to a marriage under section 23(1)(c) or 27(6)(c) or in favour of a child of the family under section 23(1)(f), (2) or (4) or 27(6)(f);

and references in this Act (except in paragraphs 17(1) and 23 of Schedule 1 below) to periodical payments orders, secured periodical payments orders, and orders for the payment of a lump sum are references to all or some of the financial provision orders requiring the sort of financial provision in question according as the context of each reference may require.

(2) The property adjustment orders for the purposes of this Act are the orders dealing with property rights available (subject to the provisions of this Act)

[1] Repealed by Domicile and Matrimonial Proceedings Act 1973 c.45 s 17 (2) Sch 6

under section 24 below for the purpose of adjusting the financial position of the parties to a marriage and any children of the family on or after the grant of a decree of divorce, nullity of marriage or judicial separation, that is to say—

(a) any order under subsection (1)(a) of that section for a transfer of property;

(b) any order under subsection (1)(b) of that section for a settlement of property; and

(c) any order under subsection (1)(c) or (d) of that section for a variation of settlement.

[Pension sharing orders

18-023 **21A.**—(1) For the purposes of this Act, a pension sharing order is an order which—

(a) provides that one party's—

(i) shareable rights under a specified pension arrangement, or

(ii) shareable state scheme rights,

be subject to pension sharing for the benefit of the other party, and

(b) specifies the percentage value to be transferred.

(2) In subsection (1) above—

(a) the reference to shareable rights under a pension arrangement is to rights in relation to which pension sharing is available under Chapter I of Part IV of the Welfare Reform and Pensions Act 1999, or under corresponding Northern Ireland legislation,

(b) the reference to shareable state scheme rights is to rights in relation to which pension sharing is available under Chapter II of Part IV of the Welfare Reform and Pensions Act 1999, or under corresponding Northern Ireland legislation, and

(c) "party" means a party to a marriage.][1]

Ancillary relief in connection with divorce proceedings, etc

Maintenance pending suit

18-024 **22.** On a petition for divorce, nullity of marriage or judicial separation, the court may make an order for maintenance pending suit, that is to say, an order requiring either party to the marriage to make to the other such periodical payments for his or her maintenance and for such term, being a term beginning not earlier than the date of the presentation of the petition and ending with the date of the determination of the suit, as the court thinks reasonable.

Financial provision orders in connection with divorce proceedings, etc

18-025 **23.**—(1) On granting a decree of divorce, a decree of nullity of marriage or a decree of judicial separation or at any time thereafter (whether, in the case of a decree of divorce or of nullity of marriage, before or after the decree is made absolute), the court may make any one or more of the following orders, that is to say—

(a) an order that either party to the marriage shall make to the other such periodical payments, for such term, as may be specified in the order;

(b) an order that either party to the marriage shall secure to the other to the satisfaction of the court such periodical payments, for such term, as may be so specified;

[1] Added by Welfare Reform and Pensions Act 1999 c.30 Sch 3 para 2

(c) an order that either party to the marriage shall pay to the other such lump sum or sums as may be so specified;
(d) an order that a party to the marriage shall make to such person as may be specified in the order for the benefit of a child of the family, or to such a child, such periodical payments, for such term, as may be so specified;
(e) an order that a party to the marriage shall secure to such person as may be so specified for the benefit of such a child, or to such a child, to the satisfaction of the court, such periodical payments, for such term, as may be so specified;
(f) an order that a party to the marriage shall pay to such person as may be so specified for the benefit of such a child, or to such a child, such lump sum as may be so specified;

subject, however, in the case of an order under paragraph (d), (e) or (f) above, to the restrictions imposed by section 29(1) and (3) below on the making of financial provision orders in favour of children who have attained the age of eighteen.

(2) The court may also, subject to those restrictions, make any one or more of the orders mentioned in subsection (1)(d), (e) and (f) above—
(a) in any proceedings for divorce, nullity of marriage or judicial separation, before granting a decree; and
(b) where any such proceedings are dismissed after the beginning of the trial, either forthwith or within a reasonable period after the dismissal.

(3) Without prejudice to the generality of subsection (1)(c) or (f) above—
(a) an order under this section that a party to a marriage shall pay a lump sum to the other party may be made for the purpose of enabling that other party to meet any liabilities or expenses reasonably incurred by him or her in maintaining himself or herself or any child of the family before making an application for an order under this section in his or her favour;
(b) an order under this section for the payment of a lump sum to or for the benefit of a child of the family may be made for the purpose of enabling any liabilities or expenses reasonably incurred by or for the benefit of that child before the making of an application for an order under this section in his favour to be met; and
(c) an order under this section for the payment of a lump sum may provide for the payment of that sum by instalments of such amount as may be specified in the order and may require the payment of the instalments to be secured to the satisfaction of the court.

(4) The power of the court under subsection (1) or (2)(a) above to make an order in favour of a child of the family shall be exercisable from time to time; and where the court makes an order in favour of a child under subsection (2)(b) above, it may from time to time, subject to the restrictions mentioned in subsection (1) above, make a further order in his favour of any of the kinds mentioned in subsection (1)(d), (e) or (f) above.

(5) Without prejudice to the power to give a direction under section 30 below for the settlement of an instrument by conveyancing counsel, where an order is made under subsection (1)(a), (b) or (c) above on or after granting a decree of divorce or nullity of marriage, neither the order nor any settlement made in pursuance of the order shall take effect unless the decree has been made absolute.

[(6) Where the court—
(a) makes an order under this section for the payment of a lump sum; and

(b) directs—

(i) that payment of that sum or any part of it shall be deferred; or

(ii) that that sum or any part of it shall be paid by instalments,

the court may order that the amount deferred or the instalments shall carry interest at such rate as may be specified by the order from such date, not earlier than the date of the order, as may be so specified, until the date when payment of it is due.][1]

Property adjustment orders in connection with divorce proceedings, etc

18-026 **24.**—(1) On granting a decree of divorce, a decree of nullity of marriage or a decree of judicial separation or at any time thereafter (whether, in the case of a decree of divorce or of nullity of marriage, before or after the decree is made absolute), the court may make any one or more of the following orders, that is to say—

(a) an order that a party to the marriage shall transfer to the other party, to any child of the family or to such person as may be specified in the order for the benefit of such a child such property as may be so specified, being property to which the first-mentioned party is entitled, either in possession or reversion;

(b) an order that a settlement of such property as may be so specified, being property to which a party to the marriage is so entitled, be made to the satisfaction of the court for the benefit of the other party to the marriage and of the children of the family or either or any of them;

(c) an order varying for the benefit of the parties to the marriage and of the children of the family or either or any of them any ante-nuptial or post-nuptial settlement (including such a settlement made by will or codicil) made on the parties to the marriage[, other than one in the form of a pension arrangement (within the meaning of section 25D below)][2];

(d) an order extinguishing or reducing the interest of either of the parties to the marriage under any such settlement[, other than one in the form of a pension arrangement (within the meaning of section 25D below)][3];

subject, however, in the case of an order under paragraph (a) above, to the restrictions imposed by section 29(1) and (3) below on the making of orders for a transfer of property in favour of children who have attained the age of eighteen.

(2) The court may make an order under subsection (1)(c) above notwithstanding that there are no children of the family.

(3) Without prejudice to the power to give a direction under section 30 below for the settlement of an instrument by conveyancing counsel, where an order is made under this section on or after granting a decree of divorce or nullity of marriage, neither the order nor any settlement made in pursuance of the order shall take effect unless the decree has been made absolute.

[Orders for sale of property

18-027 **24A.**—(1) Where the court makes under section 23 or 24 of this Act a secured periodical payments order, an order for the payment of a lump sum or a property adjustment order, then, on making that order or at any time thereafter, the court may make a further order for the sale of such property as may be specified in the order, being property in which or in the proceeds of sale of which

[1] Inserted by Administration of Justice Act 1982 c.53 ss 16, 77 (1)

[2] Words inserted by Welfare Reform and Pensions Act 1999 c.30 Sch 3 para 3

[3] Words inserted by Welfare Reform and Pensions Act 1999 c.30 Sch 3 para 3

either or both of the parties to the marriage has or have a beneficial interest, either in possession or reversion.

(2) Any order made under subsection (1) above may contain such consequential or supplementary provisions as the court thinks fit and, without prejudice to the generality of the foregoing provision, may include—

(a) provision requiring the making of a payment out of the proceeds of sale of the property to which the order relates, and

(b) provision requiring any such property to be offered for sale to a person, or class of persons, specified in the order.

(3) Where an order is made under subsection (1) above on or after the grant of a decree of divorce or nullity of marriage, the order shall not take effect unless the decree has been made absolute.

(4) Where an order is made under subsection (1) above, the court may direct that the order, or such provision thereof as the court may specify, shall not take effect until the occurrence of an event specified by the court or the expiration of a period so specified.

(5) Where an order under subsection (1) above contains a provision requiring the proceeds of sale of the property to which the order relates to be used to secure periodical payments to a party to the marriage, the order shall cease to have effect on the death or re-marriage of that person.

[(6) Where a party to a marriage has a beneficial interest in any property, or in the proceeds of sale thereof, and some other person who is not a party to the marriage also has a beneficial interest in that property or in the proceeds of sale thereof, then, before deciding whether to make an order under this section in relation to that property, it shall be the duty of the court to give that other person an opportunity to make representations with respect to the order; and any representations made by that other person shall be included among the circumstances to which the court is required to have regard under section 25(1) below.][1]][2]

[Pension sharing orders in connection with divorce proceedings etc

24B.—(1) On granting a decree of divorce or a decree of nullity of marriage or at any time thereafter (whether before or after the decree is made absolute), the court may, on an application made under this section, make one or more pension sharing orders in relation to the marriage. **18-028**

(2) A pension sharing order under this section is not to take effect unless the decree on or after which it is made has been made absolute.

(3) A pension sharing order under this section may not be made in relation to a pension arrangement which—

(a) is the subject of a pension sharing order in relation to the marriage, or

(b) has been the subject of pension sharing between the parties to the marriage.

(4) A pension sharing order under this section may not be made in relation to shareable state scheme rights if—

(a) such rights are the subject of a pension sharing order in relation to the marriage, or

(b) such rights have been the subject of pension sharing between the parties to the marriage.

(5) A pension sharing order under this section may not be made in relation to the rights of a person under a pension arrangement if there is in force a require-

[1] Inserted by Matrimonial and Family Proceedings Act 1984 c.42 ss 46 (1), 48 (3) Sch 1 para 11

[2] Inserted by Matrimonial Homes and Property Act 1981 c.24 s 7

ment imposed by virtue of section 25B or 25C below which relates to benefits or future benefits to which he is entitled under the pension arrangement.][1]

[Pension sharing orders: duty to stay

18-029 **24C.**—(1) No pension sharing order may be made so as to take effect before the end of such period after the making of the order as may be prescribed by regulations made by the Lord Chancellor.

(2) The power to make regulations under this section shall be exercisable by statutory instrument which shall be subject to annulment in pursuance of a resolution of either House of Parliament.][2]

[Pension sharing orders: apportionment of charges

18-030 **24D.** If a pension sharing order relates to rights under a pension arrangement, the court may include in the order provision about the apportionment between the parties of any charge under section 41 of the Welfare Reform and Pensions Act 1999 (charges in respect of pension sharing costs), or under corresponding Northern Ireland legislation.][3]

[Matters to which court is to have regard in deciding how to exercise its powers under ss. 23, 24 and 24A

18-031 **25.**—(1) It shall be the duty of the court in deciding whether to exercise its powers under [section 23, 24, 24A or 24B][4] above and, if so, in what manner, to have regard to all the circumstances of the case, first consideration being given to the welfare while a minor of any child of the family who has not attained the age of eighteen.

(2) As regards the exercise of the powers of the court under [section 23(1)(a), (b) or (c), 24, 24A or 24B][5] above in relation to a party to the marriage, the court shall in particular have regard to the following matters—

- (a) the income, earning capacity, property and other financial resources which each of the parties to the marriage has or is likely to have in the foreseeable future, including in the case of earning capacity any increase in that capacity which it would in the opinion of the court be reasonable to expect a party to the marriage to take steps to acquire;
- (b) the financial needs, obligations and responsibilities which each of the parties to the marriage has or is likely to have in the foreseeable future;
- (c) the standard of living enjoyed by the family before the breakdown of the marriage;
- (d) the age of each party to the marriage and the duration of the marriage;
- (e) any physical or mental disability of either of the parties to the marriage;
- (f) the contributions which each of the parties has made or is likely in the foreseeable future to make to the welfare of the family, including any contribution by looking after the home or caring for the family;
- (g) the conduct of each of the parties, if that conduct is such that it would in the opinion of the court be inequitable to disregard it;

[1] Added by Welfare Reform and Pensions Act 1999 c.30 Sch 3 para 4
[2] Added by Welfare Reform and Pensions Act 1999 c.30 Sch 3 para 4
[3] Added by Welfare Reform and Pensions Act 1999 c.30 Sch 3 para 4
[4] Words substituted by Welfare Reform and Pensions Act 1999 c.30 Sch 3 para 5 (a)
[5] Words substituted by Welfare Reform and Pensions Act 1999 c.30 Sch 3 para 5 (b)

(h) in the case of proceedings for divorce or nullity of marriage, the value to each of the parties to the marriage of any benefit [...][1] which, by reason of the dissolution or annulment of the marriage, that party will lose the chance of acquiring.

(3) As regards the exercise of the powers of the court under section 23(1)(d) or , (e) or (f), (2) (4), 24 or 24A above in relation to a child of the family, the court shall in particular have regard to the following matters—

(a) the financial needs of the child;

(b) the income, earning capacity (if any), property and other financial resources of the child;

(c) any physical or mental disability of the child;

(d) the manner in which he was being and in which the parties to the marriage expected him to be educated or trained;

(e) the considerations mentioned in relation to the parties to the marriage in paragraphs (a), (b), (c) and (e) of subsection (2) above.

(4) As regards the exercise of the powers of the court under section 23(1)(d), (e) or (f), (2) or (4), 24 or 24A above against a party to a marriage in favour of a child of the family who is not the child of that party, the court shall also have regard—

(a) to whether that party assumed any responsibility for the child's maintenance, and, if so, to the extent to which, and the basis upon which, that party assumed such responsibility and to the length of time for which that party discharged such responsibility;

(b) to whether in assuming and discharging such responsibility that party did so knowing that the child was not his or her own;

(c) to the liability of any other person to maintain the child.][2]

[Exercise of court's powers in favour of party to marriage on decree of divorce or nullity of marriage

25A.—(1) Where on or after the grant of a decree of divorce or nullity of marriage the court decides to exercise its powers under [section 23(1)(a), (b) or (c), 24, 24A or 24B][3] above in favour of a party to the marriage, it shall be the duty of the court to consider whether it would be appropriate so to exercise those powers that the financial obligations of each party towards the other will be terminated as soon after the grant of the decree as the court considers just and reasonable. **18-032**

(2) Where the court decides in such a case to make a periodical payments or secured periodical payments order in favour of a party to the marriage, the court shall in particular consider whether it would be appropriate to require those payments to be made or secured only for such term as would in the opinion of the court be sufficient to enable the party in whose favour the order is made to adjust without undue hardship to the termination of his or her financial dependence on the other party.

(3) Where on or after the grant of a decree of divorce or nullity of marriage an application is made by a party to the marriage for a periodical payments or secured periodical payments order in his or her favour, then, if the court considers that no continuing obligation should be imposed on either party to make or secure periodical payments in favour of the other, the court may dismiss the application with a direction that the applicant shall not be entitled to make

[1] Words repealed by Pensions Act 1995 c.26 Pt IV s 166 (2)
[2] Substituted by Matrimonial and Family Proceedings Act 1984 c.42 ss 3, 48 (2)
[3] Words substituted by Welfare Reform and Pensions Act 1999 c.30 Sch 3 para 6

any further application in relation to that marriage for an order under section 23(1)(a) or (b) above.][1]

[Pensions

18-033 **25B.**—(1) The matters to which the court is to have regard under section 25(2) above include—

(a) in the case of paragraph (a), any benefits under a pension [arrangement][2] which a party to the marriage has or is likely to have, and

(b) in the case of paragraph (h), any benefits under a pension [arrangement][3] which, by reason of the dissolution or annulment of the marriage, a party to the marriage will lose the chance of acquiring,

and, accordingly, in relation to benefits under a pension [arrangement][4], section 25(2)(a) above shall have effect as if "in the foreseeable future" were omitted.

(2) [...][5]

(3) The following provisions apply where, having regard to any benefits under a pension [arrangement][6], the court determines to make an order under section 23 above.

(4) To the extent to which the order is made having regard to any benefits under a pension [arrangement][7], the order may require the [person responsible for][8] the pension [arrangement][9] in question, if at any time any payment in respect of any benefits under the [arrangement][10] becomes due to the party with pension rights, to make a payment for the benefit of the other party.

[(5) The order must express the amount of any payment required to be made by virtue of subsection (4) above as a percentage of the payment which becomes due to the party with pension rights.][11]

(6) Any such payment by the [person responsible for the arrangement][12]—

(a) shall discharge so much of [his][13] liability to the party with pension rights as corresponds to the amount of the payment, and

(b) shall be treated for all purposes as a payment made by the party with pension rights in or towards the discharge of his liability under the order.

(7) Where the party with pension rights [has a right of commutation under the arrangement, the order may require him to exercise it to any extent][14]; and this section applies to [any payment due in consequence of commutation][15] in pursuance of the order as it applies to other payments in respect of benefits under the [arrangement][16].

[1] Substituted by Matrimonial and Family Proceedings Act 1984 c.42 ss 3, 48 (2)
[2] Word substituted by Welfare Reform and Pensions Act 1999 c.30 Sch 4 para 1 (2)
[3] Word substituted by Welfare Reform and Pensions Act 1999 c.30 Sch 4 para 1 (2)
[4] Word substituted by Welfare Reform and Pensions Act 1999 c.30 Sch 4 para 1 (2)
[5] Repealed by Welfare Reform and Pensions Act 1999 c.30 Sch 4 para 1 (3)
[6] Word substituted by Welfare Reform and Pensions Act 1999 c.30 Sch 4 para 1 (4)
[7] Word substituted by Welfare Reform and Pensions Act 1999 c.30 Sch 4 para 1 (5) (a)
[8] Words substituted by Welfare Reform and Pensions Act 1999 c.30 Sch 4 para 1 (5) (b)
[9] Word substituted by Welfare Reform and Pensions Act 1999 c.30 Sch 4 para 1 (5) (a)
[10] Word substituted by Welfare Reform and Pensions Act 1999 c.30 Sch 4 para 1 (5) (a)
[11] Substituted by Welfare Reform and Pensions Act 1999 c.30 Sch 4 para 1 (6)
[12] Words substituted by Welfare Reform and Pensions Act 1999 c.30 Sch 4 para 1 (7) (a)
[13] Words substituted by Welfare Reform and Pensions Act 1999 c.30 Sch 4 para 1 (7) (b)
[14] Words substituted by Welfare Reform and Pensions Act 1999 c.30 Sch 4 para 1 (8) (a)
[15] Words substituted by Welfare Reform and Pensions Act 1999 c.30 Sch 4 para 1 (8) (b)
[16] Word substituted by Welfare Reform and Pensions Act 1999 c.30 Sch 4 para 1 (8) (c)

[(7A) The power conferred by subsection (7) above may not be exercised for the purpose of commuting a benefit payable to the party with pension rights to a benefit payable to the other party.

(7B) The power conferred by subsection (4) or (7) above may not be exercised in relation to a pension arrangement which—

(a) is the subject of a pension sharing order in relation to the marriage, or

(b) has been the subject of pension sharing between the parties to the marriage.

(7C) In subsection (1) above, references to benefits under a pension arrangement include any benefits by way of pension, whether under a pension arrangement or not.][1]][2]

[Pensions: lump sums

25C.—(1) The power of the court under section 23 above to order a party to a marriage to pay a lump sum to the other party includes, where the benefits which the party with pension rights has or is likely to have under a pension [arrangement][3] include any lump sum payable in respect of his death, power to make any of the following provision by the order. **18-034**

(2) The court may—

(a) if the [person responsible for the pension arrangement in question has][4] power to determine the person to whom the sum, or any part of it, is to be paid, require [him][5] to pay the whole or part of that sum, when it becomes due, to the other party,

(b) if the party with pension rights has power to nominate the person to whom the sum, or any part of it, is to be paid, require the party with pension rights to nominate the other party in respect of the whole or part of that sum,

(c) in any other case, require the [person responsible for the pension arrangement][6] in question to pay the whole or part of that sum, when it becomes due, for the benefit of the other party instead of to the person to whom, apart from the order, it would be paid.

(3) Any payment by the [person responsible for the arrangement][7] under an order made under section 23 above by virtue of this section shall discharge so much of [his][8] liability in respect of the party with pension rights as corresponds to the amount of the payment.

[(4) The powers conferred by this section may not be exercised in relation to a pension arrangement which—

(a) is the subject of a pension sharing order in relation to the marriage, or

(b) has been the subject of pension sharing between the parties to the marriage.][9]][10]

[Pensions: supplementary

25D.—[(1) Where— **18-035**

[1] Added by Welfare Reform and Pensions Act 1999 c.30 Sch 4 para 1 (9)
[2] Added by Pensions Act 1995 c.26 Pt IV s 166 (1)
[3] Word substituted by Welfare Reform and Pensions Act 1999 c.30 Sch 4 para 2 (2)
[4] Words substituted by Welfare Reform and Pensions Act 1999 c.30 Sch 4 para 2 (3) (a) (i)
[5] Word substituted by Welfare Reform and Pensions Act 1999 c.30 Sch 4 para 2 (3) (a) (ii)
[6] Words substituted by Welfare Reform and Pensions Act 1999 c.30 Sch 4 para 2 (3) (b)
[7] Words substituted by Welfare Reform and Pensions Act 1999 c.30 Sch 4 para 2 (4) (a)
[8] Words substituted by Welfare Reform and Pensions Act 1999 c.30 Sch 4 para 2 (4) (b)
[9] Added by Welfare Reform and Pensions Act 1999 c.30 Sch 4 para 2 (5)
[10] Added by Pensions Act 1995 c.26 Pt IV s 166 (1)

(a) an order made under section 23 above by virtue of section 25B or 25C above imposes any requirement on the person responsible for a pension arrangement ("the first arrangement") and the party with pension rights acquires rights under another pension arrangement ("the new arrangement") which are derived (directly or indirectly) from the whole of his rights under the first arrangement, and

(b) the person responsible for the new arrangement has been given notice in accordance with regulations made by the Lord Chancellor,

the order shall have effect as if it had been made instead in respect of the person responsible for the new arrangement.][1]

(2) [The Lord Chancellor may by regulations][2]—

(a) in relation to any provision of sections 25B or 25C above which authorises the court making an order under section 23 above to require the [person responsible for a pension arrangement][3] to make a payment for the benefit of the other party, make provision as to the person to whom, and the terms on which, the payment is to be made,

[(ab) make, in relation to payment under a mistaken belief as to the continuation in force of a provision included by virtue of section 25B or 25C above in an order under section 23 above, provision about the rights or liabilities of the payer, the payee or the person to whom the payment was due,][4]

(b) require notices to be given in respect of changes of circumstances relevant to such orders which include provision made by virtue of sections 25B and 25C above,

[(ba) make provision for the person responsible for a pension arrangement to be discharged in prescribed circumstances from a requirement imposed by virtue of section 25B or 25C above,][5]

[(e) make provision about calculation and verification in relation to the valuation of—

(i) benefits under a pension arrangement, or

(ii) shareable state scheme rights,

for the purposes of the court's functions in connection with the exercise of any of its powers under this Part of this Act.][6][...][7]

[(2A) Regulations under subsection (2)(e) above may include—

(a) provision for calculation or verification in accordance with guidance from time to time prepared by a prescribed person, and

(b) provision by reference to regulations under section 30 or 49(4) of the Welfare Reform and Pensions Act 1999.

(2B) Regulations under subsection (2) above may make different provision for different cases.

(2C) Power to make regulations under this section shall be exercisable by statutory instrument which shall be subject to annulment in pursuance of a resolution of either House of Parliament.][8]

[(3) In this section and sections 25B and 25C above—

---

1 Substituted by Welfare Reform and Pensions Act 1999 c.30 Sch 4 para 3 (2)
2 Words substituted by Welfare Reform and Pensions Act 1999 c.30 Sch 4 para 3 (3) (a)
3 Words substituted by Welfare Reform and Pensions Act 1999 c.30 Sch 4 para 3 (3) (b)
4 Added by Welfare Reform and Pensions Act 1999 c.30 Sch 4 para 3 (3) (c)
5 Added by Welfare Reform and Pensions Act 1999 c.30 Sch 4 para 3 (3) (d)
6 Substituted by Welfare Reform and Pensions Act 1999 c.30 Sch 4 para 3 (3) (f)
7 Words repealed by Welfare Reform and Pensions Act 1999 c.30 Sch 4 para 3 (3) (g)
8 Added by Welfare Reform and Pensions Act 1999 c.30 Sch 4 para 3 (4)

"occupational pension scheme" has the same meaning as in the Pension Schemes Act 1993;

"the party with pension rights" means the party to the marriage who has or is likely to have benefits under a pension arrangement and "the other party" means the other party to the marriage;

"pension arrangement" means—

(a) an occupational pension scheme,

(b) a personal pension scheme,

(c) a retirement annuity contract,

(d) an annuity or insurance policy purchased, or transferred, for the purpose of giving effect to rights under an occupational pension scheme or a personal pension scheme, and

(e) an annuity purchased, or entered into, for the purpose of discharging liability in respect of a pension credit under section 29(1)(b) of the Welfare Reform and Pensions Act 1999 or under corresponding Northern Ireland legislation;

"personal pension scheme" has the same meaning as in the Pension Schemes Act 1993;

"prescribed" means prescribed by regulations;

"retirement annuity contract" means a contract or scheme approved under Chapter III of Part XIV of the Income and Corporation Taxes Act 1988;

"shareable state scheme rights" has the same meaning as in section 21A(1) above; and

"trustees or managers", in relation to an occupational pension scheme or a personal pension scheme, means—

(a) in the case of a scheme established under a trust, the trustees of the scheme, and

(b) in any other case, the managers of the scheme.

(4) In this section and sections 25B and 25C above, references to the person responsible for a pension arrangement are—

(a) in the case of an occupational pension scheme or a personal pension scheme, to the trustees or managers of the scheme,

(b) in the case of a retirement annuity contract or an annuity falling within paragraph (d) or (e) of the definition of "pension arrangement" above, the provider of the annuity, and

(c) in the case of an insurance policy falling within paragraph (d) of the definition of that expression, the insurer.][1]][2]

Commencement of proceedings for ancillary relief, etc

26.—(1) Where a petition for divorce, nullity of marriage or judicial separation has been presented, then, subject to subsection (2) below, proceedings for maintenance pending suit under section 22 above, for a financial provision order under section 23 above, or for a property adjustment order may be begun, subject to and in accordance with rules of court, at any time after the presentation of the petition. **18-036**

(2) Rules of court may provide, in such cases as may be prescribed by the rules—

[1] Substituted by Welfare Reform and Pensions Act 1999 c.30 Sch 4 para 3 (5)

[2] Added by Pensions Act 1995 c.26 Pt IV s 166 (1)

(a) that applications for any such relief as is mentioned in subsection (1) above shall be made in the petition or answer; and

(b) that applications for any such relief which are not so made, or are not made until after the expiration of such period following the presentation of the petition or filing of the answer as may be so prescribed, shall be made only with the leave of the court.

Financial provision in case of neglect to maintain

Financial provision orders, etc., in case of neglect by party to marriage to maintain other party or child of the family

18-037 **27.**—[(1) Either party to a marriage may apply to the court for an order under this section on the ground that the other party to the marriage (in this section referred to as the respondent)—

(a) has failed to provide reasonable maintenance for the applicant, or

(b) has failed to provide, or to make a proper contribution towards, reasonable maintenance for any child of the family.][1]

(2) The court shall not entertain an application under this section[unless—

(a) the applicant or the respondent is domiciled in England and Wales on the date of the application; or

(b) the applicant has been habitually resident there throughout the period of one year ending with that date; or

(c) the respondent is resident there on that date.][2]

[(3) Where an application under this section is made on the ground mentioned in subsection (1)(a) above, then, in deciding—

(a) whether the respondent has failed to provide reasonable maintenance for the applicant, and

(b) what order, if any, to make under this section in favour of the applicant,

the court shall have regard to all the circumstances of the case including the matters mentioned in section 25(2) above, and where an application is also made under this section in respect of a child of the family who has not attained the age of eighteen, first consideration shall be given to the welfare of the child while a minor.][3]

[(3A) Where an application under this section is made on the ground mentioned in subsection (1)(b) above then, in deciding—

(a) whether the respondent has failed to provide, or to make a proper contribution towards, reasonable maintenance for the child of the family to whom the application relates, and

(b) what order, if any, to make under this section in favour of the child,

the court shall have regard to all the circumstances of the case including the matters mentioned in [section 25(3)(a) to (e)][4] above, and where the child of the family to whom the application relates is not the child of the respondent, including also the matters mentioned in [section 25(4)][5] above.

[1] Substituted by Domestic Proceedings and Magistrates' Courts Act 1978 c.22 ss 63 (1), 89 (2)

[2] Words substituted by Domicile and Matrimonial Proceedings Act 1973 c.45 s 6 (1)

[3] Substituted by Matrimonial and Family Proceedings Act 1984 c.42 ss 4, 48 (2)

[4] Words substituted by Matrimonial and Family Proceedings Act 1984 c.42 ss 46 (1), 48 (3) Sch 1 para 12 (a)

[5] Words substituted by Matrimonial and Family Proceedings Act 1984 c.42 ss 46 (1), 48 (3) Sch 1 para 12 (a)

(3B) In relation to an application under this section on the ground mentioned in subsection (1)(a) above, [section 25(2)(c) above][1] shall have effect as if for the reference therein to the breakdown of the marriage there were substituted a reference to the failure to provide reasonable maintenance for the applicant, and in relation to an application under this section on the ground mentioned in subsection (1)(b) above, [section 25(2)(c) above (as it applies by virtue of section 25(3)(e) above)][2] shall have effect as if for the reference therein to the breakdown of the marriage there were substituted a reference to the failure to provide, or to make a proper contribution towards, reasonable maintenance for the child of the family to whom the application relates.][3]

(5) Where on an application under this section it appears to the court that the applicant or any child of the family to whom the application relates is in immediate need of financial assistance, but it is not yet possible to determine what order, if any, should be made on the application, the court may make an interim order for maintenance, that is to say, an order requiring the respondent to make to the applicant until the determination of the application such periodical payments as the court thinks reasonable.

(6) Where on an application under this section the applicant satisfies the court of any ground mentioned in subsection (1) above, the court may make [any one or more of the following orders][4], that is to say—

(a) an order that the respondent shall make to the applicant such periodical payments, for such term, as may be specified in the order;
(b) an order that the respondent shall secure to the applicant, to the satisfaction of the court, such periodical payments, for such term, as may be so specified;
(c) an order that the respondent shall pay to the applicant such lump sum as may be so specified;
(d) an order that the respondent shall make to such person as may be specified in the order for the benefit of the child to whom the application relates, or to that child, such periodical payments, for such term, as may be so specified;
(e) an order that the respondent shall secure to such person as may be so specified for the benefit of that child, or to that child, to the satisfaction of the court, such periodical payments, for such term, as may be so specified;
(f) an order that the respondent shall pay to such person as may be so specified for the benefit of that child, or to that child, such lump sum as may be so specified;

subject, however, in the case of an order under paragraph (d), (e) or (f) above, to the restrictions imposed by section 29(1) and (3) below on the making of financial provision orders in favour of children who have attained the age of eighteen.

[(6A) An application for the variation under section 31 of this Act of a periodical payments order or secured periodical payments order made under this section in favour of a child may, if the child has attained the age of sixteen, be made by the child himself.

[1] Words substituted by Matrimonial and Family Proceedings Act 1984 c.42 ss 46 (1), 48 (2) Sch 1 para 12 (b)
[2] Words substituted by Matrimonial and Family Proceedings Act 1984 c.42 ss 46 (1), 48 (2) Sch 1 para 12(b)
[3] Substituted by Domestic Proceedings and Magistrates' Courts Act 1978 c.22 ss 63 (2), 89 (2)
[4] Words substituted by Domestic Proceedings and Magistrates' Courts Act 1978 c.22 ss 63 (3), 89 (2)

[(6B) Where a periodical payments order made in favour of a child under this section ceases to have effect on the date on which the child attains the age of sixteen or at any time after that date but before or on the date on which he attains the age of eighteen, then if, on an application made to the court for an order under this subsection, it appears to the court that—

(a) the child is, will be or (if an order were made under this subsection) would be receiving instruction at an educational establishment or undergoing training for a trade, profession or vocation, whether or not he also is, will be or would be in gainful employment; or

(b) there are special circumstances which justify the making of an order under this subsection,

the court shall have power by order to revive the first mentioned order from such date as the court may specify, not being earlier than the date of the making of the application, and to exercise its power under section 31 of this Act in relation to any order so revived.][1]][2]

(7) Without prejudice to the generality of subsection (6)(c) or (f) above, an order under this section for the payment of a lump sum—

(a) may be made for the purpose of enabling any liabilities or expenses reasonably incurred in maintaining the applicant or any child of the family to whom the application relates before the making of the application to be met;

(b) may provide for the payment of that sum by instalments of such amount as may be specified in the order and may require the payment of the instalments to be secured to the satisfaction of the court.

(8) [...][3]

Additional provisions with respect to financial provision and property adjustment orders

Duration of continuing financial provision orders in favour of party to marriage, and effect of remarriage

18-038 **28.**—(1) [Subject in the case of an order made on or after the grant of a decree of divorce or nullity of marriage to the provisions of sections 25A(2) above and 31(7) below, the term to be specified in a periodical payments or secured periodical payments order in favour of a party to a marriage shall be such term as the court thinks fit, except that the term shall not begin before or extend beyond the following limits][4], that is to say—

(a) in the case of a periodical payments order, the term shall begin not earlier than the date of the making of an application for the order, and shall be so defined as not to extend beyond the death of either of the parties to the marriage or, where the order is made on or after the grant of a decree of divorce or nullity of marriage, the remarriage of the party in whose favour the order is made; and

(b) in the case of a secured periodical payments order, the term shall begin not earlier than the date of the making of an application for the order, and shall be so defined as not to extend beyond the death or, where the order is made on or after the grant of such a decree, the remarriage of the party in whose favour the order is made.

[1] Substituted by Family Law Reform Act 1987 c.42 ss 33 (1) Sch 2 para 52
[2] Inserted by Domestic Proceedings and Magistrates' Courts Act 1978 c.22 ss 63 (4), 89 (2)
[3] Repealed by Domestic Proceedings and Magistrates' Courts Act 1978 c.22 s 89 (2) Sch 3
[4] Words substituted by Matrimonial and Family Proceedings Act 1984 c.42 ss 5 (1), 48 (2)

[(1A) Where a periodical payments or secured periodical payments order in favour of a party to a marriage is made on or after the grant of a decree of divorce or nullity of marriage, the court may direct that that party shall not be entitled to apply under section 31 below for the extension of the term specified in the order][1]

(2) Where a periodical payments or secured periodical payments order in favour of a party to a marriage is made otherwise than on or after the grant of a decree of divorce or nullity of marriage, and the marriage in question is subsequently dissolved or annulled but the order continues in force, the order shall, notwithstanding anything in it, cease to have effect on the remarriage of that party, except in relation to any arrears due under it on the date of the remarriage.

(3) If after the grant of a decree dissolving or annulling a marriage either party to that marriage remarries [whether at any time before or after the commencement of this Act][2], that party shall not be entitled to apply, by reference to the grant of that decree, for a financial provision order in his or her favour, or for a property adjustment order, against the other party to that marriage.

Duration of continuing financial provision orders in favour of children, and age limit on making certain orders in their favour

18-039

Direction for settlement of instrument for securing payments or effecting property adjustment

30. Where the court decides to make a financial provision order requiring any payments to be secured or a property adjustment order— 18-040

(a) it may direct that the matter be referred to one of the conveyancing counsel of the court for him to settle a proper instrument to be executed by all necessary parties; and

(b) where the order is to be made in proceedings for divorce, nullity of marriage or judicial separation it may, if it thinks fit, defer the grant of the decree in question until the instrument has been duly executed.

Variation, discharge and enforcement of certain orders, etc

Variation, discharge, etc., of certain orders for financial relief

31.—(1) Where the court has made an order to which this section applies, then, subject to the provisions of this section [and of section 28(1A) above][3], the court shall have power to vary or discharge the order or to suspend any provision thereof temporarily and to revive the operation of any provision so suspended. 18-041

(2) This section applies to the following orders, that is to say—

(a) any order for maintenance pending suit and any interim order for maintenance;

(b) any periodical payments order;

(c) any secured periodical payments order;

(d) any order made by virtue of section 23(3)(c) or 27(7)(b) above (provision for payment of a lump sum by instalments);

[(dd) any deferred order made by virtue of section 23(1)(c) (lump sums) which includes provision made by virtue of—

[1] Inserted by Matrimonial and Family Proceedings Act 1984 c.42 ss 5 (2), 48 (2)

[2] Words inserted by Matrimonial and Family Proceedings Act 1984 c.42 ss 5 (3), 48 (2)

[3] Words inserted by Matrimonial and Family Proceedings Act 1984 c.42 ss 6 (2), 48 (2)

(i) section 25B(4), or
(ii) section 25C,
(provision in respect of pension rights)][1]
(e) any order for a settlement of property under section 24(1)(b) or for a variation of settlement under section 24(1)(c) or (d) above, being an order made on or after the grant of a decree of judicial separation.
[(f) any order made under section 24A(1) above for the sale of property][2]
[(g) a pension sharing order under section 24B above which is made at a time before the decree has been made absolute.][3]

[(2A) Where the court has made an order referred to in subsection (2)(a), (b) or (c) above, then, subject to the provisions of this section, the court shall have power to remit the payment of any arrears due under the order or of any part thereof.][4]

[(2B) Where the court has made an order referred to in subsection (2)(dd)(ii) above, this section shall cease to apply to the order on the death of either of the parties to the marriage][5]

(3) The powers exercisable by the court under this section in relation to an order shall be exercisable also in relation to any instrument executed in pursuance of the order.

(4) The court shall not exercise the powers conferred by this section in relation to an order for a settlement under section 24(1)(b) or for a variation of settlement under section 24(1)(c) or (d) above except on an application made in proceedings—
(a) for the rescission of the decree of judicial separation by reference to which the order was made, or
(b) for the dissolution of the marriage in question.

[(4A) In relation to an order which falls within paragraph (g) of subsection (2) above ("the subsection (2) order")—
(a) the powers conferred by this section may be exercised—
(i) only on an application made before the subsection (2) order has or, but for paragraph (b) below, would have taken effect; and
(ii) only if, at the time when the application is made, the decree has not been made absolute; and
(b) an application made in accordance with paragraph (a) above prevents the subsection (2) order from taking effect before the application has been dealt with.

(4B) No variation of a pension sharing order shall be made so as to take effect before the decree is made absolute.

(4C) The variation of a pension sharing order prevents the order taking effect before the end of such period after the making of the variation as may be prescribed by regulations made by the Lord Chancellor.][6]

(5) [Subject to subsections (7A) to [(7G)][7] below and without prejudice to any power exercisable by virtue of subsection (2)(d), (dd), [(e) or (g)][8] above or otherwise than by virtue of this section,][9] No property adjustment order [or

[1] Added by Pensions Act 1995 c.26 Pt IV s 166 (3) (a)
[2] Inserted by Matrimonial Homes and Property Act 1981 c.24 s 8 (2) (a)
[3] Added by Welfare Reform and Pensions Act 1999 c.30 Sch 3 para 7 (2)
[4] Inserted by Administration of Justice Act 1982 c.53 ss 51, 77 (1)
[5] Added by Pensions Act 1995 c.26 Pt IV s 166 (3) (b)
[6] Added by Welfare Reform and Pensions Act 1999 c.30 Sch 3 para 7 (3)
[7] Words substituted by Welfare Reform and Pensions Act 1999 c.30 Sch 3 para 7 (4) (a)
[8] Words substituted by Welfare Reform and Pensions Act 1999 c.30 Sch 3 para 7 (4) (b)
[9] Words added at the beginning by Family Law Act 1996 c.27 Sch 8 (I) para 16 (5) (a)

pension sharing order][1] shall be made on an application for the variation of a periodical payments or secured periodical payments order made (whether in favour of a party to a marriage or in favour of a child of the family) under section 23 above, and no order for the payment of a lump sum shall be made on an application for the variation of a periodical payments or secured periodical payments order in favour of a party to a marriage (whether made under section 23 or under section 27 above).

(6) Where the person liable to make payments under a secured periodical payments order has died, an application under this section relating to that order [(and to any order made under section 24A(1) above which requires the proceeds of sale of property to be used for securing those payments) may be made by the person entitled to payments under the periodical payments order][2] or by the personal representatives of the deceased person, but no such application shall, except with the permission of the court, be made after the end of the period of six months from the date on which representation in regard to the estate of that person is first taken out.

[(7) In exercising the powers conferred by this section the court shall have regard to all the circumstances of the case, first consideration being given to the welfare while a minor of any child of the family who has not attained the age of eighteen, and the circumstances of the case shall include any change in any of the matters to which the court was required to have regard when making the order to which the application relates, and—

(a) in the case of a periodical payments or secured periodical payments order made on or after the grant of a decree of divorce or nullity of marriage, the court shall consider whether in all the circumstances and after having regard to any such change it would be appropriate to vary the order so that payments under the order are required to be made or secured only for such further period as will in the opinion of the court be sufficient [(in the light of any proposed exercise by the court, where the marriage has been dissolved, of its powers under subsection (7B) below)][3] to enable the party in whose favour the order was made to adjust without undue hardship to the termination of those payments;

(b) in a case where the party against whom the order was made has died, the circumstances of the case shall also include the changed circumstances resulting from his or her death.][4]

[(7A) Subsection (7B) below applies where, after the dissolution of a marriage, the court—

(a) discharges a periodical payments order or secured periodical payments order made in favour of a party to the marriage; or

(b) varies such an order so that payments under the order are required to be made or secured only for such further period as is determined by the court.

(7B) The court has power, in addition to any power it has apart from this subsection, to make supplemental provision consisting of any of—

(a) an order for the payment of a lump sum in favour of a party to the marriage;

(b) one or more property adjustment orders in favour of a party to the marriage;

[1] Words inserted by Welfare Reform and Pensions Act 1999 c.30 Sch 3 para 7 (4) (c)
[2] Words substituted by Matrimonial Homes and Property Act 1981 c.24 s 8 (2) (b)
[3] Words added by Family Law Act 1996 c.27 Sch 8 (I) para 16 (6) (b)
[4] Substituted by Matrimonialand Family Proceedings Act 1984 c.42 ss 6 (3), 48 (2)

[(ba) one or more pension sharing orders;][1]

(c) a direction that the party in whose favour the original order discharged or varied was made is not entitled to make any further application for—

(i) a periodical payments or secured periodical payments order, or

(ii) an extension of the period to which the original order is limited by any variation made by the court.

(7C) An order for the payment of a lump sum made under subsection (7B) above may—

(a) provide for the payment of that sum by instalments of such amount as may be specified in the order; and

(b) require the payment of the instalments to be secured to the satisfaction of the court.

(7D) [Section 23(6)][2] above apply where the court makes an order for the payment of a lump sum under subsection (7B) above as they apply where it makes such an order under [section 23][3] above.

(7E) If under subsection (7B) above the court makes more than one property adjustment order in favour of the same party to the marriage, each of those orders must fall within a different paragraph of section 21(2) above.

(7F) Sections 24A and 30 above apply where the court makes a property adjustment order under subsection (7B) above as they apply where it makes such an order under [section 24][4] above.][5]

[(7G) Subsections (3) to (5) of section 24B above apply in relation to a pension sharing order under subsection (7B) above as they apply in relation to a pension sharing order under that section.][6]

(8) The personal representatives of a deceased person against whom a secured periodical payments order was made shall not be liable for having distributed any part of the estate of the deceased after the expiration of the period of six months referred to in subsection (6) above on the ground that they ought to have taken into account the possibility that the court might permit an application under this section to be made after that period by the person entitled to payments under the order; but this subsection shall not prejudice any power to recover any part of the estate so distributed arising by virtue of the making of an order in pursuance of this section.

(9) In considering for the purposes of subsection (6) above the question when representation was first taken out, a grant limited to settled land or to trust property shall be left out of account and a grant limited to real estate or to personal estate shall be left out of account unless a grant limited to the remainder of the estate has previously been made or is made at the same time.

[(10) Where the court, in exercise of its powers under this section, decides to vary or discharge a periodical payments or secured periodical payments order, then, subject to section 28(1) and (2) above, the court shall have power to direct that the variation or discharge shall not take effect until the expiration of such period as may be specified in the order.][7]

[(11) Where—

[1] Added by Welfare Reform and Pensions Act 1999 c.30 Sch 3 para 7 (5)
[2] Words substituted by SI 1998/2572 art 4 (a)
[3] Words substituted by SI 1998/2572 art 4 (a)
[4] Words substituted by SI 1998/2572 art 4 (b)
[5] Added by Family Law Act 1996 c.27 Sch 8 (I) para 16 (7)
[6] Added by Welfare Reform and Pensions Act 1999 c.30 Sch 3 para 7 (6)
[7] Inserted by Matrimonial and Family Proceedings Act 1984 c.42 ss 6 (4), 48 (2)

(a) a periodical payments or secured periodical payments order in favour of more than one child ("the order") is in force;

(b) the order requires payments specified in it to be made to or for the benefit of more than one child without apportioning those payments between them;

(c) a maintenance assessment ("the assessment") is made with respect to one or more, but not all, of the children with respect to whom those payments are to be made; and

(d) an application is made, before the end of the period of 6 months beginning with the date on which the assessment was made, for the variation or discharge of the order,

the court may, in exercise of its powers under this section to vary or discharge the order, direct that the variation or discharge shall take effect from the date on which the assessment took effect or any later date.

(12) Where—

(a) an order ("the child order") of a kind prescribed for the purposes of section 10(1) of the Child Support Act 1991 is affected by a maintenance assessment;

(b) on the date on which the child order became so affected there was in force a periodical payments or secured periodical payments order ("the spousal order") in favour of a party to a marriage having the care of the child in whose favour the child order was made; and

(c) an application is made, before the end of the period of 6 months beginning with the date on which the maintenance assessment was made, for the spousal order to be varied or discharged,

the court may, in exercise of its powers under this section to vary or discharge the spousal order, direct that the variation or discharge shall take effect from the date on which the child order became so affected or any later date.

(13) For the purposes of subsection (12) above, an order is affected if it ceases to have effect or is modified by or under section 10 of the Child Support Act 1991.

(14) Subsections (11) and (12) above are without prejudice to any other power of the court to direct that the variation of discharge of an order under this section shall take effect from a date earlier than that on which the order for variation or discharge was made.][1]

[(15) The power to make regulations under subsection (4C) above shall be exercisable by statutory instrument which shall be subject to annulment in pursuance of a resolution of either House of Parliament.][2]

Payment of certain arrears unenforceable without the leave of the court

32.—(1) A person shall not be entitled to enforce through the High Court or any county court the payment of any arrears due under an order for maintenance pending suit, an interim order for maintenance or any financial provision order without the leave of that court if those arrears became due more than twelve months before proceedings to enforce the payment of them are begun. **18-042**

(2) The court hearing an application for the grant of leave under this section may refuse leave, or may grant leave subject to such restrictions and conditions (including conditions as to the allowing of time for payment or the making of payment by instalments) as that court thinks proper, or may remit the payment of the arrears or of any part thereof.

[1] Added by SI 1993/623 Sch 1 para 3

[2] Added by Welfare Reform and Pensions Act 1999 c.30 Sch 3 para 7 (7)

(3) An application for the grant of leave under this section shall be made in such manner as may be prescribed by rules of court.

Orders for repayment in certain cases of sums paid under certain orders

18-043 **33.**—(1) Where on an application made under this section in relation to an order to which this section applies it appears to the court that by reason of—

(a) a change in the circumstances of the person entitled to, or liable to make, payments under the order since the order was made, or

(b) the changed circumstances resulting from the death of the person so liable,

the amount received by the person entitled to payments under the order in respect of a period after those circumstances changed or after the death of the person liable to make payments under the order, as the case may be, exceeds the amount which the person so liable or his or her personal representatives should have been required to pay, the court may order the respondent to the application to pay to the applicant such sum, not exceeding the amount of the excess, as the court thinks just.

(2) This section applies to the following orders, that is to say—

(a) any order for maintenance pending suit and any interim order for maintenance;

(b) any periodical payments order; and

(c) any secured periodical payments order.

(3) An application under this section may be made by the person liable to make payments under an order to which this section applies or his or her personal representatives and may be made against the person entitled to payments under the order or her or his personal representatives.

(4) An application under this section may be made in proceedings in the High Court or a county court for—

(a) the variation or discharge of the order to which this section applies, or

(b) leave to enforce, or the enforcement of, the payment of arrears under that order;

but when not made in such proceedings shall be made to a county court, and accordingly references in this section to the court are references to the High Court or a county court, as the circumstances require.

(5) The jurisdiction conferred on a county court by this section shall be exercisable notwithstanding that by reason of the amount claimed in the application the jurisdiction would not but for this subsection be exercisable by a county court.

(6) An order under this section for the payment of any sum may provide for the payment of that sum by instalments of such amount as may be specified in the order.

Consent orders

[Consent orders for financial provision or property adjustment

18-044 **33A.**—(1) Notwithstanding anything in the preceding provisions of this Part of this Act, on an application for a consent order for financial relief the court may, unless it has reason to think that there are other circumstances into which it ought to inquire, make an order in the terms agreed on the basis only of the prescribed information furnished with the application.

(2) Subsection (1) above applies to an application for a consent order varying or discharging an order for financial relief as it applies to an application for an order for financial relief.

(3) In this section—

'consent order', in relation to an application for an order, means an order in the terms applied for to which the respondent agrees;

'order for financial relief' means an order under any of [sections 23, 24, 24A, 24B or 27][1] above; and

'prescribed' means prescribed by rules of court.][2]

Maintenance agreements

Validity of maintenance agreements

34.—(1) If a maintenance agreement includes a provision purporting to restrict any right to apply to a court for an order containing financial arrangements, then— **18-045**

(a) that provision shall be void; but

(b) any other financial arrangements contained in the agreement shall not thereby be rendered void or unenforceable and shall, unless they are void or unenforceable for any other reason (and subject to sections 35 and 36 below), be binding on the parties to the agreement.

(2) In this section and in section 35 below—

"maintenance agreement" means any agreement in writing made, whether before or after the commencement of this Act, between the parties to a marriage, being—

(a) an agreement containing financial arrangements, whether made during the continuance or after the dissolution or annulment of the marriage; or

(b) a separation agreement which contains no financial arrangements in a case where no other agreement in writing between the same parties contains such arrangements;

"financial arrangements" means provisions governing the rights and liabilities towards one another when living separately of the parties to a marriage (including a marriage which has been dissolved or annulled) in respect of the making or securing of payments or the disposition or use of any property, including such rights and liabilities with respect to the maintenance or education of any child, whether or not a child of the family.

Alteration of agreements by court during lives of parties

35.—(1) Where a maintenance agreement is for the time being subsisting and each of the parties to the agreement is for the time being either domiciled or resident in England and Wales, then, subject to subsection (3) below, either party may apply to the court or to a magistrates' court for an order under this section. **18-046**

(2) If the court to which the application is made is satisfied either—

(a) that by reason of a change in the circumstances in the light of which any financial arrangements contained in the agreement were made or, as the case may be, financial arrangements were omitted from it (including a change foreseen by the parties when making the

[1] Words inserted by Welfare Reform and Pensions Act 1999 c.30 Sch 3 para 8

[2] Inserted by Matrimonial and Family Proceedings Act 1984 c.42 ss 7, 48 (2)

agreement), the agreement should be altered so as to make different, or, as the case may be, so as to contain, financial arrangements, or

(b) that the agreement does not contain proper financial arrangements with respect to any child of the family,

then subject to subsections (3), (4) and (5) below, that court may by order make such alterations in the agreement—

(i) by varying or revoking any financial arrangements contained in it, or

(ii) by inserting in it financial arrangements for the benefit of one of the parties to the agreement or of a child of the family,

as may appear to that court to be just having regard to all the circumstances, including, if relevant, the matters mentioned in [section 25(4)][1] above; and the agreement shall have effect thereafter as if any alteration made by the order had been made by agreement between the parties and for valuable consideration.

(3) A magistrates' court shall not entertain an application under subsection (1) above unless both the parties to the agreement are resident in England and Wales and at least one of the parties is resident [within the commission area [...][2]for which the court is appointed;][3] and shall not have power to make any order on such an application except—

(a) in a case where the agreement includes no provision for periodical payments by either of the parties, an order inserting provision for the making by one of the parties of periodical payments for the maintenance of the other party or for the maintenance of any child of the family;

(b) in a case where the agreement includes provision for the making by one of the parties of periodical payments, an order increasing or reducing the rate of, or terminating, any of those payments.

(4) Where a court decides to alter, by order under this section, an agreement by inserting provision for the making or securing by one of the parties to the agreement of periodical payments for the maintenance of the other party or by increasing the rate of the periodical payments which the agreement provides shall be made by one of the parties for the maintenance of the other, the term for which the payments or, as the case may be, the additional payments attributable to the increase are to be made under the agreement as altered by the order shall be such term as the court may specify, subject to the following limits, that is to say—

(a) where the payments will not be secured, the term shall be so defined as not to extend beyond the death of either of the parties to the agreement or the remarriage of the party to whom the payments are to be made;

(b) where the payments will be secured, the term shall be so defined as not to extend beyond the death or remarriage of that party.

(5) Where a court decides to alter, by order under this section, an agreement by inserting provision for the making or securing by one of the parties to the agreement of periodical payments for the maintenance of a child of the family or by increasing the rate of the periodical payments which the agreement provides shall be made or secured by one of the parties for the maintenance of such a child, then, in deciding the term for which under the agreement as altered by the order the payments, or as the case may be, the additional payments attributable to

[1] Words substituted by Matrimonial and Family Proceedings Act 1984 c.42 ss 46 (1), 48 (3) Sch 1 para 13 (a)

[2] Words repealed by Access to Justice Act 1999 c.22 Sch 15 (V) (1) para 1

[3] Words substituted by Matrimonial and Family Proceedings Act 1984 c.42 ss 46 (1), 48 (3) Sch 1 para 13 (b)

the increase are to be made or secured for the benefit of the child, the court shall apply the provisions of section 29(2) and (3) above as to age limits as if the order in question were a periodical payments or secured periodical payments order in favour of the child.

(6) For the avoidance of doubt it is hereby declared that nothing in this section or in section 34 above affects any power of a court before which any proceedings between the parties to a maintenance agreement are brought under any other enactment (including a provision of this Act) to make an order containing financial arrangements or any right of either party to apply for such an order in such proceedings.

Alteration of agreements by court after death of one party

36.—(1) Where a maintenance agreement within the meaning of section 34 above provides for the continuation of payments under the agreement after the death of one of the parties and that party dies domiciled in England and Wales, the surviving party or the personal representatives of the deceased party may, subject to subsections (2) and (3) below, apply to the High Court or a county court for an order under section 35 above. **18-047**

(2) An application under this section shall not, except with the permission of the High Court or a county court, be made after the end of the period of six months from the date on which representation in regard to the estate of the deceased is first taken out.

(3) A county court shall not entertain an application under this section, or an application for permission to make an application under this section, unless it would have jurisdiction by virtue of [section 22 of the Inheritance (Provision for Family and Dependants) Act 1975][1] (which confers jurisdiction on county courts in proceedings under [that Act if the value of the property mentioned in that section][2] does not exceed £5,000 or such larger sum as may be fixed by order of the Lord Chancellor) to hear and determine proceedings for an order under [section 2 of that Act][3] in relation to the deceased's estate.

(4) If a maintenance agreement is altered by a court on an application made in pursuance of subsection (1) above, the like consequences shall ensue as if the alteration had been made immediately before the death by agreement between the parties and for valuable consideration.

(5) The provisions of this section shall not render the personal representatives of the deceased liable for having distributed any part of the estate of the deceased after the expiration of the period of six months referred to in subsection (2) above on the ground that they ought to have taken into account the possibility that a court might permit an application by virtue of this section to be made by the surviving party after that period; but this subsection shall not prejudice any power to recover any part of the estate so distributed arising by virtue of the making of an order in pursuance of this section.

(6) Section 31(9) above shall apply for the purposes of subsection (2) above as it applies for the purposes of subsection (6) of section 31.

(7) Subsection (3) of [section 22 of the Inheritance (Provision for Family and Dependants) Act 1975 (which enables rules of court to provide for the transfer

[1] Words substituted by Inheritance (Provision for Family and Dependants) Act 1975 c.63 s 26 (1) (a)

[2] Words substituted by Inheritance (Provision for Family and Dependants) Act 1975 c.63 s 26 (1) (a)

[3] Words substituted by Inheritance (Provision for Family and Dependants) Act 1975 c.63 s 26 (1) (a)

from a county court to the High Court or from the High Court to a county court of proceedings for an order under section 2 of that Act) and paragraphs (a) and (b) of subsection (4)][1] of that section (provisions relating to proceedings commenced in county court before coming into force of order of the Lord Chancellor under that section) shall apply in relation to proceedings consisting of any such application as is referred to in subsection (3) above as they apply in relation to [proceedings for an order under section 2 of that Act][2].

Miscellaneous and supplemental

Avoidance of transactions intended to prevent or reduce financial relief

18-048 **37.**—(1) For the purposes of this section "financial relief" means relief under any of the provisions of [sections 22, 23, 24, 24B, 27, 31][3] (except subsection (6)) and 35 above, and any reference in this section to defeating a person's claim for financial relief is a reference to preventing financial relief from being granted to that person, or to that person for the benefit of a child of the family, or reducing the amount of any financial relief which might be so granted, or frustrating or impeding the enforcement of any order which might be or has been made at his instance under any of those provisions.

(2) Where proceedings for financial relief are brought by one person against another, the court may, on the application of the first-mentioned person—

(a) if it is satisfied that the other party to the proceedings is, with the intention of defeating the claim for financial relief, about to make any disposition or to transfer out of the jurisdiction or otherwise deal with any property, make such order as it thinks fit for restraining the other party from so doing or otherwise for protecting the claim;

(b) if it is satisfied that the other party has, with that intention, made a reviewable disposition and that if the disposition were set aside financial relief or different financial relief would be granted to the applicant, make an order setting aside the disposition;

(c) if it is satisfied, in a case where an order has been obtained under any of the provisions mentioned in subsection (1) above by the applicant against the other party, that the other party has, with that intention, made a reviewable disposition, make an order setting aside the disposition;

and an application for the purposes of paragraph (b) above shall be made in the proceedings for the financial relief in question.

(3) Where the court makes an order under subsection (2)(b) or (c) above setting aside a disposition it shall give such consequential directions as it thinks fit for giving effect to the order (including directions requiring the making of any payments or the disposal of any property).

(4) Any disposition made by the other party to the proceedings for financial relief in question (whether before or after the commencement of those proceedings) as is reviewable disposition for the purposes of subsection (2)(b) and (c) above unless it was made for valuable consideration (other than marriage) to a person who, at the time of the disposition, acted in relation to it in good faith and

[1] Words substituted by Inheritance (Provision for Family and Dependants) Act 1975 c.63 s 26 (1) (b)

[2] Words substituted by Inheritance (Provision for Family and Dependants) Act 1975 c.63 s 26 (1) (b)

[3] Figure inserted by Welfare Reform and Pensions Act 1999 c.30 Sch 3 para 9

without notice of any intention on the part of the other party to defeat the applicant's claim for financial relief.

(5) Where an application is made under this section with respect to a disposition which took place less than three years before the date of the application or with respect to a disposition or other dealing with property which is about to take place and the court is satisfied—

(a) in a case falling within subsection (2)(a) or (b) above, that the disposition or other dealing would (apart from this section) have the consequence, or

(b) in a case falling within subsection (2)(c) above, that the disposition has had the consequence,

of defeating the applicant's claim for financial relief, it shall be presumed, unless the contrary is shown, that the person who disposed of or is about to dispose of or deal with the property did so or, as the case may be, is about to do so, with the intention of defeating the applicant's claim for financial relief.

(6) In this section "disposition" does not include any provision contained in a will or codicil but, with that exception, includes any conveyance, assurance or gift of property of any description, whether made by an instrument or otherwise.

(7) This section does not apply to a disposition made before 1st January 1968.

Orders for repayment in certain cases of sums paid after cessation of order by reason of remarriage

38.—(1) Where— **18-049**

(a) a periodical payments or secured periodical payments order in favour of a party to a marriage (hereafter in this section referred to as "a payments order") has ceased to have effect by reason of the remarriage of that party, and

(b) the person liable to make payments under the order or his or her personal representatives made payments in accordance with it in respect of a period after the date of the remarriage in the mistaken belief that the order was still subsisting,

the person so liable or his or her personal representatives shall not be entitled to bring proceedings in respect of a cause of action arising out of the circumstances mentioned in paragraphs (a) and (b) above against the person entitled to payments under the order or her or his personal representatives, but may instead make an application against that person or her or his personal representatives under this section.

(2) On an application under this section the court may order the respondent to pay to the applicant a sum equal to the amount of the payments made in respect of the period mentioned in subsection (1)(b) above or, if it appears to the court that it would be unjust to make that order, it may either order the respondent to pay to the applicant such lesser sum as it thinks fit or dismiss the application.

(3) An application under this section may be made in proceedings in the High Court or a county court for leave to enforce, or the enforcement of, payment of arrears under the order in question, but when not made in such proceedings shall be made to a county court; and accordingly references in this section to the court are references to the High Court or a county court, as the circumstances require.

(4) The jurisdiction conferred on a county court by this section shall be exercisable notwithstanding that by reason of the amount claimed in the application

the jurisdiction would not but for this subsection be exercisable by a county court.

(5) An order under this section for the payment of any sum may provide for the payment of that sum by instalments of such amount as may be specified in the order.

(6) [A justices' chief executive][1] to whom any payments under a payments order are required to be made, and the collecting officer under an attachment of earnings order made to secure payments under a payments order, shall not be liable—

(a) in the case of [the justices' chief executive][2], for any act done by him in pursuance of the payments order after the date on which that order ceased to have effect by reason of the remarriage of the person entitled to payments under it, and

(b) in the case of the collecting officer, for any act done by him after that date in accordance with any enactment or rule of court specifying how payments made to him in compliance with the attachment of earnings order are to be dealt with,

if, but only if, the act was one which he would have been under a duty to do had the payments order not so ceased to have effect and the act was done before notice in writing of the fact that the person so entitled had remarried was given to him by or on behalf of that person, the person liable to make payments under the payments order or the personal representatives of either of those persons.

(7) In this section "collecting officer", in relation to an attachment of earnings order, means the officer of the High Court, the registrar of a county court or [a justices' chief executive][3] to whom a person makes payments in compliance with the order.

Settlement, etc. made in compliance with a property adjustment order may be avoided on bankruptcy of settlor

18-050 **39.** The fact that a settlement or transfer of property had to be made in order to comply with a property adjustment order shall not prevent that settlement or transfer from being [a transaction in respect of which an order may be made under [section 339 or 340 of the Insolvency Act 1986][4] (transactions at an undervalue and preferences.)][5]

Payments, etc., under order made in favour of person suffering from mental disorder

18-051 **40.** Where the court makes an order under this Part of this Act requiring payments (including a lump sum payment) to be made, or property to be transferred, to a party to a marriage and the court is satisfied that the person in whose favour the order is made is incapable, by reason of mental disorder within the meaning of the Mental Health Act 1959, of managing and administering his or her property and affairs then, subject to any order, direction or authority made or given in relation to that person under Part VIII of that Act, the court may order the payments to be made, or as the case may be, the property to be transferred, to such persons having charge of that person as the court may direct.

[1] Words substituted by Access to Justice Act 1999 c.22 Sch 13 para 82 (2) (a)
[2] Words substituted by Access to Justice Act 1999 c.22 Sch 13 para 82 (2) (b)
[3] Words substituted by Access to Justice Act 1999 c.22 Sch 13 para 82 (3)
[4] Words substituted by virtue of Insolvency Act 1986 c.45 ss 439 (2), 440, 441 Sch 14
[5] Words substituted by Insolvency Act 1985 c.65 ss 235, 236 Sch 8 para 23, Sch 9 para 11 (2)

[Appeals relating to pension sharing orders which have taken effect

40A.—(1) Subsections (2) and (3) below apply where an appeal against a pension sharing order is begun on or after the day on which the order takes effect. **18-052**

(2) If the pension sharing order relates to a person's rights under a pension arrangement, the appeal court may not set aside or vary the order if the person responsible for the pension arrangement has acted to his detriment in reliance on the taking effect of the order.

(3) If the pension sharing order relates to a person's shareable state scheme rights, the appeal court may not set aside or vary the order if the Secretary of State has acted to his detriment in reliance on the taking effect of the order.

(4) In determining for the purposes of subsection (2) or (3) above whether a person has acted to his detriment in reliance on the taking effect of the order, the appeal court may disregard any detriment which in its opinion is insignificant.

(5) Where subsection (2) or (3) above applies, the appeal court may make such further orders (including one or more pension sharing orders) as it thinks fit for the purpose of putting the parties in the position it considers appropriate.

(6) Section 24C above only applies to a pension sharing order under this section if the decision of the appeal court can itself be the subject of an appeal.

(7) In subsection (2) above, the reference to the person responsible for the pension arrangement is to be read in accordance with section 25D(4) above.][1]

PART III

PROTECTION, CUSTODY, ETC., OF CHILDREN

Restrictions on decrees for dissolution, annulment or separation affecting children

41.—(1) The Court shall not make absolute a decree of divorce or of nullity of marriage, or grant a decree of judicial separation, unless the court, by order, has declared that it is satisfied— **18-053**

(a) that for the purposes of this section there are no children of the family to whom this section applies; or

(b) that the only children who are or may be children of the family to whom this section applies are the children named in the order and that—

(i) arrangements for the welfare of every child so named have been made and are satisfactory or are the best that can be devised in the circumstances; or

(ii) it is impracticable for the party or parties appearing before the court to make any such arrangements; or

[(iii) such arrangements have been made in respect of every child named in the order except any child with respect to whom the court has made an order under section 4(5) or 5(2) of the Family Law Act 1986 (orders precluding or staying proceedings for a custody order), or][2]

(c) that there are circumstances making it desirable that the decree should be made absolute or should be granted, as the case may be, without delay notwithstanding that there are or may be children of the family to

[1] Added by Welfare Reform and Pensions Act 1999 c.30 Sch 3 para 10

[2] Inserted by Family Law Act 1986 c.55 ss 68 (1), 69 (5) Sch 1 para 13

whom this section applies and that the court is unable to make a declaration in accordance with paragraph (b) above.

(2) The court shall not make an order declaring that it is satisfied as mentioned in subsection (1)(c) above unless it has obtained a satisfactory undertaking from either or both of the parties to bring the question of the arrangements for the children named in the order before the court within a specified time.

(3) If the court makes absolute a decree of divorce or of nullity of marriage, or grants a decree of judicial separation, without having made an order under subsection (1) above the decree shall be void but, if such an order was made, no person shall be entitled to challenge the validity of the decree on the ground that the conditions prescribed by subsections (1) and (2) above were not fulfilled.

(4) If the court refuses to make an order under subsection (1) above in any proceedings for divorce, nullity of marriage or judicial separation, it shall, on an application by either party to the proceedings, make an order declaring that it is not satisfied as mentioned in that subsection.

(5) This section applies to the following children of the family, that is to say—

(a) any minor child of the family who at the date of the order under subsection (1) above is—

(i) under the age of sixteen, or

(ii) receiving instruction at an educational establishment or undergoing training for a trade, profession or vocation, whether or not he is also in gainful employment; and

(b) any other child of the family to whom the court by an order under that subsection directs that this section shall apply;

and the court may give such a direction if it is of opinion that there are special circumstances which make it desirable in the interest of the child that this section should apply to him.

(6) In this section "welfare", in relation to a child, includes the custody and education of the child and financial provision for him.

18-054 **42.** [...][1]

PART IV

MISCELLANEOUS AND SUPPLEMENTAL

Evidence

18-055 **48.**—(1) The evidence of a husband or wife shall be admissible in any proceedings to prove that marital intercourse did or did not take place between them during any period.

(2) In any proceedings for nullity of marriage, evidence on the question of sexual capacity shall be heard in camera unless in any case the judge is satisfied that in the interests of justice any such evidence ought to be heard in open court.

Parties to proceedings under this Act

18-056 **49.**—(1) Where in a petition for divorce or judicial separation, or in any other pleading praying for either form of relief, one party to a marriage alleges that the other has committed adultery, he or she shall make the person alleged to have committed adultery with the other party to the marriage a party to the proceedings unless excused by the court on special grounds from doing so.

[1] Repealed by Children Act 1989 c.41 Sch 15 para 1

(2) Rules of court may, either generally or in such cases as may be prescribed by the rules, exclude the application of subsection (1) above where the person alleged to have committed adultery with the other party to the marriage is not named in the petition or other pleading.

(3) Where in pursuance of subsection (1) above a person is made a party to proceedings for divorce or judicial separation, the court may, if after the close of the evidence on the part of the person making the allegation of adultery it is of opinion that there is not sufficient evidence against the person so made a party, dismiss him or her from the suit.

(4) Rules of court may make provision, in cases not falling within subsection (1) above, with respect to the joinder as parties to proceedings under this Act of persons involved in allegations of adultery or other improper conduct made in those proceedings, and with respect to the dismissal from such proceedings of any parties so joined; and rules of court made by virtue of this subsection may make different provision for different cases.

(5) In every case in which adultery with any party to a suit is alleged against any person not made a party to the suit or in which the court considers, in the interest of any person not already a party to the suit, that that person should be made a party to the suit, the court may if it thinks fit allow that person to intervene upon such terms, if any, as the court thinks just.

Interpretation

52.—(1) In this Act— 18-057

[...][1]

"child", in relation to one or both of the parties to a marriage, includes an illegitimate [...][2] child of that party or, as the case may be, of both parties;

"child of the family", in relation to the parties to a marriage, means—

(a) a child of both of those parties; and

(b) any other child, not being a child who has been boarded-out with those parties by a local authority or voluntary organisation, who has been treated by both of those parties as a child of their family;

"the court" (except where the context otherwise requires) means the High Court or, where a county court has jurisdiction by virtue of [Part V of the Matrimonial and Family Proceedings Act 1984][3], a county court;[...][4]

"education" includes training.

["maintenance assessment" has the same meaning as it has in the Child Support Act 1991 by virtue of section 54 of that Act as read with any regulations in force under that section.][5]

(2) In this Act—

(a) references to financial provision orders, periodical payments and secured periodical payments orders and orders for the payment of a lump sum, and references to property adjustment orders, shall be construed in accordance with section 21 above; and

[1] Definition repealed by Children Act 1975 c.72 Sch 4 Pt I

[2] Words repealed by Children Act 1975 c.72 Sch 4 Pt I

[3] Words substituted by Matrimonial and Family Proceedings Act 1984 c.42 ss 46 (1), 47 (1) (e), 48 (3) Sch 1 para 16

[4] Repealed by Children Act 1989 c.41 Sch 15 para 1

[5] Added by SI 1993/623 Sch 1 para 4

[(aa) references to pension sharing orders shall be construed in accordance with section 21A above; and.][1]

(b) references to orders for maintenance pending suit and to interim orders for maintenance shall be construed respectively in accordance with section 22 and section 27(5) above.

(3) For the avoidance of doubt it is hereby declared that references in this Act to remarriage include references to a marriage which is by law void or voidable.

(4) Except where the contrary intention is indicated, references in this Act to any enactment include references to that enactment as amended, extended or applied by or under any subsequent enactment, including this Act.

Domicile and Matrimonial Proceedings Act 1973

CHAPTER 45

PART I

DOMICILE

Husband and wife

Abolition of wife's dependent domicile

19-001 **1.**—(1) Subject to subsection (2) below, the domicile of a married woman as at any time after the coming into force of this section shall, instead of being the same as her husband's by virtue only of marriage, be ascertained by reference to the same factors as in the case of any other individual capable of having an independent domicile.

(2) Where immediately before this section came into force a woman was married and then had her husband's domicile by dependence, she is to be treated as retaining that domicile (as a domicile of choice, if it is not also her domicile of origin) unless and until it is changed by acquisition or revival of another domicile either on or after the coming into force of this section.

(3) This section extends to England and Wales, Scotland and Northern Ireland.

Minors and pupils

Age at which independent domicile can be acquired

19-002 **3.**—(1) The time at which a person first becomes capable of having an independent domicile shall be when he attains the age of sixteen or marries under that age; and in the case of a person who immediately before 1st January 1974 was incapable of having an independent domicile, but had then attained the age of sixteen or been married, it shall be that date.

(2) This section extends to England and Wales and Northern Ireland (but not to Scotland).

[1] Substituted by Welfare Reform and Pensions Act 1999 c.30 Sch 3 para 11

Dependent domicile of child not living with his father

4.—(1) Subsection (2) of this section shall have effect with respect to the dependent domicile of a child as at any time after the coming into force of this section when his father and mother are alive but living apart. **19-003**

(2) The child's domicile as at that time shall be that of his mother if—

(a) he then has his home with her and has no home with his father; or

(b) he has at any time had her domicile by virtue of paragraph (a) above and has not since had a home with his father.

(3) As at any time after the coming into force of this section, the domicile of a child whose mother is dead shall be that which she last had before she died if at her death he had her domicile by virtue of subsection (2) above and he has not since had a home with his father.

(4) Nothing in this section prejudices any existing rule of law as to the cases in which a child's domicile is regarded as being, by dependence, that of his mother.

(5) [...][1]

(6) This section extends to England and Wales, Scotland and Northern Ireland.

Inheritance (Provision for Family and Dependants) Act 1975

CHAPTER 63

Application for financial provision from deceased's estate

1.—(1) Where after the commencement of this Act a person dies domiciled in England and Wales and is survived by any of the following persons:— **20-001**

(a) the wife or husband of the deceased;

(b) a former wife or former husband of the deceased who has not remarried;

[(ba) any person (not being a person included in paragraph (a) or (b) above) to whom subsection (1A) below applies;][2]

(c) a child of the deceased;

(d) any person (not being a child of the deceased) who, in the case of any marriage to which the deceased was at any time a party, was treated by the deceased as a child of the family in relation to that marriage;

(e) any person (not being a person included in the foregoing paragraphs of this subsection) who immediately before the death of the deceased was being maintained, either wholly or partly, by the deceased;

that person may apply to the court for an order under section 2 of this Act on the ground that the disposition of the deceased's estate effected by his will or the law relating to intestacy, or the combination of his will and that law, is not such as to make reasonable financial provision for the applicant.

[(1A) This subsection applies to a person if the deceased died on or after 1st January 1996 and, during the whole of the period of two years ending immediately before the date when the deceased died, the person was living—

(a) in the same household as the deceased, and

---

[1] Repealed by Children Act 1975 c.72 s 108 (1) (b) Sch 4 Pt I

[2] Added by Law Reform (Succession) Act 1995 c.41 s 2 (2)

(b) as the husband or wife of the deceased.][1]

(2) In this Act "reasonable financial provision"—

(a) in the case of an application made by virtue of subsection (1)(a) above by the husband or wife of the deceased (except where the marriage with the deceased was the subject of a decree of judicial separation and at the date of death the decree was in force and the separation was continuing), means such financial provision as it would be reasonable in all the circumstances of the case for a husband or wife to receive, whether or not that provision is required for his or her maintenance;

(b) in the case of any other application made by virtue of subsection (1) above, means such financial provision as it would be reasonable in all the circumstances of the case for the applicant to receive for his maintenance.

(3) For the purposes of subsection (1)(e) above, a person shall be treated as being maintained by the deceased, either wholly or partly, as the case may be, if the deceased, otherwise than for full valuable consideration, was making a substantial contribution in money or money's worth towards the reasonable needs of that person.

Powers of court to make orders

20-002 **2.**—(1) Subject to the provisions of this Act, where an application is made for an order under this section, the court may, if it is satisfied that the disposition of the deceased's estate effected by his will or the law relating to intestacy, or the combination of his will and that law, is not such as to make reasonable financial provision for the applicant, make any one or more of the following orders:—

(a) an order for the making to the applicant out of the net estate of the deceased of such periodical payments and for such term as may be specified in the order;

(b) an order for the payment to the applicant out of that estate of a lump sum of such amount as may be so specified;

(c) an order for the transfer to the applicant of such property comprised in that estate as may be so specified;

(d) an order for the settlement for the benefit of the applicant of such property comprised in that estate as may be so specified;

(e) an order for the acquisition out of property comprised in that estate of such property as may be so specified and for the transfer of the property so acquired to the applicant or for the settlement thereof for his benefit;

(f) an order varying any ante-nuptial or post-nuptial settlement (including such a settlement made by will) made on the parties to a marriage to which the deceased was one of the parties, the variation being for the benefit of the surviving party to that marriage, or any child of that marriage, or any person who was treated by the deceased as a child of the family in relation to that marriage.

(2) An order under subsection (1)(a) above providing for the making out of the net estate of the deceased of periodical payments may provide for—

(a) payments of such amount as may be specified in the order,

(b) payments equal to the whole of the income of the net estate or of such portion thereof as may be so specified,

[1] Added by Law Reform (Succession) Act 1995 c.41 s 2 (3)

(c) payments equal to the whole of the income of such part of the net estate as the court may direct to be set aside or appropriated for the making out of the income thereof of payments under this section,

or may provide for the amount of the payments or any of them to be determined in any other way the court thinks fit.

(3) Where an order under subsection (1)(a) above provides for the making of payments of an amount specified in the order, the order may direct that such part of the net estate as may be so specified shall be set aside or appropriated for the making out of the income thereof of those payments; but no larger part of the net estate shall be so set aside or appropriated than is sufficient, at the date of the order, to produce by the income thereof the amount required for the making of those payments.

(4) An order under this section may contain such consequential and supplemental provisions as the court thinks necessary or expedient for the purpose of giving effect to the order or for the purpose of securing that the order operates fairly as between one beneficiary of the estate of the deceased and another and may, in particular, but without prejudice to the generality of this subsection—

(a) order any person who holds any property which forms part of the net estate of the deceased to make such payment or transfer such property as may be specified in the order;

(b) vary the disposition of the deceased's estate effected by the will or the law relating to intestacy, or by both the will and the law relating to intestacy, in such manner as the court thinks fair and reasonable having regard to the provisions of the order and all the circumstances of the case;

(c) confer on the trustees of any property which is the subject of an order under this section such powers as appear to the court to be necessary or expedient.

Matters to which court is to have regard in exercising powers under s. 2

3.—(1) Where an application is made for an order under section 2 of this Act, the court shall, in determining whether the disposition of the deceased's estate effected by his will or the law relating to intestacy, or the combination of his will and that law, is such as to make reasonable financial provision for the applicant and, if the court considers that reasonable financial provision has not been made, in determining whether and in what manner it shall exercise its powers under that section, have regard to the following matters, that is to say— **20-003**

(a) the financial resources and financial needs which the applicant has or is likely to have in the foreseeable future;

(b) the financial resources and financial needs which any other applicant for an order under section 2 of this Act has or is likely to have in the foreseeable future;

(c) the financial resources and financial needs which any beneficiary of the estate of the deceased has or is likely to have in the foreseeable future;

(d) any obligations and responsibilities which the deceased had towards any applicant for an order under the said section 2 or towards any beneficiary of the estate of the deceased;

(e) the size and nature of the net estate of the deceased;

(f) any physical or mental disability of any applicant for an order under the said section 2 or any beneficiary of the estate of the deceased;

(g) any other matter, including the conduct of the applicant or any other person, which in the circumstances of the case the court may consider relevant.

(2) Without prejudice to the generality of paragraph (g) of subsection (1) above, where an application for an order under section 2 of this Act is made by virtue of section 1(1)(a) or 1(1)(b) of this Act, the court shall, in addition to the matters specifically mentioned in paragraphs (a) to (f) of that subsection, have regard to—

(a) the age of the applicant and the duration of the marriage;

(b) the contribution made by the applicant to the welfare of the family of the deceased, including any contribution made by looking after the home or caring for the family;

and, in the case of an application by the wife or husband of the deceased, the court shall also, unless at the date of death a decree of judicial separation was in force and the separation was continuing, have regard to the provision which the applicant might reasonably have expected to receive if on the day on which the deceased died the marriage, instead of being terminated by death, had been terminated by a degree of divorce.

[(2A) Without prejudice to the generality of paragraph (g) of subsection (1) above, where an application for an order under section 2 of this Act is made by virtue of section 1(1)(ba) of this Act, the court shall, in addition to the matters specifically mentioned in paragraphs (a) to (f) of that subsection, have regard to—

(a) the age of the applicant and the length of the period during which the applicant lived as the husband or wife of the deceased and in the same household as the deceased;

(b) the contribution made by the applicant to the welfare of the family of the deceased, including any contribution made by looking after the home or caring for the family.][1]

(3) Without prejudice to the generality of paragraph (g) of subsection (1) above, where an application for an order under section 2 of this Act is made by virtue of section 1(1)(c) or 1(1)(d) of this Act, the court shall, in addition to the matters specifically mentioned in paragraphs (a) to (f) of that subsection, have regard to the manner in which the applicant was being or in which he might expect to be educated or trained, and where the application is made by virtue of section 1(1)(d) the court shall also have regard—

(a) to whether the deceased had assumed any responsibility for the applicant's maintenance and, if so, to the extent to which and the basis upon which the deceased assumed that responsibility and to the length of time for which the deceased discharged that responsibility;

(b) to whether in assuming and discharging that responsibility the deceased did so knowing that the applicant was not his own child;

(c) to the liability of any other person to maintain the applicant.

(4) Without prejudice to the generality of paragraph (g) of subsection (1) above, where an application for an order under section 2 of this Act is made by virtue of section 1(1)(e) of this Act, the court shall, in addition to the matters specifically mentioned in paragraphs (a) to (f) of that subsection, have regard to the extent to which and the basis upon which the deceased assumed responsibility for the maintenance of the applicant and to the length of time for which the deceased discharged that responsibility.

[1] Added by Law Reform (Succession) Act 1995 c.41 s 2 (4)

(5) In considering the matters to which the court is required to have rd under this section, the court shall take into account the facts as known to the court at the date of the hearing.

(6) In considering the financial resources of any person for the purposes of this section the court shall take into account his earning capacity and in considering the financial needs of any person for the purposes of this section the court shall take into account his financial obligations and responsibilities.

Time-limit for applications

4. An application for an order under section 2 of this Act shall not, except with the permission of the court, be made after the end of the period of six months from the date on which representation with respect to the estate of the deceased is first taken out. **20-004**

Variation, discharge etc. of orders for periodical payments

6.—(1) Subject to the provisions of this Act, where the court has made an order under section 2(1)(a) of this Act (in this section referred to as "the original order") for the making of periodical payments to any person (in this section referred to as "the original recipient"), the court, on an application under this section, shall have power by order to vary or discharge the original order or to suspend any provision of it temporarily and to revive the operation of any provision so suspended. **20-005**

(2) Without prejudice to the generality of subsection (1) above, an order made on an application for the variation of the original order may—

(a) provide for the making out of any relevant property of such periodical payments and for such term as may be specified in the order to any person who has applied, or would but for section 4 of this Act be entitled to apply, for an order under section 2 of this Act (whether or not, in the case of any application, an order was made in favour of the applicant);

(b) provide for the payment out of any relevant property of a lump sum of such amount as may be so specified to the original recipient or to any such person as is mentioned in paragraph (a) above;

(c) provide for the transfer of the relevant property, or such part thereof as may be so specified, to the original recipient or to any such person as is so mentioned.

(3) Where the original order provides that any periodical payments payable thereunder to the original recipient are to cease on the occurrence of an event specified in the order (other than the remarriage of a former wife or former husband) or on the expiration of a period so specified, then, if, before the end of the period of six months from the date of the occurrence of that event or of the expiration of that period, an application is made for an order under this section, the court shall have power to make any order which it would have had power to make if the application had been made before the date (whether in favour of the original recipient or any such person as is mentioned in subsection (2)(a) above and whether having effect from that date or from such later date as the court may specify).

(4) Any reference in this section to the original order shall include a reference to an order made under this section and any reference in this section to the original recipient shall include a reference to any person to whom periodical payments are required to be made by virtue of an order under this section.

(5) An application under this section may be made by any of the following persons, that is to say—

(a) any person who by virtue of section 1(1) of this Act has applied, or would but for section 4 of this Act be entitled to apply, for an order under section 2 of this Act,

(b) the personal representatives of the deceased,

(c) the trustees of any relevant property, and

(d) any beneficiary of the estate of the deceased.

(6) An order under this section may only affect—

(a) property the income of which is at the date of the order applicable wholly or in part for the making of periodical payments to any person who has applied for an order under this Act, or

(b) in the case of an application under subsection (3) above in respect of payments which have ceased to be payable on the occurrence of an event or the expiration of a period, property the income of which was so applicable immediately before the occurrence of that event or the expiration of that period, as the case may be,

and any such property as is mentioned in paragraph (a) or (b) above is in subsections (2) and (5) above referred to as "relevant property".

(7) In exercising the powers conferred by this section the court shall have regard to all the circumstances of the case, including any change in any of the matters to which the court was required to have regard when making the order to which the application relates.

(8) Where the court makes an order under this section, it may give such consequential directions as it thinks necessary or expedient having regard to the provisions of the order.

(9) No such order as is mentioned in sections 2(1)(d), (e) or (f), 9, 10 or 11 of this Act shall be made on an application under this section.

(10) For the avoidance of doubt it is hereby declared that, in relation to an order which provides for the making of periodical payments which are to cease on the occurrence of an event specified in the order (other than the remarriage of a former wife or former husband) or on the expiration of a period so specified, the power to vary an order includes power to provide for the making of periodical payments after the expiration that period or the occurrence of that event.

Payment of lump sums by instalments

20-006 7.—(1) An order under section 2(1)(b) or 6(2)(b) of this Act for the payment of a lump sum may provide for the payment of that sum by instalments of such amount as may be specified in the order.

(2) Where an order is made by virtue of subsection (1) above, the court shall have power, on an application made by the person to whom the lump sum is payable, by the personal representatives of the deceased or by the trustees of the property out of which the lump sum is payable, to vary that order by varying the number of instalments payable, the amount of any instalment and the date on which any instalment becomes payable.

Powers of court in relation to transactions intended to defeat applications for financial provision

Dispositions intended to defeat applications for financial provision

10.—(1) Where an application is made to the court for an order under section 2 of this Act, the applicant may, in the proceedings on that application, apply to the court for an order under subsection (2) below. **20-007**

(2) Where on an application under subsection (1) above the court is satisfied—

(a) that, less than six years before the date of the death of the deceased, the deceased with the intention of defeating an application for financial provision under this Act made a disposition, and

(b) that full valuable consideration for that disposition was not given by the person to whom or for the benefit of whom the disposition was made (in this section referred to as "the donee") or by any other person, and

(c) that the exercise of the powers conferred by this section would facilitate the making of financial provision for the applicant under this Act,

then, subject to the provisions of this section and of sections 12 and 13 of this Act, the court may order the donee (whether or not at the date of the order he holds any interest in the property disposed of to him or for his benefit by the deceased) to provide, for the purpose of the making of that financial provision, such sum of money or other property as may be specified in the order.

(3) Where an order is made under subsection (2) above as respects any disposition made by the deceased which consisted of the payment of money to or for the benefit of the donee, the amount of any sum of money or the value of any property ordered to be provided under that subsection shall not exceed the amount of the payment made by the deceased after deducting therefrom any capital transfer tax borne by the donee in respect of that payment.

(4) Where an order is made under subsection (2) above as respects any disposition made by the deceased which consisted of the transfer of property (other than a sum of money) to or for the benefit of the donee, the amount of any sum of money or the value of any property ordered to be provided under that subsection shall not exceed the value at the date of the death of the deceased of the property disposed of by him to or for the benefit of the donee (or if that property has been disposed of by the person to whom it was transferred by the deceased, the value at the date of that disposal thereof) after deducting therefrom any capital transfer tax borne by the donee in respect of the transfer of that property by the deceased.

(5) Where an application (in this subsection referred to as "the original application") is made for an order under subsection (2) above in relation to any disposition, then, if on an application under this subsection by the donee or by any applicant for an order under section 2 of this Act the court is satisfied—

(a) that, less than six years before the date of the death of the deceased, the deceased with the intention of defeating an application for financial provision under this Act made a disposition other than the disposition which is the subject of the original application, and

(b) that full valuable consideration for that other disposition was not given by the person to whom or for the benefit of whom that other disposition was made or by any other person, the court may exercise in relation to the person to whom or for the benefit of whom that other disposition was made the powers which the court would have had under subsection (2) above if the original application had been made in respect of that other disposition and the court had been satisfied as to the matters set out in paragraphs (a), (b) and (c) of that subsection; and where any application is made under this subsection, any reference in this section (except in subsection (2)(b) to the donee shall include a reference to the person to whom or for the benefit of whom that other disposition was made.

(6) In determining whether and in what manner to exercise its powers under this section, the court shall have regard to the circumstances in which any disposition was made and any valuable consideration which was given therefor, the relationship, if any, of the donee to the deceased, the conduct and financial resources of the donee and all the other circumstances of the case.

(7) In this section "disposition" does not include—

(a) any provision in a will, any such nomination as is mentioned in section 8(1) of this Act or any donatio mortis causa, or

(b) any appointment of property made, otherwise than by will, in the exercise of a special power of appointment,

but, subject to these exceptions, includes any payment of money (including the payment of a premium under a policy of assurance) and any conveyance, assurance, appointment or gift of property of any description, whether made by an instrument or otherwise.

(8) The provisions of this section do not apply to any disposition made before the commencement of this Act.

Contracts to leave property by will

20-008 **11.**—(1) Where an application is made to a court for an order under section 2 of this Act, the applicant may, in the proceedings on that application, apply to the court for an order under this section.

(2) Where on an application under subsection (1) above the court is satisfied—

(a) that the deceased made a contract by which he agreed to leave by his will a sum of money or other property to any person or by which he agreed that a sum of money or other property would be paid or transferred to any person out of his estate, and

(b) that the deceased made that contract with the intention of defeating an application for financial provision under this Act, and

(c) that when the contract was made full valuable consideration for that contract was not given or promised by the person with whom or for the benefit of whom the contract was made (in this section referred to as "the donee") or by any other person, and

(d) that the exercise of the powers conferred by this section would facilitate the making of financial provision for the applicant under this Act,

then, subject to the provisions of this section and of sections 12 and 13 of this Act, the court may make any one or more of the following orders, that is to say—

(i) if any money has been paid or any other property has been transferred to or for the benefit of the donee in accordance with the contract, an order directing the donee to provide, for the purpose of the making of that financial provision, such sum of money or other property as may be specified in the order;

(ii) if the money or all the money has not been paid or the property or all the property has not been transferred in accordance with the contract, an order directing the personal representatives not to make any payment or transfer any property, or not to make any further payment or transfer any further property, as the case may be, in accordance therewith or directing the personal representatives only to make such payment or transfer such property as may be specified in the order.

(3) Notwithstanding anything in subsection (2) above, the court may exercise its powers thereunder in relation to any contract made by the deceased only to the extent that the court considers that the amount of any sum of money paid or to be paid or the value of any property transferred or to be transferred in accordance with the contract exceeds the value of any valuable consideration given or to be given for that contract, and for this purpose the court shall have regard to the value of property at the date of the hearing.

(4) In determining whether and in what manner to exercise its powers under this section, the court shall have regard to the circumstances in which the contract was made, the relationship, if any, of the donee to the deceased, the conduct and financial resources of the donee and all the other circumstances of the case.

(5) Where an order has been made under subsection (2) above in relation to any contract, the rights of any person to enforce that contract or to recover damages or to obtain other relief for the breach thereof shall be subject to any adjustment made by the court under section 12(3) of this Act and shall survive to such extent only as is consistent with giving effect to the terms of that order.

(6) The provisions of this section do not apply to a contract made before the commencement of this Act.

Provisions supplementary to ss. 10 and 11

12.—(1) Where the exercise of any of the powers conferred by section 10 or 11 of this Act is conditional on the court being satisfied that a disposition or contract was made by a deceased person with the intention of defeating an application for financial provision under this Act, that condition shall be fulfilled if the court is of the opinion that, on a balance of probabilities, the intention of the deceased (though not necessarily his sole intention) in making the disposition or contract was to prevent an order for financial provision being made under this Act or to reduce the amount of the provision which might otherwise be granted by an order thereunder. **20-009**

(2) Where an application is made under section 11 of this Act with respect to any contract made by the deceased and no valuable consideration was given or promised by any person for that contract then, notwithstanding anything in subsection (1) above, it shall be presumed, unless the contrary is shown, that the deceased made that contract with the intention of defeating an application for financial provision under this Act.

(3) Where the court makes an order under section 10 or 11 of this Act it may give such consequential directions as it thinks fit (including directions requiring the making of any payment or the transfer of any property) for giving effect to the order or for securing a fair adjustment of the rights of the persons affected thereby.

(4) Any power conferred on the court by the said section 10 or 11 to order the donee, in relation to any disposition or contract, to provide any sum of money or other property shall be exercisable in like manner in relation to the personal representative of the donee, and—

(a) any reference in section 10(4) to the disposal of property by the donee shall include a reference to disposal by the personal representative of the donee, and
(b) any reference in section 10(5) to an application by the donee under that subsection shall include a reference to an application by the personal representative of the donee;

but the court shall not have power under the said section 10 or 11 to make an order in respect of any property forming part of the estate of the donee which has been distributed by the personal representative; and the personal representative shall not be liable for having distributed any such property before he has notice of the making of an application under the said section 10 or 11 on the ground that he ought to have taken into account the possibility that such an application would be made.

Provisions as to trustees in relation to ss. 10 and 11

20-010 **13.**—(1) Where an application is made for—
(a) an order under section 10 of this Act in respect of a disposition made by the deceased to any person as a trustee, or
(b) an order under section 11 of this Act in respect of any payment made or property transferred, in accordance with a contract made by the deceased, to any person as a trustee,

the powers of the court under the said section 10 or 11 to order that trustee to provide a sum of money or other property shall be subject to the following limitation (in addition, in a case of an application under section 10, to any provision regarding the deduction of capital transfer tax) namely, that the amount of any sum of money or the value of any property ordered to be provided—
(i) in the case of an application in respect of a disposition which consisted of the payment of money or an application in respect of the payment of money in accordance with a contract, shall not exceed the aggregate of so much of that money as is at the date of the order in the hands of the trustee and the value at that date of any property which represents that money or is derived therefrom and is at that date in the hands of the trustee;
(ii) in the case of an application in respect of a disposition which consisted of the transfer of property (other than a sum of money) or an application in respect of the transfer of property (other than a sum of money) in accordance with a contract, shall not exceed the aggregate of the value at the date of the order of so much of that property as is at that date in the hands of the trustee and the value at that date of any property which represents the first-mentioned property or is derived therefrom and is at that date in the hands of the trustee.

(2) Where any such application is made in respect of a disposition made to any person as a trustee or in respect of any payment made or property transferred in pursuance of a contract to any person as a trustee, the trustee shall not be liable for having distributed any money or other property on the ground that he ought to have taken into account the possibility that such an application would be made.

(3) Where any such application is made in respect of a disposition made to any person as a trustee or in respect of any payment made or property transferred in accordance with a contract to any person as a trustee, any reference in the said section 10 or 11 to the donee shall be construed as including a reference to the

trustee or trustees for the time being of the trust in question and any reference in subsection (1) or (2) above to a trustee shall be construed in the same way.

Special provisions relating to cases of divorce, separation etc

Provision as to cases where no financial relief was granted in divorce proceedings etc

14.—(1) Where, within twelve months from the date on which a decree of divorce or nullity of marriage has been made absolute or a decree of judicial separation has been granted, a party to the marriage dies and— **20-011**

(a) an application for a financial provision order under section 23 of the Matrimonial Causes Act 1973 or a property adjustment order under section 24 of that Act has not been made by the other party to that marriage, or

(b) such an application has been made but the proceedings thereon have not been determined at the time of the death of the deceased,

then, if an application for an order under section 2 of this Act is made by that other party, the court shall, notwithstanding anything in section 1 or section 3 of this Act, have power, if it thinks it just to do so, to treat that party for the purposes of that application as if the decree of divorce or nullity of marriage had not been made absolute or the decree of judicial separation had not been granted, as the case may be.

(2) This section shall not apply in relation to a decree of judicial separation unless at the date of the death of the deceased the decree was in force and the separation was continuing.

Restriction imposed in divorce proceedings etc. on application under this Act

15.—[(1) On the grant of a decree of divorce, a decree of nullity of marriage or a decree of judicial separation or at any time thereafter the court, if it considers it just to do so, may, on the application of either party to the marriage, order that the other party to the marriage shall not on the death of the applicant be entitled to apply for an order under section 2 of this Act. **20-012**

In this subsection "the court" means the High Court or, where a county court has jurisdiction by virtue of Part V of the Matrimonial and Family Proceedings Act 1984, a county court.][1]

(2) In the case of a decree of divorce or nullity of marriage an order may be made under subsection (1) above before or after the decree is made absolute, but if it is made before the decree is made absolute it shall not take effect unless the decree is made absolute.

(3) Where an order made under subsection (1) above on the grant of a decree of divorce or nullity of marriage has come into force with respect to a party to a marriage, then, on the death of the other party to that marriage, the court shall not entertain any application for an order under section 2 of this Act made by the first-mentioned party.

(4) Where an order made under subsection (1) above on the grant of a decree of judicial separation has come into force with respect to any party to a marriage, then, if the other party to that marriage dies while the decree is in force and the separation is continuing, the court shall not entertain any application for an order under section 2 of this Act made by the first-mentioned party.

[1] Substituted by Matrimonial and Family Proceedings Act 1984 c.42 s 8 (1)

Miscellaneous and supplementary provisions

Effect, duration and form of orders

20-013 **19.**—(1) Where an order is made under section 2 of this Act then for all purposes, including the purposes of the enactments relating to capital transfer tax, the will or the law relating to intestacy, or both the will and the law relating to intestacy, as the case may be, shall have effect and be deemed to have had effect as from the deceased's death subject to the provisions of the order.

(2) Any order made under section 2 or 5 of this Act in favour of—

(a) an applicant who was the former husband or former wife of the deceased, or

(b) an applicant who was the husband or wife of the deceased in a case where the marriage with the deceased was the subject of a decree of judicial separation and at the date of death the decree was in force and the separation was continuing,

shall, in so far as it provides for the making of periodical payments, cease to have effect on the remarriage of the applicant, except in relation to any arrears due under the order on the date of the remarriage.

(3) A copy of every order made under this Act [other than an order made under section 15(1) of this Act][1] shall be sent to the principal registry of the Family Division for entry and filing, and a memorandum of the order shall be endorsed on, or permanently annexed to, the probate or letters of administration under which the estate is being administered.

Provisions as to personal representatives

20-014 **20.**—(1) The provisions of this Act shall not render the personal representative of a deceased person liable for having distributed any part of the estate of the deceased, after the end of the period of six months from the date on which representation with respect to the estate of the deceased is first taken out, on the ground that he ought to have taken into account the possibility—

(a) that the court might permit the making of an application for an order under section 2 of this Act after the end of that period, or

(b) that, where an order has been made under the said section 2, the court might exercise in relation thereto the powers conferred on it by section 6 of this Act,

but this subsection shall not prejudice any power to recover, by reason of the making of an order under this Act, any part of the estate so distributed.

(2) Where the personal representative of a deceased person pays any sum directed by an order under section 5 of this Act to be paid out of the deceased's net estate, he shall not be under any liability by reason of that estate not being sufficient to make the payment, unless at the time of making the payment he has reasonable cause to believe that the estate is not sufficient.

(3) Where a deceased person entered into a contract by which the agreed to leave by his will any sum of money or other property to any person or by which he agreed that a sum of money or other property would be paid or transferred to any person out of his estate, then, if the personal representative of the deceased has reason to believe that the deceased entered into the contract with the intention of defeating an application for financial provision under this Act, he may, notwithstanding anything in that contract, postpone the payment of that sum of money or the transfer of that property until the expiration of the period of

[1] Words inserted by Administration of Justice Act 1982 c.53 s 52

six months from the date on which representation with respect to the estate of the deceased is first taken out or, if during that period an application is made for an order under section 2 of this Act, until the determination of the proceedings on that application.

Interpretation

25.—(1) In this Act— **20-015**

"beneficiary", in relation to the estate of a deceased person, means—

(a) a person who under the will of the deceased or under the law relating to intestacy is beneficially interested in the estate or would be so interested if an order had not been made under this Act, and

(b) a person who has received any sum of money or other property which by virtue of section 8(1) or 8(2) of this Act is treated as part of the net estate of the deceased or would have received that sum or other property if an order had not been made under this Act;

"child" includes an illegitimate child and a child en ventre sa mre at the death of the deceased;

"the court" means [unless the context otherwise requires][1] the High Court, or where a county court has jurisdiction by virtue of section 22 of this Act, a county court;

['former wife' or 'former husband' means a person whose marriage with the deceased was during the lifetime of the deceased either—

(a) dissolved or annulled by a decree of divorce or a decree of nullity of marriage granted under the law of any part of the British Islands, or

(b) dissolved or annulled in any country or territory outside the British Islands by a divorce or annulment which is entitled to be recognised as valid by the law of England and Wales;][2]

"net estate", in relation to a deceased person, means:—

(a) all property of which the deceased had power to dispose by his will (otherwise than by virtue of a special power of appointment) less the amount of his funeral, testamentary and administration expenses, debts and liabilities, including any capital transfer tax payable out of his estate on his death;

(b) any property in respect of which the deceased held a general power of appointment (not being a power exercisable by will) which has not been exercised;

(c) any sum of money or other property which is treated for the purposes of this Act as part of the net estate of the deceased by virtue of section 8(1) or (2) of this Act;

(d) any property which is treated for the purposes of this Act as part of the net estate of the deceased by virtue of an order made under section 9 of the Act;

(e) any sum of money or other property which is, by reason of a disposition or contract made by the deceased, ordered under section 10 or 11 of this Act to be provided for the purpose of the making of financial provision under this Act;

[1] Words inserted by Matrimonial and Family Proceedings Act 1984 c.42 s 8 (2)

[2] Definitions subtituted by Matrimonial and Family Proceedings Act 1984 c.42 s 25 (2)

"property" includes any chose in action;

"reasonable financial provision" has the meaning assigned to it by section 1 of this Act;

"valuable consideration" does not include marriage or a promise of marriage;

"will" includes codicil.

(2) For the purposes of paragraph (a) of the definition of "net estate" in subsection (1) above a person who is not of full age and capacity shall be treated as having power to dispose by will of all property of which he would have had power to dispose by will if he had been of full age and capacity.

(3) Any reference in this Act to provision out of the net estate of a deceased person includes a reference to provision extending to the whole of that estate.

(4) For the purposes of this Act any reference to a wife or husband shall be treated as including a reference to a person who in good faith entered into a void marriage with the deceased unless either—

(a) the marriage of the deceased and that person was dissolved or annulled during the lifetime of the deceased and the dissolution or annulment is recognised by the law of England and Wales, or

(b) that person has during the lifetime of the deceased entered into a later age.

(5) Any reference in this Act to remarriage or to a person who has remarried includes a reference to a marriage which is by law void or voidable or to a person who has entered into such a marriage, as the case may be, and a marriage shall be treated for the purposes of this Act as a remarriage, in relation to any party thereto, notwithstanding that the previous marriage of that party was void or voidable.

(6) Any reference in this Act to an order or decree made under the Matrimonial Causes Act 1973 or under any section of that Act shall be construed as including a reference to an order or decree which is deemed to have been made under that Act or under that section thereof, as the case may be.

(7) Any reference in this Act to any enactment is a reference to that enactment as amended by or under any subsequent enactment.

Congenital Disabilities (Civil Liability) Act 1976

CHAPTER 28

Civil liability to child born disabled

21-001 **1.**—(1) If a child is born disabled as the result of such an occurrence before its birth as is mentioned in subsection (2) below, and a person (other than the child's own mother) is under this section answerable to the child in respect of the occurrence, the child's disabilities are to be regarded as damage resulting from the wrongful act of that person and actionable accordingly at the suit of the child.

(2) An occurrence to which this section applies is one which—

(a) affected either parent of the child in his or her ability to have a normal, healthy child; or

(b) affected the mother during her pregnancy, or affected her or the child in the course of its birth, so that the child is born with disabilities which would not otherwise have been present.

(3) Subject to the following subsections, a person (here referred to as "the defendant") is answerable to the child if he was liable in tort to the parent or would, if sued in due time, have been so; and it is no answer that there could not have been such liability because the parent suffered no actionable injury, if there was a breach of legal duty which, accompanied by injury, would have given rise to the liability.

(4) In the case of an occurrence preceding the time of conception, the defendant is not answerable to the child if at that time either or both of the parents knew the risk of their child being born disabled (that is to say, the particular risk created by the occurrence); but should it be the child's father who is the defendant, this subsection does not apply if he knew of the risk and the mother did not.

(5) The defendant is not answerable to the child, for anything he did or omitted to do when responsible in a professional capacity for treating or advising the parent, if he took reasonable care having due regard to then received professional opinion applicable to the particular class of case; but this does not mean that he is answerable only because he departed from received opinion.

(6) Liability to the child under this section may be treated as having been excluded or limited by contract made with the parent affected, to the same extent and subject to the same restrictions as liability in the parent's own case; and a contract term which could have been set up by the defendant in an action by the parent, so as to exclude or limit his liability to him or her, operates in the defendant's favour to the same, but no greater, extent in an action under this section by the child.

(7) If in the child's action under this section it is shown that the parent affected shared the responsibility for the child being born disabled, the damages are to be reduced to such extent as the court thinks just and equitable having regard to the extent of the parent's responsibility.

Liability of woman driving when pregnant

2. A woman driving a motor vehicle when she knows (or ought reasonably to know) herself to be pregnant is to be regarded as being under the same duty to take care for the safety of her unborn child as the law imposes on her with respect to the safety of other people; and if in consequence of her breach of that duty her child is born with disabilities which would not otherwise have been present, those disabilities are to be regarded as damage resulting from her wrongful act and actionable accordingly at the suit of the child. **21-002**

Interpretation and other supplementary provisions

4.—(1) References in this Act to a child being born disabled or with disabilities are to its being born with any deformity, disease or abnormality, including predisposition (whether or not susceptible of immediate prognosis) to physical or mental defect in the future. **21-003**

(2) In this Act—

(a) "born" means born alive (the moment of a child's birth being when it first has a life separate from its mother), and"birth" has a corresponding meaning; and

(b) "motor vehicle" means a mechanically propelled vehicle intended or adapted for use on roads.

[and references to embryos shall be construed in accordance with section 1 of the Human Fertilisation and Embryology Act 1990][1]

(3) Liability to a child under section 1 [1A][2] or 2 of this Act is to be regarded—

(a) as respects all its incidents and any matters arising or to arise out of it; and

(b) subject to any contrary context or intention, for the purpose of construing references in enactments and documents to personal or bodily injuries and cognate matters,

as liability for personal injuries sustained by the child immediately after its birth.

(4) No damages shall be recoverable under [...][3][any][4] of those sections in respect of any loss of expectation of life, nor shall any such loss be taken into account in the compensation payable in respect of a child under the Nuclear Installations Act 1965 as extended by section 3, unless (in either case) the child lives for at least 48 hours.

[(4A) In any case where a child carried by a woman as a result of the placing in her of an embryo or of sperm and eggs or her artificial insemination is born disabled, any reference in section 1 of this Act to a parent includes a reference to a person who would be a parent but for sections 27 to 29 of the Human Fertilisation and Embryology Act 1990.][5]

(5) This Act applies in respect of births after (but not before) its passing, and in respect of any such birth it replaces any law in force before its passing, whereby a person could be liable to a child in respect of disabilities with which it might be born; but in section 1(3) of this Act the expression "liable in tort" does not include any reference to liability by virtue of this Act, or to liability by virtue of any such law.

(6) References to the Nuclear Installations Act 1965 are to that Act as amended; and for the purposes of section 28 of that Act (power by Order in Council to extend the Act to territories outside the United Kingdom) section 3 of this Act is to be treated as if it were a provision of that Act.

Legitimacy Act 1976

CHAPTER 31

Legitimacy of children of certain void marriages

22-001 **1.**—(1) The child of a void marriage, whenever born, shall, subject to subsection (2) below and Schedule 1 to this Act, be treated as the legitimate child of his parents if at the time of [the insemination resulting in the birth or, where there was no such insemination, the child's conception][6] (or at the time of the celebration of the marriage if later) both or either of the parties reasonably believed that the marriage was valid.

[1] Words inserted by Human Fertilisation and Embryology Act 1990 c.37 s 44 (2) (a)
[2] Words inserted by Human Fertilisation and Embryology Act 1990 c.37 s 44 (2) (b)
[3] Word substituted by Human Fertilisation and Embryology Act 1990 c.37 s 44 (2) (c)
[4] Word substituted by Human Fertilisation and Embryology Act 1990 c.37 s 44 (2) (c)
[5] Added by Human Fertilisation and Embryology Act 1990 c.37 s 35 (4)
[6] Words substituted by Family Law Reform Act 1987 c.42 ss 28 (1), 34 (5)

(2) This section only applies where the father of the child was domiciled in England and Wales at the time of the birth or, if he died before the birth, was so domiciled immediately before his death.

[(3) It is hereby declared for the avoidance of doubt that subsection (1) above applies notwithstanding that the belief that the marriage was valid was due to a mistake as to law.

(4) In relation to a child born after the coming into force of section 28 of the Family Law Reform Act 1987, it shall be presumed for the purposes of subsection (1) above, unless the contrary is shown, that one of the parties to the void marriage reasonably believed at the time of the insemination resulting in the birth or, where there was no such insemination, the child's conception (or at the time of the celebration of the marriage if later) that the marriage was valid.][1]

Legitimation by subsequent marriage of parents

2. Subject to the following provisions of this Act, where the parents of an illegitimate person marry one another, the marriage shall, if the father of the illegitimate person is at the date of marriage domiciled in England and Wales, render that person, if living, legitimate from the date of the marriage. **22-002**

Legitimation of adopted child

4.—(1) [Section 39 of the Adoption Act 1976][2] does not prevent an adopted child being legitimated under section 2 or 3 above if either natural parent is the sole adoptive parent. **22-003**

(2) Where an adopted child (with a sole adoptive parent) is legitimated—

(a) [subsection (2) of the said section 39][3] shall not apply after the legitimation to the natural relationship with the other natural parent, and

(b) revocation of the adoption order in consequence of the legitimation shall not affect [section 39, 41 or 42 of the Adoption Act 1976][4] as it applies to any instrument made before the date of legitimation.

Personal rights and obligations

8. A legitimated person shall have the same rights, and shall be under the same obligations in respect of the maintenance and support of himself or of any other person as if he had been born legitimate, and, subject to the provisions of this Act, the provisions of any Act relating to claims for damages, compensation, allowance, benefit or otherwise by or in respect of a legitimate child shall apply in like manner in the case of a legitimated person. **22-004**

Re-registration of birth of legitimated person

9.—(1) It shall be the duty of the parents of a legitimated person or, in cases where re-registration can be effected on information furnished by one parent and one of the parents is dead, of the surviving parent to furnish to the Registrar General information with a view to obtaining the re-registration of the birth of that person within 3 months after the date of the marriage by virtue of which he was legitimated. **22-005**

(2) The failure of the parents or either of them to furnish information as required by subjection (1) above in respect of any legitimated person shall not affect the legitimation of that person.

[1] Inserted by Family Law Reform Act 1987 c.42 ss 28 (2), 34 (5)
[2] Words substituted by Adoption Act 1976 c.36 s 73 (2) Sch 3 para 23 (a)
[3] Words substituted by Adoption Act 1976 c.36 s 73 (2) Sch 3 para 23 (b)
[4] Words substituted by Adoption Act 1976 c.36 s 73 (2) Sch 3 para 23 (c)

(3) This section does not apply in relation to a person who was legitimated otherwise than by virtue of the subsequent marriage of his parents.

(4) Any parent who fails to give information as required by this section shall be liable on summary conviction to a fine not exceeding £2.

Interpretation

22-006 **10.**—(1) In this Act, except where the context otherwise requires,—

"disposition" includes the conferring of a power of appointment and any other disposition of an interest in or right over property;

"existing", in relation to an instrument, means one made before 1st January 1976;

"legitimated person" means a person legitimated or recognised as legitimated—

(a) under section 2 or 3 above; or

(b) under section 1 or 8 of the Legitimacy Act 1926; or

(c) except in section 8, by a legitimation (whether or not by virtue of the subsequent marriage of his parents) recognised by the law of England and Wales and effected under the law of any other country;

and cognate expressions shall be construed accordingly;

"power of appointment" includes any discretionary power to transfer a beneficial interest in property without the furnishing of valuable consideration;

"void marriage" means a marriage, not being voidable only, in respect of which the High Court has or had jurisdiction to grant a decree of nullity, or would have or would have had such jurisdiction if the parties were domiciled in England and Wales.

(2) For the purposes of this Act "legitimated person" includes, where the context admits, a person legitimated, or recognised as legitimated, before the passing of the Children Act 1975.

(3) For the purpose of this Act, except where the context otherwise requires,—

(a) the death of the testator is the date at which a will or codicil is to be regarded as made;

(b) an oral disposition of property shall be deemed to be contained in an instrument made when the disposition was made.

(4) [...][1]

(5) Except in so far as the context otherwise requires, any reference in this Act to an enactment shall be construed as a reference to that enactment as amended by or under any other enactment, including this Act.

[1] Repealed by Trusts of Land and Appointment of Trustees Act 1996 c.47 Sch 4 para 1

Domestic Proceedings and Magistrates' Courts Act 1978

CHAPTER 22

PART I

MATRIMONIAL PROCEEDINGS IN MAGISTRATES' COURTS

Powers of court to make orders for financial provision for parties to a marriage and children of the family

Grounds of application for financial provision

1. Either party to a marriage may apply to a magistrates' court for an order under section 2 of this Act on the ground that the other party to the marriage [...][1]— **23-001**

(a) has failed to provide reasonable maintenance for the applicant; or
(b) has failed to provide, or to make a proper contribution towards, reasonable maintenance for any child of the family; or
(c) has behaved in such a way that the applicant cannot reasonably be expected to live with the respondent; or
(d) has deserted the applicant.

Powers of court to make orders for financial provision

2.—(1) Where on an application for an order under this section the applicant satisfies the court of any ground mentioned in section 1 of this Act, the court may, subject to the provisions of this Part of this Act, make any one or more of the following orders, that is to say— **23-002**

(a) an order that the respondent shall make to the applicant such periodical payments, and for such term, as may be specified in the order;
(b) an order that the respondent shall pay to the applicant such lump sum as may be so specified;
(c) an order that the respondent shall make to the applicant for the benefit of a child of the family to whom the application relates, or to such a child, such periodical payments, and for such term, as may be so specified;
(d) an order that the respondent shall pay to the applicant for the benefit of a child of the family to whom the application relates, or to such a child, such lump sum as may be so specified.

(2) Without prejudice to the generality of subsection (1)(b) or (d) above, an order under this section for the payment of a lump sum may be made for the purpose of enabling any liability or expenses reasonably incurred in maintaining the applicant, or any child of the family to whom the application relates, before the making of the order to be met.

[1] Words repealed by Matrimonial and Family Proceedings Act 1984 c.42 ss 46 (1), 48 (3) Sch 1 para 21

(3) The amount of any lump sum required to be paid by an order under this section shall not exceed £1000 or such larger amount as the [Lord Chancellor][1] may from time to time by order fix for the purposes of this subsection.

Any order made by the [Lord Chancellor][2] under this subsection shall be made by statutory instrument and shall be subject to annulment in pursuance of a resolution of either House of Parliament.

[Matters to which court is to have regard in exercising its powers under s. 2

23-003 **3.**—(1) Where an application is made for an order under section 2 of this Act, it shall be the duty of the court, in deciding whether to exercise its powers under that section and, if so, in what manner, to have regard to all the circumstances of the case, first consideration being given to the welfare while a minor of any child of the family who has not attained the age of eighteen.

(2) As regards the exercise of its powers under subsection (1)(a) or (b) of section 2, the court shall in particular have regard to the following matters—

(a) the income, earning capacity, property and other financial resources which each of the parties to the marriage has or is likely to have in the foreseeable future, including in the case of earning capacity any increase in that capacity which it would in the opinion of the court be reasonable to expect a party to the marriage to take steps to acquire;

(b) the financial needs, obligations and responsibilities which each of the parties to the marriage has or is likely to have in the foreseeable future;

(c) the standard of living enjoyed by the parties to the marriage before the occurrence of the conduct which is alleged as the ground of the application;

(d) the age of each party to the marriage and the duration of the marriage;

(e) any physical or mental disability of either of the parties to the marriage;

(f) the contributions which each of the parties has made or is likely in the foreseeable future to make to the welfare of the family, including any contribution by looking after the home or caring for the family;

(g) the conduct of each of the parties, if that conduct is such that it would in the opinion of the court be inequitable to disregard it.

(3) As regards the exercise of its powers under subsection (1)(c) or (d) of section 2, the court shall in particular have regard to the following matters—

(a) the financial needs of the child;

(b) the income, earning capacity (if any), property and other financial resources of the child;

(c) any physical or mental disability of the child;

(d) the standard of living enjoyed by the family before the occurrence of the conduct which is alleged as the ground of the application;

(e) the manner in which the child was being and in which the parties to the marriage expected him to be educated or trained;

(f) the matters mentioned in relation to the parties to the marriage in paragraphs (a) and (b) of subsection (2) above.

(4) As regards the exercise of its powers under section 2 in favour of a child of the family who is not the child of the respondent, the court shall also have regard—

(a) to whether the respondent has assumed any responsibility for the child's maintenance and, if he did, to the extent to which, and the basis

[1] Words substituted by SI 1992/709 Art 3 (2)
[2] Words substituted by SI 1992/709 Art 3 (2)

on which, he assumed that responsibility and to the length of time during which he discharged that responsibility;

(b) to whether in assuming and discharging that responsibility the respondent did so knowing that the child was not his own child;

(c) to the liability of any other person to maintain the child.][1]

Duration of orders for financial provision for a party to a marriage

4.—(1) The term to be specified in any order made under section 2(1)(a) of this Act shall be such term as the court thinks fit except that the term shall not begin earlier than the date of the making of the application for the order and shall not extend beyond the death of either of the parties to the marriage. **23-004**

(2) Where an order is made under the said section 2(1)(a) and the marriage of the parties affected by the order is subsequently dissolved or annulled but the order continues in force, the order shall, notwithstanding anything in it, cease to have effect on the remarriage of the party in whose favour it was made, except in relation to any arrears due under the order on the date of the remarriage.

Age limit on making orders for financial provision for children and duration of such orders

5.—(1) Subject to subsection (3) below, no order shall be made under section 2(1)(c) or (d) of this Act in favour of a child who has attained the age of eighteen. **23-005**

(2) The term to be specified in an order made under section 2(1)(c) of this Act in favour of a child may begin with the date of the making of an application for the order in question or any later date [or a date ascertained in accordance with subsection (5) or (6) below.][2] but—

(a) shall not in the first instance extend beyond the date of the birthday of the child next following his attaining the upper limit of the compulsory school age [(construed in accordance with section 8 of the Education Act 1996][3]) [unless the court considers that in the circumstances of the case the welfare of the child requires that it should extend to a later date][4]; and

(b) shall not in any event, subject to subsection (3) below, extend beyond the date of the child's eighteenth birthday.

(3) The court—

(a) may make an order under section 2(1)(c) or (d) of this Act in favour of a child who has attained the age of eighteen, and

(b) may include in an order made under section 2(1)(c) of this Act in relation to a child who has not attained that age a provision for extending beyond the date when the child will attain that age the term for which by virtue of the order any payments are to be made to or for the benefit of that child,

if it appears to the court—

(i) that the child is, or will be, or if such an order or provision were made would be, receiving instruction at an educational establishment or undergoing training for a trade, profession or vocation, whether or not he is also, or will also be, in gainful employment; or

(ii) that there are special circumstances which justify the making of the order or provision.

[1] Substituted by Matrimonial and Family Proceedings Act 1984 c.42 ss 9 (1), 48 (2)
[2] Words inserted by SI 1993/623 Sch 1 para 4
[3] Words substituted by Education Act 1996 c.56 Sch 37 (II) para 138
[4] Words substituted by Matrimonial and Family Proceedings Act 1984 c.42 ss 9 (2), 47, 48 (2)

(4) Any order made under section 2(1)(c) of this Act in favour of a child shall, notwithstanding anything in the order, cease to have effect on the death of the person liable to make payments under the order.

[Orders for payments which have been agreed by the parties

23-006 **6.**—(1) Either party to a marriage may apply to a magistrates' court for an order under this section on the ground that either the party making the application or the other party to the marriage has agreed to make such financial provision as may be specified in the application and, subject to subsection (3) below, the court on such an application may, if—

(a) it is satisfied that the applicant or the respondent, as the case may be, has agreed to make that provision, and
(b) it has no reason to think that it would be contrary to the interests of justice to exercise its powers hereunder,

order that the applicant or the respondent, as the case may be, shall make the financial provision specified in the application.

(2) In this section "financial provision" means the provision mentioned in any one or more of the following paragraphs, that is to say—

(a) the making of periodical payments by one party to the other,
(b) the payment of a lump sum by one party to the other,
(c) the making of periodical payments by one party to a child of the family or to the other party for the benefit of such a child,
(d) the payment by one party of a lump sum to a child of the family or to the other party for the benefit of such a child,

and any reference in this section to the financial provision specified in an application made under subsection (1) above or specified by the court under subsection (5) below is a reference to the type of provision specified in the application or by the court, as the case may be, to the amount so specified as the amount of any payment to be made thereunder and, in the case of periodical payments, to the term so specified as the term for which the payments are to be made.

(3) Where the financial provision specified in an application under subsection (1) above includes or consists of provision in respect of a child of the family, the court shall not make an order under that subsection unless it considers that the provision which the applicant or the respondent, as the case may be, has agreed to make in respect of that child provides for, or makes a proper contribution towards, the financial needs of the child.

(4) A party to a marriage who has applied for an order under section 2 of this Act shall not be precluded at any time before the determination of that application from applying for an order under this section; but if an order is made under this section on the application of either party and either of them has also made an application for an order under section 2 of this Act, the application made for the order under section 2 shall be treated as if it had been withdrawn.

(5) Where on an application under subsection (1) above the court decides—

(a) that it would be contrary to the interests of justice to make an order for the making of the financial provision specified in the application, or
(b) that any financial provision which the applicant or the respondent, as the case may be, has agreed to make in respect of a child of the family does not provide for, or make a proper contribution towards, the financial needs of that child,

but is of the opinion—

(i) that it would not be contrary to the interests of justice to make an order for the making of some other financial provision specified by the court, and

(ii) that, in so far as that other financial provision contains any provision for a child of the family, it provides for, or makes a proper contribution towards, the financial needs of that child,

then if both the parties agree, the court may order that the applicant or the respondent, as the case may be, shall make that other financial provision.

(6) Subject to subsection (8) below, the provisions of section 4 of this Act shall apply in relation to an order under this section which requires periodical payments to be made to a party to a marriage for his own benefit as they apply in relation to an order under section 2(1)(a) of this Act.

(7) Subject to subsection (8) below, the provisions of section 5 of this Act shall apply in relation to an order under this section for the making of financial provision in respect of a child of the family as they apply in relation to an order under section 2(1)(c) or (d) of this Act.

(8) Where the court makes an order under this section which contains provision for the making of periodical payments and, by virtue of subsection (4) above, an application for an order under section 2 of this Act is treated as if it had been withdrawn, then the term which may be specified as the term for which the payments are to be made may being with the date of the making of the application for the order under section 2 or any later date.

(9) Where the respondent is not present or represented by counsel or solicitor at the hearing of an application for an order under subsection (1) above, the court shall not make an order under this section unless there is produced to the court such evidence as may be prescribed by rules of—

(a) the consent of the respondent to the making of the order,

(b) the financial resources of the respondent, and

(c) in a case where the financial provision specified in the application includes or consists of provision in respect of a child of the family to be made by the applicant to the respondent for the benefit of the child or to the child, the financial resources of the child.][1]

Powers of court where parties are living apart by agreement

7.—(1) Where the parties to a marriage have been living apart for a continuous period exceeding three months, neither party having deserted the other, and one of the parties has been making periodical payments for the benefit of the other party or of a child of the family, that other party may apply to a magistrates' court for an order under this section, and any application made under this subsection shall specify the aggregate amount of the payments so made during the period of three months immediately preceding the date of the making of the application. **23-007**

(2) Where on an application for an order under this section the court is satisfied that the respondent has made the payments specified in the application, the court may, subject to the provisions
of this Part of this Act, make one or both of the following orders, that is to say—

(a) an order that the respondent shall make to the applicant such periodical payments, and for such term, as may be specified in the order;

[1] Substituted by Matrimonial and Family Proceedings Act 1984 c.42 ss 10, 47, 48 (2)

(b) an order that the respondent shall make to the applicant for the benefit of a child of the family to whom the application relates, or to such a child, such periodical payments, and for such term, as may be so specified.

(3) The court in the exercise of its powers under this section—

(a) shall not require the respondent to make payments which exceed in aggregate during any period of three months the aggregate amount paid by him for the 2benefit of the applicant or a child of the family during the period of three months immediately preceding the date of the making of the application;

(b) shall not require the respondent to make payments to or for the benefit of any person which exceed in amount the payments which the court considers that it would have required the respondent to make to or for the benefit of that person on an application under section 1 of this Act;

(c) shall not require payments to be made to or for the benefit of a child of the family who is not a child of the respondent unless the court considers that it would have made an order in favour of that child on an application under section 1 of this Act.

(4) Where on an application under this section the court considers that the orders which it has the power to make under this section—

(a) would not provide reasonable maintenance for the applicant, or

(b) if the application relates to a child of the family, would not provide, or make a proper contribution towards reasonable maintenance for that child,

the court shall refuse to make an order under this section, but the court may treat the application as if it were an application for an order under section 2 of this Act.

(5) The provisions of section 3 of this Act shall apply in relation to an application for an order under this section as they apply in relation to an application for an order under section 2 of this Act subject to the modification that for the reference in [subsection (2)(c)][1] of the said section 3 to the occurrence of the conduct which is alleged as the ground of the application there shall be substituted a reference to the living apart of the parties to the marriage.

(6) The provisions of section 4 of this Act shall apply in relation to an order under this section which requires periodical payments to be made to the applicant for his own benefit as they apply in relation to an order under section 2(1)(a) of this Act.

(7) The provisions of section 5 of this Act shall apply in relation to an order under this section for the making of periodical payments in respect of a child of the family as they apply in relation to an order under section 2(1)(c) of this Act.

Powers of court as to the custody etc. of children

[Restriction on making of orders under this Act: welfare of children

23-008 **8.** Where an application is made by a party to a marriage for an order under section 2, 6 or 7 of this Act, then, if there is a child of the family who is under the age of eighteen, the court shall not dismiss or make a final order on the application until it has decided whether to exercise any of its powers under the Children Act 1989 with respect to the child.][2]

[1] Words substituted by Matrimonial and Family Proceedings Act 1984 c.42 ss 46 (1), 47, 48 (3) Sch 1 para 22

[2] Substituted by Children Act 1989 c.41 s 108 Sch 13 para 36 (with Sch 14 para 1 (1))

Interim orders

19.—(1) Where an application is made for an order under section 2, 6 or 7 of this Act— **23-009**

(a) the magistrates' court at any time before making a final order on, or dismissing, the application or on refusing to make an order on the application by virtue of section 27 of this Act, and

(b) the High Court on ordering the application to be reheard by a magistrates' court (either after the refusal of an order under section 27 of this Act or on an appeal under section 29 of this Act),

shall, subject to the provisions of this Part of this Act, have the [...][1]—

(i) power to make an order (in this Part of this Act referred to as an "interim maintenance order") which requires the respondent to make to the applicant or to any child of the family who is under the age of eighteen, or to the applicant for the benefit of such a child, such periodical payments as the court thinks reasonable;

(ii) [...][2]

(2) [...][3]

(3) An interim maintenance order may provide for payments to be made from such date as the court may specify, [except that, subject to section 5(5) and (6) of this Act, the date shall not be][4] earlier than the date of the making of the application for an order under section 2, 6 or 7 of this Act; and where such an order made by the High Court on an appeal under section 29 of this Act provides for payments to be made from a date earlier than the date of the making of the order, the interim order may provide that payments made by the respondent under an order made by a magistrates' court shall, to such extent and in such manner as may be provided by the interim order, be treated as having been paid on account of any payment provided for by the interim order.

[(3A) Where an application is made for an order under section 6 of this Act by the part to the marriage who has agreed to make the financial provision specified in the application—

(a) subsection (1) shall apply as if the reference in paragraph (i) to the respondent were a reference to the applicant and the references to the applicant were references to the respondent; and

(b) [subsections (2) and][5] [subsection][6](3) shall apply accordingly.][7]

(4) [...][8]

(5) Subject to subsection (6) below, an interim order made on an application for an order under section 2, 6 or 7 of this Act shall cease to have effect on whichever of the following dates occurs first, that is to say—

(a) the date, if any, specified for the purpose in the interim order;

(b) the date of the expiration of the period of three months beginning with the date of the making of the interim order;

1 Words repealed by Children Act 1989 c.41 Sch 15 para 1
2 Repealed by Children Act 1989 c.41 Sch 15 para 1
3 Repealed by Children Act 1989 c.41 Sch 15 para 1
4 Words substituted by SI 1993/623 Sch 1 para 6
5 Word substituted by Children Act 1989 c.41 s 108 (5) Sch 13 para 37 (with Sch 14 para 1 (1))
6 Word substituted by Children Act 1989 c.41 s 108 (5) Sch 13 para 37 (with Sch 14 para 1 (1))
7 Inserted by Matrimonial and Family Proceedings Act 1984 c.42 ss 46 (1), 48 (3) Sch 1 para 24
8 Repealed by Children Act 1989 c.41 Sch 15 para 1

(c) the date on which a magistrates' court either makes a final order on or dismisses the application.

(6) Where an interim order made under subsection (1) above would, but for this subsection, cease to have effect by virtue of subsection (5)(a) or (b) above, the magistrates' court which made the order or, in the case of an interim order made by the High Court, the magistrates' court by which the application for an order under section 2, 6 or 7 of this Act is to be reheard, shall have power by order to provide that the interim order shall continue in force for a further period, and any order continued in force under this subsection shall cease to have effect on whichever of the following dates occurs first, that is to say—

(a) the date, if any, specified for the purpose in the order made under this subsection;

(b) the date of the expiration of the period of three months beginning with the date of the making of the order under this subsection or, if more than one order has been made under this subsection with respect to the application, beginning with the date of the making of the first of those orders;

(c) the date on which the court either makes a final order on, or dismisses, the application.

(7) [...][1]

(8) No appeal shall lie from the making of or refusal to make, the variation of or refusal to vary, or the revocation of or refusal to revoke, an interim maintenance order.

(9) An interim order made by the High Court under this section on ordering that an application be reheard by a magistrates' court shall, for the purpose of its enforcement and for the purposes of [...][2][section 20][3] of this Act, be treated as if it were an order of that magistrates' court and not of the High Court.

Variation, revocation and cessation of orders etc

Variation, revival and revocation of orders for periodical payments

23-010 **20.**—(1) Where a magistrates' court has made an order under section 2(1)(a) or (c) of this Act for the making of periodical payments the court shall have power, on an application made under this section, to vary or revoke that order and also to make an order under section 2(1)(b) or (d) of this Act.

[(2) Where a magistrates' court has made an order under section 6 of this Act for the making of periodical payments by a party to a marriage the court shall have power, on an application made under this section, to vary or revoke that order and also to make an order for the payment of a lump sum by that party either—

(a) to the other party to the marriage, or

(b) to a child of the family or to that other party for the benefit of that child.][4]

(3) Where a magistrates' court has made an order under section 7 of this Act for the making of periodical payments, the court shall have power, on an application made under this section, to vary or revoke that order.

(4) [...][5]

[1] Words repealed by Children Act 1989 c.41 Sch 15 para 1
[2] Words repealed by Children Act 1989 c.41 Sch 15 para 1
[3] Words repealed by Children Act 1989 c.41 Sch 15 para 1
[4] Substituted by Matrimonial and Family Proceedings Act 1984 c.42 ss 11, 48 (2)
[5] Repealed by Children Act 1989 c.41 Sch 15 para 1

(5) Where a magistrates' court has made an interim maintenance order under section 19 of this Act, the court, on an application made under this section, shall have power to vary or revoke that order, except that the court shall not by virtue of this subsection extend the period for which the order is in force.

(6) The power of the court under this section to vary an order for the making of periodical payments shall include power to suspend any provision thereof temporarily and to revive any provision so suspended.

(7) Where the court has power by virtue of this section to make an order for the payment of a lump sum, the amount of the lump sum shall not exceed the maximum amount that may at that time be required to be paid under section 2(3) of this Act, but the court may make an order for the payment of a lump sum not exceeding that amount notwithstanding that the person required to pay the lump sum was required to pay a lump sum by a previous order under this Part of this Act.

(8) Where the court has power by virtue of subsection (2) above to make an order for the payment of a lump sum and the respondent [or the applicant, as the case may be,][1] has agreed to pay a lump sum of an amount exceeding the maximum amount that may at that time be required to be paid under section 2(3) of this Act, the court may, notwithstanding anything in subsection (7) above, make an order for the payment of a lump sum of that amount.

(9) An order made by virtue of this section which varies an order for the making of periodical payments may [...][2] provide that the payments as so varied shall be made from such date as the court may specify, [except that, subject to subsections (9A) and (9B) below, the date shall not be][3] earlier than the date of the making of the application under this section.

[(9A) Where—

(a) there is in force an order ("the order")—

(i) under section 2(1)(c) of this Act,

(ii) under section 6(1) of this Act making provision of a kind mentioned in paragraph (c) of section 6(2) of this Act (regardless of whether it makes provision of any other kind mentioned in that paragraph),

(iii) under section 7(2)(b) of this Act, or

(iv) which is an interim maintenance order under which the payments are to be made to a child or to the applicant for the benefit of a child;

(b) the order requires payments specified in it to be made to or for the benefit of more than one child without apportioning those payments between them;

(c) a maintenance assessment ("the assessment") is made with respect to one or more, but not all, of the children with respect to whom those payments are to be made; and

(d) an application is made, before the end of the period of 6 months beginning with the date on which the assessment was made, for the variation or revocation of the order,

the court may, in exercise of its powers under this section to vary or revoke the order, direct that the variation or revocation shall take effect from the date on which the assessment took effect or any later date.

[1] Words inserted by Matrimonial and Family Proceedings Act 1984 c.42 ss 46 (1), 48 (3) Sch 1 para 25

[2] Words repealed by Children Act 1989 c.41 Sch 15 para 1

[3] Words substituted by SI 1993/623 Sch 1 para 7

(9B) Where—

(a) an order ("the child order") of a kind prescribed for the purposes of section 10(1) of the Child Support Act 1991 is affected by a maintenance assessment;

(b) on the date on which the child order became so affected there was in force an order ("the spousal order")—

(i) under section 2(1)(a) of this Act,

(ii) under section 6(1) of this Act making provision of a kind mentioned in section 6(2)(a) of this Act (regardless of whether it makes provision of any other kind mentioned in that paragraph),

(iii) under section 7(2)(a) of this Act, or

(iv) which is an interim maintenance order under which the payments are to be made to the applicant (otherwise than for the benefit of a child); and

(c) an application is made, before the end of the period of 6 months beginning with the date on which the maintenance assessment was made, for the spousal order to be varied or revoked,

the court may, in exercise of its powers under this section to vary or revoke the spousal order, direct that the variation or revocation shall take effect from the date on which the child order became so affected or any later date.

(9C) For the purposes of subsection (9B) above, an order is affected if it ceases to have effect or is modified by or under section 10 of the Child Support Act 1991.][1]

(10) [...][2]

(11) In exercising the powers conferred by this section the court shall, so far as it appears to the court just to do so, give effect to any agreement which has been reached between the parties in relation to the application and, if there is no such agreement or if the court decides not to give effect to the agreement, the court shall have regard to all the circumstances of the case, [first consideration being given to the welfare while a minor of any child of the family who has not attained the age of eighteen, and the circumstances of the case shall include any change][3] in any of the matters to which the court was required to have regard when making the order to which the application relates or, in the case of an application for the variation or revocation of an order made under section 6 of this Act or on an appeal under section 29 of this Act, to which the court would have been required to have regard if that order had been made under section 2 of this Act.

[(12) An application under this section may be made—

(a) where it is for the variation or revocation of an order under section 2, 6, 7 or 19 of this Act for periodical payments, by either party to the marriage in question; and

(b) where it is for the variation of an order under section 2(1)(c), 6 or 7 of this Act for periodical payments to or in respect of a child, also by the child himself, if he has attained the age of sixteen.][4]

(13) [...][5]

[1] Added by SI 1993/623 Sch 1 para 8
[2] Repealed (with saving) by Family Law Reform Act 1987 c.42 s 33 (4) Sch 4
[3] Words substituted by Matrimonial and Family Proceedings Act 1984 c.42 ss 9 (3), 48 (2)
[4] Substituted by Children Act 1989 c.41 Sch 13 para 38
[5] Repealed (with saving) by Family Law Reform Act 1987 c.42 s 33 (4) Sch 4

[Variation of orders for periodical payments: further provisions

20ZA.—(1) Subject to subsections (7) and (8) below, the power of the court under section 20 of this Act to vary an order for the making of periodical payments shall include power, if the court is satisfied that payment has not been made in accordance with the order, to exercise one of its powers under paragraphs (a) to (d) of section 59(3) of the Magistrates' Courts Act 1980. **23-011**

(2) In any case where—

(a) a magistrates' court has made an order under this Part of this Act for the making of periodical payments, and

(b) payments under the order are required to be made by any method of payment falling within section 59(6) of the Magistrates' Courts Act 1980 (standing order, etc.),

an application may be made under this subsection to the clerk to the justices for the petty sessions area for which the court is acting for the order to be varied as mentioned in subsection (3) below.

(3) Subject to subsection (5) below, where an application is made under subsection (2) above, the clerk, after giving written notice (by post or otherwise) of the application to the respondent and allowing the respondent, within the period of 14 days beginning with the date of the giving of that notice, an opportunity to make written representations, may vary the order to provide that payments under the order shall be made [to the justices' chief executive for the court][1].

(4) The clerk may proceed with an application under subsection (2) above notwithstanding that the respondent has not received written notice of the application.

(5) Where an application has been made under subsection (2) above, the clerk may, if he considers it inappropriate to exercise his power under subsection (3) above, refer the matter to the court which, subject to subsections (7) and (8) below, may vary the order by exercising one of its powers under paragraphs (a) to (d) of section 59(3) of the Magistrates' Courts Act 1980.

(6) Subsection (4) of section 59 of the Magistrates' Courts Act 1980 (power of court to order that account be opened) shall apply for the purposes of subsections (1) and (5) above as it applies for the purposes of that section.

(7) Before varying the order by exercising one of its powers under paragraphs (a) to (d) of section 59(3) of the Magistrates' Courts Act 1980, the court shall have regard to any representations made by the parties to the application.

(8) If the court does not propose to exercise its power under [paragraph (c), (cc) or (d)][2] of subsection (3) of section 59 of the Magistrates' Courts Act 1980, the court shall, unless upon representations expressly made in that behalf by the person to whom payments under the order are required to be made it is satisfied that it is undesirable to do so, exercise its power under paragraph (b) of that subsection.

(9) Subsection (12) of section 20 of this Act shall have effect for the purposes of applications under subsection (2) above as it has effect for the purposes of applications under that section.

(10) None of the powers of the court, or of the clerk to the justices, conferred by this section shall be exercisable in relation to an order under this Part of this

[1] Words substituted by Access to Justice Act 1999 c.22 Sch 13 para 91
[2] Words substituted by SI 1994/731 art 2

Act for the making of periodical payments which is not a qualifying maintenance order (within the meaning of section 59 of the Magistrates' Courts Act 1980).][1]

Variation of instalments of lump sum

23-012 **22.** Where in the exercise of its powers under [section 75 of the Magistrates' Courts Act 1980][2] a magistrates' court orders that a lump sum required to be paid under this Part of this Act shall be paid by instalments, the court, on an application made by either the person liable to pay or the person entitled to receive that sum, shall have power to vary that order by varying the number of instalments payable, the amount of any instalment payable and the date on which any instalment becomes payable.

Effect on certain orders of parties living together

23-013 **25.**—(1) Where—

(a) periodical payments are required to be made to one of the parties to a marriage (whether for his own benefit or for the benefit of a child of the family) by an order made under [section 2 or6][3] of this Act or by an interim maintenance order made under section 19 of this Act (otherwise than on an application under section 7 of this Act), [...][4]

(b) [...][5]

the order shall be enforceable notwithstanding that the parties to the marriage are living with each other at the date of the making of the order or that, although they are not living with each other at that date, they subsequently resume living with each other; but the order shall cease to have effect if after that date the parties continue to live with each other, or resume living with each other, for a continuous period exceeding six months.

(2) Where any of the following orders is made under this Part of this Act, that is to say—

(a) an order under [section 2 or 6][6] of this Act which requires periodical payments to be made to a child of the family, [or,][7]

(b) an interim maintenance order under section 19 of this Act (otherwise than on an application under section 7 of this Act) which requires periodical payments to be made to a child of the family,

(c) [...][8]

(d) [...][9]

then, unless the court otherwise directs, the order shall continue to have effect and be enforceable notwithstanding that the parties to the marriage in question are living with each other at the date of the making of the order or that, although they are not living with each other at that date, they subsequently resume living with each other.

(3) Any order made under section 7 of this Act, and any interim maintenance order made on an application for an order under that section, shall cease to have effect if the parties to the marriage resume living with each other.

[1] Added by Maintenance Enforcement Act 1991 c.17 s 5
[2] Words substituted by Magistrates' Courts Act 1980 c.43 Sch 7 para 160
[3] Words substituted by Children Act 1989 c.41 Sch 13 para 41 (1)
[4] Inserted by Children Act 1989 c.41 Sch 15 para 1
[5] Inserted by Children Act 1989 c.41 Sch 15 para 1
[6] Words substituted by Children Act 1989 c.41 Sch 13 para 41 (2) (a)
[7] Word inserted by Children Act 1989 c.41 Sch 13 para 41 (2) (b)
[8] Repealed by Children Act 1989 c.41 Sch 15 para 1
[9] Repealed by Children Act 1989 c.41 Sch 15 para 1

(4) Where an order made under this Part of this Act ceases to have effect by virtue of subsection (1) or (3) above or by virtue of a direction given under subsection (2) above, a magistrates' court may, on an application made by either party to the marriage, make an order declaring that the first mentioned order ceased to have effect from such date as the court may specify.

Reconciliation

Reconciliation

26.—(1) Where an application is made for an order under section 2 of this Act the court, before deciding whether to exercise its powers under that section, shall consider whether there is any possibility of reconciliation between the parties to the marriage in question; and if at any stage of the proceedings on that application it appears to the court that there is a reasonable possibility of such a reconciliation, the court may adjourn the proceedings for such period as it thinks fit to enable attempts to be made to effect a reconciliation. **23-014**

(2) Where the court adjourns any proceedings under subsection (1) above, it may request [an officer of the Service (within the meaning of the Criminal Justice and Court Services Act 2000)][1] or any other person to attempt to effect a reconciliation between the parties to the marriage, and where any such request is made, [that officer or][2] other person shall report in writing to the court whether the attempt has been successful or not, but shall not include in that report any other information.

Provisions relating to High Court and county court

Refusal of order in case more suitable for High Court

27. Where on hearing an application for an order under section 2 of this Act a magistrates' court is of the opinion that any of the matters in question between the parties would be more conveniently dealt with by the High Court, the magistrates' court shall refuse to make any order on the application, and no appeal shall lie from that refusal; but if in any proceedings in the High Court relating to or comprising the same subject matter as that application the High Court so orders, the application shall be reheard and determined by a magistrates' court acting for the same petty sessions area as the first mentioned court. **23-015**

Provisions relating to procedure, jurisdiction and enforcement

Enforcement etc. of orders for payment of money

32.—[(1) An order for the payment of money made by a magistrates' court under this Part of this Act shall be enforceable as a magistrates' court maintenance order.][3] **23-016**

(2) Without prejudice to [section 59 of the Magistrates' Courts Act 1980][4] (which relates to the power of a magistrates' court to direct periodical payments to be made through [a justices' chief executive][5]), a magistrates' court making an order under this Part of this Act for the making of a periodical payment by one

[1] Words substituted by Criminal Justice and Court Services Act 2000 c.43 Sch 7 (II) para 57
[2] Words substituted by Criminal Justice and Court Services Act 2000 c.43 Sch 7 (II) para 57
[3] Substituted by Family Law Reform Act 1987 c.42 s 33 (1) Sch 2 para 70
[4] Words substituted by Magistrates' Courts Act 1980 c.43 s 154 Sch 7 para 164
[5] Words substituted by Access to Justice Act 1999 c.22 Sch 13 para 92

person to another may direct that it shall be made to some third party on that other person's behalf instead of directly to that other person; and, for the purposes of any order made under this Part of this Act, [the said section 59][1] shall have effect as if, in subsection (2) thereof, for the words "the applicant for the order" there were substituted the words "the person to whom the payments under the order fall to be made".

(3) Any person for the time being under an obligation to make payments in pursuance of any order for the payment of money made under this Part of this Act shall give notice of any change of address to such person, if any, as may be specified in the order; and any person who without reasonable excuse fails to give such a notice shall be liable on summary conviction to a fine not exceeding [level 2 on the standard scale][2].

(4) A person shall not be entitled to enforce through the High Court or any county court the payment of any arrears due under an order made by virtue of this Part of this Act without the leave of that court if those arrears became due more than twelve months before proceedings to enforce the payment of them are begun.

(5) The court hearing an application for the grant of leave under subsection (4) above may refuse leave, or may grant leave subject to such restrictions and conditions (including conditions as to the allowing of time for payment or the making of payment by instalments) as that court thinks proper, or may remit the payment of such arrears or any part thereof.

(6) An application for the grant of leave under subsection (4) above shall be made in such manner as may be prescribed by rules.

PART V

SUPPLEMENTARY PROVISIONS

Interpretation

23-017 **88.**—(1) In this Act—

[...][3]

"child", in relation to one or both of the parties to a marriage, includes [a child whose father and mother were not married to each other at the time of his birth][4];

"child of the family", in relation to the parties to a marriage, means—

(a) a child of both of those parties; and

(b) any other child, not being a child who is [placed with those parties as foster parents][5] by a local authority or voluntary organisation, who has been treated by both of those parties as a child of their family;

[...][6]

["family proceedings"][7] has the meaning assigned to it by [section 65 of the Magistrates' Courts Act 1980][8];

1 Words substituted by Magistrates' Courts Act 1980 c.43 s 154 Sch 7 para 164
2 Words substituted by Criminal Justice Act 1982 c.48 s 46
3 Definition repealed by Children Act 1989 c.41 Sch 15 para 1
4 Words substituted by Children Act 1989 c.41 Sch 13 para 43 (a)
5 Words substituted by Children Act 1989 c.41 Sch 13 para 43 (b)
6 Definition repealed by Access to Justice Act 1999 c.22 Sch 15 (V) (1) para 1
7 Amended by Children Act 1989 c.41 Sch 11 (II) para 6 (a)
8 Words substituted by Magistrates' Courts Act 1980 c.43 Sch 7 para 167

"local authority" means the council of a county (other than a metropolitan county), of a metropolitan district or of a London borough, or the Common Council of the City of London;

["magistrates' court maintenance order" has the same meaning as in section 150(1) of the Magistrates' Courts Act 1980,][1]

["maintenance assessment" has the same meaning as it has in the Child Support Act 1991 by virtue of section 54 of that Act as read with any regulations in force under that section.][2]

[...][3]

[...][4]

"rules" means rules made under [section 144 of the Magistrates' Courts Act 1980][5].

(2) References in this Act to the parties to a marriage living with each other shall be construed as references to their living with each other in the same household.

(3) For the avoidance of doubt it is hereby declared that references in this Act to remarriage include references to a marriage which is by law void or voidable.

(4) Anything authorised or required by this Act to be done by, to or before the magistrates' court by, to or before which any other thing was done, or is to be done, may be done by, to or before any magistrates' court acting for the same petty sessions area as that court.

(5) Any reference in this Act to an enactment shall be construed as a reference to that enactment as amended or extended by or under any subsequent enactment, including this Act.

Magistrates' Courts Act 1980

CHAPTER 43

PART II

CIVIL JURISDICTION AND PROCEDURE

Orders for periodical payment

[Orders for periodical payment: means of payment

59.—(1) In any case where a magistrates' court orders money to be paid periodically by one person (in this section referred to as "the debtor") to another (in this section referred to as "the creditor"), then— **24-001**

(a) if the order is a qualifying maintenance order, the court shall at the same time exercise one of its powers under paragraphs (a) to (d) of subsection (3) below;

---

[1] Definition inserted by Family Law Reform Act 1987 c.42 s 33 (1) Sch 2 para 71

[2] Definition inserted by SI 1993/623 Sch 1 para 9

[3] Definition repealed by Access to Justice Act 1999 c.22 Sch 15 (V) (1) para 1

[4] Definition repealed by Access to Justice Act 1999 c.22 Sch 15 (V) (1) para 1

[5] Words substituted by Magistrates' Courts Act 1980 c.43 s 154 Sch 7 para 167

(b) if the order is not a maintenance order, the court shall at the same time exercise one of its powers under paragraphs (a) and (b) of that subsection.

(2) For the purposes of this section a maintenance order is a "qualifying maintenance order" if, at the time it is made, the debtor is ordinarily resident in England and Wales.

(3) The powers of the court are—

(a) the power to order that payments under the order be made directly by the debtor to the creditor;

(b) the power to order that payments under the order be made to [a justices' chief executive][1];

(c) the power to order that payments under the order be made by the debtor to the creditor by such method of payment falling within subsection (6) below as may be specified;

[(cc) the power to order that payments under the order be made in accordance with arrangements made by the Secretary of State for their collection;][2]

(d) the power to make an attachment of earnings order under the Attachment of Earnings Act 1971 to secure payments under the order.

[(3A) No order made by a magistrates' court under paragraphs (a) to (d) of subsection (3) above (other than one made under paragraph (cc)) shall have effect at any time when the Secretary of State is arranging for the collection of payments under the qualifying maintenance order concerned.][3]

(4) In any case where—

(a) the court proposes to exercise its power under paragraph (c) of subsection (3) above, and

(b) having given the debtor an opportunity of opening an account from which payments under the order may be made in accordance with the method of payment proposed to be ordered under that paragraph, the court is satisfied that the debtor has failed, without reasonable excuse, to open such an account,

the court in exercising its power under that paragraph may order that the debtor open such an account.

(5) In deciding, in the case of a maintenance order, which of the powers under paragraphs (a) to (d) of subsection (3) above [(other than paragraph (cc))][4] it is to exercise, the court having (if practicable) given them an opportunity to make representations shall have regard to any representations made—

(a) by the debtor,

(b) by the creditor, and

(c) if the person who applied for the maintenance order is a person other than the creditor, by that other person.

(6) The methods of payment referred to in subsection (3)(c) above are the following, that is to say—

(a) payment by standing order; or

(b) payment by any other method which requires one person to give his authority for payments of a specific amount to be made from an account of his to an account of another's on specific dates during the

---

1 Words substituted by Access to Justice Act 1999 c.22 Sch 13 para 99 (2)

2 Inserted by SI 1994/731 art 3 (2)

3 Inserted by SI 1994/731 art 3 (3)

4 Words inserted by SI 1994/731 art 3 (4)

period for which the authority is in force and without the need for any further authority from him.

(7) Where the maintenance order is an order—

(a) under the Guardianship of Minors Acts 1971 and 1973,

(b) under Part I of the Domestic Proceedings and Magistrates' Courts Act 1978, or

(c) under, or having effect as if made under, Schedule 1 to the Children Act 1989,

and the court does not propose to exercise its power under [paragraph (c), (cc) or (d)][1] of subsection (3) above, the court shall, unless upon representations expressly made in that behalf by the person who applied for the maintenance order it is satisfied that it is undesirable to do so, exercise its power under paragraph (b) of that subsection.

(8) The [Lord Chancellor][2] may by regulations confer on magistrates' courts, in addition to their powers under paragraphs (a) to (d) of subsection (3) above, the power (the "additional power") to order that payments under a qualifying maintenance order be made by the debtor to the creditor or [a justices' chief executive][3] (as the regulations may provide) by such method of payment as may be specified in the regulations.

(9) Any reference in any enactment to paragraphs (a) to (d) of subsection (3) above (but not a reference to any specific paragraph of that subsection) shall be taken to include a reference to the additional power, and the reference in subsection (10) below to the additional power shall be construed accordingly.

(10) Regulations under subsection (8) above may make provision for any enactment concerning, or connected with, payments under maintenance orders to apply, with or without modifications, in relation to the additional power.

(11) The power of the [Lord Chancellor][4] to make regulations under subsection (8) above shall be exercisable by statutory instrument and any such statutory instrument shall be subject to annulment in pursuance of a resolution of either House of Parliament.

[(12) For the purposes of this section—

(a) the reference in subsection (1) above to money paid periodically by one person to another includes, in the case of a maintenance order, a reference to a lump sum paid by instalments by one person to another; and

(b) references to arrangements made by the Secretary of State for the collection of payments are to arrangements made by him under section 30 of the Child Support Act 1991 and regulations made under that section.][5]][6]

[Orders for periodical payment: proceedings by [justices' chief executive][7]

59A.—(1) Where payments under a relevant UK order are required to be made periodically— **24-002**

(a) to or through [a justices' chief executive][8], or

(b) by any method of payment falling within section 59(6) above,

[1] Words substituted by SI 1994/731 art 3 (5)
[2] Words substituted by SI 1992/709 art 3 (2)
[3] Words substituted by Access to Justice Act 1999 c.22 Sch 13 para 99 (3)
[4] Words substituted by SI 1992/709 art 3 (2)
[5] Substituted by SI 1994/731 art 3 (6)
[6] Substituted by Maintenance Enforcement Act 1991 c.17 s 2
[7] Substituted by Access to Justice Act 1999 c.22 Sch 13 para 100 (7)
[8] Words substituted by Access to Justice Act 1999 c.22 Sch 13 para 100 (2) (a)

and any sums payable under the order are in arrear, [the relevant justices' chief executive][1] shall, if the person for whose benefit the payments are required to be made so requests in writing, and unless it appears [to that justices' chief executive][2] that it is unreasonable in the circumstances to do so, proceed in his own name for the recovery of those sums.

(2) Where payments under a relevant UK order are required to be made periodically to or through [a justices' chief executive][3], the person for whose benefit the payments are required to be made may, at any time during the period in which the payments are required to be so made, give authority in writing to [the relevant justices' chief executive for him][4] to proceed as mentioned in subsection (3) below.

(3) Where authority under subsection (2) above is given to [the relevant justices' chief executive, he][5] shall, unless it appears to him that it is unreasonable in the circumstances to do so, proceed in his own name for the recovery of any sums payable to or through him under the order in question which, on or after the date of the giving of the authority, fall into arrear.

(4) In any case where—

(a) authority under subsection (2) above has been given to [a justices' chief executive][6], and

(b) the person for whose benefit the payments are required to be made gives notice in writing to the [justices' chief executive cancelling][7] the authority,

the authority shall cease to have effect and, accordingly, the [justices' chief executive shall][8] not continue any proceedings already commenced by virtue of the authority.

(5) The person for whose benefit the payments are required to be made shall have the same liability for all the costs properly incurred in or about proceedings taken under subsection (1) above at his request or under subsection (3) above by virtue of his authority (including any costs incurred as a result of any proceedings commenced not being continued) as if the proceedings had been taken by him.

(6) Nothing in subsection (1) or (3) above shall affect any right of a person to proceed in his own name for the recovery of sums payable on his behalf under an order of any court.

(7) In this section—

["the relevant justices' chief executive", in relation to an order, means—

(a) in a case where payments under the order are required to be made to or through a justices' chief executive, that justices' chief executive;

(b) in a case where such payments are required to be made by any method of payment falling within section 59(6) above and the order was made by a magistrates' court, the justices' chief executive for that magistrates' court; and

(c) in a case where such payments are required to be made by any method of payment falling within section 59(6) above and the order was not made by a magistrates' court, the justices' chief

[1] Words substituted by Access to Justice Act 1999 c.22 Sch 13 para 100 (2) (b)
[2] Words substituted by Access to Justice Act 1999 c.22 Sch 13 para 100 (2) (c)
[3] Words substituted by Access to Justice Act 1999 c.22 Sch 13 para 100 (3) (a)
[4] Words substituted by Access to Justice Act 1999 c.22 Sch 13 para 100 (3) (b)
[5] Words substituted by Access to Justice Act 1999 c.22 Sch 13 para 100 (4)
[6] Words substituted by Access to Justice Act 1999 c.22 Sch 13 para 100 (5) (a)
[7] Words substituted by Access to Justice Act 1999 c.22 Sch 13 para 100 (5) (b)
[8] Words substituted by Access to Justice Act 1999 c.22 Sch 13 para 100 (5) (c)

executive for the magistrates' court in which the order is registered;][1]

"relevant UK order" means—

(a) an order made by a magistrates' court, other than an order made by virtue of Part II of the Maintenance Orders (Reciprocal Enforcement) Act 1972;

(b) an order made by the High Court or a county court (including an order deemed to be made by the High Court by virtue of section 1(2) of the Maintenance Orders Act 1958) and registered under Part I of that Act of 1958 in a magistrates' court; or

(c) an order made by a court in Scotland or Northern Ireland and registered under Part II of the Maintenance Orders Act 1950 in a magistrates' court;

and any reference to payments required to be made periodically includes, in the case of a maintenance order, a reference to instalments required to be paid in respect of a lump sum payable by instalments.][2]

[Revocation variation, etc. of orders for periodical payment

60.—(1) Where a magistrates' court has made an order for money to be paid periodically by one person to another, the court may, by order on complaint, revoke, revive or vary the order. **24-003**

(2) The power under subsection (1) above to vary an order shall include power to suspend the operation of any provision of the order temporarily and to revive the operation of any provision so suspended.

(3) Where the order mentioned in subsection (1) above is a maintenance order, the power under that subsection to vary the order shall include power, if the court is satisfied that payment has not been made in accordance with the order, to exercise one of its powers under paragraphs (a) to (d) of section 59(3) above.

(4) In any case where—

(a) a magistrates' court has made a maintenance order, and

(b) payments under the order are required to be made by any method of payment falling within section 59(6) above,

an interested party may apply in writing to the clerk of the court for the order to be varied as mentioned in subsection (5) below.

(5) Subject to subsection (8) below, where an application has been made under subsection (4) above, the clerk, after giving written notice (by post or otherwise) of the application to any other interested party and allowing that party, within the period of 14 days beginning with the date of the giving of that notice, an opportunity to make written representations, may vary the order to provide that payments under the order shall be made [to the justices' chief executive for the court][3].

(6) The clerk may proceed with an application under subsection (4) above notwithstanding that any such interested party as is referred to in subsection (5) above has not received written notice of the application.

(7) In subsections (4) to (6) above "interested party", in relation to a maintenance order, means —

[1] Definition substituted by Access to Justice Act 1999 c.22 Sch 13 para 100 (6)

[2] Added by Maintenance Enforcement Act 1991 c.17 s 3

[3] Words substituted by Access to Justice Act 1999 c.22 Sch 13 para 101

(a) the debtor;
(b) the creditor; and
(c) if the person who applied for the maintenance order is a person other than the creditor, that other person.

(8) Where an application has been made under subsection (4) above, the clerk may, if he considers it inappropriate to exercise his power under subsection (5) above, refer the matter to the court which may vary the order by exercising one of its powers under paragraphs (a) to (d) of section 59(3) above.

(9) Subsections (4), (5) and (7) of section 59 above shall apply for the purposes of subsections (3) and (8) above as they apply for the purposes of that section.

(10) None of the powers of the court, or of the clerk of the court, conferred by subsections (3) to (9) above shall be exercisable in relation to a maintenance order which is not a qualifying maintenance order (within the meaning of section 59 above).

(11) For the purposes of this section—
(a) "creditor" and "debtor" have the same meaning as they have in section 59 above; and
(b) the reference in subsection (1) above to money paid periodically by one person to another includes, in the case of a maintenance order, a reference to a lump sum paid by instalments by one person to another.][1]

Payments to children

Provisions as to payments required to be made to a child, etc

24-004 **62.**—(1) Where—
(a) periodical payments are required to be made, or a lump sum is required to be paid, to a child under an order made by a magistrates' court, or
(b) periodical payments are required to be made to a child under an order which is registered in a magistrates' court,

any sum required under the order to be paid to the child may be paid to the person with whom the child has his home, and that person—
(i) may proceed in his own name for the variation, revival or revocation of the order, and
(ii) may either proceed in his own name for the recovery of any sum required to be paid under the order [request or authorise the [justices' chief executive for][2] the magistrates' court under subsection (1) or subsection (2) respectively of section 59A above][3], to proceed for the recovery of that sum.

(2) Where a child has a right under any enactment to apply for the revival of an order made by a magistrates' court which provided for the making of periodical payments to or for the benefit of the child, the person with whom the child has his home may proceed in his own name for the revival of that order.

(3) Where any person by whom periodical payments are required to be paid to a child under an order made by or registered in a magistrates' court makes a complaint for the variation or revocation of that order, the person with whom the child has his home may answer the complaint in his own name.

[1] Substituted by Maintenance Enforcement Act 1991 c.17 s 4
[2] Words substituted by Access to Justice Act 1999 c.22 Sch 13 para 103
[3] Words substituted by Maintenance Enforcement Act 1991 c.17 Sch 2 para 5

(4) Nothing in subsections (1) and (2) above shall affect any right of a child to proceed in his own name for the variation, revival or revocation of an order or for the recovery of any sum payable thereunder.

(5) In this section references to the person with whom a child has his home shall be construed in accordance with Part IV of the Children Act 1975, except that, in the case of any child in the care of a local authority, the local authority shall be treated for the purposes of this section as the person with whom the child has his home.

(6) In this section any reference to an order registered in a magistrates' court is a reference to an order registered in a magistrates' court under Part II of the Maintenance Orders Act 1950 or Part I of the Maintenance Orders Act 1958.

(7) In this section "child" means a person who has not attained the age of 18.

Orders other than for payment of money

Orders other than for payment of money

63.—(1) Where under any Act passed after 31st December 1979 a magistrates' court has power to require the doing of anything other than the payment of money, or to prohibit the doing of anything, any order of the court for the purpose of exercising that power may contain such provisions for the manner in which anything is to be done, for the time within which anything is to be done, or during which anything is not to be done, and generally for giving effect to the order, as the court thinks fit. **24-005**

(2) The court may by order made on complaint suspend or rescind any such order as aforesaid.

(3) Where any person disobeys and order of a magistrates' court made under an Act passed after 31st December 1979 to do anything other than the payment of money or to abstain from doing anything the court may—

(a) order him to pay a sum not exceeding £50 for every day during which he is in default or a sum not exceeding [£5,000][1]; or

(b) commit him to custody until he has remedied his default or for a period not exceeding 2 months;

but a person who is ordered to pay a sum for every day during which he is in default or who is committed to custody until he has remedied his default shall not by virtue of this section be ordered to pay more than £1,000 or be committed for more than 2 months in all for doing or abstaining from doing the same thing contrary to the order (without prejudice to the operation of this section in relation to any subsequent default).

(4) Any sum ordered to be paid under subsection (3) above shall for the purposes of this Act be treated as adjudged to be paid by a conviction of a magistrates' court.

(5) The preceding provisions of this section shall not apply to any order for the enforcement of which provision is made by any other enactment.

Domestic proceedings

Meaning of domestic proceedings

65.—(1) In this Act ["family proceedings"][2]means proceedings under any of the following enactments, that is to say— **24-006**

[1] Word substituted by Criminal Justice Act 1991 c.53 Sch 4 (I) para 1

[2] Words substituted by Children Act 1989 c.41 Sch 11 (II) para 8 (c)

(a) the Maintenance Orders (Facilities for Enforcement) Act 1920;
(b) section 43 [...][1] of the National Assistance Act 1948;
(c) section 3 of the Marriage Act 1949;
(e) [...][2]
[(ee) section 35 of the Matrimonial Causes Act 1973;][3]
(f) Part I of the Maintenance Orders (Reciprocal Enforcement) Act 1972;
(g) [...][4]
(h) the Adoption Act 1976, except proceedings under section 34 of that Act;
(i) section 18 [...][5] of the Supplementary Benefits Act 1976;
(j) Part I of the Domestic Proceedings and Magistrates' Courts Act 1978;
(k) [...][6]
(l) section 60 of this Act;
[(m) Part I of the Civil Jurisdiction and Judgments Act 1982, so far as that Part relates to the recognition or enforcement of maintenance orders;][7]
[[(mm) section 55A of the Family Law Act 1986;][8]
(n) the Children Act 1989][9]
[(n) section 106 of the Social Security Administration Act 1992;][10]
[(o) section 20 (so far as it provides, by virtue of an order under section 45, for appeals to be made to a court) [...][11] of the Child Support Act 1991;][12]
[(p) Part IV of the Family Law Act 1996;][13]
[(q) sections 11 and 12 of the Crime and Disorder Act 1998;][14]
[(r) Council Regulation (EC) No. 44/2001 of 22nd December 2000 on jurisdiction and the recognition and enforcement of judgments in civil and commercial matters, so far as that Regulation relates to the recognition or enforcement of maintenance orders;][15]

except that, subject to subsection (2) below, it does not include—
(i) proceedings for the enforcement of any order made, confirmed or registered under any of those enactments;
(ii) proceedings for the variation of any provision for the periodical payment of money contained in an order made, confirmed or registered under any of those enactments; or
(iii) proceedings on an information in respect of the commission of an offence under any of those enactments.

(2) The court before which there fall to be heard any of the following proceedings, that is to say—

[1] Words repealed by Family Law Reform Act 1987 c.42 ss 33 (2) (4) Sch 3 paras 1, 6, Sch 4
[2] Repealed by Children Act 1989 c.41 Sch 15 para 1
[3] Inserted by Matrimonial and Family Proceedings Act 1984 c.42 s 44
[4] Repealed by Children Act 1989 c.41 Sch 15 para 1
[5] Words repealed by Family Law Reform Act 1987 c.42 s 33 (2) (4) Sch 3 paras 1, 6, Sch 4
[6] Repealed by Courts and Legal Services Act 1990 c.41 Sch 20 para 1
[7] Inserted by Civil Jurisdiction and Judgments Act 1982 c.27 s 15 (4) Sch 12 Pt I para 7 (a)
[8] Added by Child Support, Pensions and Social Security Act 2000 c.19 Sch 8 para 2 (2)
[9] Inserted by Children Act 1989 c.41 Sch 11 (II) para 8 (a)
[10] Added by Social Security (Consequential Provisions) Act 1992 c.6 Sch 2 para 60
[11] Words repealed by Child Support, Pensions and Social Security Act 2000 c.19 Sch 9 (IX) para 1
[12] Added by SI 1993/623 Sch 2 para 1
[13] Added by Family Law Act 1996 c.27 Sch 8 (III) para 49
[14] Added by Crime and Disorder Act 1998 c.37 Sch 8 para 42
[15] Added by SI 2001/3929 Sch 3 para 11 (a)

(a) proceedings (whether under this Act or any other enactment) for the enforcement of any order made, confirmed or registered under any of the enactments specified in paragraphs (a) to (k) [(m), (n)][1] [, (p) and (r)][2] of subsection (1) above;

(b) proceedings (whether under this Act or any other enactment) for the variation of any provision for the making of periodical payments contained in an order made, confirmed or registered under any of those enactments;

(c) proceedings for an attachment of earnings order to secure maintenance payments within the meaning of the Attachment of Earnings Act 1971 or for the discharge or variation of such an order; or

(d) proceedings for the enforcement of a maintenance order which is registered in a magistrates' court under Part II of the Maintenance Orders Act 1950 or Part I of the Maintenance Orders Act 1958 or for the variation of the rate of payments specified by such an order,

[(e) [proceedings under][3]section 20 (so far as it provides, by virtue of an order under section 45, for appeals to be made to a court) [...][4][of the Child Support Act 1991][5].][6]

may if it thinks fit order that those proceedings and any other proceedings being heard therewith shall, notwithstanding anything in subsection (1) above, be treated as [family proceedings][7] for the purposes of this Act.

(3) Where the same parties are parties—

(a) to proceedings which are [family proceedings][8] by virtue of subsection (1) above, and

(b) to proceedings which the court has power to treat as [family proceedings][9] by virtue of subsection (2) above,

and the proceedings are heard together by a magistrates' court, the whole of those proceedings shall be treated as [family proceedings][10] for the purposes of this Act.

(4) No appeal shall lie from the making of, or refusal to make, an order under subsection (2) above.

(5) Until the Adoption Act 1976 comes into force subsection (1) above shall have effect as if for paragraph (h) thereof there were substituted the following paragraph—

"(h) the Adoption Act 1958, the Adoption Act 1960 or Part I of the Children Act 1975, except proceedings under section 42 or 43 of the Adoption Act 1958."

(6) Until the Child Care Act 1980 comes into force subsection (1) above shall have effect as if for paragraph (k) thereof there were substituted the following paragraph—

"(k) section 87 or section 88 of the Children and Young Persons Act 1933 or section 26 of the Children Act 1948."

1 Words substituted by SI 1997/1898 art 2
2 Words substituted by SI 2001/3929 Sch 3 para 11 (b)
3 Words inserted by Child Support, Pensions and Social Security Act 2000 c.19 Sch 8 para 2 (3)
4 Words repealed by Child Support, Pensions and Social Security Act 2000 c.19 Sch 9 (IX) para 1
5 Words repealed by Child Support, Pensions and Social Security Act 2000 c.19 Sch 9 (IX) para 1
6 Added by SI 1993/623 Sch 2 para 2
7 Words substituted by Children Act 1989 c.41 Sch 11 (II) para 8 (c)
8 Words substituted by Children Act 1989 c.41 Sch 11 (II) para 8 (c)
9 Words substituted by Children Act 1989 c.41 Sch 11 (II) para 8 (c)
10 Words substituted by Children Act 1989 c.41 Sch 11 (II) para 8 (c)

[Composition of magistrates' courts for family proceedings: general

24-007 **66.**—(1) A magistrates' court when hearing family proceedings shall be composed of—

(a) two or three lay justices; or
(b) a District Judge (Magistrates' Courts) as chairman and one or two lay justices;

or, if it is not practicable for such a court to be so composed, a District Judge (Magistrates' Courts) sitting alone.

(2) Except where such a court is composed of a District Judge (Magistrates' Courts) sitting alone, it shall, so far as practicable, include both a man and a woman.

(3) In this section and section 67 below "lay justices" means justices of the peace who are not District Judges (Magistrates' Courts).][1]

PART III

SATISFACTION AND ENFORCEMENT

General provisions

Power to dispense with immediate payment

24-008 **75.**—(1) A magistrates' court by whose conviction or order a sum is adjudged to be paid may, instead of requiring immediate payment, allow time for payment, or order payment by instalments.

(2) Where a magistrates' court has allowed time for payment, the court may, on application by or on behalf of the person liable to make the payment, allow further time or order payment by instalments.

[(2A) An order under this section that a lump sum required to be paid under a maintenance order shall be paid by instalments (a "maintenance instalments order") shall be treated for the purposes of sections 59, 59B and 60 above as a maintenance order.

(2B) Subsections (5) and (7) of section 59 above (including those subsections as they apply for the purposes of section 60 above) shall have effect in relation to a maintenance instalments order—

(a) as if in subsection (5), paragraph (c) and the word "and" immediately preceding it were omitted; and
(b) as if in subsection (7)—
    (i) the reference to the maintenance order were a reference to the maintenance order in respect of which the maintenance instalments order in question is made;
    (ii) for the words "the person who applied for the maintenance order" there were substituted "the debtor".

(2C) Section 60 above shall have effect in relation to a maintenance instalments order as if in subsection (7), paragraph (c) and the word "and" immediately preceding it were omitted.][2]

(3) Where a court has ordered payment by instalments and default is made in the payment of any one instalment, proceedings may be taken as if the default had been made in the payment of all the instalments then unpaid.

[1] Substituted by Access to Justice Act 1999 c.22 Sch 11 para 27
[2] Inserted by Maintenance Enforcement Act 1991 c.17 Sch 2 para 6

Enforcement of sums adjudged to be paid

76.—(1) Subject to the following provisions of this Part of this Act, and to section 132 below [...][1], where default is made in paying a sum adjudged to be paid by a conviction or order of a magistrates' court, the court may issue a warrant of distress for the purposes of levying the sum or issue a warrant committing the defaulter to prison. **24-009**

(2) A warrant of commitment may be issued as aforesaid either—

(a) where it appears on the return to a warrant of distress that the money and goods of the defaulter are insufficient to satisfy the sum with the costs and charges of levying the sum; or

(b) instead of a warrant of distress.

(3) The period for which a person may be committed to prison under such a warrant as aforesaid shall not, subject to the provisions of any enactment passed after 31st December 1879, exceed the period applicable to the case under Schedule 4 to this Act.

[(4) Where proceedings are brought for the enforcement of a magistrates' court maintenance order under this section, the court may vary the order by exercising one of its powers under paragraphs (a) to (d) of section 59(3) above.

(5) Subsections (4), (5) and (7) of section 59 above shall apply for the purposes of subsection (4) above as they apply for the purposes of that section.

(6) Subsections (4) and (5) above shall not have effect in relation to a maintenance order which is not a qualifying maintenance order (within the meaning of section 59 above).][2]

Sums adjudged to be paid by an order

[Remission of arrears and manner in which arrears to be paid

95.—(1) On the hearing of a complaint for the enforcement, revocation, revival, variation or discharge of a magistrates' court maintenance order, a magistrates' court may remit the whole or any part of the sum due under the order. **24-010**

(2) If, on the hearing of a complaint for the enforcement, revocation, revival, variation or discharge of a magistrates' court maintenance order, a magistrates' court orders that the whole or any part of the sum due under the order be paid by instalments (an "instalments order"), then—

(a) if the maintenance order is an English maintenance order, the court shall at the same time exercise one of its powers under paragraphs (a) to (d) of section 59(3) above in relation to the instalments order;

(b) if the maintenance order is a non-English maintenance order, the court shall at the same time exercise one of its powers under subsection (3) below in relation to the instalments order.

(3) The powers of the court referred to in subsection (2)(b) above are—

(a) the power to order that payments under the order be made directly to [a justices' chief executive][3];

(b) the power to order that payments under the order be made to [a justices' chief executive][4], by such method of payment falling within section 59(6) above as may be specified;

[1] Words repealed by Criminal Justice Act 1982 c.48 s 78 Sch 16
[2] Added by Maintenance Enforcement Act 1991 c.17 s 7
[3] Words substituted by Access to Justice Act 1999 c.22 Sch 13 para 110 (a)
[4] Words substituted by Access to Justice Act 1999 c.22 Sch 13 para 110 (b)

(c) the power to make an attachment of earnings order under the Attachment of Earnings Act 1971 to secure payments under the order.

(4) The court may in the course of any proceedings concerning an instalments order or the magistrates' court maintenance order to which it relates vary the instalments order by exercising—

(a) in respect of an English maintenance order, one of the powers referred to in subsection (2)(a) above;

(b) in respect of a non-English maintenance order, one of its powers under subsection (3) above.

(5) In respect of an English maintenance order, subsections (4), (5) and (7) of section 59 above shall apply for the purposes of subsections (2)(a) and (4)(a) above as they apply for the purposes of that section.

(6) In respect of a non-English maintenance order—

(a) subsection (4) of section 59 above shall apply for the purposes of subsections (2)(b) and (4)(b) above as it applies for the purposes of that section but as if for paragraph (a) there were substituted—

"(a) the court proposes to exercise its power under paragraph (b) of section 95(3) below;"

; and

(b) in deciding which of the powers under subsection (3) above it is to exercise the court shall have regard to any representations made by the debtor (within the meaning of section 59 above).

(7) In this section—

"English maintenance order" has the same meaning as it has in section 94A above;

"non-English maintenance order" means—

(a) a maintenance order registered in, or confirmed by, a magistrates' court—

(i) under the Maintenance Orders (Facilities for Enforcement) Act 1920;

(ii) under Part II of the Maintenance Orders Act 1950;

(iii) under Part I of the Maintenance Orders (Reciprocal Enforcement) Act 1972; [...][1]

(iv) under Part I of the Civil Jurisdiction and Judgments Act 1982; [or][2]

[(v) under Council Regulation (EC) No. 44/2001 of 22nd December 2000 on jurisdiction and the recognition and enforcement of judgments in civil and commercial matters;][3]

(b) an order deemed to be made by the High Court by virtue of section 1(2) of the Maintenance Orders Act 1958 and registered under Part I of that Act in a magistrates' court; or

(c) a maintenance order made by a magistrates' court by virtue of Part II of the Maintenance Orders (Reciprocal Enforcement) Act 1972.][4]

---

[1] Word repealed by SI 2001/3929 Sch 3 para 12 (a)
[2] Word added by SI 2001/3929 Sch 3 para 12 (b)
[3] Added by SI 2001/3929 Sch 3 para 12 (c)
[4] Substituted by Maintenance Enforcement Act 1991 c.17 Sch 2 para 8

Supreme Court Act 1981

CHAPTER 54

PART II

JURISDICTION

THE HIGH COURT

Powers

Wards of court

41.—(1) Subject to the provisions of this section, no minor shall be made a ward of court except by virtue of an order to that effect made by the High Court. **25-001**

(2) Where an application is made for such an order in respect of a minor, the minor shall become a ward of court on the making of the application, but shall cease to be a ward of court at the end of such period as may be prescribed unless within that period an order has been made in accordance with the application.

[(2A) Subsection (2) does not apply with respect to a child who is the subject of a care order (as defined by section 105 of the Children Act 1989).][1]

(3) The High Court may, either upon an application in that behalf or without such an application, order that any minor who is for the time being a ward of court shall cease to be a ward of court.

British Nationality Act 1981

CHAPTER 61

PART I

BRITISH CITIZENSHIP

Acquisition after commencement

Acquisition by birth or adoption

1.—(1) A person born in the United Kingdom after commencement, [or in a qualifying territory on or after the appointed day,][2] shall be a British citizen if at the time of the birth his father or mother is— **26-001**

(a) a British citizen; or

---

[1] Added by Children Act 1989 c.41 Sch 13 para 45 (2)

[2] Words inserted by British Overseas Territories Act 2002 c.8 Sch 1 para 1 (2) (a)

(b) settled in the United Kingdom [or that territory][1].

(2) A new-born infant who, after commencement, is found abandoned in the United Kingdom, [or on or after the appointed day is found abandoned in a qualifying territory,][2] shall, unless the contrary is shown, be deemed for the purposes of subsection (1)—

(a) to have been born in the United Kingdom after commencement [or in that territory on or after the appointed day][3]; and

(b) to have been born to a parent who at the time of the birth was a British citizen or settled in the United Kingdom [or that territory][4].

(3) A person born in the United Kingdom after commencement who is not a British citizen by virtue of subsection (1) or (2) shall be entitled to be registered as a British citizen if, while he is a minor—

(a) his father or mother becomes a British citizen or becomes settled in the United Kingdom; and

(b) an application is made for his registration as a British citizen.

(4) A person born in the United Kingdom after commencement who is not a British citizen by virtue of subsection (1) or (2) shall be entitled, on an application for his registration as a British citizen made at any time after he has attained the age of ten years, to be registered as such a citizen if, as regards each of the first ten years of that person's life, the number of days on which he was absent from the United Kingdom in that year does not exceed 90.

(5) Where after commencement an order authorising the adoption of a minor who is not a British citizen is made by any court in the United Kingdom [or, on or after the appointed day, any court in a qualifying territory][5], [or where on or after the appointed day such an order is made by any court in a qualifying territory, the minor][6] shall be a British citizen as from the date on which the order is made if the adopter or, in the case of a joint adoption, one of the adopters is a British citizen on that date.

(6) Where an order in consequence of which any person became a British citizen by virtue of subsection (5) ceases to have effect, whether on annulment or otherwise, the cesser shall not affect the status of that person as a British citizen.

(7) If in the special circumstances of any particular case the Secretary of State thinks fit, he may for the purposes of subsection (4) treat the person to whom the application relates as fulfilling the requirement specified in that subsection although, as regards any one or more of the first ten years of that person's life, the number of days on which he was absent from the United Kingdom in that year or each of the years in question exceeds 90.

(8) In this section and elsewhere in this Act "settled" has the meaning given by section 50.

Acquisition by descent

26-002 **2.**—(1) A person born outside the United Kingdom [and the qualifying territories][7] after commencement shall be a British citizen if at the time of the birth his father or mother—

(a) is a British citizen otherwise than by descent; or

[1] Words inserted by British Overseas Territories Act 2002 c.8 Sch 1 para 1 (2) (b)
[2] Words inserted by British Overseas Territories Act 2002 c.8 Sch 1 para 1 (3) (a)
[3] Words inserted by British Overseas Territories Act 2002 c.8 Sch 1 para 1 (3) (b)
[4] Words inserted by British Overseas Territories Act 2002 c.8 Sch 1 para 1 (3) (c)
[5] Words inserted by British Overseas Territories Act 2002 c.8 Sch 1 para 1 (4)
[6] Word substituted by British Overseas Territories Act 2002 c.8 Sch 1 para 1 (5)
[7] Words inserted by British Overseas Territories Act 2002 c.8 Sch 1 para 2 (2) (a)

(b) is a British citizen and is serving outside the United Kingdom [and the qualifying territories][1] in service to which this paragraph applies, his or her recruitment for that service having taken place in the United Kingdom [or a qualifying territory][2]; or

(c) is a British citizen and is serving outside the United Kingdom [and the qualifying territories][3] in service under a Community institution, his or her recruitment for that service having taken place in a country which at the time of the recruitment was a member of the Communities.

(2) Paragraph (b) of subsection (1) applies to—

(a) Crown service under the government of the United Kingdom [or of a qualifying territory][4]; and

(b) service of any description for the time being designated under subsection (3).

(3) For the purposes of this section the Secretary of State may by order made by statutory instrument designate any description of service which he considers to be closely associated with the activities outside the United Kingdom [and the qualifying territories][5] of Her Majesty's government in the United Kingdom [or in a qualifying territory][6].

(4) Any order made under subsection (3) shall be subject to annulment in pursuance of a resolution of either House of Parliament.

Administration of Justice Act 1982

CHAPTER 53

PART I

DAMAGES FOR PERSONAL INJURIES ETC

Abolition of certain claims for damages etc

Abolition of actions for loss of services etc

2. No person shall be liable in tort under the law of England and Wales or the law of Northern Ireland— **27-001**

(a) to a husband on the ground only of his having deprived him of the services or society of his wife;

(b) to a parent (or person standing in the place of a parent) on the ground only of his having deprived him of the services of a child; or

(c) on the ground only—

(i) of having deprived another of the services of his menial servant;

(ii) of having deprived another of the services of his female servant by raping or seducing her; or

---

[1] Words inserted by British Overseas Territories Act 2002 c.8 Sch 1 para 2 (2) (b)
[2] Words inserted by British Overseas Territories Act 2002 c.8 Sch 1 para 2 (2) (b)
[3] Words inserted by British Overseas Territories Act 2002 c.8 Sch 1 para 2 (2) (c)
[4] Words inserted by British Overseas Territories Act 2002 c.8 Sch 1 para 2 (3)
[5] Words inserted by British Overseas Territories Act 2002 c.8 Sch 1 para 2 (4) (a)
[6] Words inserted by British Overseas Territories Act 2002 c.8 Sch 1 para 2 (4) (b)

(iii) of enticement of a servant or harbouring a servant.

Marriage Act 1983

CHAPTER 32

Marriages in England and Wales

Marriages of house-bound and detained persons in England and Wales

28-001 **1.**—(1) Subject to the provisions of this Act and the Marriage Act 1949, the marriage of a person who is house-bound or is a detained person may be solemnized in England and Wales, on the authority of [certificates of a superintendent registrar][1] issued under Part III of the Marriage Act 1949, at the place where that person usually resides.

(2) For the purposes of this section a person is house-bound if—

(a) [each notice][2] of his or her marriage given in accordance with section 27 of the Marriage Act 1949 is accompanied by a statement, made in a form prescribed under that Act by a registered medical practitioner not more than fourteen days before that notice is given, that, in his opinion—

(i) by reason of illness or disability, he or she ought not to move or be moved from his or her home or the other place where he or she is at that time, and

(ii) it is likely that it will be the case for at least the three months following the date on which the statement is made that by reason of the illness or disability he or she ought not to move or be moved from that place; and

(b) he or she is not a detained person.

(3) For the purposes of this section, a person is a detained person if he or she is for the time being detained—

(a) otherwise than by virtue of section 2, 4, 5, 35, 36 or 136 of the Mental Health Act 1983 (short term detentions), as a patient in a hospital; or

(b) in a prison or other place to which the Prison Act 1952 applies.

(4) In subsection (3) above "hospital" and "patient" have the same meanings as in Part II of the Mental Health Act 1983.

(5) For the purposes of this section, a person who is house-bound or is a detained person shall be taken, if he or she would not otherwise be, to be usually resident at the place where he or she is for the time being.

(6) Nothing in the preceding provisions of this section shall be taken to relate or have any reference to any marriage according to the usages of the Society of Friends or any marriage between two persons professing the Jewish religion according to the usages of the Jews.

[1] Words substituted by Immigration and Asylum Act 1999 c.33 Sch 14 para 77 (a)
[2] Words substituted by Immigration and Asylum Act 1999 c.33 Sch 14 para 77 (b)

(7) Schedule 1 to this Act (amendment of the Marriage Act 1949 in consequence of this section) shall have effect.

Child Abduction Act 1984

CHAPTER 37

PART I

OFFENCES UNDER LAW OF ENGLAND AND WALES

Offence of abduction of child by parent, etc

1.—(1) Subject to subsections (5) and (8) below, a person connected with a child under the age of sixteen commits an offence if he takes or sends the child out of the United Kingdom without the appropriate consent. **29-001**

[(2) A person is connected with a child for the purposes of this section if—

(a) he is a parent of the child; or

(b) in the case of a child whose parents were not married to each other at the time of his birth, there are reasonable grounds for believing that he is the father of the child; or

(c) he is a guardian of the child; or

(d) he is a person in whose favour a residence order is in force with respect to the child; or

(e) he has custody of the child.

(3) In this section 'the appropriate consent', in relation to a child, means —

(a) the consent of each of the following—

(i) the child's mother;

(ii) the child's father, if he has parental responsibility for him;

(iii) any guardian of the child;

(iv) any person in whose favour a residence order is in force with respect to the child;

(v) any person who has custody of the child; or

(b) the leave of the court granted under or by virtue of any provision of Part II of the Children Act 1989; or

(c) if any person has custody of the child, the leave of the court which awarded custody to him.

(4) A person does not commit an offence under this section by taking or sending a child out of the United Kingdom without obtaining the appropriate consent if—

(a) he is a person in whose favour there is a residence order in force with respect to the child, and

(b) he takes or sends him out of the United Kingdom for a period of less than one month.

(4A) Subsection (4) above does not apply if the person taking or sending the child out of the United Kingdom does so in breach of an order under Part II of the Children Act 1989.][1]

[1] Substituted by Children Act 1989 c.41 Sch 12 para 37 (2)

(5) A person does not commit an offence under this section by doing anything without the consent of another person whose consent is required under the foregoing provisions if—

(a) he does it in the belief that the other person—

(i) has consented; or

(ii) would consent if he was aware of all the relevant circumstances; or

(b) he has taken all reasonable steps to communicate with the other person but has been unable to communicate with him; or

(c) the other person has unreasonably refused to consent,

[(5A) Subsection (5)(c) above does not apply if—

(a) the person who refused to consent is a person—

(i) in whose favour there is a residence order in force with respect to the child; or

(ii) who has custody of the child; or

(b) the person taking or sending the child out of the United Kingdom is, by so acting, in breach of an order made by a court in the United Kingdom.][1]

(6) Where, in proceedings for an offence under this section, there is sufficient evidence to raise an issue as to the application of subsection (5) above, it shall be for the prosecution to prove that that subsection does not apply.

[(7) For the purposes of this section—

(a) 'guardian of a child', 'residence order' and 'parental responsibility' have the same meaning as in the Children Act 1989; and

(b) a person shall be treated as having custody of a child if there is in force an order of a court in the United Kingdom awarding him (whether solely or jointly with another person) custody, legal custody or care and control of the child.][2]

(8) This section shall have effect subject to the provisions of the Schedule to this Act in relation to a child who is in the care of a local authority [detained in a place of safety, remanded to a local authority accommodation or the subject of][3] proceedings or an order relating to adoption.

Offence of abduction of child by other persons

29-002 **2.**—(1) [Subject to subsection (3) below, a person, other than one mentioned in subsection (2) below.][4] commits an offence if, without lawful authority or reasonable excuse, he takes or detains a child under the age of sixteen—

(a) so as to remove him from the lawful control of any person having lawful control of the child; or

(b) so as to keep him out of the lawful control of any person entitled to lawful control of the child.

[(2) The persons are—

(a) where the father and mother of the child in question were married to each other at the time of his birth, the child's father and mother;

(b) where the father and mother of the child in question were not married to each other at the time of his birth, the child's mother; and

(c) any other person mentioned in section 1(2)(c) to (e) above.

[1] Words substituted by Children Act 1989 c.41 Sch 12 para 37 (3)
[2] Substituted by Children Act 1989 c.41 Sch 12 para 37 (4)
[3] Words substituted by Children Act 1989 c.41 Sch 12 para 37 (5)
[4] Words substituted by Children Act 1989 c.41 Sch 12 para 38 (1)

(3) In proceedings against any person for an offence under this section, it shall be a defence for that person to prove—

(a) where the father and mother of the child in question were not married to each other at the time of his birth—

(i) that he is the child's father; or

(ii) that, at the time of the alleged offence, he believed, on reasonable grounds, that he was the child's father; or

(b) that, at the time of the alleged offence, he believed that the child had attained the age of sixteen.][1]

Construction of references to taking, sending and detaining

3. For the purposes of this Part of this Act— **29-003**

(a) a person shall be regarded as taking a child if he causes or induces the child to accompany him or any other person or causes the child to be taken;

(b) a person shall be regarded as sending a child if he causes the child to be sent; [...][2]

(c) a person shall be regarded as detaining a child if he causes the child to be detained or induces the child to remain with him or any other person[; and][3]

[(d) references to a child's parents and to a child whose parents were (or were not) married to each other at the time of his birth shall be construed in accordance with section 1 of the Family Law Reform Act 1987 (which extends their meaning).][4]

Matrimonial and Family Proceedings Act 1984

CHAPTER 42

PART III

FINANCIAL RELIEF IN ENGLAND AND WALES AFTER OVERSEAS DIVORCE ETC

Applications for financial relief

Applications for financial relief after overseas divorce etc

12.—(1) Where— **30-001**

(a) a marriage has been dissolved or annulled, or the parties to a marriage have been legally separated, by means of judicial or other proceedings in an overseas country, and

(b) the divorce, annulment or legal separation is entitled to be recognised as valid in England and Wales,

---

1 Substituted by Children Act 1989 c.41 Sch 12 para 38 (2)
2 Word repealed by Children Act 1989 c.41 Sch 15 para 1
3 Added by Children Act 1989 c.41 Sch 12 para 39
4 Added by Children Act 1989 c.41 Sch 12 para 39

either party to the marriage may apply to the court in the manner prescribed by rules of court for an order for financial relief under this Part of this Act.

(2) If after a marriage has been dissolved or annulled in an overseas country one of the parties to the marriage remarries that party shall not be entitled to make an application in relation to that marriage.

(3) For the avoidance of doubt it is hereby declared that the reference in subsection (2) above to remarriage includes a reference to a marriage which is by law void or voidable.

(4) In this Part of this Act except sections 19, 23, and 24 "order for financial relief" means an order under section 17 or 22 below of a description referred to in that section.

Leave of the court required for applications for financial relief

30-002 **13.**—(1) No application for an order for financial relief shall be made under this Part of this Act unless the leave of the court has been obtained in accordance with rules of court; and the court shall not grant leave unless it considers that there is substantial ground for the making of an application for such an order.

(2) The court may grant leave under this section notwithstanding that an order has been made by a court in a country outside England and Wales requiring the other party to the marriage to make any payment or transfer any property to the applicant or a child of the family.

(3) Leave under this section may be granted subject to such conditions as the court thinks fit.

Interim orders for maintenance

30-003 **14.**—(1) Where leave is granted under section 13 above for the making of an application for an order for financial relief and it appears to the court that the applicant or any child of the family is in immediate need of financial assistance, the court may make an interim order for maintenance, that is to say, an order requiring the other party to the marriage to make to the applicant or to the child such periodical payments, and for such term, being a term beginning not earlier than the date of the grant of leave and ending with the date of the determination of the application for an order for financial relief, as the court thinks reasonable.

(2) If it appears to the court that the court has jurisdiction to entertain the application for an order for financial relief by reason only of paragraph (c) of section 15(1) below the court shall not make an interim order under this section.

(3) An interim order under subsection (1) above may be made subject to such conditions as the court thinks fit.

Jurisdiction of the court

30-004 **15.**—(1) Subject to subsection (2) below, the court shall have jurisdiction to entertain an application for an order for financial relief if any of the following jurisdictional requirements are satisfied, that is to say—

(a) either of the parties to the marriage was domiciled in England and Wales on the date of the application for leave under section 13 above or was so domiciled on the date on which the divorce, annulment or legal separation obtained in the overseas country took effect in that country; or

(b) either of the parties to the marriage was habitually resident in England and Wales throughout the period of one year ending with the date of the application for leave or was so resident throughout the period of one year ending with the date on which the divorce, annulment or legal separation obtained in the overseas country took effect in that country; or

(c) either or both of the parties to the marriage had at the date of the application for leave a beneficial interest in possession in a dwelling-house situated in England or Wales which was at some time during the marriage a matrimonial home of the parties to the marriage.

(2) Where the jurisdiction of the court to entertain proceedings under this Part of this Act would fall to be determined by reference to the jurisdictional requirements imposed by virtue of Part I of the Civil Jurisdiction and Judgments Act 1982 (implementation of certain European conventions) [or by virtue of Council Regulation (EC) No. 44/2001 of 22nd December 2000 on jurisdiction and the recognition and enforcement of judgments in civil and commercial matters or][1] then—

(a) satisfaction of the requirements of subsection (1) above shall not obviate the need to satisfy the requirements imposed by virtue of [that Regulation or][2]Part I of that Act; and

(b) satisfaction of the requirements imposed by virtue of [that Regulation or][3]Part I of that Act shall obviate the need to satisfy the requirements of subsection (1) above;

and the court shall entertain or not entertain the proceedings accordingly.

Duty of the court to consider whether England and Wales is appropriate venue for application

16.—(1) Before making an order for financial relief the court shall consider whether in all the circumstances of the case it would be appropriate for such an order to be made by a court in England and Wales, and if the court is not satisfied that it would be appropriate, the court shall dismiss the application. **30-005**

(2) The court shall in particular have regard to the following matters—

(a) the connection which the parties to the marriage have with England and Wales;

(b) the connection which those parties have with the country in which the marriage was dissolved or annulled or in which they were legally separated;

(c) the connection which those parties have with any other country outside England and Wales;

(d) any financial benefit which the applicant or a child of the family has received, or is likely to receive, in consequence of the divorce, annulment or legal separation, by virtue of any agreement or the operation of the law of a country outside England and Wales;

(e) in a case where an order has been made by a court in a country outside England and Wales requiring the other party to the marriage to make any payment or transfer any property for the benefit of the applicant or a child of the family, the financial relief given by the order and the extent to which the order has been complied with or is likely to be complied with;

(f) any right which the applicant has, or has had, to apply for financial relief from the other party to the marriage under the law of any country

[1] Words inserted by SI 2001/3929 Sch 3 para 19 (a)
[2] Words inserted by SI 2001/3929 Sch 3 para 19 (b)
[3] Words inserted by SI 2001/3929 Sch 3 para 19 (b)

outside England and Wales and if the applicant has omitted to exercise that right the reason for that omission;

(g) the availability in England and Wales of any property in respect of which an order under this Part of this Act in favour of the applicant could be made;

(h) the extent to which any order made under this Part of this Act is likely to be enforceable;

(i) the length of time which has elapsed since the date of the divorce, annulment or legal separation.

Orders for financial provision and property adjustment

Orders for financial provision and property adjustment

30-006 **17.**—[(1) Subject to section 20 below, on an application by a party to a marriage for an order for financial relief under this section, the court may—

(a) make any one or more of the orders which it could make under Part II of the 1973 Act if a decree of divorce, a decree of nullity of marriage or a decree of judicial separation in respect of the marriage had been granted in England and Wales, that is to say—

(i) any order mentioned in section 23(1) of the 1973 Act (financial provision orders); and

(ii) any order mentioned in section 24(1) of that Act (property adjustment orders); and

(b) if the marriage has been dissolved or annulled, make one or more orders each of which would, within the meaning of that Part of that Act, be a pension sharing order in relation to the marriage.][1]

(2) Subject to section 20 below, where the court makes a secured periodical payments order, an order for the payment of a lump sum or a property adjustment order under subsection (1) above, then, on making that order or at any time thereafter, the court may make any order mentioned in section 24A(1) of the 1973 Act (orders for sale of property) which the court would have power to make if the order under subsection (1) above had been made under Part II of the 1973 Act.

Matters to which the court is to have regard in exercising its powers under s. 17

30-007 **18.**—(1) In deciding whether to exercise its powers under section 17 above and, if so, in what manner the court shall act in accordance with this section.

(2) The court shall have regard to all the circumstances of the case, first consideration being given to the welfare while a minor of any child of the family who has not attained the age of eighteen.

(3) As regards the exercise of those powers in relation to a party to the marriage, the court shall in particular have regard to the matters mentioned in section 25(2)(a) to (h) of the 1973 Act and shall be under duties corresponding with those imposed by section 25A(1) and (2) of the 1973 Act where it decides to exercise under section 17 above powers corresponding with the powers referred to in those subsections.

[(3A) The matters to which the court is to have regard under subsection (3) above—

[1] Substituted by Welfare Reform and Pensions Act 1999 c.30 Sch 12 (I) para 3

(a) so far as relating to paragraph (a) of section 25(2) of the 1973 Act, include any benefits under a pension arrangement which a party to the marriage has or is likely to have (whether or not in the foreseeable future), and

(b) so far as relating to paragraph (h) of that provision, include any benefits under a pension arrangement which, by reason of the dissolution or annulment of the marriage, a party to the marriage will lose the chance of acquiring.][1]

(4) As regards the exercise of those powers in relation to a child of the family, the court shall in particular have regard to the matters mentioned in section 25(3)(a) to (e) of the 1973 Act.

(5) As regards the exercise of those powers against a party to the marriage in favour of a child of the family who is not the child of that party, the court shall also have regard to the matters mentioned in section 25(4)(a) to (c) of the 1973 Act.

(6) Where an order has been made by a court outside England and Wales for the making of payments or the transfer of property by a party to the marriage, the court in considering in accordance with this section the financial resources of the other party to the marriage or a child of the family shall have regard to the extent to which that order has been complied with or is likely to be complied with.

[(7) In this section—

(a) "pension arrangement" has the meaning given by section 25D(3) of the 1973 Act, and

(b) references to benefits under a pension arrangement include any benefits by way of pension, whether under a pension arrangement or not.][2]

Consent orders for financial provision or property adjustment

19.—(1) Notwithstanding anything in section 18 above, on an application for a consent order for financial relief the court may, unless it has reason to think that there are other circumstances into which it ought to inquire, make an order in the terms agreed on the basis only of the prescribed information furnished with the application. **30-008**

(2) Subsection (1) above applies to an application for a consent order varying or discharging an order for financial relief as it applies to an application for an order for financial relief.

(3) In this section—

"consent order", in relation to an application for an order, means an order in the terms applied for to which the respondent agrees;

"order for financial relief" means an order under section 17 above; and

"prescribed" means prescribed by rules of court.

Restriction of powers of court where jurisdiction depends on matrimonial home in England or Wales

20.—(1) Where the court has jurisdiction to entertain an application for an order for financial relief by reason only of the situation in England and Wales of a dwelling-house which was a matrimonial home of the parties, the court may make under section 17 above any one or more of the following orders (but no other)— **30-009**

[1] Added by Welfare Reform and Pensions Act 1999 c.30 Pt III s 22 (2)

[2] Added by Welfare Reform and Pensions Act 1999 c.30 Pt III s 22 (3)

(a) an order that either party to the marriage shall pay to the other such lump sum as may be specified in the order;
(b) an order that a party to the marriage shall pay to such person as may be so specified for the benefit of a child of the family, or to such a child, such lump sum as may be so specified;
(c) an order that a party to the marriage shall transfer to the other party, to any child of the family or to such person as may be so specified for the benefit of such a child, the interest of the first-mentioned party in the dwelling-house, or such part of that interest as may be so specified;
(d) an order that a settlement of the interest of a party to the marriage in the dwelling-house, or such part of that interest as may be so specified, be made to the satisfaction of the court for the benefit of the other party to the marriage and of the children of the family or either or any of them;
(e) an order varying for the benefit of the parties to the marriage and of the children of the family or either or any of them any ante-nuptial or post-nuptial settlement (including such a settlement made by will or codicil) made on the parties to the marriage so far as that settlement relates to an interest in the dwelling-house;
(f) an order extinguishing or reducing the interest of either of the parties to the marriage under any such settlement so far as that interest is an interest in the dwelling-house;
(g) an order for the sale of the interest of a party to the marriage in the dwelling-house.

(2) Where, in the circumstances mentioned in subsection (1) above, the court makes an order for the payment of a lump sum by a party to the marriage, the amount of the lump sum shall not exceed, or where more than one such order is made the total amount of the lump sums shall not exceed in aggregate, the following amount, that is to say—
(a) if the interest of that party in the dwelling-house is sold in pursuance of an order made under subsection (1)(g) above, the amount of the proceeds of the sale of that interest after deducting therefrom any costs incurred in the sale thereof;
(b) if the interest of that party is not so sold, the amount which in the opinion of the court represents the value of that interest.

(3) Where the interest of a party to the marriage in the dwelling-house is held jointly or in common with any other person or persons—
(a) the reference in subsection (1)(g) above to the interest of a party to the marriage shall be construed as including a reference to the interest of that other person, or the interest of those other persons, in the dwelling-house, and
(b) the reference in subsection (2)(a) above to the amount of the proceeds of a sale ordered under subsection (1)(g) above shall be construed as a reference to that part of those proceeds which is attributable to the interest of that party to the marriage in the dwelling-house.

Application to orders under ss. 14 and 17 of certain provisions of Part II of Matrimonial Causes Act 1973

30-010 **21.**—[(1) The following provisions of Part II of the 1973 Act (financial relief for parties to marriage and children of family) shall apply in relation to an order

[...][1] under section 14 or 17 above as they apply in relation to a like order [...][2] under that Part of that Act, that is to say—

(a) section 23(3) (provisions as to lump sums);

(b) section 24A(2), (4), (5) and (6) (provisions as to orders for sale);

[(ba) section 24B(3) to (5) (provisions about pension sharing orders in relation to divorce and nullity);

(bb) section 24C (duty to stay pension sharing orders);

(bc) section 24D (apportionment of pension sharing charges);][3]

(bd) section 25B(3) to (7B) (power, by financial provision order, to attach payments under a pension arrangement, or to require the exercise of a right of commutation under such an arrangement);

(be) section 25C (extension of lump sum powers in relation to death benefits under a pension arrangement);

(c) section 28(1) and (2) (duration of continuing financial provision orders in favour of party to marriage);

(d) section 29 (duration of continuing financial provision orders in favour of children, and age limit on making certain orders in their favour);

(e) section 30 (direction for settlement of instrument for securing payments or effecting property adjustment), except paragraph (b);

(f) section 31 (variation, discharge etc. of certain orders for financial relief), except subsection (2)(e) and subsection (4);

(g) section 32 (payment of certain arrears unenforceable without the leave of the court);

(h) section 33 (orders for repayment of sums paid under certain orders);

(i) section 38 (orders for repayment of sums paid after cessation of order by reason of remarriage);

(j) section 39 (settlements etc. made in compliance with a property adjustment order may be avoided on bankruptcy of settlor);

(k) section 40 (payments etc. under order made in favour of person suffering from mental disorder)[; and][4]

[(l) section 40A (appeals relating to pension sharing orders which have taken effect).][5]][6]

[(2) Subsection (1)(bd) and (be) above shall not apply where the court has jurisdiction to entertain an application for an order for financial relief by reason only of the situation in England or Wales of a dwelling-house which was a matrimonial home of the parties.

(3) Section 25D(1) of the 1973 Act (effect of transfers on orders relating to rights under a pension arrangement) shall apply in relation to an order made under section 17 above by virtue of subsection (1)(bd) or (be) above as it applies in relation to an order made under section 23 of that Act by virtue of section 25B or 25C of the 1973 Act.

(4) The Lord Chancellor may by regulations make for the purposes of this Part of this Act provision corresponding to any provision which may be made by him under subsections (2) to (2B) of section 25D of the 1973 Act.

1 Repealed by Welfare Reform and Pensions Act 1999 c.30 Sch 13 (II) para 1
2 Repealed by Welfare Reform and Pensions Act 1999 c.30 Sch 13 (II) para 1
3 Added by Welfare Reform and Pensions Act 1999 c.30 Sch 12 (I) para 4 (b)
4 Added by Welfare Reform and Pensions Act 1999 c.30 Sch 12 (I) para 4 (c)
5 Added by Welfare Reform and Pensions Act 1999 c.30 Sch 12 (I) para 4 (c)
6 Renumbered by Welfare Reform and Pensions Act 1999 c.30 Pt III s 22 (4)

(5) Power to make regulations under this section shall be exercisable by statutory instrument which shall be subject to annulment in pursuance of a resolution of either House of Parliament.][1]

Orders for transfer of tenancies

[Powers of court in relation to certain tenancies of dwelling-houses

30-011 **22.**—(1) This section applies if—

(a) an application is made by a party to a marriage for an order for financial relief; and

(b) one of the parties is entitled, either in his own right or jointly with the other party, to occupy a dwelling-house situated in England or Wales by virtue of a tenancy which is a relevant tenancy within the meaning of Schedule 7 to the Family Law Act 1996 (certain statutory tenancies).

(2) The court may make in relation to that dwelling-house any order which it could make under Part II of that Schedule if—

(a) a divorce order,

(b) a separation order, or

(c) a decree of nullity of marriage,

had been made or granted in England and Wales in respect of the marriage.

(3) The provision of paragraph 10, 11 and 14(1) in Part III of that Schedule apply in relation to any order under this section as they apply to any order under Part II of that Schedule.][2]

Avoidance of transactions intended to prevent or reduce financial relief

Avoidance of transactions intended to defeat applications for financial relief

30-012 **23.**—(1) For the purposes of this section "financial relief" means relief under section 14 or 17 above and any reference to defeating a claim by a party to a marriage for financial relief is a reference to preventing financial relief from being granted or reducing the amount of relief which might be granted, or frustrating or impeding the enforcement of any order which might be or has been made under either of those provisions at the instance of that party.

(2) Where leave is granted under section 13 above for the making by a party to a marriage of an application for an order for financial relief under section 17 above, the court may, on an application by that party—

(a) if it is satisfied that the other party to the marriage is, with the intention of defeating the claim for financial relief, about to make any disposition or to transfer out of the jurisdiction or otherwise deal with any property, make such order as it thinks fit for restraining the other party from so doing or otherwise for protecting the claim;

(b) if it is satisfied that the other party has, with that intention, made a reviewable disposition and that if the disposition were set aside financial relief or different financial relief would be granted to the applicant, make an order setting aside the disposition.

(3) Where an order for financial relief under section 14 or 17 above has been made by the court at the instance of a party to a marriage, then, on an application made by that party, the court may, if it is satisfied that the other party to the

[1] Added by Welfare Reform and Pensions Act 1999 c.30 Pt III s 22 (5)
[2] Substituted by Family Law Act 1996 c.27 Sch 8 (III) para 52

marriage has, with the intention of defeating the claim for financial relief, made a reviewable disposition, make an order setting aside the disposition.

(4) Where the court has jurisdiction to entertain the application for an order for financial relief by reason only of paragraph (c) of section 15(1) above, it shall not make any order under subsection (2) or (3) above in respect of any property other than the dwelling-house concerned.

(5) Where the court makes an order under subsection (2)(b) or (3) above setting aside a disposition it shall give such consequential directions as it thinks fit for giving effect to the order (including directions requiring the making of any payments or the disposal of any property).

(6) Any disposition made by the other party to the marriage (whether before or after the commencement of the application) is a reviewable disposition for the purposes of subsections (2)(b) and (3) above unless it was made for valuable consideration (other than marriage) to a person who, at the time of the disposition, acted in relation to it in good faith and without notice of any intention on the part of the other party to defeat the applicant's claim for financial relief.

(7) Where an application is made under subsection (2) or (3) above with respect to a disposition which took place less than three years before the date of the application or with respect to a disposition or other dealing with property which is about to take place and the court is satisfied—

(a) in a case falling within subsection (2)(a) or (b) above, that the disposition or other dealing would (apart from this section) have the consequence, or

(b) in a case falling within subsection (3) above, that the disposition has had the consequence,

of defeating a claim by the applicant for financial relief, it shall be presumed, unless the contrary is shown, that the person who disposed of or is about to dispose of or deal with the property did so or, as the case may be, is about to do so, with the intention of defeating the applicant's claim for financial relief.

(8) In this section "disposition" does not include any provision contained in a will or codicil but, with that exception, includes any conveyance, assurance or gift of property of any description, whether made by an instrument or otherwise.

(9) The preceding provisions of this section are without prejudice to any power of the High Court to grant injunctions under section 37 of the Supreme Court Act 1981.

Prevention of transactions intended to defeat prospective applications for financial relief

24.—(1) Where, on an application by a party to a marriage, it appears to the court— **30-013**

(a) that the marriage has been dissolved or annulled, or that the parties to the marriage have been legally separated, by means of judicial or other proceedings in an overseas country; and

(b) that the applicant intends to apply for leave to make an application for an order for financial relief under section 17 above as soon as he or she has been habitually resident in England and Wales for a period of one year; and

(c) that the other party to the marriage is, with the intention of defeating a claim for financial relief, about to make any disposition or to transfer out of the jurisdiction or otherwise deal with any property,

the court may make such order as it thinks fit for restraining the other party from taking such action as is mentioned in paragraph (c) above.

(2) For the purposes of an application under subsection (1) above—
(a) the reference to defeating a claim for financial relief shall be construed in accordance with subsection (1) of section 23 above (omitting the reference to any order which has been made); and
(b) subsections (7) and (8) of section 23 above shall apply as they apply for the purposes of an application under that section.

(3) The preceding provisions of this section are without prejudice to any power of the High Court to grant injunctions under section 37 of the Supreme Court Act 1981.

Interpretation

Interpretation of Part III

30-014 **27.** In this Part of this Act—
"the 1973 Act" means the Matrimonial Causes Act 1973;
"child of the family" has the same meaning as in section 52(1) of the 1973 Act;
"the court" means the High Court or, where a county court has jurisdiction by virtue of Part V of this Act, a county court;
"dwelling-house" includes any building or part thereof which is occupied as a dwelling, and any yard, garden, garage or outhouse belonging to the dwelling-house and occupied therewith;
"order for financial relief" has the meaning given by section 12(4) above;
"overseas country" means a country or territory outside the British Islands;
"possession" includes receipt of, or the right to receive, rents and profits;
"property adjustment order" means such an order as is specified in section 24(1)(a), (b), (c) or (d) of the 1973 Act;
"rent" does not include mortgage interest;
"secured periodical payments order" means such an order as is specified in section 23(1)(b) or (e) of the 1973 Act.

PART V

FAMILY BUSINESS: DISTRIBUTION AND TRANSFER

Preliminary

What is family business

30-015 **32.** In this Part of this Act—
"family business" means business of any description which in the High Court is for the time being assigned to the Family Division and to no other Division by or under section 61 of (and Schedule 1 to) the Supreme Court Act 1981;
"family proceedings" means proceedings which are family business;
"matrimonial cause" means an action for divorce, nullity of marriage, [or judicial separation][1];
and "the 1973 Act" means the Matrimonial Causes Act 1973.

[1] Words substituted by Family Law Act 1986 c.55 ss 68 (1), 69 (5) Sch 1 para 27

Jurisdiction of county courts in matrimonial causes and matters

Jurisdiction of county courts in matrimonial causes

33.—(1) The Lord Chancellor may by order designate any county court as a divorce county court and any court so designated shall have jurisdiction to hear and determine any matrimonial cause, except that it shall have jurisdiction to try such a cause only if it is also designated in the order as a court of trial. **30-016**

In this Part of this Act "divorce county court" means a county court so designated.

(2) The jurisdiction conferred by this section on a divorce county court shall be exercisable throughout England and Wales, but rules of court may provide for a matrimonial cause pending in one such court to be heard and determined in another or partly in that and partly in another.

(3) Every matrimonial cause shall be commenced in a divorce county court and shall be heard and determined in that or another such court unless or except to the extent it is transferred to the High Court under section 39 below or section 41 of the County Courts Act 1984 (transfer to High Court by order of High Court).

(4) The Lord Chancellor may by order designate a divorce county court as a court for the exercise of jurisdiction in matrimonial matters arising under Part III of this Act.

(5) The power to make an order under subsection (1) or (4) above shall be exercisable by statutory instrument.

Jurisdiction of divorce county courts as respects financial relief and protection of children

34.—(1) Subject to subsections (2) and (3) below, a divorce county court shall have the following jurisdiction, namely— **30-017**

(a) jurisdiction to exercise any power exercisable under Part II or Part III of the 1973 Act in connection with any petition, decree or order pending in or made by such a court and to exercise any power under section 27 or 35 of that Act;

(b) if designated by an order under section 33(4) above, jurisdiction to exercise any power under Part III of this Act.

(2) Any proceedings for the exercise of a power which a divorce county court has jurisdiction to exercise by virtue of subsection (1)(a) or (b) above shall be commenced in such divorce county court as may be prescribed by rules of court.

(3) A divorce county court shall not by virtue of subsection (1)(a) above have jurisdiction to exercise any power under section 32, 33, 36 or 38 of the 1973 Act; but nothing in this section shall prejudice the exercise by a county court of any jurisdiction conferred on county courts by any of those sections.

(4) Nothing in this section shall affect the jurisdiction of a magistrates' court under section 35 of the 1973 Act.

Consideration of agreements or arrangements

35. Any provision to be made by rules of court for the purposes of section 7 of the 1973 Act with respect to any power exercisable by the court on an application made before the presentation of a petition shall confer jurisdiction to exercise the power on divorce county courts. **30-018**

Assignment of Circuit judges to matrimonial proceedings

30-019 **36.** The jurisdiction conferred by the preceding provisions of this Part of this Act on divorce county courts, so far as it is exercisable by judges of such courts, shall be exercised by such Circuit judges as the Lord Chancellor may direct.

Distribution and transfer of family business and proceedings

Directions as to distribution and transfer of family business and proceedings

30-020 **37.** The President of the Family Division may, with the concurrence of the Lord Chancellor, give directions with respect to the distribution and transfer between the High Court and county courts of family business and family proceedings.

Transfer of family proceedings from High Court to county court

30-021 **38.**—(1) At any stage in any family proceedings in the High Court the High Court may, if the proceedings are transferable under this section, either of its own motion or on the application of any party to the proceedings, order the transfer of the whole or any part of the proceedings to a county court.

(2) The following family proceedings are transferable to a county court under this section, namely—

(a) all family proceedings commenced in the High Court which are within the jurisdiction of a county court or divorce county court;

(b) wardship proceedings, except applications for an order that a minor be made, or cease to be, a ward of court [or any other proceedings which relate to the exercise of the inherent jurisdiction of the High Court with respect to minors][1];

(c) all family proceedings transferred from a county court to the High Court under section 39 below or section 41 of the County Courts Act 1984 (transfer to High Court by order of High Court); [and][2]

[(d) all matrimonial causes and matters transferred from a county court otherwise than as mentioned in paragraph (e) above.][3]

(3) Proceedings transferred under this section shall be transferred to such county court or, in the case of a matrimonial cause or matter within the jurisdiction of a divorce county court only, such divorce county court as the High Court directs.

(4) The transfer shall not affect any right of appeal from the order directing the transfer, or the right to enforce in the High Court any judgment signed, or order made, in that Court before the transfer.

(5) Where proceedings are transferred to a county court under this section, the county court—

(a) if it has no jurisdiction apart from this paragraph, shall have jurisdiction to hear and determine those proceedings;

(b) shall have jurisdiction to award any relief which could have been awarded by the High Court.

Transfer of family proceedings to High Court from county court

30-022 **39.**—(1) At any stage in any family proceedings in a county court, the county court may, if the proceedings are transferable under this section, either of its own

[1] Words inserted by Children Act 1989 c.41 Sch 13 para 51

[2] Word inserted by Matrimonial Proceedings (Transfers) Act 1988 c.18 s 1 (1)

[3] Inserted by Matrimonial Proceedings (Transfers) Act 1988 c.18 s 1 (1)

motion or on the application of any party to the proceedings, order the transfer of the whole or any part of the proceedings to the High Court.

(2) The following family proceedings are transferable to the High Court under this section, namely—

(a) all family proceedings commenced in a county court or divorce county court; and

(b) all family proceedings transferred from the High Court to a county court or divorce county court under section 38 above.

Surrogacy Arrangements Act 1985

CHAPTER 49

Meaning of "surrogate mother", "surrogacy arrangement" and other terms

1.—(1) The following provisions shall have effect for the interpretation of this Act. **32-001**

(2) "Surrogate mother" means a woman who carries a child in pursuance of an arrangement—

(a) made before she began to carry the child, and

(b) made with a view to any child carried in pursuance of it being handed over to, and [parental responsibility being met][1] (so far as practicable) by, another person or other persons.

(3) An arrangement is a surrogacy arrangement if, were a woman to whom the arrangement relates to carry a child in pursuance of it, she would be a surrogate mother.

(4) In determining whether an arrangement is made with such a view as is mentioned in subsection (2) above regard may be had to the circumstances as a whole (and, in particular, where there is a promise or understanding that any payment will or may be made to the woman or for her benefit in respect of the carrying of any child in pursuance of the arrangement, to that promise or understanding).

(5) An arrangement may be regarded as made with such a view though subject to conditions relating to the handing over of any child.

(6) A woman who carries a child is to be treated for the purposes of subsection (2)(a) above as beginning to carry it at the time of the insemination [or of the placing in her of an embryo, of an egg in the process of fertilisation or of sperm and eggs, as the case may be,][2] that results in her carrying the child.

(7) "Body of persons" means a body of persons corporate or unincorporate.

(8) "Payment" means payment in money or money's worth.

(9) This Act applies to arrangements whether or not they are lawful [...][3]

[Surrogacy arrangements unenforceable

1A. No surrogacy arrangement is enforceable by or against any of the persons making it.][4] **32-002**

[1] Words substituted by Children Act 1989 c.41 Sch 13 para 56

[2] Words substituted by Human Fertilisation and Embryology Act 1990 c.37 s 36 (2) (a)

[3] Words repealed by Human Fertilisation and Embryology Act 1990 c.37 s 36 (2) (b)

[4] Inserted by Human Fertilisation and Embryology Act 1990 c.37 s 36 (1)

Negotiating surrogacy arrangements on a commercial basis, etc

32-003 **2.**—(1) No person shall on a commercial basis do any of the following acts in the United Kingdom, that is—

(a) initiate or take part in any negotiations with a view to the making of a surrogacy arrangement,

(b) offer or agree to negotiate the making of a surrogacy arrangement, or

(c) compile any information with a view to its use in making, or negotiating the making of, surrogacy arrangement;

and no person shall in the United Kingdom knowingly cause another to do any of those acts on a commercial basis.

(2) A person who contravenes subsection (1) above is guilty of an offence; but it is not a contravention of that subsection—

(a) for a woman, with a view to becoming a surrogate mother herself, to do any act mentioned in that subsection or to cause such an act to be done, or

(b) for any person, with a view to a surrogate mother carrying a child for him, to do such an act or to cause such an act to be done.

(3) For the purposes of this section, a person does an act on a commercial basis (subject to subsection (4) below) if—

(a) any payment is at any time received by himself or another in respect of it, or

(b) he does it with a view to any payment being received by himself or another in respect of making, or negotiating or facilitating the making of, any surrogacy arrangement.

In this subsection "payment" does not include payment to or for the benefit of a surrogate mother or prospective surrogate mother.

(4) In proceedings against a person for an offence under subsection (1) above, he is not to be treated as doing an act on a commercial basis by reason of any payment received by another in respect of the act if it is proved that—

(a) in a case where the payment was received before he did the act, he did not do the act knowing or having reasonable cause to suspect that any payment had been received in respect of the act; and

(b) in any other case, he did not do the act with a view to any payment being received in respect of it.

(5) Where—

(a) a person acting on behalf of a body of persons takes any part in negotiating or facilitating the making of a surrogacy arrangement in the United Kingdom, and

(b) negotiating or facilitating the making of surrogacy arrangements is an activity of the body,

then, if the body at any time receives any payment made by or on behalf of—

(i) a woman who carries a child in pursuance of the arrangement,

(ii) the person or persons for whom she carries it, or

(iii) any person connected with the woman or with that person or those persons,

the body is guilty of an offence.

For the purposes of this subsection, a payment received by a person connected with a body is to be treated as received by the body.

(6) In proceedings against a body for an offence under subsection (5) above, it is a defence to prove that the payment concerned was not made in respect of the arrangement mentioned in paragraph (a) of that subsection.

(7) A person who in the United Kingdom takes part in the management or control—

(a) of any body of persons, or

(b) of any of the activities of any body of persons,

is guilty of an offence if the activity described in subsection (8) below is an activity of the body concerned.

(8) The activity referred to in subsection (7) above is negotiating or facilitating the making of surrogacy arrangements in the United Kingdom, being—

(a) arrangements the making of which is negotiated or facilitated on a commercial basis, or

(b) arrangements in the case of which payments are received (or treated for the purposes of subsection (5) above as received) by the body concerned in contravention of subsection (5) above.

(9) In proceedings against a person for an offence under subsection (7) above, it is a defence to prove that he neither knew nor had reasonable cause to suspect that the activity described in subsection (8) above was an activity of the body concerned; and for the purposes of such proceedings any arrangement falling within subsection (8)(b) above shall be disregarded if it is proved that the payment concerned was not made in respect of the arrangement.

Advertisements about surrogacy

3.—(1) This section applies to any advertisement containing an indication **32-004**
(however expressed)—

(a) that any person is or may be willing to enter into a surrogacy arrangement or to negotiate or facilitate the making of a surrogacy arrangement, or

(b) that any person is looking for a woman willing to become a surrogate mother or for persons wanting a woman to carry a child as a surrogate mother.

(2) Where a newspaper or periodical containing an advertisement to which this section applies is published in the United Kingdom, any proprietor, editor or publisher of the newspaper or periodical is guilty of an offence.

(3) Where an advertisement to which this section applies is conveyed by means of a telecommunication system so as to be seen or heard (or both) in the United Kingdom, any person who in the United Kingdom causes it to be so conveyed knowing it to contain such an indication as is mentioned in subsection (1) above is guilty of an offence.

(4) A person who publishes or causes to be published in the United Kingdom an advertisement to which this section applies (not being an advertisement contained in a newspaper or periodical or conveyed by means of a telecommunication system) is guilty of an offence.

(5) A person who distributes or causes to be distributed in the United Kingdom an advertisement to which this section applies (not being an advertisement contained in a newspaper or periodical published outside the United Kingdom or an advertisement conveyed by means of a telecommunication system) knowing it to contain such an indication as is mentioned in subsection (1) above is guilty of an offence.

(6) In this section "telecommunication system" has the same meaning as in the Telecommunications Act 1984.

Offences

32-005 **4.**—(1) A person guilty of an offence under this Act shall be liable on summary conviction—

(a) in the case of an offence under section 2 to a fine not exceeding level 5 on the standard scale or to imprisonment for a term not exceeding 3 months or both,

(b) in the case of an offence under section 3 to a fine not exceeding level 5 on the standard scale.[...][1]

(2) No proceedings for an offence under this Act shall be instituted—

(a) in England and Wales, except by or with the consent of the Director of Public Prosecutions; and

(b) in Northern Ireland, except by or with the consent of the Director of Public Prosecutions for Northern Ireland.

(3) Where an offence under this Act committed by a body corporate is proved to have been committed with the consent or connivance of, or to be attributable to any neglect on the part of, any director, manager, secretary or other similar officer of the body corporate or any person who was purporting to act in any such capacity, he as well as the body corporate is guilty of the offence and is liable to be proceeded against and punished accordingly.

(4) Where the affairs of a body corporate are managed by its members, subsection (3) above shall apply in relation to the acts and defaults of a member in connection with his functions of management as if he were a director of the body corporate.

(5) In any proceedings for an offence under section 2 of this Act, proof of things done or of words written, spoken or published (whether or not in the presence of any party to the proceedings) by any person taking part in the management or control of a body of persons or of any of the activities of the body, or by any person doing any of the acts mentioned in subsection (1)(a) to (c) of that section on behalf of the body, shall be admissible as evidence of the activities of the body.

(6) In relation to an offence under this Act, section 127(1) of the Magistrates' Courts Act 1980 (information must be laid within six months of commission of offence), shall have effect as if for the reference to six months there were substituted a reference to two years.

---

[1] Words repealed by Statute Law (Repeals) Act 1993 c.50 Sch 1 (XIV) para 1

Housing Act 1985

CHAPTER 68

PART IV

SECURE TENANCIES AND RIGHTS OF SECURE TENANTS

Succession on death of tenant

Persons qualified to succeed tenant

87. A person is qualified to succeed the tenant under a secure tenancy if he occupies the dwelling-house as his only or principal home at the time of the tenant's death and either— **33-001**

(a) he is the tenant's spouse, or
(b) he is another member of the tenant's family and has resided with the tenant throughout the period of twelve months ending with the tenant's death;

unless, in either case, the tenant was himself a successor, as defined in section 88.

Supplementary provisions

Members of a person's family

113.—(1) A person is a member of another's family within the meaning of this Part if— **33-002**

(a) he is the spouse of that person, or he and that person live together as husband and wife, or
(b) he is that person's parent, grandparent, child, grandchild, brother, sister, uncle, aunt, nephew or niece.

(2) For the purpose of subsection (1)(b)—

(a) a relationship by marriage shall be treated as a relationship by blood,
(b) a relationship of the half-blood shall be treated as a relationship of the whole blood,
(c) the stepchild of a person shall be treated as his child, and
(d) an illegitimate child shall be treated as the legitimate child of his mother and reputed father.

Marriage (Prohibited Degrees of Relationship) Act 1986

CHAPTER 16

Marriage between certain persons related by affinity not to be void

34-001 **1.**—(1) A marriage solemnized after the commencement of this Act between a man and a woman who is the daughter or grand-daughter of a former spouse of his (whether the former spouse is living or not) or who is the former spouse of his father or grandfather (whether his father or grandfather is living or not) shall not be void by reason only of that relationship if both the parties have attained the age of twenty-one at the time of the marriage and the younger party has not at any time before attaining the age of eighteen been a child of the family in relation to the other party.

(2) A marriage solemnized after the commencement of this Act between a man and a woman who is the grandmother of a former spouse of his (whether the former spouse is living or not) or is a former spouse of his grandson (whether his grandson is living or not) shall not be void by reason only of that relationship.

(3) A marriage solemnized after the commencement of this Act between a man and a woman who is the mother of a former spouse of his shall not be void by reason only of that relationship if the marriage is solemnized after the death of both that spouse and the father of that spouse and after both the parties to the marriage have attained the age of twenty-one.

(4) A marriage solemnized after the commencement of this Act between a man and a woman who is a former spouse of his son shall not be void by reason only of that relationship if the marriage is solemnized after the death of both his son and the mother of his son and after both the parties to the marriage have attained the age of twenty-one.

(5) In this section "child of the family" in relation to any person, means a child who has lived in the same household as that person and been treated by that person as a child of his family.

(6) The Marriage Act 1949 shall have effect subject to the amendments specified in the Schedule to this Act, being amendments consequential on the preceding provisions of this section.

(7) Where, apart from this Act, any matter affecting the validity of a marriage would fall to be determined (in accordance with the rules of private international law) by reference to the law of a country outside England and Wales nothing in this Act shall preclude the determination of that matter in accordance with that law.

(8) Nothing in this section shall affect any marriage solemnized before the commencement of this Act.

Insolvency Act 1986

CHAPTER 45

PART IX

BANKRUPTCY

CHAPTER V

EFFECT OF BANKRUPTCY ON CERTAIN RIGHTS, TRANSACTIONS, ETC

Rights under trusts of land

[Rights under trusts of land

335A.—(1) Any application by a trustee of a bankrupt's estate under section 14 of the Trusts of Land and Appointment of Trustees Act 1996 powers of court in relation to trusts of land) for an order under that section for the sale of land shall be made to the court having jurisdiction in relation to the bankruptcy. **35-001**

(2) On such an application the court shall make such order as it thinks just and reasonable having regard to—

(a) the interests of the bankrupt's creditors,

(b) where the application is made in respect of land which includes a dwelling house which is or has been the home of the bankrupt or the bankrupt's spouse or former spouse—

(i) the conduct of the spouse or former spouse, so far as contributing to the bankruptcy,

(ii) the needs and financial resources of the spouse or former spouse, and

(iii) the needs of any children; and

(c) all the circumstances of the case other than the needs of the bankrupt.

(3) Where such an application is made after the end of the period of one year beginning with the first vesting under Chapter IV of this Part of the bankrupt's estate in a trustee, the court shall assume, unless the circumstances of the case are exceptional, that the interests of the bankrupt's creditors outweigh all other considerations.

(4) The powers conferred on the court by this section are exercisable on an application whether it is made before or after the commencement of this section.][1]

Rights of occupation

Rights of occupation etc. of bankrupt's spouse

336.—(1) Nothing occurring in the initial period of the bankruptcy (that is to say, the period beginning with the day of the presentation of the petition for the bankruptcy order and ending with the vesting of the bankrupt's estate in a **35-002**

[1] Inserted by Trusts of Land and Appointment of Trustees Act 1996 c.47 Sch 3 para 23

trustee) is to be taken as having given rise to any matrimonial home rights under Part IV of the Family Law Act 1996 in relation to a dwelling house comprised in the bankrupt's estate.

(2) Where a spouse's matrimonial home rights under the Act of 1996 are a charge on the estate or interest of the other spouse, or of trustees for the other spouse, and the other spouse is adjudged bankrupt—

(a) the charge continues to subsist notwithstanding the bankruptcy and, subject to the provisions of that Act, binds the trustee of the bankrupt's estate and persons deriving title under that trustee, and

(b) any application for an order under section 33 of that Act shall be made to the court having jurisdiction in relation to the bankruptcy.

(4) On such an application as is mentioned in subsection (2) the court shall make such order under [section 33 of the Act of 1996][1] as it thinks just and reasonable having regard to—

(a) the interests of the bankrupt's creditors,

(b) the conduct of the spouse or former spouse, so far as contributing to the bankruptcy,

(c) the needs and financial resources of the spouse or former spouse,

(d) the needs of any children, and

(e) all the circumstances of the case other than the needs of the bankrupt.

(5) Where such an application is made after the end of the period of one year beginning with the first vesting under Chapter IV of this Part of the bankrupt's estate in a trustee, the court shall assume, unless the circumstances of the case are exceptional, that the interests of the bankrupt's creditors outweigh all other considerations.

Rights of occupation of bankrupt

35-003 **337.**—(1) This section applies where—

(a) a person who is entitled to occupy a dwelling house by virtue of a beneficial estate or interest is adjudged bankrupt, and

(b) any persons under the age of 18 with whom that person had at some time occupied that dwelling house had their home with that person at the time when the bankruptcy petition was presented and at the commencement of the bankruptcy.

(2) Whether or not the bankrupt's spouse (if any) has matrimonial home rights under Part IV of the Family Law Act 1996—

(a) the bankrupt has the following rights as against the trustee of his estate—

(i) if in occupation, a right not to be evicted or excluded from the dwelling house or any part of it, except with the leave of the court,

(ii) if not in occupation, a right with the leave of the court to enter into and occupy the dwelling house, and

(b) the bankrupt's rights are a charge, having the like priority as an equitable interest created immediately before the commencement of the bankruptcy, on so much of his estate or interest in the dwelling house as vests in the trustee.

(3) The Act of 1996 has effect, with the necessary modification, as if—

(a) the rights conferred by paragraph (a) of subsection (2) were matrimonial home rights under that Act.

(b) any application for such leave as is mentioned in that paragraph were an application for an order under section 33 of that Act and

[1] Words substituted by Family Law Act 1996 c.27 Sch 8 (III) para 57 (4)

(c) any charge under paragraph (b) of that subsection on the estate or interest of the trustee were a charge under that Act on the estate or interest of a spouse."

(4) Any application for leave such as is mentioned in subsection (2)(a) or otherwise by virtue of this section for an order under [section 33 of the Act of 1996][1] shall be made to the court having jurisdiction in relation to the bankruptcy.

(5) On such an application the court shall make such order under [section 33 of the Act of 1996][2] as it thinks just and reasonable having regard to the interests of the creditors, to the bankrupt's financial resources, to the needs of the children and to all the circumstances of the case other than the needs of the bankrupt.

(6) Where such an application is made after the end of the period of one year beginning with the first vesting (under Chapter IV of this Part) of the bankrupt's estate in a trustee, the court shall assume, unless the circumstances of the case are exceptional, that the interests of the bankrupt's creditors outweigh all other considerations.

Family Law Act 1986

CHAPTER 55

PART III

DECLARATIONS OF STATUS

Declarations as to marital status

55.—(1) Subject to the following provisions of this section, any person may apply to [the High Court or a county court][3] for one or more of the following declarations in relation to a marriage specified in the application, that is to say— **36-001**

(a) a declaration that the marriage was at its inception a valid marriage;
(b) a declaration that the marriage subsisted on a date specified in the application;
(c) a declaration that the marriage did not subsist on a date so specified;
(d) a declaration that the validity of a divorce, annulment or legal separation obtained in any country outside England and Wales in respect of the marriage is entitled to recognition in England and Wales;
(e) a declaration that the validity of a divorce, annulment or legal separation so obtained in respect of the marriage is not entitled to recognition in England and Wales.

(2) A court shall have jurisdiction to entertain an application under subsection (1) above if, and only if, either of the parties to the marriage to which the application relates–

[1] Words substituted by Family Law Act 1996 c.27 Sch 8 (III) para 58 (4)
[2] Words substituted by Family Law Act 1996 c.27 Sch 8 (III) para 58 (4)
[3] Words substituted by Child Support, Pensions and Social Security Act 2000 c.19 Sch 8 para 4 (a)

(a) is domiciled in England and Wales on the date of the application, or
(b) has been habitually resident in England and Wales throughout the period of one year ending with that date, or
(c) died before that date and either—
(i) was at death domiciled in England and Wales, or
(ii) had been habitually resident in England and Wales throughout the period of one year ending with the date of death.

(3) Where an application under subsection (1) above is made [to a court][1] by any person other than a party to the marriage to which the application relates, the court shall refuse to hear the application if it considers that the applicant does not have a sufficient interest in the determination of that application.

[Declarations of parentage

36-002 **55A.**—(1) Subject to the following provisions of this section, any person may apply to the High Court, a county court or a magistrates' court for a declaration as to whether or not a person named in the application is or was the parent of another person so named.

(2) A court shall have jurisdiction to entertain an application under subsection (1) above if, and only if, either of the persons named in it for the purposes of that subsection–
(a) is domiciled in England and Wales on the date of the application, or
(b) has been habitually resident in England and Wales throughout the period of one year ending with that date, or
(c) died before that date and either–
(i) was at death domiciled in England and Wales, or
(ii) had been habitually resident in England and Wales throughout the period of one year ending with the date of death.

(3) Except in a case falling within subsection (4) below, the court shall refuse to hear an application under subsection (1) above unless it considers that the applicant has a sufficient personal interest in the determination of the application (but this is subject to section 27 of the Child Support Act 1991).

(4) The excepted cases are where the declaration sought is as to whether or not–
(a) the applicant is the parent of a named person;
(b) a named person is the parent of the applicant; or
(c) a named person is the other parent of a named child of the applicant.

(5) Where an application under subsection (1) above is made and one of the persons named in it for the purposes of that subsection is a child, the court may refuse to hear the application if it considers that the determination of the application would not be in the best interests of the child.

(6) Where a court refuses to hear an application under subsection (1) above it may order that the applicant may not apply again for the same declaration without leave of the court.

(7) Where a declaration is made by a court on an application under subsection (1) above, the prescribed officer of the court shall notify the Registrar General, in such a manner and within such period as may be prescribed, of the making of that declaration.][2]

[1] Words inserted by Child Support, Pensions and Social Security Act 2000 c.19 Sch 8 para 4 (b)
[2] Added by Child Support, Pensions and Social Security Act 2000 c.19 Pt V s 83 (2)

[Declarations of parentage, legitimacy or legitimation

56.—(1) Any person may apply to [the High Court or a county court][1] for a declaration— **36-003**

(a) [...][2]

(b) that he is the legitimate child of his parents.

(2) Any person may apply to [the High Court or a county court][3] for one (or for one or, in the alternative, the other) of the following declarations, that is to say—

(a) a declaration that he has become a legitimated person;

(b) a declaration that he has not become a legitimated person.

(3) A court shall have jurisdiction to entertain an application under this section if, and only if, the applicant—

(a) is domiciled in England and Wales on the date of the application; or

(b) has been habitually resident in England and Wales throughout the period of one year ending with that date.

(4) Where a declaration is made [by a court][4] on an application under subsection (1) above, the prescribed officer of the court shall notify the Registrar General, in such a manner and within such period as may be prescribed, of the making of that declaration.

(5) In this section 'legitimated person' means a person legitimated or recognised as legitimated—

(a) under section 2 or 3 of the Legitimacy Act 1976;

(b) under section 1 or 8 of the Legitimacy Act 1926; or

(c) by a legitimation (whether or not by virtue of the subsequent marriage of his parents) recognised by the law of England and Wales and effected under the law of another country.][5]

General provisions as to the making and effect of declarations

58.—(1) Where on an application [to a court][6] for a declaration under this Part the truth of the proposition to be declared is proved to the satisfaction of the court, the court shall make that declaration unless to do so would manifestly be contrary to public policy. **36-004**

(2) Any declaration made under this Part shall be binding on Her Majesty and all other persons.

(3) [A][7] court, on the dismissal of an application for a declaration under this Part, shall not have power to make any declaration for which an application has not been made.

(4) No declaration which may be applied for under this Part may be made otherwise than under this Part by any court.

(5) No declaration may be made by any court, whether under this Part or otherwise—

(a) that a marriage was at its inception void;

[1] Words substituted by Child Support, Pensions and Social Security Act 2000 c.19 Sch 8 para 5 (a)

[2] Repealed by Child Support, Pensions and Social Security Act 2000 c.19 Sch 9 (IX) para 1

[3] Words substituted by Child Support, Pensions and Social Security Act 2000 c.19 Sch 8 para 5 (a)

[4] Words inserted by Child Support, Pensions and Social Security Act 2000 c.19 Sch 8 para 5 (b)

[5] Substituted by Family Law Reform Act 1987 c.42 ss 22, 34 (5)

[6] Words inserted by Child Support, Pensions and Social Security Act 2000 c.19 Sch 8 para 7 (a)

[7] Word substituted by Child Support, Pensions and Social Security Act 2000 c.19 Sch 8 para 7 (b)

(b) [...][1]

(6) Nothing in this section shall effect the powers of any court to grant a decree of nullity of marriage.

Family Law Reform Act 1987

CHAPTER 42

PART I

GENERAL PRINCIPLE

General principle

37-001 **1.**—(1) In this Act and enactments passed and instruments made after the coming into force of this section, references (however expressed) to any relationship between two persons shall, unless the contrary intention appears, be construed without regard to whether or not the father and mother of either of them, or the father and mother of any person through whom the relationship is deduced, have or had been married to each other at any time.

(2) In this Act and enactments passed after the coming into force of this section, unless the contrary intention appears—

(a) references to a person whose father and mother were married to each other at the time of his birth include; and

(b) references to a person whose father and mother were not married to each other at the time of his birth do not include,

references to any person to whom subsection (3) below applies, and cognate references shall be construed accordingly.

(3) This subsection applies to any person who—

(a) is treated as legitimate by virtue of section 1 of the Legitimacy Act 1976;

(b) is a legitimated person within the meaning of section 10 of that Act;

(c) is an adopted child within the meaning of Part IV of the Adoption Act 1976; or

(d) is otherwise treated in law as legitimate.

(4) For the purpose of construing references falling within subsection (2) above, the time of a person's birth shall be taken to include any time during the period beginning with—

(a) the insemination resulting in his birth; or

(b) where there was no such insemination, his conception,

and (in either case) ending with his birth.

[1] Repealed by Child Support, Pensions and Social Security Act 2000 c.19 Sch 9 (IX) para 1

PART II

RIGHTS AND DUTIES OF PARENTS ETC

Parental rights and duties: general

Construction of enactments relating to parental rights and duties

2.—(1) In the following enactments, namely— **37-002**

(a) section 42(1) of the National Assistance Act 1948;
(b) section 6 of the Family Law Reform Act 1969;
(c) the Guardianship of Minors Act 1971 (in this Act referred to as "the 1971 Act");
(d) Part I of the Guardianship Act 1973 (in this Act referred to as "the 1973 Act");
(e) Part II of the Children Act 1975;
(f) the Child Care Act 1980 except Part I and sections 13, 24, 64 and 65;
(g) [...][1]

references (however expressed) to any relationship between two persons shall be construed in accordance with section 1 above.

PART III

PROPERTY RIGHTS

Succession on intestacy

18.—(1) In Part IV of the Administration of Estates Act 1925 (which deals with the distribution of the estate of an intestate), references (however expressed) to any relationship between two persons shall be construed in accordance with section 1 above. **37-003**

(2) For the purposes of subsection (1) above and that Part of that Act, a person whose father and mother were not married to each other at the time of his birth shall be presumed not to have been survived by his father, or by any person related to him only through his father, unless the contrary is shown.

(3) In section 50(1) of that Act (which relates to the construction of documents), the reference to Part IV of that Act, or to the foregoing provisions of that Part, shall in relation to an instrument inter vivos made, or a will or codicil coming into operation, after the coming into force of this section (but not in relation to instruments inter vivos made or wills or codicils coming into operation earlier) be construed as including references to this section.

(4) This section does not affect any rights under the intestacy of a person dying before the coming into force of this section.

Dispositions of property

19.—(1) In the following dispositions, namely— **37-004**

(a) dispositions inter vivos made on or after the date on which this section comes into force; and
(b) dispositions by will or codicil where the will or codicil is made on or after that date,

[1] Repealed by Social Security (Consequential Provisions) Act 1992 c.6 Sch 1 para 1

references (whether express or implied) to any relationship between two persons shall be construed in accordance with section 1 above.

(2) It is hereby declared that the use, without more, of the word "heir" or "heirs" or any expression [purporting to create][1] an entailed interest in real or personal property does not show a contrary intention for the purposes of section 1 as applied by subsection (1) above.

(3) In relation to the dispositions mentioned in subsection (1) above, section 33 of the Trustee Act 1925 (which specifies the trust implied by a direction that income is to be held on protective trusts for the benefit of any person) shall have effect as if any reference (however expressed) to any relationship between two persons were construed in accordance with section 1 above.

(4) Where under any disposition of real or personal property, any interest in such property is limited (whether subject to any preceding limitation or charge or not) in such a way that it would, apart from this section, devolve (as nearly as the law permits) along with a dignity or title of honour, then—

(a) whether or not the disposition contains an express reference to the dignity or title of honour; and
(b) whether or not the property or some interest in the property may in some event become severed from it,

nothing in this section shall operate to sever the property or any interest in it from the dignity or title, but the property or interest shall devolve in all respects as if this section had not been enacted.

(5) This section is without prejudice to section 42 of the Adoption Act 1976 (construction of dispositions in cases of adoption).

(6) In this section "disposition" means a disposition, including an oral disposition, of real or personal property whether inter vivos or by will or codicil.

(7) Notwithstanding any rule of law, a disposition made by will or codicil executed before the date on which this section comes into force shall not be treated for the purposes of this section as made on or after that date by reason only that the will or codicil is confirmed by a codicil executed on or after that date.

No special protection for trustees and personal representatives

37-005 **20.** Section 17 of the Family Law Reform Act 1969 (which enables trustees and personal representatives to distribute property without having ascertained that no person whose parents were not married to each other at the time of his birth, or who claims through such a person, is or may be entitled to an interest in the property) shall cease to have effect.

Entitlement to grant of probate etc

37-006 **21.**—(1) For the purpose of determining the person or persons who would in accordance with probate rules be entitled to a grant of probate or administration in respect of the estate of a deceased person, the deceased shall be presumed, unless the contrary is shown, not to have been survived—

(a) by any person related to him whose father and mother were not married to each other at the time of his birth; or
(b) by any person whose relationship with him is deduced through such a person as is mentioned in paragraph (a) above.

(2) In this section "probate rules" means rules of court made under section 127 of the Supreme Court Act 1981.

[1] Words substituted by Trusts of Land and Appointment of Trustees Act 1996 c.47 Sch 3 para 25

(3) This section does not apply in relation to the estate of a person dying before the coming into force of this section.

Housing Act 1988

CHAPTER 50

PART I

RENTED ACCOMMODATION

CHAPTER I

ASSURED TENANCIES

Miscellaneous

Succession to assured periodic tenancy by spouse

17.—(1) In any case where— 38-001

(a) the sole tenant under an assured periodic tenancy dies, and

(b) immediately before the death, the tenant's spouse was occupying the dwelling-house as his or her only or principal home, and

(c) the tenant was not himself a successor, as defined in subsection (2) or subsection (3) below,

then, on the death, the tenancy vests by virtue of this section in the spouse (and, accordingly, does not devolve under the tenant's will or intestacy).

(2) For the purposes of this section, a tenant is a successor in relation to a tenancy if—

(a) the tenancy became vested in him either by virtue of this section or under the will or intestacy of a previous tenant; or

(b) at some time before the tenant's death the tenancy was a joint tenancy held by himself and one or more other persons and, prior to his death, he became the sole tenant by survivorship; or

(c) he became entitled to the tenancy as mentioned in section 39(5) below.

(3) For the purposes of this section, a tenant is also a successor in relation to a tenancy (in this subsection referred to as "the new tenancy") which was granted to him (alone or jointly with others) if—

(a) at some time before the grant of the new tenancy, he was, by virtue of subsection (2) above, a successor in relation to an earlier tenancy of the same or substantially the same dwelling-house as is let under the new tenancy; and

(b) at all times since he became such a successor he has been a tenant (alone or jointly with others) of the dwelling-house which is let under the new tenancy or of a dwelling-house which is substantially the same as that dwelling-house.

(4) For the purposes of this section, a person who was living with the tenant as his or her wife or husband shall be treated as the tenant's spouse.

(5) If, on the death of the tenant, there is, by virtue of subsection (4) above, more than one person who fulfils the condition in subsection (1)(b) above, such one of them as may be decided by agreement or, in default of agreement, by the county court shall be treated as the tenant's spouse for the purposes of this section.

Children Act 1989

CHAPTER 41

PART I

INTRODUCTORY

Welfare of the child

39-001 **1.**—(1) When a court determines any question with respect to—

(a) the upbringing of a child; or

(b) the administration of a child's property or the application of any income arising from it,

the child's welfare shall be the court's paramount consideration.

(2) In any proceedings in which any question with respect to the upbringing of a child arises, the court shall have regard to the general principle that any delay in determining the question is likely to prejudice the welfare of the child.

(3) In the circumstances mentioned in subsection (4), a court shall have regard in particular to—

(a) the ascertainable wishes and feelings of the child concerned (considered in the light of his age and understanding);

(b) his physical, emotional and educational needs;

(c) the likely effect on him of any change in his circumstances;

(d) his age, sex, background and any characteristics of his which the [guardian ad litem][1] considers relevant;

(e) any harm which he has suffered or is at risk of suffering;

(f) how capable each of his parents, and any other person in relation to whom the [guardian ad litem][2] considers the question to be relevant, is of meeting his needs;

(g) the range of powers available to the court under this Act in the proceedings in question.

(4) The circumstances are that—

(a) the court is considering whether to make, vary or discharge a section 8 order, and the making, variation or discharge of the order is opposed by any party to the proceedings; or

(b) the court is considering whether to make, vary or discharge an order under Part IV.

(5) Where a court is considering whether or not to make one or more orders under this Act with respect to a child, it shall not make the order or any of the

[1] Words substituted by SI 1991/1247 Pt IV r 4.11

[2] Words substituted by SI 1991/1247 Pt IV r 4.11

orders unless it considers that doing so would be better for the child than making no order at all.

Parental responsibility for children

2.—(1) Where a child's father and mother were married to each other at the time of his birth, they shall each have parental responsibility for the child. **39-002**

(2) Where a child's father and mother were not married to each other at the time of his birth—

(a) the mother shall have parental responsibility for the child;

(b) the father shall not have parental responsibility for the child, unless he acquires it in accordance with the provisions of this Act.

(3) References in this Act to a child whose father and mother were, or (as the case may be) were not, married to each other at the time of his birth must be read with section 1 of the Family Law Reform Act 1987 (which extends their meaning).

(4) The rule of law that a father is the natural guardian of his legitimate child is abolished.

(5) More than one person may have parental responsibility for the same child at the same time.

(6) A person who has parental responsibility for a child at any time shall not cease to have that responsibility solely because some other person subsequently acquires parental responsibility for the child.

(7) Where more than one person has parental responsibility for a child, each of them may act alone and without the other (or others) in meeting that responsibility; but nothing in this Part shall be taken to affect the operation of any enactment which requires the consent of more than one person in a matter affecting the child.

(8) The fact that a person has parental responsibility for a child shall not entitle him to act in any way which would be incompatible with any order made with respect to the child under this Act.

(9) A person who has parental responsibility for a child may not surrender or transfer any part of that responsibility to another but may arrange for some or all of it to be met by one or more persons acting on his behalf.

(10) The person with whom any such arrangement is made may himself be a person who already has parental responsibility for the child concerned.

(11) The making of any such arrangement shall not affect any liability of the person making it which may arise from any failure to meet any part of his parental responsibility for the child concerned.

Meaning of "parental responsibility"

3.—(1) In this Act "parental responsibility" means all the rights, duties, powers, responsibilities and authority which by law a parent of a child has in relation to the child and his property. **39-003**

(2) It also includes the rights, powers and duties which a guardian of the child's estate (appointed, before the commencement of section 5, to act generally) would have had in relation to the child and his property.

(3) The rights referred to in subsection (2) include, in particular, the right of the guardian to receive or recover in his own name, for the benefit of the child, property of whatever description and wherever situated which the child is entitled to receive or recover.

(4) The fact that a person has, or does not have, parental responsibility for a child shall not affect—

(a) any obligation which he may have in relation to the child (such as a statutory duty to maintain the child); or

(b) any rights which, in the event of the child's death, he (or any other person) may have in relation to the child's property.

(5) A person who—

(a) does not have parental responsibility for a particular child; but

(b) has care of the child,

may (subject to the provisions of this Act) do what is reasonable in all the circumstances of the case for the purpose of safeguarding or promoting the child's welfare.

Acquisition of parental responsibility by father

39-004 **4.**—(1) Where a child's father and mother were not married to each other at the time of his birth—

(a) the court may, on the application of the father, order that he shall have parental responsibility for the child; or

(b) the father and mother may by agreement ("a parental responsibility agreement") provide for the father to have parental responsibility for the child.

(2) No parental responsibility agreement shall have effect for the purposes of this Act unless—

(a) it is made in the form prescribed by regulations made by the Lord Chancellor; and

(b) where regulations are made by the Lord Chancellor prescribing the manner in which such agreements must be recorded, it is recorded in the prescribed manner.

(3) Subject to section 12(4), an order under subsection (1)(a), or a parental responsibility agreement, may only be brought to an end by an order of the court made on the application—

(a) of any person who has parental responsibility for the child; or

(b) with leave of the court, of the child himself.

(4) The court may only grant leave under subsection (3)(b) if it is satisfied that the child has sufficient understanding to make the proposed application.

Appointment of guardians

39-005 **5.**—(1) Where an application with respect to a child is made to the court by any individual, the court may by order appoint that individual to be the child's guardian if—

(a) the child has no parent with parental responsibility for him; or

(b) a residence order has been made with respect to the child in favour of a parent or guardian of his who has died while the order was in force.

(2) The power conferred by subsection (1) may also be exercised in any family proceedings if the court considers that the order should be made even though no application has been made for it.

(3) A parent who has parental responsibility for his child may appoint another individual to be the child's guardian in the event of his death.

(4) A guardian of a child may appoint another individual to take his place as the child's guardian in the event of his death.

(5) An appointment under subsection (3) or (4) shall not have effect unless it is made in writing, is dated and is signed by the person making the appointment or—

(a) in the case of an appointment made by a will which is not signed by the testator, is signed at the direction of the testator in accordance with the requirements of section 9 of the Wills Act 1837; or

(b) in any other case, is signed at the direction of the person making the appointment, in his presence and in the presence of two witnesses who each attest the signature.

(6) A person appointed as a child's guardian under this section shall have parental responsibility for the child concerned.

(7) Where—

(a) on the death of any person making an appointment under subsection (3) or (4), the child concerned has no parent with parental responsibility for him; or

(b) immediately before the death of any person making such an appointment, a residence order in his favour was in force with respect to the child,

the appointment shall take effect on the death of that person.

(8) Where, on the death of any person making an appointment under subsection (3) or (4)—

(a) the child concerned has a parent with parental responsibility for him; and

(b) subsection (7)(b) does not apply,

the appointment shall take effect when the child no longer has a parent who has parental responsibility for him.

(9) Subsections (1) and (7) do not apply if the residence order referred to in paragraph (b) of those subsections was also made in favour of a surviving parent of the child.

(10) Nothing in this section shall be taken to prevent an appointment under subsection (3) or (4) being made by two or more persons acting jointly.

(11) Subject to any provision made by rules of court, no court shall exercise the High Court's inherent jurisdiction to appoint a guardian of the estate of any child.

(12) Where rules of court are made under subsection (11) they may prescribe the circumstances in which, and conditions subject to which, an appointment of such a guardian may be made.

(13) A guardian of a child may only be appointed in accordance with the provisions of this section.

Guardians: revocation and disclaimer

6.—(1) An appointment under section 5(3) or (4) revokes an earlier such appointment (including one made in an unrevoked will or codicil) made by the same person in respect of the same child, unless it is clear (whether as the result of an express provision in the later appointment or by any necessary implication) that the purpose of the later appointment is to appoint an additional guardian. **39-006**

(2) An appointment under section 5(3) or (4) (including one made in an unrevoked will or codicil) is revoked if the person who made the appointment revokes it by a written and dated instrument which is signed—

(a) by him; or

(b) at his direction, in his presence and in the presence of two witnesses who each attest the signature.

(3) An appointment under section 5(3) or (4) (other than one made in a will or codicil) is revoked if, with the intention of revoking the appointment, the person who made it—

(a) destroys the instrument by which it was made; or
(b) has some other person destroy that instrument in his presence.

[(3A) An appointment under section 5(3) or (4) (including one made in an unrevoked will or codicil) is revoked if the person appointed is the spouse of the person who made the appointment and either—

(a) a decree of a court of civil jurisdiction in England and Wales dissolves or annuls the marriage, or
(b) the marriage is dissolved or annulled and the divorce or annulment is entitled to recognition in England and Wales by virtue of Part II of the Family Law Act 1986,

unless a contrary intention appears by the appointment.][1]

(4) For the avoidance of doubt, an appointment under section 5(3) or (4) made in a will or codicil is revoked if the will or codicil is revoked.

(5) A person who is appointed as a guardian under section 5(3) or (4) may disclaim his appointment by an instrument in writing signed by him and made within a reasonable time of his first knowing that the appointment has taken effect.

(6) Where regulations are made by the Lord Chancellor prescribing the manner in which such disclaimers must be recorded, no such disclaimer shall have effect unless it is recorded in the prescribed manner.

(7) Any appointment of a guardian under section 5 may be brought to an end at any time by order of the court—

(a) on the application of any person who has parental responsibility for the child;
(b) on the application of the child concerned, with leave of the court; or
(c) in any family proceedings, if the court considers that it should be brought to an end even though no application has been made.

Welfare reports

39-007 7.—(1) A court considering any question with respect to a child under this Act may—

(a) ask [an officer of the Service][2]; or
(b) ask a local authority to arrange for—
    (i) an officer of the authority; or
    (ii) such other person (other than [an officer of the Service][3]) as the authority considers appropriate,

to report to the court on such matters relating to the welfare of that child as are required to be dealt with in the report.

(2) The Lord Chancellor may make regulations specifying matters which, unless the court orders otherwise, must be dealt with in any report under this section.

(3) The report may be made in writing, or orally, as the court requires.

(4) Regardless of any enactment or rule of law which would otherwise prevent it from doing so, the court may take account of—

(a) any statement contained in the report; and
(b) any evidence given in respect of the matters referred to in the report,

in so far as the statement or evidence is, in the opinion of the court, relevant to the question which it is considering.

[1] Added by Law Reform (Succession) Act 1995 c.41 s 4 (1)
[2] Words substituted by Criminal Justice and Court Services Act 2000 c.43 Sch 7 (II) para 88 (a)
[3] Words substituted by Criminal Justice and Court Services Act 2000 c.43 Sch 7 (II) para 88 (a)

(5) It shall be the duty of the authority or [officer of the Service][1] to comply with any request for a report under this section.

PART II

ORDERS WITH RESPECT TO CHILDREN IN FAMILY PROCEEDINGS

General

Residence, contact and other orders with respect to children

8.—(1) In this Act— 39-008

"a contact order" means an order requiring the person with whom a child lives, or is to live, to allow the child to visit or stay with the person named in the order, or for that person and the child otherwise to have contact with each other;

"a prohibited steps order" means an order that no step which could be taken by a parent in meeting his parental responsibility for a child, and which is of a kind specified in the order, shall be taken by any person without the consent of the court;

"a residence order" means an order settling the arrangements to be made as to the person with whom a child is to live; and

"a specific issue order" means an order giving directions for the purpose of determining a specific question which has arisen, or which may arise, in connection with any aspect of parental responsibility for a child.

(2) In this Act "a section 8 order" means any of the orders mentioned in subsection (1) and any order varying or discharging such an order.

(3) For the purposes of this Act "family proceedings" means any proceedings—

(a) under the inherent jurisdiction of the High Court in relation to children; and

(b) under the enactments mentioned in subsection (4),

but does not include proceedings on an application for leave under section 100(3).

(4) The enactments are—

(a) Parts I, II and IV of this Act;

(b) the Matrimonial Causes Act 1973;

(c) [...][2]

(d) the Adoption Act 1976;

(e) the Domestic Proceedings and Magistrates' Courts Act 1978;

(f) [...][3]

(g) Part III of the Matrimonial and Family Proceedings Act 1984.

[(h) the Family Law Act 1996.][4]

[(i) sections 11 and 12 of the Crime and Disorder Act 1998.][5]

[1] Words substituted by Criminal Justice and Court Services Act 2000 c.43 Sch 7 (II) para 88 (b)

[2] Repealed by Family Law Act 1996 c.27 Sch 10 para 1

[3] Repealed by Family Law Act 1996 c.27 Sch 10 para 1

[4] Added by Family Law Act 1996 c.27 Sch 8 (III) para 60 (1)

[5] Added by Crime and Disorder Act 1998 c.37 Sch 8 para 68

Restrictions on making section 8 orders

39-009 **9.**—(1) No court shall make any section 8 order, other than a residence order, with respect to a child who is in the care of a local authority.

(2) No application may be made by a local authority for a residence order or contact order and no court shall make such an order in favour of a local authority.

(3) A person who is, or was at any time within the last six months, a local authority foster parent of a child may not apply for leave to apply for a section 8 order with respect to the child unless—

(a) he has the consent of the authority;

(b) he is a relative of the child; or

(c) the child has lived with him for at least three years preceding the application.

(4) The period of three years mentioned in subsection (3)(c) need not be continuous but must have begun not more than five years before the making of the application.

(5) No court shall exercise its powers to make a specific issue order or prohibited steps order—

(a) with a view to achieving a result which could be achieved by making a residence or contact order; or

(b) in any way which is denied to the High Court (by section 100(2)) in the exercise of its inherent jurisdiction with respect to children.

(6) No court shall make any section 8 order which is to have effect for a period which will end after the child has reached the age of sixteen unless it is satisfied that the circumstances of the case are exceptional.

(7) No court shall make any section 8 order, other than one varying or discharging such an order, with respect to a child who has reached the age of sixteen unless it is satisfied that the circumstances of the case are exceptional.

Power of court to make section 8 orders

39-010 **10.**—(1) In any family proceedings in which a question arises with respect to the welfare of any child, the court may make a section 8 order with respect to the child if—

(a) an application for the order has been made by a person who—

(i) is entitled to apply for a section 8 order with respect to the child; or

(ii) has obtained the leave of the court to make the application; or

(b) the court considers that the order should be made even though no such application has been made.

(2) The court may also make a section 8 order with respect to any child on the application of a person who—

(a) is entitled to apply for a section 8 order with respect to the child;

or

(b) has obtained the leave of the court to make the application.

(3) This section is subject to the restrictions imposed by section 9.

(4) The following persons are entitled to apply to the court for any section 8 order with respect to a child—

(a) any parent or guardian of the child;

(b) any person in whose favour a residence order is in force with respect to the child.

(5) The following persons are entitled to apply for a residence or contact order with respect to a child—

(a) any party to a marriage (whether or not subsisting) in relation to whom the child is a child of the family;

(b) any person with whom the child has lived for a period of at least three years;

(c) any person who—

(i) in any case where a residence order is in force with respect to the child, has the consent of each of the persons in whose favour the order was made;

(ii) in any case where the child is in the care of a local authority, has the consent of that authority; or

(iii) in any other case, has the consent of each of those (if any) who have parental responsibility for the child.

(6) A person who would not otherwise be entitled (under the previous provisions of this section) to apply for the variation or discharge of a section 8 order shall be entitled to do so if—

(a) the order was made on his application; or

(b) in the case of a contact order, he is named in the order.

(7) Any person who falls within a category of person prescribed by rules of court is entitled to apply for any such section 8 order as may be prescribed in relation to that category of person.

(8) Where the person applying for leave to make an application for a section 8 order is the child concerned, the court may only grant leave if it is satisfied that he has sufficient understanding to make the proposed application for the section 8 order.

(9) Where the person applying for leave to make an application for a section 8 order is not the child concerned, the court shall, in deciding whether or not to grant leave, have particular regard to—

(a) the nature of the proposed application for the section 8 order;

(b) the applicant's connection with the child;

(c) any risk there might be of that proposed application disrupting the child's life to such an extent that he would be harmed by it; and

(d) where the child is being looked after by a local authority—

(i) the authority's plans for the child's future; and

(ii) the wishes and feelings of the child's parents.

(10) The period of three years mentioned in subsection (5)(b) need not be continuous but must not have begun more than five years before, or ended more than three months before, the making of the application.

General principles and supplementary provisions

11.—(1) In proceedings in which any question of making a section 8 order, or any other question with respect to such an order, arises, the court shall (in the light of any rules made by virtue of subsection (2))— **39-011**

(a) draw up a timetable with a view to determining the question without delay; and

(b) give such directions as it considers appropriate for the purpose of ensuring, so far as is reasonably practicable, that that timetable is adhered to.

(2) Rules of court may—

(a) specify periods within which specified steps must be taken in relation to proceedings in which such question arise; and

(b) make other provision with respect to such proceedings for the purpose of ensuring, so far as is reasonably practicable, that such questions are determined without delay.

(3) Where a court has power to make a section 8 order, it may do so at any time during the course of the proceedings in question even though it is not in a position to dispose finally of those proceedings.

(4) Where a residence order is made in favour of two or more persons who do not themselves all live together, the order may specify the periods during which the child is to live in the different households concerned.

(5) Where—

(a) a residence order has been made with respect to a child; and

(b) as a result of the order the child lives, or is to live, with one of two parents who each have parental responsibility for him,

the residence order shall cease to have effect if the parents live together for a continuous period of more than six months.

(6) A contact order which requires the parent with whom a child lives to allow the child to visit, or otherwise have contact with, his other parent shall cease to have effect if the parents live together for a continuous period of more than six months.

(7) A section 8 order may—

(a) contain directions about how it is to be carried into effect;

(b) impose conditions which must be complied with by any person—

(i) in whose favour the order is made;

(ii) who is a parent of the child concerned;

(iii) who is not a parent of his but who has parental responsibility for him; or

(iv) with whom the child is living,

and to whom the conditions are expressed to apply;

(c) be made to have effect for a specified period, or contain provisions which are to have effect for a specified period;

(d) make such incidental, supplemental or consequential provision as the court thinks fit.

Residence orders and parental responsibility

39-012 **12.**—(1) Where the court makes a residence order in favour of the father of a child it shall, if the father would not otherwise have parental responsibility for the child, also make an order under section 4 giving him that responsibility.

(2) Where the court makes a residence order in favour of any person who is not the parent or guardian of the child concerned that person shall have parental responsibility for the child while the residence order remains in force.

(3) Where a person has parental responsibility for a child as a result of subsection (2), he shall not have the right—

(a) to consent, or refuse to consent, to the making of an application with respect to the child under section 18 of the Adoption Act 1976;

(b) to agree, or refuse to agree, to the making of an adoption order, or an order under section 55 of the Act of 1976, with respect to the child; or

(c) to appoint a guardian for the child.

(4) Where subsection (1) requires the court to make an order under section 4 in respect of the father of a child, the court shall not bring that order to an end at any time while the residence order concerned remains in force.

Change of child's name or removal from jurisdiction

13.—(1) Where a residence order is in force with respect to a child, no person may— **39-013**

(a) cause the child to be known by a new surname; or
(b) remove him from the United Kingdom;

without either the written consent of every person who has parental responsibility for the child or the leave of the court.

(2) Subsection (1)(b) does not prevent the removal of a child, for a period of less than one month, by the person in whose favour the residence order is made.

(3) In making a residence order with respect to a child the court may grant the leave required by subsection (1)(b), either generally or for specified purposes.

Enforcement of residence orders

14.—(1) Where— **39-014**

(a) a residence order is in force with respect to a child in favour of any person; and
(b) any other person (including one in whose favour the order is also in force) is in breach of the arrangements settled by that order,

the person mentioned in paragraph (a) may, as soon as the requirement in subsection (2) is complied with, enforce the order under section 63(3) of the Magistrates' Courts Act 1980 as if it were an order requiring the other person to produce the child to him.

(2) The requirement is that a copy of the residence order has been served on the other person.

(3) Subsection (1) is without prejudice to any other remedy open to the person in whose favour the residence order is in force.

Financial relief

Orders for financial relief with respect to children

15.—(1) Schedule 1 (which consists primarily of the re-enactment, with conse- **39-015**
quential amendments and minor modifications, of provisions of [section 6 of the Family Law Reform Act 1969][1] the Guardianship of Minors Acts 1971 and 1973, the Children Act 1975 and of sections 15 and 16 of the Family Law Reform Act 1987) makes provision in relation to financial relief for children.

(2) The powers of a magistrates' court under section 60 of the Magistrates' Courts Act 1980 to revoke, revive or vary an order for the periodical payment of money [and the power of the clerk of a magistrates' court to vary such an order][2] shall not apply in relation to an order made under Schedule 1.

Family assistance orders

Family assistance orders

16.—(1) Where, in any family proceedings, the court has power to make an **39-016**
order under this Part with respect to any child, it may (whether or not it makes such an order) make an order requiring—

[1] Words added by Courts and Legal Services Act 1990 c.41 Sch 16 (I) para 10 (1)
[2] Words added by Maintenance Enforcement Act 1991 c.17 Sch 2 para 10

(a) [an officer of the Service][1] to be made available; or

(b) a local authority to make an officer of the authority available,

to advise, assist and (where appropriate) befriend any person named in the order.

(2) The persons who may be named in an order under this section ("a family assistance order") are—

(a) any parent or guardian of the child;

(b) any person with whom the child is living or in whose favour a contact order is in force with respect to the child;

(c) the child himself.

(3) No court may make a family assistance order unless—

(a) it is satisfied that the circumstances of the case are exceptional; and

(b) it has obtained the consent of every person to be named in the order other than the child.

(4) A family assistance order may direct—

(a) the person named in the order; or

(b) such of the persons named in the order as may be specified in the order,

to take such steps as may be so specified with a view to enabling the officer concerned to be kept informed of the address of any person named in the order and to be allowed to visit any such person.

(5) Unless it specifies a shorter period, a family assistance order shall have effect for a period of six months beginning with the day on which it is made.

(6) Where—

(a) a family assistance order is in force with respect to a child; and

(b) a section 8 order is also in force with respect to the child,

the officer concerned may refer to the court the question whether the section 8 order should be varied or discharged.

(7) A family assistance order shall not be made so as to require a local authority to make an officer of theirs available unless—

(a) the authority agree; or

(b) the child concerned lives or will live within their area.

(8) [...][2]

(9) [...][3]

PART III

LOCAL AUTHORITY SUPPORT FOR CHILDREN AND FAMILIES

Provision of services for children and their families

Provision of services for children in need, their families and others

39-017 **17.**—(1) It shall be the general duty of every local authority (in addition to the other duties imposed on them by this Part)—

(a) to safeguard and promote the welfare of children within their area who are in need; and

[1] Words substituted by Criminal Justice and Court Services Act 2000 c.43 Sch 7 (II) para 89 (a)

[2] Repealed by Criminal Justice and Court Services Act 2000 c.43 Sch 8 para 1

[3] Repealed by Criminal Justice and Court Services Act 2000 c.43 Sch 8 para 1

(b) so far as is consistent with that duty, to promote the upbringing of such children by their families,

by providing a range and level of services appropriate to those children's needs.

(2) For the purpose principally of facilitating the discharge of their general duty under this section, every local authority shall have the specific duties and powers set out in Part 1 of Schedule 2.

(3) Any service provided by an authority in the exercise of functions conferred on them by this section may be provided for the family of a particular child in need or for any member of his family, if it is provided with a view to safeguarding or promoting the child's welfare.

(4) The Secretary of State may by order amend any provision of Part I of Schedule 2 or add any further duty or power to those for the time being mentioned there.

(5) Every local authority—

(a) shall facilitate the provision by others (including in particular voluntary organisations) of services which the authority have power to provide by virtue of this section, or [section 18, 20, 23, 23B to 23D, 24A or 24B][1]; and

(b) may make such arrangements as they see fit for any person to act on their behalf in the provision of any such service.

(6) The services provided by a local authority in the exercise of functions conferred on them by this section may include [providing accommodation and][2] giving assistance in kind or, in exceptional circumstances, in cash.

(7) Assistance may be unconditional or subject to conditions as to the repayment of the assistance or of its value (in whole or in part).

(8) Before giving any assistance or imposing any conditions, a local authority shall have regard to the means of the child concerned and of each of his parents.

(9) No person shall be liable to make any repayment of assistance or of its value at any time when he is in receipt of income support [, [working families' tax credit][3] or][4][disabled person's tax credit][5] under the [Part VII of the Social Security Contributions and Benefits Act 1992][6][or of an income-based jobseeker's allowance][7].

(10) For the purposes of this Part a child shall be taken to be in need if—

(a) he is unlikely to achieve or maintain, or to have the opportunity of achieving or maintaining, a reasonable standard of health or development without the provision for him of services by a local authority under this Part;

(b) his health or development is likely to be significantly impaired, or further impaired, without the provision for him of such services; or

(c) he is disabled,

and "family", in relation to such a child, includes any person who has parental responsibility for the child and any other person with whom he has been living.

(11) For the purposes of this Part, a child is disabled if he is blind, deaf or dumb or suffers from mental disorder of any kind or is substantially and perma-

[1] Words substituted by Children (Leaving Care) Act 2000 c.35 s 7 (2)
[2] Words inserted by Adoption and Children Act 2002 c.38 Pt 2 s 116 (1)
[3] Words substituted by Tax Credits Act 1999 c.10 Sch 1 para 6 (d) (i)
[4] Words substituted by Disability Living Allowance and Disability Working Allowance Act 1991 c.21 Sch 3 (II) para 13
[5] Words substituted by Tax Credits Act 1999 c.10 Sch 1 para 6 (d) (i)
[6] Words substituted by Social Security (Consequential Provisions) Act 1992 c.6 Sch 2 para 108 (a)
[7] Words added by Jobseekers Act 1995 c.18 Sch 2 para 19 (2)

nently handicapped by illness, injury or congenital deformity or such other disability as may be prescribed; and in this Part—

"development" means physical, intellectual, emotional, social or behavioural development; and

"health" means physical or mental health.

[Direct payments

39-018 **17A.**—(1) Instead of providing services in the exercise of functions conferred on them by section 17, a local authority may make to a person falling within subsection (2) (if he consents) a payment of such amount as, subject to subsections (5) and (6), they think fit in respect of his securing the provision of any of the services which the local authority would otherwise have provided.

(2) The following fall within this subsection–

(a) a person with parental responsibility for a disabled child;

(b) a disabled child aged 16 or 17.

(3) A payment under subsection (1) shall be subject to the condition that the person to whom it is made shall not secure the provision of the service to which it relates by a person who is of a prescribed description.

(4) The Secretary of State may by regulations provide that the power conferred by subsection (1) is not to be exercisable in relation to the provision of residential accommodation for any person for a period exceeding a prescribed period.

(5) Except as mentioned in subsection (6) of this section, subsections (2) and (6) of section 1, and subsections (1) and (2) of section 2, of the Community Care (Direct Payments) Act 1996 apply in relation to payments under subsection (1) as they apply in relation to payments under section 1(1) of that Act, but as if–

(a) the reference to "subsection (4)" in section 1(6)(b) of that Act were a reference to subsection (3) of this section; and

(b) the references to "the relevant community care enactment" in section 2 of that Act were to Part III of the Children Act 1989.

(6) Section 1(2) of the Community Care (Direct Payments) Act 1996 does not apply in relation to payments under subsection (1) to–

(a) a person with parental responsibility for a disabled child, other than a parent of such a child under the age of sixteen, in respect of a service which would otherwise have been provided for the child; or

(b) any person who is in receipt of income support, working families' tax credit or disabled person's tax credit under Part VII of the Social Security Contributions and Benefits Act 1992 or of an income-based jobseeker's allowance,

and in those cases the amount of any payment under subsection (1) is to be at a rate equal to the local authority's estimate of the reasonable cost of securing the provision of the service concerned.][1]

Day care for pre-school and other children

39-019 **18.**—(1) Every local authority shall provide such day care for children in need within their area who are—

(a) aged five or under; and

(b) not yet attending schools,

as is appropriate.

[1] Added by Carers and Disabled Children Act 2000 c.16 s 7 (1)

(2) A local authority may provide day care for children within their area who satisfy the conditions mentioned in subsection (1)(a) and (b) even though they are not in need.

(3) A local authority may provide facilities (including training, advice, guidance and counselling) for those—

(a) caring for children in day care; or

(b) who at any time accompany such children while they are in day care.

(4) In this section "day care" means any form of care or supervised activity provided for children during the day (whether or not it is provided on a regular basis).

(5) Every local authority shall provide for children in need within their area who are attending any school such care or supervised activities as is appropriate—

(a) outside school hours; or

(b) during school holidays.

(6) A local authority may provide such care or supervised activities for children within their area who are attending any school even though those children are not in need.

(7) In this section "supervised activity" means an activity supervised by a responsible person.

Review of provision for day care, child minding etc

19.—(1) Every local authority in England and Wales shall review— **39-020**

(a) the provision which they make under section 18;

(b) the extent to which the services of child minders are available within their area with respect to children under the age of eight; and

(c) the provision for day care within their area made for children under the age of eight by persons other, than the authority, required to register under [Part XA][1].

(2) A review under subsection (1) shall be conducted—

(a) together with the appropriate local education authority; and

(b) at least once in every review period.

(3) Every local authority in Scotland shall, at least once in every review period, review—

(a) the provision for day care within their area made for children under the age of eight by the local authority and by persons required to register under section 71(1)(b); and

(b) the extent to which the services of child minders are available within their area with respect to children under the age of eight.

(4) In conducting any such review, the two authorities or, in Scotland, the authority shall have regard to the provision made with respect to children under the age of eight in relevant establishments within their area.

(5) In this section—

["relevant establishment" means–

(a) in relation to Scotland, any establishment which is mentioned in paragraphs 3 and 4 of Schedule 9 (establishments exempt from the registration requirements which apply in relation to the provision of day care in Scotland); and

(b) in relation to England and Wales, any establishment which is mentioned in paragraphs 1 and 2 of Schedule 9A (establishments

[1] Substituted by Care Standards Act 2000 c.14 Sch 4 para 14 (2)

exempt from the registration requirements which apply in relation to the provision of day care in England and Wales);][1]

"review period" means the period of one year beginning with the commencement of this section and each subsequent period of three years beginning with an anniversary of that commencement.

(6) Where a local authority have conducted a review under this section they shall publish the result of the review—

(a) as soon as is reasonably practicable;
(b) in such form as they consider appropriate; and
(c) together with any proposals they may have with respect to the matters reviewed.

(7) The authorities conducting any review under this section shall have regard to—

(a) any representations made to any one of them by any relevant [Health Authority, Special Health Authority][2] [, Primary Care Trust][3] or health board; and
(b) any other representations which they consider to be relevant.

(8) In the application of this section to Scotland, "day care" has the same meaning as in section 79 and "health board" has the same meaning as in the National Health Service (Scotland) Act 1978.

Provision of accommodation for children

Provision of accommodation for children: general

39-021 **20.**—(1) Every local authority shall provide accommodation for any child in need within their area who appears to them to require accommodation as a result of—

(a) there being no person who has parental responsibility for him;
(b) his being lost or having been abandoned; or
(c) the person who has been caring for him being prevented (whether or not permanently, and for whatever reason) from providing him with suitable accommodation or care.

(2) Where a local authority provide accommodation under subsection (1) for a child who is ordinarily resident in the area of another local authority, that other local authority may take over the provision of accommodation for the child within—

(a) three months of being notified in writing that the child is being provided with accommodation; or
(b) such other longer period as may be prescribed.

(3) Every local authority shall provide accommodation for any child in need within their area who has reached the age of sixteen and whose welfare the authority consider is likely to be seriously prejudiced if they do not provide him with accommodation.

(4) A local authority may provide accommodation for any child within their area (even though a person who has parental responsibility for him is able to provide him with accommodation) if they consider that to do so would safeguard or promote the child's welfare.

[1] Substituted by Care Standards Act 2000 c.14 Sch 4 para 14 (2)
[2] Words substituted by Health Authorities Act 1995 c.17 Sch 1 (III) para 118 (2)
[3] Words inserted by SI 2000/90 Sch 1 para 24 (2)

(5) A local authority may provide accommodation for any person who has reached the age of sixteen but is under twenty-one in any community home which takes children who have reached the age of sixteen if they consider that to do so would safeguard or promote his welfare.

(6) Before providing accommodation under this section, a local authority shall, so far as is reasonably practicable and consistent with the child's welfare—

(a) ascertain the child's wishes regarding the provision of accommodation; and

(b) give due consideration (having regard to his age and understanding) to such wishes of the child as they have been able to ascertain.

(7) A local authority may not provide accommodation under this section for any child if any person who—

(a) has parental responsibility for him; and

(b) is willing and able to—

(i) provide accommodation for him; or

(ii) arrange for accommodation to be provided for him,

objects.

(8) Any person who has parental responsibility for a child may at any time remove the child from accommodation provided by or on behalf of the local authority under this section.

(9) Subsections (7) and (8) do not apply while any person—

(a) in whose favour a residence order is in force with respect to the child; or

(b) who has care of the child by virtue of an order made in the exercise of the High Court's inherent jurisdiction with respect to children,

agrees to the child being looked after in accommodation provided by or on behalf of the local authority.

(10) Where there is more than one such person as is mentioned in subsection (9), all of them must agree.

(11) Subsections (7) and (8) do not apply where a child who has reached the age of sixteen agrees to being provided with accommodation under this section.

Provision of accommodation for children in police protection or detention or on remand, etc

21.—(1) Every local authority shall make provision for the reception and accommodation of children who are removed or kept away from home under Part V. **39-022**

(2) Every local authority shall receive, and provide accommodation for, children—

(a) in police protection whom they are requested to receive under section 46(3)(f);

(b) whom they are requested to receive under section 38(6) of the Police and Criminal Evidence Act 1984;

(c) who are—

(i) on remand under [paragraph 7(5) of Schedule 7 to the Powers of Criminal Courts (Sentencing) Act 2000 or section 23(1) of the Children and Young Persons Act 1969][1]; or

(ii) the subject of a supervision order imposing a [local authority residence requirement under paragraph 5 of Schedule 6 to that Act of 2000][2],

[1] Words substituted by Powers of Criminal Courts (Sentencing) Act 2000 c.6 Sch 9 para 126 (a)
[2] Words substituted by Powers of Criminal Courts (Sentencing) Act 2000 c.6 Sch 9 para 126 (b)

and with respect to whom they are the designated authority.

(3) Where a child has been—

(a) removed under Part V; or

(b) detained under section 38 of the Police and Criminal Evidence Act 1984,

and he is not being provided with accommodation by a local authority or in a hospital vested in the Secretary of State [[or a Primary Care Trust,][1] or otherwise made available pursuant to arrangements made by a][2][Health Authority][3][or a Primary Care Trust][4], any reasonable expenses of accommodating him shall be recoverable from the local authority in whose area he is ordinarily resident.

Duties of local authorities in relation to children looked after by them

General duty of local authority in relation to children looked after by them

39-023 **22.**—(1) In this Act, any reference to a child who is looked after by a local authority is a reference to a child who is—

(a) in their care; or

(b) provided with accommodation by the authority in the exercise of any functions (in particular those under this Act) which [are social services functions within the meaning of][5] the Local Authority Social Services Act 1970[, apart from functions under][6][sections 17, 23B and 24B][7].

(2) In subsection (1) "accommodation" means accommodation which is provided for a continuous period of more than 24 hours.

(3) It shall be the duty of a local authority looking after any child—

(a) to safeguard and promote his welfare; and

(b) to make such use of services available for children cared for by their own parents as appears to the authority reasonable in his case.

(4) Before making any decision with respect to a child whom they are looking after, or proposing to look after, a local authority shall, so far as is reasonably practicable, ascertain the wishes and feelings of—

(a) the child;

(b) his parents;

(c) any person who is not a parent of his but who has parental responsibility for him; and

(d) any other person whose wishes and feelings the authority consider to be relevant,

regarding the matter to be decided.

(5) In making any such decision a local authority shall give due consideration—

(a) having regard to his age and understanding, to such wishes and feelings of the child as they have been able to ascertain;

(b) to such wishes and feelings of any person mentioned in subsection (4)(b) to (d) as they have been able to ascertain; and

[1] Words inserted by SI 2000/90 Sch 1 para 24 (3) (a)
[2] Words inserted by National Health Service and Community Care Act 1990 c.19 s 66 (1) Sch 9 para 36 (1)
[3] Words substituted by Health Authorities Act 1995 c.17 Sch 1 (III) para 118 (3)
[4] Words inserted by SI 2000/90 Sch 1 para 24 (3) (b)
[5] Words substituted by Local Government Act 2000 c.22 Sch 5 para 19
[6] Words inserted by Children (Leaving Care) Act 2000 c.35 s 2 (2)
[7] Word inserted by Adoption and Children Act 2002 c.38 Pt 2 s 116 (2)

(c) to the child's religious persuasion, racial origin and cultural and linguistic background.

(6) If it appears to a local authority that it is necessary, for the purpose of protecting members of the public from serious injury, to exercise their powers with respect to a child whom they are looking after in a manner which may not be consistent with their duties under this section, they may do so.

(7) If the Secretary of State considers it necessary, for the purpose of protecting members of the public from serious injury, to give directions to a local authority with respect to the exercise of their powers with respect to a child whom they are looking after, he may give such directions to the authority.

(8) Where any such directions are given to an authority they shall comply with them even though doing so is inconsistent with their duties under this section.

Provision of accommodation and maintenance by local authority for children whom they are looking after

23.—(1) It shall be the duty of any local authority looking after a child— **39-024**

(a) when he is in their care, to provide accommodation for him; and

(b) to maintain him in other respects apart from providing accommodation for him.

(2) A local authority shall provide accommodation and maintenance for any child whom they are looking after by—

(a) placing him (subject to subsection (5) and any regulations made by the Secretary of State) with—

(i) a family;

(ii) a relative of his; or

(iii) any other suitable person,

on such terms as to payment by the authority and otherwise as the authority may determine;

[(aa) maintaining him in an appropriate children's home;][1]

(f) making such other arrangements as—

(i) seem appropriate to them; and

(ii) comply with any regulations made by the Secretary of State.

[(2A) Where under subsection (2)(aa) a local authority maintains a child in a home provided, equipped and maintained by the Secretary of State under section 82(5), it shall do so on such terms as the Secretary of State may from time to time determine.][2]

(3) Any person with whom a child has been placed under subsection (2)(a) is referred to in this Act as a local authority foster parent unless he falls within subsection (4).

(4) A person falls within this subsection if he is—

(a) a parent of the child;

(b) a person who is not a parent of the child but who has parental responsibility for him; or

(c) where the child is in care and there was a residence order in force with respect to him immediately before the care order was made, a person in whose favour the residence order was made.

(5) Where a child is in the care of a local authority, the authority may only allow him to live with a person who falls within subsection (4) in accordance with regulations made by the Secretary of State.

[1] Inserted by Care Standards Act 2000 c.14 Sch 4 para 14 (3)

[2] Inserted by Care Standards Act 2000 c.14 Sch 4 para 14 (3)

[(5A) For the purposes of subsection (5) a child shall be regarded as living with a person if he stays with that person for a continuous period of more than 24 hours.][1]

(6) Subject to any regulations made by the Secretary of State for the purposes of this subsection, any local authority looking after a child shall make arrangements to enable him to live with—

(a) a person falling within subsection (4); or

(b) a relative, friend or other person connected with him,

unless that would not be reasonably practicable or consistent with his welfare.

(7) Where a local authority provide accommodation for a child whom they are looking after, they shall, subject to the provisions of this Part and so far as is reasonably practicable and consistent with his welfare, secure that—

(a) the accommodation is near his home; and

(b) where the authority are also providing accommodation for a sibling of his, they are accommodated together.

(8) Where a local authority provide accommodation for a child whom they are looking after and who is disabled, they shall, so far as is reasonably practicable, secure that the accommodation is not unsuitable to his particular needs.

(9) Part II of Schedule 2 shall have effect for the purposes of making further provision as to children looked after by local authorities and in particular as to the regulations that may be made under subsections (2)(a) and (f) and (5).

[(10) In this Act–

"appropriate children's home" means a children's home in respect of which a person is registered under Part II of the Care Standards Act 2000; and

"children's home" has the same meaning as in that Act.][2]

Advice and assistance for certain children [and young persons][3]

[The responsible authority and relevant children

39-025 **23A.**—(1) The responsible local authority shall have the functions set out in section 23B in respect of a relevant child.

(2) In subsection (1) "relevant child" means (subject to subsection (3)) a child who—

(a) is not being looked after by any local authority;

(b) was, before last ceasing to be looked after, an eligible child for the purposes of paragraph 19B of Schedule 2; and

(c) is aged sixteen or seventeen.

(3) The Secretary of State may prescribe—

(a) additional categories of relevant children; and

(b) categories of children who are not to be relevant children despite falling within subsection (2).

(4) In subsection (1) the "responsible local authority" is the one which last looked after the child.

(5) If under subsection (3)(a) the Secretary of State prescribes a category of relevant children which includes children who do not fall within subsection (2)(b) (for example, because they were being looked after by a local authority in

[1] Added by Courts and Legal Services Act 1990 c.41 Sch 16 (I) para 12 (2)
[2] Inserted by Care Standards Act 2000 c.14 Sch 4 para 14 (3)
[3] Words added by Children (Leaving Care) Act 2000 c.35 s 2 (3)

Scotland), he may in the regulations also provide for which local authority is to be the responsible local authority for those children.][1]

[Additional functions of the responsible authority in respect of relevant children

23B.—(1) It is the duty of each local authority to take reasonable steps to keep in touch with a relevant child for whom they are the responsible authority, whether he is within their area or not. **39-026**

(2) It is the duty of each local authority to appoint a personal adviser for each relevant child (if they have not already done so under paragraph 19C of Schedule 2).

(3) It is the duty of each local authority, in relation to any relevant child who does not already have a pathway plan prepared for the purposes of paragraph 19B of Schedule 2—

(a) to carry out an assessment of his needs with a view to determining what advice, assistance and support it would be appropriate for them to provide him under this Part; and

(b) to prepare a pathway plan for him.

(4) The local authority may carry out such an assessment at the same time as any assessment of his needs is made under any enactment referred to in sub-paragraphs (a) to (c) of paragraph 3 of Schedule 2, or under any other enactment.

(5) The Secretary of State may by regulations make provision as to assessments for the purposes of subsection (3).

(6) The regulations may in particular make provision about—

(a) who is to be consulted in relation to an assessment;

(b) the way in which an assessment is to be carried out, by whom and when;

(c) the recording of the results of an assessment;

(d) the considerations to which the local authority are to have regard in carrying out an assessment.

(7) The authority shall keep the pathway plan under regular review.

(8) The responsible local authority shall safeguard and promote the child's welfare and, unless they are satisfied that his welfare does not require it, support him by—

(a) maintaining him;

(b) providing him with or maintaining him in suitable accommodation; and

(c) providing support of such other descriptions as may be prescribed.

(9) Support under subsection (8) may be in cash.

(10) The Secretary of State may by regulations make provision about the meaning of "suitable accommodation" and in particular about the suitability of landlords or other providers of accommodation.

(11) If the local authority have lost touch with a relevant child, despite taking reasonable steps to keep in touch, they must without delay—

(a) consider how to re-establish contact; and

(b) take reasonable steps to do so,

and while the child is still a relevant child must continue to take such steps until they succeed.

[1] Added by Children (Leaving Care) Act 2000 c.35 s 2 (4)

(12) Subsections (7) to (9) of section 17 apply in relation to support given under this section as they apply in relation to assistance given under that section.

(13) Subsections (4) and (5) of section 22 apply in relation to any decision by a local authority for the purposes of this section as they apply in relation to the decisions referred to in that section.][1]

[Continuing functions in respect of former relevant children

39-027 **23C.**—(1) Each local authority shall have the duties provided for in this section towards—

(a) a person who has been a relevant child for the purposes of section 23A (and would be one if he were under eighteen), and in relation to whom they were the last responsible authority; and

(b) a person who was being looked after by them when he attained the age of eighteen, and immediately before ceasing to be looked after was an eligible child,

and in this section such a person is referred to as a "former relevant child".

(2) It is the duty of the local authority to take reasonable steps—

(a) to keep in touch with a former relevant child whether he is within their area or not; and

(b) if they lose touch with him, to re-establish contact.

(3) It is the duty of the local authority—

(a) to continue the appointment of a personal adviser for a former relevant child; and

(b) to continue to keep his pathway plan under regular review.

(4) It is the duty of the local authority to give a former relevant child—

(a) assistance of the kind referred to in section 24B(1), to the extent that his welfare requires it;

(b) assistance of the kind referred to in section 24B(2), to the extent that his welfare and his educational or training needs require it;

(c) other assistance, to the extent that his welfare requires it.

(5) The assistance given under subsection (4)(c) may be in kind or, in exceptional circumstances, in cash.

(6) Subject to subsection (7), the duties set out in subsections (2), (3) and (4) subsist until the former relevant child reaches the age of twenty-one.

(7) If the former relevant child's pathway plan sets out a programme of education or training which extends beyond his twenty-first birthday—

(a) the duty set out in subsection (4)(b) continues to subsist for so long as the former relevant child continues to pursue that programme; and

(b) the duties set out in subsections (2) and (3) continue to subsist concurrently with that duty.

(8) For the purposes of subsection (7)(a) there shall be disregarded any interruption in a former relevant child's pursuance of a programme of education or training if the local authority are satisfied that he will resume it as soon as is reasonably practicable.

(9) Section 24B(5) applies in relation to a person being given assistance under subsection (4)(b) as it applies in relation to a person to whom section 24B(3) applies.

[1] Added by Children (Leaving Care) Act 2000 c.35 s 2 (4)

(10) Subsections (7) to (9) of section 17 apply in relation to assistance given under this section as they apply in relation to assistance given under that section.][1]

Personal advisers and pathway plans

[Personal advisers

23D.—(1) The Secretary of State may by regulations require local authorities to appoint a personal adviser for children or young persons of a prescribed description who have reached the age of sixteen but not the age of twenty-one who are not— **39-028**

(a) children who are relevant children for the purposes of section 23A;

(b) the young persons referred to in section 23C; or

(c) the children referred to in paragraph 19C of Schedule 2.

(2) Personal advisers appointed under or by virtue of this Part shall (in addition to any other functions) have such functions as the Secretary of State prescribes.][2]

[Pathway plans

23E.—(1) In this Part, a reference to a "pathway plan" is to a plan setting out— **39-029**

(a) in the case of a plan prepared under paragraph 19B of Schedule 2—

(i) the advice, assistance and support which the local authority intend to provide a child under this Part, both while they are looking after him and later; and

(ii) when they might cease to look after him; and

(b) in the case of a plan prepared under section 23B, the advice, assistance and support which the local authority intend to provide under this Part,

and dealing with such other matters (if any) as may be prescribed.

(2) The Secretary of State may by regulations make provision about pathway plans and their review.][3]

[Persons qualifying for advice and assistance

24.—(1) In this Part "a person qualifying for advice and assistance" means a person who— **39-030**

(a) is under twenty-one; and

(b) at any time after reaching the age of sixteen but while still a child was, but is no longer, looked after, accommodated or fostered.

(2) In subsection (1)(b), "looked after, accommodated or fostered" means—

(a) looked after by a local authority;

(b) accommodated by or on behalf of a voluntary organisation;

(c) accommodated in a private children's home;

(d) accommodated for a consecutive period of at least three months—

(i) by any Health Authority, Special Health Authority, Primary Care Trust or local education authority, or

(ii) in any care home or independent hospital or in any accommodation provided by a National Health Service trust; or

---

[1] Added by Children (Leaving Care) Act 2000 c.35 s 2 (4)

[2] Added by Children (Leaving Care) Act 2000 c.35 s 3

[3] Added by Children (Leaving Care) Act 2000 c.35 s 3

(e) privately fostered.

(3) Subsection (2)(d) applies even if the period of three months mentioned there began before the child reached the age of sixteen.

(4) In the case of a person qualifying for advice and assistance by virtue of subsection (2)(a), it is the duty of the local authority which last looked after him to take such steps as they think appropriate to contact him at such times as they think appropriate with a view to discharging their functions under sections 24A and 24B.

(5) In each of sections 24A and 24B, the local authority under the duty or having the power mentioned there ("the relevant authority") is—

(a) in the case of a person qualifying for advice and assistance by virtue of subsection (2)(a), the local authority which last looked after him; or

(b) in the case of any other person qualifying for advice and assistance, the local authority within whose area the person is (if he has asked for help of a kind which can be given under section 24A or 24B).][1]

[Advice and assistance

39-031 **24A.**—(1) The relevant authority shall consider whether the conditions in subsection (2) are satisfied in relation to a person qualifying for advice and assistance.

(2) The conditions are that—

(a) he needs help of a kind which they can give under this section or section 24B; and

(b) in the case of a person who was not being looked after by any local authority, they are satisfied that the person by whom he was being looked after does not have the necessary facilities for advising or befriending him.

(3) If the conditions are satisfied—

(a) they shall advise and befriend him if he was being looked after by a local authority or was accommodated by or on behalf of a voluntary organisation; and

(b) in any other case they may do so.

(4) Where as a result of this section a local authority are under a duty, or are empowered, to advise and befriend a person, they may also give him assistance.

(5) The assistance may be in kind [and, in exceptional circumstances, assistance may be given—][2]

[(a) by providing accommodation, if in the circumstances assistance may not be given in respect of the accommodation under section 24B, or

(b) in cash.][3]

(6) Subsections (7) to (9) of section 17 apply in relation to assistance given under this section or section 24B as they apply in relation to assistance given under that section.][4]

[Employment, education and training

39-032 **24B.**—(1) The relevant local authority may give assistance to any person who qualifies for advice and assistance by virtue of section 24(2)(a) by contributing to expenses incurred by him in living near the place where he is, or will be, employed or seeking employment.

[1] Substituted by Children (Leaving Care) Act 2000 c.35 s 4 (1)
[2] Substituted by Adoption and Children Act 2002 c.38 Pt 2 s 116 (3)
[3] Substituted by Adoption and Children Act 2002 c.38 Pt 2 s 116 (3)
[4] Substituted by Children (Leaving Care) Act 2000 c.35 s 4 (1)

(2) The relevant local authority may give assistance to a person to whom subsection (3) applies by—

(a) contributing to expenses incurred by the person in question in living near the place where he is, or will be, receiving education or training; or

(b) making a grant to enable him to meet expenses connected with his education or training.

(3) This subsection applies to any person who—

(a) is under twenty-four; and

(b) qualifies for advice and assistance by virtue of section 24(2)(a), or would have done so if he were under twenty-one.

(4) Where a local authority are assisting a person under subsection (2) they may disregard any interruption in his attendance on the course if he resumes it as soon as is reasonably practicable.

(5) Where the local authority are satisfied that a person to whom subsection (3) applies who is in full-time further or higher education needs accommodation during a vacation because his term-time accommodation is not available to him then, they shall give him assistance by—

(a) providing him with suitable accommodation during the vacation; or

(b) paying him enough to enable him to secure such accommodation himself.

(6) The Secretary of State may prescribe the meaning of "full-time", "further education", "higher education" and "vacation" for the purposes of subsection (5).][1]

[Information

24C.—(1) Where it appears to a local authority that a person— **39-033**

(a) with whom they are under a duty to keep in touch under section 23B, 23C or 24; or

(b) whom they have been advising and befriending under section 24A; or

(c) to whom they have been giving assistance under section 24B,

proposes to live, or is living, in the area of another local authority, they must inform that other authority.

(2) Where a child who is accommodated—

(a) by a voluntary organisation or in a private children's home;

(b) by any Health Authority, Special Health Authority, Primary Care Trust or local education authority; or

(c) in any care home or independent hospital or any accommodation provided by a National Health Service trust,

ceases to be so accommodated, after reaching the age of sixteen, the organisation, authority or (as the case may be) person carrying on the home shall inform the local authority within whose area the child proposes to live.

(3) Subsection (2) only applies, by virtue of paragraph (b) or (c), if the accommodation has been provided for a consecutive period of at least three months.][2]

[Representations: sections 23A to 24B

24D.—(1) Every local authority shall establish a procedure for considering representations (including complaints) made to them by— **39-034**

(a) a relevant child for the purposes of section 23A or a young person falling within section 23C;

[1] Substituted by Children (Leaving Care) Act 2000 c.35 s 4 (1)
[2] Substituted by Children (Leaving Care) Act 2000 c.35 s 4 (1)

(b) a person qualifying for advice and assistance; or

(c) a person falling within section 24B(2),

about the discharge of their functions under this Part in relation to him.

(2) In considering representations under subsection (1), a local authority shall comply with regulations (if any) made by the Secretary of State for the purposes of this subsection.][1]

Secure accommodation

Use of accommodation for restricting liberty

39-035 **25.**—(1) Subject to the following provisions of this section, a child who is being looked after by a local authority may not be placed, and, if placed, may not be kept, in accommodation provided for the purpose of restricting liberty ("secure accommodation") unless it appears—

(a) that—

(i) he has a history of absconding and is likely to abscond from any other description of accommodation; and

(ii) if he absconds, he is likely to suffer significant harm; or

(b) that if he is kept in any other description of accommodation he is likely to injure himself or other persons.

(2) The Secretary of State may by regulations—

(a) specify a maximum period—

(i) beyond which a child may not be kept in secure accommodation without the authority of the court; and

(ii) for which the court may authorise a child to be kept in secure accommodation;

(b) empower the court from time to time to authorise a child to be kept in secure accommodation for such further period as the regulations may specify; and

(c) provide that applications to the court under this section shall be made only by local authorities.

(3) It shall be the duty of a court hearing an application under this section to determine whether any relevant criteria for keeping a child in secure accommodation are satisfied in his case.

(4) If a court determines that any such criteria are satisfied, it shall make an order authorising the child to be kept in secure accommodation and specifying the maximum period for which he may be so kept.

(5) On any adjournment of the hearing of an application under this section, a court may make an interim order permitting the child to be kept during the period of the adjournment in secure accommodation.

(6) No court shall exercise the powers conferred by this section in respect of a child who is not legally represented in that court unless, having been informed of his right to apply for [representation funded by the Legal Services Commission as part of the Community Legal Service or Criminal Defence Service][2] and having had the opportunity to do so, he refused or failed to apply.

(7) The Secretary of State may by regulations provide that—

(a) this section shall or shall not apply to any description of children specified in the regulations;

[1] Added by Children (Leaving Care) Act 2000 c.35 s 5

[2] Words substituted by Access to Justice Act 1999 c.22 Sch 4 para 45

(b) this section shall have effect in relation to children of a description specified in the regulations subject to such modifications as may be so specified;

(c) such other provisions as may be so specified shall have effect for the purpose of determining whether a child of a description specified in the regulations may be placed or kept in secure accommodation.

(8) The giving of an authorisation under this section shall not prejudice any power of any court in England and Wales or Scotland to give directions relating to the child to whom the authorisation relates.

(9) This section is subject to section 20(8).

Supplemental

Review of cases and inquiries into representations

26.—(1) The Secretary of State may make regulations requiring the case of each child who is being looked after by a local authority to be reviewed in accordance with the provisions of the regulations. **39-036**

(2) The regulations may, in particular, make provision—

(a) as to the manner in which each case is to be reviewed;

(b) as to the considerations to which the local authority are to have regard in reviewing each case;

(c) as to the time when each case is first to be reviewed and the frequency of subsequent reviews;

(d) requiring the authority, before conducting any review, to seek the views of—

(i) the child;

(ii) his parents;

(iii) any person who is not a parent of his but who has parental responsibility for him; and

(iv) any other person whose views the authority consider to be relevant,

including, in particular, the views of those persons in relation to any particular matter which is to be considered in the course of the review;

(e) requiring the authority to consider, in the case of a child who is in their care, whether an application should be made to discharge the care order;

(f) requiring the authority to consider, in the case of a child in accommodation provided by the authority, whether the accommodation accords with the requirements of this Part;

(g) requiring the authority to inform the child, so far as is reasonably practicable, of any steps he may take under this Act;

(h) requiring the authority to make arrangements, including arrangements with such other bodies providing services as it considers appropriate, to implement any decision which they propose to make in the course, or as a result, of the review;

(i) requiring the authority to notify details of the result of the review and of any decision taken by them in consequence of the review to—

(i) the child;

(ii) his parents;

(iii) any person who is not a parent of his but who has parental responsibility for him; and

(iv) any other person whom they consider ought to be notified;

(j) requiring the authority to monitor the arrangements which they have made with a view to ensuring that they comply with the regulations.

(3) Every local authority shall establish a procedure for considering any representations (including any complaint) made to them by—

(a) any child who is being looked after by them or who is not being looked after by them but is in need;

(b) a parent of his;

(c) any person who is not a parent of his but who has parental responsibility for him;

(d) any local authority foster parent;

(e) such other person as the authority consider has a sufficient interest in the child's welfare to warrant his representations being considered by them,

about the discharge by the authority of any of their functions under this Part in relation to the child.

(4) The procedure shall ensure that at least one person who is not a member or officer of the authority takes part in—

(a) the consideration; and

(b) any discussions which are held by the authority about the action (if any) to be taken in relation to the child in the light of the consideration.

(5) In carrying out any consideration of representations under this section a local authority shall comply with any regulations made by the Secretary of State for the purpose of regulating the procedure to be followed.

(6) The Secretary of State may make regulations requiring local authorities to monitor the arrangements that they have made with a view to ensuring that they comply with any regulations made for the purposes of subsection (5).

(7) Where any representation has been considered under the procedure established by a local authority under this section, the authority shall—

(a) have due regard to the findings of those considering the representation; and

(b) take such steps as are reasonably practicable to notify (in writing)—

(i) the person making the representation;

(ii) the child (if the authority consider that he has sufficient understanding); and

(iii) such other persons (if any) as appear to the authority to be likely to be affected,

of the authority's decision in the matter and their reasons for taking that decision and of any action which they have taken, or propose to take.

(8) Every local authority shall give such publicity to their procedure for considering representations under this section as they consider appropriate.

Co-operation between authorities

39-037 **27.**—(1) Where it appears to a local authority that any authority [...][1] mentioned in subsection (3) could, by taking any specified action, help in the exercise of any of their functions under this Part, they may request the help of that other authority [...][2], specifying the action in question.

(2) An authority whose help is so requested shall comply with the request if it is compatible with their own statutory or other duties and obligations and does not unduly prejudice the discharge of any of their functions.

[1] Words repealed by Courts and Legal Services Act 1990 c.41 Sch 20 para 1
[2] Words repealed by Courts and Legal Services Act 1990 c.41 Sch 20 para 1

(3) The [authorities][1] are—

(a) any local authority;

(b) any local education authority;

(c) any local housing authority;

(d) any [[Health Authority, Special Health Authority][2] [, Primary Care Trust][3] or National Health Service trust][4]; and

(e) any person authorised by the Secretary of State for the purposes of this section.

(4) [...][5]

Consultation with local education authorities

28.—(1) Where— **39-038**

(a) a child is being looked after by a local authority; and

(b) the authority propose to provide accommodation for him in an establishment at which education is provided for children who are accommodated there,

they shall, so far as is reasonably practicable, consult the appropriate local education authority before doing so.

(2) Where any such proposal is carried out, the local authority shall, as soon as is reasonably practicable, inform the appropriate local education authority of the arrangements that have been made for the child's accommodation.

(3) Where the child ceases to be accommodated as mentioned in subsection (1)(b), the local authority shall inform the appropriate local education authority.

(4) In this section "the appropriate local education authority" means—

(a) the local education authority within whose area the local authority's area falls; or,

(b) where the child has special educational needs and a statement of his needs is maintained under [Part IV of the Education Act 1996][6], the local education authority who maintain the statement.

Recoupment of cost of providing services etc

29.—(1) Where a local authority provide any service under section 17 or 18, **39-039**
other than advice, guidance or counselling, they may recover from a person specified in subsection (4) such charge for the service as they consider reasonable.

(2) Where the authority are satisfied that that person's means are insufficient for it to be reasonably practicable for him to pay the charge, they shall not require him to pay more than he can reasonably be expected to pay.

(3) No person shall be liable to pay any charge under subsection (1) [for a service provided under section 17 or section 18(1) or (5)][7]at any time when he is in receipt of income support [under][8] [Part VII of the Social Security Contributions and Benefits Act 1992][9][, of any element of child tax credit other than the family

[1] Word substituted by Courts and Legal Services Act 1990 c.41 Sch 16 (I) para 14 (b)

[2] Words substituted by Health Authorities Act 1995 c.17 Sch 1 (III) para 118 (5)

[3] Words inserted by SI 2000/90 Sch 1 para 24 (5)

[4] Words added by Courts and Legal Services Act 1990 c.41 Sch 16 (I) para 14 (b)

[5] Repealed by Education Act 1993 c.35 Sch 21 (II) para 1

[6] Words substituted by Education Act 1996 c.56 Sch 37 (I) para 84

[7] Words inserted by Local Government Act 2000 c.22 Pt V s 103 (1)

[8] Words substituted by Tax Credits Act 2002 (c.21) s 47 Sch 3 paras 15, 18 (a)

[9] Words substituted by Social Security (Consequential Provisions) Act 1992 (c.6) s 4 Sch 2 para 108 (b)

element, of working tax credit][1] [or of an income-based jobseeker's allowance][2].

[(3A) No person shall be liable to pay any charge under subsection (1) for a service provided under section 18(2) or (6) at any time when he is in receipt of income support under Part VII of the Social Security Contributions and Benefits Act 1992 or of an income-based jobseeker's allowance.][3]

[(3B) No person shall be liable to pay any charge under subsection (1) for a service provided under section 18(2) or (6) at any time when—

(a) he is in receipt of guarantee state pension credit under section 1(3)(a) of the State Pension Credit Act 2002, or

(b) he is a member of a married or unmarried couple (within the meaning of that Act) the other member of which is in receipt of guarantee state pension credit.][4]

(4) The persons are—

(a) where the service is provided for a child under sixteen, each of his parents;

(b) where it is provided for a child who has reached the age of sixteen, the child himself; and

(c) where it is provided for a member of the child's family, that member.

(5) Any charge under subsection (1) may, without prejudice to any other method of recovery, be recovered summarily as a civil debt.

(6) Part III of Schedule 2 makes provision in connection with contributions towards the maintenance of children who are being looked after by local authorities and consists of the re-enactment with modifications of provisions in Part V of the Child Care Act 1980.

(7) Where a local authority provide any accommodation under section 20(1) for a child who was (immediately before they began to look after him) ordinarily resident within the area of another local authority, they may recover from that other authority any reasonable expenses incurred by them in providing the accommodation and maintaining him.

(8) Where a local authority provide accommodation under section 21(1) or (2)(a) or (b) for a child who is ordinarily resident within the area of another local authority and they are not maintaining him in—

(a) a community home provided by them;

(b) a controlled community home; or

(c) a hospital vested in the Secretary of State [[or a Primary Care Trust][5] or any other hospital made available pursuant to arrangements made by [a Strategic Health Authority,][6] a][7][Health Authority][8][, or a Primary Care Trust][9],

they may recover from that other authority any reasonable expenses incurred by them in providing the accommodation and maintaining him.

(9) [Except where subsection (10) applies, where][10] a local authority comply with any request under section 27(2) in relation to a child or other person who is

[1] Words inserted by Tax Credits Act 2002 (c.21) s 47 Sch 3 paras 15, 18 (b)
[2] Words inserted by Jobseekers Act 1995 s 41 (4) Sch 2 para 19 (3)
[3] Inserted by Local Government Act 2000 c.22 Pt V s 103
[4] Added by State Pension Credit Act 2002 c.16 Sch 2 (3) para 30
[5] Words added by SI 2000/90 Sch 1 para 24 (6)
[6] Words inserted by SI 2002/2469 Sch 1 (1) para 16 (2)
[7] Words inserted by National Health Service and Community Care Act 1990 c.19 s 66 (1) Sch 9 para 36 (3)
[8] Words substituted by Health Authorities Act 1995 c.17 Sch 1 (III) para 118 (6)
[9] Words added by SI 2000/90 Sch 1 para 24 (6)
[10] Added by Children (Leaving Care) Act 2000 c.35 s 7 (3)

not ordinarily resident within their area, they may recover from the local authority in whose area the child or person is ordinarily resident any [reasonable expenses][1] incurred by them in respect of that person.

[(10) Where a local authority ("authority A") comply with any request under section 27(2) from another local authority ("authority B") in relation to a child or other person—

(a) whose responsible authority is authority B for the purposes of section 23B or 23C; or

(b) whom authority B are advising or befriending or to whom they are giving assistance by virtue of section 24(5)(a),

authority A may recover from authority B any reasonable expenses incurred by them in respect of that person.][2]

Miscellaneous

30.—(1) Nothing in this Part shall affect any duty imposed on a local authority by or under any other enactment. **39-040**

(2) Any question arising under section 20(2), 21(3) or 29(7) to (9) as to the ordinary residence of a child shall be determined by agreement between the local authorities concerned or, in default of agreement, by the Secretary of State.

(3) Where the functions conferred on a local authority by this Part and the functions of a local education authority are concurrent, the Secretary of State may by regulations provide by which authority the functions are to be exercised.

(4) The Secretary of State may make regulations for determining, as respects any local education authority functions specified in the regulations, whether a child who is being looked after by a local authority is to be treated, for purposes so specified, as a child of parents of sufficient resources or as a child of parents without resources.

PART IV

CARE AND SUPERVISION

General

Care and supervision orders

31.—(1) On the application of any local authority or authorised person, the court may make an order— **39-041**

(a) placing the child with respect to whom the application is made in the care of a designated local authority; or

(b) putting him under the supervision of a designated local authority [...][3].

(2) A court may only make a care order or supervision order if it is satisfied—

(a) that the child concerned is suffering, or is likely to suffer, significant harm; and

(b) that the harm, or likelihood of harm, is attributable to—

(i) the care given to the child, or likely to be given to him if the order were not made, not being what it would be reasonable to expect a parent to give to him; or

[1] Words substituted by Courts and Legal Services Act 1990 c.41 Sch 16 (I) para 15

[2] Added by Children (Leaving Care) Act 2000 c.35 s 7 (3)

[3] Words repealed by Criminal Justice and Court Services Act 2000 c.43 Sch 8 para 1

(ii) the child's being beyond parental control.

(3) No care order or supervision order may be made with respect to a child who has reached the age of seventeen (or sixteen, in the case of a child who is married).

(4) An application under this section may be made on its own or in any other family proceedings.

(5) The court may—

(a) on an application for a care order, make a supervision order;

(b) on an application for a supervision order, make a care order.

(6) Where an authorised person proposes to make an application under this section he shall—

(a) if it is reasonably practicable to do so; and

(b) before making the application,

consult the local authority appearing to him to be the authority in whose area the child concerned is ordinarily resident.

(7) An application made by an authorised person shall not be entertained by the court if, at the time when it is made, the child concerned is—

(a) the subject of an earlier application for a care order, or supervision order, which has not been disposed of; or

(b) subject to—

(i) a care order or supervision order;

(ii) an order under [section 63(1) of the Powers of Criminal Courts (Sentencing) Act 2000][1]; or

(iii) a supervision requirement within the meaning of [Part II of the Children (Scotland) Act 1995][2].

(8) The local authority designated in a care order must be—

(a) the authority within whose area the child is ordinarily resident; or

(b) where the child does not reside in the area of a local authority, the authority within whose area any circumstances arose in consequence of which the order is being made.

(9) In this section—

"authorised person" means —

(a) the National Society for the Prevention of Cruelty to Children and any of its officers; and

(b) any person authorised by order of the Secretary of State to bring proceedings under this section and any officer of a body which is so authorised;

"harm" means ill-treatment or the impairment of health or development;

"development" means physical, intellectual, emotional, social or behavioural development;

"health" means physical or mental health; and

"ill-treatment" includes sexual abuse and forms of ill-treatment which are not physical.

(10) Where the question of whether harm suffered by a child is significant turns on the child's health or development, his health or development shall be compared with that which could reasonably be expected of a similar child.

(11) In this Act—

[1] Words substituted by Powers of Criminal Courts (Sentencing) Act 2000 c.6 Sch 9 para 127

[2] Words substituted by Children (Scotland) Act 1995 c.36 Sch 4 para 48 (2)

"a care order" means (subject to section 105(1)) an order under subsection (1)(a) and (except where express provision to the contrary is made) includes an interim care order made under section 38; and

"a supervision order" means an order under subsection (1)(b) and (except where express provision to the contrary is made) includes an interim supervision order made under section 38.

Period within which application for order under this Part must be disposed of

32.—(1) A court hearing an application for an order under this Part shall (in the light of any rules made by virtue of subsection (2))— **39-042**

(a) draw up a timetable with a view to disposing of the application without delay; and

(b) give such directions as it considers appropriate for the purpose of ensuring, so far as is reasonably practicable, that that timetable is adhered to.

(2) Rules of court may—

(a) specify periods within which specified steps must be taken in relation to such proceedings; and

(b) make other provision with respect to such proceedings for the purpose of ensuring, so far as is reasonably practicable, that they are disposed of without delay.

Care orders

Effect of care order

33.—(1) Where a care order is made with respect to a child it shall be the duty of the local authority designated by the order to receive the child into their care and to keep him in their care while the order remains in force. **39-043**

(2) Where—

(a) a care order has been made with respect to a child on the application of an authorised person; but

(b) the local authority designated by the order was not informed that that person proposed to make the application,

the child may be kept in the care of that person until received into the care of the authority.

(3) While a care order is in force with respect to a child, the local authority designated by the order shall—

(a) have parental responsibility for the child; and

(b) have the power (subject to the following provisions of this section) to determine the extent to which a parent or guardian of the child may meet his parental responsibility for him.

(4) The authority may not exercise the power in subsection (3)(b) unless they are satisfied that it is necessary to do so in order to safeguard or promote the child's welfare.

(5) Nothing in subsection (3)(b) shall prevent a parent or guardian of the child who has care of him from doing what is reasonable in all the circumstances of the case for the purpose of safeguarding or promoting his welfare.

(6) While a care order is in force with respect to a child, the local authority designated by the order shall not—

(a) cause the child to be brought up in any religious persuasion other than that in which he would have been brought up if the order had not been made; or

(b) have the right—

(i) to consent or refuse to consent to the making of an application with respect to the child under section 18 of the Adoption Act 1976;

(ii) to agree or refuse to agree to the making of an adoption order, or an order under section 55 of the Act of 1976, with respect to the child; or

(iii) to appoint a guardian for the child.

(7) While a care order is in force with respect to a child, no person may—

(a) cause the child to be known by a new surname; or

(b) remove him from the United Kingdom,

without either the written consent of every person who has parental responsibility for the child or the leave of the court.

(8) Subsection (7)(b) does not—

(a) prevent the removal of such a child, for a period of less than one month, by the authority in whose care he is; or

(b) apply to arrangements for such a child to live outside England and Wales (which are governed by paragraph 19 of Schedule 2).

(9) The power in subsection (3)(b) is subject (in addition to being subject to the provisions of this section) to any right, duty, power, responsibility or authority which a parent or guardian of the child has in relation to the child and his property by virtue of any other enactment.

Parental contact etc. with children in care

39-044 **34.**—(1) Where a child is in the care of a local authority, the authority shall (subject to the provisions of this section) allow the child reasonable contact with—

(a) his parents;

(b) any guardian of his;

(c) where there was a residence order in force with respect to the child immediately before the care order was made, the person in whose favour the order was made; and

(d) where, immediately before the care order was made, a person had care of the child by virtue of an order made in the exercise of the High Court's inherent jurisdiction with respect to children, that person.

(2) On an application made by the authority or the child, the court may make such order as it considers appropriate with respect to the contact which is to be allowed between the child and any named person.

(3) On an application made by—

(a) any person mentioned in paragraphs (a) to (d) of subsection (1); or

(b) any person who has obtained the leave of the court to make the application,

the court may make such order as it considers appropriate with respect to the contact which is to be allowed between the child and that person.

(4) On an application made by the authority or the child, the court may make an order authorising the authority to refuse to allow contact between the child and any person who is mentioned in paragraphs (a) to (d) of subsection (1) and named in the order.

(5) When making a care order with respect to a child, or in any family proceedings in connection with a child who is in the care of a local authority, the court may make an order under this section, even though no application for such an order has been made with respect to the child, if it considers that the order should be made.

(6) An authority may refuse to allow the contact that would otherwise be required by virtue of subsection (1) or an order under this section if—

(a) they are satisfied that it is necessary to do so in order to safeguard or promote the child's welfare; and

(b) the refusal—

(i) is decided upon as a matter of urgency; and

(ii) does not last for more than seven days.

(7) An order under this section may impose such conditions as the court considers appropriate.

(8) The Secretary of State may by regulations make provision as to—

(a) the steps to be taken by a local authority who have exercised their powers under subsection (6);

(b) the circumstances in which, and conditions subject to which, the terms of any order under this section may be departed from by agreement between the local authority and the person in relation to whom the order is made;

(c) notification by a local authority of any variation or suspension of arrangements made (otherwise than under an order under this section) with a view to affording any person contact with a child to whom this section applies.

(9) The court may vary or discharge any order made under this section on the application of the authority, the child concerned or the person named in the order.

(10) An order under this section may be made either at the same time as the care order itself or later.

(11) Before making a care order with respect to any child the court shall—

(a) consider the arrangements which the authority have made, or propose to make, for affording any person contact with a child to whom this section applies; and

(b) invite the parties to the proceedings to comment on those arrangements.

Supervision orders

Supervision orders

35.—(1) While a supervision order is in force it shall be the duty of the supervisor— **39-045**

(a) to advise, assist and befriend the supervised child;

(b) to take such steps as are reasonably necessary to give effect to the order; and

(c) where—

(i) the order is not wholly complied with; or

(ii) the supervisor considers that the order may no longer be necessary.

to consider whether or not to apply to the court for its variation or discharge.

(2) Parts I and II of Schedule 3 make further provision with respect to supervision orders.

Education supervision orders

39-046 **36.**—(1) On the application of any local education authority, the court may make an order putting the child with respect to whom the application is made under the supervision of a designated local education authority.

(2) In this Act "an education supervision order" means an order under subsection (1).

(3) A court may only make an education supervision order if it is satisfied that the child concerned is of compulsory school age and is not being properly educated.

(4) For the purposes of this section, a child is being properly educated only if he is receiving efficient full-time education suitable to his age, ability and aptitude and any special educational needs he may have.

(5) Where a child is—

(a) the subject of a school attendance order which is in force under [section 437 of the Education Act 1996][1] and which has not been complied with; or

(b) a registered pupil at a school which he is not attending regularly within the meaning of [section 444][2] of that Act,

then, unless it is proved that he is being properly educated, it shall be assumed that he is not.

(6) An education supervision order may not be made with respect to a child who is in the care of a local authority.

(7) The local education authority designated in an education supervision order must be—

(a) the authority within whose area the child concerned is living or will live; or

(b) where—

(i) the child is a registered pupil at a school; and

(ii) the authority mentioned in paragraph (a) and the authority within whose area the school is situated agree,

the latter authority.

(8) Where a local education authority propose to make an application for an education supervision order they shall, before making the application, consult the [...][3]appropriate local authority.

(9) The appropriate local authority is—

(a) in the case of a child who is being provided with accommodation by, or on behalf of, a local authority, that authority; and

(b) in any other case, the local authority within whose area the child concerned lives, or will live.

(10) Part III of Schedule 3 makes further provision with respect to education supervision orders.

---

[1] Words substituted by Education Act 1996 c.56 Sch 37 (I) para 85 (a)
[2] Words substituted by Education Act 1996 c.56 Sch 37 (I) para 85 (b)
[3] Words repealed by Education Act 1993 c.35 Sch 21 (II) para 1

Powers of court

Powers of court in certain family proceedings

37.—(1) Where, in any family proceedings in which a question arises with respect to the welfare of any child, it appears to the court that it may be appropriate for a care or supervision order to be made with respect to him, the court may direct the appropriate authority to undertake an investigation of the child's circumstances. **39-047**

(2) Where the court gives a direction under this section the local authority concerned shall, when undertaking the investigation, consider whether they should—

(a) apply for a care order or for a supervision order with respect to the child;

(b) provide services or assistance for the child or his family; or

(c) take any other action with respect to the child.

(3) Where a local authority undertake an investigation under this section, and decide not to apply for a care order or supervision order with respect to the child concerned, they shall inform the court of—

(a) their reasons for so deciding;

(b) any service or assistance which they have provided, or intend to provide, for the child and his family; and

(c) any other action which they have taken, or propose to take, with respect to the child.

(4) The information shall be given to the court before the end of the period of eight weeks beginning with the date of the direction, unless the court otherwise directs.

(5) The local authority named in a direction under subsection (1) must be—

(a) the authority in whose area the child is ordinarily resident; or

(b) where the child [is not ordinarily resident][1] in the area of a local authority, the authority within whose area any circumstances arose in consequence of which the direction is being given.

(6) If, on the conclusion of any investigation or review under this section, the authority decide not to apply for a care order or supervision order with respect to the child—

(a) they shall consider whether it would be appropriate to review the case at a later date; and

(b) if they decide that it would be, they shall determine the date on which that review is to begin.

Interim orders

38.—(1) Where— **39-048**

(a) in any proceedings on an application for a care order or supervision order, the proceedings are adjourned; or

(b) the court gives a direction under section 37(1),

the court may make an interim care order or an interim supervision order with respect to the child concerned.

(2) A court shall not make an interim care order or interim supervision order under this section unless it is satisfied that there are reasonable grounds for believing that the circumstances with respect to the child are as mentioned in section 31(2).

[1] Words substituted by Courts and Legal Services Act 1990 c.41 Sch 16 (I) para 16

(3) Where, in any proceedings on an application for a care order or supervision order, a court makes a residence order with respect to the child concerned, it shall also make an interim supervision order with respect to him unless satisfied that his welfare will be satisfactorily safeguarded without an interim order being made.

(4) An interim order made under or by virtue of this section shall have effect for such period as may be specified in the order, but shall in any event cease to have effect on whichever of the following events first occurs—

(a) the expiry of the period of eight weeks beginning with the date on which the order is made;
(b) if the order is the second or subsequent such order made with respect to the same child in the same proceedings, the expiry of the relevant period;
(c) in a case which falls within subsection (1)(a), the disposal of the application;
(d) in a case which falls within subsection (1)(b), the disposal of an application for a care order or supervision order made by the authority with respect to the child;
(e) in a case which falls within subsection (1)(b) and in which—
    (i) the court has given a direction under section 37(4), but
    (ii) no application for a care order or supervision order has been made with respect to the child,

the expiry of the period fixed by that direction.

(5) In subsection (4)(b) "the relevant period" means —

(a) the period of four weeks beginning with the date on which the order in question is made; or
(b) the period of eight weeks beginning with the date on which the first order was made if that period ends later than the period mentioned in paragraph (a).

(6) Where the court makes an interim care order, or interim supervision order, it may give such directions (if any) as it considers appropriate with regard to the medical or psychiatric examination or other assessment of the child; but if the child is of sufficient understanding to make an informed decision he may refuse to submit to the examination or other assessment.

(7) A direction under subsection (6) may be to the effect that there is to be—

(a) no such examination or assessment; or
(b) no such examination or assessment unless the court directs otherwise.

(8) A direction under subsection (6) may be—

(a) given when the interim order is made or at any time while it is in force; and
(b) varied at any time on the application of any person falling within any class of person prescribed by rules of court for the purposes of this subsection.

(9) Paragraphs 4 and 5 of Schedule 3 shall not apply in relation to an interim supervision order.

(10) Where a court makes an order under or by virtue of this section it shall, in determining the period for which the order is to be in force, consider whether any party who was, or might have been, opposed to the making of the order was in a position to argue his case against the order in full.

[Power to include exclusion requirement in interim care order

39-049 **38A.**—(1) Where—

(a) on being satisfied that there are reasonable grounds for believing that the circumstances with respect to a child are as mentioned in section 31(2)(a) and (b)(i), the court makes an interim care order with respect to a child, and

(b) the conditions mentioned in subsection (2) are satisfied,

the court may include an exclusion requirement in the interim care order.

(2) The conditions are—

(a) that there is reasonable cause to believe that, if a person ("the relevant person") is excluded from a dwelling-house in which the child lives, the child will cease to suffer, or cease to be likely to suffer, significant harm, and

(b) that another person living in the dwelling-house (whether a parent of the child or some other person)—

(i) is able and willing to give to the child the care which it would be reasonable to expect a parent to give him, and

(ii) consents to the inclusion of the exclusion requirement.

(3) For the purposes of this section an exclusion requirement is any one or more of the following—

(a) a provision requiring the relevant person to leave a dwelling-house in which he is living with the child,

(b) a provision prohibiting the relevant person from entering a dwelling-house in which the child lives, and

(c) a provision excluding the relevant person from a defined area in which a dwelling-house in which the child lives is situated.

(4) The court may provide that the exclusion requirement is to have effect for a shorter period than the other provisions of the interim care order.

(5) Where the court makes an interim care order containing an exclusion requirement, the court may attach a power of arrest to the exclusion requirement.

(6) Where the court attaches a power of arrest to an exclusion requirement of an interim care order, it may provide that the power of arrest is to have effect for a shorter period than the exclusion requirement.

(7) Any period specified for the purposes of subsection (4) or (6) may be extended by the court (on one or more occasions) on an application to vary or discharge the interim care order.

(8) Where a power of arrest is attached to an exclusion requirement of an interim care order by virtue of subsection (5) a constable may arrest without warrant any person whom he has reasonable cause to believe to be in breach of the requirement.

(9) Sections 47(7), (11) and (12) and 48 of, and Schedule 5 to, the Family Law Act 1996 shall have effect in relation to a person arrested under subsection (8) of this section as they have effect in relation to a person arrested under section 47(6) of that Act.

(10) If, while an interim care order containing an exclusion requirement is in force, the local authority have removed the child from the dwelling-house from which the relevant person is excluded to other accommodation for a continuous period of more than 24 hours, the interim care order shall cease to have effect in so far as it imposes the exclusion requirement.][1]

[1] Added by Family Law Act 1996 c.27 Sch 6 para 1

[Undertakings relating to interim care orders

39-050 **38B.**—(1) In any case where the court has power to include an exclusion requirement in an interim care order, the court may accept an undertaking from the relevant person.

(2) No power of arrest may be attached to any undertaking given under subsection (1).

(3) An undertaking given to a court under subsection (1)—

(a) shall be enforceable as if were an order of the court, and

(b) shall cease to have effect if, while it is in force, the local authority have removed the child from the dwelling-house from which the relevant person is excluded to other accommodation for a continuous period of more than 24 hours.

(4) This section has effect without prejudice to the powers of the High Court and county court apart from this section.

(5) In this section "exclusion requirement" and "relevant person" have the same meaning as in section 38A.][1]

Discharge and variation etc. of care orders and supervision orders

39-051 **39.**—(1) A care order may be discharged by the court on the application of—

(a) any person who has parental responsibility for the child;

(b) the child himself; or

(c) the local authority designated by the order.

(2) A supervision order may be varied or discharged by the court on the application of—

(a) any person who has parental responsibility for the child;

(b) the child himself; or

(c) the supervisor.

(3) On the application of a person who is not entitled to apply for the order to be discharged, but who is a person with whom the child is living, a supervision order may be varied by the court in so far as it imposes a requirement which affects that person.

[(3A) On the application of a person who is not entitled to apply for the order to be discharged, but who is a person to whom an exclusion requirement contained in the order applies, an interim care order may be varied or discharged by the court in so far as it imposes the exclusion requirement.

(3B) Where a power of arrest has been attached to an exclusion requirement of an interim care order, the court may, on the application of any person entitled to apply for the discharge of the order so far as it imposes the exclusion requirement, vary or discharge the order in so far as it confers a power of arrest (whether or not any application has been made to vary or discharge any other provision of the order).][2]

(4) Where a care order is in force with respect to a child the court may, on the application of any person entitled to apply for the order to be discharged, substitute a supervision order for the care order.

(5) When a court is considering whether to substitute one order for another under subsection (4) any provision of this Act which would otherwise require section 31(2) to be satisfied at the time when the proposed order is substituted or made shall be disregarded.

[1] Added by Family Law Act 1996 c.27 Sch 6 para 1
[2] Added by Family Law Act 1996 c.27 Sch 6 para 2

Orders pending appeals in cases about care or supervision orders

40.—(1) Where— 39-052

(a) a court dismisses an application for a care order; and

(b) at the time when the court dismisses the application, the child concerned is the subject of an interim care order,

the court may make a care order with respect to the child to have effect subject to such directions (if any) as the court may see fit to include in the order.

(2) Where—

(a) a court dismisses an application for a care order, or an application for a supervision order; and

(b) at the time when the court dismisses the application, the child concerned is the subject of an interim supervision order,

the court may make a supervision order with respect to the child to have effect subject to such directions (if any) as the court may see fit to include in the order.

(3) Where a court grants an application to discharge a care order or supervision order, it may order that—

(a) its decision is not to have effect; or

(b) the care order, or supervision order, is to continue to have effect but subject to such directions as the court sees fit to include in the order.

(4) An order made under this section shall only have effect for such period, not exceeding the appeal period, as may be specified in the order.

(5) Where—

(a) an appeal is made against any decision of a court under this section; or

(b) any application is made to the appellate court in connection with a proposed appeal against that decision,

the appellate court may extend the period for which the order in question is to have effect, but not so as to extend it beyond the end of the appeal period.

(6) In this section "the appeal period" means—

(a) where an appeal is made against the decision in question, the period between the making of that decision and the determination of the appeal; and

(b) otherwise, the period during which an appeal may be made against the decision.

Guardians ad litem

[Representation of child.][1]

41.—(1) For the purpose of any specified proceedings, the court shall appoint [an officer of the Service][2] for the child concerned unless satisfied that it is not necessary to do so in order to safeguard his interests. 39-053

(2) The [officer of the Service][3] shall—

(a) be appointed in accordance with rules of court; and

(b) be under a duty to safeguard the interests of the child in the manner prescribed by such rules.

(3) Where—

(a) the child concerned is not represented by a solicitor; and

(b) any of the conditions mentioned in subsection (4) is satisfied,

1 Substituted by Criminal Justice and Court Services Act 2000 c.43 Sch 7 (II) para 91 (e)

2 Words substituted by Criminal Justice and Court Services Act 2000 c.43 Sch 7 (II) para 91 (a)

3 Words substituted by Criminal Justice and Court Services Act 2000 c.43 Sch 7 (II) para 91 (b)

the court may appoint a solicitor to represent him.

(4) The conditions are that—

(a) no [officer of the Service][1] has been appointed for the child;

(b) the child has sufficient understanding to instruct a solicitor and wishes to do so;

(c) it appears to the court that it would be in the child's best interests for him to be represented by a solicitor.

(5) Any solicitor appointed under or by virtue of this section shall be appointed, and shall represent the child, in accordance with rules of court.

(6) In this section "specified proceedings" means any proceedings—

(a) on an application for a care order or supervision order;

(b) in which the court has given a direction under section 37(1) and has made, or is considering whether to make, an interim care order;

(c) on an application for the discharge of a care order or the variation or discharge of a supervision order;

(d) on an application under section 39(4);

(e) in which the court is considering whether to make a residence order with respect to a child who is the subject of a care order;

(f) with respect to contact between a child who is the subject of a care order and any other person;

(g) under Part V;

(h) on an appeal against—

(i) the making of, or refusal to make, a care order, supervision order or any order under section 34;

(ii) the making of, or refusal to make, a residence order with respect to a child who is the subject of a care order; or

(iii) the variation or discharge, or refusal of an application to vary or discharge, an order of a kind mentioned in sub-paragraph (i) or (ii);

(iv) the refusal of an application under section 39(4); or

(v) the making of, or refusal to make, an order under Part V; or

(i) which are specified for the time being, for the purposes of this section, by rules of court.

(7) [...][2]

(8) [...][3]

(9) [...][4]

(10) Rules of court may make provision as to—

(a) the assistance which any [officer of the Service][5] may be required by the court to give to it;

(b) the consideration to be given by any [officer of the Service][6], where an order of a specified kind has been made in the proceedings in question, as to whether to apply for the variation or discharge of the order;

(c) the participation of [officers of the Service][7] in reviews, of a kind specified in the rules, which are conducted by the court.

(11) Regardless of any enactment or rule of law which would otherwise prevent it from doing so, the court may take account of—

[1] Words substituted by Criminal Justice and Court Services Act 2000 c.43 Sch 7 (II) para 91 (b)
[2] Repealed by Criminal Justice and Court Services Act 2000 c.43 Sch 8 para 1
[3] Repealed by Criminal Justice and Court Services Act 2000 c.43 Sch 8 para 1
[4] Repealed by Criminal Justice and Court Services Act 2000 c.43 Sch 8 para 1
[5] Substituted by Criminal Justice and Court Services Act 2000 c.43 Sch 7 (II) para 91 (b)
[6] Substituted by Criminal Justice and Court Services Act 2000 c.43 Sch 7 (II) para 91 (b)
[7] Words substituted by Criminal Justice and Court Services Act 2000 c.43 Sch 7 (II) para 91 (c)

(a) any statement contained in a report made by [an officer of the Service][1] who is appointed under this section for the purpose of the proceedings in question; and

(b) any evidence given in respect of the matters referred to in the report,

in so far as the statement or evidence is, in the opinion of the court, relevant to the question which the court is considering.[...][2]

[Right of officer of the Service to have access to local authority records.][3]

42.—(1) Where [an officer of the Service][4] has been appointed [under section 41][5] he shall have the right at all reasonable times to examine and take copies of— **39-054**

(a) any records of, or held by, a local authority [or an authorised person][6] which were compiled in connection with the making, or proposed making, by any person of any application under this Act with respect to the child concerned; [...][7]

(b) any [...][8]records of, or held by, a local authority which were compiled in connection with any functions which stand referred to their social services committee under the Local Authority Social Services Act 1970, so far as those records relate to that child; or

[(c) any records of, or held by, an authorised person which were compiled in connection with the activities of that person, so far as those records relate to that child.][9]

(2) Where [an officer of the Service][10] takes a copy of any record which he is entitled to examine under this section, that copy or any part of it shall be admissible as evidence of any matter referred to in any—

(a) report which he makes to the court in the proceedings in question; or

(b) evidence which he gives in those proceedings.

(3) Subsection (2) has effect regardless of any enactment or rule of law which would otherwise prevent the record in question being admissible in evidence.

[(4) In this section "authorised person" has the same meaning as in section 31.][11]

PART V

PROTECTION OF CHILDREN

Child assessment orders

43.—(1) On the application of a local authority or authorised person for an order to be made under this section with respect to a child, the court may make the order if, but only if, it is satisfied that— **39-055**

---

[1] Words substituted by Criminal Justice and Court Services Act 2000 c.43 Sch 7 (II) para 91 (a)
[2] Repealed by Criminal Justice and Court Services Act 2000 c.43 Sch 8 para 1
[3] Substituted by Criminal Justice and Court Services Act 2000 c.43 Sch 7 (II) para 92 (c)
[4] Words substituted by Criminal Justice and Court Services Act 2000 c.43 Sch 7 (II) para 92 (a) (i)
[5] Words substituted by Criminal Justice and Court Services Act 2000 c.43 Sch 7 (II) para 92 (a) (ii)
[6] Words added by Courts and Legal Services Act 1990 c.41 Sch 16 (I) para 18 (2)
[7] Word repealed by Courts and Legal Services Act 1990 c.41 Sch 20 para 1
[8] Word repealed by Courts and Legal Services Act 1990 c.41 Sch 20 para 1
[9] Inserted by Courts and Legal Services Act 1990 c.41 Sch 16 (I) para 18 (3)
[10] Words substituted by Criminal Justice and Court Services Act 2000 c.43 Sch 7 (II) para 92 (b)
[11] Added by Courts and Legal Services Act 1990 c.41 Sch 16 (I) para 18 (4)

(a) the applicant has reasonable cause to suspect that the child is suffering, or is likely to suffer, significant harm;

(b) an assessment of the state of the child's health or development, or of the way in which he has been treated, is required to enable the applicant to determine whether or not the child is suffering, or is likely to suffer, significant harm; and

(c) it is unlikely that such an assessment will be made, or be satisfactory, in the absence of an order under this section.

(2) In this Act "a child assessment order" means an order under this section.

(3) A court may treat an application under this section as an application for an emergency protection order.

(4) No court shall make a child assessment order if it is satisfied—

(a) that there are grounds for making an emergency protection order with respect to the child; and

(b) that it ought to make such an order rather than a child assessment order.

(5) A child assessment order shall—

(a) specify the date by which the assessment is to begin; and

(b) have effect for such period, not exceeding 7 days beginning with that date, as may be specified in the order.

(6) Where a child assessment order is in force with respect to a child it shall be the duty of any person who is in a position to produce the child—

(a) to produce him to such person as may be named in the order; and

(b) to comply with such directions relating to the assessment of the child as the court thinks fit to specify in the order.

(7) A child assessment order authorises any person carrying out the assessment, or any part of the assessment, to do so in accordance with the terms of the order.

(8) Regardless of subsection (7), if the child is of sufficient understanding to make an informed decision he may refuse to submit to a medical or psychiatric examination or other assessment.

(9) The child may only be kept away from home—

(a) in accordance with directions specified in the order;

(b) if it is necessary for the purposes of the assessment; and

(c) for such period or periods as may be specified in the order.

(10) Where the child is to be kept away from home, the order shall contain such directions as the court thinks fit with regard to the contact that he must be allowed to have with other persons while away from home.

(11) Any person making an application for a child assessment order shall take such steps as are reasonably practicable to ensure that notice of the application is given to—

(a) the child's parents;

(b) any person who is not a parent of his but who has parental responsibility for him;

(c) any other person caring for the child;

(d) any person in whose favour a contact order is in force with respect to the child;

(e) any person who is allowed to have contact with the child by virtue of an order under section 34; and

(f) the child,

before the hearing of the application.

(12) Rules of court may make provision as to the circumstances in which—

(a) any of the persons mentioned in subsection (11); or

(b) such other person as may be specified in the rules,

may apply to the court for a child assessment order to be varied or discharged.

(13) In this section "authorised person" means a person who is an authorised person for the purposes of section 31.

Orders for emergency protection of children

44.—(1) Where any person ("the applicant") applies to the court for an order to be made under this section with respect to a child, the court may make the order if, but only if, it is satisfied that— **39-056**

(a) there is reasonable cause to believe that the child is likely to suffer significant harm if—

(i) he is not removed to accommodation provided by or on behalf of the applicant; or

(ii) he does not remain in the place in which he is then being accommodated;

(b) in the case of an application made by a local authority—

(i) enquiries are being made with respect to the child under section 47(1)(b); and

(ii) those enquiries are being frustrated by access to the child being unreasonably refused to a person authorised to seek access and that the applicant has reasonable cause to believe that access to the child is required as a matter of urgency; or

(c) in the case of an application made by an authorised person—

(i) the applicant has reasonable cause to suspect that a child is suffering, or is likely to suffer, significant harm;

(ii) the applicant is making enquiries with respect to the child's welfare; and

(iii) those enquiries are being frustrated by access to the child being unreasonably refused to a person authorised to seek access and the applicant has reasonable cause to believe that access to the child is required as a matter of urgency.

(2) In this section—

(a) "authorised person" means a person who is an authorised person for the purposes of section 31; and

(b) "a person authorised to seek access" means—

(i) in the case of an application by a local authority, an officer of the local authority or a person authorised by the authority to act on their behalf in connection with the enquiries; or

(ii) in the case of an application by an authorised person, that person.

(3) Any person—

(a) seeking access to a child in connection with enquiries of a kind mentioned in subsection (1); and

(b) purporting to be a person authorised to do so,

shall, on being asked to do so, produce some duly authenticated document as evidence that he is such a person.

(4) While an order under this section ("an emergency protection order") is in force it—

(a) operates as a direction to any person who is in a position to do so to comply with any request to produce the child to the applicant;

(b) authorises—

(i) the removal of the child at any time to accommodation provided by or on behalf of the applicant and his being kept there; or
(ii) the prevention of the child's removal from any hospital, or other place, in which he was being accommodated immediately before the making of the order; and

(c) gives the applicant parental responsibility for the child.

(5) Where an emergency protection order is in force with respect to a child, the applicant—

(a) shall only exercise the power given by virtue of subsection (4)(b) in order to safeguard the welfare of the child;
(b) shall take, and shall only take, such action in meeting his parental responsibility for the child as is reasonably required to safeguard or promote the welfare of the child (having regard in particular to the duration of the order); and
(c) shall comply with the requirements of any regulations made by the Secretary of State for the purposes of this subsection.

(6) Where the court makes an emergency protection order, it may give such directions (if any) as it considers appropriate with respect to—

(a) the contact which is, or is not, to be allowed between the child and any named person;
(b) the medical or psychiatric examination or other assessment of the child.

(7) Where any direction is given under subsection (6)(b), the child may, if he is of sufficient understanding to make an informed decision, refuse to submit to the examination or other assessment.

(8) A direction under subsection (6)(a) may impose conditions and one under subsection (6)(b) may be to the effect that there is to be—

(a) no such examination or assessment; or
(b) no such examination or assessment unless the court directs otherwise.

(9) A direction under subsection (6) may be—

(a) given when the emergency protection order is made or at any time while it is in force; and
(b) varied at any time on the application of any person falling within any class of person prescribed by rules of court for the purposes of this subsection.

(10) Where an emergency protection order is in force with respect to a child and—

(a) the applicant has exercised the power given by subsection (4)(b)(i) but it appears to him that it is safe for the child to be returned; or
(b) the applicant has exercised the power given by subsection (4)(b)(ii) but it appears to him that it is safe for the child to be allowed to be removed from the place in question,

he shall return the child or (as the case may be) allow him to be removed.

(11) Where he is required by subsection (10) to return the child the applicant shall—

(a) return him to the care of the person from whose care he was removed; or
(b) if that is not reasonably practicable, return him to the care of—
(i) a parent of his;
(ii) any person who is not a parent of his but who has parental responsibility for him; or

(iii) such other person as the applicant (with the agreement of the court) considers appropriate.

(12) Where the applicant has been required by subsection (10) to return the child, or to allow him to be removed, he may again exercise his powers with respect to the child (at any time while the emergency protection order remains in force) if it appears to him that a change in the circumstances of the case makes it necessary for him to do so.

(13) Where an emergency protection order has been made with respect to a child, the applicant shall, subject to any direction given under subsection (6), allow the child reasonable contact with—

(a) his parents;
(b) any person who is not a parent of his but who has parental responsibility for him;
(c) any person with whom he was living immediately before the making of the order;
(d) any person in whose favour a contact order is in force with respect to him;
(e) any person who is allowed to have contact with the child by virtue of an order under section 34; and
(f) any person acting on behalf of any of those persons.

(14) Wherever it is reasonably practicable to do so, an emergency protection order shall name the child; and where it does not name him it shall describe him as clearly as possible.

(15) A person shall be guilty of an offence if he intentionally obstructs any person exercising the power under subsection (4)(b) to remove, or prevent the removal of, a child.

(16) A person guilty of an offence under subsection (15) shall be liable on summary conviction to a fine not exceeding level 3 on the standard scale.

[Power to include exclusion requirement in emergency protection order

44A.—(1) Where— **39-057**

(a) on being satisfied as mentioned in section 44(1)(a), (b) or (c), the court makes an emergency protection order with respect to a child, and
(b) the conditions mentioned in subsection (2) are satisfied,

the court may include an exclusion requirement in the emergency protection order.

(2) The conditions are—

(a) that there is reasonable cause to believe that, if a person ("the relevant person") is excluded from a dwelling-house in which the child lives, then—
    (i) in the case of an order made on the ground mentioned in section 44(1)(a), the child will not be likely to suffer significant harm, even though the child is not removed as mentioned in section 44(1)(a)(i) or does not remain as mentioned in section 44(1)(a)(ii), or
    (ii) in the case of an order made on the ground mentioned in paragraph (b) or (c) of section 44(1) the enquires referred to in that paragraph will cease to be frustrated, and
(b) that another person living in the dwelling-house (whether a parent of the child or some other person)—
    (i) is able and willing to give to the child the care which it would be reasonable to expect a parent to give him, and

(ii) consents to the inclusion of the exclusion requirement.

(3) For the purposes of this section an exclusion requirement is any one or more of the following—

(a) a provision requiring the relevant person to leave a dwelling-house in which he is living with the child,

(b) a provision prohibiting the relevant person from entering a dwelling-house in which the child lives, and

(c) a provision excluding the relevant person from a defined area in which a dwelling-house in which the child lives is situated.

(4) The court may provide that the exclusion requirement is to have effect for a shorter period than the other provisions of the order.

(5) Where the court makes an emergency protection order containing an exclusion requirement, the court may attach a power of arrest to the exclusion requirement.

(6) Where the court attaches a power of arrest to an exclusion requirement of an emergency protection order, it may provide that the power of arrest is to have effect for a shorter period than the exclusion requirement.

(7) Any period specified for the purposes of subsection (4) or (6) may be extended by the court (on one or more occasions) on an application to vary or discharge the emergency protection order.

(8) Where a power of arrest is attached to an exclusion requirement of an emergency protection order by virtue of subsection (5), a constable may arrest without warrant any person whom he has reasonable cause to believe to be in breach of the requirement.

(9) Sections 47(7), (11) and (12) and 48 of, and Schedule 5 to, the Family Law Act 1996 shall have effect in relation to a person arrested under subsection (8) of this section as they have effect in relation to a person arrested under section 47(6) of that Act.

(10) If, while an emergency protection order containing an exclusion requirement is in force, the applicant has removed the child from the dwelling-house from which the relevant person is excluded to other accommodation for a continuous period of more than 24 hours, the order shall cease to have effect in so far as it imposes the exclusion requirement.][1]

[Undertakings relating to emergency protection orders

39-058 **44B.**—(1) In any case where the court has power to include an exclusion requirement in an emergency protection order, the court may accept an undertaking from the relevant person.

(2) No power of arrest may be attached to any undertaking given under subsection (1).

(3) An undertaking given to a court under subsection (1)—

(a) shall be enforceable as if it were an order of the court, and

(b) shall cease to have effect if, while it is in force, the applicant has removed the child from the dwelling-house from which the relevant person is excluded to other accommodation for a continuous period of more than 24 hours.

(4) This section has effect without prejudice to the powers of the High Court and county court apart from this section.

(5) In this section "exclusion requirement" and "relevant person" have the same meaning as in section 44A.][2]

[1] Added by Family Law Act 1996 c.27 Sch 6 para 3
[2] Added by Family Law Act 1996 c.27 Sch 6 para 3

Duration of emergency protection orders and other supplemental provisions

45.—(1) An emergency protection order shall have effect for such period, not exceeding eight days, as may be specified in the order. **39-059**

(2) Where—

(a) the court making an emergency protection order would, but for this subsection, specify a period of eight days as the period for which the order is to have effect; but

(b) the last of those eight days is a public holiday (that is to say, Christmas Day, Good Friday, a bank holiday or a Sunday),

the court may specify a period which ends at noon on the first later day which is not such a holiday.

(3) Where an emergency protection order is made on an application under section 46(7), the period of eight days mentioned in subsection (1) shall begin with the first day on which the child was taken into police protection under section 46.

(4) Any person who—

(a) has parental responsibility for a child as the result of an emergency protection order; and

(b) is entitled to apply for a care order with respect to the child,

may apply to the court for the period during which the emergency protection order is to have effect to be extended.

(5) On an application under subsection (4) the court may extend the period during which the order is to have effect by such period, not exceeding seven days, as it thinks fit, but may do so only if it has reasonable cause to believe that the child concerned is likely to suffer significant harm if the order is not extended.

(6) An emergency protection order may only be extended once.

(7) Regardless of any enactment or rule of law which would otherwise prevent it from doing so, a court hearing an application for, or with respect to, an emergency protection order may take account of—

(a) any statement contained in any report made to the court in the course of, or in connection with, the hearing; or

(b) any evidence given during the hearing,

which is, in the opinion of the court, relevant to the application.

(8) Any of the following may apply to the court for an emergency protection order to be discharged—

(a) the child;

(b) a parent of his;

(c) any person who is not a parent of his but who has parental responsibility for him; or

(d) any person with whom he was living immediately before the making of the order.

[(8A) On the application of a person who is not entitled to apply for the order to be discharged, but who is a person to whom an exclusion requirement contained in the order applies, an emergency protection order may be varied or discharged by the court in so far as it imposes the exclusion requirement.

(8B) Where a power of arrest has been attached to an exclusion requirement of an emergency protection order, the court may, on the application of any person entitled to apply for the discharge of the order so far as it imposes the exclusion requirement, vary or discharge the order in so far as it confers a power of arrest (whether or not any application has been made to vary or discharge any other provision of the order).][1]

(9) No application for the discharge of an emergency protection order shall be heard by the court before the expiry of the period of 72 hours beginning with the making of the order.

[(10) No appeal may be made against—

(a) the making of, or refusal to make, an emergency protection order;

(b) the extension of, or refusal to extend, the period during which such an order is to have effect;

(c) the discharge of, or refusal to discharge, such an order; or

(d) the giving of, or refusal to give, any direction in connection with such an order.][2]

(11) Subsection (8) does not apply—

(a) where the person who would otherwise be entitled to apply for the emergency protection order to be discharged—

(i) was given notice (in accordance with rules of court) of the hearing at which the order was made; and

(ii) was present at that hearing; or

(b) to any emergency protection order the effective period of which has been extended under subsection (5).

(12) A court making an emergency protection order may direct that the applicant may, in exercising any powers which he has by virtue of the order, be accompanied by a registered medical practitioner, registered nurse or [registered midwife][3], if he so chooses.

Removal and accommodation of children by police in cases of emergency

39-060 **46.**—(1) Where a constable has reasonable cause to believe that a child would otherwise be likely to suffer significant harm, he may—

(a) remove the child to suitable accommodation and keep him there; or

(b) take such steps as are reasonable to ensure that the child's removal from any hospital, or other place, in which he is then being accommodated is prevented.

(2) For the purposes of this Act, a child with respect to whom a constable has exercised his powers under this section is referred to as having been taken into police protection.

(3) As soon as is reasonably practicable after taking a child into police protection, the constable concerned shall—

(a) inform the local authority within whose area the child was found of the steps that have been, and are proposed to be, taken with respect to the child under this section and the reasons for taking them;

(b) give details to the authority within whose area the child is ordinarily resident ("the appropriate authority") of the place at which the child is being accommodated;

(c) inform the child (if he appears capable of understanding)—

(i) of the steps that have been taken with respect to him under this section and of the reasons for taking them; and

(ii) of the further steps that may be taken with respect to him under this section;

[1] Added by Family Law Act 1996 c.27 Sch 6 para 4
[2] Substituted by Courts and Legal Services Act 1990 c.41 Sch 16 (I) para 19
[3] Words substituted by SI 2002/253 Sch 5 para 10 (a)

(d) take such steps as are reasonably practicable to discover the wishes and feelings of the child;

(e) secure that the case is inquired into by an officer designated for the purposes of this section by the chief officer of the police area concerned; and

(f) where the child was taken into police protection by being removed to accommodation which is not provided—

(i) by or on behalf of a local authority; or

(ii) as a refuge, in compliance with the requirements of section 51,

secure that he is moved to accommodation which is so provided.

(4) As soon as is reasonably practicable after taking a child into police protection, the constable concerned shall take such steps as are reasonably practicable to inform—

(a) the child's parents;

(b) every person who is not a parent of his but who has parental responsibility for him; and

(c) any other person with whom the child was living immediately before being taken into police protection,

of the steps that he has taken under this section with respect to the child, the reasons for taking them and the further steps that may be taken with respect to him under this section.

(5) On completing any inquiry under subsection (3)(e), the officer conducting it shall release the child from police protection unless he considers that there is still reasonable cause for believing that the child would be likely to suffer significant harm if released.

(6) No child may be kept in police protection for more than 72 hours.

(7) While a child is being kept in police protection, the designated officer may apply on behalf of the appropriate authority for an emergency protection order to be made under section 44 with respect to the child.

(8) An application may be made under subsection (7) whether or not the authority know of it or agree to its being made.

(9) While a child is being kept in police protection—

(a) neither the constable concerned nor the designated officer shall have parental responsibility for him; but

(b) the designated officer shall do what is reasonable in all the circumstances of the case for the purpose of safeguarding or promoting the child's welfare (having regard in particular to the length of the period during which the child will be so protected).

(10) Where a child has been taken into police protection, the designated officer shall allow—

(a) the child's parents;

(b) any person who is not a parent of the child but who has parental responsibility for him;

(c) any person with whom the child was living immediately before he was taken into police protection;

(d) any person in whose favour a contact order is in force with respect to the child;

(e) any person who is allowed to have contact with the child by virtue of an order under section 34; and

(f) any person acting on behalf of any of those persons,

to have such contact (if any) with the child as, in the opinion of the designated officer, is both reasonable and in the child's best interests.

(11) Where a child who has been taken into police protection is in accommodation provided by, or on behalf of, the appropriate authority, subsection (10) shall have effect as if it referred to the authority rather than to the designated officer.

Local authority's duty to investigate

39-061 **47.**—(1) Where a local authority—

(a) are informed that a child who lives, or is found, in their area—

(i) is the subject of an emergency protection order; or

(ii) is in police protection; or

[(iii) has contravened a ban imposed by a curfew notice within the meaning of Chapter I of Part I of the Crime and Disorder Act 1998; or][1]

(b) have reasonable cause to suspect that a child who lives, or is found, in their area is suffering, or is likely to suffer, significant harm,

the authority shall make, or cause to be made, such enquiries as they consider necessary to enable them to decide whether they should take any action to safeguard or promote the child's welfare.

[In the case of a child falling within paragraph (a)(iii) above, the enquiries shall be commenced as soon as practicable and, in any event, within 48 hours of the authority receiving the information.][2]

(2) Where a local authority have obtained an emergency protection order with respect to a child, they shall make, or cause to be made, such enquiries as they consider necessary to enable them to decide what action they should take to safeguard or promote the child's welfare.

(3) The enquiries shall, in particular, be directed towards establishing—

(a) whether the authority should make any application to the court, or exercise any of their other powers under this Act[,or section 11 of the Crime and Disorder Act 1998 (child safety orders)][3] with respect to the child;

(b) whether, in the case of a child—

(i) with respect to whom an emergency protection order has been made; and

(ii) who is not in accommodation provided by or on behalf of the authority,

it would be in the child's best interests (while an emergency protection order remains in force) for him to be in such accommodation; and

(c) whether, in the case of a child who has been taken into police protection, it would be in the child's best interests for the authority to ask for an application to be made under section 46(7).

(4) Where enquiries are being made under subsection (1) with respect to a child, the local authority concerned shall (with a view to enabling them to determine what action, if any, to take with respect to him) take such steps as are reasonably practicable—

(a) to obtain access to him; or

(b) to ensure that access to him is obtained, on their behalf, by a person authorised by them for the purpose,

unless they are satisfied that they already have sufficient information with respect to him.

---

[1] Added by Crime and Disorder Act 1998 c.37 Pt I c I s 15 (4) (a)

[2] Words inserted by Crime and Disorder Act 1998 c.37 Pt I c I s 15 (4) (b)

[3] Words inserted by Crime and Disorder Act 1998 c.37 Sch 8 para 69

(5) Where, as a result of any such enquiries, it appears to the authority that there are matters connected with the child's education which should be investigated, they shall consult the relevant local education authority.

(6) Where, in the course of enquiries made under this section—

(a) any officer of the local authority concerned; or

(b) any person authorised by the authority to act on their behalf in connection with those enquiries—

(i) is refused access to the child concerned; or

(ii) is denied information as to his whereabouts,

the authority shall apply for an emergency protection order, a child assessment order, a care order or a supervision order with respect to the child unless they are satisfied that his welfare can be satisfactorily safeguarded without their doing so.

(7) If, on the conclusion of any enquiries or review made under this section, the authority decide not to apply for an emergency protection order, a child assessment order, a care order or a supervision order they shall—

(a) consider whether it would be appropriate to review the case at a later date; and

(b) if they decide that it would be, determine the date on which that review is to begin.

(8) Where, as a result of complying with this section, a local authority conclude that they should take action to safeguard or promote the child's welfare they shall take that action (so far as it is both within their power and reasonably practicable for them to do so).

(9) Where a local authority are conducting enquiries under this section, it shall be the duty of any person mentioned in subsection (11) to assist them with those enquiries (in particular by providing relevant information and advice) if called upon by the authority to do so.

(10) Subsection (9) does not oblige any person to assist a local authority where doing so would be unreasonable in all the circumstances of the case.

(11) The persons are—

(a) any local authority;

(b) any local education authority;

(c) any local housing authority;

(d) any [[Health Authority, Special Health Authority][1] [, Primary Care Trust][2] or National Health Service trust][3]; and

(e) any person authorised by the Secretary of State for the purposes of this section.

(12) Where a local authority are making enquiries under this section with respect to a child who appears to them to be ordinarily resident within the area of another authority, they shall consult that other authority, who may undertake the necessary enquiries in their place.

Powers to assist in discovery of children who may be in need of emergency protection

48.—(1) Where it appears to a court making an emergency protection order that adequate information as to the child's whereabouts— **39-062**

(a) is not available to the applicant for the order; but

(b) is available to another person,

[1] Words substituted by Health Authorities Act 1995 c.17 Sch 1 (III) para 118 (7)

[2] Words inserted by SI 2000/90 Sch 1 para 24 (7)

[3] Words added by Courts and Legal Services Act 1990 c.41 Sch 16 (I) para 20

it may include in the order a provision requiring that other person to disclose, if asked to do so by the applicant, any information that he may have as to the child's whereabouts.

(2) No person shall be excused from complying with such a requirement on the ground that complying might incriminate him or his spouse of an offence; but a statement or admission made in complying shall not be admissible in evidence against either of them in proceedings for any offence other than perjury.

(3) An emergency protection order may authorise the applicant to enter premises specified by the order and search for the child with respect to whom the order is made.

(4) Where the court is satisfied that there is reasonable cause to believe that there may be another child on those premises with respect to whom an emergency protection order ought to be made, it may make an order authorising the applicant to search for that other child on those premises.

(5) Where—

(a) an order has been made under subsection (4);

(b) the child concerned has been found on the premises; and

(c) the applicant is satisfied that the grounds for making an emergency protection order exist with respect to him,

the order shall have effect as if it were an emergency protection order.

(6) Where an order has been made under subsection (4), the applicant shall notify the court of its effect.

(7) A person shall be guilty of an offence if he intentionally obstructs any person exercising the power of entry and search under subsection (3) or (4).

(8) A person guilty of an offence under subsection (7) shall be liable on summary conviction to a fine not exceeding level 3 on the standard scale.

(9) Where, on an application made by any person for a warrant under this section, it appears to the court—

(a) that a person attempting to exercise powers under an emergency protection order has been prevented from doing so by being refused entry to the premises concerned or access to the child concerned; or

(b) that any such person is likely to be so prevented from exercising any such powers,

it may issue a warrant authorising any constable to assist the person mentioned in paragraph (a) or (b) in the exercise of those powers, using reasonable force if necessary.

(10) Every warrant issued under this section shall be addressed to, and executed by, a constable who shall be accompanied by the person applying for the warrant if—

(a) that person so desires; and

(b) the court by whom the warrant is issued does not direct otherwise.

(11) A court granting an application for a warrant under this section may direct that the constable concerned may, in executing the warrant, be accompanied by a registered medical practitioner, registered nurse or [registered midwife][1] if he so chooses.

(12) An application for a warrant under this section shall be made in the manner and form prescribed by rules of court.

(13) Wherever it is reasonably practicable to do so, an order under subsection (4), an application for a warrant under this section and any such warrant shall name the child; and where it does not name him it shall describe him as clearly as possible.

[1] Words substituted by SI 2002/253 Sch 5 para 10 (b)

Abduction of children in care etc

49.—(1) A person shall be guilty of an offence if, knowingly and without lawful authority or reasonable excuse, he— **39-063**

(a) takes a child to whom this section applies away from the responsible person;
(b) keeps such a child away from the responsible person; or
(c) induces, assists or incites such a child to run away or stay away from the responsible person.

(2) This section applies in relation to a child who is—

(a) in care;
(b) the subject of an emergency protection order; or
(c) in police protection,

and in this section "the responsible person" means any person who for the time being has care of him by virtue of the care order, the emergency protection order, or section 46, as the case may be.

(3) A person guilty of an offence under this section shall be liable on summary conviction to imprisonment for a term not exceeding six months, or to a fine not exceeding level 5 on the standard scale, or to both.

Recovery of abducted children etc

50.—(1) Where it appears to the court that there is reason to believe that a child to whom this section applies— **39-064**

(a) has been unlawfully taken away or is being unlawfully kept away from the responsible person;
(b) has run away or is staying away from the responsible person; or
(c) is missing,

the court may make an order under this section ("a recovery order").

(2) This section applies to the same children to whom section 49 applies and in this section "the responsible person" has the same meaning as in section 49.

(3) A recovery order—

(a) operates as a direction to any person who is in a position to do so to produce the child on request to any authorised person;
(b) authorises the removal of the child by any authorised person;
(c) requires any person who has information as to the child's whereabouts to disclose that information, if asked to do so, to a constable or an officer of the court;
(d) authorises a constable to enter any premises specified in the order and search for the child, using reasonable force if necessary.

(4) The court may make a recovery order only on the application of—

(a) any person who has parental responsibility for the child by virtue of a care order or emergency protection order; or
(b) where the child is in police protection, the designated officer.

(5) A recovery order shall name the child and—

(a) any person who has parental responsibility for the child by virtue of a care order or emergency protection order; or
(b) where the child is in police protection, the designated officer.

(6) Premises may only be specified under subsection (3)(d) if it appears to the court that there are reasonable grounds for believing the child to be on them.

(7) In this section—

"an authorised person" means—

(a) any person specified by the court;
(b) any constable;
(c) any person who is authorised—
(i) after the recovery order is made; and
(ii) by a person who has parental responsibility for the child by virtue of a care order or an emergency protection order,

to exercise any power under a recovery order

; and

"the designated officer" means the officer designated for the purposes of section 46.

(8) Where a person is authorised as mentioned in subsection (7)(c)—
(a) the authorisation shall identify the recovery order; and
(b) any person claiming to be so authorised shall, if asked to do so, produce some duty authenticated document showing that he is so authorised.

(9) A person shall be guilty of an offence if he intentionally obstructs an authorised person exercising the power under subsection (3)(b) to remove a child.

(10) A person guilty of an offence under this section shall be liable on summary conviction to a fine not exceeding level 3 on the standard scale.

(11) No person shall be excused from complying with any request made under subsection (3)(c) on the ground that complying with it might incriminate him or his spouse of an offence; but a statement or admission made in complying shall not be admissible in evidence against either of them in proceedings for an offence other than perjury.

(12) Where a child is made the subject of a recovery order whilst being looked after by a local authority, any reasonable expenses incurred by an authorised person in giving effect to the order shall be recoverable from the authority.

Refuges for children at risk

39-065 **51.**—(1) Where it is proposed to use a voluntary home or [private][1] children's home to provide a refuge for children who appear to be at risk of harm, the Secretary of State may issue a certificate under this section with respect to that home.

(2) Where a local authority or voluntary organisation arrange for a foster parent to provide such a refuge, the Secretary of State may issue a certificate under this section with respect to that foster parent.

(3) In subsection (2) "foster parent" means a person who is, or who from time to time is, a local authority foster parent or a foster parent with whom children are placed by a voluntary organisation.

(4) The Secretary of State may by regulations—
(a) make provision as to the manner in which certificates may be issued;
(b) impose requirements which must be complied with while any certificate is in force; and
(c) provide for the withdrawal of certificates in prescribed circumstances.

(5) Where a certificate is in force with respect to a home, none of the provisions mentioned in subsection (7) shall apply in relation to any person providing a refuge for any child in that home.

(6) Where a certificate is in force with respect to a foster parent, none of those provisions shall apply in relation to the provision by him of a refuge for any

[1] Words substituted by Care Standards Act 2000 c.14 Sch 4 para 14 (7)

child in accordance with arrangements made by the local authority or voluntary organisation.

(7) The provisions are—

(a) section 49;

[(b) sections 82 (recovery of certain fugitive children) and 83 (harbouring) of the Children (Scotland) Act 1995, so far as they apply in relation to anything done in England and Wales;][1]

(c) section 32(3) of the Children and Young Persons Act 1969 (compelling, persuading, inciting or assisting any person to be absent from detention, etc.), so far as it applies in relation to anything done in England and Wales;

(d) section 2 of the Child Abduction Act 1984.

Rules and regulations

52.—(1) Without prejudice to section 93 or any other power to make such rules, rules of court may be made with respect to the procedure to be followed in connection with proceedings under this Part. **39-066**

(2) The rules may, in particular make provision—

(a) as to the form in which any application is to be made or direction is to be given;

(b) prescribing the persons who are to be notified of—

(i) the making, or extension, of an emergency protection order; or

(ii) the making of an application under section 45(4) or (8) or 46(7); and

(c) as to the content of any such notification and the manner in which, and person by whom, it is to be given.

(3) The Secretary of State may by regulations provide that, where—

(a) an emergency protection order has been made with respect to a child;

(b) the applicant for the order was not the local authority within whose area the child is ordinarily resident; and

(c) that local authority are of the opinion that it would be in the child's best interests for the applicant's responsibilities under the order to be transferred to them,

that authority shall (subject to their having complied with any requirements imposed by the regulations) be treated, for the purposes of this Act, as though they and not the original applicant had applied for, and been granted, the order.

(4) Regulations made under subsection (3) may, in particular, make provision as to—

(a) the considerations to which the local authority shall have regard in forming an opinion as mentioned in subsection (3)(c); and

(b) the time at which responsibility under any emergency protection order is to be treated as having been transferred to a local authority.

PART VI

COMMUNITY HOMES

Provision of community homes by local authorities

53.—(1) Every local authority shall make such arrangements as they consider appropriate for securing that homes ("community homes") are available— **39-067**

[1] Substituted by Children (Scotland) Act 1995 c.36 Sch 4 para 48 (3)

(a) for the care and accommodation of children looked after by them; and
(b) for purposes connected with the welfare of children (whether or not looked after by them),

and may do so jointly with one or more other local authorities.

(2) In making such arrangements, a local authority shall have regard to the need for ensuring the availability of accommodation—

(a) of different descriptions; and
(b) which is suitable for different purposes and the requirements of different descriptions of children.

(3) A community home may be a home—

(a) provided, [equipped maintained and (subject to subsection (3A)) managed][1] by a local authority; or
(b) provided by a voluntary organisation but in respect of which a local authority and the organisation—
    (i) propose that, in accordance with an instrument of management, the [equipment, maintenance and (subject to subsection (3B)) management][2] of the home shall be the responsibility of the local authority; or
    (ii) so propose that the management, equipment and maintenance of the home shall be the responsibility of the voluntary organisation.

[(3A) A local authority may make arrangements for the management by another person of accommodation provided by the local authority for the purpose of restricting the liberty of children.

(3B) Where a local authority are to be responsible for the management of a community home provided by a voluntary organisation, the local authority may, with the consent of the body of managers constituted by the instrument of management for the home, make arrangements for the management by another person of accommodation provided for the purpose of restricting the liberty of children.][3]

(4) Where a local authority are to be responsible for the management of a community home provided by a voluntary organisation, the authority shall designate the home as a controlled community home.

(5) Where a voluntary organisation are to be responsible for the management of a community home provided by the organisation, the local authority shall designate the home as an assisted community home.

(6) Schedule 4 shall have effect for the purpose of supplementing the provisions of this Part.

Financial provisions applicable on cessation of controlled or assisted community home or disposal etc. of premises

39-068 **58.**—(1) Where—

(a) the instrument of management for a controlled or assisted community home is revoked or otherwise ceases to have effect under [...][4][56(3) or (4)(a) or 57(3) or (5)][5]; or
(b) any premises used for the purposes of such a home are (at any time after 13th January 1987) disposed of, or put to use otherwise than for those purposes,

[1] Words substituted by Criminal Justice and Public Order Act 1994 c.33 Pt I s 22 (2) (a) (i)
[2] Words substituted by Criminal Justice and Public Order Act 1994 c.33 Pt I s 22 (2) (a) (ii)
[3] Added by Criminal Justice and Public Order Act 1994 c.33 Pt I s 22 (2) (b)
[4] Word repealed by Care Standards Act 2000 c.14 Sch 6 para 1
[5] Word repealed by Care Standards Act 2000 c.14 Sch 6 para 1

the proprietor shall become liable to pay compensation ("the appropriate compensation") in accordance with this section.[...][1]

(2) Where the instrument of management in force at the relevant time relates—

(a) to a controlled community home; or
(b) to an assisted community home which, at any time before the instrument came into force, was a controlled community home,

the appropriate compensation is a sum equal to that part of the value of any premises which is attributable to expenditure incurred in relation to the premises, while the home was a controlled community home, by the authority who were then the responsible authority.

(3) Where the instrument of management in force at the relevant time relates—

(a) to an assisted community home; or
(b) to a controlled community home which, at any time before the instrument came into force, was an assisted community home,

the appropriate compensation is a sum equal to that part of the value of the premises which is attributable to the expenditure of money provided by way of grant under section 82, section 65 of the Children and Young Persons Act 1969 or section 82 of the Child Care Act 1980.

(4) Where the home is, at the relevant time, conducted in premises which formerly were used as an approved school or were an approved probation hostel or home, the appropriate compensation is a sum equal to that part of the value of the premises which is attributable to the expenditure—

(a) of sums paid towards the expenses of the managers of an approved school under section 104 of the Children and Young Persons Act 1933; [...][2]
(b) of sums paid under section 51(3)(c) of the Powers of Criminal Courts Act 1973 [or section 20(1)(c) of the Probation Service Act 1993][3] in relation to expenditure on approved probation hostels or homes; or
[(c) of sums paid under section 3, 5 or 9 of the Criminal Justice and Court Services Act 2000 in relation to expenditure on approved premises (within the meaning of Part I of that Act).][4]

(5) The appropriate compensation shall be paid—

(a) in the case of compensation payable under subsection (2), to the authority who were the responsible authority at the relevant time; and
(b) in any other case, to the Secretary of State.

(6) In this section—

"disposal" includes the grant of a tenancy and any other conveyance, assignment, transfer, grant, variation or extinguishment of an interest in or right over land, whether made by instrument or otherwise;

"premises" means any premises or part of premises (including land) used for the purposes of the home and belonging to the proprietor;

"the proprietor" means —

(a) the voluntary organisation by which the home is, at the relevant time, provided; or
(b) if the premises are not, at the relevant time, vested in that organisation, the persons in whom they are vested;

1 Word repealed by Care Standards Act 2000 c.14 Sch 6 para 1
2 Word repealed by Criminal Justice and Court Services Act 2000 c.43 Sch 8 para 1
3 Words added by Probation Service Act 1993 c.47 Sch 3 para 9 (2)
4 Inserted by Criminal Justice and Court Services Act 2000 c.43 Sch 7 (II) para 93 (b)

"the relevant time" means the time immediately before the liability to pay arises under subsection (1); and

"the responsible authority" means the local authority specified in the instrument of management in question.

(7) For the purposes of this section an event of a kind mentioned in subsection (1)(b) shall be taken to have occurred—

(a) in the case of a disposal, on the date on which the disposal was completed or, in the case of a disposal which is effected by a series of transactions, the date on which the last of those transactions was completed;

(b) in the case of premises which are put to different use, on the date on which they first begin to be put to their new use.

(8) The amount of any sum payable under this section shall be determined in accordance with such arrangements—

(a) as may be agreed between the voluntary organisation by which the home is, at the relevant time, provided and the responsible authority or (as the case may be) the Secretary of State; or

(b) in default of agreement, as may be determined by the Secretary of State.

(9) With the agreement of the responsible authority or (as the case may be) the Secretary of State, the liability to pay any sum under this section may be discharged, in whole or in part, by the transfer of any premises.

(10) This section has effect regardless of—

(a) anything in any trust deed for a controlled or assisted community home;

(b) the provisions of any enactment or instrument governing the disposition of the property of a voluntary organisation.

PART VII

VOLUNTARY HOMES AND VOLUNTARY ORGANISATIONS

Provision of accommodation by voluntary organisations

39-069 **59.**—(1) Where a voluntary organisation provide accommodation for a child, they shall do so by—

(a) placing him (subject to subsection (2)) with—

(i) a family;

(ii) a relative of his; or

(iii) any other suitable person,

on such terms as to payment by the organisation and otherwise as the organisation may determine;

[(aa) maintaining him in an appropriate children's home;][1]

(f) making such other arrangements (subject to subsection (3)) as seem appropriate to them.

[(1A) Where under subsection (1)(aa) a local authority maintains a child in a home provided, equipped and maintained by the Secretary of State under section

[1] Inserted by Care Standards Act 2000 c.14 Sch 4 para 14 (8)

82(5), it shall do so on such terms as the Secretary of State may from time to time determine.][1]

(2) The Secretary of State may make regulations as to the placing of children with foster parents by voluntary organisations and the regulations may, in particular, make provision which (with any necessary modifications) is similar to the provision that may be made under section 23(2)(a).

(3) The Secretary of State may make regulations as to the arrangements which may be made under subsection (1)(f) and the regulations may in particular make provision which (with any necessary modifications) is similar to the provision that may be made under section 23(2)(f).

(4) The Secretary of State may make regulations requiring any voluntary organisation who are providing accommodation for a child—

(a) to review his case; and

(b) to consider any representations (including any complaint) made to them by any person falling within a prescribed class of person,

in accordance with the provisions of the regulations.

(5) Regulations under subsection (4) may in particular make provision which (with any necessary modifications) is similar to the provision that may be made under section 26.

(6) Regulations under subsections (2) to (4) may provide that any person who, without reasonable excuse, contravenes or fails to comply with a regulation shall be guilty of an offence and liable on summary conviction to a fine not exceeding level 4 on the standard scale.

[Voluntary homes.][2]

60.—[(3) In this Act "voluntary home" means a children's home which is carried on by a voluntary organisation but does not include a community home.][3] **39-070**

(4) Schedule 5 shall have effect for the purpose of supplementing the provisions of this Part.

Duties of voluntary organisations

61.—(1) Where a child is accommodated by or on behalf of a voluntary organisation, it shall be the duty of the organisation— **39-071**

(a) to safeguard and promote his welfare;

(b) to make such use of the services and facilities available for children cared for by their own parents as appears to the organisation reasonable in his case; and

(c) to advise, assist and befriend him with a view to promoting his welfare when he ceases to be so accommodated.

(2) Before making any decision with respect to any such child the organisation shall, so far as is reasonably practicable, ascertain the wishes and feelings of—

(a) the child;

(b) his parents;

(c) any person who is not a parent of his but who has parental responsibility for him; and

(d) any other person whose wishes and feelings the organisation consider to be relevant,

regarding the matter to be decided.

[1] Inserted by Care Standards Act 2000 c.14 Sch 4 para 14 (8)
[2] Substituted by Care Standards Act 2000 c.14 Sch 4 para 14 (9)
[3] Substituted by Care Standards Act 2000 c.14 Sch 4 para 14 (9)

(3) In making any such decision the organisation shall give due consideration—

(a) having regard to the child's age and understanding, to such wishes and feelings of his as they have been able to ascertain;

(b) to such other wishes and feelings mentioned in subsection (2) as they have been able to ascertain; and

(c) to the child's religious persuasion, racial origin and cultural and linguistic background.

Duties of local authorities

39-072 **62.**—(1) Every local authority shall satisfy themselves that any voluntary organisation providing accommodation—

(a) within the authority's area for any child; or

(b) outside that area for any child on behalf of the authority,

are satisfactorily safeguarding and promoting the welfare of the children so provided with accommodation.

(2) Every local authority shall arrange for children who are accommodated within their area by or on behalf of voluntary organisations to be visited, from time to time, in the interests of their welfare.

(3) The Secretary of State may make regulations—

(a) requiring every child who is accommodated within a local authority's area, by or on behalf of a voluntary organisation, to be visited by an officer of the authority—

(i) in prescribed circumstances; and

(ii) on specified occasions or within specified periods; and

(b) imposing requirements which must be met by any local authority, or officer of a local authority, carrying out functions under this section.

(4) Subsection (2) does not apply in relation to community homes.

(5) Where a local authority are not satisfied that the welfare of any child who is accommodated by or on behalf of a voluntary organisation is being satisfactorily safeguarded or promoted they shall—

(a) unless they consider that it would not be in the best interests of the child, take such steps as are reasonably practicable to secure that the care and accommodation of the child is undertaken by—

(i) a parent of his;

(ii) any person who is not a parent of his but who has parental responsibility for him; or

(iii) a relative of his; and

(b) consider the extent to which (if at all) they should exercise any of their functions with respect to the child.

(6) Any person authorised by a local authority may, for the purpose of enabling the authority to discharge their duties under this section—

(a) enter, at any reasonable time, and inspect any premises in which children are being accommodated as mentioned in subsection (1) or (2);

(b) inspect any children there;

(c) require any person to furnish him with such records of a kind required to be kept by regulations made under [section 22 of the Care Standards Act 2000][1] (in whatever form they are held), or allow him to inspect such records, as he may at any time direct.

[1] Words substituted by Care Standards Act 2000 c.14 Sch 4 para 14 (10) (a)

(7) Any person exercising the power conferred by subsection (6) shall, if asked to do so, produce some duly authenticated document showing his authority to do so.

(8) Any person authorised to exercise the power to inspect records conferred by subsection (6)—

(a) shall be entitled at any reasonable time to have access to, and inspect and check the operation of, any computer and any associated apparatus or material which is or has been in use in connection with the records in question; and

(b) may require—

(i) the person by whom or on whose behalf the computer is or has been so used; or

(ii) any person having charge of, or otherwise concerned with the operation of, the computer, apparatus or material,

to afford him such assistance as he may reasonably require.

(9) Any person who intentionally obstructs another in the exercise of any power conferred by subsection (6) or (8) shall be guilty of an offence and liable on summary conviction to a fine not exceeding level 3 on the standard scale.

PART VIII

REGISTERED CHILDREN'S HOMES

[Private children's homes etc.][1]

63.—(1) 39-073

(2) [...][2]

(3) [...][3]

(4) [...][4]

(5) [...][5]

(7) [...][6]

(8) [...][7]

(9) [...][8]

(10) [...][9]

(11) Schedule 6 shall have effect with respect to [private][10]children's homes.

(12) Schedule 7 shall have effect for the purpose of setting out the circumstances in which a person may foster more than three children without being treated [, for the purposes of this Act and the Care Standards Act 2000,][11] as carrying on a children's home.[...][12]

[1] Substituted by Care Standards Act 2000 c.14 Sch 4 para 14 (11)
[2] Repealed by Care Standards Act 2000 c.14 Sch 6 para 1
[3] Repealed by Care Standards Act 2000 c.14 Sch 6 para 1
[4] Repealed by Care Standards Act 2000 c.14 Sch 6 para 1
[5] Repealed by Care Standards Act 2000 c.14 Sch 6 para 1
[6] Repealed by Care Standards Act 2000 c.14 Sch 6 para 1
[7] Repealed by Care Standards Act 2000 c.14 Sch 6 para 1
[8] Repealed by Care Standards Act 2000 c.14 Sch 6 para 1
[9] Repealed by Care Standards Act 2000 c.14 Sch 6 para 1
[10] Words substituted by Care Standards Act 2000 c.14 Sch 4 para 14 (11)
[11] Words substituted by Care Standards Act 2000 c.14 Sch 4 para 14 (11)
[12] Repealed by Care Standards Act 2000 c.14 Sch 6 para 1

Welfare of children in children's homes

39-074 **64.**—(1) Where a child is accommodated in a [private][1] children's home, it shall be the duty of the person carrying on the home to—

(a) safeguard and promote the child's welfare;
(b) make such use of the services and facilities available for children cared for by their own parents as appears to that person reasonable in the case of the child; and
(c) advise, assist and befriend him with a view to promoting his welfare when he ceases to be so accommodated.

(2) Before making any decision with respect to any such child the person carrying on the home shall, so far as is reasonably practicable, ascertain the wishes and feelings of—

(a) the child;
(b) his parents;
(c) any other person who is not a parent of his but who has parental responsibility for him; and
(d) any person whose wishes and feelings the person carrying on the home considers to be relevant,

regarding the matter to be decided.

(3) In making any such decision the person concerned shall give due consideration—

(a) having regard to the child's age and understanding, to such wishes and feelings of his as he has been able to ascertain;
(b) to such other wishes and feelings mentioned in subsection (2) as he has been able to ascertain; and
(c) to the child's religious persuasion, racial origin and cultural and linguistic background.

(4) Section 62, except subsection (4), shall apply in relation to any person who is carrying on a [private][2] children's home as it applies in relation to any voluntary organisation.

PART IX

PRIVATE ARRANGEMENTS FOR FOSTERING CHILDREN

Privately fostered children

39-075 **66.**—(1) In this Part—

(a) "a privately fostered child" means a child who is under the age of sixteen and who is cared for, and provided with accommodation [in their own home][3] by, someone other than—
  (i) a parent of his;
  (ii) a person who is not a parent of his but who has parental responsibility for him; or
  (iii) a relative of his

; and

(b) "to foster a child privately" means to look after the child in circumstances in which he is a privately fostered child as defined by this section.

[1] Words substituted by Care Standards Act 2000 c.14 Sch 4 para 14 (12)
[2] Words substituted by Care Standards Act 2000 c.14 Sch 4 para 14 (12)
[3] Words substituted by Care Standards Act 2000 c.14 Sch 4 para 14 (15)

(2) A child is not a privately fostered child if the person caring for and accommodating him—

(a) has done so for a period of less than 28 days; and

(b) does not intend to do so for any longer period.

(3) Subsection (1) is subject to—

(a) the provisions of section 63; and

(b) the exceptions made by paragraphs 1 to 5 of Schedule 8.

(4) In the case of a child who is disabled, subsection (1)(a) shall have effect as if for "sixteen" there were substituted "eighteen".

[(4A) The Secretary of State may by regulations make provision as to the circumstances in which a person who provides accommodation to a child is, or is not, to be treated as providing him with accommodation in the person's own home.][1]

(5) Schedule 8 shall have effect for the purposes of supplementing the provision made by this Part.

Welfare of privately fostered children

67.—(1) It shall be the duty of every local authority to satisfy themselves that the welfare of children who are privately fostered within their area is being satisfactorily safeguarded and promoted and to secure that such advice is given to those caring for them as appears to the authority to be needed. **39-076**

(2) The Secretary of State may make regulations—

(a) requiring every child who is privately fostered within a local authority's area to be visited by an officer of the authority—

(i) in prescribed circumstances; and

(ii) on specified occasions or within specified periods; and

(b) imposing requirements which are to be met by any local authority, or officer of a local authority, in carrying out functions under this section.

(3) Where any person who is authorised by a local authority to visit privately fostered children has reasonable cause to believe that—

(a) any privately fostered child is being accommodated in premises within the authority's area; or

(b) it is proposed to accommodate any such child in any such premises,

he may at any reasonable time inspect those premises and any children there.

(4) Any person exercising the power under subsection (3) shall, if so required, produce some duly authenticated document showing his authority to do so.

(5) Where a local authority are not satisfied that the welfare of any child who is privately fostered within their area is being satisfactorily safeguarded or promoted they shall—

(a) unless they consider that it would not be in the best interests of the child, take such steps as are reasonably practicable to secure that the care and accommodation of the child is undertaken by—

(i) a parent of his;

(ii) any person who is not a parent of his but who has parental responsibility for him; or

(iii) a relative of his; and

(b) consider the extent to which (if at all) they should exercise any of their functions under this Act with respect to the child.

[1] Inserted by Care Standards Act 2000 c.14 Sch 4 para 14 (15)

Persons disqualified from being private foster parents

39-077 **68.**—(1) Unless he has disclosed the fact to the appropriate local authority and obtained their written consent, a person shall not foster a child privately if he is disqualified from doing so by regulations made by the Secretary of State for the purposes of this section.

(2) The regulations may, in particular, provide for a person to be so disqualified where—

(a) an order of a kind specified in the regulations has been made at any time with respect to him;

(b) an order of a kind so specified has been made at any time with respect to any child who has been in his care;

(c) a requirement of a kind so specified has been imposed at any time with respect to any such child, under or by virtue of any enactment;

(d) he has been convicted of any offence of a kind so specified, or [a probation order has been made in respect of him or he has been][1] discharged absolutely or conditionally for any such offence;

(e) a prohibition has been imposed on him at any time under section 69 or under any other specified enactment;

(f) his rights and powers with respect to a child have at any time been vested in a specified authority under a specified enactment.

(3) Unless he has disclosed the fact to the appropriate local authority and obtained their written consent, a person shall not foster a child privately if—

(a) he lives in the same household as a person who is himself prevented from fostering a child by subsection (1); or

(b) he lives in a household at which any such person is employed.

(4) Where an authority refuse to give their consent under this section, they shall inform the applicant by a written notice which states—

(a) the reason for the refusal;

(b) the applicant's right under paragraph 8 of Schedule 8 to appeal against the refusal; and

(c) the time within which he may do so.

(5) In this section—

"the appropriate authority" means the local authority within whose area it is proposed to foster the child in question; and

"enactment" means any enactment having effect, at any time, in any part of the United Kingdom.

Power to prohibit private fostering

39-078 **69.**—(1) This section applies where a person—

(a) proposes to foster a child privately; or

(b) is fostering a child privately.

(2) Where the local authority for the area within which the child is proposed to be, or is being, fostered are of the opinion that—

(a) he is not a suitable person to foster a child;

(b) the premises in which the child will be, or is being, accommodated are not suitable; or

(c) it would be prejudicial to the welfare of the child for him to be, or continue to be, accommodated by that person in those premises,

the authority may impose a prohibition on him under subsection (3).

[1] Words substituted by Criminal Justice and Court Services Act 2000 c.43 Sch 7 (II) para 94

(3) A prohibition imposed on any person under this subsection may prohibit him from fostering privately—

(a) any child in any premises within the area of the local authority; or

(b) any child in premises specified in the prohibition;

(c) a child identified in the prohibition, in premises specified in the prohibition.

(4) A local authority who have imposed a prohibition on any person under subsection (3) may, if they think fit, cancel the prohibition—

(a) of their own motion; or

(b) on an application made by that person,

if they are satisfied that the prohibition is no longer justified.

(5) Where a local authority impose a requirement on any person under paragraph 6 of Schedule 8, they may also impose a prohibition on him under subsection (3).

(6) Any prohibition imposed by virtue of subsection (5) shall not have effect unless—

(a) the time specified for compliance with the requirement has expired; and

(b) the requirement has not been complied with.

(7) A prohibition imposed under this section shall be imposed by notice in writing addressed to the person on whom it is imposed and informing him of—

(a) the reason for imposing the prohibition;

(b) his right under paragraph 8 of Schedule 8 to appeal against the prohibition; and

(c) the time within which he may do so.

Offences

70.—(1) A person shall be guilty of an offence if— **39-079**

(a) being required, under any provision made by or under this Part, to give any notice or information—

(i) he fails without reasonable excuse to give the notice within the time specified in that provision; or

(ii) he fails without reasonable excuse to give the information within a reasonable time; or

(iii) he makes, or causes or procures another person to make, any statement in the notice or information which he knows to be false or misleading in a material particular;

(b) he refuses to allow a privately fostered child to be visited by a duly authorised officer of a local authority;

(c) he intentionally obstructs another in the exercise of the power conferred by section 67(3);

(d) he contravenes section 68;

(e) he fails without reasonable excuse to comply with any requirement imposed by a local authority under this Part;

(f) he accommodates a privately fostered child in any premises in contravention of a prohibition imposed by a local authority under this Part;

(g) he knowingly causes to be published, or publishes, an advertisement which he knows contravenes paragraph 10 of Schedule 8.

(2) Where a person contravenes section 68(3), he shall not be guilty of an offence under this section if he proves that he did not know, and had no reasonable ground for believing, that any person to whom section 68(1) applied was living or employed in the premises in question.

(3) A person guilty of an offence under subsection (1)(a) shall be liable on summary conviction to a fine not exceeding level 5 on the standard scale.

(4) A person guilty of an offence under subsection (1)(b), (c) or (g) shall be liable on summary conviction to a fine not exceeding level 3 on the standard scale.

(5) A person guilty of an offence under subsection (1)(d) or (f) shall be liable on summary conviction to imprisonment for a term not exceeding six months, or to a fine not exceeding level 5 on the standard scale, or to both.

(6) A person guilty of an offence under subsection (1)(e) shall be liable on summary conviction to a fine not exceeding level 4 on the standard scale.

(7) If any person who is required, under any provision of this Part, to give a notice fails to give the notice within the time specified in that provision, proceedings for the offence may be brought at any time within six months from the date when evidence of the offence came to the knowledge of the local authority.

(8) Subsection (7) is not affected by anything in section 127(1) of the Magistrates' Courts Act 1980 (time limit for proceedings).

PART XII

MISCELLANEOUS AND GENERAL

Notification of children accommodated in certain establishments

Children accommodated by health authorities and local education authorities

39-080 **85.**—(1) Where a child is provided with accommodation by any [[Health Authority, Special Health Authority,][1] [Primary Care Trust,][2] National Health Service trust][3] or local education authority ("the accommodating authority")—

(a) for a consecutive period of at least three months; or

(b) with the intention, on the part of that authority, of accommodating him for such a period,

the accommodating authority shall notify the responsible authority.

(2) Where subsection (1) applies with respect to a child, the accommodating authority shall also notify the responsible authority when they cease to accommodate the child.

(3) In this section "the responsible authority" means —

(a) the local authority appearing to the accommodating authority to be the authority within whose area the child was ordinarily resident immediately before being accommodated; or

(b) where it appears to the accommodating authority that a child was not ordinarily resident within the area of any local authority, the local authority within whose area the accommodation is situated.

(4) Where a local authority have been notified under this section, they shall—

(a) take such steps as are reasonably practicable to enable them to determine whether the child's welfare is adequately safeguarded and promoted while he is accommodated by the accommodating authority; and

[1] Words substituted by Health Authorities Act 1995 c.17 Sch 1 (III) para 118 (9)
[2] Words inserted by SI 2000/90 Sch 1 para 24 (9)
[3] Words inserted by National Health Service and Community Care Act 1990 c.19 s 66 (1) Sch 9 para 36 (5)

(b) consider the extent to which (if at all) they should exercise any of their functions under this Act with respect to the child.

Effect and duration of orders etc

Effect and duration of orders etc

91.—(1) The making of a residence order with respect to a child who is the subject of a care order discharges the care order. **39-081**

(2) The making of a care order with respect to a child who is the subject of any section 8 order discharges that order.

(3) The making of a care order with respect to a child who is the subject of a supervision order discharges that other order.

(4) The making of a care order with respect to a child who is a ward of court brings that wardship to an end.

(5) The making of a care order with respect to a child who is the subject of a school attendance order made under [section 437 of the Education Act 1996][1] discharges the school attendance order.

(6) Where an emergency protection order is made with respect to a child who is in care, the care order shall have effect subject to the emergency protection order.

(7) Any order made under section 4(1) or 5(1) shall continue in force until the child reaches the age of eighteen, unless it is brought to an end earlier.

(8) Any—

(a) agreement under section 4; or

(b) appointment under section 5(3) or (4),

shall continue in force until the child reaches the age of eighteen, unless it is brought to an end earlier.

(9) An order under Schedule 1 has effect as specified in that Schedule.

(10) A section 8 order shall, if it would otherwise still be in force, cease to have effect when the child reaches the age of sixteen, unless it is to have effect beyond that age by virtue of section 9(6).

(11) Where a section 8 order has effect with respect to a child who has reached the age of sixteen, it shall, if it would otherwise still be in force, cease to have effect when he reaches the age of eighteen.

(12) Any care order, other than an interim care order, shall continue in force until the child reaches the age of eighteen, unless it is brought to an end earlier.

(13) Any order made under any other provision of this Act in relation to a child shall, if it would otherwise still be in force, cease to have effect when he reaches the age of eighteen.

(14) On disposing of any application for an order under this Act, the court may (whether or not it makes any other order in response to the application) order that no application for an order under this Act of any specified kind may be made with respect to the child concerned by any person named in the order without leave of the court.

(15) Where an application ("the previous application") has been made for—

(a) the discharge of a care order;

(b) the discharge of a supervision order;

(c) the discharge of an education supervision order;

(d) the substitution of a supervision order for a care order; or

(e) a child assessment order,

[1] Words substituted by Education Act 1996 c.56 Sch 37 (I) para 90

no further application of a kind mentioned in paragraphs (a) to (e) may be made with respect to the child concerned, without leave of the court, unless the period between the disposal of the previous application and the making of the further application exceeds six months.

(16) Subsection (15) does not apply to applications made in relation to interim orders.

(17) Where—

(a) a person has made an application for an order under section 34;

(b) the application has been refused; and

(c) a period of less than six months has elapsed since the refusal,

that person may not make a further application for such an order with respect to the same child, unless he has obtained the leave of the court.

Jurisdiction and procedure etc

Jurisdiction of courts

39-082 **92.**—(1) The name "domestic proceedings", given to certain proceedings in magistrates' courts, is hereby changed to "family proceedings" and the names "domestic court" and "domestic court panel" are hereby changed to "family proceedings court" and "family panel", respectively.

(2) Proceedings under this Act shall be treated as family proceedings in relation to magistrates' courts.

(3) Subsection (2) is subject to the provisions of section 65(1) and (2) of the Magistrates' Courts Act 1980 (proceedings which may be treated as not being family proceedings), as amended by this Act.

(4) A magistrates' court shall not be competent to entertain any application, or make any order, involving the administration or application of—

(a) any property belonging to or held in trust for a child; or

(b) the income of any such property.

(5) The powers of a magistrates' court under section 63(2) of the Act of 1980 to suspend or rescind orders shall not apply in relation to any order made under this Act.

(6) Part I of Schedule 11 makes provision, including provision for the Lord Chancellor to make orders, with respect to the jurisdiction of courts and justices of the peace in relation to—

(a) proceedings under this Act; and

(b) proceedings under certain other enactments.

(7) For the purposes of this Act "the court" means the High Court, a county court or a magistrates' court.

(8) Subsection (7) is subject to the provision made by or under Part I of Schedule 11 and to any express provision as to the jurisdiction of any court made by any other provision of this Act.

(9) The Lord Chancellor may by order make provision for the principal registry of the Family Division of the High Court to be treated as if it were a county court for such purposes of this Act, or of any provision made under this Act, as may be specified in the order.

(10) Any order under subsection (9) may make such provision as the Lord Chancellor thinks expedient for the purpose of applying (with or without modifications) provisions which apply in relation to the procedure in county courts to the principal registry when it acts as if it were a county court.

(11) Part II of Schedule 11 makes amendments consequential on this section.

Appeals

94.—(1) [Subject to any express provisions to the contrary made by or under this Act, an][1] appeal shall lie to the High Court against— **39-083**

(a) the making by a magistrates' court of any order under this Act; or

(b) any refusal by a magistrates' court to make such an order.

(2) Where a magistrates' court has power, in relation to any proceedings under this Act, to decline jurisdiction because it considers that the case can more conveniently be dealt with by another court, no appeal shall lie against any exercise by that magistrates' court of that power.

(3) Subsection (1) does not apply in relation to an interim order for periodical payments made under Schedule 1.

(4) On an appeal under this section, the High Court may make such orders as may be necessary to give effect to its determination of the appeal.

(5) Where an order is made under subsection (4) the High Court may also make such incidental or consequential orders as appear to it to be just.

(6) Where an appeal from a magistrates' court relates to an order for the making of periodical payments, the High Court may order that its determination of the appeal shall have effect from such date as it thinks fit to specify in the order.

(7) The date so specified must not be earlier than the earliest date allowed in accordance with rules of court made for the purposes of this section.

(8) Where, on an appeal under this section in respect of an order requiring a person to make periodical payments, the High Court reduces the amount of those payments or discharges the order—

(a) it may order the person entitled to the payments to pay to the person making them such sum in respect of payments already made as the High Court thinks fit; and

(b) if any arrears are due under the order for periodical payments, it may remit payment of the whole, or part, of those arrears.

(9) Any order of the High Court made on an appeal under this section (other than one directing that an application be re-heard by a magistrates' court) shall, for the purposes—

(a) of the enforcement of the order; and

(b) of any power to vary, revive or discharge orders,

be treated as if it were an order of the magistrates' court from which the appeal was brought and not an order of the High Court.

(10) The Lord Chancellor may by order make provision as to the circumstances in which appeals may be made against decisions taken by courts on questions arising in connection with the transfer, or proposed transfer, of proceedings by virtue of any order under paragraph 2 of Schedule 11.

(11) Except to the extent provided for in any order made under subsection (10), no appeal may be made against any decision of a kind mentioned in that subsection.

Attendance of child at hearing under Part IV or V

95.—(1) In any proceedings in which a court is hearing an application for an order under Part IV or V, or is considering whether to make any such order, the court may order the child concerned to attend such stage or stages of the proceedings as may be specified in the order. **39-084**

[1] Words substituted by Courts and Legal Services Act 1990 c.41 Sch 16 (I) para 23

(2) The power conferred by subsection (1) shall be exercised in accordance with rules of court.

(3) Subsections (4) to (6) apply where—

(a) an order under subsection (1) has not been complied with; or

(b) the court has reasonable cause to believe that it will not be complied with.

(4) The court may make an order authorising a constable, or such person as may be specified in the order—

(a) to take charge of the child and to bring him to the court; and

(b) to enter and search any premises specified in the order if he has reasonable cause to believe that the child may be found on the premises.

(5) The court may order any person who is in a position to do so to bring the child to the court.

(6) Where the court has reason to believe that a person has information about the whereabouts of the child it may order him to disclose it to the court.

Evidence given by, or with respect to, children

39-085 **96.**—(1) Subsection (2) applies where a child who is called as a witness in any civil proceedings does not, in the opinion of the court, understand the nature of an oath.

(2) The child's evidence may be heard by the court if, in its opinion—

(a) he understands that it is his duty to speak the truth; and

(b) he has sufficient understanding to justify his evidence being heard.

(3) The Lord Chancellor may by order make provision for the admissibility of evidence which would otherwise be inadmissible under any rule of law relating to hearsay.

(4) An order under subsection (3) may only be made with respect to—

(a) civil proceedings in general or such civil proceedings, or class of civil proceedings, as may be prescribed; and

(b) evidence in connection with the upbringing, maintenance or welfare of a child.

(5) An order under subsection (3)—

(a) may, in particular, provide for the admissibility of statements which are made orally or in a prescribed form or which are recorded by any prescribed method of recording;

(b) may make different provision for different purposes and in relation to different descriptions of court; and

(c) may make such amendments and repeals in any enactment relating to evidence (other than in this Act) as the Lord Chancellor considers necessary or expedient in consequence of the provision made by the order.

(6) Subsection (5)(b) is without prejudice to section 104(4).

(7) In this section—

["civil proceedings" means civil proceeding, before any tribunal, in relation to which the strict rules of evidence apply, whether as a matter of law or by agreement of the parties, and references to "the court" shall be construed accordingly;][1]

"prescribed" means prescribed by an order under subsection (3).

[1] Substituted by Civil Evidence Act 1995 c.38 Sch 1 para 16

Privacy for children involved in certain proceedings

97.—(1) Rules made under section 144 of the Magistrates' Courts Act 1980 may make provision for a magistrates' court to sit in private in proceedings in which any powers under this Act may be exercised by the court with respect to any child. **39-086**

(2) No person shall publish any material which is intended, or likely, to identify—

(a) any child as being involved in any proceedings before [the High Court, a county court or][1] a magistrates' court in which any power under this Act may be exercised by the court with respect to that or any other child; or

(b) an address or school as being that of a child involved in any such proceedings.

(3) In any proceedings for an offence under this section it shall be a defence for the accused to prove that he did not know, and had no reason to suspect, that the published material was intended, or likely, to identify the child.

(4) The court or the [Lord Chancellor][2] may, if satisfied that the welfare of the child requires it, by order dispense with the requirements of subsection (2) to such extent as may be specified in the order.

(5) For the purposes of this section—

"publish" includes—

[(a) include in a programme service (within the meaning of the Broadcasting Act 1990);][3]

(b) cause to be published; and

"material" includes any picture or representation.

(6) Any person who contravenes this section shall be guilty of an offence and liable, on summary conviction, to a fine not exceeding level 4 on the standard scale.

(7) Subsection (1) is without prejudice to—

(a) the generality of the rule making power in section 144 of the Act of 1980; or

(b) any other power of a magistrates' court to sit in private.

(8) [Sections 69 (sittings of magistrates' courts for family proceedings) and 71 (newspaper reports of certain proceedings) of the Act of 1980][4] shall apply in relation to any proceedings [(before a magistrates' court)][5] to which this section applies subject to the provisions of this section.

Self-incrimination

98.—(1) In any proceedings in which a court is hearing an application for an order under Part IV or V, no person shall be excused from— **39-087**

(a) giving evidence on any matter; or

(b) answering any question put to him in the course of his giving evidence,

on the ground that doing so might incriminate him or his spouse of an offence.

(2) A statement or admission made in such proceedings shall not be admissible in evidence against the person making it or his spouse in proceedings for an offence other than perjury.

[1] Words added by Access to Justice Act 1999 c.22 Pt IV s 72 (a)
[2] Words substituted by SI 1992/709 art 3 (2)
[3] Paragraph substituted by Broadcasting Act 1990 c.42 s 203(1) Sch 20 para 53
[4] Words substituted by Courts and Legal Services Act 1990 c.41 Sch 16 (I) para 24
[5] Words added by Access to Justice Act 1999 c.22 Pt IV s 72 (b)

Restrictions on use of wardship jurisdiction

39-088 **100.**—(1) Section 7 of the Family Law Reform Act 1969 (which gives the High Court power to place a ward of court in the care, or under the supervision, of a local authority) shall cease to have effect.

(2) No court shall exercise the High Court's inherent jurisdiction with respect to children—

(a) so as to require a child to be placed in the care, or put under the supervision, of a local authority;

(b) so as to require a child to be accommodated by or on behalf of a local authority;

(c) so as to make a child who is the subject of a care order a ward of court; or

(d) for the purpose of conferring on any local authority power to determine any question which has arisen, or which may arise, in connection with any aspect of parental responsibility for a child.

(3) No application for any exercise of the court's inherent jurisdiction with respect to children may be made by a local authority unless the authority have obtained the leave of the court.

(4) The court may only grant leave if it is satisfied that—

(a) the result which the authority wish to achieve could not be achieved through the making of any order of a kind to which subsection (5) applies; and

(b) there is reasonable cause to believe that if the court's inherent jurisdiction is not exercised with respect to the child he is likely to suffer significant harm.

(5) This subsection applies to any order—

(a) made otherwise than in the exercise of the court's inherent jurisdiction; and

(b) which the local authority is entitled to apply for (assuming, in the case of any application which may only be made with leave, that leave is granted).

Search warrants

Power of constable to assist in exercise of certain powers to search for children or inspect premises

39-089 **102.**—(1) Where, on an application made by any person for a warrant under this section, it appears to the court—

(a) that a person attempting to exercise powers under any enactment mentioned in subsection (6) has been prevented from doing so by being refused entry to the premises concerned or refused access to the child concerned; or

(b) that any such person is likely to be so prevented from exercising any such powers,

it may issue a warrant authorising any constable to assist that person in the exercise of those powers, using reasonable force if necessary.

(2) Every warrant issued under this section shall be addressed to, and executed by, a constable who shall be accompanied by the person applying for the warrant if—

(a) that person so desires; and

(b) the court by whom the warrant is issued does not direct otherwise.

(3) A court granting an application for a warrant under this section may direct that the constable concerned may, in executing the warrant, be accompanied by a registered medical practitioner, registered nurse or [registered midwife][1] if he so chooses.

(4) An application for a warrant under this section shall be made in the manner and form prescribed by rules of court.

(5) Where—

(a) an application for a warrant under this section relates to a particular child; and

(b) it is reasonably practicable to do so,

the application and any warrant granted on the application shall name the child; and where it does not name him it shall describe him as clearly as possible.

(6) The enactments are—

(a) sections 62, 64, 67, 76, 80, 86 and 87;

(b) paragraph 8(1)(b) and (2)(b) of Schedule 3;

(c) section 33 of the Adoption Act 1976 (duty of local authority to secure that protected children are visited from time to time).

[Interpretation

105.—(1) In this Act— 39-090

"adoption agency" means a body which may be referred to as an adoption agency by virtue of section 1 of the Adoption Act 1976;

["appropriate children's home" has the meaning given by section 23;][2]

"bank holiday" means a day which is a bank holiday under the Banking and Financial Dealings Act 1971;

["care home" has the same meaning as in the Care Standards Act 2000;][3]

"care order" has the meaning given by section 31(11) and also includes any order which by or under any enactment has the effect of, or is deemed to be, a care order for the purposes of this Act; and any reference to a child who is in the care of an authority is a reference to a child who is in their care by virtue of a care order;

"child" means, subject to paragraph 16 of Schedule 1, a person under the age of eighteen;

"child assessment order" has the meaning given by section 43(2);

"child of the family", in relation to the parties to a marriage, means —

(a) a child of both of those parties;

(b) any other child, not being a child who is placed with those parties as foster parents by a local authority or voluntary organisation, who has been treated by both of those parties as a child of their family;

["children's home" has the meaning given by section 23;][4]

"community home" has the meaning given by section 53;

"contact order" has the meaning given by section 8(1);

"day care" [(except in Part XA)][5] has the same meaning as in section 18;

[1] Words substituted by SI 2002/253 Sch 5 para 10 (c)
[2] Inserted by Care Standards Act 2000 c.14 Sch 4 para 14 (23)
[3] Inserted by Care Standards Act 2000 c.14 Sch 4 para 14 (23)
[4] Inserted by Care Standards Act 2000 c.14 Sch 4 para 14 (23)
[5] Inserted by Care Standards Act 2000 c.14 Sch 4 para 14 (23)

"disabled", in relation to a child, has the same meaning as in section 17(11);[...][1]

"domestic premises" has the meaning given by section 71(12);

["dwelling-house" includes—

(a) any building or part of a building which is occupied as a dwelling;

(b) any caravan, house-boat or structure which is occupied as a dwelling;

and any yard garden, garage or outhouse belonging to it and occupied with it;][2]

"education supervision order" has the meaning given in section 36;

"emergency protection order" means an order under section 44;

"family assistance order" has the meaning given in section 16(2);

"family proceedings" has the meaning given by section 8(3);

"functions" includes powers and duties;

"guardian of a child" means a guardian (other than a guardian of the estate of a child) appointed in accordance with the provisions of section 5;

"harm" has the same meaning as in section 31(9) and the question of whether harm is significant shall be determined in accordance with section 31(10);

["Health Authority" means a Health Authority established under section 8 of the National Health Service Act 1977;][3]

"health service hospital" has the same meaning as in the National Health Service Act 1977;

"hospital" [(except in Schedule 9A)][4]has the same meaning as in the Mental Health Act 1983, except that it does not include a [hospital at which high security psychiatric services within the meaning of that Act are provided][5];

"ill-treatment" has the same meaning as in section 31(9);

["income-based jobseeker's allowance" has the same meaning as in the Jobseekers Act 1995;][6]

["independent hospital" has the same meaning as in the Care Standards Act 2000;][7]

"independent school" has the same meaning as in [the Education Act 1996][8];

"local authority" means, in relation to England [...][9], the council of a county, a metropolitan district, a London Borough or the Common Council of the City of London [, in relation to Wales, the council of a county or a county borough][10] and, in relation to Scotland, a local authority within the meaning of section 1(2) of the Social Work (Scotland) Act 1968;

"local authority foster parent" has the same meaning as in section 23(3);

---

[1] Words repealed by Health Authorities Act 1995 c.17 Sch 3 para 1
[2] Inserted by Family Law Act 1996 c.27 Sch 6 para 5
[3] Substituted by Health Authorities Act 1995 c.17 Sch 1 (III) para 118 (10) (b)
[4] Inserted by Care Standards Act 2000 c.14 Sch 4 para 14 (23)
[5] Words susbtituted by SI 2000/90 Sch 2 (I) para 5
[6] Definition inserted by Jobseekers Act 1995 c.18 Sch 2 para 19 (4)
[7] Inserted by Care Standards Act 2000 c.14 Sch 4 para 14 (23)
[8] Words substituted by Education Act 1996 c.56 Sch 37 (I) para 91
[9] Words repealed by Local Government (Wales) Act 1994 c.19 Sch 18 para 1
[10] Words inserted by Local Government (Wales) Act 1994 c.19 Sch 10 para 13

"local education authority" has the same meaning as in [the Education Act 1996][1];
"local housing authority" has the same meaning as in the Housing Act 1985;
["officer of the Service" has the same meaning as in the Criminal Justice and Court Services Act 2000;][2]
"parental responsibility" has the meaning given in section 3;
"parental responsibility agreement" has the meaning given in section 4(1);
"prescribed" means prescribed by regulations made under this Act;
[["private children's home" means a children's home in respect of which a person is registered under Part II of the Care Standards Act 2000 which is not a community home or a voluntary home;][3]
"Primary Care Trust" means a Primary Care Trust established under section 16A of the National Health Service Act 1977;][4]
"privately fostered child" and "to foster a child privately" have the same meaning as in section 66;
"prohibited steps order" has the meaning given by section 8(1);
"protected child" has the same meaning as in Part III of the Adoption Act 1976;
"registered pupil" has the same meaning as in [the Education Act 1996][5];
"relative", in relation to a child, means a grandparent, brother, sister, uncle or aunt (whether of the full blood or half blood or by affinity) or step-parent;
"residence order" has the meaning given by section 8(1);
"responsible person", in relation to a child who is the subject of a supervision order, has the meaning given in paragraph 1 of Schedule 3 ;
"school" has the same meaning as in [the Education Act 1996][6] or, in relation to Scotland, in the Education (Scotland) Act 1980;
"service" , in relation to any provision made under Part III, includes any facility;
"signed" , in relation to any person, includes the making by that person of his mark;
"special education needs" has the same meaning as in [the Education Act 1996][7];
["Special Health Authority" means a Special Health Authority established under section 11 of the National Health Service Act 1977;][8]
"specific issue order" has the meaning given by section 8(1);
"supervision order" has the meaning given by section 31(11);
"supervised child" and "supervisor", in relation to a supervision order or an education supervision order, mean respectively the child who is (or is to be) under supervision and the person under whose supervision he is (or is to be) by virtue of the order;
"upbringing" , in relation to any child, includes the care of the child but not his maintenance;
"voluntary home" has the meaning given by section 60;

[1] Words substituted by Education Act 1996 c.56 Sch 37 (I) para 91
[2] Inserted by Criminal Justice and Court Services Act 2000 c.43 Sch 7 (II) para 95
[3] Inserted by Care Standards Act 2000 c.14 Sch 4 para 14 (23)
[4] Added by SI 2000/90 Sch 1 para 24 (10)
[5] Words substituted by Education Act 1996 c.56 Sch 37 (I) para 91
[6] Words substituted by Education Act 1996 c.56 Sch 37 (I) para 91
[7] Words substituted by Education Act 1996 c.56 Sch 37 (I) para 91
[8] Substituted by Health Authorities Act 1995 c.17 Sch 1 (III) para 118 (10) (c)

"voluntary organisation" means a body (other than a public or local authority) whose activities are not carried on for profit.

(2) References in this Act to a child whose father and mother were, or (as the case may be) were not, married to each other at the time of his birth must be read with section 1 of the Family Law Reform Act 1987 (which extends the meaning of such references).

(3) References in this Act to—

(a) a person with whom a child lives, or is to live, as the result of a residence order; or

(b) a person in whose favour a residence order is in force,

shall be construed as references to the person named in the order as the person with whom the child is to live.

(4) References in this Act to a child who is looked after by a local authority have the same meaning as they have (by virtue of section 22) in Part III.

(5) References in this Act to accommodation provided by or on behalf of a local authority are references to accommodation so provided in the exercise of functions [of that or any other local authority which are social services functions within the meaning of][1] the Local Authority Social Services Act 1970.

[(5A) References in this Act to a child minder shall be construed–

(a) in relation to Scotland, in accordance with section 71;

(b) in relation to England and Wales, in accordance with section 79A.][2]

(6) In determining the "ordinary residence" of a child for any purpose of this Act, there shall be disregarded any period in which he lives in any place—

(a) which is a school or other institution;

(b) in accordance with the requirements of a supervision order under this Act or an order under [section 63(1) of the Powers of Criminal Courts (Sentencing) Act 2000][3]; or

(c) while he is being provided with accommodation by or on behalf of a local authority.

(7) References in this Act to children who are in need shall be construed in accordance with section 17.

(8) Any notice or other document required under this Act to be served on any person may be served on him by being delivered personally to him, or being sent by post to him in a registered letter or by the recorded delivery service at his proper address.

(9) Any such notice or other document required to be served on a body corporate or a firm shall be duly served if it is served on the secretary or clerk of that body or a partner of that firm.

(10) For the purposes of this section, and of section 7 of the Interpretation Act 1978 in its application to this section, the proper address of a person—

(a) in the case of a secretary or clerk of a body corporate, shall be that of the registered or principal office of that body;

(b) in the case of a partner of a firm, shall be that of the principal office of the firm; and

(c) in any other case, shall be the last known address of the person to be served.

[1] Words substituted by Local Government Act 2000 c.22 Sch 5 para 22

[2] Inserted by Care Standards Act 2000 c.14 Sch 4 para 14 (23)

[3] Words substituted by Powers of Criminal Courts (Sentencing) Act 2000 c.6 Sch 9 para 129

[SCHEDULES

Section 15(1) Schedule 1

FINANCIAL PROVISION FOR CHILDREN

Orders for financial relief against parents

1.—(1) On an application made by a parent or guardian of a child, or by any person in whose favour a residence order is in force with respect to a child, the court may— **39-091**

(a) in the case of an application to the High Court or a county court, make one or more of the orders mentioned in sub-paragraph (2);

(b) in the case of an application to a magistrates' court, make one or both of the orders mentioned in paragraphs (a) and (c) of that sub-paragraph.

(2) The orders referred to in sub-paragraph (1) are—

(a) an order requiring either or both parents of a child—

(i) to make to the applicant for the benefit of the child; or

(ii) to make to the child himself,

such periodical payments, for such term, as may be specified in the order;

(b) an order requiring either or both parents of a child—

(i) to secure to the applicant for the benefit of the child; or

(ii) to secure to the child himself,

such periodical payments, for such term, as may be so specified;

(c) an order requiring either or both parents of a child—

(i) to pay to the applicant for the benefit of the child; or

(ii) to pay to the child himself,

such lump sum as may be so specified;

(d) an order requiring a settlement to be made for the benefit of the child, and to the satisfaction of the court, of property—

(i) to which either parent is entitled (either in possession or in reversion); and

(ii) which is specified in the order;

(e) an order requiring either or both parents of a child—

(i) to transfer to the applicant, for the benefit of the child; or

(ii) to transfer to the child himself,

such property to which the parent is, or the parents are, entitled (either in possession or in reversion) as may be specified in the order.

(3) The powers conferred by this paragraph may be exercised at any time.

(4) An order under sub-paragraph (2)(a) or (b) may be varied or discharged by a subsequent order made on the application of any person by or to whom payments were required to be made under the previous order.

(5) Where a court makes an order under this paragraph—

(a) it may at any time make a further such order under sub-paragraph (2)(a), (b) or (c) with respect to the child concerned if he has not reached the age of eighteen;

(b) it may not make more than one order under sub-paragraph (2)(d) or (e) against the same person in respect of the same child.

(6) On making, varying or discharging a residence order the court may exercise any of its powers under this Schedule even though no application has been made to it under this Schedule.

[(7) Where a child is a ward of court, the court may exercise any of its powers under this Schedule even though no application has been made to it.][1]

Orders for financial relief for persons over eighteen

2.—(1) If, on an application by a person who has reached the age of eighteen, it appears to the court— **39-092**

(a) that the applicant is, will be or (if an order were made under this paragraph) would be receiving instruction at an educational establishment or undergoing training for a trade, profession or vocation, whether or not while in gainful employment; or

(b) that there are special circumstances which justify the making of an order under this paragraph,

the court may make one or both of the orders mentioned in sub-paragraph (2).

(2) The orders are—

[1] Added by Courts and Legal Services Act 1990 c.41 Sch 16 (I) para 10 (2)

(a) an order requiring either or both of the applicant's parents to pay to the applicant such periodical payments, for such term, as may be specified in the order;
(b) an order requiring either or both of the applicant's parents to pay to the applicant such lump sum as may be so specified.

(3) An application may not be made under this paragraph by any person if, immediately before he reached the age of sixteen, a periodical payments order was in force with respect to him.

(4) No order shall be made under this paragraph at a time when the parents of the applicant are living with each other in the same household.

(5) An order under sub-paragraph (2)(a) may be varied or discharged by a subsequent order made on the application of any person by or to whom payments were required to be made under the previous order.

(6) In sub-paragraph (3) "periodical payments order" means an order made under—
(a) this Schedule;
(b) [...][1]
(c) section 23 or 27 of the Matrimonial Causes Act 1973;
(d) Part I of the Domestic Proceedings and Magistrates' Courts Act 1978,
for the making or securing of periodical payments.

(7) The powers conferred by this paragraph shall be exercisable at any time.

(8) Where the court makes an order under this paragraph it may from time to time while that order remains in force make a further such order.

Duration of orders for financial relief

39-093 **3.**— (1) The term to be specified in an order for periodical payments made under paragraph 1(2)(a) or (b) in favour of a child may begin with the date of the making of an application for the order in question or any later date [or a date ascertained in accordance with sub-paragraph (5) or (6)][2] but—
(a) shall not in the first instance extend beyond the child's seventeenth birthday unless the court thinks it right in the circumstances of the case to specify a later date; and
(b) shall not in any event extend beyond the child's eighteenth birthday.

(2) Paragraph (b) of sub-paragraph (1) shall not apply in the case of a child if it appears to the court that—
(a) the child is, or will be or (if an order were made without complying with that paragraph) would be receiving instruction at an educational establishment or undergoing training for a trade, profession or vocation, whether or not while in gainful employment; or
(b) there are special circumstances which justify the making of an order without complying with that paragraph.

(3) An order for periodical payments made under paragraph 1(2)(a) or 2(2)(a) shall, notwithstanding anything in the order, cease to have effect on the death of the person liable to make payments under the order.

(4) Where an order is made under paragraph 1(2)(a) or (b) requiring periodical payments to be made or secured to the parent of a child, the order shall cease to have effect if—
(a) any parent making or securing the payments; and
(b) any parent to whom the payments are made or secured,
live together for a period of more than six months.

[(5) Where—
(a) a [maintenance calculation][3] ("the [current calculation][4]") is in force with respect to a child; and
(b) an application is made for an order under paragraph 1(2)(a) or (b) of this Schedule for periodical payments in favour of that child—
(i) in accordance with section 8 of the Child Support Act 1991; and
(ii) before the end of the period of 6 months beginning with the making of the [current calculation][5],
the term to be specified in any such order made on that application may be expressed to begin on, or at any time after, the earliest permitted date.

[1] Repealed by Child Support Act 1991 c.48 s 58 (14)
[2] Words added by SI 1993/623 Sch 1 para 10
[3] Words substituted in relation to cases specified in SI 2003/192 art.3 by Child Support, Pensions and Social Security Act 2000 c.19 Sch 3 para 10 (2) (a)
[4] Words substituted in relation to cases specified in SI 2003/192 art.3 by Child Support, Pensions and Social Security Act 2000 c.19 Sch 3 para 10 (2) (b)
[5] Words substituted in relation to cases specified in SI 2003/192 art.3 by Child Support, Pensions and Social Security Act 2000 c.19 Sch 3 para 10 (2) (b)

(6) For the purposes of subsection (5) above, "the earliest permitted date" is whichever is the later of—

(a) the date 6 months before the application is made; or

(b) the date on which the [current calculation][1] took effect or, where successive [maintenance calculations][2] have been continuously in force with respect to a child, on which the first of [those calculations][3] took effect.

(7) Where—

(a) a [maintenance calculation][4] ceases to have effect [...][5] by or under any provision of the Child Support Act 1991, and

(b) an application is made, before the end of the period of 6 months beginning with the relevant date, for an order for periodical payments under paragraph 1(2)(a) or (b) in favour of a child with respect to whom that [maintenance calculation][6] was in force immediately before it ceased to have effect [...][7],

the term to be specified in any such order, or in any interim order under paragraph 9, made on that application may begin with the date on which that [maintenance calculation][8] ceased to have effect [...][9], or any later date.

(8) In sub-paragraph (7)(b)—

(a) where the [maintenance calculation][10] ceased to have effect, the relevant date is the date on which it so ceased[...][11][.][12]

(b) [...][13]][14]

Matters to which court is to have regard in making orders for financial relief

4.—(1) In deciding whether to exercise its powers under paragraph 1 or 2, and if so in what manner, the court shall have regard to all the circumstances including— **39-094**

(a) the income, earning capacity, property and other financial resources which each person mentioned in sub-paragraph (4) has or is likely to have in the foreseeable future;

(b) the financial needs, obligations and responsibilities which each person mentioned in sub-paragraph (4) has or is likely to have in the foreseeable future;

(c) the financial needs of the child;

(d) the income, earning capacity (if any), property and other financial resources of the child;

(e) any physical or mental disability of the child;

(f) the manner in which the child was being, or was expected to be, educated or trained.

(2) In deciding whether to exercise its powers under paragraph 1 against a person who is not the mother or father of the child, and if so in what manner, the court shall in addition have regard to—

---

[1] Words substituted in relation to cases specified in SI 2003/192 art 3 by Child Support, Pensions and Social Security Act 2000 c.19 Sch 3 para 10 (2) (b)

[2] Words substituted in relation to cases specified in SI 2003/192 art 3 by Child Support, Pensions and Social Security Act 2000 c.19 Sch 3 para 10 (2) (c)

[3] Words substituted in relation to cases specified in SI 2003/192 art 3 by Child Support, Pensions and Social Security Act 2000 c.19 Sch 3 para 10 (2) (d)

[4] Words substituted in relation to cases specified in SI 2003/192 art 3 by Child Support, Pensions and Social Security Act 2000 c.19 Sch 3 para 10 (2) (a)

[5] Words repealed in relation to cases specified in SI 2003/192 art 3 by Child Support, Pensions and Social Security Act 2000 c.19 Sch 9 (I) para 1

[6] Words substituted in relation to cases specified in SI 2003/192 art 3 by Child Support, Pensions and Social Security Act 2000 c.19 Sch 3 para 10 (2) (a)

[7] Words repealed in relation to cases specified in SI 2003/192 art 3 by Child Support, Pensions and Social Security Act 2000 c.19 Sch 9 (I) para 1

[8] Words substituted in relation to cases specified in SI 2003/192 art 3 by Child Support, Pensions and Social Security Act 2000 c.19 Sch 3 para 10 (2) (a)

[9] Words repealed in relation to cases specified in SI 2003/192 art 3 by Child Support, Pensions and Social Security Act 2000 c.19 Sch 9 (I) para 1

[10] Words substituted in relation to cases specified in SI 2003/192 art 3 by Child Support, Pensions and Social Security Act 2000 c.19 Sch 3 para 10 (2) (a)

[11] Repealed in relation to cases specified in SI 2003/192 art 3 by Child Support, Pensions and Social Security Act 2000 c.19 Sch 9 (I) para 1

[12] Repealed in relation to cases specified in SI 2003/192 art 3 by Child Support, Pensions and Social Security Act 2000 c.19 Sch 9 (I) para 1

[13] Repealed in relation to cases specified in SI 2003/192 art 3 by Child Support, Pensions and Social Security Act 2000 c.19 Sch 9 (I) para 1

[14] Added by SI 1993/623 Sch 1 para 11

(a) whether that person had assumed responsibility for the maintenance of the child and, if so, the extent to which and basis on which he assumed that responsibility and the length of the period during which he met that responsibility;
(b) whether he did so knowing that the child was not his child;
(c) the liability of any other person to maintain the child.

(3) Where the court makes an order under paragraph 1 against a person who is not the father of the child, it shall record in the order that the order is made on the basis that the person against whom the order is made is not the child's father.

(4) The persons mentioned in sub-paragraph (1) are—
(a) in relation to a decision whether to exercise its powers under paragraph 1, any parent of the child;
(b) in relation to a decision whether to exercise its powers under paragraph 2, the mother and father of the child;
(c) the applicant for the order;
(d) any other person in whose favour the court proposes to make the order.

Provisions relating to lump sums

39-095 **5.**—(1) Without prejudice to the generality of paragraph 1, an order under that paragraph for the payment of a lump sum may be made for the purpose of enabling any liabilities or expenses—
(a) incurred in connection with the birth of the child or in maintaining the child; and
(b) reasonably incurred before the making of the order,
to be met.

(2) The amount of any lump sum required to be paid by an order made by a magistrates' court under paragraph 1 or 2 shall not exceed £1000 or such larger amount as the [Lord Chancellor][1] may from time to time by order fix for the purposes of this sub-paragraph.

(3) The power of the court under paragraph 1 or 2 to vary or discharge an order for the making or securing of periodical payments by a parent shall include power to make an order under that provision for the payment of a lump sum by that parent.

(4) The amount of any lump sum which a parent may be required to pay by virtue of sub-paragraph (3) shall not, in the case of an order made by a magistrates' court, exceed the maximum amount that may at the time of the making of the order be required to be paid under sub-paragraph (2), but a magistrates' court may make an order for the payment of a lump sum not exceeding that amount even though the parent was required to pay a lump sum by a previous order under this Act.

(5) An order made under paragraph 1 or 2 for the payment of a lump sum may provide for the payment of that sum by instalments.

(6) Where the court provides for the payment of a lump sum by instalments the court, on an application made either by the person liable to pay or the person entitled to receive that sum, shall have power to vary that order by varying—
(a) the number of instalments payable;
(b) the amount of any instalment payable;
(c) the date on which any instalment becomes payable.

Variation etc. of orders for periodical payments

39-096 **6.**—(1) In exercising its powers under paragraph 1 or 2 to vary or discharge an order for the making or securing of periodical payments the court shall have regard to all the circumstances of the case, including any change in any of the matters to which the court was required to have regard when making the order.

(2) The power of the court under paragraph 1 or 2 to vary an order for the making or securing of periodical payments shall include power to suspend any provision of the order temporarily and to revive any provision so suspended.

(3) Where on an application under paragraph 1 or 2 for the variation or discharge of an order for the making or securing of periodical payments the court varies the payments required to be made under that order, the court may provide that the payments as so varied shall be made from such date as the court may specify [except that, subject to sub-paragraph (9), the date shall not be][2] earlier than the date of the making of the application.

(4) An application for the variation of an order made under paragraph 1 for the making or securing of periodical payments to or for the benefit of a child may, if the child has reached the age of sixteen, be made by the child himself.

(5) Where an order for the making or securing of periodical payments made under paragraph 1 ceases to have effect on the date on which the child reaches the age of sixteen, or at any time after that

[1] Words substituted by SI 1992/709 art 3 (2)
[2] Words substituted by SI 1993/623 Sch 1 para 12

date but before or on the date on which he reaches the age of eighteen, the child may apply to the court which made the order for an order for its revival.

(6) If on such an application it appears to the court that—

(a) the child is, will be or (if an order were made under this sub-paragraph) would be receiving instruction at an educational establishment or undergoing training for a trade, profession or vocation, whether or not while in gainful employment; or

(b) there are special circumstances which justify the making of an order under this paragraph,

the court shall have power by order to revive the order from such date as the court may specify, not being earlier than the date of the making of the application.

(7) Any order which is revived by an order under sub-paragraph (5) may be varied or discharged under that provision, on the application of any person by whom or to whom payments are required to be made under the revived order.

(8) An order for the making or securing of periodical payments made under paragraph 1 may be varied or discharged, after the death of either parent, on the application of a guardian of the child concerned.

[(9) Where—

(a) an order under paragraph 1(2)(a) or (b) for the making or securing of periodical payments in favour of more than one child ("the order") is in force;

(b) the order requires payments specified in it to be made to or for the benefit of more than one child without apportioning those payments between them;

(c) a [maintenance calculation][1] ("[the calculation][2]") is made with respect to one or more, but not all, of the children with respect to whom those payments are to be made; and

(d) an application is made, before the end of the period of 6 months beginning with the date on which [the calculation][3] was made, for the variation or discharge of the order,

the court may, in exercise of its powers under paragraph 1 to vary or discharge the order, direct that the variation or discharge shall take effect from the date on which [the calculation][4] took effect or any later date.][5]

Variation of orders for periodical payments etc. made by magistrates' courts

[**6A.**— (1) Subject to sub-paragraphs (7) and (8), the power of a magistrates' court— **39-097**

(a) under paragraph 1 or 2 to vary an order for the making of periodical payments, or

(b) under paragraph 5(6) to vary an order for the payment of a lump sum by instalments,

shall include power, if the court is satisfied that payment has not been made in accordance with the order, to exercise one of its powers under paragraphs (a) to (d) of section 59(3) of the Magistrates' Courts Act 1980.

(2) In any case where—

(a) a magistrates' court has made an order under this Schedule for the making of periodical payments or for the payment of a lump sum by instalments, and

(b) payments under the order are required to be made by any method of payment falling within section 59(6) of the Magistrates' Courts Act 1980 (standing order, etc.),

any person entitled to make an application under this Schedule for the variation of the order (in this paragraph referred to as "the applicant") may apply to the clerk to the justices for the petty sessions area for which the court is acting for the order to be varied as mentioned in sub-paragraph (3).

(3) Subject to sub-paragraph (5), where an application is made under sub-paragraph (2), the clerk, after giving written notice (by post or otherwise) of the application to any interested party and allowing that party, within the period of 14 days beginning with the date of the giving of that notice, an opportunity to make written representations, may vary the order to provide that payments under the order shall be made [to the justices' chief executive for the court][6].

(4) The clerk may proceed with an application under sub-paragraph (2) notwithstanding that any such interested party as is referred to in sub-paragraph (3) has not received written notice of the application.

---

[1] Words substituted in relation to cases specified in SI 2003/192 art 3 by Child Support, Pensions and Social Security Act 2000 c.19 Sch 3 para 10 (3) (b)

[2] Words substituted in relation to cases specified in SI 2003/192 art 3 by Child Support, Pensions and Social Security Act 2000 c.19 Sch 3 para 10 (3) (a)

[3] Words substituted in relation to cases specified in SI 2003/192 art 3 by Child Support, Pensions and Social Security Act 2000 c.19 Sch 3 para 10 (3) (a)

[4] Words substituted in relation to cases specified in SI 2003/192 art 3 by Child Support, Pensions and Social Security Act 2000 c.19 Sch 3 para 10 (3) (a)

[5] Added by SI 1993/623 Sch 1 para 13

[6] Words substituted by Access to Justice Act 1999 c.22 Sch 13 para 161

(5) Where an application has been made under sub-paragraph (2), the clerk may, if he considers it inappropriate to exercise his power under sub-paragraph (3), refer the matter to the court which, subject to sub-paragraphs (7) and (8), may vary the order by exercising one of its powers under paragraphs (a) to (d) of section 59(3) of the Magistrates' Courts Act 1980.

(6) Subsection (4) of section 59 of the Magistrates' Courts Act 1980 (power of court to order that account be opened) shall apply for the purposes of sub-paragraphs (1) and (5) as it applies for the purposes of that section.

(7) Before varying the order by exercising one of its powers under paragraphs (a) to (d) of section 59(3) of the Magistrates' Courts Act 1980, the court shall have regard to any representations made by the parties to the application.

(8) If the court does not propose to exercise its power [under paragraph (c), (cc) or (d) of subsection (3) of section 59 of the Magistrates' Courts Act 1980][1], the court shall, unless upon representations expressly made in that behalf by the applicant for the order it is satisfied that it is undesirable to do so, exercise its power under paragraph (b) of that subsection.

(9) None of the powers of the court, or of the clerk to the justices, conferred by this paragraph shall be exercisable in relation to an order under this Schedule for the making of periodical payments, or for the payment of a lump sum by instalments, which is not a qualifying maintenance order (within the meaning of section 59 of the Magistrates' Courts Act 1980).

(10) In sub-paragraphs (3) and (4) "interested party", means in relation to an application made by the applicant under sub-paragraph (2), a person who would be entitled to be a party to an application for the variation of the order made by the applicant under any other provision of this Schedule if such an application were made.][2]

Variation of orders for secured periodical payments after death of parent

39-098 7.—(1) Where the parent liable to make payments under a secured periodical payments order has died, the persons who may apply for the variation or discharge of the order shall include the personal representatives of the deceased parent.

(2) No application for the variation of the order shall, except with the permission of the court, be made after the end of the period of six months from the date on which representation in regard to the estate of that parent is first taken out.

(3) The personal representatives of a deceased person against whom a secured periodical payments order was made shall not be liable for having distributed any part of the estate of the deceased after the end of the period of six months referred to in sub-paragraph (2) on the ground that they ought to have taken into account the possibility that the court might permit an application for variation to be made after that period by the person entitled to payments under the order.

(4) Sub-paragraph (3) shall not prejudice any power to recover any part of the estate so distributed arising by virtue of the variation of an order in accordance with this paragraph.

(5) Where an application to vary a secured periodical payments order is made after the death of the parent liable to make payments under the order, the circumstances to which the court is required to have regard under paragraph 6(1) shall include the changed circumstances resulting from the death of the parent.

(6) In considering for the purposes of sub-paragraph (2) the question when representation was first taken out, a grant limited to settled land or to trust property shall be left out of account and a grant limited to real estate or to personal estate shall be left out of account unless a grant limited to the remainder of the estate has previously been made or is made at the same time.

(7) In this paragraph "secured periodical payments order" means an order for secured periodical payments under paragraph 1(2)(b).

Financial relief under other enactments

39-099 **8.**—(1) This paragraph applies where a residence order is made with respect to a child at a time when there is in force an order ("the financial relief order") made under any enactment other than this Act and requiring a person to contribute to the child's maintenance.

(2) Where this paragraph applies, the court may, on the application of—

(a) any person required by the financial relief order to contribute to the child's maintenance; or

(b) any person in whose favour a residence order with respect to the child is in force,

make an order revoking the financial relief order, or varying it by altering the amount of any sum payable under that order or by substituting the applicant for the person to whom any such sum is otherwise payable under that order.

[1] Words substituted by SI 1994/731 art 4
[2] Added by Maintenance Enforcement Act 1991 c.17 s 6

Interim orders

9.—(1) Where an application is made under paragraph 1 or 2 the court may, at any time before it disposes of the application, make an interim order— **39-100**

(a) requiring either or both parents to make such periodical payments, at such times and for such term as the court thinks fit; and

(b) giving any direction which the court thinks fit.

(2) An interim order made under this paragraph may provide for payments to be made from such date as the court may specify [except that, subject to paragraph 3(5) and (6), the date shall not be][1] earlier than the date of the making of the application under paragraph 1 or 2.

(3) An interim order made under this paragraph shall cease to have effect when the application is disposed of or, if earlier, on the date specified for the purposes of this paragraph in the interim order.

(4) An interim order in which a date has been specified for the purposes of sub-paragraph (3) may be varied by substituting a later date.

Alteration of maintenance agreements

10.—(1) In this paragraph and in paragraph 11 "maintenance agreement" means any agreement in writing made with respect to a child, whether before or after the commencement of this paragraph, which— **39-101**

(a) is or was made between the father and mother of the child; and

(b) contains provision with respect to the making or securing of payments, or the disposition or use of any property, for the maintenance or education of the child,

and any such provisions are in this paragraph, and paragraph 11, referred to as "financial arrangements".

(2) Where a maintenance agreement is for the time being subsisting and each of the parties to the agreement is for the time being either domiciled or resident in England and Wales, then, either party may apply to the court for an order under this paragraph.

(3) If the court to which the application is made is satisfied either—

(a) that, by reason of a change in the circumstances in the light of which any financial arrangements contained in the agreement were made (including a change foreseen by the parties when making the agreement), the agreement should be altered so as to make different financial arrangements; or

(b) that the agreement does not contain proper financial arrangements with respect to the child,

then that court may by order make such alterations in the agreement by varying or revoking any financial arrangements contained in it as may appear to it to be just having regard to all the circumstances.

(4) If the maintenance agreement is altered by an order under this paragraph, the agreement shall have effect thereafter as if the alteration had been made by agreement between the parties and for valuable consideration.

(5) Where a court decides to make an order under this paragraph altering the maintenance agreement—

(a) by inserting provision for the making or securing by one of the parties to the agreement of periodical payments for the maintenance of the child; or

(b) by increasing the rate of periodical payments required to be made or secured by one of the parties for the maintenance of the child,

then, in deciding the term for which under the agreement as altered by the order the payments or (as the case may be) the additional payments attributable to the increase are to be made or secured for the benefit of the child, the court shall apply the provisions of sub-paragraph (1) and (2) of paragraph 3 as if the order were an order under paragraph 1(2)(a) or (b).

(6) A magistrates' court shall not entertain an application under sub-paragraph (2) unless both the parties to the agreement are resident in England and Wales and at least one of the parties is resident in the commission area [...][2]for which the court is appointed, and shall not have power to make any order on such an application except—

(a) in a case where the agreement contains no provision for periodical payments by either of the parties, an order inserting provision for the making by one of the parties of periodical payments for the maintenance of the child;

(b) in a case where the agreement includes provision for the making by one of the parties of periodical payments, an order increasing or reducing the rate of, or terminating, any of those payments.

[1] Words substituted by SI 1993/623 Sch 1 para 14

[2] Words repealed by Access to Justice Act 1999 c.22 Sch 15 (V) (1) para 1

(7) For the avoidance of doubt it is hereby declared that nothing in this paragraph affects any power of a court before which any proceedings between the parties to a maintenance agreement are brought under any other enactment to make an order containing financial arrangements or any right of either party to apply for such an order in such proceedings.

39-102 **11.**—(1) Where a maintenance agreement provides for the continuation, after the death of one of the parties, of payments for the maintenance of a child and that party dies domiciled in England and Wales, the surviving party or the personal representatives of the deceased party may apply to the High Court or a county court for an order under paragraph 10.

(2) If a maintenance agreement is altered by a court on an application under this paragraph, the agreement shall have effect thereafter as if the alteration had been made, immediately before the death, by agreement between the parties and for valuable consideration.

(3) An application under this paragraph shall not, except with leave of the High Court or a county court, be made after the end of the period of six months beginning with the day on which representation in regard to the estate of the deceased is first taken out.

(4) In considering for the purposes of sub-paragraph (3) the question when representation was first taken out, a grant limited to settled land or to trust property shall be left out of account and a grant limited to real estate or to personal estate shall be left out of account unless a grant limited to the remainder of the estate has previously been made or is made at the same time.

(5) A county court shall not entertain an application under this paragraph, or an application for leave to make an application under this paragraph, unless it would have jurisdiction to hear and determine proceedings for an order under section 2 of the Inheritance (Provision for Family and Dependants) Act 1975 in relation to the deceased's estate by virtue of section 25 of the County Courts Act 1984 (jurisdiction under the Act of 1975).

(6) The provisions of this paragraph shall not render the personal representatives of the deceased liable for having distributed any part of the estate of the deceased after the expiry of the period of six months referred to in sub-paragraph (3) on the ground that they ought to have taken into account the possibility that a court might grant leave for an application by virtue of this paragraph to be made by the surviving party after that period.

(7) Sub-paragraph (6) shall not prejudice any power to recover any part of the estate so distributed arising by virtue of the making of an order in pursuance of this paragraph.

Enforcement of orders for maintenance

39-103 **12.**—(1) Any person for the time being under an obligation to make payments in pursuance of any order for the payment of money made by a magistrates' court under this Act shall give notice of any change of address to such person (if any) as may be specified in the order.

(2) Any person failing without reasonable excuse to give such a notice shall be guilty of an offence and liable on summary conviction to a fine not exceeding level 2 on the standard scale.

(3) An order for the payment of money made by a magistrates' court under this Act shall be enforceable as a magistrates' court maintenance order within the meaning of section 150(1) of the Magistrates' Courts Act 1980.

Direction for settlement of instrument by conveyancing counsel

39-104 **13.** Where the High Court or a county court decides to make an order under this Act for the securing of periodical payments or for the transfer or settlement of property, it may direct that the matter be referred to one of the conveyancing counsel of the court to settle a proper instrument to be executed by all necessary parties.

Financial provision for child resident in country outside England and Wales

39-105 **14.**—(1) Where one parent of a child lives in England and Wales and the child lives outside England and Wales with—

(a) another parent of his;
(b) a guardian of his; or
(c) a person in whose favour a residence order is in force with respect to the child,

the court shall have power, on an application made by any of the persons mentioned in paragraphs (a) to (c), to make one or both of the orders mentioned in paragraph 1(2)(a) and (b) against the parent living in England and Wales.

(2) Any reference in this Act to the powers of the court under paragraph 1(2) or to an order made under paragraph 1(2) shall include a reference to the powers which the court has by virtue of sub-paragraph (1) or (as the case may be) to an order made by virtue of sub-paragraph (1).

Local authority contribution to child's maintenance

15.— (1) Where a child lives, or is to live, with a person as the result of a residence order, a local authority may make contributions to that person towards the cost of the accommodation and maintenance of the child. **39-106**

(2) Sub-paragraph (1) does not apply where the person with whom the child lives, or is to live, is a parent of the child or the husband or wife of a parent of the child.

Interpretation

16.— (1) In this Schedule "child" includes, in any case where an application is made under paragraph 2 or 6 in relation to a person who has reached the age of eighteen, that person. **39-107**

(2) In this Schedule, except paragraphs 2 and 15, "parent" includes any party to a marriage (whether or not subsisting) in relation to whom the child concerned is a child of the family; and for this purpose any reference to either parent or both parents shall be construed as references to any parent of his and to all of his parents.

[(3) In this Schedule, ["maintenance calculation"][1]has the same meaning as it has in the Child Support Act 1991 by virtue of section 54 of that Act as read with any regulations in force under that section.][2]

Sections 17, 23 and 29 Schedule 2

LOCAL AUTHORITY SUPPORT FOR CHILDREN AND FAMILIES

PROVISION OF SERVICES FOR FAMILIES

Identification of children in need and provision of information

1.— (1) Every local authority shall take reasonable steps to identify the extent to which there are children in need within their area. **39-108**

(2) Every local authority shall—

(a) publish information—

(i) about services provided by them under [sections 17, 18, 20, 23B to 23D, 24A and 24B][3]; and

(ii) where they consider it appropriate, about the provision by others (including, in particular, voluntary organisations) of services which the authority have power to provide under those sections; and

(b) take such steps as are reasonably practicable to ensure that those who might benefit from the services receive the information relevant to them.

[Children's services plans

1A.— (1) Every local authority shall, on or before 31st March 1997— **39-109**

(a) review their provision of services under sections 17, 20, 21, 23 and 24; and

(b) having regard to that review and to their most recent review under section 19, prepare and publish a plan for the provision of services under Part III.

(2) Every local authority—

(a) shall, from time to time review the plan prepared by them under sub-paragraph (1)(b) (as modified or last substituted under this sub-paragraph), and

(b) may, having regard to that review and to their most recent review under section 19, prepare and publish—

(i) modifications (or, as the case may be, further modifications) to the plan reviewed; or

(ii) a plan in substitution for that plan.

(3) In carrying out any review under this paragraph and in preparing any plan or modifications to a plan, a local authority shall consult—

(a) every][4]

---

[1] Words substituted in relation to cases specified in SI 2003/192 art 3 by Child Support, Pensions and Social Security Act 2000 c.19 Sch 3 para 10 (4)

[2] Added by SI 1993/623 Sch 1 para 15

[3] Words substituted by Children (Leaving Care) Act 2000 c.35 s 7 (4)

[4] Added by SI 1996/785 art 2

Maintenance of a register of disabled children

39-110 **2.**— (1) Every local authority shall open and maintain a register of disabled children within their area.

(2) The register may be kept by means of a computer.

Assessment of children's needs

39-111 **3.** Where it appears to a local authority that a child within their area is in need, the authority may assess his needs for the purposes of this Act at the same time as any assessment of his needs is made under—

(a) the Chronically Sick and Disabled Persons Act 1970;

(b) [Part IV of the Education Act 1996][1];

(c) the Disabled Persons (Services, Consultation and Representation) Act 1986; or

(d) any other enactment.

Prevention of neglect and abuse

39-112 **4.**— (1) Every local authority shall take reasonable steps, through the provision of services under Part III of this Act, to prevent children within their area suffering ill-treatment or neglect.

(2) Where a local authority believe that a child who is at any time within their area—

(a) is likely to suffer harm; but

(b) lives or proposes to live in the area of another local authority

they shall inform that other local authority.

(3) When informing that other local authority they shall specify—

(a) the harm that they believe he is likely to suffer; and

(b) (if they can) where the child lives or proposes to live.

Provision of accommodation in order to protect child

39-113 **5.**— (1) Where—

(a) it appears to a local authority that a child who is living on particular premises is suffering, or is likely to suffer, ill treatment at the hands of another person who is living on those premises; and

(b) that other person proposes to move from the premises,

the authority may assist that other person to obtain alternative accommodation.

(2) Assistance given under this paragraph may be in cash.

(3) Subsections (7) to (9) of section 17 shall apply in relation to assistance given under this paragraph as they apply in relation to assistance given under that section.

Provision for disabled children

39-114 **6.** Every local authority shall provide services designed—

(a) to minimise the effect on disabled children within their area of their disabilities; and

(b) to give such children the opportunity to lead lives which are as normal as possible.

Provision to reduce need for care proceedings etc

39-115 **7.** Every local authority shall take reasonable steps designed—

(a) to reduce the need to bring—

(i) proceedings for care or supervision orders with respect to children within their area;

(ii) criminal proceedings against such children;

(iii) any family or other proceedings with respect to such children which might lead to them being placed in the authority's care; or

(iv) proceedings under the inherent jurisdiction of the High Court with respect to children;

(b) to encourage children within their area not to commit criminal offences; and

(c) to avoid the need for children within their area to be placed in secure accommodation.

Provision for children living with their families

39-116 **8.** Every local authority shall make such provision as they consider appropriate for the following services to be available with respect to children in need within their area while they are living with their families—

(a) advice, guidance and counselling;

(b) occupational, social, cultural or recreational activities;

[1] Words substituted by Education Act 1996 c.56 Sch 37 (I) para 92

(c) home help (which may include laundry facilities);
(d) facilities for, or assistance with, travelling to and from home for the purpose of taking advantage of any other service provided under this Act or of any similar service;
(e) assistance to enable the child concerned and his family to have a holiday.

Family centres

9.—(1) Every local authority shall provide such family centres as they consider appropriate in relation to children within their area. **39-117**

(2) "Family centre" means a centre at which any of the persons mentioned in sub-paragraph (3) may—
(a) attend for occupational, social, cultural or recreational activities;
(b) attend for advice, guidance or counselling; or
(c) be provided with accommodation while he is receiving advice, guidance or counselling.

(3) The persons are—
(a) a child;
(b) his parents;
(c) any person who is not a parent of his but who has parental responsibility for him;
(d) any other person who is looking after him.

Maintenance of the family home

10. Every local authority shall take such steps as are reasonably practicable, where any child within their area who is in need and whom they are not looking after is living apart from his family— **39-118**
(a) to enable him to live with his family; or
(b) to promote contact between him and his family,
if, in their opinion, it is necessary to do so in order to safeguard or promote his welfare.

Duty to consider racial groups to which children in need belong

11. Every local authority shall, in making any arrangements— **39-119**
(a) for the provision of day care within their area; or
(b) designed to encourage persons to act as local authority foster parents,
have regard to the different racial groups to which children within their area who are in need belong.

Children Looked After by Local Authorities

Regulations as to placing of children with local authority foster parents

12. Regulations under section 23(2)(a) may, in particular, make provision— **39-120**
(a) with regard to the welfare of children placed with local authority foster parents;
(b) as to the arrangements to be made by local authorities in connection with the health and education of such children;
(c) as to the records to be kept by local authorities;
(d) for securing that a child is not placed with a local authority foster parent unless that person is for the time being approved as a local authority foster parent by such local authority as may be prescribed;
(e) for securing that where possible the local authority foster parent with whom a child is to be placed is—
(i) of the same religious persuasion as the child; or
(ii) gives an undertaking that the child will be brought up in that religious persuasion;
(f) for securing that children placed with local authority foster parents, and the premises in which they are accommodated, will be supervised and inspected by a local authority and that the children will be removed from those premises if their welfare appears to require it;
(g) as to the circumstances in which local authorities may make arrangements for duties imposed on them by the regulations to be discharged, on their behalf.

Regulations as to arrangements under section 23(2)(f)

13. Regulations under section 23(2)(f) may, in particular, make provision as to— **39-121**
(a) the persons to be notified of any proposed arrangements;
(b) the opportunities such persons are to have to make representations in relation to the arrangements proposed;
(c) the persons to be notified of any proposed changes in arrangements;
(d) the records to be kept by local authorities;

(e) the supervision by local authorities of any arrangements made.

Regulations as to conditions under which child in care is allowed to live with parent, etc

39-122 **14.** Regulations under section 23(5) may, in particular, impose requirements on a local authority as to—

(a) the making of any decision by a local authority to allow a child to live with any person falling within section 23(4) (including requirements as to those who must be consulted before the decision is made, and those who must be notified when it has been made);

(b) the supervision or medical examination of the child concerned;

(c) the removal of the child, in such circumstances as may be prescribed, from the care of the person with whom he has been allowed to live.

[(d) the records to be kept by local authorities.][1]

Promotion and maintenance of contact between child and family

39-123 **15.**— (1) Where a child is being looked after by a local authority, the authority shall, unless it is not reasonably practicable or consistent with his welfare, endeavour to promote contact between the child and—

(a) his parents;

(b) any person who is not a parent of his but who has parental responsibility for him; and

(c) any relative, friend or other person connected with him.

(2) Where a child is being looked after by a local authority—

(a) the authority shall take such steps as are reasonably practicable to secure that—

(i) his parents; and

(ii) any person who is not a parent of his but who has parental responsibility for him,

are kept informed of where he is being accommodated; and

(b) every such person shall secure that the authority are kept informed of his or her address.

(3) Where a local authority ("the receiving authority") take over the provision of accommodation for a child from another local authority ("the transferring authority") under section 20(2)—

(a) the receiving authority shall (where reasonably practicable) inform—

(i) the child's parents; and

(ii) any person who is not a parent of his but who has parental responsibility for him;

(b) sub-paragraph (2)(a) shall apply to the transferring authority, as well as the receiving authority, until at least one such person has been informed of the change; and

(c) sub-paragraph (2)(b) shall not require any person to inform the receiving authority of his address until he has been so informed.

(4) Nothing in this paragraph requires a local authority to inform any person of the whereabouts of a child if—

(a) the child is in the care of the authority; and

(b) the authority has reasonable cause to believe that informing the person would prejudice the child's welfare.

(5) Any person who fails (without reasonable excuse) to comply with sub-paragraph (2)(b) shall be guilty of an offence and liable on summary conviction to a fine not exceeding level 2 on the standard scale.

(6) It shall be a defence in any proceedings under sub-paragraph (5) to prove that the defendant was residing at the same address as another person who was the child's parent or had parental responsibility for the child and had reasonable cause to believe that the other person had informed the appropriate authority that both of them were residing at that address.

Visits to or by children: expenses

39-124 **16.**— (1) This paragraph applies where—

(a) a child is being looked after by a local authority; and

(b) the conditions mentioned in sub-paragraph (3) are satisfied.

(2) The authority may—

(a) make payments to—

(i) a parent of the child;

(ii) any person who is not a parent of his but who has parental responsibility for him; or

(iii) any relative, friend or other person connected with him,

in respect of travelling, subsistence or other expenses incurred by that person in visiting the child; or

[1] Added by Courts and Legal Services Act 1990 c.41 Sch 16 (I) para 26

(b) make payments to the child, or to any person on his behalf, in respect of travelling, subsistence or other expenses incurred by or on behalf of the child in his visiting—
(i) a parent of his;
(ii) any person who is not a parent of his but who has parental responsibility for him; or
(iii) any relative, friend or other person connected with him.

(3) The conditions are that—
(a) it appears to the authority that the visit in question could not otherwise be made without undue financial hardship; and
(b) the circumstances warrant the making of the payments.

Appointment of visitor for child who is not being visited

17.— (1) Where it appears to a local authority in relation to any child that they are looking after that— **39-125**
(a) communication between the child and—
(i) a parent of his, or
(ii) any person who is not a parent of his but who has parental responsibility for him,
has been infrequent; or
(b) he has not visited or been visited by (or lived with) any such person during the preceding twelve months,
and that it would be in the child's best interests for an independent person to be appointed to be his visitor for the purposes of this paragraph, they shall appoint such a visitor.

(2) A person so appointed shall—
(a) have the duty of visiting, advising and befriending the child; and
(b) be entitled to recover from the authority who appointed him any reasonable expenses incurred by him for the purposes of his functions under this paragraph.

(3) A person's appointment as a visitor in pursuance of this paragraph shall be determined if—
(a) he gives notice in writing to the authority who appointed him that he resigns the appointment; or
(b) the authority give him notice in writing that they have terminated it.

(4) The determination of such an appointment shall not prejudice any duty under this paragraph to make a further appointment.

(5) Where a local authority propose to appoint a visitor for a child under this paragraph, the appointment shall not be made if—
(a) the child objects to it; and
(b) the authority are satisfied that he has sufficient understanding to make an informed decision.

(6) Where a visitor has been appointed for a child under this paragraph, the local authority shall determine the appointment if—
(a) the child objects to its continuing; and
(b) the authority are satisfied that he has sufficient understanding to make an informed decision.

(7) The Secretary of State may make regulations as to the circumstances in which a person appointed as a visitor under this paragraph is to be regarded as independent of the local authority appointing him.

Power to guarantee apprenticeship deeds etc

18.— (1) While a child is being looked after by a local authority, or is a person qualifying for advice and assistance, the authority may undertake any obligation by way of guarantee under any deed of apprenticeship or articles of clerkship which he enters into. **39-126**

(2) Where a local authority have undertaken any such obligation under any deed or articles they may at any time (whether or not they are still looking after the person concerned) undertake the like obligation under any supplemental deed or articles.

Arrangements to assist children to live abroad

19.— (1) A local authority may only arrange for, or assist in arranging for, any child in their care to live outside England and Wales with the approval of the court. **39-127**

(2) A local authority may, with the approval of every person who has parental responsibility for the child arrange for, or assist in arranging for, any other child looked after by them to live outside England and Wales.

(3) The court shall not give its approval under sub-paragraph (1) unless it is satisfied that—
(a) living outside England and Wales would be in the child's best interests;
(b) suitable arrangements have been, or will be, made for his reception and welfare in the country in which he will live;

(c) the child has consented to living in that country; and

(d) every person who has parental responsibility for the child has consented to his living in that country.

(4) Where the court is satisfied that the child does not have sufficient understanding to give or withhold his consent, it may disregard sub-paragraph (3)(c) and give its approval if the child is to live in the country concerned with a parent, guardian, or other suitable person.

(5) Where a person whose consent is required by sub-paragraph (3)(d) fails to give his consent, the court may disregard that provision and give its approval if it is satisfied that that person—

(a) cannot be found;

(b) is incapable of consenting; or

(c) is withholding his consent unreasonably.

(6) Section 56 of the Adoption Act 1976 (which requires authority for the taking or sending abroad for adoption of a child who is a British subject) shall not apply in the case of any child who is to live outside England and Wales with the approval of the court given under this paragraph.

(7) Where a court decides to give its approval under this paragraph it may order that its decision is not to have effect during the appeal period.

(8) In sub-paragraph (7) "the appeal period" means —

(a) where an appeal is made against the decision, the period between the making of the decision and the determination of the appeal; and

(b) otherwise, the period during which an appeal may be made against the decision.

Preparation for ceasing to be looked after

39-128 [**19A.** It is the duty of the local authority looking after a child to advise, assist and befriend him with a view to promoting his welfare when they have ceased to look after him.][1]

39-129 [**19B.**— (1) A local authority shall have the following additional functions in relation to an eligible child whom they are looking after.

(2) In sub-paragraph (1) "eligible child" means, subject to sub-paragraph (3), a child who—

(a) is aged sixteen or seventeen; and

(b) has been looked after by a local authority for a prescribed period, or periods amounting in all to a prescribed period, which began after he reached a prescribed age and ended after he reached the age of sixteen.

(3) The Secretary of State may prescribe—

(a) additional categories of eligible children; and

(b) categories of children who are not to be eligible children despite falling within sub-paragraph (2).

(4) For each eligible child, the local authority shall carry out an assessment of his needs with a view to determining what advice, assistance and support it would be appropriate for them to provide him under this Act—

(a) while they are still looking after him; and

(b) after they cease to look after him,

and shall then prepare a pathway plan for him.

(5) The local authority shall keep the pathway plan under regular review.

(6) Any such review may be carried out at the same time as a review of the child's case carried out by virtue of section 26.

(7) The Secretary of State may be regulations make provision as to assessments for the purposes of sub-paragraph (4).

(8) The regulations may in particular provide for the matters set out in section 23B(6).][2]

Personal advisers

39-130 [**19C.** A local authority shall arrange for each child whom they are looking after who is an eligible child for the purposes of paragraph 19B to have a personal adviser.][3]

Death of children being looked after by local authorities

39-131 **20.**— (1) If a child who is being looked after by a local authority dies, the authority—

(a) shall notify the Secretary of State;

(b) shall, so far as is reasonably practicable, notify the child's parents and every person who is not a parent of his but who has parental responsibility for him;

[1] Added by Children (Leaving Care) Act 2000 c.35 s 1

[2] Added by Children (Leaving Care) Act 2000 c.35 s 1

[3] Added by Children (Leaving Care) Act 2000 c.35 s 1

(c) may, with the consent (so far as it is reasonably practicable to obtain it) of every person who has parental responsibility for the child, arrange for the child's body to be buried or cremated; and

(d) may, if the conditions mentioned in sub-paragraph (2) are satisfied, make payments to any person who has parental responsibility for the child, or any relative, friend or other person connected with the child, in respect of travelling, subsistence or other expenses incurred by that person in attending the child's funeral.

(2) The conditions are that—

(a) it appears to the authority that the person concerned could not otherwise attend the child's funeral without undue financial hardship; and

(b) that the circumstances warrant the making of the payments.

(3) Sub-paragraph (1) does not authorise cremation where it does not accord with the practice of the child's religious persuasion.

(4) Where a local authority have exercised their power under sub-paragraph (1)(c) with respect to a child who was under sixteen when he died, they may recover from any parent of the child any expenses incurred by them.

(5) Any sums so recoverable shall, without prejudice to any other method of recovery, be recoverable summarily as a civil debt.

(6) Nothing in this paragraph affects any enactment regulating or authorising the burial, cremation or anatomical examination of the body of a deceased person.

Contributions Towards Maintenance of Children Looked After by Local Authorities

Liability to contribute

21.— (1) Where a local authority are looking after a child (other than in the cases mentioned in sub-paragraph (7) they shall consider whether they should recover contributions towards the child's maintenance from any person liable to contribute ("a contributor"). **39-132**

(2) An authority may only recover contributions from a contributor if they consider it reasonable to do so.

(3) The persons liable to contribute are—

(a) where the child is under sixteen, each of his parents;

(b) where he has reached the age of sixteen, the child himself.

(4) A parent is not liable to contribute during any period when he is in receipt of income support [, [working families' tax credit][1] or][2][disabled person's tax credit][3] under the [Part VII of the Social Security Contributions and Benefits Act 1992][4][or of an income-based jobseeker's allowance][5].

(5) A person is not liable to contribute towards the maintenance of a child in the care of a local authority in respect of any period during which the child is allowed by the authority (under section 23(5)) to live with a parent of his.

(6) A contributor is not obliged to make any contribution towards a child's maintenance except as agreed or determined in accordance with this Part of this Schedule.

(7) The cases are where the child is looked after by a local authority under—

(a) section 21;

(b) an interim care order;

(c) [section 92 of the Powers of Criminal Courts (Sentencing) Act 2000][6].

Agreed contributions

22.— (1) Contributions towards a child's maintenance may only be recovered if the local authority have served a notice ("a contribution notice") on the contributor specifying— **39-133**

(a) the weekly sum which they consider that he should contribute; and

(b) arrangements for payment.

(2) The contribution notice must be in writing and dated.

(3) Arrangements for payment shall, in particular, include—

---

1 Words substituted by Tax Credits Act 1999 c.10 Sch 1 para 6 (d) (iii)

2 Words substituted by Disability Living Allowance and Disability Working Allowance Act 1991 c.21 Sch 3 (II) para 15

3 Words substituted by Tax Credits Act 1999 c.10 Sch 1 para 6 (d) (iii)

4 Words substituted by Social Security (Consequential Provisions) Act 1992 c.6 Sch 2 para 108 (c)

5 Words inserted by Jobseekers Act 1995 c.18 Sch 2 para 19 (5)

6 Words substituted by Powers of Criminal Courts (Sentencing) Act 2000 c.6 Sch 9 para 130

(a) the date on which liability to contribute begins (which must not be earlier than the date of the notice);

(b) the date on which liability under the notice will end (if the child has not before that date ceased to be looked after by the authority); and

(c) the date on which the first payment is to be made.

(4) The authority may specify in a contribution notice a weekly sum which is a standard contribution determined by them for all children looked after by them.

(5) The authority may not specify in a contribution notice a weekly sum greater than that which they consider—

(a) they would normally be prepared to pay if they had placed a similar child with local authority foster parents; and

(b) it is reasonably practicable for the contributor to pay (having regard to his means).

(6) An authority may at any time withdraw a contribution notice (without prejudice to their power to serve another).

(7) Where the authority and the contributor agree—

(a) the sum which the contributor is to contribute; and

(b) arrangements for payment,

(whether as specified in the contribution notice or otherwise) and the contributor notifies the authority in writing that he so agrees, the authority may recover summarily as a civil debt any contribution which is overdue and unpaid.

(8) A contributor may, by serving a notice in writing on the authority, withdraw his agreement in relation to any period of liability falling after the date of service of the notice.

(9) Sub-paragraph (7) is without prejudice to any other method of recovery.

Contribution orders

39-134 **23.**— (1) Where a contributor has been served with a contribution notice and has—

(a) failed to reach any agreement with the local authority as mentioned in paragraph 22(7) within the period of one month beginning with the day on which the contribution notice was served; or

(b) served a notice under paragraph 22(8) withdrawing his agreement,

the authority may apply to the court for an order under this paragraph.

(2) On such an application the court may make an order ("a contribution order") requiring the contributor to contribute a weekly sum towards the child's maintenance in accordance with arrangements for payment specified by the court.

(3) A contribution order—

(a) shall not specify a weekly sum greater than that specified in the contribution notice; and

(b) shall be made with due regard to the contributor's means.

(4) A contribution order shall not—

(a) take effect before the date specified in the contribution notice; or

(b) have effect while the contributor is not liable to contribute (by virtue of paragraph 21); or

(c) remain in force after the child has ceased to be looked after by the authority who obtained the order.

(5) An authority may not apply to the court under sub-paragraph (1) in relation to a contribution notice which they have withdrawn.

(6) Where—

(a) a contribution order is in force;

(b) the authority serve another contribution notice; and

(c) the contributor and the authority reach an agreement under paragraph 22(7) in respect of that other contribution notice,

the effect of the agreement shall be to discharge the order from the date on which it is agreed that the agreement shall take effect.

(7) Where an agreement is reached under sub-paragraph (6) the authority shall notify the court—

(a) of the agreement; and

(b) of the date on which it took effect.

(8) A contribution order may be varied or revoked on the application of the contributor or the authority.

(9) In proceedings for the variation of a contribution order, the authority shall specify—

(a) the weekly sum which, having regard to paragraph 22, they propose that the contributor should contribute under the order as varied; and

(b) the proposed arrangements for payment.

(10) Where a contribution order is varied, the order—

(a) shall not specify a weekly sum greater than that specified by the authority in the proceedings for variation; and

(b) shall be made with due regard to the contributor's means.

(11) An appeal shall lie in accordance with rules of court from any order made under this paragraph.

Enforcement of contribution orders etc

24.—(1) A contribution order made by a magistrates' court shall be enforceable as a magistrates' court maintenance order (within the meaning of section 150(1) of the Magistrates' Courts Act 1980). **39-135**

(2) Where a contributor has agreed, or has been ordered, to make contributions to a local authority, any other local authority within whose area the contributor is for the time being living may—

(a) at the request of the local authority who served the contribution notice; and

(b) subject to agreement as to any sum to be deducted in respect of services rendered,

collect from the contributor any contributions due on behalf of the authority who served the notice.

(3) In sub-paragraph (2) the reference to any other local authority includes a reference to—

(a) a local authority within the meaning of section 1(2) of the Social Work (Scotland) Act 1968; and

(b) a Health and Social Services Board established under Article 16 of the Health and Personal Social Services (Northern Ireland) Order 1972.

(4) The power to collect sums under sub-paragraph (2) includes the power to—

(a) receive and give a discharge for any contributions due; and

(b) (if necessary) enforce payment of any contributions,

even though those contributions may have fallen due at a time when the contributor was living elsewhere.

(5) Any contribution collected under sub-paragraph (2) shall be paid (subject to any agreed deduction) to the local authority who served the contribution notice.

(6) In any proceedings under this paragraph, a document which purports to be—

(a) a copy of an order made by a court under or by virtue of paragraph 23; and

(b) certified as a true copy by the [justices' chief executive for][1] the court,

shall be evidence of the order.

(7) In any proceedings under this paragraph, a certificate which—

(a) purports to be signed by the clerk or some other duly authorised officer of the local authority who obtained the contribution order; and

(b) states that any sum due to the authority under the order is overdue and unpaid,

shall be evidence that the sum is overdue and unpaid.

Regulations

25. The Secretary of State may make regulations— **39-136**

(a) as to the considerations which a local authority must take into account in deciding—

(i) whether it is reasonable to recover contributions; and

(ii) what the arrangements for payment should be;

(b) as to the procedures they must follow in reaching agreements with—

(i) contributors (under paragraphs 22 and 23); and

(ii) any other local authority (under paragraph 23).

Sections 35 and 36 Schedule 3

Supervision Orders

General

Meaning of "responsible person"

1. In this Schedule, "the responsible person", in relation to a supervised child, means — **39-137**

(a) any person who has parental responsibility for the child; and

(b) any other person with whom the child is living.

Power of supervisor to give directions to supervised child

2.—(1) A supervision order may require the supervised child to comply with any directions given from time to time by the supervisor which require him to do all or any of the following things— **39-138**

[1] Words substituted by Access to Justice Act 1999 c.22 Sch 13 para 162

(a) to live at a place or places specified in the directions for a period or periods so specified;
(b) to present himself to a person or persons specified in the directions at a place or places and on a day or days so specified;
(c) to participate in activities specified in the directions on a day or days so specified.

(2) It shall be for the supervisor to decide whether, and to what extent, he exercises his power to give directions and to decide the form of any directions which he gives.

(3) Sub-paragraph (1) does not confer on a supervisor power to give directions in respect of any medical or psychiatric examination or treatment (which are matters dealt with in paragraphs 4 and 5).

Imposition of obligations on responsible person

39-139 **3.**— (1) With the consent of any responsible person, a supervision order may include a requirement—

(a) that he take all reasonable steps to ensure that the supervised child complies with any direction given by the supervisor under paragraph 2;
(b) that he take all reasonable steps to ensure that the supervised child complies with any requirement included in the order under paragraph 4 or 5;
(c) that he comply with any directions given by the supervisor requiring him to attend at a place specified in the directions for the purpose of taking part in activities so specified.

(2) A direction given under sub-paragraph (1)(c) may specify the time at which the responsible person is to attend and whether or not the supervised child is required to attend with him.

(3) A supervision order may require any person who is a responsible person in relation to the supervised child to keep the supervisor informed of his address, if it differs from the child's.

Psychiatric and medical examinations

39-140 **4.**— (1) A supervision order may require the supervised child—

(a) to submit to a medical or psychiatric examination; or
(b) to submit to any such examination from time to time as directed by the supervisor.

(2) Any such examination shall be required to be conducted—

(a) by, or under the direction of, such registered medical practitioner as may be specified in the order;
(b) at a place specified in the order and at which the supervised child is to attend as a non-resident patient; or
(c) at—
  (i) a health service hospital; or
  (ii) in the case of a psychiatric examination, a hospital [, independent hospital or care home][1],

at which the supervised child is, or is to attend as, a resident patient.

(3) A requirement of a kind mentioned in sub-paragraph (2)(c) shall not be included unless the court is satisfied, on the evidence of a registered medical practitioner, that—

(a) the child may be suffering from a physical or mental condition that requires, and may be susceptible to, treatment; and
(b) a period as a resident patient is necessary if the examination is to be carried out properly.

(4) No court shall include a requirement under this paragraph in a supervision order unless it is satisfied that—

(a) where the child has sufficient understanding to make an informed decision, he consents to its inclusion; and
(b) satisfactory arrangements have been, or can be, made for the examination.

Psychiatric and medical treatment

39-141 **5.**— (1) Where a court which proposes to make or vary a supervision order is satisfied, on the evidence of a registered medical practitioner approved for the purposes of section 12 of the Mental Health Act 1983, that the mental condition of the supervised child—

(a) is such as requires, and may be susceptible to, treatment; but
(b) is not such as to warrant his detention in pursuance of a hospital order under Part III of that Act,

the court may include in the order a requirement that the supervised child shall, for a period specified in the order, submit to such treatment as is so specified.

(2) The treatment specified in accordance with sub-paragraph (1) must be—

(a) by, or under the direction of, such registered medical practitioner as may be specified in the order;

[1] Words substituted by Care Standards Act 2000 c.14 Sch 4 para 14 (24)

(b) as a non-resident patient at such a place as may be so specified; or

(c) as a resident patient in a hospital [, independent hospital or care home][1].

(3) Where a court which proposes to make or vary a supervision order is satisfied, on the evidence of a registered medical practitioner, that the physical condition of the supervised child is such as requires, and may be susceptible to, treatment, the court may include in the order a requirement that the supervised child shall, for a period specified in the order, submit to such treatment as is so specified.

(4) The treatment specified in accordance with sub-paragraph (3) must be—

(a) by, or under the direction of, such registered medical practitioner as may be specified in the order;

(b) as a non-resident patient at such place as may be so specified; or

(c) as a resident patient in a health service hospital.

(5) No court shall include a requirement under this paragraph in a supervision order unless it is satisfied—

(a) where the child has sufficient understanding to make an informed decision, that he consents to its inclusion; and

(b) that satisfactory arrangements have been, or can be, made for the treatment.

(6) If a medical practitioner by whom or under whose direction a supervised person is being treated in pursuance of a requirement included in a supervision order by virtue of this paragraph is unwilling to continue to treat or direct the treatment of the supervised child or is of the opinion that—

(a) the treatment should be continued beyond the period specified in the order;

(b) the supervised child needs different treatment;

(c) he is not susceptible to treatment; or

(d) he does not require further treatment,

the practitioner shall make a report in writing to that effect to the supervisor.

(7) On receiving a report under this paragraph the supervisor shall refer it to the court, and on such a reference the court may make an order cancelling or varying the requirement.

MISCELLANEOUS

Life of supervision order

6.— (1) Subject to sub-paragraph (2) and section 91, a supervision order shall cease to have effect at the end of the period of one year beginning with the date on which it was made. **39-142**

(2) A supervision order shall also cease to have effect if an event mentioned in section 25(1)(a) or (b) of the Child Abduction and Custody Act 1985 (termination of existing orders) occurs with respect to the child.

(3) Where the supervisor applies to the court to extend, or further extend, a supervision order the court may extend the order for such period as it may specify.

(4) A supervision order may not be extended so as to run beyond the end of the period of three years beginning with the date on which it was made.

Limited life of directions

7.— [...][2] **39-143**

Information to be given to supervisor etc

8.— (1) A supervision order may require the supervised child— **39-144**

(a) to keep the supervisor informed of any change in his address; and

(b) to allow the supervisor to visit him at the place where he is living.

(2) The responsible person in relation to any child with respect to whom a supervision order is made shall—

(a) if asked by the supervisor, inform him of the child's address (if it is known to him); and

(b) if he is living with the child, allow the supervisor reasonable contact with the child.

Selection of supervisor

9.— (1) A supervision order shall not designate a local authority as the supervisor unless— **39-145**

(a) the authority agree; or

(b) the supervised child lives or will live within their area.

[1] Words substituted by Care Standards Act 2000 c.14 Sch 4 para 14 (24)

[2] Repealed by Courts and Legal Services Act 1990 c.41 Sch 20 para 1

(2) [...][1]
(3) [...][2]
(4) [...][3]
(5) [...][4]

Effect of supervision order on earlier orders

39-146 **10.** The making of a supervision order with respect to any child brings to an end any earlier care or supervision order which—

(a) was made with respect to that child; and
(b) would otherwise continue in force.

Local authority functions and expenditure

39-147 **11.**—(1) The Secretary of State may make regulations with respect to the exercise by a local authority of their functions where a child has been placed under their supervision by a supervision order.

(2) Where a supervision order requires compliance with directions given by virtue of this section, any expenditure incurred by the supervisor for the purposes of the directions shall be defrayed by the local authority designated in the order.

EDUCATION SUPERVISION ORDERS

Effect of orders

39-148 **12.**—(1) Where an education supervision order is in force with respect to a child, it shall be the duty of the supervisor—

(a) to advise, assist and befriend, and give directions to—
 (i) the supervised child; and
 (ii) his parents,

in such a way as will, in the opinion of the supervisor, secure that he is properly educated;

(b) where any such directions given to—
 (i) the supervised child; or
 (ii) a parent of his,

have not been complied with, to consider what further steps to take in the exercise of the supervisor's powers under this Act.

(2) Before giving any directions under sub-paragraph (1) the supervisor shall, so far as is reasonably practicable, ascertain the wishes and feelings of—

(a) the child; and
(b) his parents,

including, in particular, their wishes as to the place at which the child should be educated.

(3) When settling the terms of any such directions, the supervisor shall give due consideration—

(a) having regard to the child's age and understanding, to such wishes and feelings of his as the supervisor has been able to ascertain; and
(b) to such wishes and feelings of the child's parents as he has been able to ascertain.

(4) Directions may be given under this paragraph at any time while the education supervision order is in force.

39-149 **13.**—(1) Where an education supervision order is in force with respect to a child, the duties of the child's parents under [sections 7 and 444 of the Education Act 1996 (duties to secure education of children and][5] to secure regular attendance of registered pupils) shall be superseded by their duty to comply with any directions in force under the education supervision order.

(2) Where an education supervision order is made with respect to a child—

(a) any school attendance order—
 (i) made under [section 437 of the Education Act 1996][6] with respect to the child; and
 (ii) in force immediately before the making of the education supervision order,

shall cease to have effect; and

[1] Repealed by Criminal Justice and Court Services Act 2000 c.43 Sch 8 para 1
[2] Repealed by Criminal Justice and Court Services Act 2000 c.43 Sch 8 para 1
[3] Repealed by Criminal Justice and Court Services Act 2000 c.43 Sch 8 para 1
[4] Repealed by Criminal Justice and Court Services Act 2000 c.43 Sch 8 para 1
[5] Words substituted by Education Act 1996 c.56 Sch 37 (I) para 93 (2) (a)
[6] Words substituted by Education Act 1996 c.56 Sch 37 (I) para 93 (2) (b) (i)

(b) while the education supervision order remains in force, the following provisions shall not apply with respect to the child—
   (i) [section 437][1] of that Act (school attendance orders);
   (ii) [section 9 of that Act][2] (pupils to be educated in accordance with wishes of their parents);
   (iii) [sections 411 and 423 of that Act][3] (parental preference and appeals against admission decisions);

(c) a supervision order made with respect to the child in criminal proceedings, while the education supervision order is in force, may not include an education requirement of the kind which could otherwise be included under [paragraph 7 of Schedule 6 to the Powers of Criminal Courts (Sentencing) Act 2000][4];

(d) any education requirement of a kind mentioned in paragraph (c), which was in force with respect to the child immediately before the making of the education supervision order, shall cease to have effect.

Effect where child also subject to supervision order

14.— (1) This paragraph applies where an education supervision order and a supervision order, or order under [section 63(1) of the Powers of Criminal Courts (Sentencing) Act 2000][5], are in force at the same time with respect to the same child. **39-150**

(2) Any failure to comply with a direction given by the supervisor under the education supervision order shall be disregarded if it would not have been reasonably practicable to comply with it without failing to comply with a direction given under the other order.

Duration of orders

15.— (1) An education supervision order shall have effect for a period of one year, beginning with the date on which it is made. **39-151**

(2) An education supervision order shall not expire if, before it would otherwise have expired, the court has (on the application of the authority in whose favour the order was made) extended the period during which it is in force.

(3) Such an application may not be made earlier than three months before the date on which the order would otherwise expire.

(4) The period during which an education supervision order is in force may be extended under sub-paragraph (2) on more than one occasion.

(5) No one extension may be for a period of more than three years.

(6) An education supervision order shall cease to have effect on—
   (a) the child's ceasing to be of compulsory school age; or
   (b) the making of a care order with respect to the child;

and sub-paragraphs (1) to (4) are subject to this sub-paragraph.

Information to be given to supervisor etc

16.— (1) An education supervision order may require the child— **39-152**
   (a) to keep the supervisor informed of any change in his address; and
   (b) to allow the supervisor to visit him at the place where he is living.

(2) A person who is the parent of a child with respect to whom an education supervision order has been made shall—
   (a) if asked by the supervisor, inform him of the child's address (if it is known to him); and
   (b) if he is living with the child, allow the supervisor reasonable contact with the child.

Discharge of orders

17.— (1) The court may discharge any education supervision order on the application of— **39-153**
   (a) the child concerned;
   (b) a parent of his; or
   (c) the local education authority concerned.

(2) On discharging an education supervision order, the court may direct the local authority within whose area the child lives, or will live, to investigate the circumstances of the child.

---

[1] Words substituted by Education Act 1996 c.56 Sch 37 (I) para 93 (2) (b) (ii)
[2] Words substituted by Education Act 1996 c.56 Sch 37 (I) para 93 (2) (b) (iii)
[3] Words substituted by Education Act 1996 c.56 Sch 37 (I) para 93 (2) (b) (iv)
[4] Words substituted by Powers of Criminal Courts (Sentencing) Act 2000 c.6 Sch 9 para 131 (2)
[5] Words substituted by Powers of Criminal Courts (Sentencing) Act 2000 c.6 Sch 9 para 131 (3)

Offences

39-154 **18.**— (1) If a parent of a child with respect to whom an education supervision order is in force persistently fails to comply with a direction given under the order he shall be guilty of an offence.

(2) It shall be a defence for any person charged with such an offence to prove that—

(a) he took all reasonable steps to ensure that the direction was complied with;
(b) the direction was unreasonable; or
(c) he had complied with—
 (i) a requirement included in a supervision order made with respect to the child; or
 (ii) directions given under such a requirement,

and that it was not reasonably practicable to comply both with the direction and with the requirement or directions mentioned in this paragraph.

(3) A person guilty of an offence under this paragraph shall be liable on summary conviction to a fine not exceeding level 3 on the standard scale.

Persistent failure of child to comply with directions

39-155 **19.**— (1) Where a child with respect to whom an education supervision order is in force persistently fails to comply with any direction given under the order, the local education authority concerned shall notify the appropriate local authority.

(2) Where a local authority have been notified under sub-paragraph (1) they shall investigate the circumstances of the child.

(3) In this paragraph "the appropriate local authority" has the same meaning as in section 36.

Miscellaneous

39-156 **20.** The Secretary of State may by regulations make provision modifying, or displacing, the provisions of any enactment about education in relation to any child with respect to whom an education supervision order is in force to such extent as appears to the Secretary of State to be necessary or expedient in consequence of the provision made by this Act with respect to such orders.

Interpretation

39-157 **21.** In this Part of this Schedule "parent" has the same meaning as in [the Education Act 1996][1].

Human Fertilisation and Embryology Act 1990

CHAPTER 37

Principal terms used

Meaning of "embryo", "gamete" and associated expressions

40-001 1.—(1) In this Act, except where otherwise stated—

(a) embryo means a live human embryo where fertilisation is complete, and

(b) references to an embryo include an egg in the process of fertilisation,

and, for this purpose, fertilisation is not complete until the appearance of a two cell zygote.

(2) This Act, so far as it governs bringing about the creation of an embryo, applies only to bringing about the creation of an embryo outside the human body; and in this Act—

(a) references to embryos the creation of which was brought about in vitro (in their application to those where fertilisation is complete) are to those where fertilisation began outside the human body whether or not it was completed there, and

---

[1] Words substituted by Education Act 1996 c.56 Sch 37 (I) para 93 (3)

(b) references to embryos taken from a woman do not include embryos whose creation was brought about in vitro.

(3) This Act, so far as it governs the keeping or use of an embryo, applies only to keeping or using an embryo outside the human body.

(4) References in this Act to gametes, eggs or sperm, except where otherwise stated, are to live human gametes, eggs or sperm but references below in this Act to gametes or eggs do not include eggs in the process of fertilisation.

Other terms

2.—(1) In this Act— **40-002**

"the Authority" means the Human Fertilisation and Embryology Authority established under section 5 of this Act,

"directions" means directions under section 23 of this Act,

"licence" means a licence under Schedule 2 to this Act and, in relation to a licence, "the person responsible" has the meaning given by section 17 of this Act, and

"treatment services" means medical, surgical or obstetric services provided to the public or a section of the public for the purpose of assisting women to carry children.

(2) References in this Act to keeping, in relation to embryos or gametes, include keeping while preserved, whether preserved by cryopreservation or in any other way; and embryos or gametes so kept are referred to in this Act as "stored" (and "store" and "storage" are to be interpreted accordingly).

(3) For the purposes of this Act, a woman is not to be treated as carrying a child until the embryo has become implanted.

Licence conditions

Conditions of licences for treatment

13.—(1) The following shall be conditions of every licence under paragraph 1 **40-003**
of Schedule 2 to this Act.

(2) Such information shall be recorded as the Authority may specify in directions about the following—

(a) the persons for whom services are provided in pursuance of the licence,

(b) the services provided for them,

(c) the persons whose gametes are kept or used for the purposes of services provided in pursuance of the licence or whose gametes have been used in bringing about the creation of embryos so kept or used,

(d) any child appearing to the person responsible to have been born as a result of treatment in pursuance of the licence,

(e) any mixing of egg and sperm and any taking of an embryo from a woman or other acquisition of an embryo, and

(f) such other matters as the Authority may specify in directions.

(3) The records maintained in pursuance of the licence shall include any information recorded in pursuance of subsection (2) above and any consent of a person whose consent is required under Schedule 3 to this Act.

(4) No information shall be removed from any records maintained in pursuance of the licence before the expiry of such period as may be specified in directions for records of the class in question.

(5) A woman shall not be provided with treatment services unless account has been taken of the welfare of any child who may be born as a result of the treatment (including the need of that child for a father), and of any other child who may be affected by the birth.

(6) A woman shall not be provided with any treatment services involving—

(a) the use of any gametes of any person, if that person's consent is required under paragraph 5 of Schedule 3 to this Act for the use in question,

(b) the use of any embryo the creation of which was brought about in vitro, or

(c) the use of any embryo taken from a woman, if the consent of the woman from whom it was taken is required under paragraph 7 of that Schedule for the use in question,

unless the woman being treated and, where she is being treated together with a man, the man, have been given a suitable opportunity to receive proper counselling about the implications of taking the proposed steps, and have been provided with such relevant information as is proper.

(7) Suitable procedures shall be maintained—

(a) for determining the persons providing gametes or from whom embryos are taken for use in pursuance of the licence, and

(b) for the purpose of securing that consideration is given to the use of practices not requiring the authority of a licence as well as those requiring such authority.

Status

Meaning of "mother"

40-004 **27.**—(1) The woman who is carrying or has carried a child as a result of the placing in her of an embryo or of sperm and eggs, and no other woman, is to be treated as the mother of the child.

(2) Subsection (1) above does not apply to any child to the extent that the child is treated by virtue of adoption as not being the child of any person other than the adopter or adopters.

(3) Subsection (1) above applies whether the woman was in the United Kingdom or elsewhere at the time of the placing in her of the embryo or the sperm and eggs.

Meaning of "father"

40-005 **28.**—(1) This section applies in the case of a child who is being or has been carried by a woman as the result of the placing in her of an embryo or of sperm and eggs or her artificial insemination.

(2) If—

(a) at the time of the placing in her of the embryo or the sperm and eggs or of her insemination, the woman was a party to a marriage, and

(b) the creation of the embryo carried by her was not brought about with the sperm of the other party to the marriage,

then, subject to subsection (5) below, the other party to the marriage shall be treated as the father of the child unless it is shown that he did not consent to the placing in her of the embryo or the sperm and eggs or to her insemination (as the case may be).

(3) If no man is treated, by virtue of subsection (2) above, as the father of the child but—

(a) the embryo or the sperm and eggs were placed in the woman, or she was artificially inseminated, in the course of treatment services provided for her and a man together by a person to whom a licence applies, and

(b) the creation of the embryo carried by her was not brought about with the sperm of that man,

then, subject to subsection (5) below, that man shall be treated as the father of the child.

(4) Where a person is treated as the father of the child by virtue of subsection (2) or (3)above, no other person is to be treated as the father of the child.

(5) Subsections (2) and (3) above do not apply—

(a) in relation to England and Wales and Northern Ireland, to any child who, by virtue of the rules of common law, is treated as the legitimate child of the parties to a marriage,

(b) in relation to Scotland, to any child who, by virtue of any enactment or other rule of law, is treated as the child of the parties to a marriage, or

(c) to any child to the extent that the child is treated by virtue of adoption as not being the child of any person other than the adopter or adopters.

(6) Where—

(a) the sperm of a man who had given such consent as is required by paragraph 5 of Schedule 3 to this Act was used for a purpose for which such consent was required, or

(b) the sperm of a man, or any embryo the creation of which was brought about with his sperm, was used after his death,

he is not to be treated as the father of the child.

(7) The references in subsection (2) above to the parties to a marriage at the time there referred to—

(a) are to the parties to a marriage subsisting at that time, unless a judicial separation was then in force, but

(b) include the parties to a void marriage if either or both of them reasonably believed at that time that the marriage was valid; and for the purposes of this subsection it shall be presumed, unless the contrary is shown, that one of them reasonably believed at that time that the marriage was valid.

(8) This section applies whether the woman was in the United Kingdom or elsewhere at the time of the placing in her of the embryo or the sperm and eggs or her artificial insemination.

(9) In subsection (7)(a) above, "judicial separation" includes a legal separation obtained in a country outside the British Islands and recognised in the United Kingdom.

Effect of sections 27 and 28

29.—(1) Where by virtue of section 27 or 28 of this Act a person is to be treated as the mother or father of a child, that person is to be treated in law as the mother or, as the case may be, father of the child for all purposes. **40-006**

(2) Where by virtue of section 27 or 28 of this Act a person is not to be treated as the mother or father of a child, that person is to be treated in law as not being the mother or, as the case may be, father of the child for any purpose.

(3) Where subsection (1) or (2) above has effect, references to any relationship between two people in any enactment, deed or other instrument or document (whenever passed or made) are to be read accordingly.

(4) In relation to England and Wales and Northern Ireland, nothing in the provisions of section 27(1) or 28(2) to (4), read with this section, affects—

(a) the succession to any dignity or title of honour or renders any person capable of succeeding to or transmitting a right to succeed to any such dignity or title, or

(b) the devolution of any property limited (expressly or not) to devolve (as nearly as the law permits) along with any dignity or title of honour.

Parental orders in favour of gamete donors

40-007 **30.**—(1) The court may make an order providing for a child to be treated in law as the child of the parties to a marriage (referred to in this section as "the husband" and "the wife") if—

(a) the child has been carried by a woman other than the wife as the result of the placing in her of an embryo or sperm and eggs or her artificial insemination,

(b) the gametes of the husband or the wife, or both, were used to bring about the creation of the embryo, and

(c) the conditions in subsections (2) to (7) below are satisfied.

(2) The husband and the wife must apply for the order within six months of the birth of the child or, in the case of a child born before the coming into force of this Act, within six months of such coming into force.

(3) At the time of the application and of the making of the order—

(a) the child's home must be with the husband and the wife, and

(b) the husband or the wife, of both of them, must be domiciled in a part of the United Kingdom or in the Channel Islands or the Isle of Man.

(4) At the time of the making of the order both the husband and the wife must have attained the age of eighteen.

(5) The court must be satisfied that both the father of the child (including a person who is the father by virtue of section 28 of this Act), where he is not the husband, and the woman who carried the child have freely, and with full understanding of what is involved, agreed unconditionally to the making of the order.

(6) Subsection (5) above does not require the agreement of a person who cannot be found or is incapable of giving agreement and the agreement of the woman who carried the child is ineffective for the purposes of that subsection if given by her less than six weeks after the child's birth.

(7) The court must be satisfied that no money or other benefit (other than for expenses reasonably incurred) has been given or received by the husband or the wife for or in consideration of—

(a) the making of the order,

(b) any agreement required by subsection (5) above,

(c) the handing over of the child to the husband and the wife, or

(d) the making of any arrangements with a view to the making of the order,

unless authorised by the court.

(8) For the purposes of an application under this section—

(a) in relation to England and Wales, section 92(7) to (10) of, and Part I of Schedule 11 to, the Children Act 1989 (jurisdiction of courts) shall apply for the purposes of this section to determine the meaning of "the court" as they apply for the purposes of that Act and proceedings on the application shall be "family proceedings" for the purposes of that Act,

(b) in relation to Scotland, "the court" means the Court of Session or the sheriff court of the sheriffdom within which the child is, and

(c) in relation to Northern Ireland, "the court" means the High Court or any county court within whose division the child is.

(9) Regulations may provide—

(a) for any provision of the enactments about adoption to have effect, with such modifications (if any) as may be specified in the regulations, in relation to orders under this section, and applications for such orders, as it has effect in relation to adoption, and applications for adoption orders, and

(b) for references in any enactment to adoption, an adopted child or an adoptive relationship to be read (respectively) as references to the effect of an order under this section, a child to whom such an order applies and a relationship arising by virtue of the enactments about adoption, as applied by the regulations, and for similar expressions in connection with adoption to be read accordingly,

and the regulations may include such incidental or supplemental provision as appears to the Secretary of State necessary or desirable in consequence of any provision made by virtue of paragraph (a) or (b) above.

(10) In this section "the enactments about adoption" means the Adoption Act 1976, the Adoption (Scotland) Act 1978 and the Adoption (Northern Ireland) Order 1987

(11) Subsection (1)(a) above applies whether the woman was in the United Kingdom or elsewhere at the time of the placing in her of the embryo or the sperm and eggs or her artificial insemination.

Information

The Authority's register of information

31.—(1) The Authority shall keep a register which shall contain any information obtained by the Authority which falls within subsection (2) below. **40-008**

(2) Information falls within this subsection if it relates to—

(a) the provision of treatment services for any identifiable individual, or

(b) the keeping or use of the gametes of any identifiable individual or of an embryo taken from any identifiable woman,

or if it shows that any identifiable individual was, or may have been, born in consequence of treatment services.

(3) A person who has attained the age of eighteen ("the applicant") may by notice to the Authority require the Authority to comply with a request under subsection (4) below, and the Authority shall do so if—

(a) the information contained in the register shows that the applicant was, or may have been, born in consequence of treatment services, and

(b) the applicant has been given a suitable opportunity to receive proper counselling about the implications of compliance with the request.

(4) The applicant may request the Authority to give the applicant notice stating whether or not the information contained in the register shows that a person other than a parent of the applicant would or might, but for sections 27 to 29 of this Act, be a parent of the applicant and, if it does show that—

(a) giving the applicant so much of that information as relates to the person concerned as the Authority is required by regulations to give (but no other information), or

(b) stating whether or not that information shows that, but for sections 27 to 29 of this Act, the applicant, and a person specified in the request as a person whom the applicant proposes to marry, would or might be related.

(5) Regulations cannot require the Authority to give any information as to the identity of a person whose gametes have been used or from whom an embryo has been taken if a person to whom a licence applied was provided with the information at a time when the Authority could not have been required to give information of the kind in question.

(6) A person who has not attained the age of eighteen ("the minor") may by notice to the Authority specifying another person ("the intended spouse") as a person whom the minor proposes to marry require the Authority to comply with a request under subsection (7) below, and the Authority shall do so if—

(a) the information contained in the register shows that the minor was, or may have been, born in consequence of treatment services, and

(b) the minor has been given a suitable opportunity to receive proper counselling about the implications of compliance with the request.

(7) The minor may request the Authority to give the minor notice stating whether or not the information contained in the register shows that, but for sections 27 to 29 of this Act, the minor and the intended spouse would or might be related.

Information to be provided to Registrar General

40-009 **32.**—(1) This section applies where a claim is made before the Registrar General that a man is or is not the father of a child and it is necessary or desirable for the purpose of any function of the Registrar General to determine whether the claim is or may be well-founded.

(2) The Authority shall comply with any request made by the Registrar General by notice to the Authority to disclose whether any information on the register kept in pursuance of section 31 of this Act tends to show that the man may be the father of the child by virtue of section 28 of this Act and, if it does, disclose that information.

(3) In this section and section 33 of this Act, "the Registrar General" means the Registrar General for England and Wales, the Registrar General of Births, Deaths and Marriages for Scotland or the Registrar General for Northern Ireland, as the case may be.

Restrictions on disclosure of information

40-010 **33.**—(1) No person who is or has been a member or employee of the Authority shall disclose any information mentioned in subsection (2) below which he holds or has held as such a member or employee.

(2) The information referred to in subsection (1) above is—

(a) any information contained or required to be contained in the register kept in pursuance of section 31 of this Act, and

(b) any other information obtained by any member or employee of the Authority on terms or in circumstances requiring it to be held in confidence.

(3) Subsection (1) above does not apply to any disclosure of information mentioned in subsection (2)(a) above made—

(a) to a person as a member or employee of the Authority,

(b) to a person to whom a licence applies for the purposes of his functions as such,

(c) so that no individual to whom the information relates can be identified,

(d) in pursuance of an order of a court under section 34 or 35 of this Act,

(e) to the Registrar General in pursuance of a request under section 32 of this Act, or

(f) in accordance with section 31 of this Act.

(4) Subsection (1) above does not apply to any disclosure of information mentioned in subsection (2)(b) above—

(a) made to a person as a member or employee of the Authority,

(b) made with the consent of the person or persons whose confidence would otherwise be protected, or

(c) which has been lawfully made available to the public before the disclosure is made.

(5) No person who is or has been a person to whom a licence applies and no person to whom directions have been given shall disclose any information falling within section 31(2) of this Act which he holds or has held as such a person.

(6) Subsection (5) above does not apply to any disclosure of information made—

(a) to a person as a member or employee of the Authority,

(b) to a person to whom a licence applies for the purposes of his functions as such,

(c) so far as it identifies a person who, but for sections 27 to 29 of this Act, would or might be a parent of a person who instituted proceedings under section 1A of the Congenital Disabilities (Civil Liability) Act 1976, but only for the purpose of defending such proceedings, or instituting connected proceedings for compensation against that parent,

(d) so that no individual to whom the information relates can be identified, [...][1]

(e) in pursuance of directions given by virtue of section 24(5) or (6) of this Act.

[(f) necessarily—

(i) for any purpose preliminary to proceedings, or

(ii) for the purposes of, or in connection with, any proceedings,

(g) for the purpose of establishing, in any proceedings relating to an application for an order under subsection (1) of section 30 of this Act, whether the condition specified in paragraph (a) or (b) of that subsection is met, or

(h) under section 3 of the Access of Health Records Act 1990 (right of access to health records).][2]

[(6A) Paragraph (f) of subsection (6) above, so far as relating to disclosure for the purposes of, or in connection with, any proceedings, does not apply—

(a) to disclosure of information enabling a person to be identified as a person whose gametes were used, in accordance with consent given under paragraph 5 of Schedule 3 to this Act, for the purposes of

[1] Word repealed by Human Fertilisation and Embryology (Disclosure of Information) Act 1992 c.54 s 1 (2)

[2] Added by Human Fertilisation and Embryology (Disclosure of Information) Act 1992 c.54 s 1 (2)

treatment services in consequence of which an identifiable individual was, or may have been, born, or

(b) to disclosure, in circumstances in which subsection (1) of section 34 of this Act applies, of information relevant to the determination of the question mentioned in that subsection.

(6B) In the case of information relating to the provision of treatment services for any identifiable individual—

(a) where one individual is identifiable, subsection (5) above does not apply to disclosure with the consent of that individual;

(b) where both a woman and a man treated together with her are identifiable, subsection (5) above does not apply—

(i) to disclosure with the consent of them both, or

(ii) if disclosure is made for the purpose of disclosing information about the provision of treatment services for one of them, to disclosure with the consent of that individual.

(6C) For the purposes of subsection (6B) above, consent must be to disclosure to a specific person, except where disclosure is to a person who needs to know—

(a) in connection with the provision of treatment services, or any other description of medical, surgical or obstetric services, for the individual giving the consent,

(b) in connection with the carrying out of an audit of clinical practice, or

(c) in connection with the auditing of accounts.

(6D) For the purposes of subsection (6B) above, consent to disclosure given at the request of another shall be disregarded unless, before it is given, the person requesting it takes reasonable steps to explain to the individual from whom it is requested the implications of compliance with the request.

(6E) In the case of information which relates to the provision of treatment services for any identifiable individual; subsection (5) above does not apply to disclosure in an emergency, that is to say, to disclosure made—

(a) by a person who is satisfied that it is necessary to make the disclosure to avert an imminent danger to the health of an individual with whose consent the information could be disclosed under subsection (6B) above, and

(b) in circumstances where it is not reasonably practicable to obtain that individual's consent.

(6F) In the case of information which shows that any identifiable individual was, or may have been, born in consequence of treatment services, subsection (5) above does not apply to any disclosure which is necessarily incidental to disclosure under subsection (6B) or (6E) above.

(6G) Regulations may provide for additional exceptions from subsection (5) above, but no exception may be made under this subsection—

(a) for disclosure of a kind mentioned in paragraph (a) or (b) of subsection (6A) above, or

(b) for disclosure, in circumstances in which section 32 of this Act applies, of information having the tendency mentioned in subsection (2) of that section.][1]

(7) This section does not apply to the disclosure to any individual of information which—

[1] Added by Human Fertilisation and Embryology (Disclosure of Information) Act 1992 c.54 s 1 (3)

(a) falls within section 31(2) of this Act by virtue of paragraph (a) or (b) of that subsection, and

(b) relates only to that individual or, in the case of an individual treated together with another, only to that individual and that other.

(8) [...][1]

[(9) In subsection (6)(f) above, references to proceedings include any formal procedure for dealing with a complaint.][2]

Disclosure in interests of justice

34.—(1) Where in any proceedings before a court the question whether a person is or is not the parent of a child by virtue of sections 27 to 29 of this Act falls to be determined, the court may on the application of any party to the proceedings make an order requiring the Authority— **40-011**

(a) to disclose whether or not any information relevant to that question is contained in the register kept in pursuance of section 31 of this Act, and

(b) if it is, to disclose so much of it as is specified in the order,

but such an order may not require the Authority to disclose any information falling within section 31(2)(b) of this Act.

(2) The court must not make an order under subsection (1) above unless it is satisfied that the interests of justice require it to do so, taking into account—

(a) any representations made by any individual who may be affected by the disclosure, and

(b) the welfare of the child, if under 18 years old, and of any other person under that age who may be affected by the disclosure.

(3) If the proceedings before the court are civil proceedings, it—

(a) may direct that the whole or any part of the proceedings on the application for an order under subsection (2) above shall be heard in camera, and

(b) if it makes such an order, may then or later direct that the whole or any part of any later stage of the proceedings shall be heard in camera.

(4) An application for a direction under subsection (3) above shall be heard in camera unless the court otherwise directs.

Disclosure in interests of justice: congenital disabilities, etc

35.—(1) Where for the purpose of instituting proceedings under section 1 of the Congenital Disabilities (Civil Liability) Act 1976 (civil liability to child born disabled) it is necessary to identify a person who would or might be the parent of a child but for sections 27 to 29 of this Act, the court may, on the application of the child, make an order requiring the Authority to disclose any information contained in the register kept in pursuance of section 31 of this Act identifying that person. **40-012**

(3) Subsections (2) to (4) of section 34 of this Act apply for the purposes of this section as they apply for the purposes of that.

(4) After section 4(4) of the Congenital Disabilities (Civil Liability) Act 1976 there is inserted—

> "(4A) In any case where a child carried by a woman as the result of the placing in her of an embryo or of sperm and eggs or her artificial insemination is born disabled, any reference in section 1 of this Act to a parent includes a reference to a person who would be a parent but for sections 27 to 29 of the Human Fertilisation and Embryology Act 1990.".

---

[1] Repealed by Data Protection Act 1998 c.29 Sch 16 (I) para 1

[2] Added by Human Fertilisation and Embryology (Disclosure of Information) Act 1992 c.54 s 1 (4)

Offences

40-013 **41.**—(1) A person who—

(a) contravenes [section 3(2), 3A or 4(1)(c)][1] of this Act, or

(b) does anything which, by virtue of section 3(3) of this Act, cannot be authorised by a licence,

is guilty of an offence and liable on conviction on indictment to imprisonment for a term not exceeding ten years or a fine or both.

(2) A person who—

(a) contravenes section 3(1) of this Act, otherwise than by doing something which, by virtue of section 3(3) of this Act, cannot be authorised by a licence,

(b) keeps or uses any gametes in contravention of section 4(1)(a) or (b) of this Act,

(c) contravenes section 4(3) of this Act, or

(d) fails to comply with any directions given by virtue of section 24(7)(a) of this Act,

is guilty of an offence.

(3) If a person—

(a) provides any information for the purposes of the grant of a licence, being information which is false or misleading in a material particular, and

(b) either he knows the information to be false or misleading in a material particular or he provides the information recklessly,

he is guilty of an offence.

(4) A person guilty of an offence under subsection (2) or (3) above is liable—

(a) on conviction on indictment, to imprisonment for a term not exceeding two years or a fine or both, and

(b) on summary conviction, to imprisonment for a term not exceeding six months or a fine not exceeding the statutory maximum or both.

(5) A person who discloses any information in contravention of section 33 of this Act is guilty of an offence and liable—

(a) on conviction on indictment, to imprisonment for a term not exceeding two years or a fine or both, and

(b) on summary conviction, to imprisonment for a term not exceeding six months or a fine not exceeding the statutory maximum or both.

(6) A person who—

(a) fails to comply with a requirement made by virtue of section 39(1)(b) or (2)(b) or 40(2)(b)(ii) or (5)(b) of this Act, or

(b) intentionally obstructs the exercise of any rights conferred by a warrant issued under section 40 of this Act,

is guilty of an offence.

(7) A person who without reasonable excuse fails to comply with a requirement imposed by regulations made by virtue of section 10(2)(a) of this Act is guilty of an offence.

(8) Where a person to whom a licence applies or the nominal licensee gives or receives any money or other benefit, not authorised by directions, in respect of any supply of gametes or embryos, he is guilty of an offence.

[1] Words inserted by Criminal Justice and Public Order Act 1994 c.33 Pt XII s 156 (3)

(9) A person guilty of an offence under subsection (6), (7) or (8) above is liable on summary conviction to imprisonment for a term not exceeding six months or a fine not exceeding level five on the standard scale or both.

(10) It is a defence for a person ("the defendant") charged with an offence of doing anything which, under section 3(1) or 4(1) of this Act, cannot be done except in pursuance of a licence to prove—

(a) that the defendant was acting under the direction of another, and

(b) that the defendant believed on reasonable grounds—

(i) that the other person was at the material time the person responsible under a licence, a person designated by virtue of section 17(2)(b) of this Act as a person to whom a licence applied, or a person to whom directions had been given by virtue of section 24(9) of this Act, and

(ii) that the defendant was authorised by virtue of the licence or directions to do the thing in question.

(11) It is a defence for a person charged with an offence under this Act to prove—

(a) that at the material time he was a person to whom a licence applied or to whom directions had been given, and

(b) that he took all such steps as were reasonable and exercised all due diligence to avoid committing the offence.

SCHEDULES

Section 12 etc Schedule 3

Consents to Use of Gametes or Embryos

Consent

1. A consent under this Schedule must be given in writing and, in this Schedule, "effective consent" means a consent under this Schedule which has not been withdrawn. **40-014**

2.— (1) A consent to the use of any embryo must specify one or more of the following purposes— **40-015**

(a) use in providing treatment services to the person giving consent, or that person and another specified person together,

(b) use in providing treatment services to persons not including the person giving consent, or

(c) use for the purposes of any project of research,

and may specify conditions subject to which the embryo may be so used.

(2) A consent to the storage of any gametes or any embryo must—

(a) specify the maximum period of storage (if less than the statutory storage period), and

(b) state what is to be done with the gametes or embryo if the person who gave the consent dies or is unable because of incapacity to vary the terms of the consent or to revoke it,

and may specify conditions subject to which the gametes or embryo may remain in storage.

(3) A consent under this Schedule must provide for such other matters as the Authority may specify in directions.

(4) A consent under this Schedule may apply—

(a) to the use or storage of a particular embryo, or

(b) in the case of a person providing gametes, to the use or storage of any embryo whose creation may be brought about using those gametes,

and in the paragraph (b) case the terms of the consent may be varied, or the consent may be withdrawn, in accordance with this Schedule either generally or in relation to a particular embryo or particular embryos.

Procedure for giving consent

3.— (1) Before a person gives consent under this Schedule— **40-016**

(a) he must be given a suitable opportunity to receive proper counselling about the implications of taking the proposed steps, and
(b) he must be provided with such relevant information as is proper.

(2) Before a person gives consent under this Schedule he must be informed of the effect of paragraph 4 below.

Variation and withdrawal of consent

40-017 **4.**—(1) The terms of any consent under this Schedule may from time to time be varied, and the consent may be withdrawn, by notice given by the person who gave the consent to the person keeping the gametes or embryo to which the consent is relevant.

(2) The terms of any consent to the use of any embryo cannot be varied, and such consent cannot be withdrawn, once the embryo has been used—
(a) in providing treatment services, or
(b) for the purposes of any project of research.

Use of gametes for treatment of others

40-018 **5.**—(1) A person's gametes must not be used for the purposes of treatment services unless there is an effective consent by that person to their being so used and they are used in accordance with the terms of the consent.

(2) A person's gametes must not be received for use for those purposes unless there is an effective consent by that person to their being so used.

(3) This paragraph does not apply to the use of a person's gametes for the purpose of that person, or that person and another together, receiving treatment services.

In vitro fertilisation and subsequent use of embryo

40-019 **6.**—(1) A person's gametes must not be used to bring about the creation of any embryo in vitro unless there is an effective consent by that person to any embryo the creation of which may be brought about with the use of those gametes being used for one or more of the purposes mentioned in paragraph 2(1) above.

(2) An embryo the creation of which was brought about in vitro must not be received by any person unless there is an effective consent by each person whose gametes were used to bring about the creation of the embryo to the use for one or more of the purposes mentioned in paragraph 2(1) above of the embryo.

(3) An embryo the creation of which was brought about in vitro must not be used for any purpose unless there is an effective consent by each person whose gametes were used to bring about the creation of the embryo to the use for that purpose of the embryo and the embryo is used in accordance with those consents.

(4) Any consent required by this paragraph is in addition to any consent that may be required by paragraph 5 above.

Embryos obtained by lavage, etc

40-020 **7.**—(1) An embryo taken from a woman must not be used for any purpose unless there is an effective consent by her to the use of the embryo for that purpose and it is used in accordance with the consent.

(2) An embryo taken from a woman must not be received by any person for use for any purpose unless there is an effective consent by her to the use of the embryo for that purpose.

(3) This paragraph does not apply to the use, for the purpose of providing a woman with treatment services, of an embryo taken from her.

Storage of gametes and embryos

40-021 **8.**—(1) A person's gametes must not be kept in storage unless there is an effective consent by that person to their storage and they are stored in accordance with the consent.

(2) An embryo the creation of which was brought about in vitro must not be kept in storage unless there is an effective consent, by each person whose gametes were used to bring about the creation of the embryo, to the storage of the embryo and the embryo is stored in accordance with those consents.

(3) An embryo taken from a woman must not be kept in storage unless there is an effective consent by her to its storage and it is stored in accordance with the consent.

Maintenance Enforcement Act 1991

CHAPTER 17

The High Court and county courts

Maintenance orders in the High Court and county courts: means of payment, attachment of earnings and revocation, variation, etc

1.—(1) Where the High Court or a county court makes a qualifying periodical maintenance order, it may at the same time exercise either of its powers under subsection (4) below in relation to the order, whether of its own motion or on an application made under this subsection by an interested party. **41-001**

(2) For the purposes of this section, a periodical maintenance order is an order—

(a) which requires money to be paid periodically by one person ("the debtor") to another ("the creditor"); and

(b) which is a maintenance order;

and such an order is a "qualifying periodical maintenance order" if, at the time it is made, the debtor is ordinarily resident in England and Wales.

(3) Where the High Court or a county court has made a qualifying periodical maintenance order, it may at any later time—

(a) on an application made under this subsection by an interested party, or

(b) of its own motion, in the course of any proceedings concerning the order,

exercise either of its powers under subsection (4) below in relation to the order.

(4) The powers mentioned in subsections (1) and (3) above are—

(a) the power to order that payments required to be made by the debtor to the creditor under the qualifying periodical maintenance order in question shall be so made by such a method of payment falling within subsection (5) below as the court may specify in the particular case; or

(b) the power, by virtue of this section, to make an attachment of earnings order under the Attachment of Earnings Act 1971 to secure payments under the qualifying periodical maintenance order in question.

(5) The methods of payment mentioned in subsection (4)(a) above are—

(a) payment by standing order; or

(b) payment by any other method which requires the debtor to give his authority for payments of a specific amount to be made from an account of his to an account of the creditor's on specific dates during the period for which the authority is in force and without the need for any further authority from the debtor.

(6) In any case where—

(a) the court proposes to exercise its power under paragraph (a) of subsection (4) above, and

(b) having given the debtor an opportunity of opening an account from which payments under the order may be made in accordance with the method of payment proposed to be ordered under that paragraph, the court is satisfied that the debtor has failed, without reasonable excuse, to open such an account, the court in exercising its power under that paragraph may order that the debtor open such an account.

(7) Where in the exercise of its powers under subsection (1) or (3) above the High Court or a county court has made in relation to a qualifying periodical maintenance order such an order as is mentioned in subsection (4)(a) above (a "means of payment order"), it may at any later time—

(a) on an application made under this subsection by an interested party, or

(b) of its own motion, in the course of any proceedings concerning the qualifying periodical maintenance order,

revoke, suspend, revive or vary the means of payment order.

(8) In deciding whether to exercise any of its powers under this section the court in question having (if practicable) given every interested party an opportunity to make representations shall have regard to any representations made by any such party.

(9) Nothing in this section shall be taken to prejudice—

(a) any power under the Attachment of Earnings Act 1971 which would, apart from this section, be exercisable by the High Court or a county court; or

(b) any right of any person to make any application under that Act;

and subsection (7) above is without prejudice to any other power of the High Court or a county court to revoke, suspend, revive or vary an order.

(10) For the purposes of this section—

"debtor" and "creditor" shall be construed in accordance with subsection (2) above;

"interested party" means any of the following, that is to say—

(a) the debtor;

(b) the creditor; and

(c) in a case where the person who applied for the qualifying periodical maintenance order in question is a person other than the creditor, that other person;

"maintenance order" means any order specified in Schedule 8 to the Administration of Justice Act 1970 and includes any such order which has been discharged, if any arrears are recoverable under it;

"qualifying periodical maintenance order" shall be construed in accordance with subsection (2) above, and the references to such an order in subsections (3) and (7) above are references to any such order, whether made before or after the coming into force of this section;

and the reference in subsection (2) above to an order requiring money to be paid periodically by one person to another includes a reference to an order requiring a lump sum to be paid by instalments by one person to another.

Child Support Act 1991

CHAPTER 48

The basic principles

The duty to maintain

1.—(1) For the purposes of this Act, each parent of a qualifying child is responsible for maintaining him. **42-001**

(2) For the purposes of this Act, an absent parent shall be taken to have met his responsibility to maintain any qualifying child of his by making periodical payments of maintenance with respect to the child of such amount, and at such intervals, as may be determined in accordance with the provisions of this Act.

(3) Where a maintenance assessment made under this Act requires the making of periodical payments, it shall be the duty of the absent parent with respect to whom the assessment was made to make those payments.

Welfare of children: the general principle

2. Where, in any case which falls to be dealt with under this Act, the Secretary of State [...][1]is considering the exercise of any discretionary power conferred by this Act, he shall have regard to the welfare of any child likely to be affected by his decision. **42-002**

Meaning of certain terms used in this Act

3.—(1) A child is a "qualifying child" if— **42-003**

(a) one of his parents is, in relation to him, an absent parent; or

(b) both of his parents are, in relation to him, absent parents.

(2) The parent of any child is [a "non-resident parent", in relation to him, if—

(a) that parent is not living in the same household with the child; and

(b) the child has his home with a person who is, in relation to him, a person with care.][2]

(3) A person is a "person with care", in relation to any child, if he is a person—

(a) with whom the child has his home;

(b) who usually provides day to day care for the child (whether exclusively or in conjunction with any other person); and

(c) who does not fall within a prescribed category of person.

(4) The Secretary of State shall not, under subsection (3)(c), prescribe as a category—

(a) parents;

(b) guardians;

(c) persons in whose favour residence orders under section 8 of the Children Act 1989 are in force;

(5) For the purposes of this Act there may be more than one person with care in relation to the same qualifying child.

---

[1] Words repealed by Social Security Act 1998 c.14 Sch 8 para 1

[2] Words substituted by Child Support, Pensions and Social Security Act 2000 c.19 Sch 3 para 11 (2)

(6) Periodical payments which are required to be paid in accordance with a maintenance assessment are referred to in this Act as "child support maintenance".

(7) Expressions are defined in this section only for the purposes of this Act.

Child support maintenance

42-004 **4.**—(1) A person who is, in relation to any qualifying child or any qualifying children, either the person with care or the absent parent may apply to the Secretary of State for a maintenance assessment to be made under this Act with respect to that child, or any of those children.

(2) Where a maintenance assessment has been made in response to an application under this section the Secretary of State may, if the person with care or absent parent with respect to whom the assessment was made applies to him under this subsection, arrange for—

(a) the collection of the child support maintenance payable in accordance with the assessment;

(b) the enforcement of the obligation to pay child support maintenance in accordance with the assessment.

(3) Where an application under subsection (2) for the enforcement of the obligation mentioned in subsection (2)(b) authorises the Secretary of State to take steps to enforce that obligation whenever he considers it necessary to do so, the Secretary of State may act accordingly.

(4) A person who applies to the Secretary of State under this section shall, so far as that person reasonably can, comply with such regulations as may be made by the Secretary of State with a view to the Secretary of State [...][1] being provided with the information which is required to enable—

(a) the absent parent to be [identified or][2] traced (where that is necessary);

(b) the amount of child support maintenance payable by the absent parent to be assessed; and

(c) that amount to be recovered from the absent parent.

(5) Any person who has applied to the Secretary of State under this section may at any time request him to cease acting under this section.

(6) It shall be the duty of the Secretary of State to comply with any request made under subsection (5) (but subject to any regulations made under subsection (8)).

(7) The obligation to provide information which is imposed by subsection (4)—

(a) shall not apply in such circumstances as may be prescribed; and

(b) may, in such circumstances as may be prescribed, be waived by the Secretary of State.

(8) The Secretary of State may by regulations make such incidental, supplemental or transitional provision as he thinks appropriate with respect to cases in which he is requested to cease to act under this section.

(9) No application may be made under this section if there is in force with respect to the person with care and absent parent in question a maintenance assessment made in response to an application [treated as made][3] under section 6.

[1] Words repealed by Social Security Act 1998 c.14 Sch 8 para 1

[2] Words added in relation to cases specified in SI 2003/192 art 3 by Child Support, Pensions and Social Security Act 2000 c.19 Sch 3 para 11 (3) (a)

[3] Words added in relation to cases specified in SI 2003/192 art 3 by Child Support, Pensions and Social Security Act 2000 c.19 Sch 3 para 11 (3) (b)

[(10) No application may be made at any time under this section with respect to a qualifying child or any qualifying children if—

(a) there is in force a written maintenance agreement made before 5th April 1993, or a maintenance order [made before a prescribed date][1], in respect of that child or those children and the person who is, at that time, the absent parent; or

[(aa) a maintenance order made on or after the date prescribed for the purposes of paragraph (a) is in force in respect of them, but has been so for less than the period of one year beginning with the date on which it was made; or][2]

(b) benefit is being paid to, or in respect of, a parent with care of that child or those children.

(11) In subsection (10) "benefit" means any benefit which is mentioned in, or prescribed by regulations under, section 6(1).][3]

Child support maintenance: supplemental provisions

5.—(1) Where— **42-005**

(a) there is more than one person with care of a qualifying child; and

(b) one or more, but not all, of them have parental responsibility for [...][4] the child;

no application may be made for a maintenance assessment with respect to the child by any of those persons who do not have parental responsibility for [...][5] the child.

(2) Where more than one application for a maintenance assessment is made with respect to the child concerned, only one of them may be proceeded with.

(3) The Secretary of State may by regulations make provision as to which of two or more applications for a maintenance assessment with respect to the same child is to be proceeded with.

[Applications by those claiming or receiving benefit

6.—(1) This section applies where income support, an income-based jobseeker's allowance or any other benefit of a prescribed kind is claimed by or in respect of, or paid to or in respect of, the parent of a qualifying child who is also a person with care of the child. **42-006**

(2) In this section, that person is referred to as "the parent".

(3) The Secretary of State may–

(a) treat the parent as having applied for a maintenance calculation with respect to the qualifying child and all other children of the non-resident parent in relation to whom the parent is also a person with care; and

(b) take action under this Act to recover from the non-resident parent, on the parent's behalf, the child support maintenance so determined.

(4) Before doing what is mentioned in subsection (3), the Secretary of State must notify the parent in writing of the effect of subsections (3) and (5) and section 46.

(5) The Secretary of State may not act under subsection (3) if the parent asks him not to (a request which need not be in writing).

---

1 Words inserted in relation to cases specified in SI 2003/192 art 3 by Child Support, Pensions and Social Security Act 2000 c.19 Pt I s 2 (2)

2 Inserted in relation to cases specified in SI 2003/192 art 3 by Child Support, Pensions and Social Security Act 2000 c.19 Pt I s 2 (3)

3 Added by Child Support Act 1995 c.34 s 18 (1)

4 Words repealed by Children (Scotland) Act 1995 c.36 Sch 5 para 1

5 Words repealed by Children (Scotland) Act 1995 c.36 Sch 5 para 1

(6) Subsection (1) has effect regardless of whether any of the benefits mentioned there is payable with respect to any qualifying child.

(7) Unless she has made a request under subsection (5), the parent shall, so far as she reasonably can, comply with such regulations as may be made by the Secretary of State with a view to the Secretary of State's being provided with the information which is required to enable–

(a) the non-resident parent to be identified or traced;

(b) the amount of child support maintenance payable by him to be calculated; and

(c) that amount to be recovered from him.

(8) The obligation to provide information which is imposed by subsection (7)–

(a) does not apply in such circumstances as may be prescribed; and

(b) may, in such circumstances as may be prescribed, be waived by the Secretary of State.

(9) If the parent ceases to fall within subsection (1), she may ask the Secretary of State to cease acting under this section, but until then he may continue to do so.

(10) The Secretary of State must comply with any request under subsection (9) (but subject to any regulations made under subsection (11)).

(11) The Secretary of State may by regulations make such incidental or transitional provision as he thinks appropriate with respect to cases in which he is asked under subsection (9) to cease to act under this section.

(12) The fact that a maintenance calculation is in force with respect to a person with care does not prevent the making of a new maintenance calculation with respect to her as a result of the Secretary of State's acting under subsection (3).][1]

Role of the courts with respect to maintenance for children

42-007 **8.**—(1) This subsection applies in any case where [the Secretary of State][2] would have jurisdiction to make a maintenance assessment with respect to a qualifying child and an absent parent of his on an application duly made [(or treated as made)][3] by a person entitled to apply for such an assessment with respect to that child.

(2) Subsection (1) applies even though the circumstances of the case are such that [the Secretary of State][4] would not make an assessment if it were applied for.

(3) [Except as provided in subsection (3A), in][5] any case where subsection (1) applies, no court shall exercise any power which it would otherwise have to make, vary or revive any maintenance order in relation to the child and absent parent concerned.

[(3A) Unless a maintenance calculation has been made with respect to the child concerned, subsection (3) does not prevent a court from varying a maintenance order in relation to that child and the non-resident parent concerned–

[1] Substituted in relation to cases specified in SI 2003/192 art 4 by Child Support, Pensions and Social Security Act 2000 c.19 Pt I s 3

[2] Words substituted by Social Security Act 1998 c.14 Sch 7 para 22

[3] Words added in relation to cases specified in SI 2003/192 art 3 by Child Support, Pensions and Social Security Act 2000 c.19 Sch 3 para 11 (5) (a)

[4] Words substituted by Social Security Act 1998 c.14 Sch 7 para 22

[5] Words added in relation to cases specified in SI 2003/192 art 3 by Child Support, Pensions and Social Security Act 2000 c.19 Sch 3 para 11 (5) (b)

(a) if the maintenance order was made on or after the date prescribed for the purposes of section 4(10)(a) or 7(10)(a); or

(b) where the order was made before then, in any case in which section 4(10) or 7(10) prevents the making of an application for a maintenance calculation with respect to or by that child.][1]

(4) Subsection (3) does not prevent a court from revoking a maintenance order.

(5) The Lord Chancellor or in relation to Scotland the Lord Advocate may by order provide that, in such circumstances as may be specified by the order, this section shall not prevent a court from exercising any power which it has to make a maintenance order in relation to a child if—

(a) a written agreement (whether or not enforceable) provides for the making, or securing, by an absent parent of the child of periodical payments to or for the benefit of the child; and

(b) the maintenance order which the court makes is, in all material respects, in the same terms as that agreement.

(6) This section shall not prevent a court from exercising any power which it has to make a maintenance order in relation to a child if—

(a) a maintenance assessment is in force with respect to the child;

[(b) the non-resident parent's net weekly income exceeds the figure referred to in paragraph 10(3) of Schedule 1 (as it has effect from time to time pursuant to regulations made under paragraph 10A(1)(b)); and][2]

(c) the court is satisfied that the circumstances of the case make it appropriate for the absent parent to make or secure the making of periodical payments under a maintenance order in addition to the child support maintenance payable by him in accordance with the maintenance assessment.

(7) This section shall not prevent a court from exercising any power which it has to make a maintenance order in relation to a child if—

(a) the child is, will be or (if the order were to be made) would be receiving instruction at an educational establishment or undergoing training for a trade, profession or vocation (whether or not while in gainful employment); and

(b) the order is made solely for the purposes of requiring the person making or securing the making of periodical payments fixed by the order to meet some or all of the expenses incurred in connection with the provision of the instruction or training.

(8) This section shall not prevent a court from exercising any power which it has to make a maintenance order in relation to a child if—

(a) a disability living allowance is paid to or in respect of him; or

(b) no such allowance is paid but he is disabled,

and the order is made solely for the purpose of requiring the person making or securing the making of periodical payments fixed by the order to meet some or all of any expenses attributable to the child's disability.

(9) For the purposes of subsection (8), a child is disabled if he is blind, deaf or dumb or is substantially and permanently handicapped by illness, injury, mental disorder or congenital deformity or such other disability as may be prescribed.

---

[1] Substituted in relation to cases specified in SI 2003/192 art 3 by Child Support, Pensions and Social Security Act 2000 c.19 Sch 3 para 11 (5) (c)

[2] Substituted in relation to cases specified in SI 2003/192 art 3 by Child Support, Pensions and Social Security Act 2000 c.19 Sch 3 para 11 (5) (d)

(10) This section shall not prevent a court from exercising any power which it has to make a maintenance order in relation to a child if the order is made against a person with care of the child.

(11) In this Act "maintenance order", in relation to any child, means an order which requires the making or securing of periodical payments to or for the benefit of the child and which is made under—

(a) Part II of the Matrimonial Causes Act 1973;
(b) the Domestic Proceedings and Magistrates' Courts Act 1978;
(c) Part III of the Matrimonial and Family Proceedings Act 1984;
(d) the Family Law (Scotland) Act 1985;
(e) Schedule 1 to the Children Act 1989; or
(f) any other prescribed enactment.

and includes any order varying or reviving such an order.

Agreements about maintenance

42-008 **9.**—(1) In this section "maintenance agreement" means any agreement for the making, or for securing the making, of periodical payments by way of maintenance, or in Scotland aliment, to or for the benefit of any child.

(2) Nothing in this Act shall be taken to prevent any person from entering into a maintenance agreement.

(3) [Subject to section 4(10)(a) and section 7(10),][1]The existence of a maintenance agreement shall not prevent any party to the agreement, or any other person, from applying for a maintenance assessment with respect to any child to or for whose benefit periodical payments are to be made or secured under the agreement.

(4) Where any agreement contains a provision which purports to restrict the right of any person to apply for a maintenance assessment, that provision shall be void.

(5) Where section 8 would prevent any court from making a maintenance order in relation to a child and an absent parent of his, no court shall exercise any power that it has to vary any agreement so as—

(a) to insert a provision requiring that absent parent to make or secure the making of periodical payments by way of maintenance, or in Scotland aliment, to or for the benefit of that child; or
(b) to increase the amount payable under such a provision.

[(6) In any case in which section 4(10) or 7(10) prevents the making of an application for a maintenance assessment, and—

[(a) no parent has been treated under section 6(3) as having applied for a maintenance calculation with respect to the child; or
(b) a parent has been so treated but no maintenance calculation has been made,][2]

subsection (5) shall have effect with the omission of paragraph (b).][3]

Relationship between maintenance assessments and certain court orders and related matters

42-009 **10.**—(1) Where an order of a kind prescribed for the purposes of this subsection is in force with respect to any qualifying child with respect to whom a maintenance assessment is made, the order—

[1] Words inserted by Child Support Act 1995 c.34 s 18 (4)
[2] Substituted in relation to cases specified in SI 2003/192 art 3 by Child Support, Pensions and Social Security Act 2000 c.19 Sch 3 para 11 (6)
[3] Added by Child Support Act 1995 c.34 s 18 (4)

(a) shall, so far as it relates to the making or securing of periodical payments, cease to have effect to such extent as may be determined in accordance with regulations made by the Secretary of State; or

(b) where the regulations so provide, shall, so far as it so relates, have effect subject to such modifications as may be so determined.

(2) Where an agreement of a kind prescribed for the purposes of this subsection is in force with respect to any qualifying child with respect to whom a maintenance assessment is made, the agreement—

(a) shall, so far as it relates to the making or securing of periodical payments, be unenforceable to such extent as may be determined in accordance with regulations made by the Secretary of State; or

(b) where the regulations so provide, shall, so far as it so relates, have effect subject to such modifications as may be so determined.

(3) Any regulations under this section may, in particular, make such provision with respect to—

(a) any case where any person with respect to whom an order or agreement of a kind prescribed for the purposes of subsection (1) or (2) has effect applies to the prescribed court, before the end of the prescribed period, for the order or agreement to be varied in the light of the maintenance assessment and of the provisions of this Act;

(b) the recovery of any arrears under the order or agreement which fell due before the coming into force of the maintenance assessment,

as the Secretary of State considers appropriate and may provide that, in prescribed circumstances, an application to any court which is made with respect to an order of a prescribed kind relating to the making or securing of periodical payments to or for the benefit of a child shall be treated by the court as an application for the order to be revoked.

(4) The Secretary of State may by regulations make provision for—

(a) notification to be given by [the Secretary of State][1] to the prescribed person in any case where [he][2] considers that the making of a maintenance assessment has affected, or is likely to affect, any order of a kind prescribed for the purposes of this subsection;

(b) notification to be given by the prescribed person to the Secretary of State in any case where a court makes an order which it considers has affected, or is likely to affect, a maintenance assessment.

(5) Rules may be made under section 144 of the Magistrates' Courts Act 1980 (rules of procedure) requiring any person who, in prescribed circumstances, makes an application to a magistrates' court for a maintenance order to furnish the court with a statement in a prescribed form, and signed by [an officer of the Secretary of State][3], as to whether or not, at the time when the statement is made, there is a maintenance assessment in force with respect to that person or the child concerned.

In this subsection—

"maintenance order" means an order of a prescribed kind for the making or securing of periodical payments to or for the benefit of a child; and

"prescribed" means prescribed by the rules.

[1] Words substituted by Social Security Act 1998 c.14 Sch 7 para 23 (1) (a)
[2] Words substituted by Social Security Act 1998 c.14 Sch 7 para 23 (1) (b)
[3] Words substituted by Social Security Act 1998 c.14 Sch 7 para 23 (2)

Maintenance assessments

[Maintenance calculations

42-010 **11.**—(1) An application for a maintenance calculation made to the Secretary of State shall be dealt with by him in accordance with the provision made by or under this Act.

(2) The Secretary of State shall (unless he decides not to make a maintenance calculation in response to the application, or makes a decision under section 12) determine the application by making a decision under this section about whether any child support maintenance is payable and, if so, how much.

(3) Where–

(a) a parent is treated under section 6(3) as having applied for a maintenance calculation; but

(b) the Secretary of State becomes aware before determining the application that the parent has ceased to fall within section 6(1),

he shall, subject to subsection (4), cease to treat that parent as having applied for a maintenance calculation.

(4) If it appears to the Secretary of State that subsection (10) of section 4 would not have prevented the parent with care concerned from making an application for a maintenance calculation under that section he shall–

(a) notify her of the effect of this subsection; and

(b) if, before the end of the period of one month beginning with the day on which notice was sent to her, she asks him to do so, treat her as having applied not under section 6 but under section 4.

(5) Where subsection (3) applies but subsection (4) does not, the Secretary of State shall notify–

(a) the parent with care concerned; and

(b) the non-resident parent (or alleged non-resident parent), where it appears to him that that person is aware that the parent with care has been treated as having applied for a maintenance calculation.

(6) The amount of child support maintenance to be fixed by a maintenance calculation shall be determined in accordance with Part I of Schedule 1 unless an application for a variation has been made and agreed.

(7) If the Secretary of State has agreed to a variation, the amount of child support maintenance to be fixed shall be determined on the basis he determines under section 28F(4).

(8) Part II of Schedule 1 makes further provision with respect to maintenance calculations.][1]

[Default and interim maintenance decisions

42-011 **12.**—(1) Where the Secretary of State–

(a) is required to make a maintenance calculation; or

(b) is proposing to make a decision under section 16 or 17,

and it appears to him that he does not have sufficient information to enable him to do so, he may make a default maintenance decision.

(2) Where an application for a variation has been made under section 28A(1) in connection with an application for a maintenance calculation (or in connection with such an application which is treated as having been made), the Secretary of State may make an interim maintenance decision.

[1] Substituted in relation to cases specified in SI 2003/192 art 3 by Child Support, Pensions and Social Security Act 2000 c.19 Pt I s 1 (1)

(3) The amount of child support maintenance fixed by an interim maintenance decision shall be determined in accordance with Part I of Schedule 1.

(4) The Secretary of State may by regulations make provision as to default and interim maintenance decisions.

(5) The regulations may, in particular, make provision as to–

(a) the procedure to be followed in making a default or an interim maintenance decision; and

(b) a default rate of child support maintenance to apply where a default maintenance decision is made.][1]

Information

Information required by Secretary of State

14.—(1) The Secretary of State may make regulations requiring any information or evidence needed for the determination of any application [made or treated as made][2] under this Act, or any question arising in connection with such an application[(or application treated as made), or needed for the making of any decision or in connection with the imposition of any condition or requirement under this Act,][3], or needed in connection with the collection or enforcement of child support or other maintenance under this Act, to be furnished— **42-012**

(a) by such persons as may be determined in accordance with regulations made by the Secretary of State; and

(b) in accordance with the regulations.

[(1A) Regulations under subsection (1) may make provision for notifying any person who is required to furnish any information or evidence under the regulations of the possible consequences of failing to do so.][4]

(2) [...][5]

(3) The Secretary of State may by regulations make provision authorising the disclosure by him [...][6], in such circumstances as may be prescribed, of such information held by [him][7] for purposes of this Act as may be prescribed.

(4) The provisions of Schedule 2 (which relate to information which is held for purposes other than those of this Act but which is required by the Secretary of State) shall have effect.

[Information-offences

14A.—(1) This section applies to– **42-013**

(a) persons who are required to comply with regulations under section 4(4) or 7(5); and

(b) persons specified in regulations under section 14(1)(a).

(2) Such a person is guilty of an offence if, pursuant to a request for information under or by virtue of those regulations–

(a) he makes a statement or representation which he knows to be false; or

---

1 Substituted in relation to cases specified in SI 2003/192 art 3 by Child Support, Pensions and Social Security Act 2000 c.19 Pt I s 4

2 Words added in relation to cases specified in SI 2003/192 art 3 by Child Support, Pensions and Social Security Act 2000 c.19 Sch 3 para 11 (7)

3 Words inserted in relation to cases specified in SI 2003/192 art 3 by Child Support, Pensions and Social Security Act 2000 c.19 Pt I s 12

4 Added by Child Support Act 1995 c.34 Sch 3 para 3 (1)

5 Repealed by Social Security Act 1998 c.14 Sch 8 para 1

6 Words repealed by Social Security Act 1998 c.14 Sch 8 para 1

7 Word substituted by Social Security Act 1998 c.14 Sch 7 para 27 (b)

(b) he provides, or knowingly causes or knowingly allows to be provided, a document or other information which he knows to be false in a material particular.

(3) Such a person is guilty of an offence if, following such a request, he fails to comply with it.

(4) It is a defence for a person charged with an offence under subsection (3) to prove that he had a reasonable excuse for failing to comply.

(5) A person guilty of an offence under this section is liable on summary conviction to a fine not exceeding level 3 on the standard scale.][1]

Powers of inspectors

42-014 **15.**—[(1) The Secretary of State may appoint, on such terms as he thinks fit, persons to act as inspectors under this section.

(2) The function of inspectors is to acquire information which the Secretary of State needs for any of the purposes of this Act.

(3) Every inspector is to be given a certificate of his appointment.

(4) An inspector has power, at any reasonable time and either alone or accompanied by such other persons as he thinks fit, to enter any premises which–

(a) are liable to inspection under this section; and

(b) are premises to which it is reasonable for him to require entry in order that he may exercise his functions under this section,

and may there make such examination and inquiry as he considers appropriate.

(4A) Premises liable to inspection under this section are those which are not used wholly as a dwelling house and which the inspector has reasonable grounds for suspecting are–

(a) premises at which a non-resident parent is or has been employed;

(b) premises at which a non-resident parent carries out, or has carried out, a trade, profession, vocation or business;

(c) premises at which there is information held by a person ("A") whom the inspector has reasonable grounds for suspecting has information about a non-resident parent acquired in the course of A's own trade, profession, vocation or business.][2]

(5) An inspector exercising his powers may question any person aged 18 or over whom he finds on the premises.

[(6) If required to do so by an inspector exercising his powers, any such person shall furnish to the inspector all such information and documents as the inspector may reasonably require.][3]

(7) No person shall be required under this section to answer any question or to give any evidence tending to incriminate himself or, in the case of a person who is married, his or her spouse.

(8) On applying for admission to any premises in the exercise of his powers, an inspector shall, if so required, produce his certificate.

(9) If any person—

(a) intentionally delays or obstructs any inspector exercising his powers; or

(b) without reasonable excuse, refuses or neglects to answer any question or furnish any information or to produce any document when required to do so under this section,

[1] Added by Child Support, Pensions and Social Security Act 2000 c.19 Pt I s 13

[2] S 15 (1)-(4A) substituted for s 15 (1)-(4) by Child Support, Pensions and Social Security Act 2000 c.19 Pt I s 14 (2)

[3] Words substituted by Child Support, Pensions and Social Security Act 2000 c.19 Pt I s 14 (3)

he shall be guilty of an offence and liable on summary conviction to a fine not exceeding level 3 on the standard scale.

(10) In this section—

"certificate" means a certificate of appointment issued under this section;

"inspector" means an inspector appointed under this section;

"powers" means powers conferred by this section;

[...][1]

[...][2]

[(11) In this section, "premises" includes–

(a) moveable structures and vehicles, vessels, aircraft and hovercraft;

(b) installations that are offshore installations for the purposes of the Mineral Workings (Offshore Installations) Act 1971; and

(c) places of all other descriptions whether or not occupied as land or otherwise,

and references in this section to the occupier of premises are to be construed, in relation to premises that are not occupied as land, as references to any person for the time being present at the place in question.][3]

Reviews and appeals

[Revision of decisions

16.—(1) Any decision [to which subsection (1A) applies][4] may be revised by the Secretary of State— **42-015**

(a) either within the prescribed period or in prescribed cases or circumstances; and

(b) either on an application made for the purpose or on his own initiative;

and regulations may prescribe the procedure by which a decision of the Secretary of State may be so revised.

[(1A) This subsection applies to–

(a) a decision of the Secretary of State under section 11, 12 or 17;

(b) a reduced benefit decision under section 46;

(c) a decision of an appeal tribunal on a referral under section 28D(1)(b).

(1B) Where the Secretary of State revises a decision under section 12(1)–

(a) he may (if appropriate) do so as if he were revising a decision under section 11; and

(b) if he does that, his decision as revised is to be treated as one under section 11 instead of section 12 (1) (and, in particular, is to be so treated for the purposes of an appeal against it under section 20).][5]

(2) In making a decision under subsection (1), the Secretary of State need not consider any issue that is not raised by the application or, as the case may be, did not cause him to act on his own initiative.

(3) Subject to subsections (4) and (5) and section 28ZC, a revision under this section shall take effect as from the date on which the original decision took (or was to take) effect.

1 Definition repealed by Child Support, Pensions and Social Security Act 2000 c.19 Sch 9 (I) para 1

2 Definition repealed by Child Support, Pensions and Social Security Act 2000 c.19 Sch 9 (I) para 1

3 Added by Child Support, Pensions and Social Security Act 2000 c.19 Pt I s 14 (4)

4 Words substituted in relation to cases specified in SI 2003/192 art 3 by Child Support, Pensions and Social Security Act 2000 c.19 Pt I s 8 (2)

5 Inserted in relation to cases specified in SI 2003/192 art 3 by Child Support, Pensions and Social Security Act 2000 c.19 Pt I s 8 (3)

(4) Regulations may provide that, in prescribed cases or circumstances, a revision under this section shall take effect as from such other date as may be prescribed.

(5) Where a decision is revised under this section, for the purpose of any rule as to the time allowed for bringing an appeal, the decision shall be regarded as made on the date on which it is so revised.

(6) Except in prescribed circumstances, an appeal against a decision of the Secretary of State shall lapse if the decision is revised under this section before the appeal is determined.][1]

[Decisions superseding earlier decisions

42-016 **17.**—(1) Subject to subsection (2), the following, namely—

(a) any decision of the Secretary of State under section 11 or 12 or this section, whether as originally made or as revised under section 16;

(b) any decision of an appeal tribunal under section 20; [...][2]

[(c) any reduced benefit decision under section 46;

(d) any decision of an appeal tribunal on a referral under section 28D(1)(b);

(e) any decision of a Child Support Commissioner on an appeal from such a decision as is mentioned in paragraph (b) or (d).][3]

may be superseded by a decision made by the Secretary of State, either on an application made for the purpose or on his own initiative.

(2) In making a decision under subsection (1), the Secretary of State need not consider any issue that is not raised by the application or, as the case may be, did not cause him to act on his own initiative.

(3) Regulations may prescribe the cases and circumstances in which, and the procedure by which, a decision may be made under this section.

[(4) Subject to subsection (5) and section 28ZC, a decision under this section shall take effect as from the beginning of the maintenance period in which it is made or, where applicable, the beginning of the maintenance period in which the application was made.

(4A) In subsection (4), a "maintenance period" is (except where a different meaning is prescribed for prescribed cases) a period of seven days, the first one beginning on the effective date of the first decision made by the Secretary of State under section 11 or (if earlier) his first default or interim maintenance decision (under section 12) in relation to the non-resident parent in question, and each subsequent one beginning on the day after the last day of the previous one.][4]

(5) Regulations may provide that, in prescribed cases or circumstances, a decision under this section shall take effect as from such other date as may be prescribed.][5]

[Appeals to appeal tribunals

42-017 **20.**—(1) A qualifying person has a right of appeal to an appeal tribunal against–

[1] Substituted by Social Security Act 1998 c.14 Pt I c III s 40

[2] Word repealed in relation to cases specified in SI 2003/192 art 3 by Child Support, Pensions and Social Security Act 2000 c.19 Sch 9 (I) para 1

[3] Paragraphs (c) to (e) substituted for paragraph (c) in relation to cases specified in SI 2003/192 art 3 by Child Support, Pensions and Social Security Act 2000 c.19 Pt I s 9 (2)

[4] Subsections (4) and (4A) substituted for subsection (4) in relation to cases specified in SI 2003/192 art 3 by Child Support, Pensions and Social Security Act 2000 c.19 Pt I s 9 (3)

[5] Remainder of s 17 and s 18 to s 19 substituted by Social Security Act 1998 c.14 Pt I c III s 41

(a) a decision of the Secretary of State under section 11, 12 or 17 (whether as originally made or as revised under section 16);
(b) a decision of the Secretary of State not to make a maintenance calculation under section 11 or not to supersede a decision under section 17;
(c) a reduced benefit decision under section 46;
(d) the imposition (by virtue of section 41A) of a requirement to make penalty payments, or their amount;
(e) the imposition (by virtue of section 47) of a requirement to pay fees.

(2) In subsection (1), "qualifying person" means–
(a) in relation to paragraphs (a) and (b)–
(i) the person with care, or non-resident parent, with respect to whom the Secretary of State made the decision, or
(ii) in a case relating to a maintenance calculation which was applied for under section 7, either of those persons or the child concerned;
(b) in relation to paragraph (c), the person in respect of whom the benefits are payable;
(c) in relation to paragraph (d), the parent who has been required to make penalty payments; and
(d) in relation to paragraph (e), the person required to pay fees.

(3) A person with a right of appeal under this section shall be given such notice as may be prescribed of–
(a) that right; and
(b) the relevant decision, or the imposition of the requirement.

(4) Regulations may make–
(a) provision as to the manner in which, and the time within which, appeals are to be brought; and
(b) such provision with respect to proceedings before appeal tribunals as the Secretary of State considers appropriate.

(5) The regulations may in particular make any provision of a kind mentioned in Schedule 5 to the Social Security Act 1998.

(6) No appeal lies by virtue of subsection (1)(c) unless the amount of the person's benefit is reduced in accordance with the reduced benefit decision; and the time within which such an appeal may be brought runs from the date of notification of the reduction.

(7) In deciding an appeal under this section, an appeal tribunal–
(a) need not consider any issue that is not raised by the appeal; and
(b) shall not take into account any circumstances not obtaining at the time when the Secretary of State made the decision or imposed the requirement.

(8) If an appeal under this section is allowed, the appeal tribunal may–
(a) itself make such decision as it considers appropriate; or
(b) remit the case to the Secretary of State, together with such directions (if any) as it considers appropriate.][1]

Child Support Commissioners

22.—(1) Her Majesty may from time to time appoint a Chief Child Support Commissioner and such number of other Child Support Commissioners as she may think fit. **42-018**

[1] Substituted in relation to cases specified in SI 2003/192 art 3 by Child Support, Pensions and Social Security Act 2000 c.19 Pt I s 10

(2) The Chief Child Support Commissioner and the other Child Support Commissioners shall be appointed from among persons who—

(a) have a 10 year general qualification; or

(b) are advocates or solicitors in Scotland of 10 years' standing.

(3) The Lord Chancellor, after consulting the Lord Advocate, may make such regulations with respect to proceedings before Child Support Commissioners as he considers appropriate.

(4) The regulations—

(a) may, in particular, make any provision of a kind mentioned in [Schedule 5 to the Social Security Act 1998][1]; and

(b) shall provide that any hearing before a Child Support Commissioner shall be in public except in so far as the Commissioner for special reasons directs otherwise.

(5) Schedule 4 shall have effect with respect to Child Support Commissioners.

[Redetermination of appeals

42-019 **23A.**—(1) This section applies where an application is made to a person under section 24(6)(a) for leave to appeal from a decision of an appeal tribunal.

(2) If the person who constituted, or was the chairman of, the appeal tribunal considers that the decision was erroneous in law, he may set aside the decision and refer the case either for redetermination by the tribunal or for determination by a differently constituted tribunal.

(3) If each of the principal parties to the case expresses the view that the decision was erroneous in point of law, the person shall set aside the decision and refer the case for determination by a differently constituted tribunal.

(4) The "principal parties" are–

(a) the Secretary of State; and

(b) those who are qualifying persons for the purposes of section 20(2) in relation to the decision in question.][2]

Appeal to Child Support Commissioner

42-020 **24.**—(1) Any person who is aggrieved by a decision of [an appeal tribunal, and the Secretary of State][3], may appeal to a Child Support Commissioner on a question of law.[...][4]

(2) Where, on an appeal under this section, a Child Support Commissioner holds that the decision appealed against was wrong in law he shall set it aside.

(3) Where a decision is set aside under subsection (2), the Child Support Commissioner may—

(a) if he can do so without making fresh or further findings of fact, give the decision which he considers should have been given by [the appeal tribunal][5];

(b) if he considers it expedient, make such findings and give such decision as he considers appropriate in the light of those findings; or

[(c) on an appeal by the Secretary of State, refer the case to [an appeal tribunal][6] with directions for its determination; or

1 Words substituted by Social Security Act 1998 c.14 Sch 7 para 29

2 Added by Child Support, Pensions and Social Security Act 2000 c.19 Pt I s 11

3 Words substituted by Social Security Act 1998 c.14 Sch 7 para 30 (1)

4 Repealed by Social Security Act 1998 c.14 Sch 8 para 1

5 Words substituted by Social Security Act 1998 c.14 Sch 7 para 30 (3) (a)

6 Words substituted by Social Security Act 1998 c.14 Sch 7 para 30 (3) (b)

(d) on any other appeal, refer the case to [the Secretary of State][1] or, if he considers it appropriate, to [an appeal tribunal][2] with directions for its determination.][3]

[(4) The reference under subsection (3) to the Secretary of State shall, subject to any direction of the Child Support Commissioner, be to an officer of his, or a person providing him with services, who has taken no part in the decision originally appealed against.][4]

(5) On a reference under subsection (3) to [an appeal tribunal][5], the tribunal shall, subject to any direction of the Child Support Commissioner, consist of persons who were not members of the tribunal which gave the decision which has been appealed against.

(6) No appeal lies under this section without the leave—

(a) of the person [who constituted, or was the chairman of, the appeal tribunal][6] when the decision appealed against was given or of [such other person][7] as may be determined in accordance with regulations made by the Lord Chancellor; or

(b) subject to and in accordance with regulations so made, of a Child Support Commissioner.

(7) The Lord Chancellor may by regulations make provision as to the manner in which, and the time within which, appeals under this section are to be brought and applications for leave under this section are to be made.

(8) Where a question which would otherwise fall to be determined by [the Secretary of State][8] first arises in the course of an appeal to a Child Support Commissioner, he may, if he thinks fit, determine it even though it has not been considered by a child support officer.

(9) Before making any regulations under subsection (6) or (7), the Lord Chancellor shall consult the Lord Advocate.

Appeal from Child Support Commissioner on question of law

25.—(1) An appeal on a question of law shall lie to the appropriate court from any decision of a Child Support Commissioner. **42-021**

(2) No such appeal may be brought except—

(a) with leave of the Child Support Commissioner who gave the decision or, where regulations made by the Lord Chancellor so provide, of a Child Support Commissioner selected in accordance with the regulations; or

(b) if the Child Support Commissioner refuses leave, with the leave of the appropriate court.

(3) An application for leave to appeal under this section against a decision of a Child Support Commissioner ("the appeal decision") may only be made by—

(a) a person who was a party to the proceedings in which the original decision, or appeal decision, was given;

(b) the Secretary of State; or

(c) any other person who is authorised to do so by regulations made by the Lord Chancellor.

---

[1] Words substituted by Social Security Act 1998 c.14 Sch 7 para 30 (3) (c)
[2] Words substituted by Social Security Act 1998 c.14 Sch 7 para 30 (3) (b)
[3] Substituted by Child Support Act 1995 c.34 Sch 3 para 7 (3)
[4] Substituted by Social Security Act 1998 c.14 Sch 7 para 30 (4)
[5] Words substituted by Social Security Act 1998 c.14 Sch 7 para 30 (5)
[6] Words substituted by Social Security Act 1998 c.14 Sch 7 para 30 (6) (a)
[7] Words substituted by Social Security Act 1998 c.14 Sch 7 para 30 (6) (b)
[8] Words substituted by Social Security Act 1998 c.14 Sch 7 para 30 (7)

[(3A) The Child Support Commissioner to whom an application for leave to appeal under this section is made shall specify as the appropriate court either the Court of Appeal or the Court of Session.

(3B) In determining the appropriate court, the Child Support Commissioner shall have regard to the circumstances of the case, and in particular the convenience of the persons who may be parties to the appeal.][1]

(4) In this section—

["appropriate court" except in subsections (3A) and (3B), means, the court specified in accordance with those subsections; and][2]

"original decision" means the decision to which the appeal decision in question relates.

(5) The Lord Chancellor may by regulations make provision with respect to—

(a) the manner in which and the time within which applications must be made to a Child Support Commissioner for leave under this section; and

(b) the procedure for dealing with such applications.

(6) Before making any regulations under subsection (2), (3) or (5), the Lord Chancellor shall consult the Lord Advocate.

Disputes about parentage

42-022 **26.**—(1) Where a person who is alleged to be a parent of the child with respect to whom an application for a maintenance assessment has been made [or treated as made][3] ("the alleged parent") denies that he is one of the child's parents, [the Secretary of State][4] shall not make a maintenance assessment on the assumption that the alleged parent is one of the child's parents unless the case falls within one of those set out in subsection (2).

(2) The Cases are—

[CASE A1

Where–

(a) the child is habitually resident in England and Wales;

(b) the Secretary of State is satisfied that the alleged parent was married to the child's mother at some time in the period beginning with the conception and ending with the birth of the child; and

(c) the child has not been adopted.

CASE A2

Where–

(a) the child is habitually resident in England and Wales;

(b) the alleged parent has been registered as father of the child under section 10 or 10A of the Births and Deaths Registration Act 1953, or in any register kept under section 13 (register of births and still-births) or section 44 (Register of Corrections Etc) of the Registration of Births, Deaths and Marriages (Scotland) Act 1965, or under Article 14 or 18(1)(b)(ii) of the Births and Deaths Registration (Northern Ireland) Order 1976; and

(c) the child has not subsequently been adopted.

CASE A3

1 Added by Child Support Act 1995 c.34 Sch 3 para 8 (1)
2 Words substituted by Child Support Act 1995 c.34 Sch 3 para 8 (2)
3 Words added in relation to cases specified in SI 2003/192 art 3 by Child Support, Pensions and Social Security Act 2000 c.19 Sch 3 para 11 (8)
4 Words substituted by Social Security Act 1998 c.14 Sch 7 para 31 (1)

Where the result of a scientific test (within the meaning of section 27A) taken by the alleged parent would be relevant to determining the child's parentage, and the alleged parent–

(a) refuses to take such a test; or

(b) has submitted to such a test, and it shows that there is no reasonable doubt that the alleged parent is a parent of the child.][1]

CASE A

Where the alleged parent is a parent of the child in question by virtue of having adopted him.

CASE B

Where the alleged parent is a parent of the child in question by virtue of an order under section 30 of the Human Fertilisation and Embryology Act 1990 (parental orders in favour of gamete donors).

[CASE B1

Where the Secretary of State is satisfied that the alleged parent is a parent of the child in question by virtue of section 27 or 28 of that Act (meaning of "mother" and of "father" respectively).][2]

CASE C

Where—

(a) either—

(i) a declaration that the alleged parent is a parent of the child in question (or a declaration which has that effect) is in force under [[section 55A or 56 of the Family Law Act 1986][3] or Article 32 of the Matrimonial and Family Proceedings (Northern Ireland) Order 1989][4] (declarations of parentage); or

(ii) a declarator by a court in Scotland that the alleged parent is a parent of the child in question (or a declarator which has that effect) is in force; and

(b) the child has not subsequently been adopted.

CASE D [...][5]

CASE E

Where—

(a) the child is habitually resident in Scotland;

(b) [the Secretary of State][6] is satisfied that one or other of the presumptions set out in section 5(1) of the Law Reform (Parent and Child) (Scotland) Act 1986 applies; and

(c) the child has not subsequently been adopted.

CASE F

Where—

(a) the alleged parent has been found, or adjudged, to be the father of the child in question—

(i) in proceedings before any court in England and Wales which are relevant proceedings for the purposes of section 12 of the Civil Evidence Act 1968 [or in proceedings before any court in Northern Ireland which are relevant proceedings for the purposes of section 8 of the Civil Evidence Act (Northern Ireland) 1971][7]; or

[1] Inserted by Child Support, Pensions and Social Security Act 2000 c.19 Pt I s 15 (1)
[2] Inserted by Child Support, Pensions and Social Security Act 2000 c.19 Pt I s 15 (2)
[3] Words inserted by Child Support, Pensions and Social Security Act 2000 c.19 Sch 8 para 12
[4] Words inserted by SI 1995/756 art 13 (a)
[5] Repealed by Child Support, Pensions and Social Security Act 2000 c.19 Sch 9 (IX) para 1
[6] Words substituted by Social Security Act 1998 c.14 Sch 7 para 31 (2)
[7] Words inserted by SI 1995/756 art 13 (b)

(ii) in affiliation proceedings before any court in the United Kingdom,(whether or not he offered any defence to the allegation of paternity) and that finding or adjudication still subsists; and

(b) the child has not subsequently been adopted.

(3) In this section—

"adopted" means adopted within the meaning of Part IV of the Adoption Act 1976 or, in relation to Scotland, Part IVof the Adoption (Scotland) Act 1978; and

"affiliation proceedings", in relation to Scotland, means any action of affiliation and aliment.

[Applications for declaration of parentage under Family Law Act 1986

42-023 **27.**—(1) This section applies where–

(a) an application for a maintenance calculation has been made (or is treated as having been made), or a maintenance calculation is in force, with respect to a person ("the alleged parent") who denies that he is a parent of a child with respect to whom the application or calculation was made or treated as made;

(b) the Secretary of State is not satisfied that the case falls within one of those set out in section 26(2); and

(c) the Secretary of State or the person with care makes an application for a declaration under section 55A of the Family Law Act 1986 as to whether or not the alleged parent is one of the child's parents.

(2) Where this section applies–

(a) if it is the person with care who makes the application, she shall be treated as having a sufficient personal interest for the purposes of subsection (3) of that section; and

(b) if it is the Secretary of State who makes the application, that subsection shall not apply.

(3) This section does not apply to Scotland.][1]

[Recovery of fees for scientific tests

42-024 **27A.**—(1) This section applies in any case where—

(a) an application for a maintenance assessment has been made [or treated as made][2] or a maintenance assessment is in force;

(b) scientific tests have been carried out (otherwise than under a direction or in response to a request) in relation to bodily samples obtained from a person who is alleged to be a parent of a child with respect to whom the application or assessment is made [or, as the case may be, treated as made][3];

(c) the results of the tests do not exclude the alleged parent from being one of the child's parents; and

(d) one of the conditions set out in subsection (2) is satisfied.

(2) The conditions are that—

(a) the alleged parent does not deny that he is one of the child's parents;

[1] Substituted by Child Support, Pensions and Social Security Act 2000 c.19 Sch 8 para 13

[2] Words added in relation to cases specified in SI 2003/192 art 3 by Child Support, Pensions and Social Security Act 2000 c.19 Sch 3 para 11 (9) (a)

[3] Words added in relation to cases specified in SI 2003/192 art 3 by Child Support, Pensions and Social Security Act 2000 c.19 Sch 3 para 11 (9) (b)

(b) in proceedings under [section 55A of the Family Law Act 1986][1], a court has made a declaration that the alleged parent is a parent of the child in in question; or

(c) in an action under section 7 of the Law Reform (Parent and Child) (Scotland) Act 1986, brought by the Secretary of State by virtue of section 28, a court has granted a decree of declarator of parentage to the effect that the alleged parent is a parent of the child in question.

(3) In any case to which this section applies, any fee paid by the Secretary of State in connection with scientific tests may be recovered by him from the alleged parent as a debt due to the Crown.

(4) In this section—

"bodily sample" means a sample of bodily fluid or bodily tissue taken for the purpose of scientific tests;

"direction" means a direction given by a court under section 20 of the Family Law Reform Act 1969 (tests to determine paternity);

"request" means a request made by a court under section 70 of the Law Reform (Miscellaneous Provisions) (Scotland) Act 1990 (blood and other samples in civil proceedings); and

"scientific tests" means scientific tests made with the object of ascertaining the inheritable characteristics of bodily fluids or bodily tissue.

(5) Any sum recovered by the Secretary of State under this section shall be paid by him into the Consolidated Fund.][2]

Decisions and appeals dependent on other cases

[Decisions involving issues that arise on appeal in other cases

28ZA.—(1) This section applies where— **42-025**

(a) a decision by the Secretary of State falls to be made under section 11, 12, 16 or 17 [or with respect to a reduced benefit decision under section 46][3]; and

[(b) an appeal is pending against a decision given in relation to a different matter by a Child Support Commissioner or a court.][4]

(2) If the Secretary of State considers it possible that the result of the appeal will be such that, if it were already determined, it would affect the decision in some way—

(a) he need not, except in such cases or circumstances as may be prescribed, make the decision while the appeal is pending;

(b) he may, in such cases or circumstances as may be prescribed, make the decision on such basis as may be prescribed.

(3) Where the Secretary of State acts in accordance with subsection (2)(b), following the determination of the appeal he shall if appropriate revise his decision (under section 16) in accordance with that determination.

(4) For the purposes of this section, an appeal against a decision is pending if—

(a) an appeal against the decision has been brought but not determined;

---

1 Words substituted by Child Support, Pensions and Social Security Act 2000 c.19 Sch 8 para 14

2 Added by Child Support Act 1995 c.34 s 21

3 Words substituted in relation to cases specified in SI 2003/192 art 3 by Child Support, Pensions and Social Security Act 2000 c.19 Sch 3 para 11 (11) (a)

4 Substituted in relation to cases specified in SI 2003/192 art 3 by Child Support, Pensions and Social Security Act 2000 c.19 Sch 3 para 11 (11) (b)

(b) an application for leave to appeal against the decision has been made but not determined; or

(c) in such circumstances as may be prescribed, an appeal against the decision has not been brought (or, as the case may be, an application for leave to appeal against the decision has not been made) but the time for doing so has not yet expired.

(5) In paragraphs (a), (b) and (c) of subsection (4), any reference to an appeal, or an application for leave to appeal, against a decision includes a reference to—

(a) an application for, or for leave to apply for, judicial review of the decision under section 31 of the Supreme Court Act 1981; or

(b) an application to the supervisory jurisdiction of the Court of Session in respect of the decision.][1]

[Appeals involving issues that arise on appeal in other cases

42-026 **28ZB.**—(1) This section applies where—

[(a) an appeal ("appeal A") in relation to a decision or the imposition of a requirement falling within section 20(1) is made to an appeal tribunal, or from an appeal tribunal to a Child Support Commissioner;][2]

(b) an appeal ("appeal B") is pending against a decision given in a different case by a Child Support Commissioner or a court.

(2) If the Secretary of State considers it possible that the result of appeal B will be such that, if it were already determined, it would affect the determination of appeal A, he may serve notice requiring the tribunal or Child Support Commissioner—

(a) not to determine appeal A but to refer it to him; or

(b) to deal with the appeal in accordance with subsection (4).

(3) Where appeal A is referred to the Secretary of State under subsection (2)(a), following the determination of appeal B and in accordance with that determination, he shall if appropriate—

(a) in a case where appeal A has not been determined by the tribunal, revise (under section 16) his decision which gave rise to that appeal; or

(b) in a case where appeal A has been determined by the tribunal, make a decision (under section 17) superseding the tribunal's decision.

(4) Where appeal A is to be dealt with in accordance with this subsection, the appeal tribunal or Child Support Commissioner shall either—

(a) stay appeal A until appeal B is determined; or

(b) if the tribunal or Child Support Commissioner considers it to be in the interests of the appellant to do so, determine appeal A as if—

(i) appeal B had already been determined; and

(ii) the issues arising on appeal B had been decided in the way that was most unfavourable to the appellant.

In this subsection "the appellant" means the person who appealed or, as the case may be, first appealed against the decision [or the imposition of the requirement][3] mentioned in subsection (1)(a).

(5) Where the appeal tribunal or Child Support Commissioner acts in accordance with subsection (4)(b)), following the determination of appeal B the Secretary of State shall, if appropriate, make a decision (under section 17) super-

[1] Inserted by Social Security Act 1998 c.14 Pt I c III s 43

[2] Substituted in relation to cases specified in SI 2003/192 art 3 by Child Support, Pensions and Social Security Act 2000 c.19 Sch 3 para 11 (12) (a)

[3] Words substituted in relation to cases specified in SI 2003/192 art 3 by Child Support, Pensions and Social Security Act 2000 c.19 Sch 3 para 11 (12) (b)

seding the decision of the tribunal or Child Support Commissioner in accordance with that determination.

(6) For the purposes of this section, an appeal against a decision is pending if—

(a) an appeal against the decision has been brought but not determined;

(b) an application for leave to appeal against the decision has been made but not determined; or

(c) in such circumstances as may be prescribed, an appeal against the decision has not been brought (or, as the case may be, an application for leave to appeal against the decision has not been made) but the time for doing so has not yet expired.

(7) In this section—

(a) the reference in subsection (1)(a) to an appeal to a Child Support Commissioner includes a reference to an application for leave to appeal to a Child Support Commissioner; and

(b) any reference in paragraph (a), (b) or (c) of subsection (6) to an appeal, or to an application for leave to appeal, against a decision includes a reference to—

(i) an application for, or for leave to apply for, judicial review of the decision under section 31 of the Supreme Court Act 1981; or

(ii) an application to the supervisory jurisdiction of the Court of Session in respect of the decision.

(8) Regulations may make provision supplementing that made by this section.][1]

Cases of error

[Restrictions on liability in certain cases of error

28ZC.—(1) Subject to subsection (2), this section applies where— **42-027**

(a) the effect of the determination, whenever made, of an appeal to a Child Support Commissioner or the court ("the relevant determination") is that the adjudicating authority's decision out of which the appeal arose was erroneous in point of law; and

(b) after the date of the relevant determination a decision falls to be made by the Secretary of State in accordance with that determination (or would, apart from this section, fall to be so made)—

(i) with respect to an application for a maintenance assessment (made after the commencement date) [or one treated as having been so made, or under section 46 as to the reduction of benefit][2];

(ii) as to whether to revise, under section 16, [any decision (made after the commencement date) referred to in section 16(1A)][3]; or

(iii) on an application under section 17 (made after the commencement date) [any decision (made after the commencement date) referred to in section 17(1)][4].

---

[1] Inserted by Social Security Act 1998 c.14 Pt I c III s 43

[2] Words added in relation to cases specified in SI 2003/192 art 3 by Child Support, Pensions and Social Security Act 2000 c.19 Sch 3 para 11 (13) (a)

[3] Words substituted in relation to cases specified in SI 2003/192 art 3 by Child Support, Pensions and Social Security Act 2000 c.19 Sch 3 para 11 (13) (b)

[4] Words substituted in relation to cases specified in SI 2003/192 art 3 by Child Support, Pensions and Social Security Act 2000 c.19 Sch 3 para 11 (13) (c)

(2) This section does not apply where the decision of the Secretary of State mentioned in subsection (1)(b)—

(a) is one which, but for section 28ZA(2)(a), would have been made before the date of the relevant determination; or

(b) is one made in pursuance of section 28ZB(3) or (5).

(3) In so far as the decision relates to a person's liability [or the reduction of a person's benefit][1] in respect of a period before the date of the relevant determination, it shall be made as if the adjudicating authority's decision had been found by the Commissioner or court not to have been erroneous in point of law.

(4) Subsection (1)(a) shall be read as including a case where—

(a) the effect of the relevant determination is that part or all of a purported regulation or order is invalid; and

(b) the error of law made by the adjudicating authority was to act on the basis that the purported regulation or order (or the part held to be invalid) was valid.

(5) It is immaterial for the purposes of subsection (1)—

(a) where such a decision as is mentioned in paragraph (b)(i) falls to be made; or

(b) where such a decision as is mentioned in paragraph (b)(ii) or (iii) falls to be made on an application under section 16 or (as the case may be) section 17,

whether the application was made before or after the date of the relevant determination.

(6) In this section—

"adjudicating authority" means the Secretary of State, or a child support officer [or, in the case of a decision made on a referral under section 28D(1)(b), an appeal tribunal][2];

"the commencement date" means the date of the coming into force of section 44 of the Social Security Act 1998; and

"the court" means the High Court, the Court of Appeal, the Court of Session, the High Court or Court of Appeal in Northern Ireland, the House of Lords or the Court of Justice of the European Community.

(7) The date of the relevant determination shall, in prescribed cases, be determined for the purposes of this section in accordance with any regulations made for that purpose.

(8) Regulations made under subsection (7) may include provision—

(a) for a determination of a higher court to be treated as if it had been made on the date of a determination of a lower court or a Child Support Commissioner; or

(b) for a determination of a lower court or a Child Support Commissioner to be treated as if it had been made on the date of a determination of a higher court.][3]

[Correction of errors and setting aside of decisions

42-028 **28ZD.**—(1) Regulations may make provision with respect to—

(a) the correction of accidental errors in any decision or record of a decision given under this Act; and

[1] Words added in relation to cases specified in SI 2003/192 art 3 by Child Support, Pensions and Social Security Act 2000 c.19 Sch 3 para 11 (13) (d)

[2] Words added in relation to cases specified in SI 2003/192 art 3 by Child Support, Pensions and Social Security Act 2000 c.19 Sch 3 para 11 (13) (e)

[3] Added by Social Security Act 1998 c.14 Pt I c III s 44

(b) the setting aside of any such decision in a case where it appears just to set the decision aside on the ground that—
   (i) a document relating to the proceedings in which the decision was given was not sent to, or was not received at an appropriate time by, a party to the proceedings or a party's representative or was not received at an appropriate time by the body or person who gave the decision; or
   (ii) a party to the proceedings or a party's representative was not present at a hearing related to the proceedings.

(2) Nothing in subsection (1) shall be construed as derogating from any power to correct errors or set aside decisions which is exercisable apart from regulations made by virtue of that subsection.][1]

Variations

[Application for variation of usual rules for calculating maintenance

28A.—(1) Where an application for a maintenance calculation is made under section 4 or 7, or treated as made under section 6, the person with care or the non-resident parent or (in the case of an application under section 7) either of them or the child concerned may apply to the Secretary of State for the rules by which the calculation is made to be varied in accordance with this Act. **42-029**

(2) Such an application is referred to in this Act as an "application for a variation".

(3) An application for a variation may be made at any time before the Secretary of State has reached a decision (under section 11 or 12(1)) on the application for a maintenance calculation (or the application treated as having been made under section 6).

(4) A person who applies for a variation–
   (a) need not make the application in writing unless the Secretary of State directs in any case that he must; and
   (b) must say upon what grounds the application is made.

(5) In other respects an application for a variation is to be made in such manner as may be prescribed.

(6) Schedule 4A has effect in relation to applications for a variation.][2]

[Preliminary consideration of applications

28B.—(1) Where an application for a variation has been duly made to the Secretary of State, he may give it a preliminary consideration. **42-030**

(2) Where he does so he may, on completing the preliminary consideration, reject the application (and proceed to make his decision on the application for a maintenance calculation without any variation) if it appears to him–
   (a) that there are no grounds on which he could agree to a variation;
   (b) that he has insufficient information to make a decision on the application for the maintenance calculation under section 11 (apart from any information needed in relation to the application for a variation), and therefore that his decision would be made under section 12(1); or
   (c) that other prescribed circumstances apply.][3]

[1] Added by Social Security Act 1998 c.14 Pt I c III s 44
[2] Substituted in relation to cases specified in SI 2003/192 art 3 by Child Support, Pensions and Social Security Act 2000 c.19 Pt I s 5 (2)
[3] Substituted in relation to cases specified in SI 2003/192 art 3 by Child Support, Pensions and Social Security Act 2000 c.19 Pt I s 5 (2)

[Imposition of regular payments condition

42-031 **28C.**—(1) Where–

(a) an application for a variation is made by the non-resident parent; and

(b) the Secretary of State makes an interim maintenance decision,

the Secretary of State may also, if he has completed his preliminary consideration (under section 28B) of the application for a variation and has not rejected it under that section, impose on the non-resident parent one of the conditions mentioned in subsection (2) (a "regular payments condition").

(2) The conditions are that–

(a) the non-resident parent must make the payments of child support maintenance specified in the interim maintenance decision;

(b) the non-resident parent must make such lesser payments of child support maintenance as may be determined in accordance with regulations made by the Secretary of State.

(3) Where the Secretary of State imposes a regular payments condition, he shall give written notice of the imposition of the condition and of the effect of failure to comply with it to–

(a) the non-resident parent;

(b) all the persons with care concerned; and

(c) if the application for the maintenance calculation was made under section 7, the child who made the application.

(4) A regular payments condition shall cease to have effect–

(a) when the Secretary of State has made a decision on the application for a maintenance calculation under section 11 (whether he agrees to a variation or not);

(b) on the withdrawal of the application for a variation.

(5) Where a non-resident parent has failed to comply with a regular payments condition, the Secretary of State may in prescribed circumstances refuse to consider the application for a variation, and instead reach his decision under section 11 as if no such application had been made.

(6) The question whether a non-resident parent has failed to comply with a regular payments condition is to be determined by the Secretary of State.

(7) Where the Secretary of State determines that a non-resident parent has failed to comply with a regular payments condition he shall give written notice of his determination to–

(a) that parent;

(b) all the persons with care concerned; and

(c) if the application for the maintenance calculation was made under section 7, the child who made the application.][1]

[Determination of applications

42-032 **28D.**—[(1) Where an application for a variation has not failed, the Secretary of State shall, in accordance with the relevant provisions of, or made under, this Act–

(a) either agree or not to a variation, and make a decision under section 11 or 12(1); or

(b) refer the application to an appeal tribunal for the tribunal to determine what variation, if any, is to be made.][2]

[1] Substituted in relation to cases specified in SI 2003/192 art 3 by Child Support, Pensions and Social Security Act 2000 c.19 Pt I s 5 (2)

[2] Substituted in relation to cases specified in SI 2003/192 art 3 by Child Support, Pensions and Social Security Act 2000 c.19 Pt I s 5 (3) (a)

(2) For the purposes of subsection (1), [an application for a variation][1] has failed if—

(a) it has [...][2]been withdrawn; or

(b) the Secretary of State has rejected it on completing a preliminary consideration under section 28B[; or][3]

[(c) the Secretary of State has refused to consider it under section 28C(5).][4]

(3) In dealing with [an application for a variation][5] which has been referred to it under subsection (1)(b), [an appeal tribunal][6] shall have the same powers, and be subject to the same duties, as would the Secretary of State if he were dealing with the application.][7]

[Matters to be taken into account

28E.—(1) In determining [whether to agree to a variation][8], the Secretary of State shall have regard both to the general principles set out in subsection (2) and to such other considerations as may be prescribed. **42-033**

(2) The general principles are that—

(a) parents should be responsible for maintaining their children whenever they can afford to do so;

(b) where a parent has more than one child, his obligation to maintain any one of them should be no less of an obligation than his obligation to maintain any other of them.

(3) In determining [whether to agree to a variation][9], the Secretary of State shall take into account any representations made to him—

(a) by the person with care or absent parent concerned; or

(b) where the application for the current assessment was made under section 7, by either of them or the child concerned.

(4) In determining [whether to agree to a variation][10], no account shall be taken of the fact that—

(a) any part of the income of the person with care concerned is, or would be if [the Secretary of State agreed to a variation][11], derived from any benefit; or

(b) some or all of any child support maintenance might be taken into account in any manner in relation to any entitlement to benefit.

(5) In this section "benefit" has such meaning as may be prescribed.][12]

---

[1] Words substituted in relation to cases specified in SI 2003/192 art 3 by Child Support, Pensions and Social Security Act 2000 c.19 Pt I s 5 (3) (b)

[2] Words repealed in relation to cases specified in SI 2003/192 art 3 by Child Support, Pensions and Social Security Act 2000 c.19 Sch 9 (I) para 1

[3] Word inserted in relation to cases specified in SI 2003/192 art 3 by Child Support, Pensions and Social Security Act 2000 c.19 Pt I s 5 (3) (c)

[4] Word inserted in relation to cases specified in SI 2003/192 art 3 by Child Support, Pensions and Social Security Act 2000 c.19 Pt I s 5 (3) (c)

[5] Words substituted in relation to cases specified in SI 2003/192 art 3 by Child Support, Pensions and Social Security Act 2000 c.19 Pt I s 5 (3) (b)

[6] Words substituted by Social Security Act 1998 c.14 Sch 7 para 36

[7] Added by Child Support Act 1995 c.34 s 4

[8] Words substituted in relation to cases specified in SI 2003/192 art 3 by Child Support, Pensions and Social Security Act 2000 c.19 Pt I s 5 (4) (a)

[9] Words substituted in relation to cases specified in SI 2003/192 art 3 by Child Support, Pensions and Social Security Act 2000 c.19 Pt I s 5 (4) (a)

[10] Words substituted in relation to cases specified in SI 2003/192 art 3 by Child Support, Pensions and Social Security Act 2000 c.19 Pt I s 5 (4) (a)

[11] Words substituted in relation to cases specified in SI 2003/192 art 3 by Child Support, Pensions and Social Security Act 2000 c.19 Pt I s 5 (4) (b)

[12] Added by Child Support Act 1995 c.34 s 5

[Agreement to a variation

42-034 **28F.**—(1) The Secretary of State may agree to a variation if–

(a) he is satisfied that the case is one which falls within one or more of the cases set out in Part I of Schedule 4B or in regulations made under that Part; and

(b) it is his opinion that, in all the circumstances of the case, it would be just and equitable to agree to a variation.

(2) In considering whether it would be just and equitable in any case to agree to a variation, the Secretary of State–

(a) must have regard, in particular, to the welfare of any child likely to be affected if he did agree to a variation; and

(b) must, or as the case may be must not, take any prescribed factors into account, or must take them into account (or not) in prescribed circumstances.

(3) The Secretary of State shall not agree to a variation (and shall proceed to make his decision on the application for a maintenance calculation without any variation) if he is satisfied that–

(a) he has insufficient information to make a decision on the application for the maintenance calculation under section 11, and therefore that his decision would be made under section 12(1); or

(b) other prescribed circumstances apply.

(4) Where the Secretary of State agrees to a variation, he shall–

(a) determine the basis on which the amount of child support maintenance is to be calculated in response to the application for a maintenance calculation (including an application treated as having been made); and

(b) make a decision under section 11 on that basis.

(5) If the Secretary of State has made an interim maintenance decision, it is to be treated as having been replaced by his decision under section 11, and except in prescribed circumstances any appeal connected with it (under section 20) shall lapse.

(6) In determining whether or not to agree to a variation, the Secretary of State shall comply with regulations made under Part II of Schedule 4B.][1]

[Variations: revision and supersession

42-035 **28G.**—(1) An application for a variation may also be made when a maintenance calculation is in force.

(2) The Secretary of State may by regulations provide for–

(a) sections 16, 17 and 20; and

(b) sections 28A to 28F and Schedules 4A and 4B,

to apply with prescribed modifications in relation to such applications.

(3) The Secretary of State may by regulations provide that, in prescribed cases (or except in prescribed cases), a decision under section 17 made otherwise than pursuant to an application for a variation may be made on the basis of a variation agreed to for the purposes of an earlier decision without a new application for a variation having to be made.][2]

[1] Substituted in relation to cases specified in SI 2003/192 art 3 by Child Support, Pensions and Social Security Act 2000 c.19 Pt I s 5 (5)

[2] Substituted by Child Support, Pensions and Social Security Act 2000 c.19 Pt I s 7

Voluntary payments

[Voluntary payments

28J.—(1) This section applies where– **42-036**

(a) a person has applied for a maintenance calculation under section 4(1) or 7(1), or is treated as having applied for one by virtue of section 6;

(b) the Secretary of State has neither made a decision under section 11 or 12 on the application, nor decided not to make a maintenance calculation; and

(c) the non-resident parent makes a voluntary payment.

(2) A "voluntary payment" is a payment–

(a) on account of child support maintenance which the non-resident parent expects to become liable to pay following the determination of the application (whether or not the amount of the payment is based on any estimate of his potential liability which the Secretary of State has agreed to give); and

(b) made before the maintenance calculation has been notified to the non-resident parent or (as the case may be) before the Secretary of State has notified the non-resident parent that he has decided not to make a maintenance calculation.

(3) In such circumstances and to such extent as may be prescribed–

(a) the voluntary payment may be set off against arrears of child support maintenance which accrued by virtue of the maintenance calculation taking effect on a date earlier than that on which it was notified to the non-resident parent;

(b) the amount payable under a maintenance calculation may be adjusted to take account of the voluntary payment.

(4) A voluntary payment shall be made to the Secretary of State unless he agrees, on such conditions as he may specify, that it may be made to the person with care, or to or through another person.

(5) The Secretary of State may by regulations make provision as to voluntary payments, and the regulations may in particular–

(a) prescribe what payments or descriptions of payment are, or are not, to count as "voluntary payments";

(b) prescribe the extent to which and circumstances in which a payment, or a payment of a prescribed description, counts.][1]

Collection and enforcement

Collection of child support maintenance

29.—(1) The Secretary of State may arrange for the collection of any child support maintenance payable in accordance with a maintenance assessment where— **42-037**

(a) the assessment is made by virtue of section 6; or

(b) an application has been made to the Secretary of State under section 4(2) or 7(3) for him to arrange for its collection.

(2) Where a maintenance assessment is made under this Act, payments of child support maintenance under the assessment shall be made in accordance with regulations made by the Secretary of State.

[1] Inserted in relation to cases specified in SI 2003/192 art 5 by Child Support, Pensions and Social Security Act 2000 c.19 Pt I s 20 (1)

(3) The regulations may, in particular, make provision—

(a) for payments of child support maintenance to be made—

(i) to the person caring for the child or children in question;

(ii) to, or through, the Secretary of State; or

(iii) to, or through, such other person as the Secretary of State may, from time to time, specify;

(b) as to the method by which payments of child support maintenance are to be made;

(c) as to the intervals at which such payments are to be made;

(d) as to the method and timing of the transmission of payments which are made, to or through the Secretary of State or any other person, in accordance with the regulations;

(e) empowering the Secretary of State to direct any person liable to make payments in accordance with the assessment—

(i) to make them by standing order or by any other method which requires one person to give his authority for payments to be made from an account of his to an account of another's on specific dates during the period for which the authority is in force and without the need for any further authority from him;

(ii) to open an account from which payments under the assessment may be made in accordance with the method of payment which that person is obliged to adopt;

(f) providing for the making of representations with respect to matters with which the regulations are concerned.

Collection and enforcement of other forms of maintenance

42-038 **30.**—(1) Where the Secretary of State is arranging for the collection of any payments under section 29 or subsection (2), he may also arrange for the collection of any periodical payments, or secured periodical payments, of a prescribed kind which are payable to or for the benefit of any person who falls within a prescribed category.

[(2) The Secretary of State may, except in prescribed cases, arrange for the collection of any periodical payments, or secured periodical payments, of a prescribed kind which are payable for the benefit of a child even though he is not arranging for the collection of child support maintenance with respect to that child.][1]

(3) Where—

(a) the Secretary of State is arranging, under this Act, for the collection of different payments ("the payments") from the same absent parent;

(b) an amount is collected by the Secretary of State from the absent parent which is less than the total amount due in respect of the payments; and

(c) the absent parent has not stipulated how that amount is to be allocated by the Secretary of State as between the payments,

the Secretary of State may allocate that amount as he sees fit.

(4) In relation to England and Wales, the Secretary of State may by regulations make provision for sections 29 and 31 to 40 to apply, with such modifications (if any) as he considers necessary or expedient, for the purpose of enabling him to enforce any obligation to pay any amount which he is authorised to collect under this section.

[1] Substituted by Child Support, Pensions and Social Security Act 2000 c.19 Sch 3 para 11 (15)

(5) In relation to Scotland, the Secretary of State may by regulations make provision for the purpose of enabling him to enforce any obligation to pay any amount which he is authorised to collect under this section—

(a) empowering him to bring any proceedings or take any other steps (other than diligence against earnings) which could have been brought or taken by or on behalf of the person to whom the periodical payments are payable;

(b) applying sections 29, 31 and 32 with such modifications (if any) as he considers necessary or expedient.

Deduction from earnings orders

31.—(1) This section applies where any person ("the liable person") is liable to make payments of child support maintenance. **42-039**

(2) The Secretary of State may make an order ("a deduction from earnings order") against a liable person to secure the payment of any amount due under the maintenance assessment in question.

(3) A deduction from earnings order may be made so as to secure the payment of—

(a) arrears of child support maintenance payable under the assessment;

(b) amounts of child support maintenance which will become due under the assessment; or

(c) both such arrears and such future amounts.

(4) A deduction from earnings order—

(a) shall be expressed to be directed at a person ("the employer") who has the liable person in his employment; and

(b) shall have effect from such date as may be specified in the order.

(5) A deduction from earnings order shall operate as an instruction to the employer to—

(a) make deductions from the liable person's earnings; and

(b) pay the amounts deducted to the Secretary of State.

(6) The Secretary of State shall serve a copy of any deduction from earnings order which he makes under this section on—

(a) the person who appears to the Secretary of State to have the liable person in question in his employment; and

(b) the liable person.

(7) Where—

(a) a deduction from earnings order has been made; and

(b) a copy of the order has been served on the liable person's employer,

it shall be the duty of that employer to comply with the order; but he shall not be under any liability for non-compliance before the end of the period of 7 days beginning with the date on which the copy was served on him.

(8) In this section and in section 32 "earnings" has such meaning as may be prescribed.

Regulations about deduction from earnings orders

32.—(1) The Secretary of State may by regulations make provision with respect to deduction from earnings orders. **42-040**

(2) The regulations may, in particular, make provision—

(a) as to the circumstances in which one person is to be treated as employed by another;

(b) requiring any deduction from earnings under an order to be made in the prescribed manner;

[(bb) for the amount or amounts which are to be deducted from the liable person's earnings not to exceed a prescribed proportion of his earnings (as determined by the employer);][1]

(c) requiring an order to specify the amount or amounts to which the order relates and the amount or amounts which are to be deducted from the liable person's earnings in order to meet his liabilities under the maintenance assessment in question;

(d) requiring the intervals between deductions to be made under an order to be specified in the order;

(e) as to the payment of sums deducted under an order to the Secretary of State;

(f) allowing the person who deducts and pays any amount under an order to deduct from the liable person's earnings a prescribed sum towards his administrative costs;

(g) with respect to the notification to be given to the liable person of amounts deducted, and amounts paid, under the order;

(h) requiring any person on whom a copy of an order is served to notify the Secretary of State in the prescribed manner and within a prescribed period if he does not have the liable person in his employment or if the liable person ceases to be in his employment;

(i) as to the operation of an order where the liable person is in the employment of the Crown;

(j) for the variation of orders;

(k) similar to that made by section 31(7), in relation to any variation of an order;

(l) for an order to lapse when the employer concerned ceases to have the liable person in his employment;

(m) as to the revival of an order in such circumstances as may be prescribed;

(n) allowing or requiring an order to be discharged;

(o) as to the giving of notice by the Secretary of State to the employer concerned that an order has lapsed or has ceased to have effect.

(3) The regulations may include provision that while a deduction from earnings order is in force—

(a) the liable person shall from time to time notify the Secretary of State, in the prescribed manner and within a prescribed period, of each occasion on which he leaves any employment or becomes employed, or re-employed, and shall include in such a notification a statement of his earnings and expected earnings from the employment concerned and of such other matters as may be prescribed;

(b) any person who becomes the liable person's employer and knows that the order is in force shall notify the Secretary of State, in the prescribed manner and within a prescribed period, that he is the liable person's employer, and shall include in such a notification a statement of the liable person's earnings and expected earnings from the employment concerned and of such other matters as may be prescribed.

(4) The regulations may include provision with respect to the priority as between a deduction from earnings order and—

(a) any other deduction from earnings order;

[1] Inserted in relation to cases specified in SI 2003/192 art 3 by Child Support, Pensions and Social Security Act 2000 c.19 Sch 3 para 11 (16)

(b) any order under any other enactment relating to England and Wales which provides for deductions from the liable person's earnings;

(c) any diligence against earnings.

(5) The regulations may include a provision that a liable person may appeal to a magistrates' court (or in Scotland to the sheriff) if he is aggrieved by the making of a deduction from earnings order against him, or by the terms of any such order, or there is a dispute as to whether payments constitute earnings or as to any other prescribed matter relating to the order.

(6) On an appeal under subsection (5) the court or (as the case may be) the sheriff shall not question the maintenance assessment by reference to which the deduction from earnings order was made.

(7) Regulations made by virtue of subsection (5) may include provision as to the powers of a magistrates' court, or in Scotland of the sheriff, in relation to an appeal (which may include provision as to the quashing of a deduction from earnings order or the variation of the terms of such an order).

(8) If any person fails to comply with the requirements of a deduction from earnings order, or with any regulation under this section which is designated for the purposes of this subsection, he shall be guilty of an offence.

(9) In subsection (8) "designated" means designated by the regulations.

(10) It shall be a defence for a person charged with an offence under subsection (8) to prove that he took all reasonable steps to comply with the requirements in question.

(11) Any person guilty of an offence under subsection (8) shall be liable on summary conviction to a fine not exceeding level two on the standard scale.

Liability orders

33.—(1) This section applies where— **42-041**

(a) a person who is liable to make payments of child support maintenance ("the liable person") fails to make one or more of those payments; and

(b) it appears to the Secretary of State that—

(i) it is inappropriate to make a deduction from earnings order against him (because, for example, he is not employed); or

(ii) although such an order has been made against him, it has proved ineffective as a means of securing that payments are made in accordance with the maintenance assessment in question.

(2) The Secretary of State may apply to a magistrates' court or, in Scotland, to the sheriff for an order ("a liability order") against the liable person.

(3) Where the Secretary of State applies for a liability order, the magistrates' court or (as the case may be) sheriff shall make the order if satisfied that the payments in question have become payable by the liable person and have not been paid.

(4) On an application under subsection (2), the court or (as the case may be) the sheriff shall not question the maintenance assessment under which the payments of child support maintenance fell to be made.

[(5) If the Secretary of State designates a liability order for the purposes of this subsection it shall be treated as a judgment entered in a county court for the purposes of section 73 of the County Courts Act 1984 (register of judgments and orders).][1]

[(6) Where regulations have been made under section 29(3)(a)–

(a) the liable person fails to make a payment (for the purposes of subsection (1)(a) of this section); and

[1] Added by Child Support Act 1995 c.34 Sch 3 para 10

(b) a payment is not paid (for the purposes of subsection (3)),

unless the payment is made to, or through, the person specified in or by virtue of those regulations for the case of the liable person in question.][1]

Enforcement of liability orders by distress

42-042 **35.**—(1) Where a liability order has been made against a person ("the liable person"), the Secretary of State may levy the appropriate amount by distress and sale of the liable person's goods.

(2) In subsection (1), "the appropriate amount" means the aggregate of—

(a) the amount in respect of which the order was made, to the extent that it remains unpaid; and

(b) an amount, determined in such manner as may be prescribed, in respect of the charges connected with the distress.

(3) The Secretary of State may, in exercising his powers under subsection (1) against the liable person's goods, seize—

(a) any of the liable person's goods except—

(i) such tools, books, vehicles and other items of equipment as are necessary to him for use personally by him in his employment, business or vocation;

(ii) such clothing, bedding, furniture, household equipment and provisions as are necessary for satisfying his basic domestic needs; and

(b) any money, banknotes, bills of exchange, promissory notes, bonds, specialties or securities for money belonging to the liable person.

(4) For the purposes of subsection (3), the liable person's domestic needs shall be taken to include those of any member of his family with whom he resides.

(5) No person levying a distress under this section shall be taken to be a trespasser—

(a) on that account; or

(b) from the beginning, on account of any subsequent irregularity in levying the distress.

(6) A person sustaining special damage by reason of any irregularity in levying a distress under this section may recover full satisfaction for the damage (and no more) by proceedings in trespass or otherwise.

(7) The Secretary of State may make regulations supplementing the provisions of this section.

(8) The regulations may, in particular—

(a) provide that a distress under this section may be levied anywhere in England and Wales;

(b) provide that such a distress shall not be deemed unlawful on account of any defect or want of form in the liability order;

(c) provide for an appeal to a magistrates' court by any person aggrieved by the levying of, or an attempt to levy, a distress under this section;

(d) make provision as to the powers of the court on an appeal (which may include provision as to the discharge of goods distrained or the payment of compensation in respect of goods distrained and sold).

[1] Added by Child Support, Pensions and Social Security Act 2000 c.19 Sch 3 para 11 (17)

Enforcement in county courts

36.—(1) Where a liability order has been made against a person, the amount in respect of which the order was made, to the extent that it remains unpaid, shall, if a county court so orders, be recoverable by means of garnishee proceedings or a charging order, as if it were payable under a county court order. **42-043**

(2) In subsection (1) "charging order" has the same meaning as in section 1 of the Charging Orders Act 1979.

[Commitment to prison and disqualification from driving

39A.—(1) Where the Secretary of State has sought– **42-044**

(a) in England and Wales to levy an amount by distress under this Act; or

(b) to recover an amount by virtue of section 36 or 38,

and that amount, or any portion of it, remains unpaid he may apply to the court under this section.

(2) An application under this section is for whichever the court considers appropriate in all the circumstances of–

(a) the issue of a warrant committing the liable person to prison; or

(b) an order for him to be disqualified from holding or obtaining a driving licence.

(3) On any such application the court shall (in the presence of the liable person) inquire as to–

(a) whether he needs a driving licence to earn his living;

(b) his means; and

(c) whether there has been wilful refusal or culpable neglect on his part.

(4) The Secretary of State may make representations to the court as to whether he thinks it more appropriate to commit the liable person to prison or to disqualify him from holding or obtaining a driving licence; and the liable person may reply to those representations.

(5) In this section and section 40B, "driving licence" means a licence to drive a motor vehicle granted under Part III of the Road Traffic Act 1988.

(6) In this section "the court" means–

(a) in England and Wales, a magistrates'court;

(b) in Scotland, the sheriff.][1]

Commitment to prison

40.—(1) [...][2] **42-045**

(2) [...][3]

(3) If, but only if, the court is of the opinion that there has been wilful refusal or culpable neglect on the part of the liable person it may—

(a) issue a warrant of commitment against him; or

(b) fix a term of imprisonment and postpone the issue of the warrant until such time and on such conditions (if any) as it thinks just.

(4) Any such warrant—

(a) shall be made in respect of an amount equal to the aggregate of—

(i) the amount mentioned in section 35(1) or so much of it as remains outstanding; and

(ii) an amount (determined in accordance with regulations made by the Secretary of State) in respect of the costs of commitment; and

[1] Added by Child Support, Pensions and Social Security Act 2000 c.19 Pt I s 16 (1)

[2] Repealed by Child Support, Pensions and Social Security Act 2000 c.19 Sch 9 (I) para 1

[3] Repealed by Child Support, Pensions and Social Security Act 2000 c.19 Sch 9 (I) para 1

(b) shall state that amount.

(5) No warrant may be issued under this section against a person who is under the age of 18.

(6) A warrant issued under this section shall order the liable person—

(a) to be imprisoned for a specified period; but

(b) to be released (unless he is in custody for some other reason) on payment of the amount stated in the warrant.

(7) The maximum period of imprisonment which may be imposed by virtue of subsection (6) shall be calculated in accordance with Schedule 4 to the Magistrates' Courts Act 1980 (maximum periods of imprisonment in default of payment) but shall not exceed six weeks.

(8) The Secretary of State may by regulations make provision for the period of imprisonment specified in any warrant issued under this section to be reduced where there is part payment of the amount in respect of which the warrant was issued.

(9) A warrant issued under this section may be directed to such person or persons as the court issuing it thinks fit.

(10) Section 80 of the Magistrates' Courts Act 1980 (application of money found on defaulter) shall apply in relation to a warrant issued under this section against a liable person as it applies in relation to the enforcement of a sum mentioned in subsection (1) of that section.

(11) The Secretary of State may by regulations make provision—

(a) as to the form of any warrant issued under this section;

(b) allowing an application under this section to be renewed where no warrant is issued or term of imprisonment is fixed;

(c) that a statement in writing to the effect that wages of any amount have been paid to the liable person during any period, purporting to be signed by or on behalf of his employer, shall be evidence of the facts stated;

(d) that, for the purposes of enabling an inquiry to be made as to the liable person's conduct and means, a justice of the peace may issue a summons to him to appear before a magistrates' court and (if he does not obey) may issue a warrant for his arrest;

(e) that for the purpose of enabling such an inquiry, a justice of the peace may issue a warrant for the liable person's arrest without issuing a summons;

(f) as to the execution of a warrant for arrest.

[(12) This section does not apply to Scotland.][1]

[Disqualification from driving: further provision

42-046 **40B.**—(1) If, but only if, the court is of the opinion that there has been wilful refusal or culpable neglect on the part of the liable person, it may–

(a) order him to be disqualified, for such period specified in the order but not exceeding two years as it thinks fit, from holding or obtaining a driving licence (a "disqualification order"); or

(b) make a disqualification order but suspend its operation until such time and on such conditions (if any) as it thinks just.

(2) The court may not take action under both section 40 and this section.

(3) A disqualification order must state the amount in respect of which it is made, which is to be the aggregate of–

[1] S 40 (12) substituted for s 40 (12)-(14) by Child Support, Pensions and Social Security Act 2000 c.19 Pt I s 17 (1)

(a) the amount mentioned in section 35(1), or so much of it as remains outstanding; and
(b) an amount (determined in accordance with regulations made by the Secretary of State) in respect of the costs of the application under section 39A.

(4) A court which makes a disqualification order shall require the person to whom it relates to produce any driving licence held by him, and its counterpart (within the meaning of section 108(1) of the Road Traffic Act 1988).

(5) On an application by the Secretary of State or the liable person, the court–

(a) may make an order substituting a shorter period of disqualification, or make an order revoking the disqualification order, if part of the amount referred to in subsection (3) (the "amount due") is paid to any person authorised to receive it; and
(b) must make an order revoking the disqualification order if all of the amount due is so paid.

(6) The Secretary of State may make representations to the court as to the amount which should be paid before it would be appropriate to make an order revoking the disqualification order under subsection (5)(a), and the person liable may reply to those representations.

(7) The Secretary of State may make a further application under section 39A if the amount due has not been paid in full when the period of disqualification specified in the disqualification order expires.

(8) Where a court–

(a) makes a disqualification order;
(b) makes an order under subsection (5); or
(c) allows an appeal against a disqualification order,

it shall send notice of that fact to the Secretary of State; and the notice shall contain such particulars and be sent in such manner and to such address as the Secretary of State may determine.

(9) Where a court makes a disqualification order, it shall also send the driving licence and its counterpart, on their being produced to the court, to the Secretary of State at such address as he may determine.

(10) Section 80 of the Magistrates' Courts Act 1980 (application of money found on defaulter) shall apply in relation to a disqualification order under this section in relation to a liable person as it applies in relation to the enforcement of a sum mentioned in subsection (1) of that section.

(11) The Secretary of State may by regulations make provision in relation to disqualification orders corresponding to the provision he may make under section 40(11).

(12) In the application to Scotland of this section–

(a) in subsection (2) for "section 40" substitute "section 40A";
(b) in subsection (3) for paragraph (a) substitute–

"(a) the appropriate amount under section 38;";

(c) subsection (10) is omitted; and
(d) for subsection (11) substitute–

"(11) The power of the Court of Session by Act of Sederunt to regulate the procedure and practice in civil proceedings in the sheriff court shall include power to make, in relation to disqualification orders, provision corresponding to that which may be made by virtue of section 40A(8)."][1]

[1] Added by Child Support, Pensions and Social Security Act 2000 c.19 Pt I s 16 (3)

Arrears of child support maintenance

42-047 **41.**—(1) This section applies where—

(a) the Secretary of State is authorised under section 4, 6 or 7 to recover child support maintenance payable by an absent parent in accordance with a maintenance assessment; and

(b) the absent parent has failed to make one or more payments of child support maintenance due from him in accordance with that assessment.

[(2) Where the Secretary of State recovers any such arrears he may, in such circumstances as may be prescribed and to such extent as may be prescribed, retain them if he is satisfied that the amount of any benefit paid to or in respect of the person with care of the child or children in question would have been less had the absent parent made the payment or payments of child support maintenance in question.

(2A) In determining for the purposes of subsection (2) whether the amount of any benefit paid would have been less at any time than the amount which was paid at that time, in a case where the maintenance assessment had effect from a date earlier than that on which it was made, the assessment shall be taken to have been in force at that time.][1]

(3) [...][2]

(4) [...][3]

(5) [...][4]

(6) Any sums retained by the Secretary of State by virtue of this section shall be paid by him into the Consolidated Fund.

[Penalty payments

42-048 **41A.**—(1) The Secretary of State may by regulations make provision for the payment to him by non-resident parents who are in arrears with payments of child support maintenance of penalty payments determined in accordance with the regulations.

(2) The amount of a penalty payment in respect of any week may not exceed 25&percent; of the amount of child support maintenance payable for that week, but otherwise is to be determined by the Secretary of State.

(3) The liability of a non-resident parent to make a penalty payment does not affect his liability to pay the arrears of child support maintenance concerned.

(4) Regulations under subsection (1) may, in particular, make provision–

(a) as to the time at which a penalty payment is to be payable;

(b) for the Secretary of State to waive a penalty payment, or part of it.

(5) The provisions of this Act with respect to–

(a) the collection of child support maintenance;

(b) the enforcement of an obligation to pay child support maintenance,

apply equally (with any necessary modifications) to penalty payments payable by virtue of regulations under this section.

[1] Substituted by Child Support Act 1995 c.34 Sch 3 para 11

[2] Repealed in relation to cases specified in SI 2003/192 art 3 by Child Support, Pensions and Social Security Act 2000 c.19 Sch 9 (I) para 1

[3] Repealed in relation to cases specified in SI 2003/192 art 3 by Child Support, Pensions and Social Security Act 2000 c.19 Sch 9 (I) para 1

[4] Repealed in relation to cases specified in SI 2003/192 art 3 by Child Support, Pensions and Social Security Act 2000 c.19 Sch 9 (I) para 1

(6) The Secretary of State shall pay penalty payments received by him into the Consolidated Fund.][1]

[Repayment of overpaid child support maintenance

41B.—(1) This section applies where it appears to the Secretary of State that an absent parent has made a payment by way of child support maintenance which amounts to an overpayment by him of that maintenance and that— **42-049**

(a) it would not be possible for the absent parent to recover the amount of the overpayment by way of an adjustment of the amount payable under a maintenance assessment; or

(b) it would be inappropriate to rely on an adjustment of the amount payable under a maintenance assessment as the means of enabling the absent parent to recover the amount of the overpayment.

[(1A) This section also applies where the non-resident parent has made a voluntary payment and it appears to the Secretary of State–

(a) that he is not liable to pay child support maintenance; or

(b) that he is liable, but some or all of the payment amounts to an overpayment,

and, in a case falling within paragraph (b), it also appears to him that subsection (1)(a) or (b) applies.][2]

(2) The Secretary of State may make such payment to the absent parent by way of reimbursement, or partial reimbursement, of the overpayment as the Secretary of State considers appropriate.

(3) Where the Secretary of State has made a payment under this section he may, in such circumstances as may be prescribed, require the relevant person to pay to him the whole, or a specified proportion, of the amount of that payment.

(4) Any such requirement shall be imposed by giving the relevant person a written demand for the amount which the Secretary of State wishes to recover from him.

(5) Any sum which a person is required to pay to the Secretary of State under this section shall be recoverable from him by the Secretary of State as a debt due to the Crown.

(6) The Secretary of State may by regulations make provision in relation to any case in which—

(a) one or more overpayments of child support maintenance are being reimbursed to the Secretary of State by the relevant person; and

(b) child support maintenance has continued to be payable by the absent parent concerned to the person with care concerned, or again becomes so payable.

[(7) For the purposes of this section–

(a) a payment made by a person under a maintenance calculation which was not validly made; and

(b) a voluntary payment made in the circumstances set out in subsection (1A)(a),

shall be treated as an overpayment of child support maintenance made by a non-resident parent.][3]

[1] Substituted in relation to cases specified in SI 2003/192 art 3 by Child Support, Pensions and Social Security Act 2000 c.19 Pt I s 18 (2)

[2] Inserted in relation to cases specified in SI 2003/192 art 5 by Child Support, Pensions and Social Security Act 2000 c.19 Pt I s 20 (3)

[3] Substituted in relation to cases specified in SI 2003/192 art 5 by Child Support, Pensions and Social Security Act 2000 c.19 Pt I s 20 (4)

(8) In this section"relevant person", in relation to an overpayment, means the person with care to whom the overpayment was made.

(9) Any sum recovered by the Secretary of State under this section shall be paid by him into the Consolidated Fund.][1]

Miscellaneous and supplemental

Regulations and orders

42-050 **52.**—(1) Any power conferred on the Lord Chancellor, the Lord Advocate or the Secretary of State by this Act to make regulations or orders (other than a deduction from earnings order) shall be exercisable by statutory instrument.

(2) No statutory instrument containing (whether alone or with other provisions) regulations made under [section 4(7), 5(3), 6(1), (9) or (10), 7(8), 12(2), 28C(2)(b), 28F(3), 30(5A), 41(2), (3) or (4), 41A, 41B(6) 42, 43(1), 46 or 47][2] or under Part I of Schedule 1 [or under Schedule 4B][3], or an order made under section 45(1) or (6), shall be made unless a draft of the instrument has been laid before Parliament and approved by a resolution of each House of Parliament.

(3) Any other statutory instrument made under this Act (except an order made under section 58(2)) shall be subject to annulment in pursuance of a resolution of either House of Parliament.

(4) Any power of a kind mentioned in subsection (1) may be exercised—

(a) in relation to all cases to which it extends, in relation to those cases but subject to specified exceptions or in relation to any specified cases or classes of case;

(b) so as to make, as respects the cases in relation to which it is exercised—

(i) the full provision to which it extends or any lesser provision (whether by way of exception or otherwise);

(ii) the same provision for all cases, different provision for different cases or classes of case or different provision as respects the same case or class of case but for different purposes of this Act;

(iii) provision which is either unconditional or is subject to any specified condition;

(c) so to provide for a person to exercise a discretion in dealing with any matter.

Meaning of "child"

42-051 **55.**—(1) For the purposes of this Act a person is a child if—

(a) he is under the age of 16;

(b) he is under the age of 19 and receiving full-time education (which is not advanced education)—

(i) by attendance at a recognised educational establishment; or

(ii) elsewhere, if the education is recognised by the Secretary of State; or

(c) he does not fall within paragraph (a) or (b) but—

(i) he is under the age of 18, and

(ii) prescribed conditions are satisfied with respect to him.

(2) A person is not a child for the purposes of this Act if he—

(a) is or has been married;

[1] Added by Child Support Act 1995 c.34 s 23

[2] Words inserted by Child Support Act 1995 c.34 Sch 3 para 15 (b)

[3] Words inserted by Child Support Act 1995 c.34 Sch 3 para 15 (c)

(b) has celebrated a marriage which is void; or

(c) has celebrated a marriage in respect of which a decree of nullity has been granted.

(3) In this section—

"advanced education" means education of a prescribed description; and

"recognised educational establishment" means an establishment recognised by the Secretary of State for the purposes of this section as being, or as comparable to, a university, college or school.

(4) Where a person has reached the age of 16, the Secretary of State may recognise education provided for him otherwise than at a recognised educational establishment only if the Secretary of State is satisfied that education was being so provided for him immediately before he reached the age of 16.

(5) The Secretary of State may provide that in prescribed circumstances education is or is not to be treated for the purposes of this section as being full-time.

(6) In determining whether a person falls within subsection (1)(b), no account shall be taken of such interruptions in his education as may be prescribed.

(7) The Secretary of State may by regulations provide that a person who ceases to fall within subsection (1) shall be treated as continuing to fall within that subsection for a prescribed period.

(8) No person shall be treated as continuing to fall within subsection (1) by virtue of regulations made under subsection (7) after the end of the week in which he reaches the age of 19.

SCHEDULES

Section 11 Schedule 1

Maintenance Assessments

Calculation of Child Support Maintenance

The maintenance requirement

1.— (1) In this Schedule "the maintenance requirement" means the amount, calculated in accordance with the formula set out in sub-paragraph (2), which is to be taken as the minimum amount necessary for the maintenance of the qualifying child or, where there is more than one qualifying child, all of them. **42-052**

(2) The formula is—

$$MR = AG - CB$$

where—

MR is the amount of the maintenance requirement;

AG is the aggregate of the amounts to be taken into account under subparagraph (3); and

CB is the amount payable by way of child benefit (or which would be so payable if the person with care of the qualifying child were an individual) or, where there is more than one qualifying child, the aggregate of the amounts so payable with respect to each of them.

(3) The amounts to be taken into account for the purpose of calculating AG are—

(a) such amount or amounts (if any), with respect to each qualifying child, as may be prescribed;

(b) such amount or amounts (if any), with respect to the person with care of the qualifying child or qualifying children, as may be prescribed; and

(c) such further amount or amounts (if any) as may be prescribed.

(4) For the purposes of calculating CB it shall be assumed that child benefit is payable with respect to any qualifying child at the basic rate.

(5) In sub-paragraph (4) "basic rate" has the meaning for the time being prescribed.

The general rule

42-053 **2.**—(1) In order to determine the amount of any maintenance assessment, first calculate—

$$(A + C) \times P$$

where—

A is the absent parent's assessable income;

C is the assessable income of the other parent, where that parent is the person with care, and otherwise has such value (if any) as may be prescribed; and

P is such number greater than zero but less than 1 as may be prescribed.

(2) Where the result of the calculation made under sub-paragraph (1) is an amount which is equal to, or less than, the amount of the maintenance requirement for the qualifying child or qualifying children, the amount of maintenance payable by the absent parent for that child or those children shall be an amount equal to—

$$A \times P$$

where—

A and P have the same values as in the calculation made under sub-paragraph (1).

(3) Where the result of the calculation made under sub-paragraph (1) is an amount which exceeds the amount of the maintenance requirement for the qualifying child or qualifying children, the amount of maintenance payable by the absent parent for that child or those children shall consist of—

(a) a basic element calculated in accordance with the provisions of paragraph 3; and
(b) an additional element calculated in accordance with the provisions of paragraph 4.

The basic element

42-054 **3.**—(1) The basic element shall be calculated by applying the formula—

$$BE = A \times G \times P$$

where—

BE is the amount of the basic element;

A and P have the same values as in the calculation made under paragraph 2(1); and

G has the value determined under sub-paragraph (2).

(2) The value of G shall be determined by applying the formula—

$$G = {}^{MR}/_{(A + C) \times P}$$

where—

MR is the amount of the maintenance requirement for the qualifying child or qualifying children; and

A, C and P have the same values as in the calculation made under paragraph 2(1).

The additional element

42-055 **4.**—(1) Subject to sub-paragraph (2), the additional element shall be calculated by applying the formula—

$$AE = (1 - G) \times A \times R$$

where—

AE is the amount of the additional element;

A has the same value as in the calculation made under paragraph 2(1);

G has the value determined under paragraph 3(2); and

R is such number greater than zero but less than 1 as may be prescribed.

(2) Where applying the alternative formula set out in sub-paragraph (3) would result in a lower amount for the additional element, that formula shall be applied in place of the formula set out in sub-paragraph (1).

(3) The alternative formula is—

$$AE = Z \times Q \times ({}^{A}/_{(A + C)})$$

where—

A and C have the same values as in the calculation made under paragraph 2(1);

Z is such number as may be prescribed; and

Q is the aggregate of—

(a) any amount taken into account by virtue of paragraph 1(3)(a) in calculating the maintenance requirement; and

(b) any amount which is both taken into account by virtue of paragraph 1(3)(c) in making that calculation and is an amount prescribed for the purposes of this paragraph.

Assessable income

5.— (1) The assessable income of an absent parent shall be calculated by applying the formula— **42-056**

$$A = N - E$$

where—

A is the amount of that parent's assessable income;

N is the amount of that parent's net income, calculated or estimated in accordance with regulations made by the Secretary of State for the purposes of this sub-paragraph; and

E is the amount of that parent's exempt income, calculated or estimated in accordance with regulations made by the Secretary of State for those purposes.

(2) The assessable income of a parent who is a person with care of the qualifying child or children shall be calculated by applying the formula—

$$C = M - F$$

where—

C is the amount of that parent's assessable income;

M is the amount of that parent's net income, calculated or estimated in accordance with regulations made by the Secretary of State for the purposes of this sub-paragraph; and

F is the amount of that parent's exempt income, calculated or estimated in accordance with regulations made by the Secretary of State for those purposes.

(3) Where the preceding provisions of this paragraph would otherwise result in a person's assessable income being taken to be a negative amount his assessable income shall be taken to be nil.

(4) Where income support [, an income-based jobseeker's allowance][1] or any other benefit of a prescribed kind is paid to or in respect of a parent who is an absent parent or a person with care that parent shall, for the purposes of this Schedule, be taken to have no assessable income.

Protected income

6.— (1) This paragraph applies where— **42-057**

(a) one or more maintenance assessments have been made with respect to an absent parent; and

(b) payment by him of the amount, or the aggregate of the amounts, so assessed would otherwise reduce his disposable income below his protected income level.

(2) The amount of the assessment, or (as the case may be) of each assessment, shall be adjusted in accordance with such provisions as may be prescribed with a view to securing so far as is reasonably practicable that payment by the absent parent of the amount, or (as the case may be) aggregate of the amounts, so assessed will not reduce his disposable income below his protected income level.

(3) Regulations made under sub-paragraph (2) shall secure that, where the prescribed minimum amount fixed by regulations made under paragraph 7 applies, no maintenance assessment is adjusted so as to provide for the amount payable by an absent parent in accordance with that assessment to be less than that amount.

(4) The amount which is to be taken for the purposes of this paragraph as an absent parent's disposable income shall be calculated, or estimated, in accordance with regulations made by the Secretary of State.

(5) Regulations made under sub-paragraph (4) may, in particular, provide that, in such circumstances and to such extent as may be prescribed—

(a) income of any child who is living in the same household with the absent parent; and

(b) where the absent parent is living together in the same household with another adult of the opposite sex (regardless of whether or not they are married), income of that other adult,

is to be treated as the absent parent's income for the purposes of calculating his disposable income.

(6) In this paragraph the "protected income level" of a particular absent parent means an amount of income calculated, by reference to the circumstances of that parent, in accordance with regulations made by the Secretary of State.

The minimum amount of child support maintenance

7.— (1) The Secretary of State may prescribe a minimum amount for the purposes of this paragraph. **42-058**

(2) Where the amount of child support maintenance which would be fixed by a maintenance assessment but for this paragraph is nil, or less than the prescribed minimum amount, the amount to be fixed by the assessment shall be the prescribed minimum amount.

[1] Words inserted by Jobseekers Act 1995 c.18 Sch 2 para 20 (7)

(3) In any case to which section 43 applies, and in such other cases (if any) as may be prescribed, sub-paragraph (2) shall not apply.

Housing costs

42-059 **8.** Where regulations under this Schedule require [the Secretary of State][1] to take account of the housing costs of any person in calculating, or estimating, his assessable income or disposable income, those regulations may make provision—

(a) as to the costs which are to be treated as housing costs for the purpose of the regulations;
(b) for the apportionment of housing costs; and
(c) for the amount of housing costs to be taken into account for prescribed purposes not to exceed such amount (if any) as may be prescribed by, or determined in accordance with, the regulations.

Regulations about income and capital

42-060 **9.** The Secretary of State may by regulations provide that, in such circumstances and to such extent as may be prescribed—

(a) income of a child shall be treated as income of a parent of his;
(b) where [the Secretary of State][2] concerned is satisfied that a person has intentionally deprived himself of a source of income with a view to reducing the amount of his assessable income, his net income shall be taken to include income from that source of an amount estimated by the child support officer;
(c) a person is to be treated as possessing capital or income which he does not possess;
(d) capital or income which a person does possess is to be disregarded;
(e) income is to be treated as capital;
(f) capital is to be treated as income.

References to qualifying children

42-061 **10.** References in this Part of this Schedule to "qualifying children" are to those qualifying children with respect to whom the maintenance assessment falls to be made.

General Provisions about Maintenance Assessments

Effective date of assessment

42-062 **11.**—(1) A maintenance assessment shall take effect on such date as may be determined in accordance with regulations made by the Secretary of State.

(2) That date may be earlier than the date on which the assessment is made.

Form of assessment

42-063 **12.** Every maintenance assessment shall be made in such form and contain such information as the Secretary of State may direct.

Assessments where amount of child support is nil

42-064 **13.** [...][3]

Consolidated applications and assessments

42-065 **14.** The Secretary of State may by regulations provide—

(a) for two or more applications for maintenance assessments to be treated, in prescribed circumstances, as a single application; and
(b) for the replacement, in prescribed circumstances, of a maintenance assessment made on the application of one person by a later maintenance assessment made on the application of that or any other person.

---

[1] Words substituted by Social Security Act 1998 c.14 Sch 7 para 48 (1)
[2] Words substituted by Social Security Act 1998 c.14 Sch 7 para 48 (2)
[3] Repealed in relation to cases specified in SI 2003/192 art 3 by Child Support, Pensions and Social Security Act 2000 c.19 Sch 9 (I) para 1

Separate assessments for different periods

15. Where [the Secretary of State][1] is satisfied that the circumstances of a case require different amounts of child support maintenance to be assessed in respect of different periods, he may make separate maintenance assessments each expressed to have effect in relation to a different specified period. **42-066**

Termination of assessments

16.— (1) A maintenance assessment shall cease to have effect— **42-067**

(a) on the death of the absent parent, or of the person with care, with respect to whom it was made;

(b) on there no longer being any qualifying child with respect to whom it would have effect;

(c) on the absent parent with respect to whom it was made ceasing to be a parent of—

(i) the qualifying child with respect to whom it was made; or

(ii) where it was made with respect to more than one qualifying child, all of the qualifying children with respect to whom it was made;

(d) where the absent parent and the person with care with respect to whom it was made have been living together for a continuous period of six months;

(e) where a new maintenance assessment is made with respect to any qualifying child with respect to whom the assessment in question was in force immediately before the making of the new assessment.

(2) A maintenance assessment made in response to an application under section 4 or 7 shall be cancelled by [the Secretary of State][2] if the person on whose application the assessment was made asks him to do so.

(3) A maintenance assessment made in response to an application under section 6 shall be cancelled by [the Secretary of State][3] if—

(a) the person on whose application the assessment was made ("the applicant") asks him to do so; and

(b) he is satisfied that the applicant has ceased to fall within subsection (1) of that section.

(4) Where [the Secretary of State][4] is satisfied that the person with care with respect to whom a maintenance assessment was made has ceased to be a person with care in relation to the qualifying child, or any of the qualifying children, with respect to whom the assessment was made, he may cancel the assessment with effect from the date on which, in his opinion, the change of circumstances took place.

[(4A) A maintenance assessment may be cancelled by [the Secretary of State][5] if he is [proposing to make a decision under section 16 or 17][6] and it appears to him—

(a) that the person with care with respect to whom the maintenance assessment in question was made has failed to provide him with sufficient information to enable him to [make the decision][7]; and

(b) where the maintenance assessment in question was made in response to an application under section 6, that the person with care with respect to whom the assessment was made has ceased to fall within subsection (1) of that section.][8]

(5) Where—

(a) at any time a maintenance assessment is in force but [the Secretary of State][9] would no longer have jurisdiction to make it if it were to be applied for at that time; and

(b) the assessment has not been cancelled, or has not ceased to have effect, under or by virtue of any other provision made by or under this Act,

it shall be taken to have continuing effect unless cancelled by [the Secretary of State][10] in accordance with such prescribed provision (including provision as to the effective date of cancellation) as the Secretary of State considers it appropriate to make.

---

[1] Words substituted by Social Security Act 1998 c.14 Sch 7 para 48 (4)
[2] Words substituted by Social Security Act 1998 c.14 Sch 7 para 48 (5) (a)
[3] Words substituted by Social Security Act 1998 c.14 Sch 7 para 48 (5) (a)
[4] Words substituted by Social Security Act 1998 c.14 Sch 7 para 48 (5) (a)
[5] Words substituted by Social Security Act 1998 c.14 Sch 7 para 48 (5) (a)
[6] Words substituted by Social Security Act 1998 c.14 Sch 7 para 48 (5) (b)
[7] Words substituted by Social Security Act 1998 c.14 Sch 7 para 48 (5) (b)
[8] Added by Child Support Act 1995 c.34 s 14 (2)
[9] Words substituted by Social Security Act 1998 c.14 Sch 7 para 48 (5) (a)
[10] Words substituted by Social Security Act 1998 c.14 Sch 7 para 48 (5) (a)

(6) Where both the absent parent and the person with care with respect to whom a maintenance assessment was made request [the Secretary of State][1] to cancel the assessment, he may do so if he is satisfied that they are living together.

(7) Any cancellation of a maintenance assessment under sub-paragraph [(4A),][2] (5) or (6) shall have effect from such date as may be determined by [the Secretary of State][3].

(8) Where [the Secretary of State][4] cancels a maintenance assessment, he shall immediately notify the absent parent and person with care, so far as that is reasonably practicable.

(9) Any notice under sub-paragraph (8) shall specify the date with effect from which the cancellation took effect.

(10) A person with care with respect to whom a maintenance assessment is in force shall provide the Secretary of State with such information, in such circumstances, as may be prescribed, with a view to assisting the Secretary of State [...][5] in determining whether the assessment has ceased to have effect, or should be cancelled.

(11) The Secretary of State may by regulations make such supplemental, incidental or transitional provision as he thinks necessary or expedient in consequence of the provisions of this paragraph.

Section 14(4) Schedule 2

PROVISION OF INFORMATION TO SECRETARY OF STATE

Inland Revenue records

42-068 **1.**— (1) This paragraph applies where the Secretary of State or the Department of Health and Social Services for Northern Ireland requires information for the purpose of tracing—

(a) the current address of an absent parent; or

(b) the current employer of an absent parent.

(2) In such a case, no obligation as to secrecy imposed by statute or otherwise on a person employed in relation to the Inland Revenue shall prevent any information obtained or held in connection with the assessment or collection of income tax from being disclosed to—

(a) the Secretary of State;

(b) the Department of Health and Social Services for Northern Ireland; or

(c) an officer of either of them authorised to receive such information in connection with the operation of this Act or of any corresponding Northern Ireland legislation.

(3) This paragraph extends only to disclosure by or under the authority of the Commissioners of Inland Revenue.

(4) Information which is the subject of disclosure to any person by virtue of this paragraph shall not be further disclosed to any person except where the further disclosure is made—

(a) to a person to whom disclosure could be made by virtue of sub-paragraph (2); or

(b) for the purposes of any proceedings (civil or criminal) in connection with the operation of this Act or of any corresponding Northern Ireland legislation.

42-069 [**1A.**— (1) This paragraph applies to any information which—

(a) relates to any earnings or other income of an absent parent in respect of a tax year in which he is or was a self-employed earner, and

(b) is required by the Secretary of State or the Department of Health and Social Services for Northern Ireland for any purposes of this Act.

(2) No obligation as to secrecy imposed by statute or otherwise on a person employed in relation to the Inland Revenue shall prevent any such information obtained or held in connection with the assessment or collection of income tax from being disclosed to—

(a) the Secretary of State;

(b) the Department of Health and Social Services for Northern Ireland; or

(c) an officer of either of them authorised to receive such information in connection with the operation of this Act.

(3) This paragraph extends only to disclosure by or under the authority of the Commissioners of Inland Revenue.

(4) Information which is the subject of disclosure to any person by virtue of this paragraph shall not be further disclosed to any person except where the further disclosure is made—

(a) to a person to whom disclosure could be made by virtue of sub-paragraph (2); or

---

[1] Words substituted by Social Security Act 1998 c.14 Sch 7 para 48 (5) (a)

[2] Words inserted by Child Support Act 1995 c.34 s 14 (3)

[3] Words substituted by Social Security Act 1998 c.14 Sch 7 para 48 (5) (c)

[4] Words substituted by Social Security Act 1998 c.14 Sch 7 para 48 (5) (a)

[5] Words repealed by Social Security Act 1998 c.14 Sch 8 para 1

(b) for the purposes of any proceedings (civil or criminal) in connection with the operation of this Act.

(5) For the purposes of this paragraph "self-employed earner" and "tax year" have the same meaning as in Parts I to VI of the Social Security Contributions and Benefits Act 1992.][1]

Local authority records

2.— [...][2] **42-070**

Section 22(5) Schedule 4

CHILD SUPPORT COMMISSIONERS

Tenure of office

1.— (1) Every Child Support Commissioner shall vacate his office [on the date on which he reaches the age of 70; but this sub-paragraph is subject to section 26(4) to (6) of the Judicial Pensions and Retirement Act 1993 (power to authorise continuance in office up to the age of 75)][3]. **42-071**

(2) [...][4]

(3) A Child Support Commissioner may be removed from office by the Lord Chancellor on the ground of misbehaviour or incapacity.

Commissioners' remuneration and their pensions

2.— (1) The Lord Chancellor may pay, or make such payments towards the provision of such remuneration, pensions, allowances or gratuities to or in respect of persons appointed as Child Support Commissioners as, with the consent of the Treasury, he may determine. **42-072**

(2) The Lord Chancellor shall pay to a Child Support Commissioner such expenses incurred in connection with his work as such a Commissioner as may be determined by the Treasury.

[(3) Sub-paragraph (1), so far as relating to pensions, allowances or gratuities, shall not have effect in relation to any person to whom Part I of the Judicial Pensions and Retirement Act 1993 applies, except to the extent provided by or under that Act.][5]

Expenses of other persons

[**2A.**— [(1) The Lord Chancellor or, in Scotland, the Secretary of State may pay to any person who attends any proceedings before a Child Support Commissioner such travelling and other allowances as he may determine.][6] **42-073**

(2) In sub-paragraph (1), references to travelling and other allowances include references to compensation for loss of remunerative time.

(3) No compensation for loss of remunerative time shall be paid to any person under this paragraph in respect of any time during which he is in receipt of other remuneration so paid.][7]

Commissioners barred from legal practice

3. Section 75 of the Courts and Legal Services Act 1990 (judges etc. barred from legal practice) shall apply to any person appointed as a Child Support Commissioner as it applies to any person holding as a full-time appointment any of the offices listed in Schedule 11 to that Act. **42-074**

Deputy Child Support Commissioners

4.— (1) The Lord Chancellor may appoint persons to act as Child Support Commissioners (but to be known as deputy Child Support Commissioners) in order to facilitate the disposal of the business of Child Support Commissioners. **42-075**

(2) A deputy Child Support Commissioner shall be appointed—

(a) from among persons who have a 10 year general qualification or are advocates or solicitors in Scotland of 10 years' standing; and

[1] Added by Welfare Reform and Pensions Act 1999 c.30 Pt V c III s 80
[2] Repealed by Social Security Act 1998 c.14 Sch 8 para 1
[3] Words substituted by Judicial Pensions and Retirement Act 1993 c.8 Sch 6 para 23 (2) (a)
[4] Repealed by Judicial Pensions and Retirement Act 1993 c.8 Sch 9 para 1
[5] Added by Judicial Pensions and Retirement Act 1993 c.8 Sch 8 para 21 (2)
[6] Substituted by Social Security Act 1998 c.14 Sch 7 para 51
[7] Added by Child Support Act 1995 c.34 Sch 3 para 18 (1)

(b) [Subject to sub-paragraph (2A)][1]for such period or on such occasions as the Lord Chancellor thinks fit.

[(2A) No appointment of a person to be a deputy Child Support Commissioner shall be such as to extend beyond the date on which he reaches the age of 70; but this sub-paragraph is subject to section 26(4) to (6) of the Judicial Pensions and Retirement Act 1993 (power to authorise continuance in office up to the age of 75).][2]

(3) Paragraph 2 applies to deputy Child Support Commissioners as if the reference to pensions were omitted and paragraph 3 does not apply to them.

Determination of questions by other officers

42-076 [**4A.**—(1) The Lord Chancellor may by regulations provide—

(a) for officers authorised—

(i) by the Lord Chancellor; or

(ii) in Scotland, by the Secretary of State,

to determine any question which is determinable by a Child Support Commissioner and which does not involve the determination of any appeal, application for leave to appeal or reference;

(b) for the procedure to be followed by any such officer in determining any such question;

(c) for the manner in which determinations of such questions by such officers may be called in question.

(2) A determination which would have the effect of preventing an appeal, application for leave to appeal or reference being determined by a Child Support Commissioner is not a determination of the appeal, application or reference for the purposes of sub-paragraph (1).][3]

Tribunals of Commissioners

42-077 **5.**—[(1) If it appears to the Chief Child Support Commissioner (or, in the case of his inability to act, to such other of the Child Support Commissioners as he may have nominated to act for the purpose) that—

(a) application for leave under section 24(6)(b); or

(b) an appeal,

falling to be heard by one of the Child Support Commissioners involves a question of law of special difficulty, he may direct [that the application or appeal][4] be dealt with by a tribunal consisting of [or more][5] of the Child Support Commissioners.][6]

(2) If the decision of such a tribunal is not unanimous, the decision of the majority shall be the decision of the tribunal[; and the presiding Child Support Commissioner shall have a casting vote if the votes are equally divided][7].

[(3) Where a direction is given under sub-paragraph (1)(a), section 24(6)(b) shall have effect as if the reference to a Child Support Commissioner were a reference to such a tribunal as is mentioned in sub-paragraph (1)][8]

Finality of decisions

42-078 **6.**—(1) Subject to section 25, the decision of any Child Support Commissioner shall be final.

[(2) If and to the extent that regulations so provide, any finding of fact or other determination which is embodied in or necessary to a decision, or on which a decision is based, shall be conclusive for the purposes of any further decision.][9]

Consultation with Lord Advocate

42-079 **7.** Before exercising any of his powers under [paragraph 1(3), 4(1) or (2)(b) or 4A(1)][10], the Lord Chancellor shall consult the Lord Advocate.

Northern Ireland

42-080 **8.** In its application to Northern Ireland this Schedule shall have effect as if—

---

[1] Words added by Judicial Pensions and Retirement Act 1993 c.8 Sch 6 para 23 (3)
[2] Added by Judicial Pensions and Retirement Act 1993 c.8 Sch 6 para 23 (3)
[3] Inserted by Child Support Act 1995 c.34 s 17 (1)
[4] Words substituted by Social Security Act 1998 c.14 Sch 7 para 52 (1) (b)
[5] Words inserted by Social Security Act 1998 c.14 Sch 7 para 52 (1) (c)
[6] Words substituted by Social Security Act 1998 c.14 Sch 7 para 52 (1) (a)
[7] Words inserted by Social Security Act 1998 c.14 Sch 7 para 52 (2)
[8] Added by Social Security Act 1998 c.14 Sch 7 para 52 (3)
[9] Substituted by Social Security Act 1998 c.14 Sch 7 para 52 (4)
[10] Words substituted by Child Support Act 1995 c.34 s 17 (2)

(a) for any reference to a Child Support Commissioner (however expressed) there were substituted a corresponding reference to a Child Support Commissioner for Northern Ireland;

(b) in paragraph 2(1), the word "pensions" were omitted;

(c) for paragraph 3, there were substituted—

"**3.** A Child Support Commissioner for Northern Ireland, so long as he holds office as such, shall not practise as a barrister or act for any remuneration to himself as arbitrator or reference or be directly or indirectly concerned in any matter as a conveyancer, notary public or solicitor."; **42-081**

(d) in paragraph 4—

(i) for paragraph (a) of sub-paragraph (2) there were substituted—

"(a) from among persons who are barristers or solicitors of not less than 10 years' standing; and";

(ii) for sub-paragraph (3) there were substituted—

"(3) Paragraph 2 applies to deputy Child Support Commissioners for Northern Ireland, but paragraph 3 does not apply to them,"; and

(e) [paragraphs 4A to 7][1] were omitted.

Schedule 4B

Departure Directions: the Cases and Controls

The Cases

General

[**1.**— (1) The cases in which a departure direction may be given are those set out in this Part of this Schedule or in regulations made under this Part. **42-082**

(2) In this Schedule"applicant" means the person whose application for a departure direction is being considered.][2]

Special expenses

[**2.**— (1) A departure direction may be given with respect to special expenses of the applicant which were not, and could not have been, taken into account in determining the current assessment in accordance with the provisions of, or made under, Part I of Schedule 1. **42-083**

(2) In this paragraph "special expenses" means the whole, or any prescribed part, of expenses which fall within a prescribed description of expenses.

(3) In prescribing descriptions of expenses for the purposes of this paragraph, the Secretary of State may, in particular, make provision with respect to—

(a) costs incurred in travelling to work;

(b) costs incurred by an absent parent in maintaining contact with the child, or with any of the children, with respect to whom he is liable to pay child support maintenance under the current assessment;

(c) costs attributable to a long-term illness or disability of the applicant or of a dependant of the applicant;

(d) debts incurred, before the absent parent became an absent parent in relation to a child with respect to whom the current assessment was made—

(i) for the joint benefit of both parents;

(ii) for the benefit of any child with respect to whom the current assessment was made; or

(iii) for the benefit of any other child falling within a prescribed category;

(e) pre-1993 financial commitments from which it is impossible for the parent concerned to withdraw or from which it would be unreasonable to expect that parent to have to withdraw;

(f) costs incurred by a parent in supporting a child who is not his child but who is part of his family.

(4) For the purposes of sub-paragraph (3)(c)—

(a) the question whether one person is a dependant of another shall be determined in accordance with regulations made by the Secretary of State;

[1] Words substituted by Child Support Act 1995 c.34 s 17 (3)

[2] Added by Child Support Act 1995 c.34 Sch 2 para 1

(b) "disability" and "illness" have such meaning as may be prescribed; and

(c) the question whether an illness or disability is long-term shall be determined in accordance with regulations made by the Secretary of State.

(5) For the purposes of sub-paragraph (3)(e), "pre-1993 financial commitments" means financial commitments of a prescribed kind entered into before 5th April 1993 in any case where—

(a) a court order of a prescribed kind was in force with respect to the absent parent and the person with care concerned at the time when they were entered into; or

(b) an agreement between them of a prescribed kind was in force at that time.

(6) For the purposes of sub-paragraph (3)(f), a child who is not the child of a particular person is a part of that person's family in such circumstances as may be prescribed.][1]

Property or capital transfers

42-084 [**3.**—(1) A departure direction may be given if—

(a) before 5th April 1993—

(i) a court order of a prescribed kind was in force with respect to the absent parent and either the person with care with respect to whom the current assessment was made or the child, or any of the children, with respect to whom that assessment was made, or

(ii) an agreement of a prescribed kind between the absent parent and any of those persons was in force;

(b) in consequence of one or more transfers of property of a prescribed kind—

(i) the amount payable by the absent parent by way of maintenance was less than would have been the case had that transfer or those transfers not been made; or

(ii) no amount was payable by the absent parent by way of maintenance; and

(c) the effect of that transfer, or those transfers, is not properly reflected in the current assessment.

(2) For the purposes of sub-paragraph (1)(b), "maintenance" means periodical payments of maintenance made (otherwise than under this Act) with respect to the child, or any of the children, with respect to whom the current assessment was made.

(3) For the purposes of sub-paragraph (1)(c), the question whether the effect of one or more transfers of property is properly reflected in the current assessment shall be determined in accordance with regulations made by the Secretary of State.][2]

42-085 [**4.**—(1) A departure direction may be given if—

(a) before 5th April 1993—

(i) a court order of a prescribed kind was in force with respect to the absent parent and either the person with care with respect to whom the current assessment was made or the child, or any of the children, with respect to whom that assessment was made, or

(ii) an agreement of a prescribed kind between the absent parent and any of those persons was in force;

(b) in pursuance of the court order or agreement, the absent parent has made one or more transfers of property of a prescribed kind;

(c) the amount payable by the absent parent by way of maintenance was not reduced as a result of that transfer or those transfers;

(d) the amount payable by the absent parent by way of child support maintenance under the current assessment has been reduced as a result of that transfer or those transfers, in accordance with provisions of or made under this Act; and

(e) it is nevertheless inappropriate, having regard to the purposes for which the transfer or transfers was or were made, for that reduction to have been made.

(2) For the purposes of sub-paragraph (1)(c), "maintenance" means periodical payments of maintenance made (otherwise than under this Act) with respect to the child, or any of the children, with respect to whom the current assessment was made.][3]

Additional cases

42-086 [**5.**—(1) The Secretary of State may by regulations prescribe other cases in which a departure direction may be given.

(2) Regulations under this paragraph may, for example, make provision with respect to cases where—

(a) assets which do not produce income are capable of producing income;

[1] Added by Child Support Act 1995 c.34 Sch 2 para 1
[2] Added by Child Support Act 1995 c.34 Sch 2 para 1
[3] Added by Child Support Act 1995 c.34 Sch 2 para 1

(b) a person's life-style is inconsistent with the level of his income;
(c) housing costs are unreasonably high;
(d) housing costs are in part attributable to housing persons whose circumstances are such as to justify disregarding a part of those costs;
(e) travel costs are unreasonably high; or
(f) travel costs should be disregarded.][1]

Regulatory Controls

[**6.**—(1) The Secretary of State may by regulations make provision with respect to the directions which may be given in a departure direction. **42-087**

(2) No directions may be given other than those which are permitted by the regulations.

(3) Regulations under this paragraph may, in particular, make provision for a departure direction to require—

(a) the substitution, for any formula set out in Part I of Schedule 1, of such other formula as may be prescribed;
(b) any prescribed amount by reference to which any calculation is to be made in fixing the amount of child support maintenance to be increased or reduced in accordance with the regulations;
(c) the substitution, for any provision in accordance with which any such calculation is to be made, of such other provision as may be prescribed.

(4) Regulations may limit the extent to which the amount of the child support maintenance fixed by a maintenance assessment made as a result of a departure direction may differ from the amount of the child support maintenance which would be fixed by a maintenance assessment made otherwise than as a result of the direction.

(5) Regulations may provide for the amount of any special expenses to be taken into account in a case falling within paragraph 2, for the purposes of a departure direction, not to exceed such amount as may be prescribed or as may be determined in accordance with the regulations.

(6) No departure direction may be given so as to have the effect of denying to an absent parent the protection of paragraph 6 of Schedule 1.

(7) Sub-paragraph (6) does not prevent the modification of the provisions of, or made under, paragraph 6 of Schedule 1 to the extent permitted by regulations under this paragraph.

(8) Any regulations under this paragraph may make different provision with respect to different levels of income.][2]

Schedule 4C

Decisions and appeals: departure directions and reduced benefit directions etc

Revision of decisions

[**1.** Section 16 shall apply in relation to— **42-088**

(a) any decision of the Secretary of State with respect to a departure direction, a reduced benefit direction or a person's liability under section 43;
(b) any decision of the Secretary of State under section 17 as extended by paragraph 2; and
(c) any decision of an appeal tribunal on a referral under section 28D(1)(b),

as it applies in relation to any decision of the Secretary of State under section 11,12 or 17.][3]

Decisions superseding earlier decisions

[**2.**—(1) Section 17 shall apply in relation to— **42-089**

(a) any decision of the Secretary of State with respect to a departure direction, a reduced benefit direction or a person's liability under section 43;
(b) any decision of the Secretary of State under section 17 as extended by this sub-paragraph; and
(c) any decision of an appeal tribunal on a referral under section 28D(1)(b),

whether as originally made or as revised under section 16 as extended by paragraph 1, as it applies in relation to any decision of the Secretary of State under section 11, 12 or 17, whether as originally made or as revised under section 16.

[1] Added by Child Support Act 1995 c.34 Sch 2 para 1
[2] Added by Child Support Act 1995 c.34 Sch 2 para 1
[3] Added by Social Security Act 1998 c.14 Sch 7 para 54

(2) Section 17 shall apply in relation to any decision of an appeal tribunal under section 20 as extended by paragraph 3 as it applies in relation to any decision of an appeal tribunal under section 20.][1]

Appeals to appeal tribunals

42-090 [**3.**— (1) Subject to sub-paragraphs (2) and (3), section 20 shall apply—

(a) in relation to a qualifying person who is aggrieved by any decision of the Secretary of State with respect to a departure direction; and

(b) in relation to any person who is aggrieved by a decision of the Secretary of State—

(i) with respect to a reduced benefit direction; or

(ii) with respect to a person's liability under section 43,

as it applies in relation to a person whose application for a maintenance assessment is refused or to such a person as is mentioned in subsection (2) of section 20.

(2) On an appeal under section 20 as extended by sub-paragraph (1)(a), the appeal tribunal shall—

(a) consider the matter—

(i) as if it were exercising the powers of the Secretary of State in relation to the application in question; and

(ii) as if it were subject to the duties imposed on him in relation to that application;

(b) have regard to any representations made to it by the Secretary of State; and

(c) confirm the decision or replace it with such decision as the tribunal considers appropriate.

(3) No appeal shall lie under section 20 as extended by sub-paragraph (1)(b)(i) unless the amount of the person's benefit is reduced in accordance with the reduced benefit direction; and the time within which such an appeal may be brought shall run from the date of the notification of the reduction.

(4) In sub-paragraph (1) "qualifying person" means—

(a) the person with care, or absent parent, with respect to whom the current assessment was made; or

(b) where the application for the current assessment was made under section 7, either of those persons or the child concerned.][2]

Decisions and appeals dependent on other cases

42-091 [**4.**— (1) Section 28ZA shall also apply where—

(a) a decision falls to be made—

(i) with respect to a departure direction, a reduced benefit direction or a person's liability under section 43, by the Secretary of State; or

(ii) with respect to a departure direction, by an appeal tribunal on a referral under section 28D(1)(b); and

(b) an appeal is pending against a decision given with respect to a different direction by a Child Support Commissioner or a court.

(2) Section 28ZA as it applies by virtue of sub-paragraph (1) shall have effect as if the reference in subsection (3) to section 16 were a reference to that section as extended by paragraph 1.

(3) Section 28ZA as it applies by virtue of sub-paragraph (1)(a)(ii) shall have effect as if—

(a) in subsection (2)—

(i) for the words "the Secretary of State" there were substituted the words "the appeal tribunal" and

(ii) for the word "he", in both places where it occurs, there were substituted the word "it"; and

(b) in subsection (3)—

(i) for the words "the Secretary of State" there were substituted the words "the appeal tribunal";

(ii) for the word "he" there were substituted the words "the Secretary of State"; and

(iii) for the word "his" there were substituted the words "the tribunal's".][3]

42-092 [**5.**— (1) Section 28ZB shall also apply where—

(a) an appeal is made to an appeal tribunal under section 20 as extended by paragraph 3; and

(b) an appeal is pending against a decision given in a different case by a Child Support Commissioner or a court.

[1] Added by Social Security Act 1998 c.14 Sch 7 para 54
[2] Added by Social Security Act 1998 c.14 Sch 7 para 54
[3] Added by Social Security Act 1998 c.14 Sch 7 para 54

(2) Section 28ZB as it applies by virtue of sub-paragraph (1) shall have effect as if any reference to section 16 or section 17 were a reference to that section as extended by paragraph 1 or, as the case may be, paragraph 2.][1]

Cases of error

[**6.**—(1) Subject to sub-paragraph (2) below, section 28ZC shall also apply where— **42-093**

(a) the effect of the determination, whenever made, of an appeal to a Child Support Commissioner or the court ("the relevant determination") is that the adjudicating authority's decision out of which the appeal arose was erroneous in point of law; and

(b) after the date of the relevant determination a decision falls to be made by the Secretary of State in accordance with that determination (or would, apart from this paragraph, fall to be so made)—

(i) in relation to an application for a departure direction (made after the commencement date);

(ii) as to whether to revise, under section 16 as extended by paragraph 1, a decision (made after the commencement date) in relation to a departure direction, a reduced benefit direction or a person's liability under section 43; or

(iii) on an application made under section 17 as extended by paragraph 2 before the date of the relevant determination (but after the commencement date) for a decision in relation to a departure direction, a reduced benefit direction or a person's liability under section 43 to be superseded.

(2) Section 28ZC shall not apply where the decision of the Secretary of State mentioned in sub-paragraph (1)(b) above—

(a) is one which, but for section 28ZA(2)(a) as it applies by virtue of paragraph 4(1), would have been made before the date of the relevant determination; or

(b) is one made in pursuance of section 28ZB(3) or (5) as it applies by virtue of paragraph 5(1).

(3) Section 28ZC as it applies by virtue of sub-paragraph (1) shall have effect as if in subsection (4), in the definition of "adjudicating authority", at the end there were inserted the words "or, in the case of a decision made on a referral under section 28D(1)(b), an appeal tribunal".

(4) In this paragraph "adjudicating authority", "the commencement date" and "the court" have the same meanings as in section 28ZC.][2]

Social Security Administration Act 1992

CHAPTER 5

PART III

OVERPAYMENTS AND ADJUSTMENTS OF BENEFIT

Adjustments of benefits

[Payment of benefit where maintenance payments collected by Secretary of State

74A.—(1) This section applies where— **43-001**

(a) a person ("the claimant") is entitled to a benefit to which this section applies;

(b) the Secretary of State is collecting periodical payments of child or spousal maintenance made in respect of the claimant or a member of the claimant's family; and

---

[1] Added by Social Security Act 1998 c.14 Sch 7 para 54

[2] Added by Social Security Act 1998 c.14 Sch 7 para 54

(c) the inclusion of any such periodical payment in the claimant's relevant income would, apart from this section, have the effect of reducing the amount of the benefit to which the claimant is entitled.

(2) The Secretary of State may, to such extent as he considers appropriate, treat any such periodical payment as not being relevant income for the purposes of calculating the amount of benefit to which the claimant is entitled.

(3) The Secretary of State may, to the extent that any periodical payment collected by him is treated as not being relevant income for those purposes, retain the whole or any part of that payment.

(4) Any sum retained by the Secretary of State under subsection (3) shall be paid by him into the Consolidated Fund.

(5) In this section—

"child" means a person under the age of 16;

"child maintenance", "spousal maintenance" and "relevant income"have such meaning as may be prescribed;

"family" means —

(a) a married or unmarried couple;

(b) a married or unmarried couple and a member of the same household for whom one of them is, or both are, responsible and who is a child or a person of a prescribed description;

(c) except in prescribed circumstances, a person who is not a member of a married or unmarried couple and a member of the same household for whom that person is responsible and who is a child or a person of a prescribed description;

"married couple" means a man and woman who are married to each other and are members of the same household; and

"unmarried couple" means a man and woman who are not married to each other but are living together as husband and wife otherwise than in prescribed circumstances.

(6) For the purposes of this section, the Secretary of State may by regulations make provision as to the circumstances in which—

(a) persons are to be treated as being or not being members of the same household;

(b) one person is to be treated as responsible or not responsible for another.

(7) The benefits to which this section applies are income support, an income-based jobseeker's allowance and such other benefits (if any) as may be prescribed.][1]

Social fund awards

Recovery of social fund awards

43-002 **78.**—(1) A social fund award which is repayable shall be recoverable by the Secretary of State.

(2) Without prejudice to any other method of recovery, the Secretary of State may recover an award by deduction from prescribed benefits.

(3) The Secretary of State may recover an award—

(a) from the person to or for the benefit of whom it was made;

[1] Added by Child Support Act 1995 c.34 s 25

(b) where that person is a member of a married or unmarried couple, from the other member of the couple;

(c) from a person who is liable to maintain the person by or on behalf of whom the application for the award was made or any person in relation to whose needs the award was made.

[(3A) Where—

(a) a jobseeker's allowance is payable to a person from whom an award is recoverable under subsection (3) above; and

(b) that person is subject to a bankruptcy order,

a sum deducted from that benefit under subsection (2) above shall not be treated as income of his for the purposes of the Insolvency Act 1986.

(3B) Where—

(a) a jobseeker's allowance is payable to a person from whom an award is recoverable under subsection (3) above; and

(b) the estate of that person is sequestrated,

a sum deducted from that benefit under subsection (2) above shall not be treated as income of his for the purposes of the Bankruptcy (Scotland) Act 1985.][1]

(5) In this section—

"married couple" means a man and woman who are married to each other and are members of the same household;

"unmarried couple" means a man and woman who are not married to each other but are living together as husband and wife otherwise than in circumstances prescribed under section 132 of the Contributions and Benefits Act.

(6) For the purposes of this section—

(a) a man shall be liable to maintain his wife and any children of whom he is the father;

(b) a woman shall be liable to maintain her husband and any children of whom she is the mother;

(c) a person shall be liable to maintain another person throughout any period in respect of which the first-mentioned person has, on or after 23rd May 1980 (the date of the passing of the Social Security Act 1980) and either alone or jointly with a further person, given an undertaking in writing in pursuance of immigration rules within the meaning of the Immigration Act 1971 to be responsible for the maintenance and accommodation of the other person; and

(d) "child" includes a person who has attained the age of 16 but not the age of 19 and in respect of whom either parent, or some person acting in the place of either parent, is receiving income support or an income-based jobseeker's allowance.

(7) Any reference in subsection (6) above to children of whom the man or the woman is the father or the mother shall be construed in accordance with section 1 of the Family Law Reform Act 1987.

[1] Added by Jobseekers Act 1995 c.18 Pt III s 32 (2)

PART V

INCOME SUPPORT AND THE DUTY TO MAINTAIN

Failure to maintain-general

43-003 **105.**—(1) If—

(a) any person persistently refuses or neglects to maintain himself or any person whom he is liable to maintain; and

(b) in consequence of his refusal or neglect income support or an income-based jobseeker's allowance is paid to or in respect of him or such a person,

he shall be guilty of an offence and liable on summary conviction to imprisonment for a term not exceeding 3 months or to a fine of an amount not exceeding level 4 on the standard scale or to both.

(2) For the purposes of subsection (1) above a person shall not be taken to refuse or neglect to maintain himself or any other person by reason only of anything done or omitted in furtherance of a trade dispute.

(3) Subject to subsection (4) below. Subsections (6) to (9) of section 78 above shall have effect for the purposes of this Part of this Act as they have effect for the purposes of that section.

[(4) For the purposes of this section, in its application to an income-based jobseeker's allowance, a person is liable to maintain another if that other person is his or her spouse.][1]

Recovery of expenditure on benefit from person liable for maintenance

43-004 **106.**—(1) Subject to the following provisions of this section, if income support is claimed by or in respect of a person whom another person is liable to maintain or paid to or in respect of such a person, the Secretary of State may make a complaint against the liable person to a magistrates' court for an order under this section.

(2) On the hearing of a complaint under this section the court shall have regard to all the circumstances and, in particular, to the income of the liable person, and may order him to pay such sum, weekly or otherwise, as it may consider appropriate, except that in a case falling within section 78(6)(c) above that sum shall not include any amount which is not attributable to income support (whether paid before or after the making of the order).

(3) In determining whether to order any payments to be made in respect of income support for any period before the complaint was made, or the amount of any such payments, the court shall disregard any amount by which the liable person's income exceeds the income which was his during that period.

(4) Any payments ordered to be made under this section shall be made—

(a) to the Secretary of State in so far as they are attributable to any income support (whether paid before or after the making of the order);

(b) to the person claiming income support or (if different) the dependant; or

(c) to such other person as appears to the court expedient in the interests of the dependant.

(5) [...][2]

[1] Added by Jobseekers Act 1995 c.18 Sch 2 para 53 (4)
[2] Provision omitted by Social Security Administration Act 1992 c.5 Pt V s 106 (6)

Recovery of expenditure on income support: additional amounts and transfer of orders

107.—(1) In any case where— 43-005

(a) the claim for income support referred to in section 106(1) above is or was made by the parent of one or more children in respect of both himself and those children; and

(b) the other parent is liable to maintain those children but, by virtue of not being the claimant's husband or wife, is not liable to maintain the claimant,

the sum which the court may order that other parent to pay under subsection (2) of that section may include an amount, determined in accordance with regulations, in respect of any income support paid to or for the claimant by virtue of such provisions as may be prescribed.

(2) Where the sum which a court orders a person to pay under section 106 above includes by virtue of subsection (1) above an amount (in this section referred to as a "personal allowance element") in respect of income support by virtue of paragraph 1(2) of Schedule 2 to the Income Support (General) Regulations 1987 (personal allowance for lone parent) the order shall separately identify the amount of the personal allowance element.

(3) In any case where—

(a) there is in force an order under subsection (2) of section 106 above made against a person ("the liable parent") who is the parent of one or more children, in respect of the other parent or the children; and

(b) payments under the order fall to be made to the Secretary of State by virtue of subsection (4)(a) of that section; and

(c) that other parent ("the dependent parent") ceases to claim income support,

the Secretary of State may, by giving notice in writing to the court which made the order and to the liable parent and the dependent parent, transfer to the dependent parent the right to receive the payments under the order, exclusive of any personal allowance element, and to exercise the relevant rights in relation to the order, except so far as relating to that element.

(4) Notice under subsection (3) above shall not be given (and if purportedly given, shall be of no effect) at a time when there is in force a maintenance order made against the liable parent—

(a) in favour of the dependent parent or one or more of the children; or

(b) in favour of some other person for the benefit of the dependent parent or one or more of the children;

and if such a maintenance order is made at any time after notice under that subsection has been given, the order under section 106(2) above shall cease to have effect.

(5) In any case where—

(a) notice is given to a magistrates'court under subsection (3) above,

(b) payments under the order are required to be made by any method of payment falling within section 59(6) of the Magistrates' Courts Act 1980 (standing order, etc.), and

(c) the clerk to the justices for the petty sessions area for which the court is acting decides that payment by that method is no longer possible, the clerk shall amend the order to provide that payments under the order shall be made by the liable parent [to the justices' chief executive for the court][1].

(6) Except as provided by subsections (8) and (12) below, where the Secretary of State gives notice under subsection (3) above, he shall cease to be entitled—

(a) to receive any payment under the order in respect of any personal allowance element; or

(b) to exercise the relevant rights, so far as relating to any such element,

notwithstanding that the dependent parent does not become entitled to receive any payment in respect of that element or to exercise the relevant rights so far as so relating.

(7) If, in a case where the Secretary of State gives notice under subsection (3) above, a payment under the order is or has been made to him wholly or partly in respect of the whole or any part of the period beginning with the day on which the transfer takes effect and ending with the day on which the notice under subsection (3) above is given to the liable parent, the Secretary of State shall—

(a) repay to or for the liable parent so much of the payment as is referable to any personal allowance element in respect of that period or, as the case may be, the part of it in question; and

(b) pay to or for the dependent parent so much of any remaining balance of the payment as is referable to that period or part;

and a payment under paragraph (b) above shall be taken to discharge, to that extent, the liability of the liable parent to the dependent parent under the order in respect of that period or part.

(8) If, in a case where the Secretary of State has given notice under subsection (3) above, the dependent parent makes a further claim for income support, then—

(a) the Secretary of State may, by giving a further notice in writing to the court which made the order and to the liable parent and the dependent parent, transfer back from the dependent parent to himself the right to receive the payments and to exercise the relevant rights; and

(b) that transfer shall revive the Secretary of State's right to receive payment under the order in respect of any personal allowance element and to exercise the relevant rights so far as relating to any such element.

(9) Subject to subsections (10) and (11) below, in any case where—

(a) notice is given to a magistrates' court under subsection (8) above, and

(b) the method of payment under the order which subsists immediately before the day on which the transfer under subsection (8) above takes effect differs from the method of payment which subsisted immediately before the day on which the transfer under subsection (3) above (or, if there has been more than one such transfer, the last such transfer) took effect,

the clerk to the justices for the petty sessions area for which the court is acting shall amend the order by reinstating the method of payment under the order which subsisted immediately before the day on which the transfer under subsection (3) above (or, as the case may be, the last such transfer) took effect.

(10) The clerk shall not amend the order under subsection (9) above if the Secretary of State gives notice in writing to the clerk, on or before the day on which the notice under subsection (8) above is given, that the method of payment

[1] Words substituted by Access to Justice Act 1999 c.22 Sch 13 para 168

under the order which subsists immediately before the day on which the transfer under subsection (8) above takes effect is to continue.

(11) In any case where—

(a) notice is given to a magistrates' court under subsection (8) above,

(b) the method of payment under the order which subsisted immediately before the day on which the transfer under subsection (3) above (or, if there has been more than one such transfer, the last such transfer) took effect was any method of payment falling within section 59(6) of the Magistrates' Courts Act 1980 (standing order, etc.), and

(c) the clerk decides that payment by that method is no longer possible,

the clerk shall amend the order to provide that payments under the order shall be made by the liable parent to the justices' chief executive for the court.

(12) A transfer under subsection (3) or (8) above does not transfer or otherwise affect the right of any person—

(a) to receive a payment which fell due to him at a time before the transfer took effect; or

(b) to exercise the relevant rights in relation to any such payment;

and, where notice is given under subsection (3), subsection (6) above does not deprive the Secretary of State of his right to receive such a payment in respect of any personal allowance element or to exercise the relevant rights in relation to such a payment.

(13) For the purposes of this section—

(a) a transfer under subsection (3) above takes effect on the day on which the dependent parent ceases to be in receipt of income support in consequence of the cessation referred to in paragraph (c) of that subsection, and

(b) a transfer under subsection (8) above takes effect on—

(i) the first day in respect of which the dependent parent receives income support after the transfer under subsection (3) above took effect, or

(ii) such later day as may be specified for the purpose in the notice under subsection (8),

irrespective of the day on which notice under the subsection in question is given.

(14) Any notice required to be given to the liable parent under subsection (3) or (8) above shall be taken to have been given if it has been sent to his last known address.

(15) In this section—

"child" means a person under the age of 16, notwithstanding section 78(6)(d) above;

"court" shall be construed in accordance with section 106 above;

"maintenance order"—

(a) in England and Wales, means—

(i) any order for the making of periodical payments or for the payment of a lump sum which is, or has at any time been, a maintenance order within the meaning of the Attachment of Earnings Act 1971;

(ii) any order under Part III of the Matrimonial and Family Proceedings Act 1984 (overseas divorce) for the making of periodical payments or for the payment of a lump sum;

"the relevant rights", in relation to an order under section 106(2) above, means the right to bring any proceedings, take any steps or do any other thing under or in relation to the order which the Secretary of State could have brought, taken or done apart from any transfer under this section.

Reduction of expenditure on income support: certain maintenance orders to be enforceable by the Secretary of State

43-006 **108.**—(1) This section applies where—

(a) a person ("the claimant") who is the parent of one or more children is in receipt of income support either in respect of those children or in respect of both himself and those children; and

(b) there is in force a maintenance order made against the other parent ("the liable person")—

(i) in favour of the claimant or one or more of the children, or

(ii) in favour of some other person for the benefit of the claimant or one or more of the children;

and in this section "the primary recipient" means the person in whose favour that maintenance order was made.

(2) If, in a case where this section applies, the liable person fails to comply with any of the terms of the maintenance order—

(a) the Secretary of State may bring any proceedings or take any other steps to enforce the order that could have been brought or taken by or on behalf of the primary recipient; and

(b) any court before which proceedings are brought by the Secretary of State by virtue of paragraph (a) above shall have the same powers in connection with those proceedings as it would have had if they had been brought by the primary recipient.

(3) The Secretary of State's powers under this section are exercisable at his discretion and whether or not the primary recipient or any other person consents to their exercise; but any sums recovered by virtue of this section shall be payable to or for the primary recipient, as if the proceedings or steps in question had been brought or taken by him or on his behalf.

(4) The powers conferred on the Secretary of State by subsection (2)(a) above include power—

(a) to apply for the registration of the maintenance order under—

(i) section 17 of the Maintenance Orders Act 1950;

(ii) section 2 of the Maintenance Orders Act 1958; [...][1]

(iii) the Civil Jurisdiction and Judgments Act 1982; [or][2]

[(iv) Council Regulation (EC) No. 44/2001 of 22nd December 2000 on jurisdiction and the recognition and enforcement of judgments in civil and commercial matters; and][3]

(b) to make an application under section 2 of the Maintenance Orders (Reciprocal Enforcement) Act 1972 (application for enforcement in reciprocating country).

(5) Where this section applies, the prescribed person shall in prescribed circumstances give the Secretary of State notice of any application—

(a) to alter, vary, suspend, discharge, revoke, revive or enforce the maintenance order in question; or

(b) to remit arrears under that maintenance order;

and the Secretary of State shall be entitled to appear and be heard on the application.

[1] Word repealed by SI 2001/3929 Sch 3 para 24 (a)
[2] Word substituted by SI 2001/3929 Sch 3 para 24 (b)
[3] Added by SI 2001/3929 Sch 3 para 24 (c)

(6) Where, by virtue of this section, the Secretary of State commences any proceedings to enforce a maintenance order, he shall, in relation to those proceedings, be treated for the purposes of any enactment or instrument relating to maintenance orders as if he were a person entitled to payment under the maintenance order in question (but shall not thereby become entitled to any such payment).

(8) In this section "maintenance order" has the same meaning as it has in section 107 above but does not include any such order for the payment of a lump sum.

Criminal Justice and Public Order Act 1994

CHAPTER 33

PART XII

MISCELLANEOUS AND GENERAL

Harassment, alarm or distress

Offence of causing intentional harassment, alarm or distress

154. In Part I of the Public Order Act 1986 (offences relating to public order), after section 4, there shall be inserted the following section— **44-001**

"Intentional harassment, alarm or distress

(1) A person is guilty of an offence if, with intent to cause a person harassment, alarm or distress, he— **44-002**

(a) uses threatening, abusive or insulting words or behaviour, or disorderly behaviour, or

(b) displays any writing, sign or other visible representation which is threatening, abusive or insulting,

thereby causing that or another person harassment, alarm or distress.

(2) An offence under this section may be committed in a public or a private place, except that no offence is committed where the words or behaviour are used, or the writing, sign or other visible representation is displayed, by a person inside a dwelling and the person who is harassed, alarmed or distressed is also inside that or another dwelling.

(3) It is a defence for the accused to prove—

(a) that he was inside a dwelling and had no reason to believe that the words or behaviour used, or the writing, sign or other visible representation displayed, would be heard or seen by a person outside that or any other dwelling, or

(b) that his conduct was reasonable.

(4) A constable may arrest without warrant anyone he reasonably suspects is committing an offence under this section.

(5) A person guilty of an offence under this section is liable on summary conviction to imprisonment for a term not exceeding 6 months or a fine not exceeding level 5 on the standard scale or both.".

Pensions Act 1995

CHAPTER 26

PART IV

MISCELLANEOUS AND GENERAL

Pensions on divorce, etc

Pensions on divorce etc

45-001 **166.**—(4) Nothing in the provisions mentioned in subsection (5) applies to a court exercising its powers under section 23 of the Matrimonial Causes Act 1973 (financial provision in connection with divorce proceedings, etc.) in respect of any benefits under a pension [arrangement][1] (within the meaning of section 25B(1) of the Matrimonial Causes Act 1973) which a party to the marriage has or is likely to have.

(5) The provisions referred to in subsection (4) are—

(a) section 203(1) and (2) of the Army Act 1955, 203(1) and (2) of the Air Force Act 1955, 128G(1) and (2) of the Naval Discipline Act 1957 or 159(4) and (4A) of the Pension Schemes Act 1993 (which prevent assignment, or orders being made restraining a person from receiving anything which he is prevented from assigning),

(b) section 91 of this Act,

(c) any provision of any enactment (whether passed or made before or after this Act is passed) corresponding to any of the enactments mentioned in paragraphs (a) and (b), and

(d) any provision of the [arrangement][2] in question corresponding to any of those enactments.

(6) Subsections (3) to (7) of section 25B, and section 25C of the Matrimonial Causes Act 1973, as inserted by this section, do not affect the powers of the court under section 31 of that Act (variation, discharge, etc.) in relation to any order made before the commencement of this section.

---

1 Words substituted by Welfare Reform and Pensions Act 1999 c.30 Sch 12 (I) para 62 (2)
2 Substituted by Welfare Reform and Pensions Act 1999 c.30 Sch 12 (I) para 62 (3)

Child Support Act 1995

CHAPTER 34

Miscellaneous

Deferral of right to apply for maintenance assessment

18.—(6) Neither section 4(10) nor section 7(10) of the 1991 Act shall apply in relation to a maintenance order made in the circumstances mentioned in subsection (7) or (8) of section 8 of the 1991 Act. **46-001**

(7) The Secretary of State may by regulations make provision for section 4(10), or section 7(10), of the 1991 Act not to apply in relation to such other cases as may be prescribed.

Family Law Act 1996

CHAPTER 27

PART I

PRINCIPLES OF PARTS II AND III

The general principles underlying Parts II and III

1. The court and any person, in exercising functions under or in consequence of Parts II and III, shall have regard to the following general principles— **47-001**

(a) that the institution of marriage is to be supported;

(b) that the parties to a marriage which may have broken down are to be encouraged to take all practicable steps, whether by marriage counselling or otherwise, to save the marriage;

(c) that a marriage which has irretrievably broken down and is being brought to an end should be brought to an end—

  (i) with minimum distress to the parties and to the children affected;

  (ii) with questions dealt with in a manner designed to promote as good a continuing relationship between the parties and any children affected as is possible in the circumstances; and

  (iii) without costs being unreasonably incurred in connection with the procedures to be followed in bringing the marriage to an end; and

(d) that any risk to one of the parties to a marriage, and to any children, of violence from the other party should, so far as reasonably practicable, be removed or diminished.

PART II

DIVORCE AND SEPARATION

Marriage support services

Funding for marriage support services

47-002 **22.**—(1) The Lord Chancellor may, with the approval of the Treasury, make grants in connection with—

(a) the provision of marriage support services;

(b) research into the causes of marital breakdown;

(c) research into ways of preventing marital breakdown.

(2) Any grant under this section may be made subject to such conditions as the Lord Chancellor considers appropriate.

(3) In exercising his power to make grants in connection with the provision of marriage support services, the Lord Chancellor is to have regard, in particular, to the desirability of services of that kind being available when they are first needed.

PART IV

FAMILY HOMES AND DOMESTIC VIOLENCE

Rights to occupy matrimonial home

Rights concerning matrimonial home where one spouse has no estate, etc

47-003 **30.**—(1) This section applies if—

(a) one spouse is entitled to occupy a dwelling-house by virtue of—

(i) a beneficial estate or interest or contract; or

(ii) any enactment giving that spouse the right to remain in occupation; and

(b) the other spouse is not so entitled.

(2) Subject to the provisions of this Part, the spouse not so entitled has the following rights ("matrimonial home rights")—

(a) if in occupation, a right not to be evicted or excluded from the dwelling-house or any part of it by the other spouse except with the leave of the court given by an order under section 33;

(b) if not in occupation, a right with the leave of the court so given to enter into and occupy the dwelling-house.

(3) If a spouse is entitled under this section to occupy a dwelling-house or any part of a dwelling-house, any payment or tender made or other thing done by that spouse in or towards satisfaction of any liability of the other spouse in respect of rent, mortgage payments or other outgoings affecting the dwelling-house is, whether or not it is made or done in pursuance of an order under section 40, as good as if made or done by the other spouse.

(4) A spouse's occupation by virtue of this section—

(a) is to be treated, for the purposes of the Rent (Agriculture) Act 1976 and the Rent Act 1977 (other than Part V and sections 103 to 106 of that Act), as occupation by the other spouse as the other spouse's residence, and

(b) if the spouse occupies the dwelling-house as that spouse's only or principal home, is to be treated, for the purposes of the Housing Act 1985 [, Part I of the Housing Act 1988 and Chapter I of Part V of the Housing Act 1996][1], as occupation by the other spouse as the other spouse's only or principal home.

(5) If a spouse ("the first spouse")—

(a) is entitled under this section to occupy a dwelling-house or any part of a dwelling-house, and

(b) makes any payment in or towards satisfaction of any liability of the other spouse ("the second spouse") in respect of mortgage payments affecting the dwelling-house,

the person to whom the payment is made may treat it as having been made by the second spouse, but the fact that that person has treated any such payment as having been so made does not affect any claim of the first spouse against the second spouse to an interest in the dwelling-house by virtue of the payment.

(6) If a spouse is entitled under this section to occupy a dwelling-house or part of a dwelling-house by reason of an interest of the other spouse under a trust, all the provisions of subsections (3) to (5) apply in relation to the trustees as they apply in relation to the other spouse.

(7) This section does not apply to a dwelling-house which has at no time been, and which was at no time intended by the spouse to be, a matrimonial home of theirs.

(8) A spouse's matrimonial home rights continue—

(a) only so long as the marriage subsists, except to the extent that an order under section 33(5) otherwise provides; and

(b) only so long as the other spouse is entitled as mentioned in subsection (1) to occupy the dwelling-house, except where provision is made by section 31 for those rights to be a charge on an estate or interest in the dwelling-house.

(9) It is hereby declared that a spouse—

(a) who has an equitable interest in a dwelling-house or in its proceeds of sale, but

(b) is not a spouse in whom there is vested (whether solely or as joint tenant) a legal estate in fee simple or a legal term of years absolute in the dwelling-house,

is to be treated, only for the purpose of determining whether he has matrimonial home rights, as not being entitled to occupy the dwelling-house by virtue of that interest.

Effect of matrimonial home rights as charge on dwelling-house

31.—(1) Subsections (2) and (3) apply if, at any time during a marriage, one spouse is entitled to occupy a dwelling-house by virtue of a beneficial estate or interest. **47-004**

(2) The other spouse's matrimonial home rights are a charge on the estate or interest.

(3) The charge created by subsection (2) has the same priority as if it were an equitable interest created at whichever is the latest of the following dates—

(a) the date on which the spouse so entitled acquires the estate or interest;

(b) the date of the marriage; and

(c) 1st January 1968 (the commencement date of the Matrimonial Homes Act 1967.

[1] Words substituted by SI 1997/74 Sch 1 para 10 (a)

(4) Subsections (5) and (6) apply if, at any time when a spouse's matrimonial home rights are a charge on an interest of the other spouse under a trust, there are, apart from either of the spouses, no persons, living or unborn, who are or could become beneficiaries under the trust.

(5) The rights are a charge also on the estate or interest of the trustees for the other spouse.

(6) The charge created by subsection (5) has the same priority as if it were an equitable interest created (under powers overriding the trusts) on the date when it arises.

(7) In determining for the purposes of subsection (4) whether there are any persons who are not, but could become, beneficiaries under the trust, there is to be disregarded any potential exercise of a general power of appointment exercisable by either or both of the spouses alone (whether or not the exercise of it requires the consent of another person).

(8) Even though a spouse's matrimonial home rights are a charge on an estate or interest in the dwelling-house, those rights are brought to an end by—

(a) the death of the other spouse, or

(b) the termination (otherwise than by death) of the marriage,

unless the court directs otherwise by an order made under section 33(5).

(9) If—

(a) a spouse's matrimonial home rights are a charge on an estate or interest in the dwelling-house, and

(b) that estate or interest is surrendered to merge in some other estate or interest expectant on it in such circumstances that, but for the merger, the person taking the estate or interest would be bound by the charge,

the surrender has effect subject to the charge and the persons thereafter entitled to the other estate or interest are, for so long as the estate or interest surrendered would have endured if not so surrendered, to be treated for all purposes of this Part as deriving title to the other estate or interest under the other spouse or, as the case may be, under the trustees for the other spouse, by virtue of the surrender.

(10) If the title to the legal estate by virtue of which a spouse is entitled to occupy a dwelling-house (including any legal estate held by trustees for that spouse) is registered under the Land Registration Act 1925 or any enactment replaced by that Act—

(a) registration of a land charge affecting the dwelling-house by virtue of this Part is to be effected by registering a notice under that Act; and

(b) a spouse's matrimonial home rights are not an overriding interest within the meaning of that Act affecting the dwelling-house even though the spouse is in actual occupation of the dwelling-house.

(11) A spouse's matrimonial home rights (whether or not constituting a charge) do not entitle that spouse to lodge a caution under section 54 of the Land Registration Act 1925.

(12) If—

(a) a spouse's matrimonial home rights are a charge on the estate of the other spouse or of trustees of the other spouse, and

(b) that estate is the subject of a mortgage,

then if, after the date of the creation of the mortgage ("the first mortgage"), the charge is registered under section 2 of the Land Charges Act 1972, the charge is, for the purposes of section 94 of the Law of Property Act 1925 (which regulates the rights of mortgagees to make further advances ranking in priority to subsequent mortgages), to be deemed to be a mortgage subsequent in date to the first mortgage.

(13) It is hereby declared that a charge under subsection (2) or (5) is not registrable under subsection (10) or under section 2 of the Land Charges Act 1972 unless it is a charge on a legal estate.

Further provisions relating to matrimonial home rights

32. Schedule 4 re-enacts with consequential amendments and minor modifi- **47-005**
cations provisions of the Matrimonial Homes Act 1983.

Occupation orders

Occupation orders where applicant has estate or interest etc. or has matrimonial home rights

33.—(1) If— **47-006**

(a) a person ("the person entitled")—
 (i) is entitled to occupy a dwelling-house by virtue of a beneficial estate or interest or contract or by virtue of any enactment giving him the right to remain in occupation, or
 (ii) has matrimonial home rights in relation to a dwelling-house, and
(b) the dwelling-house—
 (i) is or at any time has been the home of the person entitled and of another person with whom he is associated, or
 (ii) was at any time intended by the person entitled and any such other person to be their home,

the person entitled may apply to the court for an order containing any of the provisions specified in subsections (3), (4) and (5).

(2) If an agreement to marry is terminated, no application under this section may be made by virtue of section 62(3)(e) by reference to that agreement after the end of the period of three years beginning with the day on which it is terminated.

(3) An order under this section may—
(a) enforce the applicant's entitlement to remain in occupation as against the other person ("the respondent");
(b) require the respondent to permit the applicant to enter and remain in the dwelling-house or part of the dwelling-house;
(c) regulate the occupation of the dwelling-house by either or both parties;
(d) if the respondent is entitled as mentioned in subsection (1)(a)(i), prohibit, suspend or restrict the exercise by him of his right to occupy the dwelling-house.
(e) if the respondent has matrimonial home rights in relation to the dwelling-house and the applicant is the other spouse, restrict or terminate those rights;
(f) require the respondent to leave the dwelling-house or part of the dwelling-house; or
(g) exclude the respondent from a defined area in which the dwelling-house is included.

(4) An order under this section may declare that the applicant is entitled as mentioned in subsection (1)(a)(i) or has matrimonial home rights.

(5) If the applicant has matrimonial home rights and the respondent is the other spouse, an order under this section made during the marriage may provide that those rights are not brought to an end by—

(a) the death of the other spouse; or
(b) the termination (otherwise than by death) of the marriage.

(6) In deciding whether to exercise its powers under subsection (3) and (if so) in what manner, the court shall have regard to all the circumstances including—

(a) the housing needs and housing resources of each of the parties and of any relevant child;
(b) the financial resources of each of the parties;
(c) the likely effect of any order, or of any decision by the court not to exercise its powers under subsection (3), on the health, safety or well-being of the parties and of any relevant child; and
(d) the conduct of the parties in relation to each other and otherwise.

(7) If it appears to the court that the applicant or any relevant child is likely to suffer significant harm attributable to conduct of the respondent if an order under this section containing one or more of the provisions mentioned in subsection (3) is not made, the court shall make the order unless it appears to it that—

(a) the respondent or any relevant child is likely to suffer significant harm if the order is made; and
(b) the harm likely to be suffered by the respondent or child in that event is as great as, or greater than, the harm attributable to conduct of the respondent which is likely to be suffered by the applicant or child if the order is not made.

(8) The court may exercise its powers under subsection (5) in any case where it considers that in all the circumstances it is just and reasonable to do so.

(9) An order under this section—

(a) may not be made after the death of either of the parties mentioned in subsection (1); and
(b) except in the case of an order made by virtue of subsection (5)(a), ceases to have effect on the death of either party.

(10) An order under this section may, in so far as it has continuing effect, be made for a specified period, until the occurrence of a specified event or until further order.

Effect of order under s. 33 where rights are charge on dwelling-house

47-007 **34.**—(1) If a spouse's matrimonial home rights are a charge on the estate or interest of the other spouse or of trustees for the other spouse—

(a) an order under section 33 against the other spouse has, except so far as a contrary intention appears, the same effect against persons deriving title under the other spouse or under the trustees and affected by the charge, and
(b) sections 33(1), (3), (4) and (10) and 30(3) to (6) apply in relation to any person deriving title under the other spouse or under the trustees and affected by the charge as they apply in relation to the other spouse.

(2) The court may make an order under section 33 by virtue of subsection (1)(b) if it considers that in all the circumstances it is just and reasonable to do so.

One former spouse with no existing right to occupy

47-008 **35.**—(1) This section applies if—

(a) one former spouse is entitled to occupy a dwelling-house by virtue of a beneficial estate or interest or contract, or by virtue of any enactment giving him the right to remain in occupation;
(b) the other former spouse is not so entitled; and
(c) the dwelling-house was at any time their matrimonial home or was at any time intended by them to be their matrimonial home.

(2) The former spouse not so entitled may apply to the court for an order under this section against the other former spouse ("the respondent").

(3) If the applicant is in occupation, an order under this section must contain provision—
(a) giving the applicant the right not to be evicted or excluded form the dwelling-house or any part of it by the respondent for the period specified in the order; and
(b) prohibiting the respondent from exciting or excluding the applicant during that period.

(4) If the applicant is not in occupation, an order under this section must contain provision—
(a) giving the applicant the right to enter into and occupy the dwelling-house for the period specified in the order; and
(b) requiring the respondent to permit the exercise of that right.

(5) An order under this section may also—
(a) regulate the occupation of the dwelling-house by either or both of the parties;
(b) prohibit, suspend or restrict the exercise by the respondent of his right to occupy the dwelling-house;
(c) require the respondent to leave the dwelling-house or part of the dwelling-house; or
(d) exclude the respondent from a defined area in which the dwelling-house is included.

(6) In deciding whether to make an order under this section containing provision of the kind mentioned in subsection (3) or (4) and (if so) in what manner, the court shall have regard to all the circumstances including—
(a) the housing needs and housing resources of each of the parties and of any relevant child;
(b) the financial resources of each of the parties;
(c) the likely effect of any order, or of any decision by the court not to exercise its powers under subsection (3) or (4), on the health, safety or well-being of the parties and of any relevant child;
(d) the conduct of the parties in relation to each other and otherwise;
(e) the length of time that has elapsed since the parties ceased to live together;
(f) the length of time that has elapsed since the marriage was dissolved or annulled; and
(g) the existence of any pending proceedings between the parties—
  (i) for an order under section 23A or 24 of the Matrimonial Causes Act 1973 (property adjustment orders in connection with divorce proceedings etc.);
  (ii) for an order under paragraph 1(2)(d) or (e) of Schedule 1 to the Children Act 1989 (orders for financial relief against parents); or
  (iii) relating to the legal or beneficial ownership of the dwelling-house.

(7) In deciding whether to exercise its power to include one or more of the provisions referred to in subsection (5) ("a subsection (5) provision") and (if so) in

what manner, the court shall have regard to all the circumstances including the matters mentioned in subsection (6)(a) to (e).

(8) If the court decides to make an order under this section and it appears to it that, if the order does not include a subsection (5) provision, the applicant or any relevant child is likely to suffer significant harm attributable to conduct of the respondent, the court shall include the subsection (5) provision in the order unless it appears to the court that—

(a) the respondent or any relevant child is likely to suffer significant harm if the provision is included in the order; and
(b) the harm likely to be suffered by the respondent or child in that event is as great as or greater than the harm attributable to conduct of the respondent which is likely to be suffered by the applicant or child if the provision is not included.

(9) An order under this section—

(a) may not be made after the death of either of the former spouses; and
(b) ceases to have effect on the death of either of them.

(10) An order under this section must be limited so as to have effect for a specified period not exceeding six months, but may be extended on one or more occasions for a further specified period not exceeding six months.

(11) A former spouse who has an equitable interest in the dwelling-house or in the proceeds of sale of the dwelling-house but in whom there is not vested (whether solely or as joint tenant) a legal estate in fee simple or a legal term of years absolute in the dwelling-house is to be treated (but only for the purpose of determining whether he is eligible to apply under this section) as not being entitled to occupy the dwelling-house by virtue of that interest.

(12) Subsection (11) does not prejudice any right of such a former spouse to apply for an order under section 33.

(13) So long as an order under this section remains in force, subsections (3) to (6) of section 30 apply in relation to the applicant—

(a) as if he were the spouse entitled to occupy the dwelling-house by virtue of that section; and
(b) as if the respondent were the other spouse.

One cohabitant or former cohabitant with no existing right to occupy

47-009 **36.**—(1) This section applies if—

(a) one cohabitant or former cohabitant is entitled to occupy a dwelling-house by virtue of a beneficial estate or interest or contract or by virtue of any enactment giving him the right to remain in occupation;
(b) the other cohabitant or former cohabitant is not so entitled; and
(c) that dwelling-house is the home in which they live together as husband and wife or a home in which they at any time so lived together or intended so to live together.

(2) The cohabitant or former cohabitant not so entitled may apply to the court for an order under this section against the other cohabitant or former cohabitant ("the respondent").

(3) If the applicant is in occupation, an order under this section must contain provision—

(a) giving the applicant the right not to be evicted or excluded from the dwelling-house or any part of it by the respondent for the period specified in the order; and
(b) prohibiting the respondent from evicting or excluding the applicant during that period.

(4) If the applicant is not in occupation, an order under this section must contain provision—

(a) giving the applicant the right to enter into and occupy the dwelling-house for the period specified in the order; and

(b) requiring the respondent to permit the exercise of that right.

(5) An order under this section may also—

(a) regulate the occupation of the dwelling-house by either or both of the parties;

(b) prohibit, suspend or restrict the exercise by the respondent of his right to occupy the dwelling-house;

(c) require the respondent to leave the dwelling-house or part of the dwelling-house; or

(d) exclude the respondent from a defined area in which the dwelling-house is included.

(6) In deciding whether to make an order under this section containing provision of the kind mentioned in subsection (3) or (4) and (if so) in what manner, the court shall have regard to all the circumstances including—

(a) the housing needs and housing resources of each of the parties and of any relevant child;

(b) the financial resources of each of the parties;

(c) the likely effect of any order, or of any decision by the court not to exercise its powers under subsection (3) or (4), on the health, safety or well-being of the parties and of any relevant child;

(d) the conduct of the parties in relation to each other and otherwise;

(e) the nature of the parties' relationship;

(f) the length of time during which they have lived together as husband and wife;

(g) whether there are or have been any children who are children of both parties or for whom both parties have or have had parental responsibility;

(h) the length of time that has elapsed since the parties ceased to live together; and

(i) the existence of any pending proceedings between the parties—

(i) for an order under paragraph 1(2)(d) or (e) of Schedule 1 to the Children Act 1989 (orders for financial relief against parents); or

(ii) relating to the legal or beneficial ownership of the dwelling-house.

(7) In deciding whether to exercise its powers to include one or more of the provisions referred to in subsection (5) ("a subsection (5) provision") and (if so) in what manner, the court shall have regard to all the circumstances including—

(a) the matters mentioned in subsection (6)(a) to (d); and

(b) the questions mentioned in subsection (8).

(8) The questions are—

(a) whether the applicant or any relevant child is likely to suffer significant harm attributable to conduct of the respondent if the subsection (5) provision is not included in the order; and

(b) whether the harm likely to be suffered by the respondent or child if the provision is included is as great as or greater than the harm attributable to conduct of the respondent which is likely to be suffered by the applicant or child if the provision is not included.

(9) An order under this section—

(a) may not be made after the death of either of the parties; and

(b) ceases to have effect on the death of either of them.

(10) An order under this section must be limited so as to have effect for a specified period not exceeding six months, but may be extended on one occasion for a further specified period not exceeding six months.

(11) A person who has an equitable interest in the dwelling-house or in the proceeds of sale of the dwelling-house but in whom there is not vested (whether solely or as joint tenant) a legal estate in fee simple or a legal term of years absolute in the dwelling-house is to be treated (but only for the purpose of determining whether he is eligible to apply under this section) as not being entitled to occupy the dwelling-house by virtue of that interest.

(12) Subsection (11) does not prejudice any right of such a person to apply for an order under section 33.

(13) So long as the order remains in force, subsections (3) to (6) of section 30 apply in relation to the applicant—

(a) as if he were a spouse entitled to occupy the dwelling-house by virtue of that section; and

(b) as if the respondent were the other spouse.

Neither spouse entitled to occupy

47-010 **37.**—(1) This section applies if—

(a) one spouse or former spouse and the other spouse or former spouse occupy a dwelling-house which is or was the matrimonial home; but

(b) neither of them is entitled to remain in occupation—

(i) by virtue of a beneficial estate or interest or contract; or

(ii) by virtue of any enactment giving him the right to remain in occupation.

(2) Either of the parties may apply to the court for an order against the other under this section.

(3) An order under this section may—

(a) require the respondent to permit the applicant to enter and remain in the dwelling-house or part of the dwelling-house;

(b) regulate the occupation of the dwelling-house by either or both of the spouses;

(c) require the respondent to leave the dwelling-house or part of the dwelling-house; or

(d) exclude the respondent from a defined area in which the dwelling-house is included.

(4) Subsections (6) and (7) of section 33 apply to the exercise by the court of its powers under this section as they apply to the exercise by the court of its powers under subsection (3) of that section.

(5) An order under this section must be limited so as to have effect for a specified period not exceeding six months, but may be extended on one or more occasions for a further specified period not exceeding six months.

Neither cohabitant or former cohabitant entitled to occupy

47-011 **38.**—(1) This section applies if—

(a) one cohabitant or former cohabitant and the other cohabitant or former cohabitant occupy a dwelling-house which is the home in which they live or lived together as husband and wife; but

(b) neither of them is entitled to remain in occupation—

(i) by virtue of a beneficial estate or interest or contract; or

(ii) by virtue of any enactment giving him the right to remain in occupation.

(2) Either of the parties may apply to the court for an order against the other under this section.

(3) An order under this section may—

(a) require the respondent to permit the applicant to enter and remain in the dwelling-house or part of the dwelling-house;

(b) regulate the occupation of the dwelling-house by either or both of the parties;

(c) require the respondent to leave the dwelling-house or part of the dwelling-house; or

(d) exclude the respondent from a defined area in which the dwelling-house is included.

(4) In deciding whether to exercise its powers to include one or more of the provisions referred to in subsection (3) ("a subsection (3) provision") and (if so) in what manner, the court shall have regard to all the circumstances including—

(a) the housing needs and housing resources of each of the parties and of any relevant child;

(b) the financial resources of each of the parties;

(c) the likely effect of any order, or of any decision by the court not to exercise its powers under subsection (3), on the health, safety or well-being of the parties and of any relevant child;

(d) the conduct of the parties in relation to each other and otherwise; and

(e) the question mentioned in subsection (5).

(5) The questions are—

(a) whether the applicant or any relevant child is likely to suffer significant harm attributable to conduct of the respondent if the subsection (3) provision is not included in the order; and

(b) whether the harm likely to be suffered by the respondent or child if the provision is included is as great as or greater than the harm attributable to conduct of the respondent which is likely to be suffered by the applicant or child if the provision is not included.

(6) An order under this section shall be limited so as to have effect for a specified period not exceeding six months, but may be extended on one occasion for a further specified period not exceeding six months.

Supplementary provisions

39.—(1) In this Part an "occupation order" means an order under section 33, 35, 36, 37 or 38. **47-012**

(2) An application for an occupation order may be made in other family proceedings or without any other family proceedings being instituted.

(3) If—

(a) an application for an occupation order is made under section 33, 35, 36, 37 or 38, and

(b) the court considers that it has no power to make the order under the section concerned, but that it has power to make an order under one of the other sections,

the court may make an order under that other section.

(4) The fact that a person has applied for an occupation order under sections 35 to 38, or that an occupation order has been made, does not affect the right of any person to claim a legal or equitable interest in any property in any subsequent proceedings (including subsequent proceedings under this Part).

Additional provisions that may be included in certain occupation orders

47-013 **40.**—(1) The court may on, or at any time after, making an occupation order under section 33, 35 or 36—

(a) impose on either party obligations as to—

(i) the repair and maintenance of the dwelling-house; or

(ii) the discharge of rent, mortgage payments or other outgoings affecting the dwelling-house;

(b) order a party occupying the dwelling-house or any part of it (including a party who is entitled to do so by virtue of a beneficial estate or interest or contract or by virtue of any enactment giving him the right to remain in occupation) to make periodical payments to the other party in respect of the accommodation, if the other party would (but for the order) be entitled to occupy the dwelling-house by virtue of a beneficial estate or interest or contract or by virtue of any such enactment;

(c) grant either party possession or use of furniture or other contents of the dwelling-house;

(d) order either party to take reasonable care of any furniture or other contents of the dwelling-house;

(e) order either party to take reasonable steps to keep the dwelling-house and any furniture or other contents secure.

(2) In deciding whether and, if so, how to exercise its powers under this section, the court shall have regard to all the circumstances of the case including—

(a) the financial needs and financial resources of the parties; and

(b) the financial obligations which they have, or are likely to have in the foreseeable future, including financial obligations to each other and to any relevant child.

(3) An order under this section ceases to have effect when the occupation order to which it relates ceases to have effect.

Additional considerations if parties are cohabitants or former cohabitants

47-014 **41.**—(1) This section applies if the parties are cohabitants or former cohabitants.

(2) Where the court is required to consider the nature of the parties' relationship, it is to have regard to the fact that they have not given each other the commitment involved in marriage.

Non-molestation orders

Non-molestation orders

47-015 **42.**—(1) In this Part a "non-molestation order" means an order containing either or both of the following provisions—

(a) provision prohibiting a person ("the respondent") from molesting another person who is associated with the respondent;

(b) provision prohibiting the respondent from molesting a relevant child

(2) The court may make a non-molestation order—

(a) if an application for the order has been made (whether in other family proceedings or without any other family proceedings being instituted) by a person who is associated with the respondent; or

(b) if in any family proceedings to which the respondent is a party the court considers that the order should be made for the benefit of any other party to the proceedings or any relevant child even though no such application has been made.

(3) In subsection (2) "family proceedings" includes proceedings in which the court has made an emergency protection order under section 44 of the Children Act 1989 which includes an exclusion requirement (as defined in section 44A(3) of that Act).

(4) Where an agreement to marry is terminated, no application under subsection (2)(a) may be made by virtue of section 62(3)(e) by reference to that agreement after the end of the period of three years beginning with the day on which it is terminated.

(5) In deciding whether to exercise its powers under this section and, if so, in what manner, the court shall have regard to all the circumstances including the need to secure the health, safety and well-being—

(a) of the applicant or, in a case falling within subsection (2)(b), the person for whose benefit the order would be made; and

(b) of any relevant child.

(6) A non-molestation order may be expressed so as to refer to molestation in general, to particular acts of molestation, or to both.

(7) A non-molestation order may be made for a specified period or until further order.

(8) A non-molestation order which is made in other family proceedings ceases to have effect if those proceedings are withdrawn or dismissed.

Further provisions relating to occupation and non-molestation orders

Leave of court required for applications by children under sixteen

43.—(1) A child under the age of sixteen may not apply for an occupation order or a non-molestation order except with the leave of the court. **47-016**

(2) The court may grant leave for the purposes of subsection (1) only if it is satisfied that the child has sufficient understanding to make the proposed application for the occupation order or non-molestation order.

Evidence of agreement to marry

44.—(1) Subject to subsection (2), the court shall not make an order under section 33 or 42 by virtue of section 62(3)(e) unless there is produced to it evidence in writing of the existence of the agreement to marry. **47-017**

(2) Subsection (1) does not apply if the court is satisfied that the agreement to marry was evidenced by—

(a) the gift of an engagement ring by one party to the agreement to the other in contemplation of their marriage, or

(b) a ceremony entered into by the parties in the presence of one or more other persons assembled for the purpose of witnessing the ceremony.

Ex parte orders

45.—(1) The court may, in any case where it considers that it is just and convenient to do so, make an occupation order or a non-molestation order even though the respondent has not been given such notice of the proceedings as would otherwise be required by rules of court. **47-018**

(2) In determining whether to exercise its powers under subsection (1), the court shall have regard to all the circumstances including—

(a) any risk of significant harm to the applicant or a relevant child, attributable to conduct of the respondent, if the order is not made immediately;
(b) whether it is likely that the applicant will be deterred or prevented from pursuing the application if an order is not made immediately; and
(c) whether there is reason to believe that the respondent is aware of the proceedings but is deliberately evading service and that the applicant or a relevant child will be seriously prejudiced by the delay involved—
(i) where the court is a magistrates' court, in effecting service of proceedings; or
(ii) in any other case, in effecting substituted service.

(3) If the court makes an order by virtue of subsection (1) it must afford the respondent an opportunity to make representations relating to the order as soon as just and convenient at a full hearing.

(4) If, at a full hearing, the court makes an occupation order ("the full order"), then—
(a) for the purposes of calculating the maximum period for which the full order may be made to have effect, the relevant section is to apply as if the period for which the full order will have effect began on the date on which the initial order first had effect; and
(b) the provisions of section 36(10) or 38(6) as to the extension of orders are to apply as if the full order and the initial order were a single order.

(5) In this section—
"full hearing" means a hearing of which notice has been given to all the parties in accordance with rules of court;
"initial order" means an occupation order made by virtue of subsection (1); and
"relevant section" means section 33(10), 35(10), 36(10), 37(5) or 38(6).

Undertakings

47-019 **46.**—(1) In any case where the court has power to make an occupation order or non-molestation order, the court may accept an undertaking from any party to the proceedings.

(2) No power of arrest may be attached to any undertaking given under subsection (1).

(3) The court shall not accept an undertaking under subsection (1) in any case where apart from this section a power of arrest would be attached to the order.

(4) An undertaking given to a court under subsection (1) is enforceable as if it were an order of the court.

(5) This section has effect without prejudice to the powers of the High Court and the county court apart from this section.

Arrest for breach of order

47-020 **47.**—(1) In this section "a relevant order" means an occupation order or a non-molestation order.

(2) If—
(a) the court makes a relevant order; and
(b) it appears to the court that the respondent has used or threatened violence against the applicant or a relevant child.

it shall attach a power of arrest to one or more provisions of the order unless satisfied that in all the circumstances of the case the applicant or child will be adequately protected without such a power of arrest.

(3) Subsection (2) does not apply in any case where the relevant order is made by virtue of section 45(1), but in such a case the court may attach a power of arrest to one or more provisions of the order if it appears to it—

(a) that the respondent has used or threatened violence against the applicant or a relevant child; and

(b) that there is a risk of significant harm to the applicant or child, attributable to conduct of the respondent, if the power of arrest is not attached to those provisions immediately.

(4) If, by virtue of subsection (3), the court attaches a power of arrest to any provisions of a relevant order, it may provide that the power of arrest is to have effect for a shorter period than the other provisions of the order.

(5) Any period specified for the purposes of subsection (4) may be extended by the court (on one or more occasions) on an application to vary or discharge the relevant order.

(6) If, by virtue of subsection (2) or (3), a power of arrest is attached to certain provisions of an order, a constable may arrest without warrant a person whom he has reasonable cause for suspecting to be in breach of any such provision.

(7) If a power of arrest is attached under subsection (2) or (3) to certain provisions of the order and the respondent is arrested under subsection (6)—

(a) he must be brought before the relevant judicial authority within the period of 24 hours beginning at the time of his arrest; and

(b) if the matter is not then disposed of forthwith, the relevant judicial authority before whom he is brought may remand him.

In reckoning for the purposes of this subsection any period of 24 hours, no account is to be taken of Christmas Day, Good Friday or any Sunday.

(8) If the court has made a relevant order but—

(a) has not attached a power of arrest under subsection (2) or (3) to any provisions of the order, or

(b) has attached that power only to certain provisions of the order,

then, if at any time the applicant considers that the respondent has failed to comply with the order, he may apply to the relevant judicial authority for the issue of a warrant for the arrest of the respondent.

(9) The relevant judicial authority shall not issue a warrant on an application under subsection (8) unless—

(a) the application is substantiated on oath; and

(b) the relevant judicial authority has reasonable grounds for believing that the respondent has failed to comply with the order.

(10) If a person is brought before a court by virtue of a warrant issued under subsection (9) and the court does not dispose of the matter forthwith, the court may remand him.

(11) Schedule 5 (which makes provision corresponding to that applying in magistrates' courts in civil cases under sections 128 and 129 of the Magistrates' Courts Act 1980), has effect in relation to the powers of the High Court and a county court to remand a person by virtue of this section.

(12) If a person remanded under this section is granted bail (whether in the High Court or a county court under Schedule 5 or in a magistrates' court under section 128 or 129 of the Magistrates' Courts Act 1980), he may be required by the relevant judicial authority to comply, before release on bail or later, with such

requirements as appear to that authority to be necessary to secure that he does not interfere with witnesses or otherwise obstruct the course of justice.

Remand for medical examination and report

47-021 **48.**—(1) If the relevant judicial authority has reason to consider that a medical report will be required, any power to remand a person under section 47(7)(b) or (10) may be exercised for the purpose of enabling a medical examination and report to be made.

(2) If such a power is so exercised, the adjournment must not be for more than 4 weeks at a time unless the relevant judicial authority remands the accused in custody.

(3) If the relevant judicial authority so remands the accused, the adjournment must not be for more than 3 weeks at a time.

(4) If there is reason to suspect that a person who has been arrested—

(a) under section 47(6), or

(b) under a warrant issued on an application made under section 47(8),

is suffering from mental illness or severe mental impairment, the relevant judicial authority has the same power to make an order under section 35 of the Mental Health Act 1983 (remand for report on accused's mental condition) as the Crown Court has under section 35 of the Act of 1983 in the case of an accused person within the meaning of that section.

Variation and discharge of orders

47-022 **49.**—(1) An occupation order or non-molestation order may be varied or discharged by the court on an application by—

(a) the respondent, or

(b) the person on whose application the order was made.

(2) In the case of a non-molestation order made by virtue of section 42(2)(b), the order may be varied or discharged by the court even though no such application has been made.

(3) If a spouse's matrimonial home rights are a charge on the estate or interest of the other spouse or of trustees for the other spouse, an order under section 33 against the other spouse may also be varied or discharged by the court on an application by any person deriving title under the other spouse or under the trustees and affected by the charge.

(4) If, by virtue of section 47(3), a power of arrest has been attached to certain provisions of an occupation order or non-molestation order, the court may vary or discharge the order under subsection (1) in so far as it confers a power of arrest (whether or not any application has been made to vary or discharge any other provision of the order).

Enforcement powers of magistrates' courts

Power of magistrates' court to suspend execution of committal order

47-023 **50.**—(1) If, under section 63(3) of the Magistrates' Courts Act 1980, a magistrates' court has power to commit a person to custody for breach of a relevant requirement, the court may by order direct that the execution of the order of committal is to be suspended for such period or on such terms and conditions as it may specify.

(2) In subsection (1) "a relevant requirement" means—

(a) an occupation order or non-molestation order;

(b) an exclusion requirement included by virtue of section 38A of the Children Act 1989 in an interim care order made under section 38 of that Act; or

(c) an exclusion requirement included by virtue of section 44A of the Children Act 1989 in an emergency protection order under section 44 of that Act.

Power of magistrates' court to order hospital admission or guardianship

51.—(1) A magistrates' court has the same power to make a hospital order or guardianship order under section 37 of the Mental Health Act 1983 or an interim hospital order under section 38 of that Act in the case of a person suffering from mental illness or severe mental impairment who could otherwise be committed to custody for breach of a relevant requirement as a magistrates' court has under those sections in the case of a person convicted of an offence punishable on summary conviction with imprisonment. **47-024**

(2) In subsection (1) "a relevant requirement" has the meaning given by section 50(2).

Interim care orders and emergency protection orders

Amendments of Children Act 1989

52. Schedule 6 makes amendments of the provisions of the Children Act 1989 relating to interim care orders and emergency protection orders. **47-025**

Transfer of tenancies

Transfer of certain tenancies

53. Schedule 7 makes provision in relation to the transfer of certain tenancies on divorce etc. or on separation of cohabitants. **47-026**

Dwelling-house subject to mortgage

Actions by mortgagees: joining connected persons as parties

55.—(1) This section applies if a mortgagee of land which consists of or includes a dwelling-house brings an action in any court for the enforcement of his security. **47-027**

(2) A connected person who is not already a party to the action is entitled to be made a party in the circumstances mentioned in subsection (3).

(3) The circumstances are that—

(a) the connected person is enabled by section 30(3) or (6) (or by section 30(3) or (6) as applied by section 35(13) or 36(13), to meet the mortgagor's liabilities under the mortgage:

(b) he has applied to the court before the action is finally disposed of in that court; and

(c) the court sees no special reason against his being made a party to the action and is satisfied—

(i) that he may be expected to make such payments or do such other things in or towards satisfaction of the mortgagor's liabilities or obligations as might affect the outcome of the proceedings; or

(ii) that the expectation of it should be considered under section 36 of the Administration of Justice Act 1970

(4) In this section "connected person" has the same meaning as in section 54.

Actions by mortgagees: service of notice on certain persons

47-028 **56.**—(1) This section applies if a mortgagee of land which consists, or substantially consists, of a dwelling-house brings an action for the enforcement of his security, and at the relevant time there is—

(a) in the case of unregistered land, a land charge of Class F registered against the person who is the estate owner at the relevant time or any person who, where the estate owner is a trustee, preceded him as trustee during the subsistence of the mortgage; or

(b) in the case of registered land, a subsisting registration of—

(i) a notice under section 31(10).

(ii) a notice under section 2(8) of the Matrimonial Homes Act 1983; or

(iii) a notice or caution under section 2(7) of the Matrimonial Homes Act 1967.

(2) If the person on whose behalf—

(a) the land charge is registered, or

(b) the notice or caution is entered,

is not a party to the action, the mortgagee must serve notice of the action on him.

(3) If—

(a) an official search has been made on behalf of the mortgagee which would disclose any land charge of Class F, notice or caution within subsection (1)(a) or (b),

(b) a certificate of the result of the search has been issued, and

(c) the action is commenced within the priority period,

the relevant time is the date of the certificate.

(4) In any other case the relevant time is the time when the action is commenced.

(5) The priority period is, for both registered and unregistered land, the period for which, in accordance with section 11(5) and (6) of the Land Charges Act 1972, a certificate on an official search operates in favour of a purchaser.

Jurisdiction and procedure etc

Jurisdiction of courts

47-029 **57.**—(1) For the purposes of this Part "the court" means the High Court, a county court or a magistrates' court.

(2) Subsection (1) is subject to the provision made by or under the following provisions of this section, to section 59 and to any express provision as to the jurisdiction of any court made by any other provision of this Part.

(3) The Lord Chancellor may by order specify proceedings under this Part which may only be commenced in—

(a) a specified level of court;

(b) a court which falls within a specified class of court; or

(c) a particular court determined in accordance with, or specified in, the order.

(4) The Lord Chancellor may by order specify circumstances in which specified proceedings under this Part may only be commenced in—

(a) a specified level of court;
(b) a court which falls within a specified class of court; or
(c) a particular court determined in accordance with, or specified in, the order.

(5) The Lord Chancellor may by order provide that in specified circumstances the whole, or any specified part of any specified proceedings under this Part is to be transferred to—

(a) a specified level of court;
(b) a court which falls within a specified class of court: or
(c) a particular court determined in accordance with, or specified in, the order.

(6) An order under subsection (5) may provide for the transfer to be made at any stage, or specified stage, or specified stage , of the proceedings and whether or not the proceedings, or any part of them, have already been transferred.

(7) An order under subsection (5) may make such provision as the Lord Chancellor thinks appropriate for excluding specified proceedings from the operation of section 38 or 39 of the Matrimonial and Family Proceedings Act 1984 (transfer of family proceedings) or any other enactment which would otherwise govern the transfer of those proceedings, or any part of them.

(8) For the purposes of subsections (3), (4) and (5), there are three levels of court—

(a) the High Court;
(b) any county court; and
(c) any magistrates' court.

(9) The Lord Chancellor may by order make provision for the principal registry of the Family Division of the High Court to be treated as if it were a county court for specified purposes of this Part, or of any provision made under this Part.

(10) Any order under subsection (9) may make such provision as the Lord Chancellor thinks expedient for the purpose of applying (with or without modifications) provisions which apply in relation to the procedure in county courts to the principal registry when it acts as if it were a county court.

(11) In this section "specified" means specified by an order under this section.

Contempt proceedings

58. The powers of the court in relation to contempt of court arising out of a person's failure to comply with an order under this Part may be exercised by the relevant judicial authority. **47-030**

Magistrates' courts

59.—(1) A magistrates' court shall not be competent to entertain any application, or make any order, involving any disputed question as to a party's entitlement to occupy any property by virtue of a beneficial estate or interest or contract or by virtue of any enactment giving him the right to remain in occupation, unless it is unnecessary to determine the question in order to deal with the application or make the order. **47-031**

(2) A magistrates' court may decline jurisdiction in any proceedings under this Part if it considers that the case can more conveniently be dealt with by another court.

(3) The powers of a magistrates' court under section 63(2) of the Magistrates' Courts Act 1980 to suspend or rescind orders shall not apply in relation to any order made under this Part.

Provision for third parties to act on behalf of victims of domestic violence

47-032 **60.**—(1) Rules of court may provide for a prescribed person, or any person in a prescribed category, ("a representative") to act on behalf of another in relation to proceedings to which this Part applies.

(2) Rules made under this section may, in particular, authorise a representative to apply for an occupation order or for a non-molestation order for which the person on whose behalf the representative is acting could have applied.

(3) Rules made under this section may prescribe—

(a) conditions to be satisfied before a representative may make an application to the court on behalf of another; and

(b) considerations to be taken into account by the court in determining whether, and if so how, to exercise any of its powers under this Part when a representative is acting on behalf of another.

(4) Any rules made under this section may be made so as to have effect for a specified period and may make consequential or transitional provision with respect to the expiry of the specified period.

(5) Any such rules may be replaced by further rules made under this section

Appeals

47-033 **61.**—(1) An appeal shall lie to the High Court against—

(a) the making by a magistrates' court of any order under this Part, or

(b) any refusal by a magistrates' court to make such an order,

but no appeal shall lie against any exercise by a magistrates' court of the power conferred by section 59(2).

(2) On an appeal under this section, the High Court may make such orders as may be necessary to give effect to its determination of the appeal.

(3) Where an order is made under subsection (2), the High Court may also make such incidental or consequential orders as appear to it to be just.

(4) Any order of the High Court made on an appeal under this section (other than one directing that an application be re-heard by a magistrates' court) shall, for the purposes—

(a) of the enforcement of the order, and

(b) of any power to vary, revive or discharge orders,

be treated as if it were an order of the magistrates' court from which the appeal was brought and not an order of the High Court.

(5) The Lord Chancellor may by order make provision as to the circumstances in which appeals may be made against decisions taken by courts on questions arising in connection with the transfer, or proposed transfer, of proceedings by virtue of any order under section 57(5).

(6) Except to the extent provided for in any order made under subsection (5), no appeal may be made against any decision of a kind mentioned in that subsection.

General

Meaning of "cohabitants", "relevant child" and "associated persons"

47-034 **62.**—(1) For the purposes of this Part—

(a) "cohabitants" are a man and a woman who, although not married to each other, are living together as husband and wife; and
(b) "former cohabitants" is to be read accordingly, but does not include cohabitants who have subsequently married each other.

(2) In this Part, "relevant child", in relation to any proceedings under this Part, means—
(a) any child who is living with or might reasonably be expected to live with either party to the proceedings;
(b) any child in relation to whom an order under the Adoption Act 1976 or the Children Act 1989 is in question in the proceedings; and
(c) any other child whose interests the court considers relevant.

(3) For the purposes of this Part, a person is associated with another person if—
(a) they are or have been married to each other;
(b) they are cohabitants or former cohabitants;
(c) they live or have lived in the same household, otherwise than merely by reason of one of them being the other's employee, tenant, lodger or boarder;
(d) they are relatives;
(e) they have agreed to marry one another (whether or not that agreement has been terminated);
(f) in relation to any child, they are both persons falling within subsection (4); or
(g) they are parties to the same family proceedings (other than proceedings under this Part).

(4) A person falls within this subsection in relation to a child if—
(a) he is a parent of the child; or
(b) he has or has had parental responsibility for the child.

(5) If a child has been adopted or has been freed for adoption by virtue of any of the enactments mentioned in section 16(1) of the Adoption Act 1976 two persons are also associated with each other for the purposes of this Part if—
(a) one is a natural parent of the child or a parent of such a natural parent; and
(b) the other is the child or any person—
(i) who has become a parent of the child by virtue of an adoption order or has applied for an adoption order, or
(ii) with whom the child has at any time been placed for adoption.

(6) A body corporate and another person are not, by virtue of subsection (3)(f) or (g), to be regarded for the purposes of this Part as associated with each other.

Interpretation of Part IV

63.—(1) In this Part— **47-035**

"adoption order" has the meaning given by section 72(1) of the Adoption Act 1976;
"associated", in relation to a person, is to be read with section 62(3) to (6);
"child" means a person under the age of eighteen years;
"cohabitant" and "former cohabitant" have the meaning given by section 62(1);
"the court" is to be read with section 57;
"development" means physical, intellectual, emotional, social or behavioural development;

"dwelling-house" includes (subject to subsection (4))—
(a) any building or part of a building which is occupied as a dwelling,
(b) any caravan, house-boat or structure which is occupied as a dwelling,
and any yard, garden, garage or outhouse belonging to it and occupied with it;
"family proceedings" means any proceedings—
(a) under the inherent jurisdiction of the High Court in relation to children; or
(b) under the enactments mentioned in subsection (2);

"harm"—
(a) in relation to a person who has reached the age of eighteen years, means ill-treatment or the impairment of health; and
(b) in relation to a child, means ill-treatment or the impairment of health or development;
"health" includes physical or mental health;
"ill-treatment" includes forms of ill-treatment which are not physical and, in relation to a child, includes sexual abuse;
"matrimonial home rights" has the meaning given by section 30;
"mortgage", "mortgagor" and "mortgagee" have the same meaning as in the Law of Property Act 1925;
"mortgage payments" includes any payments which, under the terms of the mortgage, the mortgagor is required to make to any person;
"non-molestation order" has the meaning given by section 42(1);
"occupation order" has the meaning given by section 39;
"parental responsibility" has the same meaning as in the Children Act 1989;
"relative", in relation to a person, means—
(a) the father, mother, stepfather, stepmother, son, daughter, stepson, stepdaughter, grandmother, grandfather grandson or granddaughter of that person or of that person spouse or former spouse, or
(b) the brother, sister, uncle, aunt, niece or nephew (whether of the full blood or of the half blood or by affinity) of that person or of that person's spouse or former spouse,
and includes, in relation to a person who is living or has lived with another person as husband and wife, any person who would fall within paragraph (a) or (b) if the parties were married to each other;
"relevant child", in relation to any proceedings under this Part, has the meaning given by section 62(2);
"the relevant judicial authority", in relation to any order under this Part, means—
(a) where the order was made by the High Court, a judge of that court;
(b) where the order was made by a county court, a judge or district judge of that or any other county court; or
(c) where the order was made by a magistrates' court, any magistrates' court.

(2) The enactments referred to in the definition of "family proceedings" are—
(a) Part II;

(b) this Part;
(c) the Matrimonial Causes Act 1973;
(d) the Adoption Act 1976,
(e) the Domestic Proceedings and Magistrates' Courts Act 1978;
(f) Part III of the Matrimonial and Family Proceedings Act 1984;
(g) Parts I, II and IV of the Children Act 1989;
(h) section 30 of the Human Fertilisation and Embryology Act 1990.

(3) Where the question of whether harm suffered by a child is significant turns on the child's health or development, his health or development shall be compared with that which could reasonably be expected of a similar child.

(4) For the purposes of sections 31, 32, 53 and 54 and such other provisions of this Part (if any) as may be prescribed, this Part is to have effect as if paragraph (b) of the definition of "dwelling-house" were omitted.

(5) It is hereby declared that this Part applies as between the parties to a marriage even though either of them is, or has at any time during the marriage been, married to more than one person.

PART V

SUPPLEMENTAL

Provision for separate representation for children

64.—(1) The Lord Chancellor may by regulations provide for the separate representation of children in proceedings in England and Wales which relate to any matter in respect of which a question has arisen, or may arise, under— **47-036**

(a) Part II;
(b) Part IV;
(c) the 1973 Act; or
(d) the Domestic Proceedings and Magistrates' Courts Act 1978.

(2) The regulations may provide for such representation only in specified circumstances.

SCHEDULES

Section 32 Schedule 4

PROVISIONS SUPPLEMENTARY TO SECTIONS 30 AND 31

Interpretation

1.— (1) In this Schedule— **47-037**

(a) any reference to a solicitor includes a reference to a licensed conveyancer or a recognised body, and
(b) any reference to a person's solicitor includes a reference to a licensed conveyancer or recognised body acting for that person.

(2) In sub-paragraph (1)—

"licensed conveyancer" has the meaning given by section 11(2) of the Administration of Justice Act 1985;

"recognised body" means a body corporate for the time being recognised under section 9(incorporated practices) or section 32 (provision of conveyancing by recognised bodies) of that Act.

Restriction on registration where spouse entitled to more than one charge

47-038 2. Where one spouse is entitled by virtue of section 31 to a registrable charge in respect of each of two or more dwelling-houses, only one of the charges to which that spouse is so entitled shall be registered under section 31(10) or under section 2 of the Land Charges Act 1972 at any one time, and if any of those charges is registered under either of those provisions the Chief Land Registrar, on being satisfied that any other of them is so registered, shall cancel the registration of the charge first registered.

Contract for sale of house affected by registered charge to include term requiring cancellation of registration before completion

47-039 3.—(1) Where one spouse is entitled by virtue of section 31 to a charge on an estate in a dwelling-house and the charge is registered under section 31(10) or section 2 of the Land Charges Act 1972 it shall be a term of any contract for the sale of that estate whereby the vendor agrees to give vacant possession of the dwelling-house on completion of the contract that the vendor will before such completion procure the cancellation of the registration of the charge at his expense.

(2) Sub-paragraph (1) shall not apply to any such contract made by a vendor who is entitled to sell the estate in the dwelling-house freed from any such charge.

(3) If, on the completion of such a contract as is referred to in sub-paragraph (1) there is delivered to the purchaser or his solicitor an application by the spouse entitled to the charge for the cancellation of the registration of that charge, the term of the contract for which sub-paragraph (1) provides shall be deemed to have been performed.

(4) This paragraph applies only if and so far as a contrary intention is not expressed in the contract.

(5) This paragraph shall apply to a contract for exchange as it applies to a contract for sale.

(6) This paragraph shall, with the necessary modifications, apply to a contract for the grant of a lease or underlease of a dwelling-house as it applies to a contract for the sale of an estate in a dwelling-house.

Cancellation of registration after termination of marriage, etc

47-040 4.—(1) Where a spouse's matrimonial home rights are a charge on an estate in the dwelling-house and the charge is registered under section 31(10) or under section 2 of the Land Charges Act 1972 the Chief Land Registrar shall, subject to sub-paragraph (2), cancel the registration of the charge if he is satisfied—

(a) by the production of a certificate or other sufficient evidence, that either spouse is dead, or

(b) by the production of an official copy of a decree or order of a court, that the marriage in question has been terminated otherwise than by death, or

(c) by the production of an order of the court, that the spouse's matrimonial home rights constituting the charge have been terminated by the order.

(2) Where—

(a) the marriage in question has been terminated by the death of the spouse entitled to an estate in the dwelling-house or otherwise than by death, and

(b) an order affecting the charge of the spouse not so entitled had been made under section 33(5).

then if, after the making of the order, registration of the charge was renewed or the charge registered in pursuance of sub-paragraph (3), the Chief Land Registrar shall not cancel the registration of the charge in accordance with sub-paragraph (1) unless he is also satisfied that the order has ceased to have effect.

(3) Where such an order has been made, then, for the purposes of sub-paragraph (2), the spouse entitled to the charge affected by the order may—

(a) if before the date of the order the charge was registered under section 31(10) or under section 2 of the Land Charges Act 1972, renew the registration of the charge, and

(b) if before the said date the charge was not so registered, register the charge under section 31(10) or under section 2 of the Land Charges Act 1972.

(4) Renewal of the registration of a charge in pursuance of sub-paragraph (3) shall be effected in such manner as may be prescribed, and an application for such renewal or for registration of a charge in pursuance of that sub-paragraph shall contain such particulars of any order affecting the charge made under section 33(5) as may be prescribed.

(5) The renewal in pursuance of sub-paragraph (3) of the registration of a charge shall not affect the priority of the charge.

(6) In this paragraph "prescribed" means prescribed by rules made under section 16 of the Land Charges Act 1972 or section 144 of the Land Registration Act 1925, as the circumstances of the case required.

Release of matrimonial home rights

5.—(1) A spouse entitled to matrimonial home rights may by a release in writing release those rights or release them as respects part only of the dwelling-house affected by them. **47-041**

(2) Where a contract is made for the sale of an estate or interest in a dwelling-house, or for the grant of a lease or underlease of a dwelling-house, being (in either case) a dwelling-house affected by a charge registered under section 31(10) or under section 2 of the Land Charges Act 1972, then, without prejudice to sub-paragraph (1), the matrimonial home rights constituting the charge shall be deemed to have been released on the happening of whichever of the following events first occurs—

(a) the delivery to the purchaser or lessee, as the case may be, or his solicitor on completion of the contract of an application by the spouse entitled to the charge for the cancellation of the registration of the charge; or

(b) the lodging of such an application at Her Majesty's Land Registry.

Postponement of priority of charge

6. A spouse entitled by virtue of section 31 to a charge on an estate or interest may agree in writing that any other charge on, or interest in, that estate or interest shall rank in priority to the charge to which that spouse is so entitled. **47-042**

Section 47(11) Schedule 5

Powers of High Court and County Court to Remand

Interpretation

1. In this Schedule"the court" means the High Court or a county court and includes— **47-043**

(a) in relation to the High Court, a judge of that court, and

(b) in relation to a county court, a judge or district judge of that court.

Remand in custody or on bail

2.—(1) Where a court has power to remand a person under section 47, the court may— **47-044**

(a) remand him in custody, that is to say, commit him to custody to be brought before the court at the end of the period of remand or at such earlier time as the court may require, or

(b) remand him on bail—

(i) by taking from him a recognizance (with or without sureties) conditioned as provided in sub-paragraph (3) or

(ii) by fixing the amount of the recognizances with a view to their being taken subsequently in accordance with paragraph 4 and in the meantime committing the person to custody in accordance with paragraph (a),

(2) Where a person is brought before the court after remand, the court may further remand him.

(3) Where a person is remanded on bail under sub-paragraph (1), the court may direct that his recognizance be conditioned for his appearance—

(a) before that court at the end of the period of remand, or

(b) at every time and place to which during the course of the proceedings the hearing may from time to time be adjourned.

(4) Where a recognizance is conditioned for a person's appearance in accordance with sub-paragraph (1)(b), the fixing of any time for him next to appear shall be deemed to be a remand; but nothing in this sub-paragraph or sub-paragraph (3) shall deprive the court of power at any subsequent hearing to remand him afresh.

(5) Subject to paragraph 3 the court shall not remand a person under this paragraph for a period exceeding 8 clear days, except that—

(a) if the court remands him on bail, it may remand him for a longer period if he and the other party consent, and

(b) if the court adjourns a case under section 48(1), the court may remand him for the period of the adjournment.

(6) Where the court has power under this paragraph to remand a person in custody it may, if the remand is for a period not exceeding 3 clear days, commit him to the custody of a constable.

Further remand

47-045 **3.**—(1) If the court is satisfied that any person who has been remanded under paragraph 2 is unable by reason of illness or accident to appear or be brought before the court at the expiration of the period for which he was remanded, the court may, in his absence, remand him for a further time; and paragraph 2(5) shall not apply.

(2) Notwithstanding anything in paragraph 2(1) the power of the court under sub-paragraph (1) to remand a person on bail for a further time may be exercised by enlarging his recognizance and those of any sureties for him to a later time.

(3) Where a person remanded on bail under paragraph 2 is bound to appear before the court at any time and the court has no power to remand him under sub-paragraph (1), the court may in his absence enlarge his recognizance and those of any sureties for him to a later time; and the enlargement of his recognizance shall be deemed to be a further remand.

Postponement of taking of recognizance

47-046 **4.** Where under paragraph 2(1)(b)(ii) the court fixes the amount in which the principal and his sureties, if any, are to be bound, the recognizance may thereafter be taken by such person as may be prescribed by rules of court, and the same consequences shall follow as if it had been entered into before the court.

Section 53. Schedule 7

Transfer of Certain Tenancies on Divorce Etc, or on Separation of Cohabitants

General

Interpretation

47-047 **1.** In this Schedule—

"cohabitant" except in paragraph 3 includes (where the context requires) former cohabitant;

"the court" does not include a magistrates' court,

"landlord" includes—

(a) any person from time to time deriving title under the original landlord; and

(b) in relation to any dwelling-house, any person other than the tenant who is, or (but for Part VII of the Rent Act 1977 or Part II of the Rent (Agriculture) Act 1976 would be, entitled to possession of the dwelling-house;

"Part II order" means an order under Part II of this Schedule;

"a relevant tenancy" means—

(a) a protected tenancy or statutory tenancy within the meaning of the Rent Act 1977;

(b) a statutory tenancy within the meaning of the Rent (Agriculture) Act 1976;

(c) a secure tenancy within the meaning of section 79 of the Housing Act 1985; [...][1]

(d) an assured tenancy or assured agricultural occupancy within the meaning of Part I of the Housing Act 1988; [or][2]

[(e) an introductory tenancy within the meaning of Chapter I of Part V of the Housing Act 1996;][3]

"spouse", except in paragraph 2, includes (where the context requires) former spouse; and "tenancy" includes sub-tenancy.

Cases in which the court may make an order

47-048 **2.**—(1) This paragraph applies if one spouse is entitled, either in his own right or jointly with the other spouse, to occupy a dwelling-house by virtue of a relevant tenancy.

(2) At any time when it has power to make a property adjustment order under section 23A (divorce or separation) or 24 (nullity) of the Matrimonial Causes Act 1973 with respect to the marriage, the court may make a Part II order.

---

[1] Word repealed by SI 1997/74 Sch 1 para 10 (b) (i)

[2] Added by SI 1997/74 Sch 1 para 10 (b) (i)

[3] Added by SI 1997/74 Sch 1 para 10 (b) (i)

3.—(1) This paragraph applies if one cohabitant is entitled, either in his own right or jointly with the other cohabitant, to occupy a dwelling-house by virtue of a relevant tenancy. **47-049**

(2) If the cohabitants cease to live together as husband and wife, the court may make a Part II order.

4. The court shall not make a Part II order unless the dwelling-house is or was— **47-050**

(a) in the case of spouses, a matrimonial home; or
(b) in the case of cohabitants, a home in which they lived together as husband and wife.

Matters to which the court must have regard

5. In determining whether to exercise its powers under Part II of this Schedule and, if so, in what manner, the court shall have regard to all the circumstances of the case including— **47-051**

(a) the circumstances in which the tenancy was granted to either or both of the spouses or cohabitants or, as the case requires, the circumstances in which either or both of them became tenant under the tenancy;
(b) the matters mentioned in section 33(6)(a), (b) and (c) and, where the parties are cohabitants and only one of them is entitled to occupy the dwelling-house by virtue of the relevant tenancy, the further matters mentioned in section 36(6)(e), (f), (g) and (h); and
(c) the suitability of the parties as tenants.

ORDERS THAT MAY BE MADE

References to entitlement to occupy

6. References in this Part of this Schedule to a spouse or a cohabitant being entitled to occupy a dwelling-house by virtue of a relevant tenancy apply whether that entitlement is in his own right or jointly with the other spouse or cohabitant. **47-052**

Protected, secure or assured tenancy or assured agricultural occupancy

7.—(1) If a spouse or cohabitant is entitled to occupy the dwelling-house by virtue of a protected tenancy within the meaning of the Rent Act 1977, a secure tenancy within the meaning of the Housing Act 1985 [, an assured tenancy][1] or assured agricultural occupancy within the meaning of Part I of the Housing Act 1988 [or an introductory tenancy within the meaning of Chapter I of Part V of the Housing Act 1996][2], the court may by order direct that, as from such date as may be specified in the order, there shall, by virtue of the order and without further assurance, be transferred to, and vested in, the other spouse or cohabitant— **47-053**

(a) the estate or interest which the spouse or cohabitant so entitled had in the dwelling-house immediately before that date by virtue of the lease or agreement creating the tenancy and any assignment of that lease or agreement, with all rights, privileges and appurtenances attaching to that estate or interest but subject to all covenants, obligations, liabilities and incumbrances to which it is subject; and
(b) where the spouse or cohabitant so entitled is an assignee of such lease or agreement, the liability of that spouse or cohabitant under any covenant of indemnity by the assignee express or implied in the assignment of the lease or agreement to that spouse or cohabitant.

(2) If an order is made under this paragraph, any liability or obligation to which the spouse or cohabitant so entitled is subject under any covenant having reference to the dwelling-house in the lease or agreement, being a liability or obligation falling due to be discharged or performed on or after the date so specified, shall not be enforceable against that spouse or cohabitant.

(3) If the spouse so entitled is a successor within the meaning of Part IV of the Housing Act 1985, his former spouse or former cohabitant (or, if a separation order is in force, his spouse) shall be deemed also to be a successor within the meaning of that Part.

[(3A) If the Spouse or cohabitant so entitled is a successor within the meaning of section 132 of the Housing Act 1996, his former spouse or former cohabitant (or, if a separation order is in force, his spouse) shall be deemed also to be a successor within the meaning of that section.][3]

(4) If the spouse or cohabitant so entitled is for the purpose of section 17 of the Housing Act 1988 a successor in relation to the tenancy or occupancy, his former spouse or former cohabitant (or, if a separation order is in force, his spouse) is to be deemed to be successor in relation to the tenancy or occupancy for the purposes of that section.

[1] Words substituted by SI 1997/74 Sch 1 para 10 (b) (ii)
[2] Words inserted by SI 1997/74 Sch 1 para 10 (b) (ii)
[3] Added by SI 1997/74 Sch 1 para 10 (b) (iii)

(5) If the transfer under sub-paragraph (1) is of an assured agricultural occupancy, then, for the purposes of Chapter III of Part I of the Housing Act 1988—

(a) the agricultural worker condition is fulfilled with respect to the dwelling-house while the spouse or cohabitant to whom the assured agricultural occupancy is transferred continues to be the occupier under that occupancy, and

(b) that condition is to be treated as so fulfilled by virtue of the same paragraph of Schedule 3 to the Housing Act 1988 as was applicable before the transfer.

(6) In this paragraph, references to a separation order being in force include references to there being a judicial separation in force.

Statutory tenancy within the meaning of the Rent Act 1977

47-054 **8.**—(1) This paragraph applies if the spouse or cohabitant is entitled to occupy the dwelling-house by virtue of a statutory tenancy within the meaning of the Rent Act 1977.

(2) The court may by order direct that, as from the date specified in the order—

(a) that spouse or cohabitant is to cease to be entitled to occupy the dwelling-house; and

(b) the other spouse or cohabitant is to be deemed to be the tenant or, as the case may be, the sole tenant under that statutory tenancy.

(3) The question whether the provisions of paragraphs 1 to 3, or (as the case may be) paragraphs 5 to 7 of Schedule 1 to the Rent Act 1977, as to the succession by the surviving spouse of a deceased tenant, or by a member of the deceased tenant's family, to the right to retain possession are capable of having effect in the event of the death of the person deemed by an order under this paragraph to be the tenant or sole tenant under the statutory tenancy is to be determined according as those provisions have or have not already had effect in relation to the statutory tenancy.

Statutory tenancy within the meaning of the Rent (Agriculture) Act 1976

47-055 **9.**—(1) This paragraph applies if the spouse or cohabitant is entitled to occupy the dwelling-house by virtue of a statutory tenancy within the meaning of the Rent (Agriculture) Act 1976.

(2) The court may by order direct that, as from such date as may be specified in the order—

(a) that spouse or cohabitant is to cease to be entitled to occupy the dwelling-house; and

(b) the other spouse or cohabitant is to be deemed to be the tenant or, as the case may be, the sole tenant under that statutory tenancy.

(3) A spouse or cohabitant who is deemed under this paragraph to be the tenant under a statutory tenancy is (within the meaning of that Act) a statutory tenant in his own right, or a statutory tenant by succession, according as the other spouse or cohabitant was a statutory tenant in his own right or a statutory tenant by succession.

Supplementary Provisions

Compensation

47-056 **10.**—(1) If the court makes a Part II order, it may by the order direct the making of a payment by the spouse or cohabitant to whom the tenancy is transferred ("the transferee") to the other spouse or cohabitant ("the transferor").

(2) Without prejudice to that, the court may, on making an order by virtue of sub-paragraph (1) for the payment of a sum—

(a) direct that payment of that sum or any part of it is to be deferred until a specified date or until the occurrence of a specified event, or

(b) direct that that sum or any part of it is to be paid by instalments.

(3) Where an order has been made by virtue of sub-paragraph (1) the court may, on the application of the transferee or the transferor—

(a) exercise its powers under sub-paragraph (2), or

(b) vary any direction previously given under that sub-paragraph,

at any time before the sum whose payment is required by the order is paid in full.

(4) In deciding whether to exercise its powers under this paragraph and, if so, in what manner, the court shall have regard to all the circumstances including—

(a) the financial loss that would otherwise be suffered by the transferor as a result of the order;

(b) the financial needs and financial resources of the parties; and

(c) the financial obligations which the parties have, or are likely to have in the foreseeable future, including financial obligations to each other and to any relevant child.

(5) The court shall not give any direction under sub-paragraph (2) unless it appears to it that immediate payment of the sum required by the order would cause the transferee financial hardship

which is greater than any financial hardship that would be caused to the transferor if the direction were given.

Liabilities and obligations in respect of the dwelling-house

11.— (1) If the court makes a Part II order, it may by the order direct that both spouses or cohabitants are to be jointly and severally liable to discharge or perform any or all of the liabilities and obligations in respect of the dwelling-house (whether arising under the tenancy or otherwise) which— **47-057**

(a) have at the date of the order fallen due to be discharged or performed by one only of them; or

(b) but for the direction, would before the date specified as the date on which the order is to take effect fall due to be discharged or performed by one only of them.

(2) If the court gives such a direction, it may further direct that either spouse or cohabitant is to be liable to indemnify the other in whole or in part against any payment made or expenses incurred by the other in discharging or performing any such liability or obligation.

Date when order made between spouses is to take effect

12.— (1) In the case of a decree of nullity of marriage, the date specified in a Part II order as the date on which the order is to take effect must not be earlier than the date on which the decree is made absolute. **47-058**

(2) In the case of divorce proceedings or separation proceedings, the date specified in a Part II order as the date on which the order is to take effect is to be determined as if the court were making a property adjustment order under section 23A of the Matrimonial Causes Act 1973 (regard being had to the restrictions imposed by section 23B of that Act).

Remarriage of either spouse

13.— (1) If after the making of a divorce order or the grant of a decree annulling a marriage either spouse remarries, that spouse is not entitled to apply, by reference to the making of that order or the grant of that decree, for a Part II order. **47-059**

(2) For the avoidance of doubt it is hereby declared that the reference in sub-paragraph (1) to remarriage includes a reference to a marriage which is by law void or voidable.

Rules of court

14.— (1) Rules of court shall be made requiring the court, before it makes an order under this Schedule to give the landlord of the dwelling-house to which the order will relate an opportunity of being heard. **47-060**

(2) Rules of court may provide that an application for a Part II order by reference to an order or decree may not, without the leave of the court by which that order was made or decree was granted, be made after the expiration of such period from the order or grant as may be prescribed by the rules.

Saving for other provisions of Act

15.— (1) If a spouse is entitled to occupy a dwelling-house by virtue of a tenancy, this Schedule does not affect the operation of section 30 and 31 in relation to the other spouse's matrimonial home rights. **47-061**

(2) If a spouse or cohabitant is entitled to occupy a dwelling-house by virtue of a tenancy, the court's powers to make orders under this Schedule are additional to those conferred by sections 33, 35 and 36.

Housing Act 1996

CHAPTER 52

PART V

CONDUCT OF TENANTS

CHAPTER I

INTRODUCTORY TENANCIES

Succession on death of tenant

Persons qualified to succeed tenant

48-001 **131.** A person is qualified to succeed the tenant under an introductory tenancy if he occupies the dwelling-house as his only or principal home at the time of the tenant's death and either—

(a) he is the tenant's spouse, or

(b) he is another member of the tenant's family and has resided with the tenant throughout the period of twelve months ending with the tenant's death;

unless, in either case, the tenant was himself a successor, as defined in section 132.

Cases where the tenant is a successor

48-002 **132.**—(1) The tenant is himself a successor if—

(a) the tenancy vested in him by virtue of section 133 (succession to introductory tenancy),

(b) he was a joint tenant and has become the sole tenant,

(c) he became the tenant on the tenancy being assigned to him (but subject to subsections (2) and (3)), or

(d) he became the tenant on the tenancy being vested in him on the death of the previous tenant.

(2) A tenant to whom the tenancy was assigned in pursuance of an order under section 24 of the Matrimonial Causes Act 1973 (property adjustment orders in connection with matrimonial proceedings) or section 17(1) of the Matrimonial and Family Proceedings Act 1984 (property adjustment orders after overseas divorce, &c.) is a successor only if the other party to the marriage was a successor.

(3) Where within six months of the coming to an end of an introductory tenancy ("the former tenancy") the tenant becomes a tenant under another introductory tenancy, and—

(a) the tenant was a successor in relation to the former tenancy, and

(b) under the other tenancy either the dwelling-house or the landlord, or both, are the same as under the former tenancy,

the tenant is also a successor in relation to the other tenancy unless the agreement creating that tenancy otherwise provides.

Succession to introductory tenancy

133.—(1) This section applies where a tenant under an introductory tenancy dies. **48-003**

(2) Where there is a person qualified to succeed the tenant, the tenancy vests by virtue of this section in that person, or if there is more than one such person in the one to be preferred in accordance with the following rules—

(a) the tenant's spouse is to be preferred to another member of the tenant's family;

(b) of two or more other members of the tenant's family such of them is to be preferred as may be agreed between them or as may, where there is no such agreement, be selected by the landlord.

(3) Where there is no person qualified to succeed the tenant, the tenancy ceases to be an introductory tenancy—

(a) when it is vested or otherwise disposed of in the course of the administration of the tenant's estate, unless the vesting or other disposal is in pursuance of an order made under—

(i) section 24 of the Matrimonial Causes Act 1973 (property adjustment orders made in connection with matrimonial proceedings),

(ii) section 17(1) of the Matrimonial and Family Proceedings Act 1984 (property adjustment orders after overseas divorce, &c.), or

(iii) Paragraph 1 of Schedule 1 to the Children Act 1989 (orders for financial relief against parents); or

(b) when it is known that when the tenancy is so vested or disposed of it will not be in pursuance of such an order.

Assignment

Assignment in general prohibited

134.—(1) An introductory tenancy is not capable of being assigned except in the cases mentioned in subsection (2). **48-004**

(2) The exceptions are—

(a) an assignment in pursuance of an order made under—

(i) section 24 of the Matrimonial Causes Act 1973 (property adjustment orders in connection with matrimonial proceedings),

(ii) section 17(1) of the Matrimonial and Family Proceedings Act 1984 (property adjustment orders after overseas divorce, &c.), or

(iii) paragraph 1 of Schedule 1 to the Children Act 1989 (orders for financial relief against parents);

(b) an assignment to a person who would be qualified to succeed the tenant if the tenant died immediately before the assignment.

(3) Subsection (1) also applies to a tenancy which is not an introductory tenancy but would be if the tenant, or where the tenancy is a joint tenancy, at least one of the tenants, were occupying or continuing to occupy the dwelling-house as his only or principal home.

Supplementary

Members of a person's family: Chapter I

140.—(1) A person is a member of another's family within the meaning of this Chapter if— **48-005**

(a) he is the spouse of that person, or he and that person live together as husband and wife, or

(b) he is that person's parent, grandparent, child, grandchild, brother, sister, uncle, aunt, nephew or niece.

(2) For the purpose of subsection (1)(b)—

(a) a relationship by marriage shall be treated as a relationship by blood,

(b) a relationship of the half-blood shall be treated as a relationship of the whole blood, and

(c) the stepchild of a person shall be treated as his child.

CHAPTER II

REPOSSESSION, &C.: SECURE AND ASSURED TENANCIES

PART VII

HOMELESSNESS

Homelessness and threatened homelessness

Homelessness and threatened homelessness

48-006 **175.**—(1) A person is homeless if he has no accommodation available for his occupation, in the United Kingdom or elsewhere, which he—

(a) is entitled to occupy by virtue of an interest in it or by virtue of an order of a court,

(b) has an express or implied licence to occupy, or

(c) occupies as a residence by virtue of any enactment or rule of law giving him the right to remain in occupation or restricting the right of another person to recover possession.

(2) A person is also homeless if he has accommodation but—

(a) he cannot secure entry to it, or

(b) it consists of a moveable structure, vehicle or vessel designed or adapted for human habitation and there is no place where he is entitled or permitted both to place it and to reside in it.

(3) A person shall not be treated as having accommodation unless it is accommodation which it would be reasonable for him to continue to occupy.

(4) A person is threatened with homelessness if it is likely that he will become homeless within 28 days.

Meaning of accommodation available for occupation

48-007 **176.** Accommodation shall be regarded as available for a person's occupation only if it is available for occupation by him together with—

(a) any other person who normally resides with him as a member of his family, or

(b) any other person who might reasonably be expected to reside with him.

References in this Part to securing that accommodation is available for a person's occupation shall be construed accordingly.

Whether it is reasonable to continue to occupy accommodation

177.—(1) It is not reasonable for a person to continue to occupy accommodation if it is probable that this will lead to domestic violence [or other violence][1] against him, or against— **48-008**

(a) a person who normally resides with him as a member of his family, or

(b) any other person who might reasonably be expected to reside with him.

[(1A) For this purpose "violence" means—

(a) violence from another person; or

(b) threats of violence from another person which are likely to be carried out;

and violence is "domestic violence" if it is from a person who is associated with the victim.][2]

(2) In determining whether it would be, or would have been, reasonable for a person to continue to occupy accommodation, regard may be had to the general circumstances prevailing in relation to housing in the district of the local housing authority to whom he has applied for accommodation or for assistance in obtaining accommodation.

(3) The Secretary of State may by order specify—

(a) other circumstances in which it is to be regarded as reasonable or not reasonable for a person to continue to occupy accommodation, and

(b) other matters to be taken into account or disregarded in determining whether it would be, or would have been, reasonable for a person to continue to occupy accommodation.

Meaning of associated person

178.—(1) For the purposes of this Part, a person is associated with another person if— **48-009**

(a) they are or have been married to each other;

(b) they are cohabitants or former cohabitants;

(c) they live or have lived in the same household;

(d) they are relatives;

(e) they have agreed to marry one another (whether or not that agreement has been terminated);

(f) in relation to a child, each of them is a parent of the child or has, or has had, parental responsibility for the child.

(2) If a child has been adopted or has been freed for adoption by virtue of any of the enactments mentioned in section 16(1) of the Adoption Act 1976, two persons are also associated with each other for the purposes of this Part if—

(a) one is a natural parent of the child or a parent of such a natural parent, and

(b) the other is the child or a person—

(i) who has become a parent of the child by virtue of an adoption order or who has applied for an adoption order, or

(ii) with whom the child has at any time been placed for adoption.

(3) In this section—

"adoption order" has the meaning given by section 72(1) of the Adoption Act 1976;

"child" means a person under the age of 18 years;

[1] Words inserted by Homelessness Act 2002 c.7 s 10

[2] Inserted by Homelessness Act 2002 c.7 s 10

"cohabitants" means a man and a woman who, although not married to each other, are living together as husband and wife, and "former cohabitants" shall be construed accordingly;

"parental responsibility" has the same meaning as in the Children Act 1989; and

"relative", in relation to a person, means—

(a) the father, mother, stepfather, stepmother, son, daughter, stepson, stepdaughter, grandmother, grandfather, grandson or granddaughter of that person or of that person's spouse or former spouse, or

(b) the brother, sister, uncle, aunt, niece or nephew (whether of the full blood or of the half blood or by affinity) of that person or of that person's spouse or former spouse,

and includes, in relation to a person who is living or has lived with another person as husband and wife, a person who would fall within paragraph (a) or (b) if the parties were married to each other.

Interim duty to accommodate

Interim duty to accommodate in case of apparent priority need

48-010 **188.**—(1) If the local housing authority have reason to believe that an applicant may be homeless, eligible for assistance and have a priority need, they shall secure that accommodation is available for his occupation pending a decision as to the duty (if any) owed to him under the following provisions of this Part.

(2) The duty under this section arises irrespective of any possibility of the referral of the applicant's case to another local housing authority (see sections 198 to 200).

(3) The duty ceases when the authority's decision is notified to the applicant, even if the applicant requests a review of the decision (see section 202).

The authority may [secure][1] that accommodation is available for the applicant's occupation pending a decision on a review.

Priority need for accommodation

48-011 **189.**—(1) The following have a priority need for accommodation—

(a) a pregnant woman or a person with whom she resides or might reasonably be expected to reside;

(b) a person with whom dependent children reside or might reasonably be expected to reside;

(c) a person who is vulnerable as a result of old age, mental illness or handicap or physical disability or other special reason, or with whom such a person resides or might reasonably be expected to reside;

(d) a person who is homeless or threatened with homelessness as a result of an emergency such as flood, fire or other disaster.

(2) The Secretary of State may by order—

(a) specify further descriptions of persons as having a priority need for accommodation, and

(b) amend or repeal any part of subsection (1).

[1] Words substituted by Homelessness Act 2002 c.7 Sch 1 para 8

(3) Before making such an order the Secretary of State shall consult such associations representing relevant authorities, and such other persons, as he considers appropriate.

(4) No such order shall be made unless a draft of it has been approved by resolution of each House of Parliament.

Duties to persons found to be homeless or threatened with homelessness

Duties to persons becoming homeless intentionally

190.—(1) This section applies where the local housing authority are satisfied that an applicant is homeless and is eligible for assistance but are also satisfied that he became homeless intentionally. **48-012**

(2) If the authority are satisfied that the applicant has a priority need, they shall—

(a) secure that accommodation is available for his occupation for such period as they consider will give him a reasonable opportunity of securing accommodation for his occupation, and

(b) provide him with [(or secure that he is provided with) advice and assistance][1] in any attempts he may make to secure that accommodation becomes available for his occupation.

(3) If they are not satisfied that he has a priority need, they shall provide him with [(or secure that he is provided with) advice and assistance][2] in any attempts he may make to secure that accommodation becomes available for his occupation.

[(4) The applicant's housing needs shall be assessed before advice and assistance is provided under subsection (2)(b) or (3).

(5) The advice and assistance provided under subsection (2)(b) or (3) must include information about the likely availability in the authority's district of types of accommodation appropriate to the applicant's housing needs (including, in particular, the location and sources of such types of accommodation).][3]

Becoming homeless intentionally

191.—(1) A person becomes homeless intentionally if he deliberately does or fails to do anything in consequence of which he ceases to occupy accommodation which is available for his occupation and which it would have been reasonable for him to continue to occupy. **48-013**

(2) For the purposes of subsection (1) an act or omission in good faith on the part of a person who was unaware of any relevant fact shall not be treated as deliberate.

(3) A person shall be treated as becoming homeless intentionally if—

(a) he enters into an arrangement under which he is required to cease to occupy accommodation which it would have been reasonable for him to continue to occupy, and

(b) the purpose of the arrangement is to enable him to become entitled to assistance under this Part,

and there is no other good reason why he is homeless.

(4) [...][4]

[1] Words substituted by Homelessness Act 2002 c.7 Sch 1 para 9
[2] Words substituted by Homelessness Act 2002 c.7 Sch 1 para 9
[3] Added by Homelessness Act 2002 c.7 Sch 1 para 10
[4] Repealed by Homelessness Act 2002 c.7 Sch 2 para 1

Duty to persons not in priority need who are not homeless intentionally

48-014 **192.**—(1) This section applies where the local housing authority—

(a) are satisfied that an applicant is homeless and eligible for assistance, and

(b) are not satisfied that he became homeless intentionally,

but are not satisfied that he has a priority need.

(2) The authority shall provide the applicant with [(or secure that he is provided with) advice and assistance][1] in any attempts he may make to secure that accommodation becomes available for his occupation.

[(3) The authority may secure that accommodation is available for occupation by the applicant.][2]

[(4) The applicant's housing needs shall be assessed before advice and assistance is provided under subsection (2).

(5) The advice and assistance provided under subsection (2) must include information about the likely availability in the authority's district of types of accommodation appropriate to the applicant's housing needs (including, in particular, the location and sources of such types of accommodation).][3]

Duty to persons with priority need who are not homeless intentionally

48-015 **193.**—(1) This section applies where the local housing authority are satisfied that an applicant is homeless, eligible for assistance and has a priority need, and are not satisfied that he became homeless intentionally.[...][4]

(2) Unless the authority refer the application to another local housing authority (see section 198), they shall secure that accommodation is available for occupation by the applicant.

[(3) The authority are subject to the duty under this section until it ceases by virtue of any of the following provisions of this section.][5]

(5) The local housing authority shall cease to be subject to the duty under this section if the applicant, having been informed by the authority of the possible consequence of refusal [and of his right to request a review of the suitability of the accommodation][6], refuses an offer of accommodation which the authority are satisfied is suitable for him and the authority notify him that they regard themselves as having discharged their duty under this section.

(6) The local housing authority shall cease to be subject to the duty under this section if the applicant—

(a) ceases to be eligible for assistance,

(b) becomes homeless intentionally from the accommodation made available for his occupation,

(c) accepts an offer of accommodation under Part VI (allocation of housing), or

[(cc) accepts an offer of an assured tenancy (other than an assured shorthold tenancy) from a private landlord,][7]

(d) otherwise voluntarily ceases to occupy as his only or principal home the accommodation made available for his occupation.

[1] Words substituted by Homelessness Act 2002 c.7 Sch 1 para 11
[2] Inserted by Homelessness Act 2002 c.7 s 5 (1)
[3] Added by Homelessness Act 2002 c.7 Sch 1 para 12
[4] Words repealed in relation to Wales by Homelessness Act 2002 c.7 Sch 2 para 1
[5] S 193 (3) substituted for s 193 (3)-(4) in relation to Wales by Homelessness Act 2002 c.7 s 6 (1)
[6] Words inserted by Homelessness Act 2002 c.7 s 8 (1)
[7] Inserted by Homelessness Act 2002 c.7 s 7

[(7) The local housing authority shall also cease to be subject to the duty under this section if the applicant, having been informed of the possible consequence of refusal and of his right to request a review of the suitability of the accommodation, refuses a final offer of accommodation under Part 6.

(7A) An offer of accommodation under Part 6 is a final offer for the purposes of subsection (7) if it is made in writing and states that it is a final offer for the purposes of subsection (7).

(7B) The authority shall also cease to be subject to the duty under this section if the applicant accepts a qualifying offer of an assured shorthold tenancy which is made by a private landlord in relation to any accommodation which is, or may become, available for the applicant's occupation.

(7C) The applicant is free to reject a qualifying offer without affecting the duty owed to him under this section by the authority.

(7D) For the purposes of subsection (7B) an offer of an assured shorthold tenancy is a qualifying offer if—

- (a) it is made, with the approval of the authority, in pursuance of arrangements made by the authority with the landlord with a view to bringing the authority's duty under this section to an end;
- (b) the tenancy being offered is a fixed term tenancy (within the meaning of Part 1 of the Housing Act 1988 (c. 50)); and
- (c) it is accompanied by a statement in writing which states the term of the tenancy being offered and explains in ordinary language that—
  - (i) there is no obligation to accept the offer, but
  - (ii) if the offer is accepted the local housing authority will cease to be subject to the duty under this section in relation to the applicant.

(7E) An acceptance of a qualifying offer is only effective for the purposes of subsection (7B) if the applicant signs a statement acknowledging that he has understood the statement mentioned in subsection (7D).

(7F) The local housing authority shall not—

- (a) make a final offer of accommodation under Part 6 for the purposes of subsection (7); or
- (b) approve an offer of an assured shorthold tenancy for the purposes of subsection (7B),

unless they are satisfied that the accommodation is suitable for the applicant and that it is reasonable for him to accept the offer.][1]

(8) For the purposes of [subsection (7F)][2] an applicant may reasonably be expected to accept an offer even though he is under contractual or other obligations in respect of his existing accommodation, provided he is able to bring those obligations to an end before he is required to take up the offer.

(9) A person who ceases to be owed the duty under this section may make a fresh application to the authority for accommodation or assistance in obtaining accommodation.

Duties in case of threatened homelessness

195.—(1) This section applies where the local housing authority are satisfied that an applicant is threatened with homelessness and is eligible for assistance. **48-016**

(2) If the authority—

- (a) are satisfied that he has a priority need, and
- (b) are not satisfied that he became threatened with homelessness intentionally,

[1] Inserted by Homelessness Act 2002 c.7 s 7
[2] Words substituted by Homelessness Act 2002 c.7 s 7

they shall take reasonable steps to secure that accommodation does not cease to be available for his occupation.[...][1]

(3) Subsection (2) does not affect any right of the authority, whether by virtue of a contract, enactment or rule of law, to secure vacant possession of any accommodation.

[(3A) The authority shall, on becoming subject to the duty under this section, give the applicant a copy of the statement included in their allocation scheme by virtue of section 167(1A) (policy on offering choice to people allocated housing accommodation under Part 6).][2]

(4) Where in pursuance of the duty under subsection (2) the authority secure that accommodation other than that occupied by the applicant when he made his application is available for occupation by him, the provisions of section 193(3) to (9) (period for which duty owed) [...][3] apply, with any necessary modifications, in relation to the duty under this section as they apply in relation to the duty under section 193.

(5) If the authority—

(a) are not satisfied that the applicant has a priority need, or

(b) are satisfied that he has a priority need but are also satisfied that he became threatened with homelessness intentionally,

they shall [provide him with (or secure that he is provided with) advice and assistance][4] in any attempts he may make to secure that accommodation does not cease to be available for his occupation.

[(6) The applicant's housing needs shall be assessed before advice and assistance is provided under subsection (5).

(7) The advice and assistance provided under subsection (5) must include information about the likely availability in the authority's district of types of accommodation appropriate to the applicant's housing needs (including, in particular, the location and sources of such types of accommodation).

(8) If the authority decide that they owe the applicant the duty under subsection (5) by virtue of paragraph (b) of that subsection, they may, pending a decision on a review of that decision—

(a) secure that accommodation does not cease to be available for his occupation; and

(b) if he becomes homeless, secure that accommodation is so available.][5]

[(9) If the authority—

(a) are not satisfied that the applicant has a priority need; and

(b) are not satisfied that he became threatened with homelessness intentionally,

the authority may take reasonable steps to secure that accommodation does not cease to be available for the applicant's occupation.][6]

[1] Words repealed by Homelessness Act 2002 c.7 Sch 2 para 1
[2] Inserted by Homelessness Act 2002 c.7 Sch 1 para 14
[3] Words repealed in relation to Wales by Homelessness Act 2002 c.7 Sch 2 para 1
[4] Words substituted by Homelessness Act 2002 c.7 Sch 1 para 14
[5] Substituted by Homelessness Act 2002 c.7 Sch 1 para 14
[6] Added by Homelessness Act 2002 c.7 s 5 (2)

Supplementary provisions

[Co-operation in certain cases involving children

213A—(1) This section applies where a local housing authority have reason to believe that an applicant with whom a person under the age of 18 normally resides, or might reasonably be expected to reside— **48-017**

(a) may be ineligible for assistance;

(b) may be homeless and may have become so intentionally; or

(c) may be threatened with homelessness intentionally.

(2) A local housing authority shall make arrangements for ensuring that, where this section applies—

(a) the applicant is invited to consent to the referral of the essential facts of his case to the social services authority for the district of the housing authority (where that is a different authority); and

(b) if the applicant has given that consent, the social services authority are made aware of those facts and of the subsequent decision of the housing authority in respect of his case.

(3) Where the local housing authority and the social services authority for a district are the same authority (a "unitary authority"), that authority shall make arrangements for ensuring that, where this section applies—

(a) the applicant is invited to consent to the referral to the social services department of the essential facts of his case; and

(b) if the applicant has given that consent, the social services department is made aware of those facts and of the subsequent decision of the authority in respect of his case.

(4) Nothing in subsection (2) or (3) affects any power apart from this section to disclose information relating to the applicant's case to the social services authority or to the social services department (as the case may be) without the consent of the applicant.

(5) Where a social services authority—

(a) are aware of a decision of a local housing authority that the applicant is ineligible for assistance, became homeless intentionally or became threatened with homelessness intentionally, and

(b) request the local housing authority to provide them with advice and assistance in the exercise of their social services functions under Part 3 of the Children Act 1989,

the local housing authority shall provide them with such advice and assistance as is reasonable in the circumstances.

(6) A unitary authority shall make arrangements for ensuring that, where they make a decision of a kind mentioned in subsection (5)(a), the housing department provide the social services department with such advice and assistance as the social services department may reasonably request.

(7) In this section, in relation to a unitary authority—

"the housing department" means those persons responsible for the exercise of their housing functions; and "the social services department" means those persons responsible for the exercise of their social services functions under Part 3 of the Children Act 1989.][1]

Education Act 1996

CHAPTER 56

PART I

GENERAL

CHAPTER I

THE STATUTORY SYSTEM OF EDUCATION

General

Duty of parents to secure education of children of compulsory school age

49-001 **7.** The parent of every child of compulsory school age shall cause him to receive efficient full-time education suitable—

(a) to his age, ability and aptitude, and

(b) to any special educational needs he may have,

either by regular attendance at school or otherwise.

Compulsory education

Pupils to be educated in accordance with parents' wishes

49-002 **9.** In exercising or performing all their respective powers and duties under the Education Acts, the Secretary of [State and local education authorities][2] shall have regard to the general principle that pupils are to be educated in accordance with the wishes of their parents, so far as that is compatible with the provision of efficient instruction and training and the avoidance of unreasonable public expenditure.

[1] Added by Homelessness Act 2002 c.7 s 12

[2] Words substituted by School Standards and Framework Act 1998 c.31 Sch 30 para 61

PART V

THE CURRICULUM

CHAPTER IV

MISCELLANEOUS AND SUPPLEMENTARY PROVISIONS

Sex education

Sex education: manner of provision

403.—(1) The governing body and head teacher shall take such steps as are reasonably practicable to secure that where sex education is given to any registered pupils at a maintained school, it is given in such a manner as to encourage those pupils to have due regard to moral considerations and the value of family life. **49-003**

[(1A) The Secretary of State must issue guidance designed to secure that when sex education is given to registered pupils at maintained schools–

(a) they learn the nature of marriage and its importance for family life and the bringing up of children, and

(b) they are protected from teaching and materials which are inappropriate having regard to the age and the religious and cultural background of the pupils concerned.

(1B) In discharging their functions under subsection (1) governing bodies and head teachers must have regard to the Secretary of State's guidance.

(1C) Guidance under subsection (1A) must include guidance about any material which may be produced by NHS bodies for use for the purposes of sex education in schools.

(1D) The Secretary of State may at any time revise his guidance under subsection (1A).][1]

[(2) In this section "maintained school" includes a community or foundation special school established in a hospital and"NHS body" has the same meaning as in section 22 of the National Health Service Act 1977.][2]

Exemption from sex education

405. If the parent of any pupil in attendance at a maintained school requests that he may be wholly or partly excused from receiving sex education at the school, the pupil shall, except so far as such education is comprised in the National Curriculum, be so excused accordingly until the request is withdrawn. **49-004**

[1] Inserted by Learning and Skills Act 2000 c.21 Pt V s 148
[2] Substituted by Learning and Skills Act 2000 c.21 Pt V s 148

PART VI

SCHOOL ADMISSIONS, ATTENDANCE AND CHARGES

CHAPTER II

SCHOOL ATTENDANCE

School attendance orders

School attendance orders

49-005 **437.**—(1) If it appears to a local education authority that a child of compulsory school age in their area is not receiving suitable education, either by regular attendance at school or otherwise, they shall serve a notice in writing on the parent requiring him to satisfy them within the period specified in the notice that the child is receiving such education.

(2) That period shall not be less than 15 days beginning with the day on which the notice is served.

(3) If—

(a) a parent on whom a notice has been served under subsection (1) fails to satisfy the local education authority, within the period specified in the notice, that the child is receiving suitable education, and

(b) in the opinion of the authority it is expedient that the child should attend school,

the authority shall serve on the parent an order (referred to in this Act as a "school attendance order"), in such form as may be prescribed, requiring him to cause the child to become a registered pupil at a school named in the order.

(4) A school attendance order shall (subject to any amendment made by the local education authority) continue in force for so long as the child is of compulsory school age, unless—

(a) it is revoked by the authority, or

(b) a direction is made in respect of it under section 443(2) or 447(5).

(5) Where a maintained school is named in a school attendance order, the local education authority shall inform the governing body and the head teacher.

(6) Where a maintained school is named in a school attendance order, the governing body (and, in the case of a maintained school, the local education authority) shall admit the child to the school.

(7) Subsection (6) does not affect any power to exclude from a school a pupil who is already a registered pupil there.

(8) In this Chapter—

["maintained school" means any community, foundation or voluntary school or any community or foundation special school not established in a hospital; and][1]

"suitable education", in relation to a child, means efficient full-time education suitable to his age, ability and aptitude and to any special educational needs he may have.

[1] Substituted by School Standards and Framework Act 1998 c.31 Sch 30 para 113 (b)

Choice of school: child without statement of special educational needs

438.—(1) This section applies where a local education authority are required by virtue of section 437(3) to serve a school attendance order in respect of a child, other than a child for whom they maintain a statement under section 324. **49-006**

(2) Before serving the order, the authority shall serve on the parent a notice in writing—

(a) informing him of their intention to serve the order,

(b) specifying the school which the authority intend to name in the order and, if they think fit, one or more other schools which they regard as suitable alternatives, and

(c) stating the effect of subsections (3) to (6).

(3) If the notice specifies one or more alternative schools and the parent selects one of them within the period of 15 days beginning with the day on which the notice is served, the school selected by him shall be named in the order.

(4) If—

(a) within the period mentioned in subsection (3) the parent applies for the child to be admitted to a school maintained by a local education authority and, where that authority are not the authority by whom the notice was served, notifies the latter authority of the application, and,

(b) the child is offered a place at the school as a result of the application,

that school shall be named in the order.

(5) If—

(a) within the period mentioned in subsection (3), the parent applies to the local education authority by whom the notice was served for education to be provided at a school which is not a school maintained by a local education authority, and

(b) the child is offered a place at the school under arrangements made by the authority under which the fees payable in respect of the education provided at the school are to be paid by them under section 517,

that school shall be named in the order.

(6) If, within the period mentioned in subsection (3)—

(a) the parent—

(i) applies for the child to be admitted to a school which is not maintained by a local education authority[...][1], and in respect of which no application is made under subsection (5), and

(ii) notifies the local education authority by whom the notice was served of the application,

(b) the child is offered a place at the school as a result of the application, and

(c) the school is suitable to his age, ability and aptitude and to any special educational needs he may have,

that school shall be named in the order.

School attendance: offences and education supervision orders

Offence: failure to comply with school attendance order

443.—(1) If a parent on whom a school attendance order is served fails to comply with the requirements of the order, he is guilty of an offence, unless he proves that he is causing the child to receive suitable education otherwise than at school. **49-007**

[1] Words repealed by School Standards and Framework Act 1998 c.31 Sch 31 para 1

(2) If, in proceedings for an offence under this section, the parent is acquitted, the court may direct that the school attendance order shall cease to be in force.

(3) A direction under subsection (2) does not affect the duty of the local education authority to take further action under section 437 if at any time the authority are of the opinion that, having regard to any change of circumstances, it is expedient to do so.

(4) A person guilty of an offence under this section is liable on summary conviction to a fine not exceeding level 3 on the standard scale.

Offence: failure to secure regular attendance at school of registered pupil

49-008 **444.**—(1) If a child of compulsory school age who is a registered pupil at a school fails to attend regularly at the school, his parent is guilty of an offence.

(1A) If in the circumstances mentioned in subsection (1) the parent knows that his child is failing to attend regularly at the school and fails without reasonable justification to cause him to do so, he is guilty of an offence.

(2) Subsections (3) to (6) below apply in proceedings for an offence under this section in respect of a child who is not a boarder at the school at which he is a registered pupil.

(3) The child shall not be taken to have failed to attend regularly at the school by reason of his absence from the school—

(a) with leave,
(b) at any time when he was prevented from attending by reason of sickness or any unavoidable cause, or
(c) on any day exclusively set apart for religious observance by the religious body to which his parent belongs.

(4) The child shall not be taken to have failed to attend regularly at the school if the parent proves—

(a) that the school at which the child is a registered pupil is not within walking distance of the child's home, and
(b) that no suitable arrangements have been made by the local education authority for any of the following—
  (i) his transport to and from the school,
  (ii) boarding accommodation for him at or near the school, or
  (iii) enabling him to become a registered pupil at a school nearer to his home.

(5) In subsection (4) "walking distance"—

(a) in relation to a child who is under the age of eight, means 3.218688 kilometres (two miles), and
(b) in relation to a child who has attained the age of eight, means 4.828032 kilometres (three miles),

in each case measured by the nearest available route.

(6) If it is proved that the child has no fixed abode, subsection (4) shall not apply, but the parent shall be acquitted if he proves—

(a) that he is engaged in a trade or business of such a nature as to require him to travel from place to place,
(b) that the child has attended at a school as a registered pupil as regularly as the nature of that trade or business permits, and
(c) if the child has attained the age of six, that he has made at least 200 attendances during the period of 12 months ending with the date on which the proceedings were instituted.

(7) In proceedings for an offence under this section in respect of a child who is a boarder at the school at which he is a registered pupil, the child shall be taken to have failed to attend regularly at the school if he is absent from it without leave during any part of the school term at a time when he was not prevented from being present by reason of sickness or any unavoidable cause.

(8) A person guilty of an offence under subsection (1) is liable on summary conviction to a fine not exceeding level 3 on the standard scale.

[(8A) A person guilty of an offence under subsection (1A) is liable on summary conviction—

(a) to a fine not exceeding level 4 on the standard scale, or

(b) to imprisonment for a term not exceeding three months,

or both.

(8B) If, on the trial of an offence under subsection (1A), the court finds the defendant not guilty of that offence but is satisfied that he is guilty of an offence under subsection (1), the court may find him guilty of that offence.][1]

(9) In this section "leave", in relation to a school, means leave granted by any person authorised to do so by the governing body or proprietor of the school.

Education supervision orders

447.—(1) Before instituting proceedings for an offence under section 443 or 444, a local education authority shall consider whether it would be appropriate (instead of or as well as instituting the proceedings) to apply for an education supervision order with respect to the child. **49-009**

(2) The court—

(a) by which a person is convicted of an offence under section 443, or

(b) before which a person is charged with an offence under section 444,

may direct the local education authority instituting the proceedings to apply for an education supervision order with respect to the child unless the authority, having consulted the appropriate local authority, decide that the child's welfare will be satisfactorily safeguarded even though no education supervision order is made.

(3) Where, following such a direction, a local education authority decide not to apply for an education supervision order, they shall inform the court of the reasons for their decision.

(4) Unless the court has directed otherwise, the information required under subsection (3) shall be given to the court before the end of the period of eight weeks beginning with the date on which the direction was given.

(5) Where—

(a) a local education authority apply for an education supervision order with respect to a child who is the subject of a school attendance order, and

(b) the court decides that section 36(3) of the Children Act 1989 (education supervision orders) prevents it from making the order,

the court may direct that the school attendance order shall cease to be in force.

(6) In this section—

"the appropriate local authority" has the same meaning as in section 36(9) of the Children Act 1989, and

"education supervision order" means an education supervision order under that Act.

[1] Added by Criminal Justice and Court Services Act 2000 c.43 Pt IV c I s 72 (1) (c)

PART X

MISCELLANEOUS AND GENERAL

Chapter II

[PUNISHMENT AND RESTRAINT OF PUPILS
Corporal punishment][1]

No right to give corporal punishment

49-010 **548.**—(1) Corporal punishment given by, or on the authority of, a member of staff to a child—

(a) for whom education is provided at any school, or

(b) for whom education is provided, otherwise than at school, under any arrangements made by a local education authority, or

(c) for whom specified nursery education is provided otherwise than at school,

cannot be justified in any proceedings on the ground that it was given in pursuance of a right exercisable by the member of staff by virtue of his position as such.

(2) Subsection (1) applies to corporal punishment so given to a child at any time, whether at the school or other place at which education is provided for the child, or elsewhere.

(3) The following provisions have effect for the purposes of this section.

(4) Any reference to giving corporal punishment to a child is to doing anything for the purpose of punishing that child (whether or not there are other reasons for doing it) which, apart from any justification, would constitute battery.

(5) However, corporal punishment shall not be taken to be given to a child by virtue of anything done for reasons that include averting—

(a) an immediate danger of personal injury to, or

(b) an immediate danger to the property of, any person (including the child himself).

(6) "Member of staff", in relation to the child concerned, means —

(a) any person who works as a teacher at the school or other place at which education is provided for the child, or

(b) any other person who (whether in connection with the provision of education for the child or otherwise)—

(i) works at that school or place, or—

(ii) otherwise provides his services there (whether or not for payment),

and has lawful control or charge of the child.

(7) "Child" (except in subsection (8)) means a person under the age of 18.

(8) "Specified nursery education" means full-time or part-time education suitable for children who have not attained compulsory school age which is provided—

(a) by a local education authority; or

(b) by any other person—

(i) who is (or is to be) in receipt of financial assistance given by such an authority and whose provision of nursery education is taken

[1] Substituted by Education Act 1997 c.44 Sch 7 para 38

into account by the authority in formulating proposals for the purposes of section 120(2)(a) of the School Standards and Framework Act 1998, or

(ii) who is (or is to be) in receipt of grants under section 1 of the Nursery Education and Grant-Maintained Schools Act 1996; or

(c) (otherwise than as mentioned in paragraph (a) or (b)) in any educational institution which would fall within section 4(1) above (definition of "school") but for the fact that it provides part-time, rather than full-time, primary education.

Detention

[Power of members of staff to restrain pupils

550A.—(1) A member of the staff of a school may use, in relation to any pupil at the school, such force as is reasonable in the circumstances for the purpose of preventing the pupil from doing (or continuing to do) any of the following, namely— **49-011**

(a) committing any offence,

(b) causing personal injury to, or damage to the property of, any person (including the pupil himself), or

(c) engaging in any behaviour prejudicial to the maintenance of good order and discipline at the school or among any of its pupils, whether that behaviour occurs during a teaching session or otherwise.

(2) subsection (1) applies where a member of the staff of a school is—

(a) on the premises of the school, or

(b) elsewhere at a time when, as a member of its staff, he has lawful control or charge of the pupil concerned;

but it does not authorise anything to be done in relation to a pupil which constitutes the giving of corporal punishment within the meaning of section 548.

(3) Subsection (1) shall not be taken to prevent any person from relying on any defence available to him otherwise than by virtue of this section.

(4) In this section—

"member of the staff", in relation to a school, means any teacher who works at the school and any other person who, with the authority of the head teacher, has lawful control or charge of pupils at the school;

"offence" includes anything that would be an offence but for the operation of any presumption that a person under a particular age is incapable of committing an offence.][1]

Power to restrain pupils

[Detention outside school hours lawful despite absence of parental consent

550B.—(1) Where a pupil to whom this section applies is required on disciplinary grounds to spend a period of time in detention at his school after the end of any school session, his detention shall not be rendered unlawful by virtue of the absence of his parent's consent to it if the conditions set out in subsection (3) are satisfied. **49-012**

(2) This section applies to any pupil who has not attained the age of 18 and is attending—

(a) a school maintained by a local education authority; or

[1] Added by Education Act 1997 c.44 Pt II s 4

(c) a city technology college, city college for the technology of the arts or [Academy][1].

(3) The conditions referred to in subsection (1) are as follows—

(a) the head teacher of the school must have previously determined, and have—

(i) made generally known within the school, and

(ii) taken steps to bring to the attention of the parent of every person who is for the time being a registered pupil there,

that the detention of pupils after the end of a school session is one of the measures that may be taken with a view to regulating the conduct of pupils;

(b) the detention must be imposed by the head teacher or by another teacher at the school specifically or generally authorised by him for the purpose;

(c) the detention must be reasonable in all the circumstances; and

(d) the pupil's parent must have been given at least 24 hours' notice in writing that the detention was due to take place.

(4) In determining for the purposes of subsection (3)(c) whether a pupil's detention is reasonable, the following matters in particular shall be taken into account—

(a) whether the detention constitutes a proportionate punishment in the circumstances of the case; and

(b) any special circumstances relevant to its imposition on the pupil which are known to the person imposing it (or of which he ought reasonably to be aware) including in particular—

(i) the pupil's age,

(ii) any special educational needs he may have,

(iii) any religious requirements affecting him, and

(iv) where arrangements have to be made for him to travel from the school to his home, whether suitable alternative arrangements can reasonably be made by his parent.

(5) Section 572 which provides for the methods by which notices may be served under this Act, does not preclude a notice from being given to a pupil's parent under this section by any other effective method.][2]

Protection from Harassment Act 1997

CHAPTER 40

England and Wales

Prohibition of harassment

50-001 **1.**—(1) A person must not pursue a course of conduct—

(a) which amounts to harassment of another, and

(b) which he knows or ought to know amounts to harassment of the other.

---

[1] Words substituted by Education Act 2002 c.32 Sch 7 (2) para 6 (7)

[2] Added by Education Act 1997 c.44 Pt II s 4

(2) For the purposes of this section, the person whose course of conduct is in question ought to know that it amounts to harassment of another if a reasonable person in possession of the same information would think the course of conduct amounted to harassment of the other.

(3) Subsection (1) does not apply to a course of conduct if the person who pursued it shows—

(a) that it was pursued for the purpose of preventing or detecting crime,

(b) that it was pursued under any enactment or rule of law or to comply with any condition or requirement imposed by any person under any enactment, or

(c) that in the particular circumstances the pursuit of the course of conduct was reasonable.

Offence of harassment

2.—(1) A person who pursues a course of conduct in breach of section 1 is guilty of an offence. **50-002**

(2) A person guilty of an offence under this section is liable on summary conviction to imprisonment for a term not exceeding six months, or a fine not exceeding level 5 on the standard scale, or both.

(3) [...][1]

Civil remedy

3.—(1) An actual or apprehended breach of section 1 may be the subject of a claim in civil proceedings by the person who is or may be the victim of the course of conduct in question. **50-003**

(2) On such a claim, damages may be awarded for (among other things) any anxiety caused by the harassment and any financial loss resulting from the harassment.

(3) Where—

(a) in such proceedings the High Court or a county court grants an injunction for the purpose of restraining the defendant from pursuing any conduct which amounts to harassment, and

(b) the plaintiff considers that the defendant has done anything which he is prohibited from doing by the injunction,

the plaintiff may apply for the issue of a warrant for the arrest of the defendant.

(4) An application under subsection (3) may be made—

(a) where the injunction was granted by the High Court, to a judge of that court, and

(b) where the injunction was granted by a county court, to a judge or district judge of that or any other county court.

(5) The judge or district judge to whom an application under subsection (3) is made may only issue a warrant if—

(a) the application is substantiated on oath, and

(b) the judge or district judge has reasonable grounds for believing that the defendant has done anything which he is prohibited from doing by the injunction.

(6) Where—

(a) the High Court or a county court grants an injunction for the purpose mentioned in subsection (3)(a), and

[1] Repealed by Police Reform Act 2002 c.30 Sch 8 para 1

(b) without reasonable excuse the defendant does anything which he is prohibited from doing by the injunction,

he is guilty of an offence.

(7) Where a person is convicted of an offence under subsection (6) in respect of any conduct, that conduct is not punishable as a contempt of court.

(8) A person cannot be convicted of an offence under subsection (6) in respect of any conduct which has been punished as a contempt of court.

(9) A person guilty of an offence under subsection (6) is liable—

(a) on conviction on indictment, to imprisonment for a term not exceeding five years, or a fine, or both, or

(b) on summary conviction, to imprisonment for a term not exceeding six months, or a fine not exceeding the statutory maximum, or both.

Putting people in fear of violence

50-004 **4.**—(1) A person whose course of conduct causes another to fear, on at least two occasions, that violence will be used against him is guilty of an offence if he knows or ought to know that his course of conduct will cause the other so to fear on each of those occasions.

(2) For the purposes of this section, the person whose course of conduct is in question ought to know that it will cause another to fear that violence will be used against him on any occasion if a reasonable person in possession of the same information would think the course of conduct would cause the other so to fear on that occasion.

(3) It is a defence for a person charged with an offence under this section to show that—

(a) his course of conduct was pursued for the purpose of preventing or detecting crime,

(b) his course of conduct was pursued under any enactment or rule of law or to comply with any condition or requirement imposed by any person under any enactment, or

(c) the pursuit of his course of conduct was reasonable for the protection of himself or another or for the protection of his or another's property.

(4) A person guilty of an offence under this section is liable—

(a) on conviction on indictment, to imprisonment for a term not exceeding five years, or a fine, or both, or

(b) on summary conviction, to imprisonment for a term not exceeding six months, or a fine not exceeding the statutory maximum, or both.

(5) If on the trial on indictment of a person charged with an offence under this section the jury find him not guilty of the offence charged, they may find him guilty of an offence under section 2.

(6) The Crown Court has the same powers and duties in relation to a person who is by virtue of subsection (5) convicted before it of an offence under section 2 as a magistrates' court would have on convicting him of the offence.

Restraining orders

50-005 **5.**—(1) A court sentencing or otherwise dealing with a person ("the defendant") convicted of an offence under section 2 or 4 may (as well as sentencing him or dealing with him in any other way) make an order under this section.

(2) The order may, for the purpose of protecting the victim of the offence, or any other person mentioned in the order, from further conduct which—

(a) amounts to harassment, or

(b) will cause a fear of violence,
prohibit the defendant from doing anything described in the order.

(3) The order may have effect for a specified period or until further order.

(4) The prosecutor, the defendant or any other person mentioned in the order may apply to the court which made the order for it to be varied or discharged by a further order.

(5) If without reasonable excuse the defendant does anything which he is prohibited from doing by an order under this section, he is guilty of an offence.

(6) A person guilty of an offence under this section is liable—

(a) on conviction on indictment, to imprisonment for a term not exceeding five years, or a fine, or both, or

(b) on summary conviction, to imprisonment for a term not exceeding six months, or a fine not exceeding the statutory maximum, or both.

Interpretation of this group of sections

7.—(1) This section applies for the interpretation of sections 1 to 5. **50-006**

(2) References to harassing a person include alarming the person or causing the person distress.

(3) A"course of conduct"must involve conduct on at least two occasions.

[(3A) A person's conduct on any occasion shall be taken, if aided, abetted, counselled or procured by another–

(a) to be conduct on that occasion of the other (as well as conduct of the person whose conduct it is); and

(b) to be conduct in relation to which the other's knowledge and purpose, and what he ought to have known, are the same as they were in relation to what was contemplated or reasonably foreseeable at the time of the aiding, abetting, counselling or procuring.][1]

(4) "Conduct"includes speech.

School Standards and Framework Act 1998

CHAPTER 31

PART II

NEW FRAMEWORK FOR MAINTAINED SCHOOLS

CHAPTER VI

RELIGIOUS EDUCATION AND WORSHIP

Religious education

Duty to secure due provision of religious education

69.—(1) Subject to section 71, in relation to any community, foundation or voluntary school— **51-001**

[1] Added by Criminal Justice and Police Act 2001 c.16 Pt 1 c 3 s 44 (1)

(a) the local education authority and the governing body shall exercise their functions with a view to securing, and
(b) the head teacher shall secure,

that religious education is given in accordance with the provision for such education included in the school's basic curriculum by virtue of [section 80(1)(a) or 101(1)(a) of the Education Act 2002][1].

(2) Schedule 19 has effect for determining the provision for religious education which is required by [section 80(1)(a) or 101(1)(a)][2] of that Act to be included in the basic curriculum of schools within each of the following categories, namely—

(a) community schools and foundation and voluntary schools which do not have a religious character,
(b) foundation and voluntary controlled schools which have a religious character, and
(c) voluntary aided schools which have a religious character.

(3) For the purposes of this Part a foundation or voluntary school has a religious character if it is designated as a school having such a character by an order made by the Secretary of State.

(4) An order under subsection (3) shall state, in relation to each school designated by the order, the religion or religious denomination in accordance with whose tenets religious education is, or may be, required to be provided at the school in accordance with Schedule 19 (or, as the case may be, each such religion or religious denomination).

(5) The procedure to be followed in connection with—

(a) the designation of a school in an order under subsection (3), and
(b) the inclusion in such an order, in relation to a school, of the statement required by subsection (4),

shall be specified in regulations.

Religious worship

Requirements relating to collective worship

51-002 **70.**—(1) Subject to section 71, each pupil in attendance at a community, foundation or voluntary school shall on each school day take part in an act of collective worship.

(2) Subject to section 71, in relation to any community, foundation or voluntary school—

(a) the local education authority and the governing body shall exercise their functions with a view to securing, and
(b) the head teacher shall secure,

that subsection (1) is complied with.

(3) Schedule 20 makes further provision with respect to the collective worship required by this section, including provision relating to—

(a) the arrangements which are to be made in connection with such worship, and
(b) the nature of such worship.

---
[1] Substituted by Education Act 2002 c.32 Sch 21 para 104
[2] Substituted by Education Act 2002 c.32 Sch 21 para 104

Exceptions and special arrangements etc

Exceptions and special arrangements; provision for special schools

71.—(1) If the parent of a pupil at a community, foundation or voluntary school requests that he may be wholly or partly excused— **51-003**

(a) from receiving religious education given in the school in accordance with the school's basic curriculum,

(b) from attendance at religious worship in the school, or

(c) both from receiving such education and from such attendance,

the pupil shall be so excused until the request is withdrawn.

(2) In subsection (1)—

(a) the reference to religious education given in accordance with the school's basic curriculum is to such education given in accordance with the provision included in the school's basic curriculum by virtue of [section 80(1)(a) or 101(1)(a) of the Education Act 2002][1], and

(b) the reference to religious worship in the school includes religious worship which by virtue of paragraph 2(6) of Schedule 20 takes place otherwise than on the school premises.

(3) Where in accordance with subsection (1) a pupil has been wholly or partly excused from receiving religious education or from attendance at religious worship and the local education authority are satisfied—

(a) that the parent of the pupil desires him to receive religious education of a kind which is not provided in the school during the periods of time during which he is so excused,

(b) that the pupil cannot with reasonable convenience be sent to another community, foundation or voluntary school where religious education of the kind desired by the parent is provided, and

(c) that arrangements have been made for him to receive religious education of that kind during school hours elsewhere,

the pupil may be withdrawn from the school during such periods of time as are reasonably necessary for the purpose of enabling him to receive religious education in accordance with the arrangements.

(4) A pupil may not be withdrawn from school under subsection (3) unless the local education authority are satisfied that the arrangements there mentioned are such as will not interfere with the attendance of the pupil at school on any day except at the beginning or end of a school session (or, if there is only one, the school session) on that day.

(5) Where the parent of a pupil who is a boarder at a community, foundation or voluntary school requests that the pupil be permitted—

(a) to receive religious education in accordance with the tenets of a particular religion or religious denomination outside school hours, or

(b) to attend worship in accordance with such tenets on Sundays or other days exclusively set apart for religious observance by the religious body to which his parent belongs,

the governing body shall make arrangements for giving the pupil reasonable opportunities for doing so.

(6) Arrangements under subsection (5) may provide for making facilities for such education or worship available on the school premises, but any expenditure entailed by the arrangements shall not be met from the school's budget share or otherwise by the local education authority.

[1] Substituted by Education Act 2002 c.32 Sch 21 para 105

(7) Regulations shall make provision for securing that, so far as practicable, every pupil attending a community or foundation special school—

(a) receives religious education and attends religious worship, or

(b) is withdrawn from receiving such education or from attendance at such worship in accordance with the wishes of his parent.

PART III

SCHOOL ADMISSIONS

CHAPTER I

ADMISSION ARRANGEMENTS

Parental preferences

Parental preferences

51-004 **86.**—(1) A local education authority shall make arrangements for enabling the parent of a child in the area of the authority—

(a) to express a preference as to the school at which he wishes education to be provided for his child in the exercise of the authority's functions, and

(b) to give reasons for his preference.

(2) Subject to subsections (3) and (6) and section 87 (children excluded from two or more schools), a local education authority and the governing body of a maintained school shall comply with any preference expressed in accordance with arrangements made under subsection (1).

(3) The duty imposed by subsection (2) does not apply—

(a) if compliance with the preference would prejudice the provision of efficient education or the efficient use of resources;

(b) if the preferred school is a foundation or voluntary aided school and compliance with the preference would be incompatible with any special arrangements under section 91 (admission arrangements to preserve the religious character of a foundation or voluntary aided school); or

(c) if the arrangements for admission to the preferred school—

(i) are wholly based on selection by reference to ability or aptitude, and

(ii) are so based with a view to admitting only pupils with high ability or with aptitude,

and compliance with the preference would be incompatible with selection under those arrangements.

(4) For the purposes of subsection (3)(a) prejudice of the kind referred to in that provision may arise by reason of measures required to be taken in order to ensure compliance with the duty imposed by section 1(6) (duty of local education authority and governing body to comply with limit on infant class sizes).

(5) No prejudice shall, however, be taken to arise for the purposes of subsection (3)(a) from the admission to a maintained school in a school year of a number of pupils in a relevant age group which does not exceed—

(a) the relevant standard number, or

(b) the admission number fixed in accordance with section 93, whichever is the greater.

(6) Where—

(a) the admission arrangements for two or more maintained schools provide for co-ordinated admissions on the part of those schools, and

(b) they are approved by the Secretary of State for the purposes of this subsection,

they shall have effect in relation to each of those schools despite anything in subsection (2).

(7) Where the arrangements for the admission of pupils to a maintained school provide for applications for admission to be made to (or to a person acting on behalf of) the governing body of the school, a parent who makes such an application shall be regarded for the purposes of this section as having expressed a preference for that school in accordance with arrangements made under subsection (1).

(8) The duty imposed by subsection (2) in relation to a preference expressed in accordance with arrangements made under subsection (1) shall apply also in relation to—

(a) any application for the admission to a maintained school of a child who is not in the area of the authority maintaining the school, and

(b) any application made by a parent as mentioned in section 438(4) or 440(2) of the Education Act 1996 (application for a particular school to be named in a school attendance order);

and references in subsection (3) to a preference and a preferred school shall be construed accordingly.

(9) Where admission arrangements for a school provide for all pupils admitted to the school to be selected by reference to ability or aptitude, those arrangements shall be taken for the purposes of this section to be wholly based on selection by reference to ability or aptitude, whether or not they also provide for the use of additional criteria in circumstances where the number of children in a relevant age group who are assessed to be of the requisite ability or aptitude is greater than the number of pupils which it is intended to admit to the school in that age group.

PART V

NURSERY EDUCATION

Nursery education

Definition of "nursery education"

117. In this part "nursery education" means full-time or part-time education suitable for children who have not attained compulsory school age (whether provided at schools or elsewhere). **51-005**

General duty of local education authority

Duty of LEA as respects availability of nursery education

118.—(1) A local education authority shall secure that the provision (whether or not by them) of nursery education for children who— **51-006**

(a) have not attained compulsory school age, but

(b) have attained such age as may be prescribed, is sufficient for their area.

(2) In determining for the purposes of subsection (1) whether the provision of such education is sufficient for their area a local education authority—
   (a) may have regard to any facilities which they expect to be available outside their area for providing such education; and
   (b) shall have regard to any guidance given from time to time by the Secretary of State.

Crime and Disorder Act 1998

CHAPTER 37

PART I

PREVENTION OF CRIME AND DISORDER

CHAPTER I

ENGLAND AND WALES

Youth crime and disorder

Parenting orders

52-001 **8.**—(1) This section applies where, in any court proceedings—
   (a) a child safety order is made in respect of a child;
   (b) an anti-social behaviour order or sex offender order is made in respect of a child or young person;
   (c) a child or young person is convicted of an offence; or
   (d) a person is convicted of an offence under section 443 (failure to comply with school attendance order) or section 444 (failure to secure regular attendance at school of registered pupil) of the Education Act 1996.

(2) Subject to subsection (3) and section 9(1) below [and to section 19(5) of, and paragraph 13(5) of Schedule 1 to, the Powers of Criminal Courts (Sentencing) Act 2000][1], if in the proceedings the court is satisfied that the relevant condition is fulfilled, it may make a parenting order in respect of a person who is a parent or guardian of the child or young person or, as the case may be, the person convicted of the offence under section 443 or 444 ("the parent").

(3) A court shall not make a parenting order unless it has been notified by the Secretary of State that arrangements for implementing such orders are available in the are in which it appears to the court that the parent resides or will reside and the notice has not been withdrawn.

(4) A parenting order is an order which requires the parent—
   (a) to comply, for a period not exceeding twelve months, with such requirements as are specified in the order; and
   (b) subject to subsection (5) below, to attend, for a concurrent period not exceeding three months and not more than once in any week, such

[1] Words substituted by Powers of Criminal Courts (Sentencing) Act 2000 c.6 Sch 9 para 194

counselling or guidance sessions as may be specified in directions given by the responsible officer;

and in this subsection "week" means a period of seven days beginning with a Sunday.

(5) A parenting order may, but need not, include such a requirement as is mentioned in subsection (4)(b) above in any case where such an order has been made in respect of the parent on a previous occasion.

(6) The relevant condition is that the parenting order would be desirable in the interests of preventing—

(a) in a case falling within paragraph (a) or (b) of subsection (1) above, any repetition of the kind of behaviour which led to the child safety order, anti-social behaviour order or sex offender order being made;

(b) in a case falling within paragraph (c) of that subsection, the commission of any further offence by the child or young person;

(c) in a case falling within paragraph (d) of that subsection, the commission of any further offence under section 443 or 444 of the Education Act 1996.

(7) The requirements that may be specified under subsection (4)(a) above are those which the court considers desirable in the interests of preventing any such repetition or, as the case may be, the commission of any such further offence.

(8) In this section and section 9 below "responsible officer", in relation to a parenting order, means one of the following who is specified in the order, namely—

(a) [an officer of a local probation board][1];

(b) a social worker of a local authority social services department; and

(c) a member of a youth offending team.

Parenting orders: supplemental

9.—(1) Where a person under the age of 16 is convicted of an offence, the court by or before which he is so convicted— **52-002**

(a) if it is satisfied that the relevant condition is fulfilled, shall make a parenting order; and

(b) if it is not so satisfied, shall state in open court that it is not and why it is not.

[(1A) Subsection (1) above has effect subject to [section 19(5) of, and paragraph 13(5) of Schedule 1 to, the Powers of Criminal Courts (Sentencing) Act 2000][2].][3]

(2) Before making a parenting order—

(a) in a case falling within paragraph (a) of subsection (1) of section 8 above;

(b) in a case falling within paragraph (b) or (c) of that subsection, where the person concerned is under the age of 16; or

(c) in a case falling within paragraph (d) of that subsection, where the person to whom the offence related is under that age,

a court shall obtain and consider information about the person's family circumstances and the likely effect of the order on those circumstances.

(3) Before making a parenting order, a court shall explain to the parent in ordinary language—

[1] Words substituted by Criminal Justice and Court Services Act 2000 c.43 Sch 7 (I) para 4 (1)

[2] Words substituted by Powers of Criminal Courts (Sentencing) Act 2000 c.6 Sch 9 para 195

[3] Added by Youth Justice and Criminal Evidence Act 1999 c.23 Sch 4 para 27

(a) the effect of the order and of the requirements proposed to be included in it;
(b) the consequences which may follow (under subsection (7) below) if he fails to comply with any of those requirements; and
(c) that the court has power (under subsection (5) below) to review the order on the application either of the parent or of the responsible officer.

(4) Requirements specified in, and directions given under, a parenting order shall, as far as practicable, be such as to avoid—
(a) any conflict with the parent's religious beliefs; and
(b) any interference with the times, if any, at which he normally works or attends an educational establishment.

(5) If while a parenting order is in force it appears to the court which made it, on the application of the responsible officer or the parent, that it is appropriate to make an order under this subsection, the court may make an order discharging the parenting order or varying it—
(a) by cancelling any provision included in it; or
(b) by inserting in it (either in addition to or in substitution for any of its provisions) any provision that could have been included in the order if the court had then had power to make it and were exercising the power.

(6) Where an application under subsection (5) above for the discharge of a parenting order is dismissed, no further application for its discharge shall be made under that subsection by any person except with the consent of the court which made the order.

(7) If while a parenting order is in force the parent without reasonable excuse fails to comply with any requirement included in the order, or specified in directions given by the responsible officer, he shall be liable on summary conviction to a fine not exceeding level 3 on the standard scale.

Appeals against parenting orders

52-003 **10.**—(1) An appeal shall lie—
(a) to the High Court against the making of a parenting order by virtue of paragraph (a) of subsection (1) of section 8 above; and
(b) to the Crown Court against the making of a parenting order by virtue of paragraph (b) of that subsection.

(2) On an appeal under subsection (1) above the High Court or the Crown Court—
(a) may make such orders as may be necessary to give effect to its determination of the appeals; and
(b) may also make such incidental or consequential orders as appear to it to be just.

(3) Any order of the High Court or the Crown Court made on an appeal under subsection (1) above (other than one directing that an application be re-heard by a magistrates' court) shall, for the purposes of subsections (5) to (7) of section 9 above, be treated as if it were an order of the court from which the appeal was brought and not an order of the High Court or the Crown Court.

(4) A person in respect of whom a parenting order is made by virtue of section 8(1)(c) above shall have the same right of appeal against the making of the order as if—
(a) the offence that led to the making of the order were an offence committed by him; and

(b) the order were a sentence passed on him for the offence.

(5) A person in respect of whom a parenting order is made by virtue of section 8(1)(d) above shall have the same right of appeal against the making of the order as if the order were a sentence passed on him for the offence that led to the making of the order.

Child safety orders

11.—(1) Subject to subsection (2) below, if a magistrates' court, on the application of a local authority, is satisfied that one or more of the conditions specified in subsection (3) below are fulfilled with respect to a child under the age of 10, it may make an order (a "child safety' order") which— **52-004**

(a) places the child, for a period (not exceeding the permitted maximum) specified in the order, under the supervision of the responsible officer; and

(b) requires the child to comply with such requirements as are so specified.

(2) A court shall not make a child safety order unless it has been notified by the Secretary of State that arrangements for implementing such orders are available in the area in which it appears that the child resides or will reside and the notice has not been withdrawn.

(3) The conditions are—

(a) that the child has committed an act which, if he had been aged 10 or over, would have constituted an offence;

(b) that a child safety order is necessary for the purpose of preventing the commission by the child of such an act as is mentioned in paragraph (a) above;

(c) that the child has contravened a ban imposed by a curfew notice; and

(d) that the child has acted in a manner that caused or was likely to cause harassment, alarm or distress to one or more persons not of the same household as himself.

(4) The maximum period permitted for the purposes of subsection (1)(a) above is three months or, where the court is satisfied that the circumstances of the case are exceptional, 12 months.

(5) The requirements that may be specified under subsection (1)(b) above are those which the court considers desirable in the interests of—

(a) securing that the child receives appropriate care, protection and support and is subject to proper control; or

(b) preventing any repetition of the kind of behaviour which led to the child safety order being made.

(6) Proceedings under this section or section 12 below shall be family proceedings for the purposes of the 1989 Act or section 65 of the Magistrates' Courts Act 1980 ("the 1980 Act"); and the standard of proof applicable to such proceedings shall be that applicable to civil proceedings.

(7) In this section "local authority" has the same meaning as in the 1989 Act.

(8) In this section and section 12 below, "responsible officer", in relation to a child safety order, means one of the following who is specified in the order, namely—

(a) a social worker of a local authority social services department; and

(b) a member of a youth offending team.

Child safety orders: supplemental

52-005 **12.**—(1) Before making a child safety order, a magistrates' court shall obtain and consider information about the child's family circumstances and the likely effect of the order on those circumstances.

(2) Before making a child safety order, a magistrates' court shall explain to the parent or guardian of the child in ordinary language—

(a) the effect of the order and of the requirements proposed to be included in it;
(b) the consequences which may follow (under subsection (6) below) if the child fails to comply with any of those requirements; and
(c) that the court has power (under subsection (4) below) to review the order on the application either of the parent or guardian or of the responsible officer.

(3) Requirements included in a child safety order shall, as far as practicable, be such as to avoid—

(a) any conflict with the parent's religious beliefs; and
(b) any interference with the times, if any, at which the child normally attends school.

(4) If while a child safety order is in force in respect of a child it appears to the court which made it, on the application of the responsible officer or a parent or guardian of the child, that it is appropriate to make an order under this subsection, the court may make an order discharging the child safety order or varying it—

(a) by cancelling any provision included in it; or
(b) by inserting in it (either in addition to or in substitution for any of its provisions) any provision that could have been included in the order if the court had then had power to make it and were exercising the power.

(5) Where an application under subsection (4) above for the discharge of a child safety order is dismissed, no further application for its discharge shall be made under that subsection by any person except with the consent of the court which made the order.

(6) Where a child safety order is in force and it is proved to the satisfaction of the court which made it or another magistrates' court acting for the same petty sessions area, on the application of the responsible officer, that the child has failed to comply with any requirement included in the order, the court—

(a) may discharge the order and make in respect of him a care order under subsection (1)(a) of section 31 of the 1989 Act; or
(b) may make an order varying the order—
    (i) by cancelling any provision included in it; or
    (ii) by inserting in it (either in addition to or in substitution for any of its provisions) any provision that could have been included in the order if the court had then had power to make it and were exercising the power.

(7) Subsection (6)(a) above applies whether or not the court is satisfied that the conditions mentioned in section 31(2) of the 1989 Act are fulfilled.

Appeals against child safety orders

52-006 **13.**—(1) An appeal shall lie to the High Court against the making by a magistrates' court of a child safety order; and on such an appeal the High Court—

(a) may make such orders as may be necessary to give effect to its determination of the appeal; and
(b) may also make such incidental or consequential orders as appear to it to be just.

(2) Any order of the High Court made on an appeal under this section (other than one directing that an application be re-heard by a magistrates' court) shall, for the purposes of subsections (4) to (6) of section 12 above, be treated as if it were an order of the magistrates' court from which the appeal was brought and not an order of the High Court.

(3) Subsections (6) and (7) of section 10 above shall apply for the purposes of subsection (1) above as they apply for the purposes of subsection (1)(a) of that section.

Local child curfew schemes

14.—(1) A local authority [or a chief officer of police][1]may make a scheme (a **52-007**
"local child curfew scheme") for enabling the authority [or (as the case may be) the officer][2]—
(a) subject to and in accordance with the provisions of the scheme; and
(b) if, after such consultation as is required by the scheme, the authority [or (as the case may be) the officer][3]considers it necessary to do so for the purpose of maintaining order,

to give a notice imposing, for a specified period (not exceeding 90 days), a ban to which subsection (2) below applies.

(2) This subsection applies to a ban on children of specified ages ([under 16][4]) being in a public place within a specified area—
(a) during specified hours (between 9 pm and 6 am); and
(b) otherwise than under the effective control of a parent or a responsible person aged 18 or over.

(3) Before making a local child curfew scheme, a local authority shall consult—
(a) every chief officer of police any part of whose police area lies within its area; and
(b) such other persons or bodies as it considers appropriate.

[(3A) Before making a local child curfew scheme, a chief officer of police shall consult–
(a) every local authority any part of whose area lies within the area to be specified; and
(b) such other persons or bodies as he considers appropriate.][5]

[(4) A local child curfew scheme shall, if made by a local authority, be made under the common seal of the authority.

(4A) A local child curfew scheme shall not have effect until it is confirmed by the Secretary of State.][6]

(5) The Secretary of State—
(a) may confirm, or refuse to confirm, a local child curfew scheme submitted under this section for confirmation; and
(b) may fix the date on which such a scheme is to come into operation;

[1] Words inserted by Criminal Justice and Police Act 2001 c.16 Pt 1 c 3 s 49 (2)
[2] Words inserted by Criminal Justice and Police Act 2001 c.16 Pt 1 c 3 s 49 (2)
[3] Words inserted by Criminal Justice and Police Act 2001 c.16 Pt 1 c 3 s 49 (2)
[4] Words substituted by Criminal Justice and Police Act 2001 c.16 Pt 1 c 3 s 48
[5] Added by Criminal Justice and Police Act 2001 c.16 Pt 1 c 3 s 49 (3)
[6] Subsections (4) and (4A) substituted for subsection (4) by Criminal Justice and Police Act 2001 c.16 Pt 1 c 3 s 49 (4)

and if no date is so fixed, the scheme shall come into operation at the end of the period of one month beginning with the date of its confirmation.

(6) A notice given under a local child curfew scheme (a "curfew notice") may specify different hours in relation to children of different ages.

(7) A curfew notice shall be given—

(a) by posting the notice in some conspicuous place or places within the specified area; and

(b) in such other manner, if any, as appears to the local authority [or (as the case may be) the chief officer of police][1]to be desirable for giving publicity to the notice.

(8) In this section—

"local authority" means—

(a) in relation to England, the council of a district or London brought, the Common Council of the City of London, the Council of the Isle of Wight and the Council of the Isles of Scilly;

(b) in relation to Wales, the council of a county or county borough;

"public place" has the same meaning as in Part II of the Public Order Act 1986.

Contravention of curfew notices

52-008 **15.**—(1) Subsections (2) and (3) below apply where a constable has reasonable cause to believe that a child is in contravention of a ban imposed by a curfew notice.

(2) The constable shall, as soon as practicable, inform the local authority for the area that the child has contravened the ban.

(3) The constable may remove the child to the child's place of residence unless he has reasonable cause to believe that the child would, if removed to that place, be likely to suffer significant harm.

Removal of truants to designated premises etc

52-009 **16.**—(1) This section applies where a local authority—

(a) designates premises in a police area ("designated premises") as premises to which children and young persons of compulsory school age may be removed under this section; and

(b) notifies the chief officer of police for that area of the designation.

(2) A police officer of or above the rank of superintendent may direct that the powers conferred on a constable by subsection (3) below—

(a) shall be exercisable as respects any area falling within the police area and specified in the direction; and

(b) shall be so exercisable during a period so specified;

and references in that subsection to a specified area and a specified period shall be construed accordingly.

(3) If a constable has reasonable cause to believe that a child or young person found by him in a public place in a specified area during a specified period—

(a) is of compulsory school age; and

(b) is absent from a school without lawful authority,

the constable may remove the child or young person to designated premises, or to the school from which he is so absent.

[1] Words inserted by Criminal Justice and Police Act 2001 c.16 Pt 1 c 3 s 49 (5)

[(3A) The power of a police officer of or above the rank of superintendent under subsection (2) to specify any area falling within a police area shall be exercisable by such an officer who is a member of the British Transport Police as if the reference in that subsection to an area in the police area were a reference to—

(a) any area in or in the vicinity of any policed premises; or

(b) the whole or any part of any such premises;

and references in subsection (3) to the specified area shall have effect accordingly.][1]

(4) A child's or young person's absence from a school shall be taken to be without lawful authority unless it falls within subsection (3) (leave, sickness, unavoidable cause or day set apart for religious observance) of section 444 of the Education Act 1996.

(5) In this section—

['British Transport Police' means the force of constables appointed under section 53 of the British Transport Commission Act 1949 (c. xxix);][2]

"local authority" means—

(a) in relation to England, a county council, a district council whose district does not form part of an area that has a county council, a London borough council or the Common Council of the City of London;

(b) in relation to Wales, a county council or a county borough council;

['policed premises' has the meaning given by section 53(3) of the British Transport Commission Act 1949;][3]

"public place" has the same meaning as in section 14 above;

"school" has the same meaning as in the Education Act 1996.

Miscellaneous and supplemental

Interpretation etc. of Chapter I

18.—(1) In this Chapter— 52-010

"anti-social behaviour order" has the meaning given by section 1(4) above;

"chief officer of police" has the meaning given by section 101(1) of the Police Act 1996;

"child safety order" has the meaning given by section 11(1) above;

"curfew notice" has the meaning given by section 14(6) above;

"local child curfew scheme" has the meaning given by section 14(1) above;

"parenting order" has the meaning given by section 8(4) above;

"police area" has the meaning given by section 1(2) of the Police Act 1996;

"police authority" has the meaning given by section 101(1) of that Act;

"responsible officer"—

(a) in relation to a parenting order, has the meaning given by section 8(8) above;

(b) in relation to a child safety order, has the meaning given by section 11(8) above;

"sex offender order" has the meaning given by section 2(3) above.

---

1 Added by Police Reform Act 2002 c.30 Pt 4 c 2 s 75 (1)

2 Definition inserted by Police Reform Act 2002 c.30 Pt 4 c 2 s 75 (2) (a)

3 Definition inserted by Police Reform Act 2002 c.30 Pt 4 c 2 s 75 (2) (b)

[(2) In this Chapter, "protecting the public from serious harm" shall be construed in accordance with section 161(4) of the Powers of Criminal Courts (Sentencing) Act 2000.][1]

(3) Where directions under a parenting order are to be given by [an officer of a local probation board][2], [the officer of a local probation board][3] shall be an officer appointed for or assigned to the petty sessions area within which it appears to the court that the child or, as the case may be, the parent resides or will reside.

(4) Where the supervision under a child safety order is to be provided, or directions under a parenting order are to be given, by—

(a) a social worker of a local authority social services department; or

(b) a member of a youth offending team,

the social worker or member shall be a social worker of, or a member of a youth offending team established by, the local authority within whose area it appears to the court that the child or, as the case may be, the parent resides or will reside.

Human Rights Act 1998

CHAPTER 42

Introduction

The Convention Rights

53-001 **1.**—(1) In this Act "the Convention rights" means the rights and fundamental freedoms set out in—

(a) Articles 2 to 12 and 14 of the Convention,

(b) Articles 1 to 3 of the First Protocol, and

(c) Articles 1 and 2 of the Sixth Protocol,

as read with Articles 16 to 18 of the Convention.

(2) Those Articles are to have effect for the purposes of this Act subject to any designated derogation or reservation (as to which see sections 14 and 15).

(3) The Articles are set out in Schedule 1.

(4) The [Lord Chancellor][4] may by order make such amendments to this Act as he considers appropriate to reflect the effect, in relation to the United Kingdom, of a protocol.

(5) In subsection (4) "protocol" means a protocol to the Convention—

(a) which the United Kingdom has ratified; or

(b) which the United Kingdom has signed with a view to ratification.

(6) No amendment may be made by an order under subsection (4) so as to come into force before the protocol concerned is in force in relation to the United Kingdom.

---

1 Substituted by Powers of Criminal Courts (Sentencing) Act 2000 c.6 Sch 9 para 196
2 Words substituted by Criminal Justice and Court Services Act 2000 c.43 Sch 7 (I) para 4 (1)
3 Words substituted by Criminal Justice and Court Services Act 2000 c.43 Sch 7 (I) para 4 (1)
4 Words substituted by SI 2001/3500 Sch 2 (I) para 7 (a)

Legislation

Interpretation of legislation

3.—(1) So far as it is possible to do so, primary legislation and subordinate legislation must be read and given effect in a way which is compatible with the Convention rights. **53-002**

(2) This section—

(a) applies to primary legislation and subordinate legislation whenever enacted;

(b) does not affect the validity, continuing operation or enforcement of any incompatible primary legislation; and

(c) does not affect the validity, continuing operation or enforcement of any incompatible subordinate legislation if (disregarding any possibility of revocation) primary legislation prevents removal of the incompatibility.

Declaration of incompatibility

4.—(1) Subsection (2) applies in any proceedings in which a court determines whether a provision of primary legislation is compatible with a Convention right. **53-003**

(2) If the court is satisfied that the provision is incompatible with a Convention right, it may make a declaration of that incompatibility.

(3) Subsection (4) applies in any proceedings in which a court determines whether a provision of subordinate legislation, made in the exercise of a power conferred by primary legislation, is compatible with a Convention right.

(4) If the court is satisfied—

(a) that the provision is incompatible with a Convention right, and

(b) that (disregarding any possibility of revocation) the primary legislation concerned prevents removal of the incompatibility,

it may make a declaration of that incompatibility.

(5) In this section "court" means —

(a) the House of Lords;

(b) the Judicial Committee of the Privy Council;

(c) the Courts-Martial Appeal Court;

(d) in Scotland, the High Court of Justiciary sitting otherwise than as a trial court or the Court of Session;

(e) in England and Wales or Northern Ireland, the High Court or the Court of Appeal.

(6) A declaration under this section ("a declaration of incompatibility")—

(a) does not affect the validity, continuing operation or enforcement of the provision in respect of which it is given; and

(b) is not binding on the parties to the proceedings in which it is made.

Public authorities

Acts of public authorities

6.—(1) It is unlawful for a public authority to act in a way which is incompatible with a Convention right. **53-004**

(2) Subsection (1) does not apply to an act if—

(a) as the result of one or more provisions of primary legislation, the authority could not have acted differently; or

(b) in the case of one or more provisions of, or made under, primary legislation which cannot be read or given effect in a way which is compatible with the Convention rights, the authority was acting so as to give effect to or enforce those provisions.

(3) In this section "public authority" includes—

(a) a court or tribunal, and

(b) any person certain of whose functions are functions of a public nature,

but does not include either House of Parliament or a person exercising functions in connection with proceedings in Parliament.

(4) In subsection (3) "Parliament" does not include the House of Lords in its judicial capacity.

(5) In relation to a particular act, a person is not a public authority by virtue only of subsection (3)(b) if the nature of the act is private.

(6) "An act" includes a failure to act but does not include a failure to—

(a) introduce in, or lay before, Parliament a proposal for legislation; or

(b) make any primary legislation or remedial order.

Proceedings

53-005 7.—(1) A person who claims that a public authority has acted (or proposes to act) in a way which is made unlawful by section 6(1) may—

(a) bring proceedings against the authority under this Act in the appropriate court or tribunal, or

(b) rely on the Convention right or rights concerned in any legal proceedings,

but only if he is (or would be) a victim of the unlawful act.

(2) In subsection (1)(a) "appropriate court or tribunal" means such court or tribunal as may be determined in accordance with rules; and proceedings against an authority include a counterclaim or similar proceedings.

(3) If the proceedings are brought on an application for judicial review, the applicant is to be taken to have a sufficient interest in relation to the unlawful act only if he is, or would be, a victim of that act.

(4) If the proceedings are made by way of a petition for judicial review in Scotland, the applicant shall be taken to have title and interest to sue in relation to the unlawful act only if he is, or would be, a victim of that act.

(5) Proceedings under subsection (1)(a) must be brought before the end of—

(a) the period of one year beginning with the date on which the act complained of took place; or

(b) such longer period as the court or tribunal considers equitable having regard to all the circumstances,

but that is subject to any rule imposing a stricter time limit in relation to the procedure in question.

(6) In subsection (1)(b) "legal proceedings" includes—

(a) proceedings brought by or at the instigation of a public authority; and

(b) an appeal against the decision of a court or tribunal.

(7) For the purposes of this section, a person is a victim of an unlawful act only if he would be a victim for the purposes of Article 34 of the Convention if proceedings were brought in the European Court of Human Rights in respect of that act.

(8) Nothing in this Act creates a criminal offence.

(9) In this section "rules" means —

(a) in relation to proceedings before a court or tribunal outside Scotland, rules made by the Lord Chancellor or the Secretary of State for the purposes of this section or rules of court,
(b) in relation to proceedings before a court or tribunal in Scotland, rules made by the Secretary of State for those purposes,
(c) in relation to proceedings before a tribunal in Northern Ireland—
(i) which deals with transferred matters; and
(ii) for which no rules made under paragraph (a) are in force,
rules made by a Northern Ireland department for those purposes,

and includes provision made by order under section 1 of the Courts and Legal Services Act 1990.

(10) In making rules, regard must be had to section 9.

(11) The Minister who has power to make rules in relation to a particular tribunal may, to the extent he considers it necessary to ensure that the tribunal can provide an appropriate remedy in relation to an act (or proposed act) of a public authority which is (or would be) unlawful as a result of section 6(1), by order add to—
(a) the relief or remedies which the tribunal may grant; or
(b) the grounds on which it may grant any of them.

(12) An order made under subsection (11) may contain such incidental, supplemental, consequential or transitional provision as the Minister making it considers appropriate.

(13) "The Minister" includes the Northern Ireland department concerned.

Judicial remedies

8.—(1) In relation to any act (or proposed act) of a public authority which **53-006**
the court finds is (or would be) unlawful, it may grant such relief or remedy, or make such order, within its powers as it considers just and appropriate.

(2) But damages may be awarded only by a court which has power to award damages, or to order the payment of compensation, in civil proceedings.

(3) No award of damages is to be made unless, taking account of all the circumstances of the case, including—
(a) any other relief or remedy granted, or order made, in relation to the act in question (by that or any other court), and
(b) the consequences of any decision (of that or any other court) in respect of that act,

the court is satisfied that the award is necessary to afford just satisfaction to the person in whose favour it is made.

(4) In determining—
(a) whether to award damages, or
(b) the amount of an award,

the court must take into account the principles applied by the European Court of Human Rights in relation to the award of compensation under Article 41 of the Convention.

(5) A public authority against which damages are awarded is to be treated—
(a) in Scotland, for the purposes of section 3 of the Law Reform (Miscellaneous Provisions) (Scotland) Act 1940 as if the award were made in an action of damages in which the authority has been found liable in respect of loss or damage to the person to whom the award is made;
(b) for the purposes of the Civil Liability (Contribution) Act 1978 as liable in respect of damage suffered by the person to whom the award is made.

(6) In this section—

"court" includes a tribunal;

"damages" means damages for an unlawful act of a public authority; and

"unlawful" means unlawful under section 6(1).

Judicial acts

53-007 **9.**—(1) Proceedings under section 7(1)(a) in respect of a judicial act may be brought only—

(a) by exercising a right of appeal;

(b) on an application (in Scotland a petition) for judicial review; or

(c) in such other forum as may be prescribed by rules.

(2) That does not affect any rule of law which prevents a court from being the subject of judicial review.

(3) In proceedings under this Act in respect of a judicial act done in good faith, damages may not be awarded otherwise than to compensate a person to the extent required by Article 5(5) of the Convention.

(4) An award of damages permitted by subsection (3) is to be made against the Crown; but no award may be made unless the appropriate person, if not a party to the proceedings, is joined.

(5) In this section—

"appropriate person" means the Minister responsible for the court concerned, or a person or government department nominated by him;

"court" includes a tribunal;

"judge" includes a member of a tribunal, a justice of the peace and a clerk or other officer entitled to exercise the jurisdiction of a court;

"judicial act" means a judicial act of a court and includes an act done on the instructions, or on behalf, of a judge; and

"rules" has the same meaning as in section 7(9).

SCHEDULES

Section 1(3) Schedule 1

THE ARTICLES

THE CONVENTION

RIGHTS AND FREEDOMS

Right to life

53-008 **Article 2**—1. Everyone's right to life shall be protected by law. No one shall be deprived of his life intentionally save in the execution of a sentence of a court following his conviction of a crime for which this penalty is provided by law.

2. Deprivation of life shall not be regarded as inflicted in contravention of this Article when it results from the use of force which is no more than absolutely necessary:

(a) in defence of any person from unlawful violence;

(b) in order to effect a lawful arrest or to prevent the escape of a person lawfully detained;

(c) in action lawfully taken for the purpose of quelling a riot or insurrection.

Prohibition of torture

Article 3 No one shall be subjected to torture or to inhuman or degrading treatment or punishment. **53-009**

Prohibition of slavery and forced labour

Article 4—1. No one shall be held in slavery or servitude. **53-010**

2. No one shall be required to perform forced or compulsory labour.
3. For the purpose of this Article the term "forced or compulsory labour" shall not include:
   (a) any work required to be done in the ordinary course of detention imposed according to the provisions of Article 5 of this Convention or during conditional release from such detention;
   (b) any service of a military character or, in case of conscientious objectors in countries where they are recognised, service exacted instead of compulsory military service;
   (c) any service exacted in case of an emergency or calamity threatening the life or well-being of the community;
   (d) any work or service which forms part of normal civic obligations.

Right to liberty and security

Article 5—1. Everyone has the right to liberty and security of a person. No one shall be deprived **53-011**
of his liberty save in the following cases and in accordance with a procedure prescribed by law:
   (a) the lawful detention of a person after conviction by a competent court;
   (b) the lawful arrest or detention of a person for non-compliance with the lawful order of a court or in order to secure the fulfilment of any obligation prescribed by law;
   (c) the lawful arrest or detention of a person effected for the purpose of bringing him before the competent legal authority on reasonable suspicion of having committed an offence or when it is reasonably considered necessary to prevent his committing an offence or fleeing after having done so;
   (d) the detention of a minor by lawful order for the purpose of educational supervision or his lawful detention for the purpose of bringing him before the competent legal authority;
   (e) the lawful detention of persons for the prevention of the spreading of infectious diseases, of persons of unsound mind, alcoholics or drug addicts or vagrants;
   (f) the lawful arrest or detention of a person to prevent his effecting an unauthorised entry into the country or of a person against whom action is being taken with a view to deportation or extradition.

2. Everyone who is arrested shall be informed promptly, in a language which he understands, of the reasons for his arrest and of any charge against him.

3. Everyone arrested or detained in accordance with the provisions of paragraph 1(c) of this Article shall be brought promptly before a judge or other officer authorised by law to exercise judicial power and shall be entitled to trial within a reasonable time or to release pending trial. Release may be conditioned by guarantees to appear for trial.

4. Everyone who is deprived of his liberty by arrest or detention shall be entitled to take proceedings by which the lawfulness of his detention shall be decided speedily by a court and his release ordered if the detention is not lawful.

5. Everyone who has been the victim of arrest or detention in contravention of the provisions of this Article shall have an enforceable right to compensation.

Right to a fair trial

Article 6—1. In the determination of his civil rights and obligations or of any criminal charge **53-012**
against him, everyone is entitled to a fair and public hearing within a reasonable time by an independent and impartial tribunal established by law. Judgment shall be pronounced publicly but the press and public may be excluded from all or part of the trial in the interest of morals, public order or national security in a democratic society, where the interests of juveniles or the protection of the private life of the parties so require, or to the extent strictly necessary in the opinion of the court in special circumstances where publicity would prejudice the interests of justice.

2. Everyone charged with a criminal offence shall be presumed innocent until proved guilty according to law.

3. Everyone charged with a criminal offence has the following minimum rights:

(a) to be informed promptly, in a language which he understands and in detail, of the nature and cause of the accusation against him;

(b) to have adequate time and facilities for the preparation of his defence;

(c) to defend himself in person or through legal assistance of his own choosing or, if he has not sufficient means to pay for legal assistance, to be given it free when the interests of justice so require;

(d) to examine or have examined witnesses against him and to obtain the attendance and examination of witnesses on his behalf under the same conditions as witnesses against him;

(e) to have the free assistance of an interpreter if he cannot understand or speak the language used in court.

No punishment without law

53-013 **Article 7**—1. No one shall be held guilty of any criminal offence on account of any act or omission which did not constitute a criminal offence under national or international law at the time when it was committed. Nor shall a heavier penalty be imposed than the one that was applicable at the time the criminal offence was committed.

2. This Article shall not prejudice the trial and punishment of any person for any act or omission which, at the time when it was committed, was criminal according to the general principles of law recognised by civilised nations.

Right to respect for private and family life

53-014 **Article 8**—1. Everyone has the right to respect for his private and family life, his home and his correspondence.

2. There shall be no interference by a public authority with the exercise of this right except such as is in accordance with the law and is necessary in a democratic society in the interests of national security, public safety or the economic well-being of the country, for the prevention of disorder or crime, for the protection of health or morals, or for the protection of the rights and freedoms of others.

Freedom of thought, conscience and religion

53-015 **Article 9**—1. Everyone has the right to freedom of thought, conscience and religion, this right includes freedom to change his religion or belief and freedom, either alone or in community with others and in public or private, to manifest his religion or belief, in worship, teaching, practice and observance.

2. Freedom to manifest one's religion or beliefs shall be subject only to such limitation as are prescribed by law and are necessary in a democratic society in the interests of public safety, for the protection of public order, health or morals, or for the protection of the rights and freedoms of others.

Freedom of expression

53-016 **Article 10**—1. Everyone has the right to freedom of expression. This right shall include freedom to hold opinions and to receive and impart information and ideas without interference by public authority and regardless of frontiers. This Article shall not prevent States from requiring the licensing of broadcasting, television or cinema enterprises.

2. The exercise of these freedoms, since it carries with it duties and responsibilities, may be subject to such formalities, conditions, restrictions or penalties as are prescribed by law and are necessary in a democratic society, in the interests of national security, territorial integrity or public safety, for the prevention of disorder or crime, for the protection of health or morals, for the protection of the reputation or rights of others, for preventing the disclosure of information received in confidence, or for maintaining the authority and impartiality of the judiciary.

Freedom of assembly and association

Article 11—1. Everyone has the right to freedom of peaceful assembly and to freedom of association with others, including the right to form and to join trade unions for the protection of his interests. **53-017**

2. No restrictions shall be placed on the exercise of these rights other than such as are prescribed by law and are necessary in a democratic society in the interests of national security or public safety, for the prevention of disorder or crime, for the protection of health or morals or for the protection of the rights and freedoms of others. This Article shall not prevent the imposition of lawful restrictions on the exercise of these rights by members of the armed forces, of the police or of the administration of the State.

Right to marry

Article 12 Men and women of marriageable age have the right to marry and to found a family, according to the national laws governing the exercise of this right. **53-018**

Prohibition of discrimination

Article 14 The enjoyment of the rights and freedoms set forth in this Convention shall be secured without discrimination on any ground such as sex, race, colour, language, religion, political or other opinion, national or social origin, association with a national minority, property, birth or other status. **53-019**

Restrictions on political activity of aliens

Article 16 Nothing in Articles 10, 11 and 14 shall be regarded as preventing the High Contracting Parties from imposing restrictions on the political activity of aliens. **53-020**

Prohibition of abuse of rights

Article 17 Nothing in this Convention may be interpreted as implying for any State, group or person any right to engage in any activity or perform any act aimed at the destruction of any of the rights and freedoms set forth herein or at their limitation to a greater extent than is provided for in the Convention. **53-021**

Limitation on use of restrictions on rights

Article 18 The restrictions permitted under this Convention to the said rights and freedoms shall not be applied for any purpose other than those for which they have been prescribed. **53-022**

THE FIRST PROTOCOL

Protection of property

Article 1 Every natural or legal person is entitled to the peaceful enjoyment of his possessions. No one shall be deprived of his possessions except in the public interest and subject to the conditions provided for by law and by the general principles of international law. **53-023**

The preceding provisions shall not, however, in any way impair the right of a State to enforce such laws as it deems necessary to control the use of property in accordance with the general interest or to secure the payment of taxes or other contributions or penalties.

Right to education

Article 2 No person shall be denied the right to education. In the exercise of any functions which it assumes in relation to education and to teaching, the State shall respect the right of parents to ensure such education and teaching in conformity with their own religious and philosophical convictions. **53-024**

Right to free elections

53-025 **Article 3** The High Contracting Parties undertake to hold free elections at reasonable intervals by secret ballot, under conditions which will ensure the free expression of the opinion of the people in the choice of the legislature.

THE SIXTH PROTOCOL

Abolition of the death penalty

53-026 **Article 1** The death penalty shall be abolished. No one shall be condemned to such penalty or executed.

Death penalty in time of war

53-027 **Article 2** A State may make provision in its law for the death penalty in respect of acts committed in time of war or of imminent threat of war; such penalty shall be applied only in the instances laid down in the law and in accordance with its provisions. The State shall communicate to the Secretary General of the Council of Europe the relevant provisions of that law.

Protection of Children Act 1999

CHAPTER 14

Department of Health list

Duty of Secretary of State to keep list

54-001 **1.**—(1) The Secretary of State shall keep a list of individuals who are considered unsuitable to work with children.

(2) An individual shall not be included in the list unless—

(a) he has been referred to the Secretary of State under [section 2 or 2A or 2D][1] below;

[(aa) he has been included in the list under section 2B below; or][2]

(b) he is transferred to the list from the Consultancy Service Index under section 3 below.

(3) The Secretary of State may at any time remove an individual from the list if he is satisfied that the individual should not have been included in it.

General

Effect of inclusion in either list

54-002 **7.**—[(1) Where a child care organisation proposes to offer an individual employment in a child care position, the organisation–

(a) shall ascertain whether the individual is included in–

(i) the list kept under section 1 above;

(ii) the list kept for the purposes of regulations made under section 218(6) of the 1988 Act ("the 1988 Act list"); or

[1] Words added by Care Standards Act 2000 c.14 Pt VII s 95 (2)

[2] Added by Care Standards Act 2000 c.14 Pt VII s 96 (2)

(iii) any list kept by the Secretary of State or the National Assembly for Wales of persons disqualified under section 470 or 471 of the Education Act 1996 ("the 1996 Act list"); and

(b) if he is included in any of those lists, shall not offer him employment in such a position.][1]

[[(1A) Where–

(a) a person ("the recipient") employs, or proposes to employ, an individual to provide care for a child; and

(b) a local authority proposes to make a payment to the recipient under section 17A of the Children Act 1989 (direct payments) in respect of his securing the provision of the care,

the authority shall, if the recipient asks it to do so, ascertain whether the individual is included in any of the lists mentioned in subsection (1) above.][2]

(1A) Where a child care organisation discovers that an individual employed by it in a child care position is included in any of the lists mentioned in subsection (1) above, it shall cease to employ him in a child care position.

For the purposes of this subsection an individual is not employed in a child care position if he has been suspended or provisionally transferred to a position which is not a child care position.][3]

(2) Where a child care organisation proposes to offer employment in a child care position to an individual who has been supplied by an organisation which carries on an employment agency [or an employment business][4], or an agency for the supply of nurses, there is a sufficient compliance with subsection (1) above if the child care organisation—

(a) satisfies itself that, on a date within the last 12 months, the other organisation ascertained whether the individual was included in [any of the lists mentioned in subsection (1) above][5];

(b) obtains written confirmation of the facts as ascertained by that organisation; and

(c) if the individual was included in [any of those lists][6] on that date, does not offer him employment in a child care position.

[(2A) Where a local authority is required under subsection (1A) above to ascertain whether an individual who has been supplied as mentioned in subsection (2) above is included in any of the lists there mentioned, there is sufficient compliance with subsection (1A) above if the authority–

(a) satisfies itself that, on a date within the last 12 months, the organisation which supplied the individual ascertained whether he was included in any of those lists; and

(b) obtains written confirmation of the facts as ascertained by the organisation.][7]

(3) It is immaterial for the purposes of subsection (1) or (2) above whether the individual is already employed by the child care organisation.

[(4) In this section–

(a) any reference to inclusion in the 1988 Act list is a reference to inclusion in that list on the grounds mentioned in section 218(6ZA)(c) of the 1988 Act; and

---

[1] Substituted by Care Standards Act 2000 c.14 Pt VII s 101 (2)
[2] Added by Care Standards Act 2000 c.14 Pt VII s 98
[3] Added by Care Standards Act 2000 c.14 Sch 4 para 26 (2i) (a)
[4] Words inserted by Care Standards Act 2000 c.14 Sch 4 para 26 (2i) (b)
[5] Words substituted by Care Standards Act 2000 c.14 Pt VII s 101 (3) (a)
[6] Words substituted by Care Standards Act 2000 c.14 Pt VII s 101 (3) (b)
[7] Added by Care Standards Act 2000 c.14 Pt VII s 98

(b) any reference to inclusion in the 1996 Act list is a reference to inclusion in that list as a person disqualified on the grounds mentioned in section 469(1)(d)(i) of the Education Act 1996.][1]

Youth Justice and Criminal Evidence Act 1999

CHAPTER 23

PART II

GIVING OF EVIDENCE OR INFORMATION FOR PURPOSES OF CRIMINAL PROCEEDINGS

CHAPTER I

SPECIAL MEASURES DIRECTIONS IN CASE OF VULNERABLE AND INTIMIDATED WITNESSES

Preliminary

Witnesses eligible for assistance on grounds of age or incapacity

55-001 **16.**—(1) For the purposes of this Chapter a witness in criminal proceedings (other than the accused) is eligible for assistance by virtue of this section—

(a) if under the age of 17 at the time of the hearing; or

(b) if the court considers that the quality of evidence given by the witness is likely to be diminished by reason of any circumstances falling within subsection (2).

(2) The circumstances falling within this subsection are—

(a) that the witness—

(i) suffers from mental disorder within the meaning of the Mental Health Act 1983, or

(ii) otherwise has a significant impairment of intelligence and social functioning;

(b) that the witness has a physical disability or is suffering from a physical disorder.

(3) In subsection (1)(a) "the time of the hearing", in relation to a witness, means the time when it falls to the court to make a determination for the purposes of section 19(2) in relation to the witness.

(4) In determining whether a witness falls within subsection (1)(b) the court must consider any views expressed by the witness.

(5) In this Chapter references to the quality of a witness's evidence are to its quality in terms of completeness, coherence and accuracy; and for this purpose "coherence" refers to a witness's ability in giving evidence to give answers which address the questions put to the witness and can be understood both individually and collectively.

[1] Substituted by Care Standards Act 2000 c.14 Pt VII s 101 (4)

Witnesses eligible for assistance on grounds of fear or distress about testifying

17.—(1) For the purposes of this Chapter a witness in criminal proceedings (other than the accused) is eligible for assistance by virtue of this subsection if the court is satisfied that the quality of evidence given by the witness is likely to be diminished by reason of fear or distress on the part of the witness in connection with testifying in the proceedings. **55-002**

(2) In determining whether a witness falls within subsection (1) the court must take into account, in particular—

(a) the nature and alleged circumstances of the offence to which the proceedings relate;

(b) the age of the witness;

(c) such of the following matters as appear to the court to be relevant, namely—

(i) the social and cultural background and ethnic origins of the witness,

(ii) the domestic and employment circumstances of the witness, and

(iii) any religious beliefs or political opinions of the witness;

(d) any behaviour towards the witness on the part of—

(i) the accused,

(ii) members of the family or associates of the accused, or

(iii) any other person who is likely to be an accused or a witness in the proceedings.

(3) In determining that question the court must in addition consider any views expressed by the witness.

(4) Where the complainant in respect of a sexual offence is a witness in proceedings relating to that offence (or to that offence and any other offences), the witness is eligible for assistance in relation to those proceedings by virtue of this subsection unless the witness has informed the court of the witness' wish not to be so eligible by virtue of this subsection.

Special measures available to eligible witnesses

18.—(1) For the purposes of this Chapter— **55-003**

(a) the provision which may be made by a special measures direction by virtue of each of sections 23 to 30 is a special measure available in relation to a witness eligible for assistance by virtue of section 16; and

(b) the provision which may be made by such a direction by virtue of each of sections 23 to 28 is a special measure available in relation to a witness eligible for assistance by virtue of section 17;

but this subsection has effect subject to subsection (2).

(2) Where (apart from this subsection) a special measure would, in accordance with subsection (1)(a) or (b), be available in relation to a witness in any proceedings, it shall not be taken by a court to be available in relation to the witness unless—

(a) the court has been notified by the Secretary of State that relevant arrangements may be made available in the area in which it appears to the court that the proceedings will take place, and

(b) the notice has not been withdrawn.

(3) In subsection (2) "relevant arrangements" means arrangements for implementing the measure in question which cover the witness and the proceedings in question.

(4) The withdrawal of a notice under that subsection relating to a special measure shall not affect the availability of that measure in relation to a witness if a special measures direction providing for that measure to apply to the witness's evidence has been made by the court before the notice is withdrawn.

(5) The Secretary of State may by order make such amendments of this Chapter as he considers appropriate for altering the special measures which, in accordance with subsection (1)(a) or (b), are available in relation to a witness eligible for assistance by virtue of section 16 or (as the case may be) section 17, whether—

(a) by modifying the provisions relating to any measure for the time being available in relation to such a witness,
(b) by the addition—
   (i) (with or without modifications) of any measure which is for the time being available in relation to a witness eligible for assistance by virtue of the other of those sections, or
   (ii) of any new measure, or
(c) by the removal of any measure.

Special measures directions

Special provisions relating to child witnesses

55-004 **21.**—(1) For the purposes of this section—

(a) a witness in criminal proceedings is a "child witness" if he is an eligible witness by reason of section 16(1)(a) (whether or not he is an eligible witness by reason of any other provision of section 16 or 17);
(b) a child witness is "in need of special protection" if the offence (or any of the offences) to which the proceedings relate is—
   (i) an offence falling within section 35(3)(a) (sexual offences etc.), or
   (ii) an offence falling within section 35(3)(b), (c) or (d) (kidnapping, assaults etc.); and
(c) a "relevant recording", in relation to a child witness, is a video recording of an interview of the witness made with a view to its admission as evidence in chief of the witness.

(2) Where the court, in making a determination for the purposes of section 19(2), determines that a witness in criminal proceedings is a child witness, the court must—

(a) first have regard to subsections (3) to (7) below; and
(b) then have regard to section 19(2);

and for the purposes of section 19(2), as it then applies to the witness, any special measures required to be applied in relation to him by virtue of this section shall be treated as if they were measures determined by the court, pursuant to section 19(2)(a) and (b)(i), to be ones that (whether on their own or with any other special measures) would be likely to maximise, so far as practicable, the quality of his evidence.

(3) The primary rule in the case of a child witness is that the court must give a special measures direction in relation to the witness which complies with the following requirements—

(a) it must provide for any relevant recording to be admitted under section 27 (video recorded evidence in chief); and
(b) it must provide for any evidence given by the witness in the proceedings which is not given by means of a video recording (whether in chief or

otherwise) to be given by means of a live link in accordance with section 24.

(4) The primary rule is subject to the following limitations—

(a) the requirement contained in subsection (3)(a) or (b) has effect subject to the availability (within the meaning of section 18(2)) of the special measure in question in relation to the witness;

(b) the requirement contained in subsection (3)(a) also has effect subject to section 27(2); and

(c) the rule does not apply to the extent that the court is satisfied that compliance with it would not be likely to maximise the quality of the witness's evidence so far as practicable (whether because the application to that evidence of one or more other special measures available in relation to the witness would have that result or for any other reason).

(5) However, subsection (4)(c) does not apply in relation to a child witness in need of special protection.

(6) Where a child witness is in need of special protection by virtue of subsection (1)(b)(i), any special measures direction given by the court which complies with the requirement contained in subsection (3)(a) must in addition provide for the special measure available under section 28 (video recorded cross-examination or re-examination) to apply in relation to—

(a) any cross-examination of the witness otherwise than by the accused in person, and

(b) any subsequent re-examination.

(7) The requirement contained in subsection (6) has effect subject to the following limitations—

(a) it has effect subject to the availability (within the meaning of section 18(2)) of that special measure in relation to the witness; and

(b) it does not apply if the witness has informed the court that he does not want that special measure to apply in relation to him.

(8) Where a special measures direction is given in relation to a child witness who is an eligible witness by reason only of section 16(1)(a), then—

(a) subject to subsection (9) below, and

(b) except where the witness has already begun to give evidence in the proceedings,

the direction shall cease to have effect at the time when the witness attains the age of 17.

(9) Where a special measures direction is given in relation to a child witness who is an eligible witness by reason only of section 16(1)(a) and—

(a) the direction provides—

(i) for any relevant recording to be admitted under section 27 as evidence in chief of the witness, or

(ii) for the special measure available under section 28 to apply in relation to the witness, and

(b) if it provides for that special measure to so apply, the witness is still under the age of 17 when the video recording is made for the purposes of section 28,

then, so far as it provides as mentioned in paragraph (a)(i) or (ii) above, the direction shall continue to have effect in accordance with section 20(1) even though the witness subsequently attains that age.

Extension of provisions of section 21 to certain witnesses over 17

22.—(1) For the purposes of this section—

(a) a witness in criminal proceedings (other than the accused) is a "qualifying witness" if he—
   (i) is not an eligible witness at the time of the hearing (as defined by section 16(3)), but
   (ii) was under the age of 17 when a relevant recording was made;

(b) a qualifying witness is "in need of special protection" if the offence (or any of the offences) to which the proceedings relate is—
   (i) an offence falling within section 35(3)(a) (sexual offences etc.), or
   (ii) an offence falling within section 35(3)(b), (c) or (d) (kidnapping, assaults etc.); and

(c) a "relevant recording", in relation to a witness, is a video recording of an interview of the witness made with a view to its admission as evidence in chief of the witness.

(2) Subsections (2) to (7) of section 21 shall apply as follows in relation to a qualifying witness—

(a) subsections (2) to (4), so far as relating to the giving of a direction complying with the requirement contained in subsection (3)(a), shall apply to a qualifying witness in respect of the relevant recording as they apply to a child witness (within the meaning of that section);

(b) subsection (5), so far as relating to the giving of such a direction, shall apply to a qualifying witness in need of special protection as it applies to a child witness in need of special protection (within the meaning of that section); and

(c) subsections (6) and (7) shall apply to a qualifying witness in need of special protection by virtue of subsection (1)(b)(i) above as they apply to such a child witness as is mentioned in subsection (6).

Special measures

Screening witness from accused

55-006 **23.**—(1) A special measures direction may provide for the witness, while giving testimony or being sworn in court, to be prevented by means of a screen or other arrangement from seeing the accused.

(2) But the screen or other arrangement must not prevent the witness from being able to see, and to be seen by—

(a) the judge or justices (or both) and the jury (if there is one);

(b) legal representatives acting in the proceedings; and

(c) any interpreter or other person appointed (in pursuance of the direction or otherwise) to assist the witness.

(3) Where two or more legal representatives are acting for a party to the proceedings, subsection (2)(b) is to be regarded as satisfied in relation to those representatives if the witness is able at all material times to see and be seen by at least one of them.

Evidence by live link

55-007 **24.**—(1) A special measures direction may provide for the witness to give evidence by means of a live link.

(2) Where a direction provides for the witness to give evidence by means of a live link, the witness may not give evidence in any other way without the permission of the court.

(3) The court may give permission for the purposes of subsection (2) if it appears to the court to be in the interests of justice to do so, and may do so either—

(a) on an application by a party to the proceedings, if there has been a material change of circumstances since the relevant time, or

(b) of its own motion.

(4) In subsection (3) "the relevant time" means —

(a) the time when the direction was given, or

(b) if a previous application has been made under that subsection, the time when the application (or last application) was made.

(5) Where in proceedings before a magistrates' court—

(a) evidence is to be given by means of a live link in accordance with a special measures direction, but

(b) suitable facilities for receiving such evidence are not available at any petty-sessional court-house in which that court can (apart from this subsection) lawfully sit,

the court may sit for the purposes of the whole or any part of those proceedings at a place where such facilities are available and which has been appointed for the purposes of this subsection by the justices acting for the petty sessions area for which the court acts.

(6) A place appointed under subsection (5) may be outside the petty sessions area for which it is appointed; but (if so) it is to be regarded as being in that area for the purpose of the jurisdiction of the justices acting for that area.

(7) In this section "petty-sessional court-house" has the same meaning as in the Magistrates' Courts Act 1980 and "petty sessions area" has the same meaning as in the Justices of the Peace Act 1997.

(8) In this Chapter "live link" means a live television link or other arrangement whereby a witness, while absent from the courtroom or other place where the proceedings are being held, is able to see and hear a person there and to be seen and heard by the persons specified in section 23(2)(a) to (c).

Powers of Criminal Courts (Sentencing) Act 2000

CHAPTER 6

PART VI

FINANCIAL PENALTIES AND ORDERS

Young offenders

Power to order parent or guardian to pay fine, costs or compensation

137.—(1) Where— **56-001**

(a) a child or young person (that is to say, any person aged under 18) is convicted of any offence for the commission of which a fine or costs may be imposed or a compensation order may be made, and

(b) the court is of the opinion that the case would best be met by the imposition of a fine or costs or the making of such an order, whether with or without any other punishment,

the court shall order that the fine, compensation or costs awarded be paid by the parent or guardian of the child or young person instead of by the child or young person himself, unless the court is satisfied—

(i) that the parent or guardian cannot be found; or

(ii) that it would be unreasonable to make an order for payment, having regard to the circumstances of the case.

(2) Where but for this subsection a court would impose a fine on a child or young person under—

(a) paragraph 4(1)(a) or 5(1)(a) of Schedule 3 to this Act (breach of curfew, probation, community service, combination or drug treatment and testing order),

(b) paragraph 2(1)(a) of Schedule 5 to this Act (breach of attendance centre order or attendance centre rules),

(c) paragraph 2(2)(a) of Schedule 7 to this Act (breach of supervision order),

(d) paragraph 2(2)(a) of Schedule 8 to this Act (breach of action plan order or reparation order),

(e) section 104(3)(b) above (breach of requirements of supervision under a detention and training order), or

(f) section 4(3)(b) of the Criminal Justice and Public Order Act 1994 (breach of requirements of supervision under a secure training order),

the court shall order that the fine be paid by the parent or guardian of the child or young person instead of by the child or young person himself, unless the court is satisfied—

(i) that the parent or guardian cannot be found; or

(ii) that it would be unreasonable to make an order for payment, having regard to the circumstances of the case.

(3) In the case of a young person aged 16 or over, subsections (1) and (2) above shall have effect as if, instead of imposing a duty, they conferred a power to make such an order as is mentioned in those subsections.

(4) Subject to subsection (5) below, no order shall be made under this section without giving the parent or guardian an opportunity of being heard.

(5) An order under this section may be made against a parent or guardian who, having been required to attend, has failed to do so.

(6) A parent or guardian may appeal to the Crown Court against an order under this section made by a magistrates' court.

(7) A parent or guardian may appeal to the Court of Appeal against an order under this section made by the Crown Court, as if he had been convicted on indictment and the order were a sentence passed on his conviction.

(8) In relation to a child or young person for whom a local authority have parental responsibility and who—

(a) is in their care, or

(b) is provided with accommodation by them in the exercise of any functions (in particular those under the Children Act 1989) which [are social services functions within the meaning of][1] the Local Authority Social Services Act 1970,

references in this section to his parent or guardian shall be construed as references to that authority.

[1] Words inserted by SI 2002/808 art 34

(9) In subsection (8) above "local authority" and "parental responsibility" have the same meanings as in the Children Act 1989.

Fixing of fine or compensation to be paid by parent or guardian

138.—(1) For the purposes of any order under section 137 above made against the parent or guardian of a child or young person— **56-002**

(a) section 128 above (fixing of fines) shall have effect as if any reference in subsections (1) to (4) to the financial circumstances of the offender were a reference to the financial circumstances of the parent or guardian, and as if subsection (5) were omitted;

(b) section 130(11) above (determination of compensation order) shall have effect as if any reference to the means of the person against whom the compensation order is made were a reference to the financial circumstances of the parent or guardian; and

(c) section 130(12) above (preference to be given to compensation if insufficient means to pay both compensation and a fine) shall have effect as if the reference to the offender were a reference to the parent or guardian;

but in relation to an order under section 137 made against a local authority this subsection has effect subject to subsection (2) below.

(2) For the purposes of any order under section 137 above made against a local authority, sections 128(1) (duty to inquire into financial circumstances) and 130(11) above shall not apply.

(3) For the purposes of any order under section 137 above, where the parent or guardian of an offender who is a child or young person—

(a) has failed to comply with an order under section 136 above, or

(b) has otherwise failed to co-operate with the court in its inquiry into his financial circumstances,

and the court considers that it has insufficient information to make a proper determination of the parent's or guardian's financial circumstances, it may make such determination as it thinks fit.

(4) Where a court has, in fixing the amount of a fine, determined the financial circumstances of a parent or guardian under subsection (3) above, subsections (2) to (4) of section 129 above (remission of fines) shall (so far as applicable) have effect as they have effect in the case mentioned in section 129(1), but as if the reference in section 129(2) to the offender's financial circumstances were a reference to the financial circumstances of the parent or guardian.

(5) In this section "local authority" has the same meaning as in the Children Act 1989.

PART VII

FURTHER POWERS OF COURTS

Young offenders

Binding over of parent or guardian

150.—(1) Where a child or young person (that is to say, any person aged under 18) is convicted of an offence, the powers conferred by this section shall be exercisable by the court by which he is sentenced for that offence, and where the offender is aged under 16 when sentenced it shall be the duty of that court— **56-003**

(a) to exercise those powers if it is satisfied, having regard to the circumstances of the case, that their exercise would be desirable in the interests of preventing the commission by him of further offences; and

(b) if it does not exercise them, to state in open court that it is not satisfied as mentioned in paragraph (a) above and why it is not so satisfied;

but this subsection has effect subject to section 19(5) above and paragraph 13(5) of Schedule 1 to this Act (cases where referral orders made or extended).

(2) The powers conferred by this section are as follows—

(a) with the consent of the offender's parent or guardian, to order the parent or guardian to enter into a recognizance to take proper care of him and exercise proper control over him; and

(b) if the parent or guardian refuses consent and the court considers the refusal unreasonable, to order the parent or guardian to pay a fine not exceeding £1,000;

and where the court has passed a community sentence on the offender, it may include in the recognizance a provision that the offender's parent or guardian ensure that the offender complies with the requirements of that sentence.

(3) An order under this section shall not require the parent or guardian to enter into a recognizance for an amount exceeding £1,000.

(4) An order under this section shall not require the parent or guardian to enter into a recognizance—

(a) for a period exceeding three years; or

(b) where the offender will attain the age of 18 in a period shorter than three years, for a period exceeding that shorter period.

(5) Section 120 of the Magistrates' Courts Act 1980 (forfeiture of recognizances) shall apply in relation to a recognizance entered into in pursuance of an order under this section as it applies in relation to a recognizance to keep the peace.

(6) A fine imposed under subsection (2)(b) above shall be deemed, for the purposes of any enactment, to be a sum adjudged to be paid by a conviction.

(7) In fixing the amount of a recognizance under this section, the court shall take into account among other things the means of the parent or guardian so far as they appear or are known to the court; and this subsection applies whether taking into account the means of the parent or guardian has the effect of increasing or reducing the amount of the recognizance.

(8) A parent or guardian may appeal to the Crown Court against an order under this section made by a magistrates' court.

(9) A parent or guardian may appeal to the Court of Appeal against an order under this section made by the Crown Court, as if he had been convicted on indictment and the order were a sentence passed on his conviction.

(10) A court may vary or revoke an order made by it under this section if, on the application of the parent or guardian, it appears to the court, having regard to any change in the circumstances since the order was made, to be in the interests of justice to do so.

(11) For the purposes of this section, taking "care" of a person includes giving him protection and guidance and "control" includes discipline.

Care Standards Act 2000

CHAPTER 14

PART I

INTRODUCTORY

Preliminary

Children's homes

1.—(1) Subsections (2) to (6) have effect for the purposes of this Act. **57-001**

(2) An establishment is a children's home (subject to the following provisions of this section) if it provides care and accommodation wholly or mainly for children.

(3) An establishment is not a children's home merely because a child is cared for and accommodated there by a parent or relative of his or by a foster parent.

(4) An establishment is not a children's home if it is–

(a) a health service hospital;

(b) an independent hospital or an independent clinic; or

(c) a residential family centre,

or if it is of a description excepted by regulations.

(5) Subject to subsection (6), an establishment is not a children's home if it is a school.

(6) A school is a children's home at any time if at that time accommodation is provided for children at the school and either–

(a) in each year that fell within the period of two years ending at that time, accommodation was provided for children, either at the school or under arrangements made by the proprietor of the school, for more than 295 days; or

(b) it is intended to provide accommodation for children, either at the school or under arrangements made by the proprietor of the school, for more than 295 days in any year;

and in this subsection "year" means a period of twelve months.

But accommodation shall not for the purposes of paragraph (a) be regarded as provided to children for a number of days unless there is at least one child to whom it is provided for that number of days; and paragraph (b) shall be construed accordingly.

(7) For the purposes of this section a person is a foster parent in relation to a child if–

(a) he is a local authority foster parent in relation to the child;

(b) he is a foster parent with whom a child has been placed by a voluntary organisation under section 59(1)(a) of the 1989 Act; or

(c) he fosters the child privately.

Other basic definitions

4.—(1) This section has effect for the purposes of this Act. **57-002**

(2) "Residential family centre" means, subject to subsection (6), any establishment at which–

(a) accommodation is provided for children and their parents;
(b) the parents' capacity to respond to the children's needs and to safeguard their welfare is monitored or assessed; and
(c) the parents are given such advice, guidance or counselling as is considered necessary.

In this subsection "parent", in relation to a child, includes any person who is looking after him.

(4) "Fostering agency" means, subject to subsection (6)–
(a) an undertaking which consists of or includes discharging functions of local authorities in connection with the placing of children with foster parents; or
(b) a voluntary organisation which places children with foster parents under section 59(1) of the 1989 Act.

(6) The definitions in subsections (2) to (5) do not include any description of establishment, undertaking or organisation excepted from those definitions by regulations.

(7) "Voluntary adoption agency" means an adoption society within the meaning of the Adoption Act 1976 which is a voluntary organisation within the meaning of that Act.

(8) Below in this Act–
(a) any reference to a description of establishment is a reference to a children's home, an independent hospital, an independent hospital in which treatment or nursing (or both) are provided for persons liable to be detained under the Mental Health Act 1983, an independent clinic, a care home or a residential family centre;
(b) a reference to any establishment is a reference to an establishment of any of those descriptions.

(9) Below in this Act–
(a) any reference to a description of agency is a reference to an independent medical agency, a domiciliary care agency, a nurses agency, a fostering agency or a voluntary adoption agency;
(b) a reference to any agency is a reference to an agency of any of those descriptions.

Registration authorities

Registration authorities

57-003 **5.** For the purposes of this Act–
(a) the registration authority in relation to England is the National Care Standards Commission;
(b) the registration authority in relation to Wales is the National Assembly for Wales (referred to in this Act as "the Assembly").

National Care Standards Commission

57-004 **6.**—(1) There shall be a body corporate, to be known as the National Care Standards Commission (referred to in this Act as "the Commission"), which shall exercise in relation to England the functions conferred on it by or under this Act or any other enactment.

(2) The Commission shall, in the exercise of its functions, act–
(a) in accordance with any directions in writing given to it by the Secretary of State; and

(b) under the general guidance of the Secretary of State.

PART II

ESTABLISHMENTS AND AGENCIES

Regulations and standards

Regulation of establishments and agencies

22.—(1) Regulations may impose in relation to establishments and agencies any requirements which the appropriate Minister thinks fit for the purposes of this Part and may in particular make any provision such as is mentioned in subsection (2), (7) or (8). **57-005**

(2) Regulations may–

(a) make provision as to the persons who are fit to carry on or manage an establishment or agency;

(b) make provision as to the persons who are fit to work at an establishment or for the purposes of an agency;

(c) make provision as to the fitness of premises to be used as an establishment or for the purposes of an agency;

(d) make provision for securing the welfare of persons accommodated in an establishment or provided with services by an establishment, an independent medical agency or a domiciliary care agency;

(e) make provision for securing the welfare of children placed, under section 23(2)(a) of the 1989 Act, by a fostering agency;

(f) make provision as to the management and control of the operations of an establishment or agency;

(g) make provision as to the numbers of persons, or persons of any particular type, working at an establishment or for the purposes of an agency;

(h) make provision as to the management and training of such persons;

(i) impose requirements as to the financial position of an establishment or agency;

(j) make provision requiring the person carrying on an establishment or agency to appoint a manager in prescribed circumstances.

(3) Regulations under subsection (2)(a) may, in particular, make provision for prohibiting persons from managing an establishment or agency unless they are registered in, or in a particular part of, one of the registers maintained under section 56(1).

(4) Regulations under subsection (2)(b) may, in particular, make provision for prohibiting persons from working in such positions as may be prescribed at an establishment, or for the purposes of an agency, unless they are registered in, or in a particular part of, one of the registers maintained under section 56(1).

(5) Regulations under paragraph (d) of subsection (2) may, in particular, make provision–

(a) as to the promotion and protection of the health of persons such as are mentioned in that paragraph;

(b) as to the control and restraint of adults accommodated in, or provided with services by, an establishment;

(c) as to the control, restraint and discipline of children accommodated in, or provided with services by, an establishment.

(6) Regulations under paragraph (e) of subsection (2) may, in particular, make provision–

(a) as to the promotion and protection of the health of children such as are mentioned in that paragraph;

(b) as to the control, restraint and discipline of such children.

(7) Regulations may make provision as to the conduct of establishments and agencies, and such regulations may in particular–

(a) make provision as to the facilities and services to be provided in establishments and by agencies;

(j) make provision requiring arrangements to be made by the person who carries on, or manages, an establishment or agency for dealing with complaints made by or on behalf of those seeking, or receiving, any of the services provided in the establishment or by the agency and requiring that person to take steps for publicising the arrangements;

(8) Regulations may make provision–

(a) requiring the approval of the appropriate Minister for the provision and use of accommodation for the purpose of restricting the liberty of children in children's homes;

(b) imposing other requirements (in addition to those imposed by section 25 of the 1989 Act (use of accommodation for restricting liberty)) as to the placing of a child in accommodation provided for the purpose mentioned in paragraph (a), including a requirement to obtain the permission of any local authority who are looking after the child;

(c) as to the facilities which are to be provided for giving religious instruction to children in children's homes.

(10) References in this section to agencies do not include references to voluntary adoption agencies.

National minimum standards

57-006 **23.**—(1) The appropriate Minister may prepare and publish statements of national minimum standards applicable to establishments or agencies.

(2) The appropriate Minister shall keep the standards set out in the statements under review and may publish amended statements whenever he considers it appropriate to do so.

(3) Before issuing a statement, or an amended statement which in the opinion of the appropriate Minister effects a substantial change in the standards, the appropriate Minister shall consult any persons he considers appropriate.

(4) The standards shall be taken into account–

(a) in the making of any decision by the registration authority under this Part;

(b) in any proceedings for the making of an order under section 20;

(c) in any proceedings on an appeal against such a decision or order; and

(d) in any proceedings for an offence under regulations under this Part.

PART III

LOCAL AUTHORITY SERVICES

Introductory

57-007 **43.**—(1) This section has effect for the purposes of this Part.

(2) "Relevant functions", in relation to a local authority, means relevant adoption functions and relevant fostering functions.

(3) In relation to a local authority–
(a) "relevant adoption functions" means functions under the Adoption Act 1976 of making or participating in arrangements for the adoption of children; and
(b) "relevant fostering functions" means functions under section 23(2)(a) of the 1989 Act or regulations under any of paragraphs (a), (b) or (d) to (f) of paragraph 12 of Schedule 2 to that Act.

General powers of the Commission

44. The Commission may at any time give advice to the Secretary of State on– **57-008**
(a) any changes which the Commission thinks should be made, for the purpose of securing improvement in the quality of services provided by local authorities in England in the exercise of relevant functions, in the standards set out in statements under section 49; and
(b) any other matter connected with the exercise by local authorities in England of relevant functions.

Inspection by registration authority of adoption and fostering services

45.—(1) Subject to section 47(6)– **57-009**
(a) the registration authority may at any time require a local authority to provide it with any information relating to the discharge by the local authority of relevant functions which the registration authority considers it necessary or expedient to have for the purposes of its functions under this Part;
(b) a person authorised to do so by the registration authority may at any time enter and inspect premises which are used, or which he has reasonable cause to believe to be used, by a local authority in its discharge of relevant functions.

(2) A person authorised by virtue of this section to enter and inspect premises may–
(a) inspect and take copies of any documents or records relating to the discharge by the local authority of relevant functions;
(b) interview in private any employee of the local authority.

(3) The powers under subsection (2)(a) include–
(a) power to require the local authority to produce any documents or records, wherever kept, for inspection on the premises; and
(b) in relation to records which are kept by means of a computer, power to require the records to be produced in a form in which they are legible and can be taken away.

(4) Subject to section 47(6), the Secretary of State may by regulations require the Commission to arrange for premises which are used by a local authority in its discharge of relevant functions to be inspected on such occasions or at such intervals as may be prescribed.

Regulation of the exercise of relevant fostering functions

48.—(1) Regulations may make provision about the exercise by local authorities of relevant fostering functions, and may in particular make provision– **57-010**
(a) as to the persons who are fit to work for local authorities in connection with the exercise of such functions;
(b) as to the fitness of premises to be used by local authorities in their exercise of such functions;

(c) as to the management and control of the operations of local authorities in their exercise of such functions;
(d) as to the numbers of persons, or persons of any particular type, working for local authorities in connection with the exercise of such functions;
(e) as to the management and training of such persons.

(2) Regulations under subsection (1)(a) may, in particular, make provision for prohibiting persons from working for local authorities in such positions as may be prescribed unless they are registered in, or in a particular part of, one of the registers maintained under section 56(1).

Carers and Disabled Children Act 2000

CHAPTER 16

Right of carers to assessment

58-001 **1.**—(1) If an individual aged 16 or over ("the carer")–
(a) provides or intends to provide a substantial amount of care on a regular basis for another individual aged 18 or over ("the person cared for"); and
(b) asks a local authority to carry out an assessment of his ability to provide and to continue to provide care for the person cared for,

the local authority must carry out such an assessment if it is satisfied that the person cared for is someone for whom it may provide or arrange for the provision of community care services.

(2) For the purposes of such an assessment, the local authority may take into account, so far as it considers it to be material, an assessment under section 1(1) of the Carers (Recognition and Services) Act 1995.

(3) Subsection (1) does not apply if the individual provides or will provide the care in question–
(a) by virtue of a contract of employment or other contract with any person; or
(b) as a volunteer for a voluntary organisation.

(4) The Secretary of State (or, in relation to Wales, the National Assembly for Wales) may give directions as to the manner in which an assessment under subsection (1) is to be carried out or the form it is to take.

(5) Subject to any such directions, it is to be carried out in such manner, and is to take such form, as the local authority considers appropriate.

(6) In this section, "voluntary organisation" has the same meaning as in the National Assistance Act 1948.

Services for carers

58-002 **2.**—(1) The local authority must consider the assessment and decide–
(a) whether the carer has needs in relation to the care which he provides or intends to provide;
(b) if so, whether they could be satisfied (wholly or partly) by services which the local authority may provide; and

(c) if they could be so satisfied, whether or not to provide services to the carer.

(2) The services referred to are any services which–

(a) the local authority sees fit to provide; and

(b) will in the local authority's view help the carer care for the person cared for,

and may take the form of physical help or other forms of support.

(3) A service, although provided to the carer–

(a) may take the form of a service delivered to the person cared for if it is one which, if provided to him instead of to the carer, could fall within community care services and they both agree it is to be so delivered; but

(b) if a service is delivered to the person cared for it may not, except in prescribed circumstances, include anything of an intimate nature.

(4) Regulations may make provision about what is, or is not, of an intimate nature for the purposes of subsection (3).

Assessments: persons with parental responsibility for disabled children

6.—(1) If a person with parental responsibility for a disabled child– **58-003**

(a) provides or intends to provide a substantial amount of care on a regular basis for the child; and

(b) asks a local authority to carry out an assessment of his ability to provide and to continue to provide care for the child,

the local authority must carry out such an assessment if it is satisfied that the child and his family are persons for whom it may provide or arrange for the provision of services under section 17 of the Children Act 1989 ("the 1989 Act").

(2) For the purposes of such an assessment, the local authority may take into account, so far as it considers it to be material, an assessment under section 1(2) of the Carers (Recognition and Services) Act 1995.

(3) The Secretary of State (or, in relation to Wales, the National Assembly for Wales) may give directions as to the manner in which an assessment under subsection (1) is to be carried out or the form it is to take.

(4) Subject to any such directions, it is to be carried out in such manner, and is to take such form, as the local authority considers appropriate.

(5) The local authority must take the assessment into account when deciding what, if any, services to provide under section 17 of the 1989 Act.

(6) Terms used in this section have the same meaning as in Part III of the 1989 Act.

Children (Leaving Care) Act 2000

CHAPTER 35

Exclusion from benefits

6.—(1) No person is entitled to income-based jobseekers allowance under the Jobseekers Act 1995, or to income support or housing benefit under the Social Security Contributions and Benefits Act 1992, while he is a person to whom this section applies. **59-001**

(2) Subject to subsection (3), this section applies to—
(a) an eligible child for the purposes of paragraph 19B of Schedule 2 to the Children Act 1989;
(b) a relevant child for the purposes of section 23A of that Act; and
(c) any person of a description prescribed in regulations under subsection (4).

(8) Powers to make regulations under this section are exercisable by statutory instrument.

Criminal Justice and Court Services Act 2000

CHAPTER 43

PART I

THE NEW SERVICES

CHAPTER II

CHILDREN AND FAMILY COURT ADVISORY AND SUPPORT SERVICE

Establishment of the Service

60-001 **11.**—(1) There shall be a body corporate to be known as the Children and Family Court Advisory and Support Service (referred to in this Part as the Service) which is to exercise the functions conferred on it by virtue of this Act and any other enactment.

(2) Schedule 2 (which makes provision about the constitution of the Service, its powers and other matters relating to it) is to have effect.

(3) References in this Act or any other enactment to an officer of the Service are references to—
(a) any member of the staff of the Service appointed under paragraph 5(1)(a) of that Schedule, and
(b) any other individual exercising functions of an officer of the Service by virtue of section 13(2) or (4).

Principal functions of the Service

60-002 **12.**—(1) In respect of family proceedings in which the welfare of children is or may be in question, it is a function of the Service to—
(a) safeguard and promote the welfare of the children,
(b) give advice to any court about any application made to it in such proceedings,
(c) make provision for the children to be represented in such proceedings,
(d) provide information, advice and other support for the children and their families.

(2) The Service must also make provision for the performance of any functions conferred on officers of the Service by virtue of this Act or any other

enactment (whether or not they are exercisable for the purposes of the functions conferred on the Service by subsection (1)).

(3) Regulations may provide for grants to be paid by the Service to any person for the purpose of furthering the performance of any of the Service's functions.

(4) The regulations may provide for the grants to be paid on conditions, including conditions—

(a) regulating the purposes for which the grant or any part of it may be used,

(b) requiring repayment to the Service in specified circumstances.

(5) In this section, "family proceedings" has the same meaning as in the Matrimonial and Family Proceedings Act 1984 and also includes any other proceedings which are family proceedings for the purposes of the Children Act 1989, but—

(a) references to family proceedings include (where the context allows) family proceedings which are proposed or have been concluded, and

(b) for the purposes of paragraph (a), where a supervision order (within the meaning of the Children Act 1989) is made in family proceedings, the proceedings are not to be treated as concluded until the order has ceased to have effect.

Other powers of the Service

13.—(1) The Service may make arrangements with organisations under which the organisations perform functions of the Service on its behalf. **60-003**

(2) Arrangements under subsection (1) may provide for the organisations to designate individuals who may perform functions of officers of the Service.

(3) But the Service may only make an arrangement under subsection (1) if it is of the opinion—

(a) that the functions in question will be performed efficiently and to the required standard, and

(b) that the arrangement represents good value for money.

(4) The Service may make arrangements with individuals under which they may perform functions of officers of the Service.

(5) The Service may commission, or assist the conduct of, research by any person into matters concerned with the exercise of its functions.

Provision of staff or services to other organisations

14.—(1) The Service may make arrangements with an organisation or individual under which staff of the Service may work for the organisation or individual. **60-004**

(2) The Service may make arrangements with an organisation or individual under which any services provided to the Service by its staff are also made available to the organisation or individual.

(3) The Service may charge for anything done under arrangements under this section.

Right to conduct litigation and right of audience

15.—(1) The Service may authorise an officer of the Service of a prescribed description— **60-005**

(a) to conduct litigation in relation to any proceedings in any court,

(b) to exercise a right of audience in any proceedings before any court,

in the exercise of his functions.

(2) An officer of the Service exercising a right to conduct litigation by virtue of subsection (1)(a) who would otherwise have such a right by virtue of section 28(2)(a) of the Courts and Legal Services Act 1990 is to be treated as having acquired that right solely by virtue of this section.

(3) An officer of the Service exercising a right of audience by virtue of subsection (1)(b) who would otherwise have such a right by virtue of section 27(2)(a) of the Courts and Legal Services Act 1990 is to be treated as having acquired that right solely by virtue of this section.

(4) In this section and section 16, "right to conduct litigation" and "right of audience" have the same meanings as in section 119 of the Courts and Legal Services Act 1990.

Cross-examination of officers of the Service

60-006 **16.**—(1) An officer of the Service may, subject to rules of court, be cross-examined in any proceedings to the same extent as any witness.

(2) But an officer of the Service may not be cross-examined merely because he is exercising a right to conduct litigation or a right of audience granted in accordance with section 15.

PART II

PROTECTION OF CHILDREN

Disqualification orders

Meaning of "offence against a child"

60-007 **26.**—(1) For the purposes of this Part, an individual commits an offence against a child if—

(a) he commits any offence mentioned in paragraph 1 of Schedule 4,
(b) he commits against a child any offence mentioned in paragraph 2 of that Schedule, or
(c) he falls within paragraph 3 of that Schedule,

and references to being convicted of, or charged with, an offence against a child are to be read accordingly.

(2) The Secretary of State may by order amend Schedule 4 so as to add, modify or omit any entry.

Disqualification from working with children: adults

60-008 **28.**—(1) This section applies where either of the conditions set out below is satisfied in the case of an individual.

(2) The first condition is that—

(a) the individual is convicted of an offence against a child committed when he was aged 18 or over, and
(b) a qualifying sentence is imposed by a senior court in respect of the conviction.

(3) The second condition is that—

(a) the individual is charged with an offence against a child committed when he was aged 18 or over, and
(b) a relevant order is made by a senior court in respect of the act or omission charged against him as the offence.

(4) Subject to subsection (5), the court must order the individual to be disqualified from working with children.

(5) An order shall not be made under this section if the court is satisfied, having regard to all the circumstances, that it is unlikely that the individual will commit any further offence against a child.

(6) If the court does not make an order under this section, it must state its reasons for not doing so and cause those reasons to be included in the record of the proceedings.

Disqualification from working with children: juveniles

29.—(1) This section applies where either of the conditions set out below is satisfied in the case of an individual. **60-009**

(2) The first condition is that—

(a) the individual is convicted of an offence against a child committed at a time when the individual was under the age of 18, and

(b) a qualifying sentence is imposed by a senior court in respect of the conviction.

(3) The second condition is that—

(a) the individual is charged with an offence against a child committed at a time when the individual was under the age of 18, and

(b) a relevant order is made by a senior court in respect of the act or omission charged against him as the offence.

(4) If the court is satisfied, having regard to all the circumstances, that it is likely that the individual will commit a further offence against a child, it must order the individual to be disqualified from working with children.

(5) If the court makes an order under this section, it must state its reasons for doing so and cause those reasons to be included in the record of the proceedings.

Sections 28 and 29: supplemental

30.—(1) In sections 28 and 29 and this section— **60-010**

"guardianship order" means a guardianship order within the meaning of the Army Act 1955, the Air Force Act 1955, the Naval Discipline Act 1957 or the Mental Health Act 1983,

"qualifying sentence" means—

(a) a sentence of imprisonment for a term of 12 months or more,

(b) a sentence of detention in a young offender institution for a term of 12 months or more,

(c) a sentence of detention during Her Majesty's pleasure,

(d) a sentence of detention for a period of 12 months or more under section 91 of the Powers of Criminal Courts (Sentencing) Act 2000 (offenders under 18 convicted of certain serious offences),

(e) a detention and training order for a term of 12 months or more,

(f) a sentence of detention for a term of 12 months or more imposed by a court-martial or the Courts-Martial Appeal Court,

(g) a hospital order within the meaning of the Mental Health Act 1983, or

(h) a guardianship order,

"relevant order" means—

(a) an order made by the Crown Court, the Court of Appeal, a court-martial or the Courts-Martial Appeal Court that the individual in question be admitted to hospital, or
(b) a guardianship order,

"senior court" means the Crown Court, the Court of Appeal, a court-martial or the Courts-Martial Appeal Court.

Human Reproductive Cloning Act 2001

CHAPTER 23

The offence

61-001 **1.**—(1) A person who places in a woman a human embryo which has been created otherwise than by fertilisation is guilty of an offence.

(2) A person who is guilty of the offence is liable on conviction on indictment to imprisonment for a term not exceeding 10 years or a fine or both.

(3) No proceedings for the offence may be instituted–

(a) in England and Wales, except with the consent of the Director of Public Prosecutions;

Adoption and Children Act 2002

CHAPTER 38

PART 1

ADOPTION

CHAPTER I

INTRODUCTORY

Considerations applying to the exercise of powers

62-001 **1.**—(1) This section applies whenever a court or adoption agency is coming to a decision relating to the adoption of a child.

(2) The paramount consideration of the court or adoption agency must be the child's welfare, throughout his life.

(3) The court or adoption agency must at all times bear in mind that, in general, any delay in coming to the decision is likely to prejudice the child's welfare.

(4) The court or adoption agency must have regard to the following matters (among others)—

(a) the child's ascertainable wishes and feelings regarding the decision (considered in the light of the child's age and understanding),
(b) the child's particular needs,
(c) the likely effect on the child (throughout his life) of having ceased to be a member of the original family and become an adopted person,
(d) the child's age, sex, background and any of the child's characteristics which the court or agency considers relevant,
(e) any harm (within the meaning of the Children Act 1989 (c. 41)) which the child has suffered or is at risk of suffering,
(f) the relationship which the child has with relatives, and with any other person in relation to whom the court or agency considers the relationship to be relevant, including—
  (i) the likelihood of any such relationship continuing and the value to the child of its doing so,
  (ii) the ability and willingness of any of the child's relatives, or of any such person, to provide the child with a secure environment in which the child can develop, and otherwise to meet the child's needs,
  (iii) the wishes and feelings of any of the child's relatives, or of any such person, regarding the child.

(5) In placing the child for adoption, the adoption agency must give due consideration to the child's religious persuasion, racial origin and cultural and linguistic background.

(6) The court or adoption agency must always consider the whole range of powers available to it in the child's case (whether under this Act or the Children Act 1989); and the court must not make any order under this Act unless it considers that making the order would be better for the child than not doing so.

(7) In this section, "coming to a decision relating to the adoption of a child", in relation to a court, includes—
(a) coming to a decision in any proceedings where the orders that might be made by the court include an adoption order (or the revocation of such an order), a placement order (or the revocation of such an order) or an order under section 26 (or the revocation or variation of such an order),
(b) coming to a decision about granting leave in respect of any action (other than the initiation of proceedings in any court) which may be taken by an adoption agency or individual under this Act,

but does not include coming to a decision about granting leave in any other circumstances.

(8) For the purposes of this section—
(a) references to relationships are not confined to legal relationships,
(b) references to a relative, in relation to a child, include the child's mother and father.

CHAPTER 2

THE ADOPTION SERVICE

The Adoption Service

Basic definitions

62-002 **2.**—(1) The services maintained by local authorities under section 3(1) may be collectively referred to as "the Adoption Service", and a local authority or registered adoption society may be referred to as an adoption agency.

(2) In this Act, "registered adoption society" means a voluntary organisation which is an adoption society registered under Part 2 of the Care Standards Act 2000 (c. 14); but in relation to the provision of any facility of the Adoption Service, references to a registered adoption society or to an adoption agency do not include an adoption society which is not registered in respect of that facility.

(3) A registered adoption society is to be treated as registered in respect of any facility of the Adoption Service unless it is a condition of its registration that it does not provide that facility.

(4) No application for registration under Part 2 of the Care Standards Act 2000 may be made in respect of an adoption society which is an unincorporated body.

(5) In this Act—

"the 1989 Act" means the Children Act 1989 (c. 41),

"adoption society" means a body whose functions consist of or include making arrangements for the adoption of children,

"voluntary organisation" means a body other than a public or local authority the activities of which are not carried on for profit.

(6) In this Act, "adoption support services" means—

(a) counselling, advice and information, and

(b) any other services prescribed by regulations,

in relation to adoption.

(7) The power to make regulations under subsection (6)(b) is to be exercised so as to secure that local authorities provide financial support.

(8) In this Chapter, references to adoption are to the adoption of persons, wherever they may be habitually resident, effected under the law of any country or territory, whether within or outside the British Islands.

Maintenance of Adoption Service

62-003 **3.**—(1) Each local authority must continue to maintain within their area a service designed to meet the needs, in relation to adoption, of—

(a) children who may be adopted, their parents and guardians,

(b) persons wishing to adopt a child, and

(c) adopted persons, their parents, natural parents and former guardians;

and for that purpose must provide the requisite facilities.

(2) Those facilities must include making, and participating in, arrangements—

(a) for the adoption of children, and

(b) for the provision of adoption support services.

(3) As part of the service, the arrangements made for the purposes of subsection (2)(b)—

(a) must extend to the provision of adoption support services to persons who are within a description prescribed by regulations,
(b) may extend to the provision of those services to other persons.

(4) A local authority may provide any of the requisite facilities by securing their provision by—
(a) registered adoption societies, or
(b) other persons who are within a description prescribed by regulations of persons who may provide the facilities in question.

(5) The facilities of the service must be provided in conjunction with the local authority's other social services and with registered adoption societies in their area, so that help may be given in a co-ordinated manner without duplication, omission or avoidable delay.

(6) The social services referred to in subsection (5) are the functions of a local authority which are social services functions within the meaning of the Local Authority Social Services Act 1970 (c. 42) (which include, in particular, those functions in so far as they relate to children).

Assessments etc. for adoption support services

4.—(1) A local authority must at the request of— 62-004
(a) any of the persons mentioned in paragraphs (a) to (c) of section 3(1), or
(b) any other person who falls within a description prescribed by regulations (subject to subsection (7)(a)),

carry out an assessment of that person's needs for adoption support services.

(2) A local authority may, at the request of any person, carry out an assessment of that person's needs for adoption support services.

(3) A local authority may request the help of the persons mentioned in paragraph (a) or (b) of section 3(4) in carrying out an assessment.

(4) Where, as a result of an assessment, a local authority decide that a person has needs for adoption support services, they must then decide whether to provide any such services to that person.

(5) If—
(a) a local authority decide to provide any adoption support services to a person, and
(b) the circumstances fall within a description prescribed by regulations,

the local authority must prepare a plan in accordance with which adoption support services are to be provided to the person and keep the plan under review.

(6) Regulations may make provision about assessments, preparing and reviewing plans, the provision of adoption support services in accordance with plans and reviewing the provision of adoption support services.

(7) The regulations may in particular make provision—
(a) as to the circumstances in which a person mentioned in paragraph (b) of subsection (1) is to have a right to request an assessment of his needs in accordance with that subsection,
(b) about the type of assessment which, or the way in which an assessment, is to be carried out,
(c) about the way in which a plan is to be prepared,
(d) about the way in which, and time at which, a plan or the provision of adoption support services is to be reviewed,
(e) about the considerations to which a local authority are to have regard in carrying out an assessment or review or preparing a plan,

(f) as to the circumstances in which a local authority may provide adoption support services subject to conditions,

(g) as to the consequences of conditions imposed by virtue of paragraph (f) not being met (including the recovery of any financial support provided by a local authority),

(h) as to the circumstances in which this section may apply to a local authority in respect of persons who are outside that local authority's area,

(i) as to the circumstances in which a local authority may recover from another local authority the expenses of providing adoption support services to any person.

(8) A local authority may carry out an assessment of the needs of any person under this section at the same time as an assessment of his needs is made under any other enactment.

(9) If at any time during the assessment of the needs of any person under this section, it appears to a local authority that—

(a) there may be a need for the provision of services to that person by a Primary Care Trust (in Wales, a Health Authority or Local Health Board), or

(b) there may be a need for the provision to him of any services which fall within the functions of a local education authority (within the meaning of the Education Act 1996 (c. 56)),

the local authority must notify that Primary Care Trust, Health Authority, Local Health Board or local education authority.

(10) Where it appears to a local authority that another local authority could, by taking any specified action, help in the exercise of any of their functions under this section, they may request the help of that other local authority, specifying the action in question.

(11) A local authority whose help is so requested must comply with the request if it is consistent with the exercise of their functions.

Local authority plans for adoption services

62-005 **5.**—(1) Each local authority must prepare a plan for the provision of the services maintained under section 3(1) and secure that it is published.

(2) The plan must contain information of a description prescribed by regulations (subject to subsection (4)(b)).

(3) The regulations may make provision requiring local authorities—

(a) to review any plan,

(b) in the circumstances prescribed by the regulations, to modify that plan and secure its publication or to prepare a plan in substitution for that plan and secure its publication.

(4) The appropriate Minister may direct—

(a) that a plan is to be included in another document specified in the direction,

(b) that the requirements specified in the direction as to the description of information to be contained in a plan are to have effect in place of the provision made by regulations under subsection (2).

(5) Directions may be given by the appropriate Minister for the purpose of making provision in connection with any duty imposed by virtue of this section including, in particular, provision as to—

(a) the form and manner in which, and the time at which, any plan is to be published,

(b) the description of persons who are to be consulted in the preparation of any plan,

(c) the time at which any plan is to be reviewed.

(6) Subsections (2) to (5) apply in relation to a modified or substituted plan (or further modified or substituted plan) as they apply in relation to a plan prepared under subsection (1).

(7) Directions given under this section may relate—

(a) to a particular local authority,

(b) to any class or description of local authorities, or

(c) except in the case of a direction given under subsection (4)(b), to local authorities generally,

and accordingly different provision may be made in relation to different local authorities or classes or descriptions of local authorities.

Arrangements on cancellation of registration

6. Where, by virtue of the cancellation of its registration under Part 2 of the Care Standards Act 2000 (c. 14), a body has ceased to be a registered adoption society, the appropriate Minister may direct the body to make such arrangements as to the transfer of its functions relating to children and other transitional matters as seem to him expedient. **62-006**

Supplemental

Inspection of premises etc

15.—(1) The appropriate Minister may arrange for any premises in which— **62-007**

(a) a child is living with a person with whom the child has been placed by an adoption agency, or

(b) a child in respect of whom a notice of intention to adopt has been given under section 44 is, or will be, living,

to be inspected from time to time.

(2) The appropriate Minister may require an adoption agency—

(a) to give him any information, or

(b) to allow him to inspect any records (in whatever form they are held),

relating to the discharge of any of its functions in relation to adoption which the appropriate Minister specifies.

(3) An inspection under this section must be conducted by a person authorised by the appropriate Minister.

(4) An officer of a local authority may only be so authorised with the consent of the authority.

(5) A person inspecting any premises under subsection (1) may—

(a) visit the child there,

(b) make any examination into the state of the premises and the treatment of the child there which he thinks fit.

(6) A person authorised to inspect any records under this section may at any reasonable time have access to, and inspect and check the operation of, any computer (and associated apparatus) which is being or has been used in connection with the records in question.

(7) A person authorised to inspect any premises or records under this section may—

(a) enter the premises for that purpose at any reasonable time,

(b) require any person to give him any reasonable assistance he may require.

(8) A person exercising a power under this section must, if required to do so, produce a duly authenticated document showing his authority.

(9) Any person who intentionally obstructs another in the exercise of a power under this section is guilty of an offence and liable on summary conviction to a fine not exceeding level 3 on the standard scale.

CHAPTER 3

PLACEMENT FOR ADOPTION AND ADOPTION ORDERS

Placement of children by adoption agency for adoption

Placement for adoption by agencies

62-008 **18.**—(1) An adoption agency may—

(a) place a child for adoption with prospective adopters, or

(b) where it has placed a child with any persons (whether under this Part or not), leave the child with them as prospective adopters,

but, except in the case of a child who is less than six weeks old, may only do so under section 19 or a placement order.

(2) An adoption agency may only place a child for adoption with prospective adopters if the agency is satisfied that the child ought to be placed for adoption.

(3) A child who is placed or authorised to be placed for adoption with prospective adopters by a local authority is looked after by the authority.

(4) If an application for an adoption order has been made by any persons in respect of a child and has not been disposed of—

(a) an adoption agency which placed the child with those persons may leave the child with them until the application is disposed of, but

(b) apart from that, the child may not be placed for adoption with any prospective adopters.

"Adoption order" includes a Scottish or Northern Irish adoption order.

(5) References in this Act (apart from this section) to an adoption agency placing a child for adoption—

(a) are to its placing a child for adoption with prospective adopters, and

(b) include, where it has placed a child with any persons (whether under this Act or not), leaving the child with them as prospective adopters;

and references in this Act (apart from this section) to a child who is placed for adoption by an adoption agency are to be interpreted accordingly.

(6) References in this Chapter to an adoption agency being, or not being, authorised to place a child for adoption are to the agency being or (as the case may be) not being authorised to do so under section 19 or a placement order.

(7) This section is subject to sections 30 to 35 (removal of children placed by adoption agencies).

Placing children with parental consent

62-009 **19.**—(1) Where an adoption agency is satisfied that each parent or guardian of a child has consented to the child—

(a) being placed for adoption with prospective adopters identified in the consent, or

(b) being placed for adoption with any prospective adopters who may be chosen by the agency,

and has not withdrawn the consent, the agency is authorised to place the child for adoption accordingly.

(2) Consent to a child being placed for adoption with prospective adopters identified in the consent may be combined with consent to the child subsequently being placed for adoption with any prospective adopters who may be chosen by the agency in circumstances where the child is removed from or returned by the identified prospective adopters.

(3) Subsection (1) does not apply where—

(a) an application has been made on which a care order might be made and the application has not been disposed of, or

(b) a care order or placement order has been made after the consent was given.

(4) References in this Act to a child placed for adoption under this section include a child who was placed under this section with prospective adopters and continues to be placed with them, whether or not consent to the placement has been withdrawn.

(5) This section is subject to section 52 (parental etc. consent).

Advance consent to adoption

20.—(1) A parent or guardian of a child who consents to the child being **62-010**
placed for adoption by an adoption agency under section 19 may, at the same or any subsequent time, consent to the making of a future adoption order.

(2) Consent under this section—

(a) where the parent or guardian has consented to the child being placed for adoption with prospective adopters identified in the consent, may be consent to adoption by them, or

(b) may be consent to adoption by any prospective adopters who may be chosen by the agency.

(3) A person may withdraw any consent given under this section.

(4) A person who gives consent under this section may, at the same or any subsequent time, by notice given to the adoption agency—

(a) state that he does not wish to be informed of any application for an adoption order, or

(b) withdraw such a statement.

(5) A notice under subsection (4) has effect from the time when it is received by the adoption agency but has no effect if the person concerned has withdrawn his consent.

(6) This section is subject to section 52 (parental etc. consent).

Placement orders

21.—(1) A placement order is an order made by the court authorising a local **62-011**
authority to place a child for adoption with any prospective adopters who may be chosen by the authority.

(2) The court may not make a placement order in respect of a child unless—

(a) the child is subject to a care order,

(b) the court is satisfied that the conditions in section 31(2) of the 1989 Act (conditions for making a care order) are met, or

(c) the child has no parent or guardian.

(3) The court may only make a placement order if, in the case of each parent or guardian of the child, the court is satisfied—

(a) that the parent or guardian has consented to the child being placed for adoption with any prospective adopters who may be chosen by the local authority and has not withdrawn the consent, or

(b) that the parent's or guardian's consent should be dispensed with.

This subsection is subject to section 52 (parental etc. consent).

(4) A placement order continues in force until—

(a) it is revoked under section 24,

(b) an adoption order is made in respect of the child, or

(c) the child marries or attains the age of 18 years.

"Adoption order" includes a Scottish or Northern Irish adoption order.

Applications for placement orders

62-012 **22.**—(1) A local authority must apply to the court for a placement order in respect of a child if—

(a) the child is placed for adoption by them or is being provided with accommodation by them,

(b) no adoption agency is authorised to place the child for adoption,

(c) the child has no parent or guardian or the authority consider that the conditions in section 31(2) of the 1989 Act are met, and

(d) the authority are satisfied that the child ought to be placed for adoption.

(2) If—

(a) an application has been made (and has not been disposed of) on which a care order might be made in respect of a child, or

(b) a child is subject to a care order and the appropriate local authority are not authorised to place the child for adoption,

the appropriate local authority must apply to the court for a placement order if they are satisfied that the child ought to be placed for adoption.

(3) If—

(a) a child is subject to a care order, and

(b) the appropriate local authority are authorised to place the child for adoption under section 19,

the authority may apply to the court for a placement order.

(4) If a local authority—

(a) are under a duty to apply to the court for a placement order in respect of a child, or

(b) have applied for a placement order in respect of a child and the application has not been disposed of,

the child is looked after by the authority.

(5) Subsections (1) to (3) do not apply in respect of a child—

(a) if any persons have given notice of intention to adopt, unless the period of four months beginning with the giving of the notice has expired without them applying for an adoption order or their application for such an order has been withdrawn or refused, or

(b) if an application for an adoption order has been made and has not been disposed of.

"Adoption order" includes a Scottish or Northern Irish adoption order.

(6) Where—

(a) an application for a placement order in respect of a child has been made and has not been disposed of, and

(b) no interim care order is in force,

the court may give any directions it considers appropriate for the medical or psychiatric examination or other assessment of the child; but a child who is of sufficient understanding to make an informed decision may refuse to submit to the examination or other assessment.

(7) The appropriate local authority—

(a) in relation to a care order, is the local authority in whose care the child is placed by the order, and

(b) in relation to an application on which a care order might be made, is the local authority which makes the application.

Varying placement orders

23.—(1) The court may vary a placement order so as to substitute another local authority for the local authority authorised by the order to place the child for adoption. **62-013**

(2) The variation may only be made on the joint application of both authorities.

Revoking placement orders

24.—(1) The court may revoke a placement order on the application of any person. **62-014**

(2) But an application may not be made by a person other than the child or the local authority authorised by the order to place the child for adoption unless—

(a) the court has given leave to apply, and

(b) the child is not placed for adoption by the authority.

(3) The court cannot give leave under subsection (2)(a) unless satisfied that there has been a change in circumstances since the order was made.

(4) If the court determines, on an application for an adoption order, not to make the order, it may revoke any placement order in respect of the child.

(5) Where—

(a) an application for the revocation of a placement order has been made and has not been disposed of, and

(b) the child is not placed for adoption by the authority,

the child may not without the court's leave be placed for adoption under the order.

Parental responsibility

25.—(1) This section applies while— **62-015**

(a) a child is placed for adoption under section 19 or an adoption agency is authorised to place a child for adoption under that section, or

(b) a placement order is in force in respect of a child.

(2) Parental responsibility for the child is given to the agency concerned.

(3) While the child is placed with prospective adopters, parental responsibility is given to them.

(4) The agency may determine that the parental responsibility of any parent or guardian, or of prospective adopters, is to be restricted to the extent specified in the determination.

Contact

26.—(1) On an adoption agency being authorised to place a child for adoption, or placing a child for adoption who is less than six weeks old, any provision for contact under the 1989 Act ceases to have effect. **62-016**

(2) While an adoption agency is so authorised or a child is placed for adoption—

(a) no application may be made for any provision for contact under that Act, but

(b) the court may make an order under this section requiring the person with whom the child lives, or is to live, to allow the child to visit or stay with the person named in the order, or for the person named in the order and the child otherwise to have contact with each other.

(3) An application for an order under this section may be made by—

(a) the child or the agency,

(b) any parent, guardian or relative,

(c) any person in whose favour there was provision for contact under the 1989 Act which ceased to have effect by virtue of subsection (1),

(d) if a residence order was in force immediately before the adoption agency was authorised to place the child for adoption or (as the case may be) placed the child for adoption at a time when he was less than six weeks old, the person in whose favour the order was made,

(e) if a person had care of the child immediately before that time by virtue of an order made in the exercise of the High Court's inherent jurisdiction with respect to children, that person,

(f) any person who has obtained the court's leave to make the application.

(4) When making a placement order, the court may on its own initiative make an order under this section.

(5) This section does not prevent an application for a contact order under section 8 of the 1989 Act being made where the application is to be heard together with an application for an adoption order in respect of the child.

(6) In this section, "provision for contact under the 1989 Act" means a contact order under section 8 of that Act or an order under section 34 of that Act (parental contact with children in care).

Contact: supplementary

62-017 **27.**—(1) An order under section 26—

(a) has effect while the adoption agency is authorised to place the child for adoption or the child is placed for adoption, but

(b) may be varied or revoked by the court on an application by the child, the agency or a person named in the order.

(2) The agency may refuse to allow the contact that would otherwise be required by virtue of an order under that section if—

(a) it is satisfied that it is necessary to do so in order to safeguard or promote the child's welfare, and

(b) the refusal is decided upon as a matter of urgency and does not last for more than seven days.

(3) Regulations may make provision as to—

(a) the steps to be taken by an agency which has exercised its power under subsection (2),

(b) the circumstances in which, and conditions subject to which, the terms of any order under section 26 may be departed from by agreement between the agency and any person for whose contact with the child the order provides,

(c) notification by an agency of any variation or suspension of arrangements made (otherwise than under an order under that section) with a view to allowing any person contact with the child.

(4) Before making a placement order the court must—
(a) consider the arrangements which the adoption agency has made, or proposes to make, for allowing any person contact with the child, and
(b) invite the parties to the proceedings to comment on those arrangements.

(5) An order under section 26 may provide for contact on any conditions the court considers appropriate.

Further consequences of placement

28.—(1) Where a child is placed for adoption under section 19 or an adoption agency is authorised to place a child for adoption under that section— **62-018**
(a) a parent or guardian of the child may not apply for a residence order unless an application for an adoption order has been made and the parent or guardian has obtained the court's leave under subsection (3) or (5) of section 47,
(b) if an application has been made for an adoption order, a guardian of the child may not apply for a special guardianship order unless he has obtained the court's leave under subsection (3) or (5) of that section.

(2) Where—
(a) a child is placed for adoption under section 19 or an adoption agency is authorised to place a child for adoption under that section, or
(b) a placement order is in force in respect of a child,

then (whether or not the child is in England and Wales) a person may not do either of the following things, unless the court gives leave or each parent or guardian of the child gives written consent.

(3) Those things are—
(a) causing the child to be known by a new surname, or
(b) removing the child from the United Kingdom.

(4) Subsection (3) does not prevent the removal of a child from the United Kingdom for a period of less than one month by a person who provides the child's home.

Further consequences of placement orders

29.—(1) Where a placement order is made in respect of a child and either— **62-019**
(a) the child is subject to a care order, or
(b) the court at the same time makes a care order in respect of the child,

the care order does not have effect at any time when the placement order is in force.

(2) On the making of a placement order in respect of a child, any order mentioned in section 8(1) of the 1989 Act, and any supervision order in respect of the child, ceases to have effect.

(3) Where a placement order is in force—
(a) no prohibited steps order, residence order or specific issue order, and
(b) no supervision order or child assessment order,

may be made in respect of the child.

(4) Subsection (3)(a) does not apply in respect of a residence order if—
(a) an application for an adoption order has been made in respect of the child, and
(b) the residence order is applied for by a parent or guardian who has obtained the court's leave under subsection (3) or (5) of section 47 or by any other person who has obtained the court's leave under this subsection.

(5) Where a placement order is in force, no special guardianship order may be made in respect of the child unless—

(a) an application has been made for an adoption order, and

(b) the person applying for the special guardianship order has obtained the court's leave under this subsection or, if he is a guardian of the child, has obtained the court's leave under section 47(5).

(6) Section 14A(7) of the 1989 Act applies in respect of an application for a special guardianship order for which leave has been given as mentioned in subsection (5)(b) with the omission of the words "the beginning of the period of three months ending with".

(7) Where a placement order is in force—

(a) section 14C(1)(b) of the 1989 Act (special guardianship: parental responsibility) has effect subject to any determination under section 25(4) of this Act,

(b) section 14C(3) and (4) of the 1989 Act (special guardianship: removal of child from UK etc.) does not apply.

Removal of children who are or may be placed by adoption agencies

General prohibitions on removal

62-020 **30.**—(1) Where—

(a) a child is placed for adoption by an adoption agency under section 19, or

(b) a child is placed for adoption by an adoption agency and either the child is less than six weeks old or the agency has at no time been authorised to place the child for adoption,

a person (other than the agency) must not remove the child from the prospective adopters.

(2) Where—

(a) a child who is not for the time being placed for adoption is being provided with accommodation by a local authority, and

(b) the authority have applied to the court for a placement order and the application has not been disposed of,

only a person who has the court's leave (or the authority) may remove the child from the accommodation.

(3) Where subsection (2) does not apply, but—

(a) a child who is not for the time being placed for adoption is being provided with accommodation by an adoption agency, and

(b) the agency is authorised to place the child for adoption under section 19 or would be so authorised if any consent to placement under that section had not been withdrawn,

a person (other than the agency) must not remove the child from the accommodation.

(4) This section is subject to sections 31 to 33 but those sections do not apply if the child is subject to a care order.

(5) This group of sections (that is, this section and those sections) apply whether or not the child in question is in England and Wales.

(6) This group of sections does not affect the exercise by any local authority or other person of any power conferred by any enactment, other than section 20(8) of the 1989 Act (removal of children from local authority accommodation).

(7) This group of sections does not prevent the removal of a child who is arrested.

(8) A person who removes a child in contravention of this section is guilty of an offence and liable on summary conviction to imprisonment for a term not exceeding three months, or a fine not exceeding level 5 on the standard scale, or both.

Recovery by parent etc. where child not placed or is a baby

31.—(1) Subsection (2) applies where— **62-021**

(a) a child who is not for the time being placed for adoption is being provided with accommodation by an adoption agency, and

(b) the agency would be authorised to place the child for adoption under section 19 if consent to placement under that section had not been withdrawn.

(2) If any parent or guardian of the child informs the agency that he wishes the child to be returned to him, the agency must return the child to him within the period of seven days beginning with the request unless an application is, or has been, made for a placement order and the application has not been disposed of.

(3) Subsection (4) applies where—

(a) a child is placed for adoption by an adoption agency and either the child is less than six weeks old or the agency has at no time been authorised to place the child for adoption, and

(b) any parent or guardian of the child informs the agency that he wishes the child to be returned to him,

unless an application is, or has been, made for a placement order and the application has not been disposed of.

(4) The agency must give notice of the parent's or guardian's wish to the prospective adopters who must return the child to the agency within the period of seven days beginning with the day on which the notice is given.

(5) A prospective adopter who fails to comply with subsection (4) is guilty of an offence and liable on summary conviction to imprisonment for a term not exceeding three months, or a fine not exceeding level 5 on the standard scale, or both.

(6) As soon as a child is returned to an adoption agency under subsection (4), the agency must return the child to the parent or guardian in question.

Recovery by parent etc. where child placed and consent withdrawn

32.—(1) This section applies where— **62-022**

(a) a child is placed for adoption by an adoption agency under section 19, and

(b) consent to placement under that section has been withdrawn,

unless an application is, or has been, made for a placement order and the application has not been disposed of.

(2) If a parent or guardian of the child informs the agency that he wishes the child to be returned to him—

(a) the agency must give notice of the parent's or guardian's wish to the prospective adopters, and

(b) the prospective adopters must return the child to the agency within the period of 14 days beginning with the day on which the notice is given.

(3) A prospective adopter who fails to comply with subsection (2)(b) is guilty of an offence and liable on summary conviction to imprisonment for a term not

exceeding three months, or a fine not exceeding level 5 on the standard scale, or both.

(4) As soon as a child is returned to an adoption agency under this section, the agency must return the child to the parent or guardian in question.

(5) Where a notice under subsection (2) is given, but—

(a) before the notice was given, an application for an adoption order (including a Scottish or Northern Irish adoption order), special guardianship order or residence order, or for leave to apply for a special guardianship order or residence order, was made in respect of the child, and

(b) the application (and, in a case where leave is given on an application to apply for a special guardianship order or residence order, the application for the order) has not been disposed of,

the prospective adopters are not required by virtue of the notice to return the child to the agency unless the court so orders.

Recovery by parent etc. where child placed and placement order refused

62-023 **33.**—(1) This section applies where—

(a) a child is placed for adoption by a local authority under section 19,

(b) the authority have applied for a placement order and the application has been refused, and

(c) any parent or guardian of the child informs the authority that he wishes the child to be returned to him.

(2) The prospective adopters must return the child to the authority on a date determined by the court.

(3) A prospective adopter who fails to comply with subsection (2) is guilty of an offence and liable on summary conviction to imprisonment for a term not exceeding three months, or a fine not exceeding level 5 on the standard scale, or both.

(4) As soon as a child is returned to the authority, they must return the child to the parent or guardian in question.

Placement orders: prohibition on removal

62-024 **34.**—(1) Where a placement order in respect of a child—

(a) is in force, or

(b) has been revoked, but the child has not been returned by the prospective adopters or remains in any accommodation provided by the local authority,

a person (other than the local authority) may not remove the child from the prospective adopters or from accommodation provided by the authority.

(2) A person who removes a child in contravention of subsection (1) is guilty of an offence.

(3) Where a court revoking a placement order in respect of a child determines that the child is not to remain with any former prospective adopters with whom the child is placed, they must return the child to the local authority within the period determined by the court for the purpose; and a person who fails to do so is guilty of an offence.

(4) Where a court revoking a placement order in respect of a child determines that the child is to be returned to a parent or guardian, the local authority must return the child to the parent or guardian as soon as the child is returned to the authority or, where the child is in accommodation provided by the authority, at once.

(5) A person guilty of an offence under this section is liable on summary conviction to imprisonment for a term not exceeding three months, or a fine not exceeding level 5 on the standard scale, or both.

(6) This section does not affect the exercise by any local authority or other person of a power conferred by any enactment, other than section 20(8) of the 1989 Act.

(7) This section does not prevent the removal of a child who is arrested.

(8) This section applies whether or not the child in question is in England and Wales.

Return of child in other cases

35.—(1) Where a child is placed for adoption by an adoption agency and the prospective adopters give notice to the agency of their wish to return the child, the agency must— **62-025**

(a) receive the child from the prospective adopters before the end of the period of seven days beginning with the giving of the notice, and

(b) give notice to any parent or guardian of the child of the prospective adopters' wish to return the child.

(2) Where a child is placed for adoption by an adoption agency, and the agency—

(a) is of the opinion that the child should not remain with the prospective adopters, and

(b) gives notice to them of its opinion,

the prospective adopters must, not later than the end of the period of seven days beginning with the giving of the notice, return the child to the agency.

(3) If the agency gives notice under subsection (2)(b), it must give notice to any parent or guardian of the child of the obligation to return the child to the agency.

(4) A prospective adopter who fails to comply with subsection (2) is guilty of an offence and liable on summary conviction to imprisonment for a term not exceeding three months, or a fine not exceeding level 5 on the standard scale, or both.

(5) Where—

(a) an adoption agency gives notice under subsection (2) in respect of a child,

(b) before the notice was given, an application for an adoption order (including a Scottish or Northern Irish adoption order), special guardianship order or residence order, or for leave to apply for a special guardianship order or residence order, was made in respect of the child, and

(c) the application (and, in a case where leave is given on an application to apply for a special guardianship order or residence order, the application for the order) has not been disposed of,

prospective adopters are not required by virtue of the notice to return the child to the agency unless the court so orders.

(6) This section applies whether or not the child in question is in England and Wales.

Removal of children in non-agency cases

Restrictions on removal

62-026 **36.**—(1) At any time when a child's home is with any persons ("the people concerned") with whom the child is not placed by an adoption agency, but the people concerned—

(a) have applied for an adoption order in respect of the child and the application has not been disposed of,
(b) have given notice of intention to adopt, or
(c) have applied for leave to apply for an adoption order under section 42(6) and the application has not been disposed of,

a person may remove the child only in accordance with the provisions of this group of sections (that is, this section and sections 37 to 40).
The reference to a child placed by an adoption agency includes a child placed by a Scottish or Northern Irish adoption agency.

(2) For the purposes of this group of sections, a notice of intention to adopt is to be disregarded if—

(a) the period of four months beginning with the giving of the notice has expired without the people concerned applying for an adoption order, or
(b) the notice is a second or subsequent notice of intention to adopt and was given during the period of five months beginning with the giving of the preceding notice.

(3) For the purposes of this group of sections, if the people concerned apply for leave to apply for an adoption order under section 42(6) and the leave is granted, the application for leave is not to be treated as disposed of until the period of three days beginning with the granting of the leave has expired.

(4) This section does not prevent the removal of a child who is arrested.

(5) Where a parent or guardian may remove a child from the people concerned in accordance with the provisions of this group of sections, the people concerned must at the request of the parent or guardian return the child to the parent or guardian at once.

(6) A person who—

(a) fails to comply with subsection (5), or
(b) removes a child in contravention of this section,

is guilty of an offence and liable on summary conviction to imprisonment for a term not exceeding three months, or a fine not exceeding level 5 on the standard scale, or both.

(7) This group of sections applies whether or not the child in question is in England and Wales.

Applicants for adoption

62-027 **37.** If section 36(1)(a) applies, the following persons may remove the child—

(a) a person who has the court's leave,
(b) a local authority or other person in the exercise of a power conferred by any enactment, other than section 20(8) of the 1989 Act.

Local authority foster parents

62-028 **38.**—(1) This section applies if the child's home is with local authority foster parents.

(2) If—

(a) the child has had his home with the foster parents at all times during the period of five years ending with the removal and the foster parents have given notice of intention to adopt, or

(b) an application has been made for leave under section 42(6) and has not been disposed of,

the following persons may remove the child.

(3) They are—

(a) a person who has the court's leave,

(b) a local authority or other person in the exercise of a power conferred by any enactment, other than section 20(8) of the 1989 Act.

(4) If subsection (2) does not apply but—

(a) the child has had his home with the foster parents at all times during the period of one year ending with the removal, and

(b) the foster parents have given notice of intention to adopt,

the following persons may remove the child.

(5) They are—

(a) a person with parental responsibility for the child who is exercising the power in section 20(8) of the 1989 Act,

(b) a person who has the court's leave,

(c) a local authority or other person in the exercise of a power conferred by any enactment, other than section 20(8) of the 1989 Act.

Partners of parents

39.—(1) This section applies if a child's home is with a partner of a parent and the partner has given notice of intention to adopt. **62-029**

(2) If the child's home has been with the partner for not less than three years (whether continuous or not) during the period of five years ending with the removal, the following persons may remove the child—

(a) a person who has the court's leave,

(b) a local authority or other person in the exercise of a power conferred by any enactment, other than section 20(8) of the 1989 Act.

(3) If subsection (2) does not apply, the following persons may remove the child—

(a) a parent or guardian,

(b) a person who has the court's leave,

(c) a local authority or other person in the exercise of a power conferred by any enactment, other than section 20(8) of the 1989 Act.

Other non-agency cases

40.—(1) In any case where sections 37 to 39 do not apply but— **62-030**

(a) the people concerned have given notice of intention to adopt, or

(b) the people concerned have applied for leave under section 42(6) and the application has not been disposed of,

the following persons may remove the child.

(2) They are—

(a) a person who has the court's leave,

(b) a local authority or other person in the exercise of a power conferred by any enactment, other than section 20(8) of the 1989 Act.

Breach of restrictions on removal

Recovery orders

62-031 **41.**—(1) This section applies where it appears to the court—

(a) that a child has been removed in contravention of any of the preceding provisions of this Chapter or that there are reasonable grounds for believing that a person intends to remove a child in contravention of those provisions, or

(b) that a person has failed to comply with section 31(4), 32(2), 33(2), 34(3) or 35(2).

(2) The court may, on the application of any person, by an order—

(a) direct any person who is in a position to do so to produce the child on request to any person mentioned in subsection (4),

(b) authorise the removal of the child by any person mentioned in that subsection,

(c) require any person who has information as to the child's whereabouts to disclose that information on request to any constable or officer of the court,

(d) authorise a constable to enter any premises specified in the order and search for the child, using reasonable force if necessary.

(3) Premises may only be specified under subsection (2)(d) if it appears to the court that there are reasonable grounds for believing the child to be on them.

(4) The persons referred to in subsection (2) are—

(a) any person named by the court,

(b) any constable,

(c) any person who, after the order is made under that subsection, is authorised to exercise any power under the order by an adoption agency which is authorised to place the child for adoption.

(5) A person who intentionally obstructs a person exercising a power of removal conferred by the order is guilty of an offence and liable on summary conviction to a fine not exceeding level 3 on the standard scale.

(6) A person must comply with a request to disclose information as required by the order even if the information sought might constitute evidence that he had committed an offence.

(7) But in criminal proceedings in which the person is charged with an offence (other than one mentioned in subsection (8))—

(a) no evidence relating to the information provided may be adduced, and

(b) no question relating to the information may be asked,

by or on behalf of the prosecution, unless evidence relating to it is adduced, or a question relating to it is asked, in the proceedings by or on behalf of the person.

(8) The offences excluded from subsection (7) are—

(a) an offence under section 2 or 5 of the Perjury Act 1911 (c. 6) (false statements made on oath otherwise than in judicial proceedings or made otherwise than on oath),

(b) an offence under section 44(1) or (2) of the Criminal Law (Consolidation) (Scotland) Act 1995 (c. 39) (false statements made on oath or otherwise than on oath).

(9) An order under this section has effect in relation to Scotland as if it were an order made by the Court of Session which that court had jurisdiction to make.

Preliminaries to adoption

Child to live with adopters before application

42.—(1) An application for an adoption order may not be made unless— **62-032**

(a) if subsection (2) applies, the condition in that subsection is met,

(b) if that subsection does not apply, the condition in whichever is applicable of subsections (3) to (5) applies.

(2) If—

(a) the child was placed for adoption with the applicant or applicants by an adoption agency or in pursuance of an order of the High Court, or

(b) the applicant is a parent of the child,

the condition is that the child must have had his home with the applicant or, in the case of an application by a couple, with one or both of them at all times during the period of ten weeks preceding the application.

(3) If the applicant or one of the applicants is the partner of a parent of the child, the condition is that the child must have had his home with the applicant or, as the case may be, applicants at all times during the period of six months preceding the application.

(4) If the applicants are local authority foster parents, the condition is that the child must have had his home with the applicants at all times during the period of one year preceding the application.

(5) In any other case, the condition is that the child must have had his home with the applicant or, in the case of an application by a couple, with one or both of them for not less than three years (whether continuous or not) during the period of five years preceding the application.

(6) But subsections (4) and (5) do not prevent an application being made if the court gives leave to make it.

(7) An adoption order may not be made unless the court is satisfied that sufficient opportunities to see the child with the applicant or, in the case of an application by a couple, both of them together in the home environment have been given—

(a) where the child was placed for adoption with the applicant or applicants by an adoption agency, to that agency,

(b) in any other case, to the local authority within whose area the home is.

(8) In this section and sections 43 and 44(1)—

(a) references to an adoption agency include a Scottish or Northern Irish adoption agency,

(b) references to a child placed for adoption by an adoption agency are to be read accordingly.

Reports where child placed by agency

43. Where an application for an adoption order relates to a child placed for adoption by an adoption agency, the agency must— **62-033**

(a) submit to the court a report on the suitability of the applicants and on any other matters relevant to the operation of section 1, and

(b) assist the court in any manner the court directs.

Notice of intention to adopt

44.—(1) This section applies where persons (referred to in this section as "proposed adopters") wish to adopt a child who is not placed for adoption with them by an adoption agency. **62-034**

(2) An adoption order may not be made in respect of the child unless the proposed adopters have given notice to the appropriate local authority of their intention to apply for the adoption order (referred to in this Act as a "notice of intention to adopt").

(3) The notice must be given not more than two years, or less than three months, before the date on which the application for the adoption order is made.

(4) Where—

(a) if a person were seeking to apply for an adoption order, subsection (4) or (5) of section 42 would apply, but

(b) the condition in the subsection in question is not met,

the person may not give notice of intention to adopt unless he has the court's leave to apply for an adoption order.

(5) On receipt of a notice of intention to adopt, the local authority must arrange for the investigation of the matter and submit to the court a report of the investigation.

(6) In particular, the investigation must, so far as practicable, include the suitability of the proposed adopters and any other matters relevant to the operation of section 1 in relation to the application.

(7) If a local authority receive a notice of intention to adopt in respect of a child whom they know was (immediately before the notice was given) looked after by another local authority, they must, not more than seven days after the receipt of the notice, inform the other local authority in writing that they have received the notice.

(8) Where—

(a) a local authority have placed a child with any persons otherwise than as prospective adopters, and

(b) the persons give notice of intention to adopt,

the authority are not to be treated as leaving the child with them as prospective adopters for the purposes of section 18(1)(b).

(9) In this section, references to the appropriate local authority, in relation to any proposed adopters, are—

(a) in prescribed cases, references to the prescribed local authority,

(b) in any other case, references to the local authority for the area in which, at the time of giving the notice of intention to adopt, they have their home,

and "prescribed" means prescribed by regulations.

Suitability of adopters

62-035 **45.**—(1) Regulations under section 9 may make provision as to the matters to be taken into account by an adoption agency in determining, or making any report in respect of, the suitability of any persons to adopt a child.

(2) In particular, the regulations may make provision for the purpose of securing that, in determining the suitability of a couple to adopt a child, proper regard is had to the need for stability and permanence in their relationship.

The making of adoption orders

Adoption orders

46.—(1) An adoption order is an order made by the court on an application under section 50 or 51 giving parental responsibility for a child to the adopters or adopter. **62-036**

(2) The making of an adoption order operates to extinguish—

(a) the parental responsibility which any person other than the adopters or adopter has for the adopted child immediately before the making of the order,

(b) any order under the 1989 Act or the Children (Northern Ireland) Order 1995 (S.I. 1995/755 (N.I. 2)),

(c) any order under the Children (Scotland) Act 1995 (c. 36) other than an excepted order, and

(d) any duty arising by virtue of an agreement or an order of a court to make payments, so far as the payments are in respect of the adopted child's maintenance or upbringing for any period after the making of the adoption order.

"Excepted order" means an order under section 9, 11(1)(d) or 13 of the Children (Scotland) Act 1995 or an exclusion order within the meaning of section 76(1) of that Act.

(3) An adoption order—

(a) does not affect parental responsibility so far as it relates to any period before the making of the order, and

(b) in the case of an order made on an application under section 51(2) by the partner of a parent of the adopted child, does not affect the parental responsibility of that parent or any duties of that parent within subsection (2)(d).

(4) Subsection (2)(d) does not apply to a duty arising by virtue of an agreement—

(a) which constitutes a trust, or

(b) which expressly provides that the duty is not to be extinguished by the making of an adoption order.

(5) An adoption order may be made even if the child to be adopted is already an adopted child.

(6) Before making an adoption order, the court must consider whether there should be arrangements for allowing any person contact with the child; and for that purpose the court must consider any existing or proposed arrangements and obtain any views of the parties to the proceedings.

Conditions for making adoption orders

47.—(1) An adoption order may not be made if the child has a parent or guardian unless one of the following three conditions is met; but this section is subject to section 52 (parental etc. consent). **62-037**

(2) The first condition is that, in the case of each parent or guardian of the child, the court is satisfied—

(a) that the parent or guardian consents to the making of the adoption order,

(b) that the parent or guardian has consented under section 20 (and has not withdrawn the consent) and does not oppose the making of the adoption order, or

(c) that the parent's or guardian's consent should be dispensed with.

(3) A parent or guardian may not oppose the making of an adoption order under subsection (2)(b) without the court's leave.

(4) The second condition is that—

(a) the child has been placed for adoption by an adoption agency with the prospective adopters in whose favour the order is proposed to be made,

(b) either—

(i) the child was placed for adoption with the consent of each parent or guardian and the consent of the mother was given when the child was at least six weeks old, or

(ii) the child was placed for adoption under a placement order, and

(c) no parent or guardian opposes the making of the adoption order.

(5) A parent or guardian may not oppose the making of an adoption order under the second condition without the court's leave.

(6) The third condition is that the child is free for adoption by virtue of an order made—

(a) in Scotland, under section 18 of the Adoption (Scotland) Act 1978 (c. 28), or

(b) in Northern Ireland, under Article 17(1) or 18(1) of the Adoption (Northern Ireland) Order 1987 (S.I. 1987/2203 (N.I. 22)).

(7) The court cannot give leave under subsection (3) or (5) unless satisfied that there has been a change in circumstances since the consent of the parent or guardian was given or, as the case may be, the placement order was made.

(8) An adoption order may not be made in relation to a person who is or has been married.

(9) An adoption order may not be made in relation to a person who has attained the age of 19 years.

Restrictions on making adoption orders

62-038 **48.**—(1) The court may not hear an application for an adoption order in relation to a child, where a previous application to which subsection (2) applies made in relation to the child by the same persons was refused by any court, unless it appears to the court that, because of a change in circumstances or for any other reason, it is proper to hear the application.

(2) This subsection applies to any application—

(a) for an adoption order or a Scottish or Northern Irish adoption order, or

(b) for an order for adoption made in the Isle of Man or any of the Channel Islands.

Applications for adoption

62-039 **49.**—(1) An application for an adoption order may be made by—

(a) a couple, or

(b) one person,

but only if it is made under section 50 or 51 and one of the following conditions is met.

(2) The first condition is that at least one of the couple (in the case of an application under section 50) or the applicant (in the case of an application under section 51) is domiciled in a part of the British Islands.

(3) The second condition is that both of the couple (in the case of an application under section 50) or the applicant (in the case of an application under

section 51) have been habitually resident in a part of the British Islands for a period of not less than one year ending with the date of the application.

(4) An application for an adoption order may only be made if the person to be adopted has not attained the age of 18 years on the date of the application.

(5) References in this Act to a child, in connection with any proceedings (whether or not concluded) for adoption, (such as "child to be adopted" or "adopted child") include a person who has attained the age of 18 years before the proceedings are concluded.

Adoption by couple

50.—(1) An adoption order may be made on the application of a couple where both of them have attained the age of 21 years. **62-040**

(2) An adoption order may be made on the application of a couple where—

(a) one of the couple is the mother or the father of the person to be adopted and has attained the age of 18 years, and

(b) the other has attained the age of 21 years.

Adoption by one person

51.—(1) An adoption order may be made on the application of one person who has attained the age of 21 years and is not married. **62-041**

(2) An adoption order may be made on the application of one person who has attained the age of 21 years if the court is satisfied that the person is the partner of a parent of the person to be adopted.

(3) An adoption order may be made on the application of one person who has attained the age of 21 years and is married if the court is satisfied that—

(a) the person's spouse cannot be found,

(b) the spouses have separated and are living apart, and the separation is likely to be permanent, or

(c) the person's spouse is by reason of ill-health, whether physical or mental, incapable of making an application for an adoption order.

(4) An adoption order may not be made on an application under this section by the mother or the father of the person to be adopted unless the court is satisfied that—

(a) the other natural parent is dead or cannot be found,

(b) by virtue of section 28 of the Human Fertilisation and Embryology Act 1990 (c. 37), there is no other parent, or

(c) there is some other reason justifying the child's being adopted by the applicant alone,

and, where the court makes an adoption order on such an application, the court must record that it is satisfied as to the fact mentioned in paragraph (a) or (b) or, in the case of paragraph (c), record the reason.

Placement and adoption: general

Parental etc. consent

52.—(1) The court cannot dispense with the consent of any parent or guardian of a child to the child being placed for adoption or to the making of an adoption order in respect of the child unless the court is satisfied that— **62-042**

(a) the parent or guardian cannot be found or is incapable of giving consent, or

(b) the welfare of the child requires the consent to be dispensed with.

(2) The following provisions apply to references in this Chapter to any parent or guardian of a child giving or withdrawing—

(a) consent to the placement of a child for adoption, or

(b) consent to the making of an adoption order (including a future adoption order).

(3) Any consent given by the mother to the making of an adoption order is ineffective if it is given less than six weeks after the child's birth.

(4) The withdrawal of any consent to the placement of a child for adoption, or of any consent given under section 20, is ineffective if it is given after an application for an adoption order is made.

(5) "Consent" means consent given unconditionally and with full understanding of what is involved; but a person may consent to adoption without knowing the identity of the persons in whose favour the order will be made.

(6) "Parent" (except in subsections (9) and (10) below) means a parent having parental responsibility.

(7) Consent under section 19 or 20 must be given in the form prescribed by rules, and the rules may prescribe forms in which a person giving consent under any other provision of this Part may do so (if he wishes).

(8) Consent given under section 19 or 20 must be withdrawn—

(a) in the form prescribed by rules, or

(b) by notice given to the agency.

(9) Subsection (10) applies if—

(a) an agency has placed a child for adoption under section 19 in pursuance of consent given by a parent of the child, and

(b) at a later time, the other parent of the child acquires parental responsibility for the child.

(10) The other parent is to be treated as having at that time given consent in accordance with this section in the same terms as those in which the first parent gave consent.

Modification of 1989 Act in relation to adoption

62-043 **53.**—(1) Where—

(a) a local authority are authorised to place a child for adoption, or

(b) a child who has been placed for adoption by a local authority is less than six weeks old,

regulations may provide for the following provisions of the 1989 Act to apply with modifications, or not to apply, in relation to the child.

(2) The provisions are—

(a) section 22(4)(b), (c) and (d) and (5)(b) (duty to ascertain wishes and feelings of certain persons),

(b) paragraphs 15 and 21 of Schedule 2 (promoting contact with parents and parents' obligation to contribute towards maintenance).

(3) Where a registered adoption society is authorised to place a child for adoption or a child who has been placed for adoption by a registered adoption society is less than six weeks old, regulations may provide—

(a) for section 61 of that Act to have effect in relation to the child whether or not he is accommodated by or on behalf of the society,

(b) for subsections (2)(b) to (d) and (3)(b) of that section (duty to ascertain wishes and feelings of certain persons) to apply with modifications, or not to apply, in relation to the child.

(4) Where a child's home is with persons who have given notice of intention to adopt, no contribution is payable (whether under a contribution order or

otherwise) under Part 3 of Schedule 2 to that Act (contributions towards maintenance of children looked after by local authorities) in respect of the period referred to in subsection (5).

(5) That period begins when the notice of intention to adopt is given and ends if—

(a) the period of four months beginning with the giving of the notice expires without the prospective adopters applying for an adoption order, or

(b) an application for such an order is withdrawn or refused.

(6) In this section, "notice of intention to adopt" includes notice of intention to apply for a Scottish or Northern Irish adoption order.

Disclosing information during adoption process

54. Regulations under section 9 may require adoption agencies in prescribed circumstances to disclose in accordance with the regulations prescribed information to prospective adopters. **62-044**

Revocation of adoptions on legitimation

55.—(1) Where any child adopted by one natural parent as sole adoptive parent subsequently becomes a legitimated person on the marriage of the natural parents, the court by which the adoption order was made may, on the application of any of the parties concerned, revoke the order. **62-045**

(2) In relation to an adoption order made by a magistrates' court, the reference in subsection (1) to the court by which the order was made includes a court acting for the same petty sessions area.

Disclosure of information in relation to a person's adoption

Information to be kept about a person's adoption

56.—(1) In relation to an adopted person, regulations may prescribe— **62-046**

(a) the information which an adoption agency must keep in relation to his adoption,

(b) the form and manner in which it must keep that information.

(2) Below in this group of sections (that is, this section and sections 57 to 65), any information kept by an adoption agency by virtue of subsection (1)(a) is referred to as section 56 information.

(3) Regulations may provide for the transfer in prescribed circumstances of information held, or previously held, by an adoption agency to another adoption agency.

Restrictions on disclosure of protected etc. information

57.—(1) Any section 56 information kept by an adoption agency which— **62-047**

(a) is about an adopted person or any other person, and

(b) is or includes identifying information about the person in question,

may only be disclosed by the agency to a person (other than the person the information is about) in pursuance of this group of sections.

(2) Any information kept by an adoption agency—

(a) which the agency has obtained from the Registrar General on an application under section 79(5) and any other information which would enable the adopted person to obtain a certified copy of the record of his birth, or

(b) which is information about an entry relating to the adopted person in the Adoption Contact Register,

may only be disclosed to a person by the agency in pursuance of this group of sections.

(3) In this group of sections, information the disclosure of which to a person is restricted by virtue of subsection (1) or (2) is referred to (in relation to him) as protected information.

(4) Identifying information about a person means information which, whether taken on its own or together with other information disclosed by an adoption agency, identifies the person or enables the person to be identified.

(5) This section does not prevent the disclosure of protected information in pursuance of a prescribed agreement to which the adoption agency is a party.

(6) Regulations may authorise or require an adoption agency to disclose protected information to a person who is not an adopted person.

Disclosure of other information

62-048 **58.**—(1) This section applies to any section 56 information other than protected information.

(2) An adoption agency may for the purposes of its functions disclose to any person in accordance with prescribed arrangements any information to which this section applies.

(3) An adoption agency must, in prescribed circumstances, disclose prescribed information to a prescribed person.

Offence

62-049 **59.** Regulations may provide that a registered adoption society which discloses any information in contravention of section 57 is to be guilty of an offence and liable on summary conviction to a fine not exceeding level 5 on the standard scale.

Disclosing information to adopted adult

62-050 **60.**—(1) This section applies to an adopted person who has attained the age of 18 years.

(2) The adopted person has the right, at his request, to receive from the appropriate adoption agency—

(a) any information which would enable him to obtain a certified copy of the record of his birth, unless the High Court orders otherwise,

(b) any prescribed information disclosed to the adopters by the agency by virtue of section 54.

(3) The High Court may make an order under subsection (2)(a), on an application by the appropriate adoption agency, if satisfied that the circumstances are exceptional.

(4) The adopted person also has the right, at his request, to receive from the court which made the adoption order a copy of any prescribed document or prescribed order relating to the adoption.

(5) Subsection (4) does not apply to a document or order so far as it contains information which is protected information.

Disclosing protected information about adults

62-051 **61.**—(1) This section applies where—

(a) a person applies to the appropriate adoption agency for protected information to be disclosed to him, and

(b) none of the information is about a person who is a child at the time of the application.

(2) The agency is not required to proceed with the application unless it considers it appropriate to do so.

(3) If the agency does proceed with the application it must take all reasonable steps to obtain the views of any person the information is about as to the disclosure of the information about him.

(4) The agency may then disclose the information if it considers it appropriate to do so.

(5) In deciding whether it is appropriate to proceed with the application or disclose the information, the agency must consider—

(a) the welfare of the adopted person,

(b) any views obtained under subsection (3),

(c) any prescribed matters,

and all the other circumstances of the case.

(6) This section does not apply to a request for information under section 60(2) or to a request for information which the agency is authorised or required to disclose in pursuance of regulations made by virtue of section 57(6).

Disclosing protected information about children

62.—(1) This section applies where— **62-052**

(a) a person applies to the appropriate adoption agency for protected information to be disclosed to him, and

(b) any of the information is about a person who is a child at the time of the application.

(2) The agency is not required to proceed with the application unless it considers it appropriate to do so.

(3) If the agency does proceed with the application, then, so far as the information is about a person who is at the time a child, the agency must take all reasonable steps to obtain—

(a) the views of any parent or guardian of the child, and

(b) the views of the child, if the agency considers it appropriate to do so having regard to his age and understanding and to all the other circumstances of the case,

as to the disclosure of the information.

(4) And, so far as the information is about a person who has at the time attained the age of 18 years, the agency must take all reasonable steps to obtain his views as to the disclosure of the information.

(5) The agency may then disclose the information if it considers it appropriate to do so.

(6) In deciding whether it is appropriate to proceed with the application, or disclose the information, where any of the information is about a person who is at the time a child—

(a) if the child is an adopted child, the child's welfare must be the paramount consideration,

(b) in the case of any other child, the agency must have particular regard to the child's welfare.

(7) And, in deciding whether it is appropriate to proceed with the application or disclose the information, the agency must consider—

(a) the welfare of the adopted person (where subsection (6)(a) does not apply),

(b) any views obtained under subsection (3) or (4),

(c) any prescribed matters,

and all the other circumstances of the case.

(8) This section does not apply to a request for information under section 60(2) or to a request for information which the agency is authorised or required to disclose in pursuance of regulations made by virtue of section 57(6).

Counselling

62-053 **63.**—(1) Regulations may require adoption agencies to give information about the availability of counselling to persons—

(a) seeking information from them in pursuance of this group of sections,

(b) considering objecting or consenting to the disclosure of information by the agency in pursuance of this group of sections, or

(c) considering entering with the agency into an agreement prescribed for the purposes of section 57(5).

(2) Regulations may require adoption agencies to make arrangements to secure the provision of counselling for persons seeking information from them in prescribed circumstances in pursuance of this group of sections.

(3) The regulations may authorise adoption agencies—

(a) to disclose information which is required for the purposes of such counselling to the persons providing the counselling,

(b) where the person providing the counselling is outside the United Kingdom, to require a prescribed fee to be paid.

(4) The regulations may require any of the following persons to provide counselling for the purposes of arrangements under subsection (2)—

(a) a local authority, a council constituted under section 2 of the Local Government etc. (Scotland) Act 1994 (c. 39) or a Health and Social Services Board established under Article 16 of the Health and Personal Social Services (Northern Ireland) Order 1972 (S.I. 1972/1265 (N.I. 14)),

(b) a registered adoption society, an organisation within section 144(3)(b) or an adoption society which is registered under Article 4 of the Adoption (Northern Ireland) Order 1987 (S.I. 1987/2203 (N.I. 22)),

(c) an adoption support agency in respect of which a person is registered under Part 2 of the Care Standards Act 2000 (c. 14).

(5) For the purposes of subsection (4), where the functions of a Health and Social Services Board are exercisable by a Health and Social Services Trust, the reference in sub-paragraph (a) to a Board is to be read as a reference to the Health and Social Services Trust.

Other provision to be made by regulations

62-054 **64.**—(1) Regulations may make provision for the purposes of this group of sections, including provision as to—

(a) the performance by adoption agencies of their functions,

(b) the manner in which information may be received, and

(c) the matters mentioned below in this section.

(2) Regulations may prescribe—

(a) the manner in which agreements made by virtue of section 57(5) are to be recorded,

(b) the information to be provided by any person on an application for the disclosure of information under this group of sections.

(3) Regulations may require adoption agencies—

(a) to give to prescribed persons prescribed information about the rights or opportunities to obtain information, or to give their views as to its disclosure, given by this group of sections,

(b) to seek prescribed information from, or give prescribed information to, the Registrar General in prescribed circumstances.

(4) Regulations may require the Registrar General—

(a) to disclose to any person (including an adopted person) at his request any information which the person requires to assist him to make contact with the adoption agency which is the appropriate adoption agency in the case of an adopted person specified in the request (or, as the case may be, in the applicant's case),

(b) to disclose to the appropriate adoption agency any information which the agency requires about any entry relating to the adopted person on the Adoption Contact Register.

(5) Regulations may provide for the payment of a prescribed fee in respect of the disclosure in prescribed circumstances of any information in pursuance of section 60, 61 or 62; but an adopted person may not be required to pay any fee in respect of any information disclosed to him in relation to any person who (but for his adoption) would be related to him by blood (including half-blood) or marriage.

(6) Regulations may provide for the payment of a prescribed fee by an adoption agency obtaining information under subsection (4)(b).

Sections 56 to 65: interpretation

65.—(1) In this group of sections— **62-055**

"appropriate adoption agency", in relation to an adopted person or to information relating to his adoption, means—

(a) if the person was placed for adoption by an adoption agency, that agency or (if different) the agency which keeps the information in relation to his adoption,

(b) in any other case, the local authority to which notice of intention to adopt was given,

"prescribed" means prescribed by subordinate legislation,

"regulations" means regulations under section 9,

"subordinate legislation" means regulations or, in relation to information to be given by a court, rules.

(2) But—

(a) regulations under section 63(2) imposing any requirement on a council constituted under section 2 of the Local Government etc. (Scotland) Act 1994 (c. 39), or an organisation within section 144(3)(b), are to be made by the Scottish Ministers,

(b) regulations under section 63(2) imposing any requirement on a Health and Social Services Board established under Article 16 of the Health and Personal Social Services (Northern Ireland) Order 1972 (S.I. 1972/1265 (N.I. 14)), or an adoption society which is registered under Article 4 of the Adoption (Northern Ireland) Order 1987 (S.I. 1987/2203 (N.I. 22)), are to be made by the Department of Health, Social Services and Public Safety.

(3) The power of the Scottish Ministers or of the Department of Health, Social Services and Public Safety to make regulations under section 63(2) includes power to make—

(a) any supplementary, incidental or consequential provision,
(b) any transitory, transitional or saving provision,
which the person making the regulations considers necessary or expedient.

(4) Regulations prescribing any fee by virtue of section 64(6) require the approval of the Chancellor of the Exchequer.

(5) Regulations making any provision as to the manner in which any application is to be made for the disclosure of information by the Registrar General require his approval.

CHAPTER 4

STATUS OF ADOPTED CHILDREN

Meaning of adoption in Chapter 4

62-056 **66.**—(1) In this Chapter "adoption" means—

(a) adoption by an adoption order or a Scottish or Northern Irish adoption order,
(b) adoption by an order made in the Isle of Man or any of the Channel Islands,
(c) an adoption effected under the law of a Convention country outside the British Islands, and certified in pursuance of Article 23(1) of the Convention (referred to in this Act as a "Convention adoption"),
(d) an overseas adoption, or
(e) an adoption recognised by the law of England and Wales and effected under the law of any other country;

and related expressions are to be interpreted accordingly.

(2) But references in this Chapter to adoption do not include an adoption effected before the day on which this Chapter comes into force (referred to in this Chapter as "the appointed day").

(3) Any reference in an enactment to an adopted person within the meaning of this Chapter includes a reference to an adopted child within the meaning of Part 4 of the Adoption Act 1976 (c. 36).

Status conferred by adoption

62-057 **67.**—(1) An adopted person is to be treated in law as if born as the child of the adopters or adopter.

(2) An adopted person is the legitimate child of the adopters or adopter and, if adopted by—

(a) a couple, or
(b) one of a couple under section 51(2),

is to be treated as the child of the relationship of the couple in question.

(3) An adopted person—

(a) if adopted by one of a couple under section 51(2), is to be treated in law as not being the child of any person other than the adopter and the other one of the couple, and
(b) in any other case, is to be treated in law, subject to subsection (4), as not being the child of any person other than the adopters or adopter;

but this subsection does not affect any reference in this Act to a person's natural parent or to any other natural relationship.

(4) In the case of a person adopted by one of the person's natural parents as sole adoptive parent, subsection (3)(b) has no effect as respects entitlement to

property depending on relationship to that parent, or as respects anything else depending on that relationship.

(5) This section has effect from the date of the adoption.

(6) Subject to the provisions of this Chapter and Schedule 4, this section—

(a) applies for the interpretation of enactments or instruments passed or made before as well as after the adoption, and so applies subject to any contrary indication, and

(b) has effect as respects things done, or events occurring, on or after the adoption.

Adoptive relatives

68.—(1) A relationship existing by virtue of section 67 may be referred to as an adoptive relationship, and— **62-058**

(a) an adopter may be referred to as an adoptive parent or (as the case may be) as an adoptive father or adoptive mother,

(b) any other relative of any degree under an adoptive relationship may be referred to as an adoptive relative of that degree.

(2) Subsection (1) does not affect the interpretation of any reference, not qualified by the word "adoptive", to a relationship.

(3) A reference (however expressed) to the adoptive mother and father of a child adopted by—

(a) a couple of the same sex, or

(b) a partner of the child's parent, where the couple are of the same sex,

is to be read as a reference to the child's adoptive parents.

Rules of interpretation for instruments concerning property

69.—(1) The rules of interpretation contained in this section apply (subject to any contrary indication and to Schedule 4) to any instrument so far as it contains a disposition of property. **62-059**

(2) In applying section 67(1) and (2) to a disposition which depends on the date of birth of a child or children of the adoptive parent or parents, the disposition is to be interpreted as if—

(a) the adopted person had been born on the date of adoption,

(b) two or more people adopted on the same date had been born on that date in the order of their actual births;

but this does not affect any reference to a person's age.

(3) Examples of phrases in wills on which subsection (2) can operate are—

1. Children of A "living at my death or born afterwards".

2. Children of A "living at my death or born afterwards before any one of such children for the time being in existence attains a vested interest and who attain the age of 21 years".

3. As in example 1 or 2, but referring to grandchildren of A instead of children of A.

4. A for life "until he has a child", and then to his child or children.

Note. Subsection (2) will not affect the reference to the age of 21 years in example 2.

(4) Section 67(3) does not prejudice—

(a) any qualifying interest, or

(b) any interest expectant (whether immediately or not) upon a qualifying interest.

"Qualifying interest" means an interest vested in possession in the adopted person before the adoption.

(5) Where it is necessary to determine for the purposes of a disposition of property effected by an instrument whether a woman can have a child—

(a) it must be presumed that once a woman has attained the age of 55 years she will not adopt a person after execution of the instrument, and

(b) if she does so, then (in spite of section 67) that person is not to be treated as her child or (if she does so as one of a couple) as the child of the other one of the couple for the purposes of the instrument.

(6) In this section, "instrument" includes a private Act settling property, but not any other enactment.

Dispositions depending on date of birth

62-060 **70.**—(1) Where a disposition depends on the date of birth of a person who was born illegitimate and who is adopted by one of the natural parents as sole adoptive parent, section 69(2) does not affect entitlement by virtue of Part 3 of the Family Law Reform Act 1987 (c. 42) (dispositions of property).

(2) Subsection (1) applies for example where—

(a) a testator dies in 2001 bequeathing a legacy to his eldest grandchild living at a specified time,

(b) his unmarried daughter has a child in 2002 who is the first grandchild,

(c) his married son has a child in 2003,

(d) subsequently his unmarried daughter adopts her child as sole adoptive parent.

In that example the status of the daughter's child as the eldest grandchild of the testator is not affected by the events described in paragraphs (c) and (d).

Protection of trustees and personal representatives

62-061 **72.**—(1) A trustee or personal representative is not under a duty, by virtue of the law relating to trusts or the administration of estates, to enquire, before conveying or distributing any property, whether any adoption has been effected or revoked if that fact could affect entitlement to the property.

(2) A trustee or personal representative is not liable to any person by reason of a conveyance or distribution of the property made without regard to any such fact if he has not received notice of the fact before the conveyance or distribution.

(3) This section does not prejudice the right of a person to follow the property, or any property representing it, into the hands of another person, other than a purchaser, who has received it.

Meaning of disposition

62-062 **73.**—(1) This section applies for the purposes of this Chapter.

(2) A disposition includes the conferring of a power of appointment and any other disposition of an interest in or right over property; and in this subsection a power of appointment includes any discretionary power to transfer a beneficial interest in property without the furnishing of valuable consideration.

(3) This Chapter applies to an oral disposition as if contained in an instrument made when the disposition was made.

(4) The date of death of a testator is the date at which a will or codicil is to be regarded as made.

(5) The provisions of the law of intestate succession applicable to the estate of a deceased person are to be treated as if contained in an instrument executed by him (while of full capacity) immediately before his death.

Miscellaneous enactments

74.—(1) Section 67 does not apply for the purposes of— **62-063**

(a) the table of kindred and affinity in Schedule 1 to the Marriage Act 1949 (c. 76),

(b) sections 10 and 11 of the Sexual Offences Act 1956 (c. 69) (incest), or

(c) section 54 of the Criminal Law Act 1977 (c. 45) (inciting a girl to commit incest).

(2) Section 67 does not apply for the purposes of any provision of—

(a) the British Nationality Act 1981 (c. 61),

(b) the Immigration Act 1971 (c. 77),

(c) any instrument having effect under an enactment within paragraph (a) or (b), or

(d) any other provision of the law for the time being in force which determines British citizenship, British overseas territories citizenship, the status of a British National (Overseas) or British Overseas citizenship.

Pensions

75. Section 67(3) does not affect entitlement to a pension which is payable to **62-064**
or for the benefit of a person and is in payment at the time of the person's adoption.

Insurance

76.—(1) Where a child is adopted whose natural parent has effected an **62-065**
insurance with a friendly society or a collecting society or an industrial insurance company for the payment on the death of the child of money for funeral expenses, then—

(a) the rights and liabilities under the policy are by virtue of the adoption transferred to the adoptive parents, and

(b) for the purposes of the enactments relating to such societies and companies, the adoptive parents are to be treated as the person who took out the policy.

(2) Where the adoption is effected by an order made by virtue of section 51(2), the references in subsection (1) to the adoptive parents are to be read as references to the adopter and the other one of the couple.

Chapter 5

The Registers

Adopted Children Register etc

Adopted Children Register

77.—(1) The Registrar General must continue to maintain in the General **62-066**
Register Office a register, to be called the Adopted Children Register.

(2) The Adopted Children Register is not to be open to public inspection or search.

(3) No entries may be made in the Adopted Children Register other than entries—

(a) directed to be made in it by adoption orders, or

(b) required to be made under Schedule 1.

(4) A certified copy of an entry in the Adopted Children Register, if purporting to be sealed or stamped with the seal of the General Register Office, is to be received as evidence of the adoption to which it relates without further or other proof.

(5) Where an entry in the Adopted Children Register contains a record—

(a) of the date of birth of the adopted person, or

(b) of the country, or the district and sub-district, of the birth of the adopted person,

a certified copy of the entry is also to be received, without further or other proof, as evidence of that date, or country or district and sub-district, (as the case may be) in all respects as if the copy were a certified copy of an entry in the registers of live-births.

(6) Schedule 1 (registration of adoptions and the amendment of adoption orders) is to have effect.

Searches and copies

62-067 **78.**—(1) The Registrar General must continue to maintain at the General Register Office an index of the Adopted Children Register.

(2) Any person may—

(a) search the index,

(b) have a certified copy of any entry in the Adopted Children Register.

(3) But a person is not entitled to have a certified copy of an entry in the Adopted Children Register relating to an adopted person who has not attained the age of 18 years unless the applicant has provided the Registrar General with the prescribed particulars.

"Prescribed" means prescribed by regulations made by the Registrar General with the approval of the Chancellor of the Exchequer.

(4) The terms, conditions and regulations as to payment of fees, and otherwise, applicable under the Births and Deaths Registration Act 1953 (c. 20), and the Registration Service Act 1953 (c. 37), in respect of—

(a) searches in the index kept in the General Register Office of certified copies of entries in the registers of live-births,

(b) the supply from that office of certified copies of entries in those certified copies,

also apply in respect of searches, and supplies of certified copies, under subsection (2).

Connections between the register and birth records

62-068 **79.**—(1) The Registrar General must make traceable the connection between any entry in the registers of live-births or other records which has been marked "Adopted" and any corresponding entry in the Adopted Children Register.

(2) Information kept by the Registrar General for the purposes of subsection (1) is not to be open to public inspection or search.

(3) Any such information, and any other information which would enable an adopted person to obtain a certified copy of the record of his birth, may only be disclosed by the Registrar General in accordance with this section.

(4) In relation to a person adopted before the appointed day the court may, in exceptional circumstances, order the Registrar General to give any information mentioned in subsection (3) to a person.

(5) On an application made in the prescribed manner by the appropriate adoption agency in respect of an adopted person a record of whose birth is kept

by the Registrar General, the Registrar General must give the agency any information relating to the adopted person which is mentioned in subsection (3).

"Appropriate adoption agency" has the same meaning as in section 65.

(6) In relation to a person adopted before the appointed day, Schedule 2 applies instead of subsection (5).

(7) On an application made in the prescribed manner by an adopted person a record of whose birth is kept by the Registrar General and who—

(a) is under the age of 18 years, and

(b) intends to be married,

the Registrar General must inform the applicant whether or not it appears from information contained in the registers of live-births or other records that the applicant and the person whom the applicant intends to marry may be within the prohibited degrees of relationship for the purposes of the Marriage Act 1949 (c. 76).

(8) Before the Registrar General gives any information by virtue of this section, any prescribed fee which he has demanded must be paid.

(9) In this section—

"appointed day" means the day appointed for the commencement of sections 56 to 65,

"prescribed" means prescribed by regulations made by the Registrar General with the approval of the Chancellor of the Exchequer.

Adoption Contact Register

Adoption Contact Register

80.—(1) The Registrar General must continue to maintain at the General Register Office in accordance with regulations a register in two Parts to be called the Adoption Contact Register. **62-069**

(2) Part 1 of the register is to contain the prescribed information about adopted persons who have given the prescribed notice expressing their wishes as to making contact with their relatives.

(3) The Registrar General may only make an entry in Part 1 of the register for an adopted person—

(a) a record of whose birth is kept by the Registrar General,

(b) who has attained the age of 18 years, and

(c) who the Registrar General is satisfied has such information as is necessary to enable him to obtain a certified copy of the record of his birth.

(4) Part 2 of the register is to contain the prescribed information about persons who have given the prescribed notice expressing their wishes, as relatives of adopted persons, as to making contact with those persons.

(5) The Registrar General may only make an entry in Part 2 of the register for a person—

(a) who has attained the age of 18 years, and

(b) who the Registrar General is satisfied is a relative of an adopted person and has such information as is necessary to enable him to obtain a certified copy of the record of the adopted person's birth.

(6) Regulations may provide for—

(a) the disclosure of information contained in one Part of the register to persons for whom there is an entry in the other Part,

(b) the payment of prescribed fees in respect of the making or alteration of entries in the register and the disclosure of information contained in the register.

Adoption Contact Register: supplementary

62-070 **81.**—(1) The Adoption Contact Register is not to be open to public inspection or search.

(2) In section 80, "relative", in relation to an adopted person, means any person who (but for his adoption) would be related to him by blood (including half-blood) or marriage.

(3) The Registrar General must not give any information entered in the register to any person except in accordance with subsection (6)(a) of that section or regulations made by virtue of section 64(4)(b).

(4) In section 80, "regulations" means regulations made by the Registrar General with the approval of the Chancellor of the Exchequer, and "prescribed" means prescribed by such regulations.

General

Interpretation

62-071 **82.**—(1) In this Chapter—

"records" includes certified copies kept by the Registrar General of entries in any register of births,

"registers of live-births" means the registers of live-births made under the Births and Deaths Registration Act 1953 (c. 20).

(2) Any register, record or index maintained under this Chapter may be maintained in any form the Registrar General considers appropriate; and references (however expressed) to entries in such a register, or to their amendment, marking or cancellation, are to be read accordingly.

Chapter 6

Adoptions with a Foreign Element

Bringing children into and out of the United Kingdom

Restriction on bringing children in

62-072 **83.**—(1) This section applies where a person who is habitually resident in the British Islands (the "British resident")—

(a) brings, or causes another to bring, a child who is habitually resident outside the British Islands into the United Kingdom for the purpose of adoption by the British resident, or

(b) at any time brings, or causes another to bring, into the United Kingdom a child adopted by the British resident under an external adoption effected within the period of six months ending with that time.

The references to adoption, or to a child adopted, by the British resident include a reference to adoption, or to a child adopted, by the British resident and another person.

(2) But this section does not apply if the child is intended to be adopted under a Convention adoption order.

(3) An external adoption means an adoption, other than a Convention adoption, of a child effected under the law of any country or territory outside the British Islands, whether or not the adoption is—

(a) an adoption within the meaning of Chapter 4, or

(b) a full adoption (within the meaning of section 88(3)).

(4) Regulations may require a person intending to bring, or to cause another to bring, a child into the United Kingdom in circumstances where this section applies—

(a) to apply to an adoption agency (including a Scottish or Northern Irish adoption agency) in the prescribed manner for an assessment of his suitability to adopt the child, and

(b) to give the agency any information it may require for the purpose of the assessment.

(5) Regulations may require prescribed conditions to be met in respect of a child brought into the United Kingdom in circumstances where this section applies.

(6) In relation to a child brought into the United Kingdom for adoption in circumstances where this section applies, regulations may—

(a) provide for any provision of Chapter 3 to apply with modifications or not to apply,

(b) if notice of intention to adopt has been given, impose functions in respect of the child on the local authority to which the notice was given.

(7) If a person brings, or causes another to bring, a child into the United Kingdom at any time in circumstances where this section applies, he is guilty of an offence if—

(a) he has not complied with any requirement imposed by virtue of subsection (4), or

(b) any condition required to be met by virtue of subsection (5) is not met,

before that time, or before any later time which may be prescribed.

(8) A person guilty of an offence under this section is liable—

(a) on summary conviction to imprisonment for a term not exceeding six months, or a fine not exceeding the statutory maximum, or both,

(b) on conviction on indictment, to imprisonment for a term not exceeding twelve months, or a fine, or both.

(9) In this section, "prescribed" means prescribed by regulations and "regulations" means regulations made by the Secretary of State, after consultation with the Assembly.

Giving parental responsibility prior to adoption abroad

84.—(1) The High Court may, on an application by persons who the court is satisfied intend to adopt a child under the law of a country or territory outside the British Islands, make an order giving parental responsibility for the child to them. **62-073**

(2) An order under this section may not give parental responsibility to persons who the court is satisfied meet those requirements as to domicile, or habitual residence, in England and Wales which have to be met if an adoption order is to be made in favour of those persons.

(3) An order under this section may not be made unless any requirements prescribed by regulations are satisfied.

(4) An application for an order under this section may not be made unless at all times during the preceding ten weeks the child's home was with the applicant or, in the case of an application by two people, both of them.

(5) Section 46(2) to (4) has effect in relation to an order under this section as it has effect in relation to adoption orders.

(6) Regulations may provide for any provision of this Act which refers to adoption orders to apply, with or without modifications, to orders under this section.

(7) In this section, "regulations" means regulations made by the Secretary of State, after consultation with the Assembly.

Restriction on taking children out

62-074 **85.**—(1) A child who—

(a) is a Commonwealth citizen, or

(b) is habitually resident in the United Kingdom,

must not be removed from the United Kingdom to a place outside the British Islands for the purpose of adoption unless the condition in subsection (2) is met.

(2) The condition is that—

(a) the prospective adopters have parental responsibility for the child by virtue of an order under section 84, or

(b) the child is removed under the authority of an order under section 49 of the Adoption (Scotland) Act 1978 (c. 28) or Article 57 of the Adoption (Northern Ireland) Order 1987 (S.I. 1987/2203 (N.I. 22)).

(3) Removing a child from the United Kingdom includes arranging to do so; and the circumstances in which a person arranges to remove a child from the United Kingdom include those where he—

(a) enters into an arrangement for the purpose of facilitating such a removal of the child,

(b) initiates or takes part in any negotiations of which the purpose is the conclusion of an arrangement within paragraph (a), or

(c) causes another person to take any step mentioned in paragraph (a) or (b).

An arrangement includes an agreement (whether or not enforceable).

(4) A person who removes a child from the United Kingdom in contravention of subsection (1) is guilty of an offence.

(5) A person is not guilty of an offence under subsection (4) of causing a person to take any step mentioned in paragraph (a) or (b) of subsection (3) unless it is proved that he knew or had reason to suspect that the step taken would contravene subsection (1).

But this subsection only applies if sufficient evidence is adduced to raise an issue as to whether the person had the knowledge or reason mentioned.

(6) A person guilty of an offence under this section is liable—

(a) on summary conviction to imprisonment for a term not exceeding six months, or a fine not exceeding the statutory maximum, or both,

(b) on conviction on indictment, to imprisonment for a term not exceeding twelve months, or a fine, or both.

(7) In any proceedings under this section—

(a) a report by a British consular officer or a deposition made before a British consular officer and authenticated under the signature of that officer is admissible, upon proof that the officer or the deponent cannot be found in the United Kingdom, as evidence of the matters stated in it, and

(b) it is not necessary to prove the signature or official character of the person who appears to have signed any such report or deposition.

Overseas adoptions

Overseas adoptions

87.—(1) In this Act, "overseas adoption"— **62-075**

(a) means an adoption of a description specified in an order made by the Secretary of State, being a description of adoptions effected under the law of any country or territory outside the British Islands, but

(b) does not include a Convention adoption.

(2) Regulations may prescribe the requirements that ought to be met by an adoption of any description effected after the commencement of the regulations for it to be an overseas adoption for the purposes of this Act.

(3) At any time when such regulations have effect, the Secretary of State must exercise his powers under this section so as to secure that subsequently effected adoptions of any description are not overseas adoptions for the purposes of this Act if he considers that they are not likely within a reasonable time to meet the prescribed requirements.

(4) In this section references to this Act include the Adoption Act 1976 (c. 36).

(5) An order under this section may contain provision as to the manner in which evidence of any overseas adoption may be given.

(6) In this section—

"adoption" means an adoption of a child or of a person who was a child at the time the adoption was applied for,

"regulations" means regulations made by the Secretary of State after consultation with the Assembly.

Miscellaneous

Modification of section 67 for Hague Convention adoptions

88.—(1) If the High Court is satisfied, on an application under this section, **62-076**
that each of the following conditions is met in the case of a Convention adoption, it may direct that section 67(3) does not apply, or does not apply to any extent specified in the direction.

(2) The conditions are—

(a) that under the law of the country in which the adoption was effected, the adoption is not a full adoption,

(b) that the consents referred to in Article 4(c) and (d) of the Convention have not been given for a full adoption or that the United Kingdom is not the receiving State (within the meaning of Article 2 of the Convention),

(c) that it would be more favourable to the adopted child for a direction to be given under subsection (1).

(3) A full adoption is an adoption by virtue of which the child is to be treated in law as not being the child of any person other than the adopters or adopter.

(4) In relation to a direction under this section and an application for it, sections 59 and 60 of the Family Law Act 1986 (c. 55) (declarations under Part 3

of that Act as to marital status) apply as they apply in relation to a direction under that Part and an application for such a direction.

Annulment etc. of overseas or Hague Convention adoptions

62-077 **89.**—(1) The High Court may, on an application under this subsection, by order annul a Convention adoption or Convention adoption order on the ground that the adoption is contrary to public policy.

(2) The High Court may, on an application under this subsection—

(a) by order provide for an overseas adoption or a determination under section 91 to cease to be valid on the ground that the adoption or determination is contrary to public policy or that the authority which purported to authorise the adoption or make the determination was not competent to entertain the case, or

(b) decide the extent, if any, to which a determination under section 91 has been affected by a subsequent determination under that section.

(3) The High Court may, in any proceedings in that court, decide that an overseas adoption or a determination under section 91 is to be treated, for the purposes of those proceedings, as invalid on either of the grounds mentioned in subsection (2)(a).

(4) Subject to the preceding provisions, the validity of a Convention adoption, Convention adoption order or overseas adoption or a determination under section 91 cannot be called in question in proceedings in any court in England and Wales.

Section 89: supplementary

62-078 **90.**—(1) Any application for an order under section 89 or a decision under subsection (2)(b) or (3) of that section must be made in the prescribed manner and within any prescribed period.

"Prescribed" means prescribed by rules.

(2) No application may be made under section 89(1) in respect of an adoption unless immediately before the application is made—

(a) the person adopted, or

(b) the adopters or adopter,

habitually reside in England and Wales.

(3) In deciding in pursuance of section 89 whether such an authority as is mentioned in section 91 was competent to entertain a particular case, a court is bound by any finding of fact made by the authority and stated by the authority to be so made for the purpose of determining whether the authority was competent to entertain the case.

Overseas determinations and orders

62-079 **91.**—(1) Subsection (2) applies where any authority of a Convention country (other than the United Kingdom) or of the Channel Islands, the Isle of Man or any British overseas territory has power under the law of that country or territory—

(a) to authorise, or review the authorisation of, an adoption order made in that country or territory, or

(b) to give or review a decision revoking or annulling such an order or a Convention adoption.

(2) If the authority makes a determination in the exercise of that power, the determination is to have effect for the purpose of effecting, confirming or termi-

nating the adoption in question or, as the case may be, confirming its termination.

(3) Subsection (2) is subject to section 89 and to any subsequent determination having effect under that subsection.

CHAPTER 7

MISCELLANEOUS

Restrictions

Restriction on arranging adoptions etc

92.—(1) A person who is neither an adoption agency nor acting in pursuance of an order of the High Court must not take any of the steps mentioned in subsection (2). **62-080**

(2) The steps are—

(a) asking a person other than an adoption agency to provide a child for adoption,

(b) asking a person other than an adoption agency to provide prospective adopters for a child,

(c) offering to find a child for adoption,

(d) offering a child for adoption to a person other than an adoption agency,

(e) handing over a child to any person other than an adoption agency with a view to the child's adoption by that or another person,

(f) receiving a child handed over to him in contravention of paragraph (e),

(g) entering into an agreement with any person for the adoption of a child, or for the purpose of facilitating the adoption of a child, where no adoption agency is acting on behalf of the child in the adoption,

(h) initiating or taking part in negotiations of which the purpose is the conclusion of an agreement within paragraph (g),

(i) causing another person to take any of the steps mentioned in paragraphs (a) to (h).

(3) Subsection (1) does not apply to a person taking any of the steps mentioned in paragraphs (d), (e), (g), (h) and (i) of subsection (2) if the following condition is met.

(4) The condition is that—

(a) the prospective adopters are parents, relatives or guardians of the child (or one of them is), or

(b) the prospective adopter is the partner of a parent of the child.

(5) References to an adoption agency in subsection (2) include a prescribed person outside the United Kingdom exercising functions corresponding to those of an adoption agency, if the functions are being exercised in prescribed circumstances in respect of the child in question.

(6) The Secretary of State may, after consultation with the Assembly, by order make any amendments of subsections (1) to (4), and any consequential amendments of this Act, which he considers necessary or expedient.

(7) In this section—

(a) "agreement" includes an arrangement (whether or not enforceable),

(b) "prescribed" means prescribed by regulations made by the Secretary of State after consultation with the Assembly.

Offence of breaching restrictions under section 92

62-081 **93.**—(1) If a person contravenes section 92(1), he is guilty of an offence; and, if that person is an adoption society, the person who manages the society is also guilty of the offence.

(2) A person is not guilty of an offence under subsection (1) of taking the step mentioned in paragraph (f) of section 92(2) unless it is proved that he knew or had reason to suspect that the child was handed over to him in contravention of paragraph (e) of that subsection.

(3) A person is not guilty of an offence under subsection (1) of causing a person to take any of the steps mentioned in paragraphs (a) to (h) of section 92(2) unless it is proved that he knew or had reason to suspect that the step taken would contravene the paragraph in question.

(4) But subsections (2) and (3) only apply if sufficient evidence is adduced to raise an issue as to whether the person had the knowledge or reason mentioned.

(5) A person guilty of an offence under this section is liable on summary conviction to imprisonment for a term not exceeding six months, or a fine not exceeding £10,000, or both.

Prohibition of certain payments

62-082 **95.**—(1) This section applies to any payment (other than an excepted payment) which is made for or in consideration of—

(a) the adoption of a child,
(b) giving any consent required in connection with the adoption of a child,
(c) removing from the United Kingdom a child who is a Commonwealth citizen, or is habitually resident in the United Kingdom, to a place outside the British Islands for the purpose of adoption,
(d) a person (who is neither an adoption agency nor acting in pursuance of an order of the High Court) taking any step mentioned in section 92(2),
(e) preparing, causing to be prepared or submitting a report the preparation of which contravenes section 94(1).

(2) In this section and section 96, removing a child from the United Kingdom has the same meaning as in section 85.

(3) Any person who—

(a) makes any payment to which this section applies,
(b) agrees or offers to make any such payment, or
(c) receives or agrees to receive or attempts to obtain any such payment,

is guilty of an offence.

(4) A person guilty of an offence under this section is liable on summary conviction to imprisonment for a term not exceeding six months, or a fine not exceeding £10,000, or both.

Excepted payments

62-083 **96.**—(1) A payment is an excepted payment if it is made by virtue of, or in accordance with provision made by or under, this Act, the Adoption (Scotland) Act 1978 (c. 28) or the Adoption (Northern Ireland) Order 1987 (S.I. 1987/2203 (N.I. 22)).

(2) A payment is an excepted payment if it is made to a registered adoption society by—

(a) a parent or guardian of a child, or
(b) a person who adopts or proposes to adopt a child,

in respect of expenses reasonably incurred by the society in connection with the adoption or proposed adoption of the child.

(3) A payment is an excepted payment if it is made in respect of any legal or medical expenses incurred or to be incurred by any person in connection with an application to a court which he has made or proposes to make for an adoption order, a placement order, or an order under section 26 or 84.

(4) A payment made as mentioned in section 95(1)(c) is an excepted payment if—

(a) the condition in section 85(2) is met, and
(b) the payment is made in respect of the travel and accommodation expenses reasonably incurred in removing the child from the United Kingdom for the purpose of adoption.

Sections 92 to 96: interpretation

97. In sections 92 to 96— **62-084**

(a) "adoption agency" includes a Scottish or Northern Irish adoption agency,
(b) "payment" includes reward,
(c) references to adoption are to the adoption of persons, wherever they may be habitually resident, effected under the law of any country or territory, whether within or outside the British Islands.

Information

Pre-commencement adoptions: information

98.—(1) Regulations under section 9 may make provision for the purpose of— **62-085**

(a) assisting persons adopted before the appointed day who have attained the age of 18 to obtain information in relation to their adoption, and
(b) facilitating contact between such persons and their relatives.

(2) For that purpose the regulations may confer functions on—

(a) registered adoption support agencies,
(b) the Registrar General,
(c) adoption agencies.

(3) For that purpose the regulations may—

(a) authorise or require any person mentioned in subsection (2) to disclose information,
(b) authorise or require the disclosure of information contained in records kept under section 8 of the Public Records Act 1958 (c. 51) (court records),

and may impose conditions on the disclosure of information, including conditions restricting its further disclosure.

(4) The regulations may authorise the charging of prescribed fees by any person mentioned in subsection (2) or in respect of the disclosure of information under subsection (3)(b).

(5) An authorisation or requirement to disclose information by virtue of subsection (3)(a) has effect in spite of any restriction on the disclosure of information in Chapter 5.

(6) The making of regulations by virtue of subsections (2) to (4) which relate to the Registrar General requires the approval of the Chancellor of the Exchequer.

(7) In this section—

"appointed day" means the day appointed for the commencement of sections 56 to 65,

"registered adoption support agency" means an adoption support agency in respect of which a person is registered under Part 2 of the Care Standards Act 2000 (c. 14),

"relative", in relation to an adopted person, means any person who (but for his adoption) would be related to him by blood (including half-blood) or marriage.

Proceedings

Privacy

62-086 **101.**—(1) Proceedings under this Act in the High Court or a County Court may be heard and determined in private.

(2) In section 12 of the Administration of Justice Act 1960 (c. 65) (publication of information relating to proceedings in private), in subsection (1)(a)(ii), after "1989" there is inserted "or the Adoption and Children Act 2002".

(3) In section 97 of the 1989 Act (privacy for children involved in certain proceedings), after "this Act" in subsections (1) and (2) there is inserted "or the Adoption and Children Act 2002".

The Children and Family Court Advisory and Support Service

Officers of the Service

62-087 **102.**—(1) For the purposes of—

(a) any relevant application,

(b) the signification by any person of any consent to placement or adoption,

rules must provide for the appointment in prescribed cases of an officer of the Children and Family Court Advisory and Support Service ("the Service").

(2) The rules may provide for the appointment of such an officer in other circumstances in which it appears to the Lord Chancellor to be necessary or expedient to do so.

(3) The rules may provide for the officer—

(a) to act on behalf of the child upon the hearing of any relevant application, with the duty of safeguarding the interests of the child in the prescribed manner,

(b) where the court so requests, to prepare a report on matters relating to the welfare of the child in question,

(c) to witness documents which signify consent to placement or adoption,

(d) to perform prescribed functions.

(4) A report prepared in pursuance of the rules on matters relating to the welfare of a child must—

(a) deal with prescribed matters (unless the court orders otherwise), and

(b) be made in the manner required by the court.

(5) A person who—

(a) in the case of an application for the making, varying or revocation of a placement order, is employed by the local authority which made the application,

(b) in the case of an application for an adoption order in respect of a child who was placed for adoption, is employed by the adoption agency which placed him, or

(c) is within a prescribed description,

is not to be appointed under subsection (1) or (2).

(6) In this section, "relevant application" means an application for—

(a) the making, varying or revocation of a placement order,

(b) the making of an order under section 26, or the varying or revocation of such an order,

(c) the making of an adoption order, or

(d) the making of an order under section 84.

(7) Rules may make provision as to the assistance which the court may require an officer of the Service to give to it.

Right of officers of the Service to have access to adoption agency records

103.—(1) Where an officer of the Service has been appointed to act under section 102(1), he has the right at all reasonable times to examine and take copies of any records of, or held by, an adoption agency which were compiled in connection with the making, or proposed making, by any person of any application under this Part in respect of the child concerned. **62-088**

(2) Where an officer of the Service takes a copy of any record which he is entitled to examine under this section, that copy or any part of it is admissible as evidence of any matter referred to in any—

(a) report which he makes to the court in the proceedings in question, or

(b) evidence which he gives in those proceedings.

(3) Subsection (2) has effect regardless of any enactment or rule of law which would otherwise prevent the record in question being admissible in evidence.

Evidence

Evidence of consent

104.—(1) If a document signifying any consent which is required by this Part to be given is witnessed in accordance with rules, it is to be admissible in evidence without further proof of the signature of the person by whom it was executed. **62-089**

(2) A document signifying any such consent which purports to be witnessed in accordance with rules is to be presumed to be so witnessed, and to have been executed and witnessed on the date and at the place specified in the document, unless the contrary is proved.

General

Avoiding delay

109.—(1) In proceedings in which a question may arise as to whether an adoption order or placement order should be made, or any other question with respect to such an order, the court must (in the light of any rules made by virtue of subsection (2))— **62-090**

(a) draw up a timetable with a view to determining such a question without delay, and

(b) give such directions as it considers appropriate for the purpose of ensuring that the timetable is adhered to.

(2) Rules may—

(a) prescribe periods within which prescribed steps must be taken in relation to such proceedings, and
(b) make other provision with respect to such proceedings for the purpose of ensuring that such questions are determined without delay.

PART 3

MISCELLANEOUS AND FINAL PROVISIONS

CHAPTER 1

MISCELLANEOUS

Advertisements in the United Kingdom

Restriction on advertisements etc

62-091 **123.**—(1) A person must not—
(a) publish or distribute an advertisement or information to which this section applies, or
(b) cause such an advertisement or information to be published or distributed.

(2) This section applies to an advertisement indicating that—
(a) the parent or guardian of a child wants the child to be adopted,
(b) a person wants to adopt a child,
(c) a person other than an adoption agency is willing to take any step mentioned in paragraphs (a) to (e), (g) and (h) and (so far as relating to those paragraphs) (i) of section 92(2),
(d) a person other than an adoption agency is willing to receive a child handed over to him with a view to the child's adoption by him or another, or
(e) a person is willing to remove a child from the United Kingdom for the purposes of adoption.

(3) This section applies to—
(a) information about how to do anything which, if done, would constitute an offence under section 85 or 93, section 11 or 50 of the Adoption (Scotland) Act 1978 (c. 28) or Article 11 or 58 of the Adoption (Northern Ireland) Order 1987 (S.I. 1987/2203 (N.I. 22)) (whether or not the information includes a warning that doing the thing in question may constitute an offence),
(b) information about a particular child as a child available for adoption.

(4) For the purposes of this section and section 124—
(a) publishing or distributing an advertisement or information means publishing it or distributing it to the public and includes doing so by electronic means (for example, by means of the internet),
(b) the public includes selected members of the public as well as the public generally or any section of the public.

(5) Subsection (1) does not apply to publication or distribution by or on behalf of an adoption agency.

(6) The Secretary of State may by order make any amendments of this section which he considers necessary or expedient in consequence of any devel-

opments in technology relating to publishing or distributing advertisements or other information by electronic or electro-magnetic means.

(7) References to an adoption agency in this section include a prescribed person outside the United Kingdom exercising functions corresponding to those of an adoption agency, if the functions are being exercised in prescribed circumstances.

"Prescribed" means prescribed by regulations made by the Secretary of State.

(8) Before exercising the power conferred by subsection (6) or (7), the Secretary of State must consult the Scottish Ministers, the Department of Health, Social Services and Public Safety and the Assembly.

(9) In this section—

(a) "adoption agency" includes a Scottish or Northern Irish adoption agency,

(b) references to adoption are to the adoption of persons, wherever they may be habitually resident, effected under the law of any country or territory, whether within or outside the British Islands.

Offence of breaching restriction under section 123

124.—(1) A person who contravenes section 123(1) is guilty of an offence. **62-092**

(2) A person is not guilty of an offence under this section unless it is proved that he knew or had reason to suspect that section 123 applied to the advertisement or information.

But this subsection only applies if sufficient evidence is adduced to raise an issue as to whether the person had the knowledge or reason mentioned.

(3) A person guilty of an offence under this section is liable on summary conviction to imprisonment for a term not exceeding three months, or a fine not exceeding level 5 on the standard scale, or both.

Adoption and Children Act Register

Adoption and Children Act Register

125.—(1) Her Majesty may by Order in Council make provision for the **62-093** Secretary of State to establish and maintain a register, to be called the Adoption and Children Act Register, containing—

(a) prescribed information about children who are suitable for adoption and prospective adopters who are suitable to adopt a child,

(b) prescribed information about persons included in the register in pursuance of paragraph (a) in respect of things occurring after their inclusion.

(2) For the purpose of giving assistance in finding persons with whom children may be placed for purposes other than adoption, an Order under this section may—

(a) provide for the register to contain information about such persons and the children who may be placed with them, and

(b) apply any of the other provisions of this group of sections (that is, this section and sections 126 to 131), with or without modifications.

(3) The register is not to be open to public inspection or search.

(4) An Order under this section may make provision about the retention of information in the register.

(5) Information is to be kept in the register in any form the Secretary of State considers appropriate.

Use of an organisation to establish the register

62-094 **126.**—(1) The Secretary of State may make an arrangement with an organisation under which any function of his under an Order under section 125 of establishing and maintaining the register, and disclosing information entered in, or compiled from information entered in, the register to any person is performed wholly or partly by the organisation on his behalf.

(2) The arrangement may include provision for payments to be made to the organisation by the Secretary of State.

(3) If the Secretary of State makes an arrangement under this section with an organisation, the organisation is to perform the functions exercisable by virtue of this section in accordance with any directions given by the Secretary of State and the directions may be of general application (or general application in any part of Great Britain) or be special directions.

(4) An exercise of the Secretary of State's powers under subsection (1) or (3) requires the agreement of the Scottish Ministers (if the register applies to Scotland) and of the Assembly (if the register applies to Wales).

(5) References in this group of sections to the registration organisation are to any organisation for the time being performing functions in respect of the register by virtue of arrangements under this section.

Use of an organisation as agency for payments

62-095 **127.**—(1) An Order under section 125 may authorise an organisation with which an arrangement is made under section 126 to act as agent for the payment or receipt of sums payable by adoption agencies to other adoption agencies and may require adoption agencies to pay or receive such sums through the organisation.

(2) The organisation is to perform the functions exercisable by virtue of this section in accordance with any directions given by the Secretary of State; and the directions may be of general application (or general application in any part of Great Britain) or be special directions.

(3) An exercise of the Secretary of State's power to give directions under subsection (2) requires the agreement of the Scottish Ministers (if any payment agency provision applies to Scotland) and of the Assembly (if any payment agency provision applies to Wales).

Supply of information for the register

62-096 **128.**—(1) An Order under section 125 may require adoption agencies to give prescribed information to the Secretary of State or the registration organisation for entry in the register.

(2) Information is to be given to the Secretary of State or the registration organisation when required by the Order and in the prescribed form and manner.

(3) An Order under section 125 may require an agency giving information which is entered on the register to pay a prescribed fee to the Secretary of State or the registration organisation.

(4) But an adoption agency is not to disclose any information to the Secretary of State or the registration organisation—

(a) about prospective adopters who are suitable to adopt a child, or persons who were included in the register as such prospective adopters, without their consent,

(b) about children suitable for adoption, or persons who were included in the register as such children, without the consent of the prescribed person.

(5) Consent under subsection (4) is to be given in the prescribed form.

Disclosure of information

129.—(1) Information entered in the register, or compiled from information entered in the register, may only be disclosed under subsection (2) or (3). **62-097**

(2) Prescribed information entered in the register may be disclosed by the Secretary of State or the registration organisation—

(a) where an adoption agency is acting on behalf of a child who is suitable for adoption, to the agency to assist in finding prospective adopters with whom it would be appropriate for the child to be placed,

(b) where an adoption agency is acting on behalf of prospective adopters who are suitable to adopt a child, to the agency to assist in finding a child appropriate for adoption by them.

(3) Prescribed information entered in the register, or compiled from information entered in the register, may be disclosed by the Secretary of State or the registration organisation to any prescribed person for use for statistical or research purposes, or for other prescribed purposes.

(4) An Order under section 125 may prescribe the steps to be taken by adoption agencies in respect of information received by them by virtue of subsection (2).

(5) Subsection (1) does not apply—

(a) to a disclosure of information with the authority of the Secretary of State, or

(b) to a disclosure by the registration organisation of prescribed information to the Scottish Ministers (if the register applies to Scotland) or the Assembly (if the register applies to Wales).

(6) Information disclosed to any person under subsection (2) or (3) may be given on any prescribed terms or conditions.

(7) An Order under section 125 may, in prescribed circumstances, require a prescribed fee to be paid to the Secretary of State or the registration organisation—

(a) by a prescribed adoption agency in respect of information disclosed under subsection (2), or

(b) by a person to whom information is disclosed under subsection (3).

(8) If any information entered in the register is disclosed to a person in contravention of subsection (1), the person disclosing it is guilty of an offence.

(9) A person guilty of an offence under subsection (8) is liable on summary conviction to imprisonment for a term not exceeding three months, or a fine not exceeding level 5 on the standard scale, or both.

Territorial application

130.—(1) In this group of sections, "adoption agency" means— **62-098**

(a) a local authority in England,

(b) a registered adoption society whose principal office is in England.

(2) An Order under section 125 may provide for any requirements imposed on adoption agencies in respect of the register to apply—

(a) to Scottish local authorities and to voluntary organisations providing a registered adoption service,

(b) to local authorities in Wales and to registered adoption societies whose principal offices are in Wales,

and, in relation to the register, references to adoption agencies in this group of sections include any authorities or societies mentioned in paragraphs (a) and (b) to which an Order under that section applies those requirements.

(3) For the purposes of this group of sections, references to the register applying to Scotland or Wales are to those requirements applying as mentioned in paragraph (a) or, as the case may be, (b) of subsection (2).

(4) An Order under section 125 may apply any provision made by virtue of section 127—

(a) to Scottish local authorities and to voluntary organisations providing a registered adoption service,

(b) to local authorities in Wales and to registered adoption societies whose principal offices are in Wales.

(5) For the purposes of this group of sections, references to any payment agency provision applying to Scotland or Wales are to provision made by virtue of section 127 applying as mentioned in paragraph (a) or, as the case may be, (b) of subsection (4).

Supplementary

62-099 **131.**—(1) In this group of sections—

(a) "organisation" includes a public body and a private or voluntary organisation,

(b) "prescribed" means prescribed by an Order under section 125,

(c) "the register" means the Adoption and Children Act Register,

(d) "Scottish local authority" means a local authority within the meaning of the Regulation of Care (Scotland) Act 2001 (asp 4),

(e) "voluntary organisation providing a registered adoption service" has the same meaning as in section 144(3).

(2) For the purposes of this group of sections—

(a) a child is suitable for adoption if an adoption agency is satisfied that the child ought to be placed for adoption,

(b) prospective adopters are suitable to adopt a child if an adoption agency is satisfied that they are suitable to have a child placed with them for adoption.

(3) Nothing authorised or required to be done by virtue of this group of sections constitutes an offence under section 93, 94 or 95.

(4) No recommendation to make an Order under section 125 is to be made to Her Majesty in Council unless a draft has been laid before and approved by resolution of each House of Parliament.

(5) If any provision made by an Order under section 125 would, if it were included in an Act of the Scottish Parliament, be within the legislative competence of that Parliament, no recommendation to make the Order is to be made to Her Majesty in Council unless a draft has been laid before, and approved by resolution of, the Parliament.

(6) No recommendation to make an Order under section 125 containing any provision in respect of the register is to be made to Her Majesty in Council if the register applies to Wales or the Order would provide for the register to apply to Wales, unless a draft has been laid before, and approved by resolution of, the Assembly.

(7) No recommendation to make an Order under section 125 containing any provision by virtue of section 127 is to be made to Her Majesty in Council if any

payment agency provision applies to Wales or the Order would provide for any payment agency provision to apply to Wales, unless a draft has been laid before, and approved by resolution of, the Assembly.

CHAPTER 2

FINAL PROVISIONS

General interpretation etc

144.—(1) In this Act— **62-100**

"appropriate Minister" means—

(a) in relation to England, Scotland or Northern Ireland, the Secretary of State,

(b) in relation to Wales, the Assembly,

and in relation to England and Wales means the Secretary of State and the Assembly acting jointly,

"the Assembly" means the National Assembly for Wales,

"body" includes an unincorporated body,

"by virtue of" includes "by" and "under",

"child", except where used to express a relationship, means a person who has not attained the age of 18 years,

"the Convention" means the Convention on Protection of Children and Co-operation in respect of Intercountry Adoption, concluded at the Hague on 29th May 1993,

"Convention adoption order" means an adoption order which, by virtue of regulations under section 1 of the Adoption (Intercountry Aspects) Act 1999 (c. 18) (regulations giving effect to the Convention), is made as a Convention adoption order,

"Convention country" means a country or territory in which the Convention is in force,

"court" means, subject to any provision made by virtue of Part 1 of Schedule 11 to the 1989 Act, the High Court, a county court or a magistrates' court,

"enactment" includes an enactment comprised in subordinate legislation,

"fee" includes expenses,

"guardian" has the same meaning as in the 1989 Act and includes a special guardian within the meaning of that Act,

"information" means information recorded in any form,

"local authority" means any unitary authority, or any county council so far as they are not a unitary authority,

"Northern Irish adoption agency" means an adoption agency within the meaning of Article 3 of the Adoption (Northern Ireland) Order 1987 (S.I. 1987/2203 (N.I. 22)),

"Northern Irish adoption order" means an order made, or having effect as if made, under Article 12 of the Adoption (Northern Ireland) Order 1987,

"notice" means a notice in writing,

"registration authority" (in Part 1) has the same meaning as in the Care Standards Act 2000 (c. 14),

"regulations" means regulations made by the appropriate Minister, unless they are required to be made by the Lord Chancellor, the Secretary of State or the Registrar General,

"relative", in relation to a child, means a grandparent, brother, sister, uncle or aunt, whether of the full blood or half-blood or by marriage,

"rules" means rules made under section 141(1) or made by virtue of section 141(2) under section 144 of the Magistrates' Courts Act 1980 (c. 43),

"Scottish adoption order" means an order made, or having effect as if made, under section 12 of the Adoption (Scotland) Act 1978 (c. 28),

"subordinate legislation" has the same meaning as in the Interpretation Act 1978 (c. 30),

"unitary authority" means—

(a) the council of any county so far as they are the council for an area for which there are no district councils,

(b) the council of any district comprised in an area for which there is no county council,

(c) the council of a county borough,

(d) the council of a London borough,

(e) the Common Council of the City of London.

(2) Any power conferred by this Act to prescribe a fee by Order in Council or regulations includes power to prescribe—

(a) a fee not exceeding a prescribed amount,

(b) a fee calculated in accordance with the Order or, as the case may be, regulations,

(c) a fee determined by the person to whom it is payable, being a fee of a reasonable amount.

(3) In this Act, "Scottish adoption agency" means—

(a) a local authority, or

(b) a voluntary organisation providing a registered adoption service;

but in relation to the provision of any particular service, references to a Scottish adoption agency do not include a voluntary organisation unless it is registered in respect of that service or a service which, in Scotland, corresponds to that service. Expressions used in this subsection have the same meaning as in the Regulation of Care (Scotland) Act 2001 (asp 4) and "registered" means registered under Part 1 of that Act.

(4) In this Act, a couple means—

(a) a married couple, or

(b) two people (whether of different sexes or the same sex) living as partners in an enduring family relationship.

(5) Subsection (4)(b) does not include two people one of whom is the other's parent, grandparent, sister, brother, aunt or uncle.

(6) References to relationships in subsection (5)—

(a) are to relationships of the full blood or half blood or, in the case of an adopted person, such of those relationships as would exist but for adoption, and

(b) include the relationship of a child with his adoptive, or former adoptive, parents,

but do not include any other adoptive relationships.

(7) For the purposes of this Act, a person is the partner of a child's parent if the person and the parent are a couple but the person is not the child's parent.

SCHEDULES

Section 79(6) Schedule 2

Disclosure of Birth Records by Registrar General

1. On an application made in the prescribed manner by an adopted person— 62-101

(a) a record of whose birth is kept by the Registrar General, and

(b) who has attained the age of 18 years,

the Registrar General must give the applicant any information necessary to enable the applicant to obtain a certified copy of the record of his birth.

"Prescribed" means prescribed by regulations made by the Registrar General with the approval of the Chancellor of the Exchequer.

2. (1) Before giving any information to an applicant under paragraph 1, the Registrar General must inform the applicant that counselling services are available to the applicant— 62-102

(a) from a registered adoption society, an organisation within section 144(3)(b) or an adoption society which is registered under Article 4 of the Adoption (Northern Ireland) Order 1987 (S.I. 1987/2203 (N.I. 22)),

(b) if the applicant is in England and Wales, at the General Register Office or from any local authority or registered adoption support agency,

(c) if the applicant is in Scotland, from any council constituted under section 2 of the Local Government etc. (Scotland) Act 1994 (c. 39),

(d) if the applicant is in Northern Ireland, from any Board.

(2) In sub-paragraph (1)(b), "registered adoption support agency" means an adoption support agency in respect of which a person is registered under Part 2 of the Care Standards Act 2000 (c. 14).

(3) In sub-paragraph (1)(d), "Board" means a Health and Social Services Board established under Article 16 of the Health and Personal Social Services (Northern Ireland) Order 1972 (S.I. 1972/1265 (N.I. 14)); but where the functions of a Board are exercisable by a Health and Social Services Trust, references in that sub-paragraph to a Board are to be read as references to the Health and Social Services Trust.

(4) If the applicant chooses to receive counselling from a person or body within sub-paragraph (1), the Registrar General must send to the person or body the information to which the applicant is entitled under paragraph 1.

3. (1) Where an adopted person who is in England and Wales— 62-103

(a) applies for information under paragraph 1 or Article 54 of the Adoption (Northern Ireland) Order 1987, or

(b) is supplied with information under section 45 of the Adoption (Scotland) Act 1978 (c. 28),

the persons and bodies mentioned in sub-paragraph (2) must, if asked by the applicant to do so, provide counselling for the applicant.

(2) Those persons and bodies are—

(a) the Registrar General,

(b) any local authority,

(c) a registered adoption society, an organisation within section 144(3)(b) or an adoption society which is registered under Article 4 of the Adoption (Northern Ireland) Order 1987.

4. (1) Where a person— 62-104

(a) was adopted before 12th November 1975, and

(b) applies for information under paragraph 1,

the Registrar General must not give the information to the applicant unless the applicant has attended an interview with a counsellor arranged by a person or body from whom counselling services are available as mentioned in paragraph 2.

(2) Where the Registrar General is prevented by sub-paragraph (1) from giving information to a person who is not living in the United Kingdom, the Registrar General may give the information to any body which—

(a) the Registrar General is satisfied is suitable to provide counselling to that person, and

(b) has notified the Registrar General that it is prepared to provide such counselling.

UNITED NATIONS CONVENTION ON THE RIGHTS OF THE CHILD

Part I

Article 1

For the purposes of the present Convention, a child means every human being below the age of eighteen years unless under the law applicable to the child, majority is attained earlier. **A–001**

Article 2

1. States Parties shall respect and ensure the rights set forth in the present Convention to each child within their jurisdiction without discrimination of any kind, irrespective of the child's or his or her parent's or legal guardian's race, colour, sex, language, religion, political or other opinion, national, ethnic or social origin, property, disability, birth or other status. **A–002**

2. States Parties shall take all appropriate measures to ensure that the child is protected against all forms of discrimination or punishment on the basis of the status, activities, expressed opinions, or beliefs of the child's parents, legal guardians, or family members.

Article 3

1. In all actions concerning children, whether undertaken by public or private social welfare institutions, courts of law, administrative authorities or legislative bodies, the best interests of the child shall be a primary consideration. **A–003**

2. States Parties undertake to ensure the child such protection and care as is necessary for his or her well-being, taking into account the rights and duties of his or her parents, legal guardians, or other individuals legally responsible for him or her, and, to this end, shall take all appropriate legislative and administrative measures.

3. States Parties shall ensure that the institutions, services and facilities responsible for the care or protection of children shall conform with the standards established by competent authorities, particularly in the areas of safety, health, in the number and suitability of their staff, as well as competent supervision.

Article 4

States Parties shall undertake all appropriate legislative, administrative, and other measures for the implementation of the rights recognized in the present Convention. With regard to economic, social and cultural rights, States Parties shall undertake such measures to the maximum extent of their available resources and, where needed, within the framework of international co-operation. **A–004**

Article 5

A–005 States Parties shall respect the responsibilities, rights and duties of parents or, where applicable, the members of the extended family or community as provided for by local custom, legal guardians or other persons legally responsible for the child, to provide, in a manner consistent with the evolving capacities of the child, appropriate direction and guidance in the exercise by the child of the rights recognized in the present Convention.

Article 6

A–006 1. States Parties recognize that every child has the inherent right to life.

2. States Parties shall ensure to the maximum extent possible the survival and development of the child.

Article 7

A–007 1. The child shall be registered immediately after birth and shall have the right from birth to a name, the right to acquire a nationality and as far as possible, the right to know and be cared for by his or her parents.

2. States Parties shall ensure the implementation of these rights in accordance with their national law and their obligations under the relevant international instruments in this field, in particular where the child would otherwise be stateless.

Article 8

A–008 1. States Parties undertake to respect the right of the child to preserve his or her identity, including nationality, name and family relations as recognized by law without unlawful interference.

2. Where a child is illegally deprived of some or all of the elements of his or her identity, States Parties shall provide appropriate assistance and protection, with a view to re-establishing speedily his or her identity.

Article 9

A–009 1. States Parties shall ensure that a child shall not be separated from his or her parents against their will, except when competent authorities subject to judicial review determine, in accordance with applicable law and procedures, that such separation is necessary for the best interests of the child. Such determination may be necessary in a particular case such as one involving abuse or neglect of the child by the parents, or one where the parents are living separately and a decision must be made as to the child's place of residence.

2. In any proceedings pursuant to paragraph 1 of the present article, all interested parties shall be given an opportunity to participate in the proceedings and make their views known.

3. States Parties shall respect the right of the child who is separated from one or both parents to maintain personal relations and direct contact with both parents on a regular basis, except if it is contrary to the child's best interests.

4. Where such separation results from any action initiated by a State Party, such as the detention, imprisonment, exile, deportation or death (including death arising from any cause while the person is in the custody of the State) of one or both parents or of the child, that State Party shall, upon request,

provide the parents, the child or, if appropriate, another member of the family with the essential information concerning the whereabouts of the absent member(s) of the family unless the provision of the information would be detrimental to the well-being of the child. States Parties shall further ensure that the submission of such a request shall of itself entail no adverse consequences for the person(s) concerned.

Article 10

1. In accordance with the obligation of States Parties under Article 9, paragraph 1, applications by a child or his or her parents to enter or leave a State Party for the purpose of family reunification shall be dealt with by States Parties in a positive, humane and expeditious manner. States Parties shall further ensure that the submission of such a request shall entail no adverse consequences for the applicants and for the members of their family. **A–010**

2. A child whose parents reside in different States shall have the right to maintain on a regular basis, save in exceptional circumstances personal relations and direct contacts with both parents. Towards that end and in accordance with the obligation of States Parties under Article 9, paragraph 1, States Parties shall respect the right of the child and his or her parents to leave any country, including their own, and to enter their own country. The right to leave any country shall be subject only to such restrictions as are prescribed by law and which are necessary to protect the national security, public order (ordre public), public health or morals or the rights and freedoms of others and are consistent with the other rights recognized in the present Convention.

Article 12

1. States Parties shall assure to the child who is capable of forming his or her own views the right to express those views freely in all matters affecting the child, the views of the child being given due weight in accordance with the age and maturity of the child. **A–011**

2. For this purpose, the child shall in particular be provided the opportunity to be heard in any judicial and administrative proceedings affecting the child, either directly, or through a representative or an appropriate body, in a manner consistent with the procedural rules of national law.

Article 13

1. The child shall have the right to freedom of expression; this right shall include freedom to seek, receive and impart information and ideas of all kinds, regardless of frontiers, either orally, in writing or in print, in the form of art, or through any other media of the child's choice. **A–012**

2. The exercise of this right may be subject to certain restrictions, but these shall only be such as are provided by law and are necessary:
(a) For respect of the rights or reputations of others; or
(b) For the protection of national security or of public order (ordre public), or of public health or morals.

Article 14

1. States Parties shall respect the right of the child to freedom of thought, conscience and religion. **A-014**

2. States Parties shall respect the rights and duties of the parents and, when applicable, legal guardians, to provide direction to the child in the exercise of his or her right in a manner consistent with the evolving capacities of the child.

3. Freedom to manifest one's religion or beliefs may be subject only to such limitations as are prescribed by law and are necessary to protect public safety, order, health or morals, or the fundamental rights and freedoms of others.

Article 15

A–014 1. States Parties recognize the rights of the child to freedom of association and to freedom of peaceful assembly.

2. No restrictions may be placed on the exercise of these rights other than those imposed in conformity with the law and which are necessary in a democratic society in the interests of national security or public safety, public order (ordre public), the protection of public health or morals or the protection of the rights and freedoms of others.

Article 16

A–015 1. No child shall be subjected to arbitrary or unlawful interference with his or her privacy, family, home or correspondence, nor to unlawful attacks on his or her honour and reputation.

2. The child has the right to the protection of the law against such interference or attacks.

Article 18

A–016 1. States Parties shall use their best efforts to ensure recognition of the principle that both parents have common responsibilities for the upbringing and development of the child. Parents or, as the case may be, legal guardians, have the primary responsibility for the upbringing and development of the child. The best interests of the child will be their basic concern.

2. For the purpose of guaranteeing and promoting the rights set forth in the present Convention, States Parties shall render appropriate assistance to parents and legal guardians in the performance of their child-rearing responsibilities and shall ensure the development of institutions, facilities and services for the care of children.

3. States Parties shall take all appropriate measures to ensure that children of working parents have the right to benefit from child-care services and facilities for which they are eligible.

Article 19

A–017 1. States Parties shall take all appropriate legislative, administrative, social and educational measures to protect the child from all forms of physical or mental violence, injury or abuse, neglect or negligent treatment, maltreatment or exploitation, including sexual abuse, while in the care of parent(s), legal guardian(s) or any other person who has the care of the child.

2. Such protective measures should, as appropriate, include effective procedures for the establishment of social programmes to provide necessary support for the child and for those who have the care of the child, as well as for

other forms of prevention and for identification, reporting, referral, investigation, treatment and follow-up of instances of child maltreatment described heretofore, and, as appropriate, for judicial involvement.

Article 20

1. A child temporarily or permanently deprived of his or her family environment, or in whose own best interests cannot be allowed to remain in that environment, shall be entitled to special protection and assistance provided by the State. **A–018**

2. States Parties shall in accordance with their national laws ensure alternative care for such a child.

3. Such care could include, inter alia, foster placement, kafalah of Islamic law, adoption or if necessary placement in suitable institutions for the care of children. When considering solutions, due regard shall be paid to the desirability of continuity in a child's upbringing and to the child's ethnic, religious, cultural and linguistic background.

Article 21

States Parties that recognize and/or permit the system of adoption shall ensure that the best interests of the child shall be the paramount consideration and they shall: **A–019**

(a) Ensure that the adoption of a child is authorized only by competent authorities who determine, in accordance with applicable law and procedures and on the basis of all pertinent and reliable information, that the adoption is permissible in view of the child's status concerning parents, relatives and legal guardians and that, if required, the persons concerned have given their informed consent to the adoption on the basis of such counselling as may be necessary;

(b) Recognize that inter-country adoption may be considered as an alternative means of child's care, if the child cannot be placed in a foster or an adoptive family or cannot in any suitable manner be cared for in the child's country of origin;

(c) Ensure that the child concerned by inter-country adoption enjoys safeguards and standards equivalent to those existing in the case of national adoption;

(d) Take all appropriate measures to ensure that, in inter-country adoption, the placement does not result in improper financial gain for those involved in it;

(e) Promote, where appropriate, the objectives of the present article by concluding bilateral or multilateral arrangements or agreements, and endeavour, within this framework, to ensure that the placement of the child in another country is carried out by competent authorities or organs.

Article 22

1. States Parties shall take appropriate measures to ensure that a child who is seeking refugee status or who is considered a refugee in accordance with applicable international or domestic law and procedures shall, whether unaccompanied or accompanied by his or her parents or by any other person, receive appropriate protection and humanitarian assistance in the enjoyment **A–020**

of applicable rights set forth in the present Convention and in other international human rights or humanitarian instruments to which the said States are Parties.
2. For this purpose, States Parties shall provide, as they consider appropriate, co-operation in any efforts by the United Nations and other competent intergovernmental organizations or non-governmental organizations co-operating with the United Nations to protect and assist such a child and to trace the parents or other members of the family of any refugee child in order to obtain information necessary for reunification with his or her family. In cases where no parents or other members of the family can be found, the child shall be accorded the same protection as any other child permanently or temporarily deprived of his or her family environment for any reason , as set forth in the present Convention.

Article 23

A–021 1. States Parties recognize that a mentally or physically disabled child should enjoy a full and decent life, in conditions which ensure dignity, promote self-reliance and facilitate the child's active participation in the community.

2. States Parties recognize the right of the disabled child to special care and shall encourage and ensure the extension, subject to available resources, to the eligible child and those responsible for his or her care, of assistance for which application is made and which is appropriate to the child's condition and to the circumstances of the parents or others caring for the child.

3. Recognizing the special needs of a disabled child, assistance extended in accordance with paragraph 2 of the present article shall be provided free of charge, whenever possible, taking into account the financial resources of the parents or others caring for the child, and shall be designed to ensure that the disabled child has effective access to and receives education, training, health care services, rehabilitation services, preparation for employment and recreation opportunities in a manner conducive to the child's achieving the fullest possible social integration and individual development, including his or her cultural and spiritual development

4. States Parties shall promote, in the spirit of international cooperation, the exchange of appropriate information in the field of preventive health care and of medical, psychological and functional treatment of disabled children, including dissemination of and access to information concerning methods of rehabilitation, education and vocational services, with the aim of enabling States Parties to improve their capabilities and skills and to widen their experience in these areas. In this regard, particular account shall be taken of the needs of developing countries.

Article 24

A–022 1. States Parties recognize the right of the child to the enjoyment of the highest attainable standard of health and to facilities for the treatment of illness and rehabilitation of health. States Parties shall strive to ensure that no child is deprived of his or her right of access to such health care services.

2. States Parties shall pursue full implementation of this right and, in particular, shall take appropriate measures:
(a) To diminish infant and child mortality;

(b) To ensure the provision of necessary medical assistance and health care to all children with emphasis on the development of primary health care;
(c) To combat disease and malnutrition, including within the framework of primary health care, through, inter alia, the application of readily available technology and through the provision of adequate nutritious foods and clean drinking-water, taking into consideration the dangers and risks of environmental pollution;
(d) To ensure appropriate pre-natal and post-natal health care for mothers;
(e) To ensure that all segments of society, in particular parents and children, are informed, have access to education and are supported in the use of basic knowledge of child health and nutrition, the advantages of breastfeeding, hygiene and environmental sanitation and the prevention of accidents;
(f) To develop preventive health care, guidance for parents and family planning education and services.

3. States Parties shall take all effective and appropriate measures with a view to abolishing traditional practices prejudicial to the health of children.

4. States Parties undertake to promote and encourage international co-operation with a view to achieving progressively the full realization of the right recognized in the present article. In this regard, particular account shall be taken of the needs of developing countries.

Article 25

States Parties recognize the right of a child who has been placed by the competent authorities for the purposes of care, protection or treatment of his or her physical or mental health, to a periodic review of the treatment provided to the child and all other circumstances relevant to his or her placement. **A–023**

Article 26

1. States Parties shall recognize for every child the right to benefit from social security, including social insurance, and shall take the necessary measures to achieve the full realization of this right in accordance with their national law. **A–024**

2. The benefits should, where appropriate, be granted, taking into account the resources and the circumstances of the child and persons having responsibility for the maintenance of the child, as well as any other consideration relevant to an application for benefits made by or on behalf of the child.

Article 27

1. States Parties recognize the right of every child to a standard of living adequate for the child's physical, mental, spiritual, moral and social development. **A–025**

2. The parent(s) or others responsible for the child have the primary responsibility to secure, within their abilities and financial capacities, the conditions of living necessary for the child's development.

3. States Parties, in accordance with national conditions and within their means, shall take appropriate measures to assist parents and others responsible for the child to implement this right and shall in case of need provide material assistance and support programmes, particularly with regard to nutrition, clothing and housing.

4. States Parties shall take all appropriate measures to secure the recovery of maintenance for the child from the parents or other persons having financial responsibility for the child, both within the State Party and from abroad. In particular, where the person having financial responsibility for the child lives in a State different from that of the child, States Parties shall promote the accession to international agreements or the conclusion of such agreements, as well as the making of other appropriate arrangements.

Article 28

A–026 1. States Parties recognize the right of the child to education, and with a view to achieving this right progressively and on the basis of equal opportunity, they shall, in particular:

(a) Make primary education compulsory and available free to all;
(b) Encourage the development of different forms of secondary education, including general and vocational education, make them available and accessible to every child, and take appropriate measures such as the introduction of free education and offering financial assistance in case of need;
(c) Make higher education accessible to all on the basis of capacity by every appropriate means;
(d) Make educational and vocational information and guidance available and accessible to all children;
(e) Take measures to encourage regular attendance at schools and the reduction of drop-out rates.

2. States Parties shall take all appropriate measures to ensure that school discipline is administered in a manner consistent with the child's human dignity and in conformity with the present Convention.

3. States Parties shall promote and encourage international cooperation in matters relating to education, in particular with a view to contributing to the elimination of ignorance and illiteracy throughout the world and facilitating access to scientific and technical knowledge and modern teaching methods. In this regard, particular account shall be taken of the needs of developing countries.

Article 29

A–027 1. States Parties agree that the education of the child shall be directed to:

(a) The development of the child's personality, talents and mental and physical abilities to their fullest potential;
(b) The development of respect for human rights and fundamental freedoms, and for the principles enshrined in the Charter of the United Nations;
(c) The development of respect for the child's parents, his or her own cultural identity, language and values, for the national values of the country in which the child is living, the country from which he or she may originate, and for civilizations different from his or her own;
(d) The preparation of the child for responsible life in a free society, in the spirit of understanding, peace, tolerance, equality of sexes, and friendship among all peoples, ethnic, national and religious groups and persons of indigenous origin;
(e) The development of respect for the natural environment.

2. No part of the present Article or Article 28 shall be construed so as to interfere with the liberty of individuals and bodies to establish and direct educational institutions, subject always to the observance of the principle set forth in paragraph 1 of the present article and to the requirements that the education given in such institutions shall conform to such minimum standards as may be laid down by the State.

Article 30

In those States in which ethnic, religious or linguistic minorities or persons of indigenous origin exist, a child belonging to such a minority or who is indigenous shall not be denied the right, in community with other members of his or her group, to enjoy his or her own culture, to profess and practise his or her own religion, or to use his or her own language. **A–028**

Article 31

1. States Parties recognize the right of the child to rest and leisure, to engage in play and recreational activities appropriate to the age of the child and to participate freely in cultural life and the arts. **A–029**

2. States Parties shall respect and promote the right of the child to participate fully in cultural and artistic life and shall encourage the provision of appropriate and equal opportunities for cultural, artistic, recreational and leisure activity.

Article 32

1. States Parties recognize the right of the child to be protected from economic exploitation and from performing any work that is likely to be hazardous or to interfere with the child's education, or to be harmful to the child's health or physical, mental, spiritual, moral or social development. **A–030**

2. States Parties shall take legislative, administrative, social and educational measures to ensure the implementation of the present article. To this end, and having regard to the relevant provisions of other international instruments, States Parties shall in particular:
(a) Provide for a minimum age or minimum ages for admission to employment;
(b) Provide for appropriate regulation of the hours and conditions of employment;
(c) Provide for appropriate penalties or other sanctions to ensure the effective enforcement of the present article.

Article 33

States Parties shall take all appropriate measures, including legislative, administrative, social and educational measures, to protect children from the illicit use of narcotic drugs and psychotropic substances as defined in the relevant international treaties, and to prevent the use of children in the illicit production and trafficking of such substances. **A–031**

Article 34

States Parties undertake to protect the child from all forms of sexual exploitation and sexual abuse. For these purposes, States Parties shall in particular take all appropriate national, bilateral and multilateral measures to prevent: **A–032**

(a) The inducement or coercion of a child to engage in any unlawful sexual activity;
(b) The exploitative use of children in prostitution or other unlawful sexual practices;
(c) The exploitative use of children in pornographic performances and materials.

Article 35

A–033 States Parties shall take all appropriate national, bilateral and multilateral measures to prevent the abduction of, the sale of or traffic in children for any purpose or in any form.

Article 36

A–034 States Parties shall protect the child against all other forms of exploitation prejudicial to any aspects of the child's welfare.

Article 37

A–035 States Parties shall ensure that:
(a) No child shall be subjected to torture or other cruel, inhuman or degrading treatment or punishment. Neither capital punishment nor life imprisonment without possibility of release shall be imposed for offences committed by persons below eighteen years of age;
(b) No child shall be deprived of his or her liberty unlawfully or arbitrarily. The arrest, detention or imprisonment of a child shall be in conformity with the law and shall be used only as a measure of last resort and for the shortest appropriate period of time;
(c) Every child deprived of liberty shall be treated with humanity and respect for the inherent dignity of the human person, and in a manner which takes into account the needs of persons of his or her age. In particular, every child deprived of liberty shall be separated from adults unless it is considered in the child's best interest not to do so and shall have the right to maintain contact with his or her family through correspondence and visits, save in exceptional circumstances;
(d) Every child deprived of his or her liberty shall have the right to prompt access to legal and other appropriate assistance, as well as the right to challenge the legality of the deprivation of his or her liberty before a court or other competent, independent and impartial authority, and to a prompt decision on any such action.

Article 38

A–036 1. States Parties undertake to respect and to ensure respect for rules of international humanitarian law applicable to them in armed conflicts which are relevant to the child.

2. States Parties shall take all feasible measures to ensure that persons who have not attained the age of fifteen years do not take a direct part in hostilities.

3. States Parties shall refrain from recruiting any person who has not attained the age of fifteen years into their armed forces. In recruiting among those persons who have attained the age of fifteen years but who have not attained the age of eighteen years, States Parties shall endeavour to give priority to those who are oldest.

4. In accordance with their obligations under international humanitarian law to protect the civilian population in armed conflicts, States Parties shall take all feasible measures to ensure protection and care of children who are affected by an armed conflict.

Article 39

States Parties shall take all appropriate measures to promote physical and psychological recovery and social reintegration of a child victim of: any form of neglect, exploitation, or abuse; torture or any other form of cruel, inhuman or degrading treatment or punishment; or armed conflicts. Such recovery and reintegration shall take place in an environment which fosters the health, self-respect and dignity of the child. **A–037**

Article 40

1. States Parties recognize the right of every child alleged as, accused of, or recognized as having infringed the penal law to be treated in a manner consistent with the promotion of the child's sense of dignity and worth, which reinforces the child's respect for the human rights and fundamental freedoms of others and which takes into account the child's age and the desirability of promoting the child's reintegration and the child's assuming a constructive role in society. **A–038**

2. To this end, and having regard to the relevant provisions of international instruments, States Parties shall, in particular, ensure that:

(a) No child shall be alleged as, be accused of, or recognized as having infringed the penal law by reason of acts or omissions that were not prohibited by national or international law at the time they were committed;

(b) Every child alleged as or accused of having infringed the penal law has at least the following guarantees:

- (i) To be presumed innocent until proven guilty according to law;
- (ii) To be informed promptly and directly of the charges against him or her, and, if appropriate, through his or her parents or legal guardians, and to have legal or other appropriate assistance in the preparation and presentation of his or her defence;
- (iii) To have the matter determined without delay by a competent, independent and impartial authority or judicial body in a fair hearing according to law, in the presence of legal or other appropriate assistance and, unless it is considered not to be in the best interest of the child, in particular, taking into account his or her age or situation, his or her parents or legal guardians;
- (iv) Not to be compelled to give testimony or to confess guilt; to examine or have examined adverse witnesses and to obtain the participation and examination of witnesses on his or her behalf under conditions of equality;
- (v) If considered to have infringed the penal law, to have this decision and any measures imposed in consequence thereof reviewed by a higher competent, independent and impartial authority or judicial body according to law;
- (vi) To have the free assistance of an interpreter if the child cannot understand or speak the language used;

(vii) To have his or her privacy fully respected at all stages of the proceedings.

3. States Parties shall seek to promote the establishment of laws, procedures, authorities and institutions specifically applicable to children alleged as, accused of, or recognized as having infringed the penal law, and, in particular:

(a) The establishment of a minimum age below which children shall be presumed not to have the capacity to infringe the penal law;
(b) Whenever appropriate and desirable, measures for dealing with such children without resorting to judicial proceedings, providing that human rights and legal safeguards are fully respected.

4. A variety of dispositions, such as care, guidance and supervision orders; counselling; probation; foster care; education and vocational training programmes and other alternatives to institutional care shall be available to ensure that children are dealt with in a manner appropriate to their well-being and proportionate both to their circumstances and the offence.

INDEX